An Inexplicable Deception

A State Corruption of Justice

Volume I

by
Anant Kumar Tripati LLM, Merit

An Inexplicable Deception
A State Corruption of Justice

Volume I

Copyright © 2017 By Anant Kumar Tripati

Anant Kumar Tripati LLM, Merit
Post Office Box 14961
Santa Rosa, California 95402
E-mail: tripati@sbcglobal.net

Library of Congress Cataloging-in-Publication Data
An Inexplicable Deformity.

ISBN: 9781947170001

This book has been published and made available as an e-book.

FOREWARD

This book has been painstakingly researched and written in hopes of enabling the basic humane treatment for all those incarcerated in the United States today and in the future.

THE AUTHOR

ANANT KUMAR TRIPATI LLM, Merit (2014)
UNIVERSITY OF LONDON
UNIVERSITY COLLEGE LONDON
QUEEN MARY UNIVERSITY OF LONDON

Mr. Tripati has specializations in Public International Law (2014), Public Law (2014), and European Law (2013).

INTRODUCTION

FRAUD UPON THE COURT IN CRIMINAL CASES

Though traditionally used in civil cases there is no reason why criminal cases cannot be challenged pursuant to the doctrine of fraud upon the court. It is an unconscionable plan or scheme which is designed to improperly influence the court in its decision so that the judicial machinery cannot perform in the usual manner its impartial task of adjudging cases that are presented for adjudication when a prosecutor fails to disclose:

- It is the norm for appointed PCR counsel not to raise all federal claims;
- It is common practice for lawyers to have their clients provide false testimony to state courts thereby preventing a fair trial;
- It is common practice for lawyers not to fairly present their federal claims to state courts thereby preventing federal habeas review;
- It is very common for lawyers and the state not to disclose to the court all relevant facts in order to convict thereby convicting the incompetent;
- Counsel fail to advise inmates the time frames for filing federal habeas and paralegals do not assist inmates by policy;
- These same lawyers as a matter of routine practice file briefs asserting there are no appealable issues. The appellate courts refuse to take judicial notice of their own records which records show that lawyers who represented the defendants in the trial court as a matter of routine fail to make the necessary record and do not subject the state's case to a meaningful testing. These same lawyers surface again and again engaging in exactly the same conduct. As it was never their intent to subject the state's case to a meaningful adversarial process, when viewed in the totality, and not in isolation, this should constitute fraud upon the court by these lawyers;

- Law enforcement officers consistently engage in warrantless searches; Officers often manufacture their pretext to stop;
- The same law enforcement officers consistently engage in warrantless searches; Officers often manufacture their pretext to stop such as "meandering" rather than walking;
- Law enforcement officers consistently manufacture consent and courts allow this;
- The state has the tendency to release/destroy evidence, not investigate thoroughly, and again the same police/prosecutors are involved;
- Consistently police do not conduct thorough investigations and witnesses are unable to identify the defendants;
- As a matter of regular practice prosecutors consistently when they realize they may not prevail, engage in misconduct, to provoke mistrials, and State courts do nothing;
- It is the norm for prosecutors to present false evidence to convict and rarely are they penalized;
- Prosecutors, improperly vouch for their witnesses, appeal to the passions of the jury thereby preventing a meaningful defense;
- For appointed PCR counsel not to raise all federal claims;
- The state consistently changes the charges to meet its end;
- The same police and prosecutors consistently argue that there are confidential informants who will be jeopardized if disclosed, but do not provide case/fact specific evidence. By so doing they prevent examination;

PROSECUTORS CONSISTENTLY PREVENT EVIDENCE OF THIRD PARTIES WHO COMMITTED CRIMES FROM BEING PRESENTED THEREBY PREVENTING A MEANINGFUL DEFENSE.

As the minister of justice the goal of the prosecutor is to do justice and not to convict. A prosecutor "may prosecute with earnestness and vigor - indeed, he should do so. But, while he may strike hard blows, he is not at liberty to strike foul ones." Berger v. United States, 295 U.S. 78, 88, 55 S. Ct. 629, 79 L. Ed. 1314 (1935). "A prosecutor's actions constitute misconduct if they 'so infected the trial with unfairness as to make the resulting conviction a denial of due process.'" Wood v. Ryan, 693 F.3d 1104, 1113 (9th Cir. 2012) (quoting Darden v. Wainwright, 477 U.S. 168, 181, 106 S. Ct. 2464, 91 L. Ed. 2d 144 (1986)). "[I]n order to set aside a judgment or order because of fraud upon the court.... it is necessary to show an unconscionable plan or scheme which is designed to improperly influence the court in its decision." England v. Doyle, supra, 281 F.2d at 309. See also United States v. Standard Oil Co. of California, 73 F.R.D. 612, 615 (N.D. Cal. 1977).

Fraud upon the court "embraces only that species of fraud which does, or attempts to defile the court itself, or is a fraud perpetrated by officers of the court so that the judicial machinery cannot perform in the usual manner its impartial task of adjudging cases that are presented for adjudication......while an attorney "should represent his client with singular loyalty that loyalty obviously does not demand that he act dishonestly or fraudulently; on the contrary his loyalty to the court, as an officer thereof, demands integrity and honest dealing with the court. Kupferman v Consolidated Research Mfg., Corp., 459 F.2d 1072, 1078 (2nd. Cir. 1972) (emphasis added) And when he departs from that standard in the conduct of a case he perpetrates a fraud upon the court."." Hadges v. Yonkers Racing Corp., 48 F.3d 1320, 1325 (2d Cir. 1995) (emphasis added) (quotation omitted).

In United States v. International Telephone & Tel. Corp., 349 F. Supp. 22, 29 (D. Conn. 1972), aff'd without opinion, 410 U.S. 919, (1973), the trial court explained:

The elements of fraud on the court include conduct: 1) on the part of an officer of the court; 2) that is directed at the judicial machinery itself; 3) that is intentionally false, willfully blind to the truth, or is in reckless disregard for the truth; 4) that is a positive averment or a concealment when one is under a duty to disclose; and 5) that deceives the court. See Demjanjuk v. Petrovsky, 10 F.3d 338, 348 (6th Cir. 1993). See Alley v. Bell, 405 F.3d 371, 373 (6th Cir. 2005) (en banc) (Cole, J. concurring) ("Perhaps Alley's allegations of fraud are true, and perhaps they are not—obviously it will be up to the district court to consider the Rule 60(b) motion and determine if fraud actually occurred."). Workman's entitlement to a stay instead turns on whether he has shown a likelihood of success in arguing that he is entitled to an evidentiary hearing to prove his fraud claims. This in turn depends on whether the allegedly fraudulent conduct of State officials during trial can be imputed to the State's federal habeas counsel.

Hazel-Atlas Co. v. Hartford Co., 322 U.S. 238 (1944), overruled on other grounds by Standard Oil Co. of Cal. v. United States, 429 U.S. 17 (1976) Hazel-Atlas addressed the power of a federal court to set aside a judgment obtained by fraud despite the untimeliness of the action brought for that purpose. Hazel-Atlas, 322 U.S. at 239, 244. The time limit at issue was the term of court. Id. at 244. As the Supreme Court explained, "[f]ederal courts, both trial and appellate, long ago established the general rule that they would not alter or set aside their judgments after the expiration of the term at which the judgments were finally entered." Id. at 244. The general rule was not, however, without exception:

From the beginning there has existed alongside the term rule a rule of equity to the effect that under certain circumstances, one of which is after-discovered fraud, relief will be granted against judgments regardless of the term of their entry. This equity rule, which was firmly established in English practice long before the foundation of our Republic, the courts have developed and fashioned to fulfill a universally recognized need for correcting injustices which, in certain instances, are deemed sufficiently gross to demand a departure from rigid adherence to the term rule . . .. [I]n cases where courts have exercised the power, the relief granted has taken several forms: setting aside the judgment to permit a new trial, altering the terms of the judgment, or restraining the beneficiaries of the judgment from taking any benefit whatever from it. But whatever form the relief has taken in particular cases, the net result in every case has been the same: where the situation has required, the court has, in some manner, devitalized the judgment even though the term at which it was entered had long since passed away. Id. at 244-45 (citations and footnote omitted).

It has been noted that the "fraud exception for untimely requests" recognized in Hazel-Atlas "never included garden-variety fraud" claims such as suspected perjury by a witness. Geo. P. Reintjes Co., Inc. v. Riley Stoker Corp., 71 F.3d 44, 47-48 (1st Cir. 1995). The Hazel-Atlas Court stated that the case before it was "not simply a case of a judgment obtained with the aid of a witness who, on the basis of after-discovered evidence, is believed possibly to have been guilty of perjury." Hazel-Atlas, 322 U.S. at 245. Rather, it involved "a deliberately planned and carefully executed scheme to defraud not only the Patent Office but the Circuit Court of Appeals." Id. at 245-46.

THE FRAUD UPON THE COURT LANDSCAPE IN CIVIL CASES:

Kupferman v Consolidated Research Mfg., Corp., 459 F.2d 1072, 1078 (2nd. Cir. 1972) (emphasis added) fraud upon the court "embraces only that species of fraud which does, or attempts to defile the court itself, or is a fraud perpetrated by officers of the court so that the judicial machinery cannot perform in the usual manner its impartial task of adjudging cases that are presented for adjudication......while an attorney "should represent his client with singular loyalty that loyalty obviously does not demand that he act dishonestly or fraudulently; on the contrary his loyalty to the court, as an officer thereof, demands integrity and honest dealing with the court. And when he departs from that standard in the conduct of a case he perpetrates a fraud upon the court."." Hadges v. Yonkers Racing Corp., 48 F.3d 1320, 1325 (2d Cir. 1995) (emphasis added) (quotation omitted). Thus, consistent with the First Circuit's observation that fraud on the court does not encompass "garden-variety fraud," Geo. P. Reintjes, 71 F.3d at 48, "[p]erjury constitutes fraud on the court only in special situations, such as when an officer of the court commits the perjury." Myser v. Tangen, No. C14-0608JLR, 2015 WL 502316, at *6 (W.D. Wash. Feb. 5, 2015).

When the unsuccessful party is kept away from the court by a false promise of compromise, or such conduct as prevents a real trial upon the issues involved, or any other act or omission which procures the absence of the unsuccessful party at the trial. Further, it consists of fraud by the other party to the suit which prevents the losing party either from knowing about his rights or defenses, or from having a fair opportunity to present them upon the trial. In United States v. International Telephone & Tel. Corp., 349 F. Supp. 22, 29 (D. Conn. 1972), aff'd without opinion, 410 U.S. 919, (1973), the trial court explained:

Generally speaking, only the most egregious misconduct, such as bribery of a judge or members of a jury, or the fabrication of evidence by a party in which an attorney is implicated, will constitute a fraud on the court. See Hazel-Atlas Glass Co. v. Hartford-Empire Co., 322 U.S. 238, 64 S. Ct. 997, 88 L. Ed. 1250 (1944); Root Refin. Co. v. Universal Oil Products, 169 F.2d 514 (3d Cir. 1948); 7 J. W. Moore, Federal Practice, para. 60.33 at 510-11. Less egregious misconduct, such as nondisclosure to the court of facts allegedly pertinent to the matter before it will not ordinarily rise to the level of fraud on the court. See Kupferman v. Consolidated Research & Mfg. Co., 459 F.2d 1072 (2d Cir. 1972); see also England v. Doyle, 281 F.2d 304, 310 (9th Cir. 1960). "[I]n order to set aside a judgment or order because of fraud upon the court under Rule 60(b). it is necessary to show an unconscionable plan or scheme which is designed to improperly influence the court in its decision." England v. Doyle, supra, 281 F.2d at 309. See also United States v. Standard Oil Co. of California, 73 F.R.D. 612, 615 (N.D. Cal. 1977).

The treatment of perjured testimony is less clear. Perjury by a witness may constitute grounds for a new trial under the statute providing that a new trial may be granted when, due to accident, mistake or misfortune, justice has not been done. See Rasquin v. Cohen, 92 N.H. 440, 441 (1943); see RSA 526:1 (2007) (current version of statute cited in Rasquin). A petition under that statute, however, must be brought within three years of the tainted judgment. See RSA 526:4 (2007). Perjurious testimony of witness and the other exculpatory evidence amount to a fraud on the court by the State Attorney General during the habeas proceedings The elements of fraud on the court include conduct: 1) on the part of an officer of the court; 2) that is directed at the judicial machinery itself; 3) that is intentionally false, willfully blind to the truth, or is in reckless disregard for the truth; 4) that is a positive averment or a concealment when one is under a duty to disclose; and 5) that deceives the court. See Demjanjuk v. Petrovsky, 10 F.3d 338, 348 (6th Cir. 1993). See Alley v. Bell, 405 F.3d 371, 373 (6th Cir. 2005) (en banc) (Cole, J. concurring) ("Perhaps Alley's allegations of fraud are true, and perhaps they are not—obviously it will be up to the district court to consider the Rule 60(b) motion and determine if fraud actually occurred."). Workman's entitlement to a stay instead turns on whether he has shown a likelihood of success in arguing that he is entitled to an evidentiary hearing to prove his fraud claims. This in turn depends on whether the allegedly fraudulent conduct of State officials during trial can be imputed to the State's federal habeas counsel.

Hazel-Atlas Co. v. Hartford Co., 322 U.S. 238 (1944), overruled on other grounds by Standard Oil Co. of Cal. v. United States, 429 U.S. 17 (1976) Hazel-Atlas addressed the power of a federal court to set aside a judgment obtained by fraud despite the untimeliness of the action brought for that purpose. Hazel-Atlas, 322 U.S. at 239, 244. The time limit at issue was the term of court. Id. at 244. As the Supreme Court explained, "[f]ederal courts, both trial and appellate, long ago established the general rule that they would not alter or set aside their judgments after the expiration of the term at which the judgments were finally entered." Id. at 244. The general rule was not, however, without exception:

From the beginning there has existed alongside the term rule a rule of equity to the effect that under certain circumstances, one of which is after-discovered fraud, relief will be granted against judgments regardless of the term of their entry. This equity rule, which was firmly established in English practice long before the foundation of our Republic, the courts have developed and fashioned to fulfill a universally recognized need for correcting injustices which, in certain instances, are deemed sufficiently gross to demand a departure from rigid adherence to the term rule . . .. [I]n cases where courts have exercised the power, the relief granted has taken several forms: setting aside the judgment to permit a new trial, altering the terms of the judgment, or restraining the beneficiaries of the judgment from taking any benefit whatever from it. But whatever form the relief has taken in particular cases, the net result in every case has been the same: where the situation has required, the court has, in some manner, devitalized the judgment even though the term at which it was entered had long since passed away.

Id. at 244-45 (citations and footnote omitted).

It has been noted that the "fraud exception for untimely requests" recognized in Hazel-Atlas "never included garden-variety fraud" claims such as suspected perjury by a witness. Geo. P. Reintjes Co., Inc. v. Riley Stoker Corp., 71 F.3d 44, 47-48 (1st Cir. 1995). The Hazel-Atlas Court stated that the case before it was "not simply a case of a judgment obtained with the aid of a witness who, on the basis of after-discovered evidence, is believed possibly to have been guilty of perjury." Hazel-Atlas, 322 U.S. at 245. Rather, it involved "a deliberately planned and carefully executed scheme to defraud not only the Patent Office but the Circuit Court of Appeals." Id. at 245-46.

All courts have not explicitly addressed whether, or under what circumstances, a judgment may be set aside or a new trial granted, on grounds of perjury, long after the original judgment was rendered. In cases where perjury has been used to vitiate a judgment, the action, however it was brought, would seem to have been, under any measure, timely. See Craft v. Thompson, 51 N.H. 536 (1872) (arbitrators' 1870 award set aside in equity in 1872 when defendant's pleadings effectively admitted the award was obtained through his perjury); G.F.M.C. v. Mathes, 5 N.H. 574 (1832) (perjury of witness given as alternate grounds for new trial in 1832 when tainted trial held in 1830); cf. Hadges, 48 F.3d at 1325 (noting, under federal law, that "the type of fraud necessary to sustain an independent action attacking the finality of a judgment is narrower in scope than that which is sufficient for relief by timely motion" (quotation omitted)). On the other hand, in cases where courts have set aside a judgment long after it was rendered, the fraud was of a kind other than perjury. See Adams, 51 N.H. at 400 (1864 divorce decree set aside in 1872 for fraudulent failure to notify libellee of the divorce action); cf. Bussey v. Bussey, 95 N.H. 349, 350 (1949) (affirming dismissal of petition brought in 1946 to vacate 1927 divorce decree as within trial court's discretion and noting that although trial court unquestionably had the power to vacate the decree, "[a]fter a long lapse of time and change in status of persons upon faith in the validity of the decree, this power will always be exercised with great caution" (quotation omitted)).

The motion to set aside on this ground is addressed to the sound discretion of the trial court. Title v. United States, 263 F.2d 28 (9th Cir. 1959); Siberell v. United States, 268 F.2d 61 (9th Cir. 1959). And the burden is on the moving party to establish fraud by clear and convincing evidence. Atchison, Topeka & Santa Fe Railway Co. v. Barrett, 246 F.2d 846 (9th Cir. 1957). England v. Doyle, 281 F.2d 304, 309-310 (9th Cir. 1960).

Fraud on the Court as a Basis for Dismissal with Prejudice or Default: An Old Remedy Has New Teeth by John T. Kolinski February, 2004 Volume LXXVIII, No. 2 reads in part" That cheaters should not be allowed to prosper has long been central to the moral fabric of our society and one of the underpinnings of our legal system. The requisite fraud on the court occurs where "it can be demonstrated, clearly and convincingly, that a party has sentiently set in motion some unconscionable scheme calculated to interfere with the judicial system's ability impartially to adjudicate a matter by improperly influencing the trier of fact or unfairly hampering the presentation of the opposing party's claim or defense." Aoude v. Mobil Oil Corp., 892 F.2d 1115, 1118 (1st Cir. 1989) . . . .. The trial court has the inherent authority, within the exercise of sound judicial discretion, to dismiss an action when a plaintiff has perpetrated a fraud on the court, or where a party refuses to comply with court orders. Kornblum v. Schneider, 609 So. 2d 138, 139 (Fla. 4th DCA 1992).

As a general proposition, substantive misconduct is more likely to result in an affirmed dismissal with prejudice or default than procedural misconduct, precisely because substantive misconduct more clearly and directly subverts the judicial process. The integrity of the judicial system is rarely challenged sufficiently by willful disobedience to a court order or even multiple procedural shortcomings so as to warrant the ultimate sanction of dismissal, thus depriving the offending litigant of an adjudication on the merits. This distinction between substantive and procedural misconduct is in carefully balanc[ing] a policy favoring adjudication on the merits with competing policies to maintain the integrity of the judicial system.

Additionally, whether substantive or procedural misconduct is the basis for the sanction, the trial court must hold an evidentiary hearing before dismissing a case with prejudice,8 and must make an express finding that the conduct forming the basis for the dismissal was willful or done in bad faith or was deliberate and in contumacious disregard of the court's authority. Appellate courts do not hesitate to reverse and remand for noncompliance with these requirements.

Substantive misconduct is and should be subject to less tolerance before dismissal with prejudice is warranted. Lying about facts central to the case, including the nature and extent of one's own injuries, simply cannot be tolerated and, frequently, cannot be remedied by any lesser sanction than dismissal with prejudice.

Regrettably, many people do not consider lying under oath about the nature and extent of their injuries or other facts pertinent to their lawsuits to be egregious misconduct. To many, it is simply the way the game is played. "Everybody does it," according to this questionable train of thought, "so how bad can it possibly be?" While never overtly agreeing with this premise, many trial and appellate courts find it difficult to dismiss claims with prejudice or default defendants for such behavior. There are typically two prongs to their analysis. First, although the misconduct should not go unpunished, a "lesser sanction" than dismissal will be fashioned and meted out if possible. Secondly, the jury, as trier of fact, can mete out any punishment it deems appropriate—from an adverse verdict to a reduced or enhanced verdict—in the event it determines that misconduct by a litigant has occurred.

Simply allowing the opposing party to bring the transgression to the attention of the jury is hardly a "sanction." That is nothing more than allowing highly relevant evidence to be heard by the jury. At a minimum, the court should be able to assure the aggrieved party that the guilty party's misconduct will not be repeated and that the guilty party will not be allowed to profit by its misconduct. One possibility is to exclude from the trial the precise damage claim or defense pertinent to the offending testimony or conduct. Another is to subject the claim or defense involved to a higher standard of proof. Rarely will the assessment of a monetary sanction be sufficient to remedy the type of significant misconduct which approaches fraud on the court.

For example, in Jacob, it would certainly appear appropriate to disallow any recovery for future pain and suffering to plaintiff, while allowing her to recover damages for past medical expenses. Similarly, the court might limit any recovery for future medical expenses to those which can be proven by "clear and convincing evidence," that is, something more than plaintiff's suspect testimony and the opinion of her treating physician based on plaintiff's subjective symptoms. Additionally, the court may give a jury instruction informing the jury about the offending conduct. Although the credibility of the witnesses is and must remain within the sole province of the jury, it hardly seems offensive to that principle to have the court instruct the jury that plaintiff or defendant gave false testimony or deliberately omitted relevant information during discovery, if the trial court has in fact made that adjudication based upon clear and convincing evidence. Trial courts have broad discretion to fashion such remedies and sanctions. This discretion is fully warranted where a party has been found by clear and convincing evidence to have perpetrated a fraud on the court and the court has, nevertheless, allowed the case to proceed.

The plaintiff's false or misleading statement given under oath concerning issues central to her case amounted to fraud. See Cox v. Burke, 706 So. 2d 43, 47 (Fla. 5th DCA 1998).

The notion that "intent" must be coupled with "acts" and "bad consequences" to gauge the seriousness of the offense and the punishment is sound to a point, but has less application in cases of "substantive fraud" than "procedural misconduct." Missing a court ordered deadline for filing a pretrial stipulation rarely, if ever, warrants dismissal with prejudice no matter how willful it is found to be. Lying under oath at deposition or trial about a fact directly bearing on liability or damages can be sufficient, in and of itself, to warrant dismissal with prejudice. In the case of such substantive fraud, the success of the fraud should play less of a role, if any role whatsoever

The integrity of the litigation process depends on truthful disclosure of facts. A system that depends on an adversary's ability to uncover falsehoods is doomed to failure, which is why this kind of conduct must be discouraged in the strongest possible way. Although Cox insists on her constitutional right to have her case heard, she can, by her own conduct, forfeit that right. This is an area where the trial court is and should be vested with discretion to fashion the apt remedy. While this court might have imposed a lesser sanction, the question in this case is close enough that we cannot declare the lower court to have abused its discretion.

In the best of circumstances, the adversarial process embodied in civil litigation can be contentious. Hard fought litigation sometimes breeds suspicion and distrust among adversaries and their counsel. Using the word "liar" to refer to an adverse party at trial has always been one of the surest ways to incur a trial or appellate court's wrath despite being entirely proper assuming there is record evidence to support the inference. Fraud on the court requires more than name-calling. It requires proving to the court clearly and convincingly that your adversary is deliberately not being forthright with you or the court and that its refusal to do so is subverting the administration of justice in your case to your client's severe prejudice.

Prosecutorial misconduct and vindictive prosecution constitute fraud upon the court Hazel-Atlas Glass Co. v. Hartford Empire Co., 64 S. Ct. 997 (1944) states fraud corrupted the very integrity of the judicial machinery. A cause of action for fraud on the court may be brought at any time, and any order, judgment or decree, obtained by fraud upon the court may be recalled and set aside at any time, whether entered in a civil or criminal case. See, State v. Booker, 314 So. 2d 136 (Fla. 1975). Burton stands for the proposition that an order produced by fraud upon the court, including an order denying a motion for post conviction relief, may be set aside at any time. See, Booker v. State, 503 So. 2d 888 (Fla. 1987).

U.S. v. Velsicol Chem. Corp., 498 F. Supp. 1255 (D.D.C. 1980). The Court ruled that due process would not tolerate judicial vindictiveness or retaliation for pursuit of a statutory right. "(Since) the fear of such vindictiveness may unconstitutionally deter a defendant's exercise of the right to appeal or collaterally attack his first conviction, due process also requires that a defendant be freed of apprehension of such a retaliatory motivation on the part of the sentencing judge." 395 U.S. at 725, 89 S. Ct. at 2080. The vindictive prosecution doctrine reaches all prosecutions "that pose a realistic likelihood of "vindictiveness,' " Perry, 417 U.S. at 27, 94 S. Ct. at 2102, whether or not the prosecutor acted out of vindictiveness in fact. "(T) he evil to which Pearce is directed is the apprehension on the defendant's part of receiving a vindictively-imposed penalty for the assertion of rights." U.S. v. Jamison, 164 U.S. App. D.C. 300, 505 F.2d 407, 415 (D.C.Cir.1974). The Ninth Circuit has also ruled in a number of situations that the apprehension or appearance of prosecutorial vindictiveness is sufficient to warrant a dismissal when a defendant is thwarted in the exercise of his rights. The "mere appearance of vindictiveness is enough to place the burden on the prosecution (to show a legitimate motive)." U.S. v. RuesgaMartinez, 534 F.2d 1367, 1369 (9th Cir. 1976). "Later, in U.S. v. Groves, 571 F.2d

450 (9th Cir. 1978), that court, relying in part on Jamison, ruled that the government bore the "heavy burden of proving that any increase in the severity of the alleged charges was not motivated by a vindictive purpose." Thus, in addition to mere appearances, this proceeding involves an explicit threat, the gravamen of which is an intent to retaliate for the exercise of a right. That threat was carried out in the felony indictment presently before the Court. The limits of acceptable exercise of prosecutorial discretion in charging decisions are exceeded when, as in this case, the prosecutor threatens defendant with increased charges and then "ups-the-ante" without adequate justification. As the district court in U.S. v. DeMarco so aptly stated, "(t)he day our Constitution permits prosecutors to deter defendants from exercising any and all of their guaranteed rights by threatening them with new charges fortunately has not yet arrived." 401 F. Supp. 505, 510 (C.D.Cal.1975), aff'd 550 F.2d 1224 (9th Cir.), cert. denied, 434 U.S. 827, 98 S. Ct. 105, 54 L. Ed. 2d 85 (1977). The prosecutorial vindictiveness motion warrants a dismissal of the present indictment against Velsicol and the individual defendants. U.S. v. Alvarado-Sandoval, 557 F.2d 645 (9th Cir. 1977) ("appearance of vindictiveness, not vindictiveness itself, is the touchstone..."); U.S. v. DeMarco, 550 F.2d 1224, 1227 (9th Cir. 1977) ("apprehension of vindictiveness and the "appearance of vindictiveness' are adequate to bring this case squarely within Blackledge (v. Perry).") (citation omitted). The circuit courts of appeal have developed a number of standards for examining prosecutorial decision making for impermissible motives. See discussion and cases cited in U.S. v. Andrews, 612 F.2d 235, 249-254 (6th Cir. 1979) (Keith, J. dissenting). Actual vindictiveness, however, is always regarded as an impermissible factor in prosecutorial decision making. See e.g., Hardwick v. Doolittle, 558 F.2d 292, 299-300 (5th Cir. 1977), cert. denied, 434 U.S. 1049, 98 S. Ct. 897, 54 L. Ed. 2d 801 (1978).

Atchak v. State, 640 P.2d 135, (Ak App., 1981.). Existence of prosecutorial vindictiveness must be established by an objective standard, on the basis of the totality of the circumstances in each case; the subjective belief of defendant is not determinative; on the other hand, it is not necessary that actual malice or retaliatory motivation exist on the part of the prosecution. Determining the strength of the appearance of prosecutorial vindictiveness is a process which involves, first, an inquiry as to the prosecution's "stake" in deterring the exercise of the specific right asserted by defendant, and, second, scrutiny of the state's conduct for a connection between assertion of a right by defendant and an increase or threatened increase in charges by the state. Prosecutorial mistake, negligence or misunderstanding will not suffice to rebut a prima facie showing of prosecutorial vindictiveness. It is not appropriate, where apparent prosecutorial vindictiveness would result, to allow the state to alter an initial charging decision which amounted to a calculated risk, rather than an exercise of prosecutorial discretion made for legitimate, strategic reasons. Explanation offered by the State in the record and in its argument on appeal was inadequate to dispel the strong appearance of prosecutorial vindictiveness which led to defendant's abandonment of any attempt to challenge the validity of his original and superseding indictments; the prosecutor admitted creating a situation in which defendant was forced to choose between a possible manslaughter charge and waiver of his right to challenge the indictments against him for leaving the scene of an accident involving injury without stopping to render aid. Court should not hesitate to reverse a conviction when a substantial flaw in the underlying indictment is found, regardless of the strength of the evidence against the accused or the fairness of the trial leading to conviction. While we realize that prosecutorial independence is a vital consideration involved in all cases dealing with the Pearce/Blackledge rule, our solicitude for the independent discretion of the state diminishes significantly when, in increasing or threatening to increase a charge, the prosecution simply attempts to alter, without significant intervening circumstances, a fully informed decision which it previously made. As held in Hardwick v. Doolittle, 558 F.2d 292, 301 (5th Cir. 1977), cert. denied, 434 U.S. 1049, 98 S.Ct. 897, 54 L.Ed.2d 801 (1978) (citation omitted): We recognize that there is a broad ambit to prosecutorial discretion, most of which is not subject to judicial control. But if Blackledge teaches any lesson, it is that a prosecutor's discretion to reindict a defendant is constrained by the due process clause.... (O)nce a prosecutor exercises his discretion to bring certain charges against the defendant, neither he nor his successor may, without explanation, increase the number of or severity of those charges in circumstances which suggest that the increase is retaliation for the defendant's assertion of statutory or constitutional rights. As stated in U.S. v. Ruesga-Martinez, 534 F.2d at 1369 (footnotes and citations omitted; emphasis in original): Pearce and Blackledge ... establish, beyond doubt, that when the prosecution has occasion to reindict the accused because the accused has exercised some procedural right, the prosecution bears a heavy burden of proving that any increase in the severity of the alleged charges was not motivated by a vindictive motive. We do not question the prosecutor's authority to bring the felony charges in the first instance, nor do we question the prosecutor's discretion in choosing which charges to bring against a particular defendant. But when, as here, there is a significant possibility that such discretion may have been exercised with a vindictive motive or purpose, the reason for the increase in the gravity of the charges must be made to appear. We do not intend by our opinion to impugn the actual motives of the (prosecution) in any way. But Pearce and Blackledge seek to reduce or eliminate apprehension on the part of an accused that he may be subjected to retaliatory or vindictive punishment by the prosecution only for attempting to exercise his procedural rights. Hence, the mere appearance of vindictiveness is enough to place the burden on the prosecution. We note that previous cases have invoked the Pearce/Blackledge doctrine despite affirmative findings of a lack of malice or improper motivation on the part of the prosecution. See, e.g., U.S. v. Groves, 571 F.2d at 453; U.S. v. Ruesga-Martinez, 534 F.2d at 1369-70. The Alaska Supreme Court has consistently held that courts should not hesitate to reverse a conviction when a substantial flaw in the underlying indictment is found, regardless of the strength of the evidence against the accused or the fairness of the trial leading to the conviction. Keith v. State, 612 P.2d 977, 980-81 (Alaska 1980); Adams v. State, 598 P.2d 503, 510 (Alaska 1979).

Berger v. U.S., 55 S. Ct. 629, 295 U.S. 78 (U.S. 1935). Justice Sutherland best explained the duties and obligations of prosecutors: "The U.S. Attorney is the representative not of an ordinary party to a controversy, but of a sovereignty whose obligation to govern impartially is as compelling as its obligation to govern at all; and whose interest, therefore, in a criminal prosecution is not that it shall win a case, but that justice shall be done. As such, he is in a peculiar and very definite sense the servant of the law, the twofold aim of which is that guilt shall not escape or innocence suffer. He may prosecute with earnestness and vigor -- indeed; he should do so. But, while he may strike hard blows, he is not at liberty to strike foul ones. It is as much his duty to refrain from improper methods calculated to produce a wrongful conviction as it is to use every legitimate means to bring about a just one." 295 U.S. at 88, 55 S. Ct. 633. And, as Justice Douglas more figuratively described this same duty: "The function of the prosecutor under the federal Constitution is not to tack as many skins of victims as possible against the wall. His function is to vindicate the rights of the people as expressed in the laws and give those accused of crime a fair trial." Donnelly v. De Christoforo, 416 U.S. 637, 648-649, 94 S. Ct. 1868, 1874, 40 L. Ed. 2d 431 (1974) (Douglas J., dissenting).

Jackson v. Walker, 585 F2d 139 (5th Cir. 1978). Three months later we decided Hardwick v. Doolittle, 558 F.2d 292 (5th Cir. 1977). Hardwick, which interpreted Blackledge and related cases, makes it clear that in some cases the apprehension of vindictiveness is sufficient only to establish a prima facie showing of unconstitutional vindictiveness. Upon this showing, the burden shifts to the state to demonstrate that the reason for the increase in charging was other than to retaliate against the defendant for the exercise of her legal rights. If the state fails to meet this burden, the court must find actual vindictiveness and a violation of the due process clause. In Blackledge the Supreme Court made clear that a prosecutor's discretion to reindict a defendant is limited by the due process clause. In that case the defendant, convicted of an assault misdemeanor in a state court, claimed his right to a trial De novo in a higher court. The prosecutor then obtained a superseding indictment charging the defendant with a felony, assault with intent to kill, based on the same act as the earlier charge. Significantly, the Court stated that it saw no evidence that the prosecutor in this case acted in bad faith or maliciously in seeking a felony indictment against Perry. The rationale of our judgment ..., however, (is) not grounded upon the proposition that actual retaliatory motivation must inevitably exist. Rather, ... "since the fear of such vindictiveness may unconstitutionally deter a defendant's exercise of the right to appeal or collaterally attack his first conviction, due process also requires that a defendant be freed of apprehension of such a retaliatory motivation on the part of the (prosecutor).' 417 U.S. at 28, 94 S. Ct. at 2102, quoting North Carolina v. Pearce, 395 U.S. 711, 725, 89 S. Ct. 2072, 2080, 23 L. Ed. 2d 656. In effect Blackledge sets up a per se rule for some situations. It lays down the principle that in some situations a due process violation can be established by a showing that defendants might have a reasonable apprehension of prosecutorial vindictiveness, without a showing that the prosecutor actually had a vindictive or retaliatory motive to deter appeals. There are at least two reasons for such a per se rule. First, it is difficult to prove in court the actual state of mind of a prosecutor during his exercise of discretion. And second, reindictments that look vindictive, even though they are not, may still make future defendants so apprehensive about the vindictiveness of prosecutors that they will be deterred from appealing their convictions. Hardwick and other cases speak in terms of "actual malice" or "actual vindictiveness." In one sense these terms are misleading. For a prosecution to be unconstitutional, it is not necessary that the prosecutor bear any ill will toward the particular defendant in the case. The unconstitutional motive may be simply the prosecutor's intent to discourage other criminal appeals in the future by "upping the ante" in the current appeal, even though he feels no particular malice for the current defendant. Of course, a prosecutor may also intend to punish the current defendant for appealing. The terms "malice" and "vindictiveness" more accurately describe only the latter motive, but the due process clause proscribes both motivations.

U.S. v. Alvarado-Sandoval, 557 F.2d 645 (9th Cir. 1977). Defense counsel was not prepared at that time to enter a plea because he wished to investigate the possibility of raising a question about the legality of the search. The magistrate stated from the bench that he understood defendant's position concerning the possibility of motions and set the case for further proceedings. Thereafter, the U.S. Attorney advised the court and defense counsel that the Government would be considering the case for a possible felony indictment. On June 17, 1976 a two-count indictment was filed in the U.S. District Court charging appellant with felony violations of 8 U.S.C. §§ 1325 and 1326. On August 5, 1976 appellant moved the court to dismiss the indictment as the product of a violation of the principles established in Blackledge v. Perry, 417 U.S. 21, 94 S. Ct. 2098, 40 L. Ed. 2d 628 (1974); North Carolina v. Pearce, 395 U.S. 711, 89 S. Ct. 2072, 23 L. Ed. 2d 656 (1969); and U.S.

v. Ruesga-Martinez, 534 F.2d 1367 (9th Cir. 1976). The district court denied the motion. Appellant was subsequently tried and convicted of the felony charges. Appearance of vindictiveness, not vindictiveness in fact, is the touchstone of Blackledge, Pearce and Ruesga-Martinez. The Government attempts to distinguish Ruesga-Martinez, which is otherwise identical, on the ground that the appellant in this case did not affirmatively assert a right which then precipitated a "raising of the ante" by the Government. The failure to interpose a formal motion before the magistrate, does not effectively distinguish this case from Ruesga-Martinez. Appellant's counsel made plain his intention to proceed under the misdemeanor charge. Here, as in Ruesga-Martinez, the appearance of vindictiveness existed. It was only after the appellant, through his counsel, indicated that no plea would be entered and only after the understanding of possible motions was referred to by the magistrate, that the assistant U.S. Attorney indicated that a felony indictment would be considered. All of the information about appellant's prior record was known to the U.S. Attorney's office before these events occurred. It is immaterial that, due to a failure of communication within the office, the assistant U.S. Attorney who initially appeared was not personally aware of that record.

U.S. v. Basurto, 497 F.2d 781 (9th Cir. 1974). With that great power and authority there is a correlative duty, and that is not to permit a person to stand trial when he knows that perjury permeates the indictment. At the point at which he learned of the perjury before the grand jury, the prosecuting attorney was under a duty to notify the court and the grand jury, to correct the cancer of justice that had become apparent to him. To permit the appellants to stand trial when the prosecutor knew of the perjury before the grand jury only allowed the cancer to grow. We also note that jeopardy had not attached at the time the prosecutor learned of the perjured testimony, nor had the statute of limitations for the offenses charged run. Under Illinois v.

Somerville, 410 U.S. 458, 35 L. Ed. 2d 425, 93 S. Ct. 1066 (1973), if the prosecutor had brought the perjury to the court's attention before the trial commenced and the indictments had been dismissed, the Double Jeopardy Clause of the Fifth Amendment would not have barred trial under a new indictment. We hold that the Due Process Clause of the Fifth Amendment is violated when a defendant has to stand trial on an indictment which the government knows is based partially on perjured testimony, when the perjured testimony is material, and when jeopardy has not attached. Whenever the prosecutor learns of any perjury committed before the grand jury, he is under a duty to immediately inform the court and opposing counsel -- and, if the perjury may be material, also the grand jury -- in order that appropriate action may be taken. We base our decision on a long line of cases which recognize the existence of a duty of good faith on the part of the prosecutor with respect to the court, the grand jury, and the defendant. While the facts of these cases may not exactly parallel those of the instant case, we hold that their rulings regarding the consequences of a violation or abuse of this prosecutorial duty must be applied where the prosecutor has knowledge that testimony before the grand jury was perjured. See Mooney v. Holohan, 294 U.S. 103, 79 L. Ed. 791, 55 S. Ct. 340 (1935); Giles v. Maryland, 386 U.S. 66, 17 L. Ed. 2d 737, 87 S. Ct. 793 (1967); Napue v. Illinois, 360 U.S. 264, 3 L. Ed. 2d 1217, 79 S. Ct. 1173 (1959); Alcorta v. Texas, 355 U.S. 28, 2 L. Ed. 2d 9, 78 S. Ct. 103 (1957); Hysler v. Florida, 315 U.S. 411, 86 L. Ed. 932, 62 S. Ct. 688 (1942); Pyle v. Kansas, 317 U.S. 213, 87 L. Ed. 214, 63 S. Ct. 177 (1942). In Napue v. Illinois, supra, the Supreme Court reaffirmed the principle stated in many of its prior decisions that "a conviction obtained through use of false evidence, known to be such by representatives of the State, must fall under the Fourteenth Amendment, [citations]. The same result obtains when the State, although not soliciting false evidence, allows it to go uncorrected when it appears. [Citations.]" 360 U.S. at 269. The Court reiterated "the principle that a State may not knowingly use false evidence, including false testimony, to obtain a tainted conviction, implicit in any concept of ordered liberty..." Id. See Giles v. Maryland, supra, at 74. The Court held in Napue that the prosecution's use of known false testimony at trial required a reversal of the petitioner's conviction. The same result must obtain when the government allows a defendant to stand trial on an indictment which it knows to be based in part upon perjured testimony.

The consequences to the defendant of perjured testimony given before the grand jury are no less severe than those of perjured testimony given at trial, and in fact may be more severe. The defendant has no effective means of cross-examining or rebutting perjured testimony given before the grand jury, as he might in court. In Mesarosh v. U.S., 352 U.S. 1, 1 L. Ed. 2d 1, 77 S. Ct. 1 (1956), while a review of the petitioners' convictions was pending in the Supreme Court, the Solicitor General informed the Court of indications he had just received that one of the government's witnesses at trial had testified falsely in other proceedings. While the government believed that the witness' testimony at trial "was entirely truthful and credible," it suggested a remand to the district court for a determination of the credibility of the witness' testimony. Solely on the basis of the government's representations, the Supreme Court reversed the convictions and directed that petitioners be granted a new trial. The Court stated, inter alia, that "Mazzei [the witness], by his testimony, has poisoned the water in this reservoir, and the reservoir cannot be cleansed without first draining it of all impurity... Pollution having taken place here, the condition should be remedied at the earliest opportunity. "'The untainted administration of justice is certainly one of the most cherished aspects of our institutions. Its observance is one of our proudest boasts... Fastidious regard for the honor of the administration of justice requires the Court to make certain that the doing of justice be made so manifest that only irrational or perverse claims of its disregard can be asserted.' Communist Party v. Subversive Activities Control Board, 351 U.S. 115, 124, 100 L. Ed. 1003, 76 S. Ct. 663." 352 U.S. at 14. Permitting a defendant to stand trial on an indictment which the government knows is based on perjured testimony cannot comport with this "fastidious regard for the honor of the administration of justice." Because the prosecuting attorney did not take appropriate action to cure the indictment upon discovery of the perjured grand jury testimony, we reverse appellants' convictions.

The Court relied upon Justice Holmes' statement in Silverthorne Lumber Co. v. U.S., 251 U.S. 385, 392, 40 S. Ct. 182, 64 L. Ed. 319 (1920), that "the essence of a provision forbidding the acquisition of evidence in a certain way is that not merely evidence so acquired shall not be used before the Court but that it shall not be used at all..." Thus, the test that should have been used in this case is that any statements made by Basurto that related to or were prompted by any inadmissible evidence, or that would not have been made but for the possession of such evidence by the government agents, were the "fruits" of, were derived from, such evidence and should have been excluded.

Murphy v. Waterfront Comm'n, 378 U.S. 52 (1964) U.S. Supreme Court: "[A] state witness may not be compelled to give testimony which may be incriminating under federal law unless the compelled testimony and its fruits cannot be used in any manner by federal officials in connection with a criminal prosecution against him. We conclude, moreover, that in order to implement this constitutional rule and accommodate the interests of the State and Federal Governments in investigating and prosecuting crime, the Federal Government must be prohibited from making any such use of compelled testimony and its fruits." 378 U.S.79.

U.S. Supreme Court Mesarosh V. U.S., 352 U.S. 1 (1956). The witness's credibility has been wholly discredited by the disclosures of the Solicitor General; the dignity of the U.S. Government will not permit the conviction of any person on tainted testimony; this conviction is tainted; and justice requires that petitioners be accorded a new trial. In this case, it cannot be determined conclusively by any court that the testimony of this discredited witness before a jury was insignificant in the general case against petitioners; it has tainted the trial as to all petitioners. Mazzei, by his testimony, has poisoned the water in this reservoir, and the reservoir cannot be cleansed without first draining it of all impurity. This is a federal criminal case, and this Court has supervisory jurisdiction over the proceedings of the federal courts. If it has any duty to perform in this regard, it is to see that the waters of justice are not polluted. Pollution having taken place here, the condition should be remedied at the earliest opportunity.

"The untainted administration of justice is certainly one of the most cherished aspects of our institutions. Its observance is one of our proudest boasts. This Court is charged with supervisory functions in relation to proceedings in the federal courts. See McNabb v. U.S., 318 U.S. 332. Therefore, fastidious regard for the honor of the administration of justice requires the Court to make certain that the doing of justice be made so manifest that only irrational or perverse claims of its disregard can be asserted." Communist Party v. Subversive Activities Control Board, 351 U.S. 115, 124.

The government of a strong and free nation does not need convictions based upon such testimony. It cannot afford to abide with them. The interests of justice call for a reversal of the judgments below with direction to grant the petitioners a new trial.

U.S. v. Carrillo, 709 F.2d 35 (9th Cir. 1983). In as much as an obligation to testify did not become a condition and because Carrillo fulfilled all other obligations under the agreement, under settled notions of fundamental fairness the government was bound to uphold its end of the bargain. See U.S.

v. Irwin, 612 F.2d 1182, 1189-91 (9th Cir. 1980) (recognition of enforceability of cooperation agreements); U.S. v. Garcia, 519 F.2d at 1345 & n.2 (same); cf. Johnson v. Mabry, 707 F.2d 323 (8th Cir. 1983) (constitutional right to fairness requires that government be scrupulously fair when negotiating plea agreements and that government honor terms of its proposal even in the absence of defendant's detrimental reliance); U.S. v. Minnesota Mining & Mfg. Co., 551 F.2d at 1111 (where defendants fully discharge their obligations under plea agreement government is bound to fulfill its promise to forego future criminal prosecution); U.S. v. Hallam, 472 F.2d 168, 169 (9th Cir. 1973) (same). The remedy for the breach of this promise rests within the sound discretion of the trial court. See Santobello v. New York, 404 U.S. 257, 263, 92 S. Ct. 495, 30 L. Ed. 2d 427 (1971); U.S. v. Minnesota Mining & M F.2d at 1112. By dismissing the indictment, the district court effectively enforced the agreement. The remedy granted was not outside the district court's discretion. Id.

The court in Ray H. Chewning, Jr., Appellant, vs. Ford Motor Company, David J. Bickerstaff, and David J. Bickerstaff and Associates, Inc., Defendants, THE STATE OF SOUTH CAROLINA In The Court of Appeals

States.

In April 1990, Chewning suffered injuries in a rollover crash of his Ford Bronco II. He filed a products liability claim against Ford and the car dealership that sold him the automobile. After a sixteen-day trial in 1993, a jury returned a verdict in favor of Ford. The trial court denied Chewning's motion for judgment notwithstanding the verdict or a new trial.

Within one year of the judgment, Chewning sought relief pursuant to Rule 60(b)(1) and (3), SCRCP, on the grounds of newly discovered evidence and fraud, alleging Bickerstaff, the former design engineer for Ford's Light Truck Engineering Department and one of Ford's witnesses, committed perjury during the trial. This motion was denied.

In 1998, Chewning brought this independent action, asserting several causes of action including fraud upon the court. The Defendants removed the case to the United States District Court for South Carolina. The district court dismissed all of Chewning's claims except his action for fraud upon the court. Chewning v. Ford Motor Co., 35 F. Supp. 2d 487 (D.S.C. 1998). The district court remanded the fraud upon the court claim together with "such other related claims in equity, if any, as the state court may allow to be added by amendment." Id. at 492.

Chewning refiled his case in the circuit court asserting causes of action for fraud upon the court and an independent action in equity for fraud. In his amended complaint, Chewning alleged the judgment in the original products liability case should be vacated because:

(1) Defendants' and Ford's attorneys knowingly purchased and used the false testimony of BICKERSTAFF in favor of FORD during FORD'S defense of the BRONCO II CASES and concealed this from Plaintiffs and

(2) FORD fraudulently concealed, hid and misrepresented to the Plaintiffs and the Courts about the existence and location of documents . . . that provide evidence that was favorable to Plaintiffs' cases and evidence that FORD knew, or should have known, would harm Plaintiffs' defense.

Among other allegations, Chewning contends Ford and its attorneys bought favorable and untruthful testimony from Bickerstaff. While at Ford, Bickerstaff criticized the Bronco II and recommended certain unimplemented corrective measures. Curiously, when litigation arose concerning the Bronco II, Bickerstaff, then a member of an engineering consulting firm, agreed to testify as a witness "in Ford's favor" in exchange for large sums of money. Chewning alleges this scheme persisted through multiple trials and depositions until a memo detailing Ford's and Chewning's arrangement was discovered.

The Defendants successfully filed a motion to dismiss under Rule 12(b)(6), SCRCP. This appeal follows.

Chewning argues the circuit court erred in dismissing his claim as untimely. We agree. Under Rule 60(b), SCRCP, a party may seek to set aside a final judgment for fraud upon the court. This right is independent of the Rule 60(b)(3) ground for relief for fraud, misrepresentation, or other misconduct by an adverse party. Relief for fraud upon the court is not subject to the one-year limit placed on relief under Rule 60(b)(3). See H. Lightsey & J. Flanagan, South Carolina Civil Procedure 407 (2d ed. 1985). Therefore, we find the circuit court erred in dismissing Chewning's claim as untimely under Rule 60(b)(3).

Chewning also argues the circuit court erred in its application of the law of extrinsic and intrinsic fraud. We agree because we find the facts asserted in the amended complaint constitute a valid claim for relief for fraud upon the court.

Fraud upon the court is "fraud which . . . subvert[s] the integrity of the Court itself, or is a fraud perpetrated by officers of the court so that the judicial machinery cannot perform in the usual manner its impartial task of adjudging cases that are presented for adjudication." Evans v. Gunter, 294 S.C. 525, 529, 366 S.E.2d 44, 46 (Ct. App. 1988) (emphasis added) (quoting Lightsey & Flanagan, supra, at 408). It has also been defined as "fraud that does, or at least attempts to, defile the court itself . . . ." 12 Moore's Federal Practice § 60.21[4][a] (3d. ed. 2000). Historically, after the period to claim relief under Rule 60(b)(1) through (3), SCRCP, has expired, courts have required a showing of extrinsic fraud to vacate a judgment. See Hagy v. Pruitt, 339 S.C. 425, 430, 529 S.E.2d 714, 717 (2000); Evans, 294 S.C. at 529, 366 S.E.2d at 46.

South Carolina law maintains a distinction between intrinsic and extrinsic fraud. Mr. G v. Mrs. G, 320 S.C. 305, 307-08, 465 S.E.2d 101, 102-03 (Ct. App. 1995) (Hearn, J. dissenting). "Intrinsic fraud refers to fraud presented and considered in the judgment assailed, including perjury and forged documents presented at trial." Evans, 294 S.C. at

529, 366 S.E.2d at 46. It is fraud which "goes to the merits of the prior proceeding which the moving party should have guarded against at the time." City of San Francisco v. Cartagena, 41 Cal. Rptr. 2d 797, 801 (Cal. Ct. App. 1995), quoted with approval in Mr. G, 320 S.C. at 308, 465 S.E.2d at 103. By contrast, extrinsic fraud "refers to frauds collateral or external to the matter tried such as bribery or other misleading acts which prevent the movant from presenting all of his case or deprives one of the opportunity to be heard." Lightsey & Flanagan, supra, at 486; see also Hilton Head Ctr., Inc. v. Pub. Serv. Comm'n, 294 S.C. 9, 11, 362 S.E.2d 176, 177 (1987) ("Extrinsic fraud is fraud that induces a person not to present a case or deprives a person of the opportunity to be heard.").

Here, Chewning alleges that Ford's attorneys collaborated in a deliberate scheme to purchase testimony in a series of cases involving Bronco II rollovers. Ordinarily, perjury is intrinsic, rather than extrinsic, fraud. Hagy, 339 S.C. at 432, 529 S.E.2d at 718 (2000); Rycroft v. Tanguay, 279 S.C. 76, 79, 302 S.E.2d 327, 329 (1983); Corley v. Centennial Constr. Co., 247 S.C. 179, 189, 146 S.E.2d 609, 614 (1966). Chewning argues, however, that because he alleges Ford's attorneys suborned the perjured testimony, it is in fact extrinsic fraud and thus a basis to set aside the underlying verdict. We agree.

This court has previously refused to carve out an attorney fraud exception to the intrinsic/extrinsic fraud rule. Bankers Trust Co. v. Braten, 317 S.C. 547, 552, 455 S.E.2d 199, 202 (Ct. App. 1995). However, Chewning's inability to present his full case at trial distinguishes this case from Bankers Trust. There, the alleged attorney fraud was discovered during the pendency of the original trial, and the falsity of the statement in question was argued at the summary judgment stage and on appeal. Id. We decline to apply the reasoning of Bankers Trust to this case because when the complaint is viewed in the light most favorable to Chewning, it does not appear he had the opportunity to litigate the issue of attorney involvement in perjury at trial.

Chewning alleges a scheme of perjury and failure to produce documents perpetuated by attorneys. In Davis v. Davis, 236 S.C. 277, 113 S.E.2d 819 (1960), fraud on the court, specifically distinguished from fraud as now contemplated by Rule 60(b)(3), was found where an attorney in a divorce action did not file the opposing side's answer and then represented to the court that the opposing party was in default. Affirming the trial court's decision to vacate the default decree, the court found, "This reasonably may be held to have been extrinsic fraud upon her and upon the court." Id. at 281, 113 S.E.2d 821. This holding is consistent with attorney disciplinary opinions finding attorney misrepresentations to be fraud upon the court. See, e.g., In re Celsor, 330 S.C. 497, 501, 499 S.E.2d 809, 811 (1998) (finding improper signature without valid power of attorney, notarization of that signature, and misrepresentation to court to be fraud upon the court); In re Jennings, 321 S.C. 440, 446, 468 S.E.2d 869, 873 (1996) (holding forgery of signature on court document is fraud upon the court). Therefore, we find Chewning has alleged sufficient facts to show extrinsic fraud upon the court.

Moreover, federal jurisprudence supports this holding. Because Rule 60(b), SCRCP was modeled after Rule 60(b), FRCP, we take instruction from federal cases discussing fraud upon the court. The seminal case on this topic is Hazel-Atlas Glass Co. v. Hartford-Empire Co., 322 U.S. 238 (1944). In Hazel-Atlas, the Supreme Court set aside a judgment after more than one year because it found a party and its attorneys engaged in "a deliberately planned and carefully executed scheme to defraud" the patent office and the circuit court of appeals. Id. at 245. As a result, the Court held it would be manifestly unconscionable to allow the judgment to stand. Id.

Although perjury alone will not serve to vacate a judgment, it is considered fraud upon the court when it involves or is suborned by an attorney. See generally Moore's Federal Practice, supra, at § 60.21[4][b] & [c]. "Involvement of an attorney, as an officer of the court, in a scheme to suborn perjury would certainly be considered fraud on the court." Great Coastal Express, Inc. v. Int'l Bhd. of Teamsters, 675 F.2d 1349, 1357 (4th Cir. 1982); see also Meindl v. Genesys Pac. Techs., Inc., 204 F.3d 124, 130 (4th Cir.) ("[F]raud upon the court includes fraud by bribing a judge, or tampering with a jury, or fraud by an officer of the court, including an attorney."); Cleveland Demolition Co. v. Azcon Scrap Corp., 827 F.2d 984, 986 (4th Cir. 1987) ("A verdict may be set aside for fraud on the court if an attorney and a witness have conspired to present perjured testimony."). In Great Coastal, the court did not find fraud upon the court because it determined the behavior complained of involved primarily the two parties and did not show either a plan to subvert the judicial process or a threat of public injury. Here, the complaint alleges an ongoing plot between Ford, Ford's attorneys, and a witness to hide the truth in a series of products liability cases. If proven, these facts would constitute a scheme resulting in harm to the public at large and would result in the type of fraud envisioned in Hazel-Atlas and Great Coastal.

As an additional sustaining ground, the trial court found that Chewning's amended complaint did not satisfy Rule 9(b), SCRCP, because Chewning did not "identify any alleged perjured testimony by Bickerstaff in the underlying products liability trial, only subsequent testimony from cases after Chewning's." We disagree. After a careful analysis of the complaint, we find that Chewning did plead with specificity that Bickerstaff gave untruthful testimony at Chewning's trial that the Bronco II "was designed in a safe and reliable manner." Therefore, we find the trial judge erred in finding this as an additional sustaining ground.

In considering relief from a final judgment, "the balance is drawn between finality of judgments, on the one hand, and preserving the court's fundamental purpose of providing a fair and just resolution of disputes, on the other." Hagy, 331 S.C. at 221, 500 S.E.2d at 172. Based on Davis and federal jurisprudence, we find Chewning's complaint states a claim for fraud upon the court. If Chewning's allegations are true, it would be manifestly unjust for the original judgment to stand. Accordingly, we reverse the circuit judge's dismissal order and remand the fraud upon the court claim for proceedings consistent with this opinion.

CITES AND AUTHORITIES

CHRISTOPHER TODD OLSON, PETITIONER, V. CHARLES L. RYAN, ET AL., RESPONDENTS.

No. CV-12-02578-PHX-SMM (BSB) UNITED STATES DISTRICT COURT FOR THE DISTRICT OF ARIZONA

(Text added/modified for emphasis). The Attorney General failed to disclose that in Arizona it is the norm for appointed PCR counsel not to raise all federal claims. Failure to disclose this systemic problem is fraud upon the court.

COUNSEL: Christopher Todd Olson, also named as: Chris Olson and Christopher T. Olson, Petitioner, Pro se, BUCKEYE, AZ. For Attorney General of the State of Arizona, Charles L Ryan, named as Chuck Ryan, Respondents: Linley Sarah Wilson, LEAD ATTORNEY, Office of the Attorney General - Phoenix, Phoenix, AZ.

2. Grounds Three and Four

In Ground Three, Petitioner argues that trial counsel Sonia Martinez (Nayeri) provided ineffective assistance of counsel in violation of the *Sixth Amendment* because she "let the court [] have jury trial without [him when Petitioner] tried to get a day off because [he] was sick," did not get a plea bargain for Petitioner, and "let the court [] use priors over 10 years old" at sentencing. (Doc. 5 at 9.) Petitioner also asserts that his initial post-conviction attorney, Pamela Eaton, "wasted a year of [his] time." (*Id.*) Eaton was appointed as post-conviction counsel in September 2011. (Doc. 16, Ex. J.) The trial court later removed her and appointed Janelle MacEachern to represent Petitioner. (Doc. 16, Ex. K.) At the time of Petitioner's trial, his counsel went by the last name Nayeri. (Doc. 16, Exs. B-D.) She later went by the last name Martinez. (*Id.*, Ex. E.)

Petitioner did not raise these claims of ineffective assistance of trial counsel and post-conviction counsel in any state court. Although he made some allegations that post conviction counsel MacEachern was "lazy" (Doc. 16, Ex. N, Doc. 16-1 at 118), he did not argue that trial counsel Martinez, or his initial post-conviction attorney Eaton, were ineffective on the grounds that he now asserts in his Amended Petition. Moreover, even if Petitioner's claim that post-conviction counsel Eaton was ineffective was properly exhausted and could provide a basis for *§ 2254* relief, he would not be entitling to relief based on his allegation that Eaton "wasted a year of [his] time." Petitioner's unsupported, conclusory allegations are not sufficient to support a claim for federal habeas relief. *See Jones v. Gomez, 66 F.3d 199, 204-05 (9th Cir.*

1995) (stating that conclusory allegations with no reference to the record or other evidence do not warrant habeas relief). Even if Eaton wasted time, Petitioner has not shown that he was prejudiced because the trial court appointed Petitioner new post-conviction counsel, and Petitioner ultimately filed a pro per petition asserting his claims for review.

Even if the Court were to construe Plaintiff's allegation that post-conviction counsel MacEachern was "lazy" as a claim of ineffective assistance of counsel, that claim is not the same as the ineffective assistance of counsel claims that he now asserts in Ground Three of the Amended Petition. Ineffective assistance of counsel claims is highly fact-dependent. *Hemmerle v. Arizona, 495 F.3d 1069, 1075 (9th Cir. 2007)*. Thus, a petitioner's assertion in state court that he received ineffective assistance does not satisfy the fair presentation requirement unless the petitioner alleges ineffective assistance of counsel on the same grounds in his federal habeas petition. *See Moormann v. Schriro, 426 F.3d 1044, 1056 (9th Cir. 2005)* (finding that the petitioner "did not present these claims of ineffective assistance in state court, and we cannot address them on habeas review"). Because Petitioner did not present the same claims of ineffective assistance in state court that he asserts in Ground Three, he did not properly exhaust those claims.

....

1. Ineffective Assistance of Post-Conviction Counsel

To establish "cause" to overcome the procedural bar of his claims, Petitioner argues that he was denied the effective assistance of counsel on post-conviction review. (Doc. 19 at 5-7.) Petitioner relies on the Supreme Court's decision in *Martinez v. Ryan, U.S. , 132 S. Ct. 1309, 1315, 182 L. Ed. 2d 272 (2012)*, which held that the ineffective assistance of post-conviction counsel, while not stating a constitutional claim itself, can be a sufficient equitable reason, or a "cause," to excuse defaulted claims of ineffective assistance of trial counsel when a post-conviction proceeding represents the first opportunity under state law for a petitioner to raise claims of ineffective assistance of trial counsel.

Thus, under *Martinez*, the procedural default may be excused if there is "cause" for the default. The Court in *Martinez* established a four-part test to determine whether the ineffective assistance of post-conviction counsel will excuse the procedural default of a claim of ineffective assistance of trial counsel. "Cause" is established under *Martinez* when:

> (1) the claim of "ineffective assistance of trial counsel" was a "substantial" claim; (2) the "cause" consisted of there being "no counsel" or only "ineffective" counsel during the state collateral review proceeding; (3) the state collateral review proceeding was the "initial" review proceeding in respect to the "ineffective-assistance-of-trial-counsel claim"; and (4) state law requires that an "ineffective assistance of trial counsel [claim] . . . be raised in an initial-review collateral review proceeding.

Trevino v. Thaler, U.S., 133 S. Ct. 1911, 1918, 185 L. Ed. 2d 1044 (2013) (alterations in original).

Because *Martinez* applies only to defaulted ineffective assistance of counsel claims, it is potentially applicable only to Petitioner's claim of ineffective assistance of trial counsel asserted in Ground Three. *See Ha Van Nguyen v. Curry, 736 F.3d 1287, 1296 (9th Cir. 2013)* (holding that "the *Martinez* standard for cause applies to all *Sixth Amendment* ineffective-assistance claims, both to trial and appellate, that have been procedurally defaulted by ineffective counsel in the initial-review state-court collateral proceeding."). As discussed below, Petitioner has not established cause under *Martinez*.

2. *Martinez* Analysis of Ground Three

Under the *Martinez* test, Petitioner must first show a "substantial" underlying ineffective assistance of trial counsel claim. A "substantial" claim is a claim that "has some merit." *Martinez, 132 S. Ct. at 1318*. Similar to the standard for issuing a certificate of appealability, "substantially" requires the petitioner to demonstrate that "reasonable jurists could debate whether . . . the petition should have been resolved in a different manner or that the issues presented were adequate to deserve encouragement to proceed further." *Detrich v. Ryan, 740 F.3d 1237, 1245 (9th Cir. 2013)* (internal quotations omitted).

Whether Petitioner's claims of ineffective assistance are analyzed on the merits, or for substantiality under the first prong of *Martinez*, the result is the same: Petitioner's claims have no substantial merit. To prevail on a claim of ineffective assistance of counsel, Petitioner must (1) show that counsel's performance fell below objective standards of reasonableness and was "outside the wide range of professionally competent assistance," and (2) establish that counsel's performance prejudiced him by creating "a reasonable probability that absent the errors the fact finder would have had a reasonable doubt respecting guilt." *Strickland v. Washington, 466 U.S. 668, 687-94, 104 S. Ct. 2052, 80 L. Ed. 2d 674 (1984).*

In Ground Three, Petitioner argues that trial counsel was ineffective for "let[ting]" the court proceed with the jury trial in Petitioner's absence. As discussed below in Section III(B), the trial court did not err in continuing trial when Petitioner absented himself due to an illness. Accordingly, any objection to the court's decision to proceed in Petitioner's absence would have been futile. Failure to take futile action does not constitute deficient performance. *See Rupe v. Wood, 93 F.3d 1434, 1445 (9th Cir. 1996); Sexton v. Cozner, 679 F.3d 1150, 1157 (9th Cir. 2012).* "The failure to raise a meritless legal argument does not constitute ineffective assistance of counsel." *Baumann v. United States, 692 F.2d 565, 572 (9th Cir. 1982).* Accordingly, Petitioner does not have a substantial claim that he was prejudiced by trial counsel's alleged error in failing to object to the trial proceeding in his absence, and *Martinez* does not excuse his default of that ineffective assistance of counsel claim.

Petitioner also claims that trial counsel was ineffective for failing to obtain a plea bargain. The negotiation of a plea bargain is "'a critical phase of litigation for purposes of the *Sixth Amendment* right to effective assistance of counsel.'" *Missouri v. Frye, U.S., 132 S. Ct. 1399, 1406, 182 L. Ed. 2d 379 (2012)* (quoting *Padilla v. Kentucky, 559 U.S. 356, 373, 130 S. Ct. 1473, 176 L. Ed. 2d 284 (2010)).* If counsel has misadvised a defendant about the law during a plea negotiation, or improperly coerced a defendant to accept a plea bargain, counsel's performance may be found deficient. *See Lafler v. Cooper, U.S., 132 S. Ct. 1376, 1384, 182 L. Ed. 2d 398 (2012)* (counsel's erroneous legal advice about possibility of conviction that led to rejection of plea offer constituted deficient performance). Additionally, "[i]f a plea bargain has been offered, a defendant has the right to effective assistance of counsel in considering whether to accept it." *Id. at 1387.*

To show prejudice from ineffective assistance of counsel "where a plea offer has lapsed or been rejected because of counsel's deficient performance, [a petitioner] must demonstrate a reasonable probability" that (1) he "would have accepted the earlier plea offer," and (2) "the plea would have been entered without the prosecution canceling it or the trial court refusing to accept it, if they had the authority to exercise that discretion under state law." *Frye, 132 S. Ct. at 1409.* Here, while Petitioner argues that trial counsel was ineffective for failing to obtain a plea bargain, he does not allege that a plea was offered, that counsel failed to communicate a plea offer, or that counsel gave him erroneous advice about any particular plea offer. (Doc. 5 at 9.) Petitioner's "conclusory suggestions that his trial . . . counsel provided ineffective assistance fall far short of stating a valid claim of constitutional violation." *See Jones, 66 F.3d at 205.*

Finally, Petitioner asserts that trial counsel was ineffective for failing to object to the court's use of prior convictions that were over ten years old. As the post-conviction court found, Petitioner admitted that he had four prior felony convictions at the time of sentencing. (Doc. 16, Ex. X at 3-14.) Thus, he was sentenced under *Ariz. Rev. Stat. § 13-105(22) (d)*, which defines "historical prior felony conviction" to include "[a]ny felony conviction that is a third or more prior felony conviction," without regard to the date of those convictions.

Because Petitioner had four prior felony convictions, the trial court correctly assessed Petitioner with two historical prior felonies. *See State v. Provenzino, 221 Ariz. 364, 212 P.3d 56, 58 n.4 (Ariz. Ct. App. 2009)* (noting that the definition of a historical prior felony conviction includes any felony conviction that is a third or more prior felony conviction). Thus, the trial court properly considered Petitioner's third and fourth prior convictions, even though they otherwise would have been too old to be considered as prior historical felonies under other subsections of the statute. *See Ariz. Rev. Stat. § 13-105(22) (b) and (c).* Thus, trial counsel was not ineffective for failing to object to Petitioner's sentence on that basis and Petitioner has not presented a substantial claim of ineffective assistance of counsel.

Accordingly, the ineffective assistance of post-conviction counsel does not excuse Petitioner's procedural default of his claims of ineffective assistance of trial counsel. Because Petitioner's ineffective assistance of counsel claims in Ground Three do not satisfy the first prong of the *Martinez* test, the Court does not address the remaining prongs of the test.

BEAU JOHN GREENE, PETITIONER, VS. CHARLES L. RYAN, ET AL., RESPONDENTS.

No. CV-03-605-TUC-FRZ UNITED STATES DISTRICT COURT FOR THE DISTRICT OF ARIZONA

(Text added/modified for emphasis) It is common practice in Arizona for lawyers to have their clients provide false testimony to state courts thereby preventing a fair trial. Aware of the existence of this practice the Attorney general perpetrates fraud upon the court by asking federal courts to preclude review and not making this disclosure.

COUNSEL: For Beau John Greene, Petitioner: Jennifer Y Garcia, LEAD ATTORNEY, Federal Public Defenders Office, Phoenix, AZ; Leticia Marquez, LEAD ATTORNEY, Federal Public Defenders Office, Tucson, AZ. For Dora Schriro, Director Arizona Department of Corrections, Charles Goldsmith, Warden, Arizona State Prison - Eyman Complex, Respondents: Kent E Cattani, LEAD ATTORNEY, Office of the Attorney General, Criminal Appeals Section, Phoenix, AZ.

..

Claim 4: Ineffective Assistance of Counsel

Petitioner alleges that trial counsel performed ineffectively by calling him as a witness and advising him to testify untruthfully (Claim 4-A); by failing to file a motion to vacate the judgment after two witnesses came forward to support Petitioner's defense (4-B); and by failing to present expert evidence in mitigation at sentencing (4-C (3)).

Clearly established federal law

Claims of ineffective assistance of counsel are governed by the principles set forth in *Strickland v. Washington, 466 U.S. 668, 104 S. Ct. 2052, 80 L. Ed. 2d 674 (1984)*. To prevail under *Strickland,* a petitioner must show that counsel's representation fell below an objective standard of reasonableness and that the deficiency prejudiced the defense. *Id. at 687-88.*

The inquiry under *Strickland* is highly deferential, and "every effort [must] be made to eliminate the distorting effects of hindsight, to reconstruct the circumstances of counsel's challenged conduct, and to evaluate the conduct from counsel's perspective at the time." *Id. at 689; see Wong v. Belmontes, U.S., 130 S. Ct. 383, 384, 175 L. Ed. 2d 328 (2009)* (per curiam); *Bobby v. Van Hook, U.S., 130 S. Ct. 13, 16, 175 L. Ed. 2d 255 (2009)* (per curiam). Thus, to satisfy *Strickland's first* prong, a defendant must overcome "the presumption that, under the circumstances, the challenged action might be considered sound trial strategy." *Id.* "The test has nothing to do with what the best lawyers would have done. Nor is the test even what best lawyers would have done. We ask only whether some reasonable lawyer at the trial could have acted, in the circumstances, as defense counsel acted at trial." *Id. at 687-88.*

With respect to *Strickland's* second prong, a petitioner must affirmatively prove prejudice by "show[ing] that there is a reasonable probability that, but for counsel's unprofessional errors, the result of the proceeding would have been different. A reasonable probability is a probability sufficient to undermine confidence in the outcome." *Strickland, 466 U.S. at 694.*

Because an ineffective assistance of counsel claim must satisfy both prongs of *Strickland,* the reviewing court "need not determine whether counsel's performance was deficient before examining the prejudice suffered by the defendant as a result of the alleged deficiencies." *Id. at 697* ("if it is easier to dispose of an ineffectiveness claim on the ground of lack of sufficient prejudice . . . that course should be followed").

Under the AEDPA, this Court's review of the state court's decision is subject to another level of deference. *Bell v. Cone, 535 U.S. 685, 698-99, 122 S. Ct. 1843, 152 L. Ed. 2d 914 (2002); see Knowles v. Mirzayance, 129 S. Ct. 1411, 1420, 173 L. Ed. 2d 251 (2009)* (noting that a "doubly deferential" standard applies to *Strickland* claims under the AEDPA).

Therefore, to prevail on this claim, Petitioner must make the additional showing that the state court, in ruling that counsel was not ineffective, applied *Strickland* in an objectively unreasonable manner. *28 U.S.C. § 2254(d)(1)*.

Claim 4-A

Petitioner alleges that counsel performed ineffectively by presenting his testimony and advising him to testify untruthfully regarding the manner in which he killed the victim. (Dkt. 82 at 72-76.) Petitioner contends that this element of counsel's performance prejudiced him at both the guilt and sentencing stages of trial. Petitioner also alleged in Claim 4-A that counsel performed ineffectively by failing to present expert testimony during the guilt phase of trial. The Court found that this aspect of the claim was procedurally barred. (Dkt. 86 at 17.) In Claim 4-C (3) below, the Court addresses Petitioner's challenge to counsel's [*14] handling of expert testimony at sentencing.

Background

At trial and sentencing Petitioner was represented by Jill Thorpe and David Darby, with Darby as lead counsel. (RT 9/9/02 at 12, 17.) Thorpe was primarily responsible for the sentencing stage of trial. (*Id.* at 12.) A third attorney, Julie Duval, also assisted the defense. (*Id.* at 86-87.)

....

Petitioner raised claims of ineffective assistance of counsel in his PCR petition. The court held an evidentiary hearing. Petitioner's trial counsel testified, along with a *Strickland* expert. Petitioner also testified.

At the hearing, Thorpe testified that prior to his trial testimony Petitioner informed defense counsel that he had struck Johnson with a weighted, lead-lined "sap glove." (*Id.* at 18, 44-46; *see id.* at 90, 128.) Thorpe testified that Petitioner's story about the sap glove was the "third or fourth version" he had given as to how he killed Johnson. (*Id.* at 16.) Petitioner also provided the information about the sap glove to Dr. Philip Kanof, a toxicologist retained by the defense. (*Id.* at 18-19, 128.) According to Thorpe, Dr. Kanof orally informed her that he was prepared to testify that Petitioner was suffering from methamphetamine-induced psychosis at the time of the murder. (*Id.* at 19.)

Darby testified that his goal in defending Petitioner was to avoid a first-degree murder conviction. (*Id.* at 70.) He was convinced there was a good chance Petitioner would be convicted of second-degree murder and confident Petitioner would not be sentenced to death. (*Id.* at 53, 65, 70, 11.) Darby also believed Petitioner would be granted a new trial or relief on appeal based on the trial court's failure to provide lesser-included murder instructions. (*Id.* at 20-22.) Darby and Thorpe concluded that evidence showing Petitioner used a weapon to kill the victim would be harmful to the defense because it indicated premeditation. (*Id.* at 48, 53, 71.) It would also provide support for the cruel, heinous, or depraved aggravating factor. (*Id.* at 29.) Finally, in counsel's view, the evidence would potentially jeopardize the defense on retrial. (*Id.* at 21-22.) Because Dr. Kanof was aware that Petitioner had used a weapon to kill the victim, Darby chose not to present his testimony at trial or at sentencing and risk the possible negative consequences resulting from disclosure of the sap glove evidence. (*Id.* at 52-53.) Co-counsel Thorpe agreed with this strategy, and drafted a memorandum documenting their decision, which Petitioner signed after discussing the matter with counsel. (*Id.* at 20-24, 52-53; *see* Petition for Review, 3/17/03, Ex. E.)

However, counsel also determined that Petitioner's testimony was necessary to support the defense theory that Petitioner did not act with premeditation, but reacted spontaneously to the victim's homosexual advances. (*Id.* at 33, 60-61, 77.) According to Darby, Petitioner testified willingly. (*Id.* at 75.) Darby advised Petitioner not to volunteer information about the sap glove but to answer truthfully if the question was raised on cross-examination. (*Id.* at 46, 48, 56, 131.)

Petitioner's *Strickland* expert, a criminal defense attorney named Bret Huggins, testified that Darby performed at a constitutionally deficient level. (*Id.* at 98.) Huggins stated that he could see no benefit to calling Petitioner as a witness at the guilt phase of trial. (*Id.* at 101-02.) Petitioner's testimony that he struck the victim with his bare hand was discredited by the evidence from the medical examiner; as a result, the jury saw Petitioner as a liar. (*Id.* at 101) Huggins conceded, however, that the outcome of the guilt stage of trial would not have changed if

Petitioner's testimony had been omitted. (*Id.* at 119.) Huggins also testified that counsel performed ineffectively at sentencing by failing to call Dr. Kanof, whose testimony would have supported the impaired capacity statutory mitigating factor. (*Id.* at 103.) Huggins also testified that he would not have recommended that Petitioner testify more forthcoming and reveal that he had used a sap glove to strike the victim. (*Id.* at 101-02.)

According to Petitioner's testimony at the evidentiary hearing, he was under the impression that he would not testify at trial because counsel had never discussed the issue with him. (*Id.* at 129, 132.) Petitioner stated that the night before he testified Darby and Thorpe met with him for an hour or less. (*Id.* at 130.) They told him he needed to testify in order to avoid a first-degree murder conviction and death sentence. (*Id.*) It was only at this point, according to Petitioner, that Darby asked him about the facts of the murder. (*Id.*) When Petitioner told him about using the sap glove, Darby explained that such information would be damaging and that Petitioner should simply testify that he struck the victim with his hand. (*Id.* at 131.) According to Petitioner, Darby told him that such testimony would be technically true and Petitioner would not be testifying falsely, as long as the prosecutor did not ask him if he had anything on his hand. (*Id.* at 131-32.) Petitioner had confidence in his attorneys and followed their advice. (*Id.* at 132.) When asked at the evidentiary hearing what alternative strategy the defense should have pursued, Petitioner responded: "I could have not testified. I could have gotten on the stand and told a different story. I could have lied in a different fashion. I could have had my attorney try to fight the testimony of the State's witnesses." (*Id.* at 154.)

The PCR court rejected Petitioner's claim that counsel performed ineffectively by presenting his testimony. The court, noting that Petitioner's own *Strickland* expert testified that there was no reasonable probability of a different verdict if Petitioner had not testified falsely, found that Petitioner had not been prejudiced by counsel's performance. (ME 1/10/03 at 2.) The court further explained:

> The basic problem with Defendant's argument is its logic. A defendant who falsely claims to have killed a victim in a rage does not thereby provide a jury with sufficient evidence to

convict him of killing with premeditation. Such a conviction must be established, as it was in this case, by evidence other than that of the Defendant's lies. Accordingly, the Court finds that Defendant's false testimony played no role in his convictions.

Similarly, his false testimony did not influence the Court's sentencing decisions. . .. The Court arrived at its decision to sentence Petitioner to death based solely on the aggravating and mitigating evidence. Defendant's untruthful testimony neither established aggravation nor rebutted mitigation. Accordingly, the Court finds that Defendant's false testimony played no role in its choice of sentences.

. . . Defendant argues that his trial counsel was ineffective for even calling him to testify. . .. As noted above, the Court finds no connection between Defendant's untruthful testimony and his convictions and sentence. He thus fails to prove that he was prejudiced by his decision to testify. In any event, the decision to testify was his, not his counsel's, though the decision was made with counsel's advice.

(*Id.* at 3-4.) Because the PCR court's ruling focused on *Strickland's* prejudice prong, and given the *Strickland* court's instruction to dispose of ineffective assistance claims based on lack of prejudice where it is easier to do so, *466 U.S. at 697*, this Court will not make a determination as to the reasonableness of counsel's strategic decisions.

Analysis

The PCR court's rejection of this claim was not based on an unreasonable application of *Strickland.* Petitioner's testimony did not prejudice him at the guilt stage of trial. As the state court noted, Petitioner's false version of events did not provide support for a finding of premeditation. Nor was there a reasonable probability of a different verdict if Petitioner had testified truthfully about the weapon used to kill the victim or if he had remained silent and left uncontested the evidence suggesting he acted with premeditation and for pecuniary gain in attacking the victim and taking his car and wallet. Moreover, without

Petitioner's testimony, the jury would have been left with no information about Petitioner's condition at the time of the crime, including the fact that he was suffering the effects of withdrawal after a nearly week-long methamphetamine binge.

The cases Petitioner relies on are distinguishable. For example, in *Johnson v. Baldwin, 114 F.3d 835 (9th Cir. 1997)*, the defendant provided uncorroborated and unconvincing testimony that he was not present at the scene of the crime. The court found that counsel's failure to investigate the defendant's "incredibly lame" alibi and confront him with the "difficulties of his story" constituted ineffective assistance of counsel. *Id. at 838.* If counsel had conducted such an investigation and challenged the defendant with its results, the defendant "probably would not have elected to lie to the jury." *Id. at 840.* Counsel's performance was prejudicial because the State's case against the defendant was "extremely weak" and the jury's "adverse credibility determination . . . probably tipped the scale against him." *Id.* In Petitioner's case, by contrast, there was no failure to investigate; counsel was aware of Petitioner's latest version of the killing. In addition, the case against Petitioner was not weak; he admitted killing the victim, and it was only his testimony that provided any alternative to the State's evidence that the killing was premeditated. *See Carter v. Lee, 283 F.3d 240, 249-53 (4th Cir. 2002)* (rejecting ineffective assistance claim based on petitioner's contention that he was "forced" to testify when counsel advised him that his testimony was necessary to support diminished capacity defense, and finding no prejudice where case against petitioner was strong); *United States v. Sanchez-Cervantes, 282 F.3d 664, 672 (9th Cir. 2002)* (advising defendant to testify was not an objectively unreasonable strategic decision and there was no prejudice because evidence against defendant was strong).

Another reason the Court cannot find prejudice is because Petitioner has offered alternate versions of what his truthful testimony would have been. According to the memorandum he signed for trial counsel, as well as an affidavit drafted for the PCR proceedings, Petitioner told counsel and Dr. Kanof that when the victim placed his hand on Petitioner's knee, he reached into his "fanny pack," grabbed the sap glove, and struck Johnson repeatedly. (Petition for Review,

3/17/93, Ex. C.) At the PCR evidentiary hearing, however, Petitioner testified that he donned the glove when he stepped outside the vehicle to use the restroom; he intended to use the glove to threaten Johnson if he refused to drive him back to town. (RT 9/9/02 at 158-60.) Petitioner argues that instead of presenting either version of his truthful testimony, the strategically better alternative would have been not to call Petitioner to testify on his own behalf. Again, this would have left the jury with no explanation for the crime beyond the most damaging version presented through the State's evidence.

ABRAAN RENE ORTIZ, PETITIONER, VS. CHARLES L. RYAN, ET AL., RESPONDENTS.

No. CV-11-626-TUC-FRZ-DTF UNITED STATES DISTRICT COURT FOR THE DISTRICT OF ARIZONA

(Text added/modified for emphasis) It is common practice in Arizona for lawyers not to fairly present their federal claims to state courts thereby preventing federal habeas review. Aware of the existence of this practice the Attorney general perpetrates fraud upon the court by asking federal courts to preclude review and not making this disclosure.

COUNSEL: Abraan Rene Ortiz, Petitioner, Pro se, TUCSON, AZ. For Charles L Ryan, Respondent: Laura Patrice Chiasson, LEAD ATTORNEY, Office of the Attorney General, Tucson, AZ.

MERITS ANALYSIS

Standard for Ineffective Assistance of Counsel Claims
The governing federal standard for claims of ineffective assistance of counsel is set forth in *Strickland v. Washington, 466 U.S. 668, 686, 104 S. Ct. 2052, 80 L. Ed. 2d 674 (1984)*, which recognizes a right to "effective assistance of counsel" arising under the *Sixth Amendment*. The *Strickland* standard for IAC has two components. A defendant must first demonstrate that counsel's performance was deficient, *i.e.*, that

counsel made errors so serious that counsel was not functioning as the "counsel" guaranteed a defendant by the *Sixth Amendment*. *466 U.S. at 687*. It requires the defendant to show that counsel's conduct "fell below an objective standard of reasonableness." *Id. at 687-88*. Counsel's performance is strongly presumed to fall within the ambit of reasonable conduct unless petitioner can show otherwise. *Id. at 689-90*. Second, a defendant must show that the mistakes made were "prejudicial to the defense," that is, the mistakes created a "reasonable probability that, but for [the] unprofessional errors, the result of the proceeding would have been different." *Id. at 694*. A court need not address both prongs of an ineffectiveness claim, if it is easier to dispose of it solely by assessing prejudice, the court is free to do so. *Id. at 697*.

Claim 1(b)
Petitioner alleges that trial and appellate counsel failed to challenge the search on the proper grounds. The PCR court set forth the following background relevant to this claim:

> On November 30th, two TPD officers approached a parked vehicle with a temporary license plate. The officers had noticed that the lights to the vehicle were off and that there were two passengers inside. When one of the officers approached the vehicle, the occupants rolled down the window and the officer encountered a strong odor of unburnt marijuana. The second officer then approached and also detected the odor and the occupants were asked to exit the vehicle. When the occupants had exited the vehicle Officer Currier informed the Defendant of his intention to search the vehicle. The officers searched the car for marijuana including a lunch box that was in the back seat of the vehicle. Inside the lunch box the officers found what appeared to be cocaine, a measuring spoon, an air freshener, and a small scale.

(Doc. 10, Ex. F at 1-2.) The Court then addressed Petitioner's claim that counsel was ineffective for failing to challenge the search of the lunch box.

With respect to trial counsel, the PCR court found he had made the argument that Petitioner was alleging he failed to make. After the close of testimony at the suppression hearing, counsel argued that Officer Currier did not have permission to search the car and "certainly didn't have permission to search in the lunch box, which is another container, and he specified that the odor wasn't emanating from the container." (*Id.* at 3.) The court followed up with the prosecution, asking, "even though they are searching the vehicle, is there -- do they not need to get a search warrant just to search the lunch container. I mean, that is going -- it's not going anywhere." (*Id.*) The court further inquired, "but do you believe that the lunch box is part of the vehicle search." (*Id.*) Based on these facts, the court found that counsel had made the argument in question and that the trial court understood that counsel was asking for suppression specifically as to the lunch box search; therefore, it found Petitioner had not satisfied either prong of the *Strickland* standard. (*Id.* at 3-4.) The appellate court similarly found that the trial court considered the propriety of the search of the lunchbox. (Doc. 10, Ex. I at 6.) The court found, therefore, that Petitioner was not prejudiced by counsel's actions. (*Id.*)

This Court must defer to facts as found by the state court, unless rebutted by clear and convincing evidence. *28 U.S.C. § 2254(e)(1).* The state courts' fact finding is dispositive of this claim. The state courts found that the trial judge ruled on the question Petitioner argued his counsel failed to raise. Petitioner has not argued that this finding was in error nor presented any evidence to rebut it. The Court reviewed the transcript from the suppression hearing, including the court's ruling, and concludes that the state courts' fact finding was not unreasonable in light of the record, *see 28 U.S.C. § 2254(d)(2).* Because the trial court addressed the claim, even if not clearly raised by counsel, Petitioner was not prejudiced. The state courts' denial of this claim, as to trial counsel, was not an unreasonable application of *Strickland.*

With respect to appellate counsel, Petitioner alleges she should have argued that, even if there was probable cause to search the car, there was not probable cause to search the lunch box. Because this claim was denied by the state court on the merits but without any rationale (Doc. 10, Ex. I), the Court independently reviews the record but defers to the state court's ultimate decision to deny the claim, *see Pirtle v. Morgan, 313 F.3d 1160, 1167 (9th Cir. 2002)*.

In evaluating prejudice, the Court assesses whether there is a reasonable probability that the claim would have been successful if counsel had raised it on appeal. *See Moormann v. Ryan, 628 F.3d 1102, 1106 (9th Cir. 2010)*. "If probable cause justifies the search of a lawfully stopped vehicle, it justifies the search of every part of the vehicle and its contents that may conceal the object of the search." *United States v. Ross, 456 U.S. 798, 825, 102 S. Ct. 2157, 72 L. Ed. 2d 572 (1982)*. Thus, the scope of an automobile search is "defined by the object of the search and the places in which there is probable cause to believe that it may be found." *Id. at 824*. For example, if there is probable cause to believe undocumented aliens are being transported in a van, that will not justify a warrantless search of a suitcase. *Id.*

Petitioner argues that the search of the lunchbox lacked probable cause because an officer testified that the scent of marijuana was not emanating from the lunch box. Officer Currier testified that a strong odor of unburnt marijuana was coming from the interior of the car. (Doc. 10, Ex. U at 19.) On cross-examination, he responded with "No" to the question, "Now, the odor was not emanating from the lunch box; correct?" (*Id.* at 21.)

The lunchbox was in the passenger compartment of the car, which is where the odor was detected by two officers. Thus, there was probable cause to search that area of the car. Further, some quantity of marijuana could fit inside a lunchbox. Therefore, there was probable cause to search the box. Trial counsel did not establish if Officer Currier determined there was no scent of marijuana emanating from the lunchbox prior to opening it. His testimony could readily be interpreted as indicating that he did not find marijuana in the lunchbox, thus, it was not producing the odor. Petitioner was not prejudiced because there was not a reasonable probability that, if this claim had been raised on appeal, it would have been successful. This conclusion is bolstered by the fact that the Arizona Court of Appeals denied Petitioner's claim as to appellate counsel.

SANJAY BABULAL GOHEL, PETITIONER -VS- CHARLES L. RYAN, RESPONDENT.

CV-10-0001-PHX-FJM (JFM)

UNITED STATES DISTRICT COURT FOR THE DISTRICT OF ARIZONA

(Text added/modified for emphasis) It is common practice in Arizona for lawyers not to fairly present their federal claims to state courts thereby preventing federal habeas review. Aware of the existence of this practice the Attorney general perpetrates fraud upon the court by asking federal courts to preclude review and not making this disclosure.

COUNSEL: For Sanjay Babulal Gohel, also named as: Sanjay B. Gohel, Petitioner: Christine Corey Whalin, LEAD ATTORNEY, David Michael Cantor, Law Offices of David Michael Cantor PC, Phoenix, AZ; John Richard Gustafson, Law Offices of David Michael Cantor PC, Tempe, AZ. For Charles L Ryan, Director of the Arizona Department of Corrections, Terry L Goddard, The Attorney General of the State of Arizona, Respondents: Amy M Thorson, Office of the Attorney General, Tucson, AZ.

II. RELEVANT FACTUAL & PROCEDURAL BACKGROUND

A. FACTUAL BACKGROUND

As summarized by the Arizona Court of Appeals on direct appeal, evidence at trial showed that on four separate occasions, Petitioner tried to hire someone to kill his wife, Jaimini. The first three attempts fell through, but in June 1997 Petitioner asked co-inductee Falcon, a frequent shopper in Petitioner's grocery store, to kill her. Falcon offered to find someone else to commit the murder for the $8000 offered by Petitioner. This person was Falcon's co-worker Munoz, known as "El Gato." Over the next month, Petitioner made periodic payments to Falcon and Munoz, drove them to both his home in Peoria and his wife's place of business, showed them his wife's car, invited Munoz to his grocery store at a time his wife would be there so Munoz could identify her, and provided Munoz with the handheld remote for entry to his wife's car. (Pet. Exhibit 3, Mem. Dec. 3/27/03 at 2.) Exhibits numbered 1 through 23 (Doc. 4) to the Original Petition (Doc. 1) (which are incorporated by reference in the Amended Petition (Doc. 12) (*see* Doc. 13 at 2)), Exhibits numbered 24 through 27 (Doc. 13) to the Amended Petition (Doc. 12), and Exhibits numbered 28 through 30 to the Reply (Doc. 21) are numbered sequentially, and are referenced herein as "Pet. Exhibit." Exhibits to Respondents' Answer (Doc. 15) are referenced herein as "Resp. Exhibit." Exhibits to Respondents' Supplemental Answer (Docs. 26, 27 and 28) are labeled, and are referenced herein as "Supp. Exhibit."

In the early morning of July 31, 1997, Munoz used the remote control to enter Petitioner's wife's car, which was parked in the driveway of Petitioner's home. He then hid under a coat in the back seat, provided by Petitioner for this purpose. When Petitioner's wife entered the vehicle to drive to work, she began backing out of the driveway. Munoz shot her twice in the head, killing her. A neighbor called 9-1-1 after hearing the noise and witnessing a Hispanic male run from the scene. (*Id.*at 3.)

B. PROCEEDINGS AT TRIAL

Falcon and Petitioner were eventually indicted for their parts in the crime. Falcon entered into a plea agreement and pled guilty to one count of manslaughter.

Munoz was never located, and Petitioner filed, *inter alia*, a successful Motion in Limine (Pet. Exhibit 28) to prevent Falcon from testifying to statements by Munoz.

After selection of a jury, Petitioner proceeded to trial on September 27, 2000. The trial included the following testimony:

Benny Hays -- Mr. Hays testified that he was a neighbor of Petitioner, and on the morning of the shooting he was outside having coffee at about 5:30 a.m. when he heard a loud noise, walked to the end of his drive and back and heard another loud noise a minute or two later. He then saw a man, 20-25 years old, running down the street.

Then, a neighbor came and told him a lady had driven a car through a short block fence. He called 911, to report the accident. He and the neighbor, Hank, walked to the scene and saw that the car had backed across the street into the fence. The front passenger door was open, and the lady was slumped over in the driver's seat. They decided not to try to move the victim to avoid injuring her.

They went to Petitioner's house and he answered the door in his night clothes. Petitioner said he recognized the car and they walked across the street. He did not see Petitioner try to assist the driver. An officer arrived in a few minutes, and he told the officer his story. He did not think either loud noise sounded like a gunshot. He did not see any blood on the victim, and did not look closely at her. He is not familiar with the sound of gunfire, and was not certain about the elapsed time. (Supp. Exhibit I, R.T. 9/27/00 at 53-76.)

Neil Morse -- Officer Morse testified that he responded to the scene of the shooting, and created a diagram of the scene. The car had backed across the street into a block wall. There was minimal damage to the vehicle suggesting a low impact speed. The car was in line with the driveway across the street. The victim had already been removed when he arrived. Although he responded at 6:00 a.m., he was first patrolling the neighborhood and did not arrive at the scene for several hours. (Supp. Exhibit I, R.T. 9/27/00 at 77-87.)

Mary Stephaniak -- Officer Stephaniak testified that she was called to the scene at about 5:30 a.m., and was the first responder. About five people were standing around the car, and Petitioner flagged her down. She approached Petitioner and he said "She's my wife." Petitioner appeared concerned but not upset, and was not crying. The front passenger door was open. She checked the victim for a pulse, found a slight pulse and saw a large amount of blood. The victim's purse was on the passenger side floorboard, and appeared undisturbed. A bag of fruit was on the passenger seat. She called for the fire department. She asked Petitioner if identification would be in the victim's wallet, and she noticed the wallet was in the purse on the top with the clasp closed. She and another officer removed the victim from the car and began CPR. Then the fire department arrived and transported her to the hospital. As they moved her and did CPR, blood spattered on the pavement and outside the car.

She spoke with Petitioner who told her the victim was going to work, and had said goodbye, but he had fallen back to sleep, until the neighbor knocked on the door. Petitioner said he had not heard anything.

The victim had a gold colored bracelet on her right wrist. She looked for a wound, but couldn't find it because of the blood matted in the victim's hair. The other officer found a bullet hole in the driver's side windshield. So, she checked the victim's hands and around her for signs that the wound was self-inflicted. She found nothing, and there was no weapon in the car.

When she first responded to the scene, she did not believe there was an emergency. Petitioner's hair was disheveled. She couldn't determine the location or nature of the victim's wound because of the blood. They did not determine the victim had been shot until the other officer arrived. Petitioner had been pacing around the car, and had not been told the victim had been shot. She requested the fire department twice, and the other officer had done so once. Petitioner had asked where the ambulance was. Petitioner had started to assist them in removing the victim, but Stephaniak stopped him. She questioned Petitioner while the ambulance crew worked on the victim, but he was unresponsive. Petitioner's father offered to answer her questions. Petitioner and his father both said they had not heard anything.

The victim was transported by helicopter. When she was put on the gurney, Petitioner began to cry, and his father had to restrain him from going to his wife. Petitioner's legs began to buckle and they sat him on the sidewalk.

Petitioner was in a T-shirt and shorts. When she told him it looked like the victim had been shot, his demeanor did not change. (Supp. Exhibit I, R.T. 9/27/00 at 88-116.)

Douglas Maurer - Mr. Maurer testified that his grandmother shopped at the Wittmann grocery store owned by Petitioner's father. His grandmother bought on credit, and he would borrow money from Petitioner. His sister-in-law worked for Petitioner, and he installed gravel and put in a security light for Petitioner. He had felony convictions and had problems with drugs. In late 1996, Petitioner approached him and asked what would happen if he put nitroglycerin in someone's drink, whether it would kill them. Petitioner mentioned his wife had been in a car accident and had seizures. Maurer didn't know, but agreed to find out. Petitioner later got angry with him when Petitioner heard that he was asking around about nitroglycerin.

In February, 1997, Petitioner approached him about putting a hit on his wife, because he wanted out of the marriage. Maurer suggested some ways Petitioner could kill her, and Petitioner talked about staging a robbery in Las Vegas, or hiding in her car and cutting her throat or shooting her. Petitioner brought the subject up again a week later, and they discussed Maurer following them to Las Vegas on a bus, and killing her with a knife at a motel. Petitioner was going to pay him in cash and credit. He agreed to do it for money for drugs. He talked about the plan with his brother's current wife, Tammy, and decided it wasn't smart.

In March, 1997, Maurer asked Deputy Baker about who would be believed if a businessman hired a drug addict to kill their wife. He told the officer the businessman was Petitioner, who had asked him to kill Petitioner's wife. He told defense counsel he had not identified Petitioner to Deputy Baker. The officer did not believe him. His criminal problems would have been helped by being an informant when he talked to Deputy Baker about Petitioner.

He had talked with Deputy Baker about being an informant about drug suppliers, and assumed they paid informants. But Baker's supervisors wouldn't let him become an informant. He did not think he would be paid for telling about the conversations with Petitioner.

In the spring of 1997, he was facing a criminal prosecution for escape, and a potential probation violation on a prior Georgia conviction. He had escaped from a police car, and eventually turned himself into Deputy Baker on April 22, 1997 because officers had told his grandmother he would be shot.

Later, Petitioner brought up the subject again, suggesting Maurer use a gun, and asked him to test fire a gun. Maurer got the gun from Petitioner in May, 1997. He was supposed to kill the victim in Arizona. He was to be paid the same amount. Maurer test fired the gun and then traded the gun for drugs, telling Petitioner that he had ditched it because an officer was following him.

Petitioner found out about the gun, and banned Maurer from the store. On a later occasion, Maurer was walking past the store and he and Petitioner got in an argument over Maurer owing him for the gun. Petitioner claimed Maurer had stolen the gun.

On June 23, 1997, he was placed on probation. Within a couple of days, he went on a crystal meth binge with Tammy Goad, in violation of his probation. He was home on drugs on July 2nd and July 4th, but went and bought shoes and applied for a job on July 3rd. The purchase and application documented his whereabouts on July 3, the date of the murder. He was arrested on July 7th on a probation violation, and Peoria police interviewed him, and he told them the same information... The police officers interviewed him on July 9th and twice on July 23. Between the two conversations on the 23rd they had inspected his sneakers and when they told him they matched the imprint in the car, he refused to talk further. When he spoke with Peoria police he referred to Petitioner as a "sand nigger." In the time period he was talking with Petitioner, he would wear camouflage clothing.

He is 5 feet, 9 inches tall, and at the time of the murder he weighed about 135 pounds.

He was using crystal methamphetamine and marijuana in 1996, but only methamphetamine by late 1996, and in increasing amounts through the summer of 1997. He was suffering from anxiety, depression, and hearing voices at the time, and had attempted suicide. He was discharged from the Navy due to a personality disorder, but eventually received a disability. He would hear voices when he had been without sleep for weeks at a time.

Tammy Goad was a drug addict, and had relationships with Maurer and his brother, and would be with Maurer when he had money for drugs. She eventually married his brother.

During one of his conversations with Petitioner, Maurer recorded the conversation. He didn't take the tapes to the police because he planned to blackmail Petitioner. Tammy stole the tape recorder and tape. Tammy told him she listened to the tape and didn't hear anything incriminating on it. They had planned for him to escape to avoid his criminal problems, and Tammy would handle the blackmail. The tapes of Petitioner had recorded, but were erased by Tammy's brother.

Maurer testified he was losing money by testifying at trial. The drugs did not affect his memory, and Petitioner asked him to kill his wife in 1996 and 1997. At the time, he did not care what happened to him, whether his probation was violated. His attitude changed in 1998 when his grandmother died. He completed intensive probation, graduated college, and got into a drug treatment program.

Maurer testified he had nothing to do with the victim's murder. His conversations with Deputy Baker about the killing did not have any effect on his pending charges.

(Supp. Exhibit J, R.T. 10/2/00 at 3-135.)

Isidro Falcon -- Mr. Falcon testified that in 1997 he weighed 199, and was five feet and five or six inches tall. He lived two blocks from Wittmann grocery. Alfonso Munoz, known as El Gato, lived 60 feet from the store, with his sister-in-law, Paula Hernandez. He had known Petitioner for about eight years, having met him at the store they owned in Surprise. He cannot read, and completed the sixth grade, and worked in agriculture and landscaping, and was working at a golf course.

About three weeks before the murder, Petitioner had started a conversation about having his wife killed. Falcon had been buying groceries on credit. Petitioner said he had a job for Falcon, who thought it was for landscaping. Petitioner said he wanted his wife killed, Falcon responded that he didn't want to do it. Petitioner asked if he knew someone who could do it. He offered $2,000, but Falcon told him the trigger man wanted more, so they discussed $8,000, $2,000 down and payments.

When he first talked with Petitioner about wanting to have his wife killed, Petitioner told him it was because she spent a lot of money when she went to California. Falcon couldn't believe he wanted to kill her. Petitioner said his wife had a disease and blamed him for giving it to her, and that he had it but blamed her.

After talking with Petitioner, he asked El Gato who claimed to have killed for money in Mexico. They discussed $2,000, but El Gato wanted $8,000. The next day, he told Petitioner that El Gato would do it. Petitioner knew El Gato.

About a week before the murder, El Gato told him that the victim was going to be killed soon. Petitioner had told him that he wanted her killed before their anniversary, when they had a trip planned to go to California.

Petitioner gave him $2,000 in cash in a white envelope, and a gun, a .380 chrome pistol with a brown handle in a holster. That same day, which was a couple of days before the murder, he gave the pistol to El Gato, and he didn't see it again. He gave El Gato the pistol to commit the murder. He gave El Gato $1,000 and Petitioner was supposed to make payments through Colin Head for the balance.

Falcon had never been to Petitioner's house. The first plan was to kill her in the parking lot at her workplace, Del Webb Hospital. Petitioner drove Falcon and El Gato there. Falcon translated for El Gato, who did not speak any English. Petitioner then decided he wanted her killed in front of his house, because he had been "burned" by Doug Maurer and Colin, who he had given stuff to kill her but they hadn't followed through. Petitioner wanted to watch through the window. He told Falcon and El Gato this while driving them to his house the Friday before the murder.

They had arranged to meet at Peter Piper Pizza in Peoria, where Falcon was taking his family. Petitioner and El Gato got him out of the restaurant, and they drove to Petitioner's house. Petitioner told them the days his wife worked, and what time she left, which was early in the morning, around 5:00 or 5:30. Petitioner gave Falcon a remote to the victim's car. Falcon gave the remote to El Gato, and Petitioner showed him how to use it. El Gato was to cover himself up with a coat in the floor of the back of the car, and kill her with the gun.

Three days before the murder, Petitioner arranged for the victim to come to the store, and then called Falcon on pretense of reviewing landscaping plans. Falcon and El Gato went to the store and saw the victim. Petitioner showed Falcon her car. Petitioner knew El Gato was to be the one to actually murder the victim.

On July 3, 1997 he got a ride to work from El Gato, arrived at 4:20 and left at about 1:00 or 1:30. On the day of the murder, El Gato was dressed in two pair of army pants, an army shirt, and had sweats and a sweatshirt on. He was wearing white tennis shoes.

He rode home with another worker. He loaned his car to El Gato and expected him to pick him up, but he never arrived. He saw El Gato later that day when it was getting dark, and El Gato said "he had done what he had to do." [1] (*Id.* at 142-149.)

---

1 Objections were raised to this testimony. (Supp. Exhibit J, R.T. 10/2/00 at 149, *et seq.*)

The car, a 1976 Toyota, had been bought by Petitioner, and Falcon was driving it to decide whether to buy it. A week before they first discussed the murder, Petitioner sold him the car for $1,000, to be paid $100 every two weeks. Petitioner gave him the car, the key and the title. He took it to Flagstaff but it didn't have enough power so he told Petitioner he didn't want it. Petitioner insisted on the sale. In between, they discussed Petitioner wanting his wife murdered. He never paid anything on the car. El Gato had never borrowed his car before. After the murder, he told Petitioner he did not want the car because it had been used in a murder. Petitioner told him to keep it and start making the payments. He eventually sold the car.

He got another $1,000 in a white envelope from Colin, which he delivered to El Gato. El Gato threatened to come after Falcon if he ever got caught. He told El Gato that Petitioner wanted the murder done before his anniversary.

After the murder, one of Petitioner's employees, Don Mecham, took him to get the car. He paid him $5 for gas. El Gato said something to him so he knew where to find his car after the murder. The car was parked two blocks from Petitioner's house on a residential street. The car wouldn't start, so they had to jump it. The key was in the ignition. There was a white envelope in the car. He took the car home. When he went to pick up the car after the murder, the windows were down and the key was in the ignition.

He went to talk to Petitioner the next day. Petitioner asked if everything was fine, and he said yes. He said he didn't know they were going to use his car, and he didn't want it. Petitioner told him to do whatever he wanted with it. He sold the car a couple of days later.

With the money he got, he bought his kids some clothes and put a down payment on some land. He did not finish paying for it because he was arrested on the murder in December, 1997. He was charged with murder and conspiracy to commit murder, and pled guilty to manslaughter. He was awaiting sentencing, in a range of 7 to 18 years. He agreed to testify and assist in the investigation as part of the plea agreement.

After he told Colin Head to take away the envelope with money after the murder, he did not receive anything further from Petitioner. A couple of days after the murder, El Gato came to his house and asked for money to go to Mexico. He told El Gato he had no money and he should go talk to Petitioner. He has not seen El Gato since then.

At the time of the events, he was drinking 12 to 18 beers per evening, and would smoke marijuana on a nightly basis. Before his plea agreement he was facing charges for murder and conspiracy to commit murder, and the state had filed a notice of intent to seek the death penalty.

He told his friend Ron Wallace about the murder, but discovered that Wallace had been wearing a wire and had set him up.

(Supp. Exhibit K, R.T. 10/3/00 at 9-167.)

William Moore -- Mr. Moore testified that he had lived in Wittman, Arizona, and knew Petitioner since 1991 or 1992. Petitioner owned Wittman Grocery. Moore bought from the store and did work for Petitioner as a sign maker. He knew Petitioner's father who ran the liquor store. Moore was in prison for three years in Nevada on possession of a stolen vehicle.

In February of 1997, Moore's nephew, who worked for Petitioner, told Moore that Petitioner wanted to see him about some signs. Don Mecham lived with Moore. Petitioner asked about Moore's legal troubles in Nevada, and then asked him "what if I needed somebody to disappear." Moore responded that nothing could be that bad.

Moore knew Isidro Falcon. In June of 1997, he saw Falcon talking with Petitioner at the store. Later in June, he saw Petitioner talking to Falcon outside by Petitioner's truck.

In December, 1997 he had a conversation with Petitioner about rumors surrounding the murder. Moore denied talking about Petitioner, and Petitioner said the rumors were told by Leslie. Moore had heard Leslie say that Petitioner had gotten Falcon to kill his wife. Moore asked Petitioner why he didn't just divorce his wife. Petitioner responded that he would lose everything if he had. Petitioner expressed a lack of trust in Falcon, and concern if Falcon was arrested and said anything, Petitioner would be harmed. He offered Moore $10,000, $5,000 for Moore and $5,000 for somebody from Nevada, to kill Falcon. Moore expressed dissatisfaction that Petitioner had involved Don Mecham, by having him take Falcon to the scene to pick up the car.

He was aware at the time of this conversation in December that the victim had been murdered, although he was in California when it occurred.

He did not report any of this to law enforcement until two weeks later, in December, 1997 when he was in jail on class two felony charges of fraudulent schemes and artifices arising in Tucson. Those charges arose out of a $100 deposit he had taken as a licensed sign painter and hadn't done the job. He expected it to be dropped to a misdemeanor, with six months' sentence. He had his wife contact Detective Lopez' office. He was aware at that time that Petitioner and Falcon had been arrested. If convicted, he faced the possibility of a substantial prison sentence because of his extensive prior criminal history. Those charges were dismissed after a request by the prosecutor in Petitioner's case in exchange for testimony from Moore.

In addition, theft charges from Maricopa County were dismissed along with the Tucson charges when Detective Lane said that it should be dismissed because of his cooperation. Also, a seven-year-old charge in Mohave County was dismissed.

At the time of trial, Moore faced probation violations in Kingman and Maricopa County. He pled guilty to another theft charge in Kingman, and was awaiting sentencing to prison or reinstatement on probation. A good word from the prosecutor in this case would be helpful to him.

He had been convicted on two counts of theft in Maricopa County, each class three felonies, and placed on probation. He faced sentencing on violation of that probation, either by reinstatement or prison sentences of up to two 8.5 year consecutive sentences. He had a total of eleven prior convictions.

He got good deals in exchange for his agreement to testify in another conspiracy/murder for hire case in Pima County. There was a verdict in that case. He violated his probation because he received a threat on his life.

He had no agreements about his current cases concerning his testimony in this case.

In March, 1998 he had a conversation with Detective Lopez about the conspiracy with regard to the Petitioner, and contrasted it to the situation in Pima County.

He believed Petitioner approached him about killing his wife and Falcon because Petitioner knew about his extensive criminal history, and he knew people who could do something like that. (Supp. Exhibit L, R.T. 10/4/00 at 21-45; Supp. Exhibit Q, R.T. 10/16/00 at 37-75.)

Mark Fischione -- Dr. Fischione, an employee of the medical examiner's office, testified that he had performed the autopsy on the victim, and determined that her death was a homicide, the result of two gunshot wounds to the back of her head. One shot was in an upward, right to left trajectory, hit the top of the skull and bounced back within the brain. The second shot was in the same general trajectory, but only grazed across the scalp without penetrating into the scalp. The two gunshots appeared to be from some distance other than direct contact. The soot and stippling which could indicate the range would have been caught by the victim's hair. The hair was sent for examination, but he did not do the testing or get the results. (Supp. Exhibit L, R.T. 10/4/00 at 54-85.)

Lewis Roane -- Mr. Roane, a crime scene technician with the Peoria police department, testified that he responded to the scene. He took various pictures as directed by a detective. (Supp. Exhibit L, R.T. 10/4/00 at 86-91.)

Robert Sanders -- Sergeant Sanders, of the Peoria police department, testified that he responded to the scene of the murder which he first believed to be the scene of an injury accident. He arrived at 5:39 a.m., and saw a vehicle that had backed into and over a small block fence. The vehicle was running and the front passenger door was open. The driver's window was halfway down, and the radio station was playing extremely loudly. Officer Stefaniak was present.

He spoke with Benny Hays and then instructed units to circulate in the area to look for a person running from the scene, giving a description of a Hispanic male wearing a green military jacket, blue pants and a white shirt, five-seven, 160 pounds.

He could see blood on the right side of the victim's head. Officer Stefaniak reported that the victim still had a pulse. They removed the victim from the car and placed her on the ground, and began performing life-saving efforts...

He noticed a bullet hole in the windshield and advised Stefaniak that they might have a gunshot victim. The bullet hole was made from the inside out. There was brain matter, hair, tissue, and blood on the inside of the windshield and dashboard. There were no signs of forced entry into the vehicle.

The fire department arrived after 15 to 18 minutes.

He looked for a gun in the vehicle, but found none. He found a charcoal black sweatshirt with silver cuffs and a sunscreen in the back of the car. In the front, there was a black purse on the front passenger floorboard, and a plastic baggie of fruit on the passenger seat. In the rear of the car there was a key and a remote control for a keyless entry or car alarm behind the passenger seat. Behind the driver's seat there was a shell casing. The purse did not look ransacked. He did not find a second shell casing.

When he first looked in the car, the victim was slumped over to the right side. When he looked in the car after determining there was a bullet hole in the windshield, he saw a lot more blood. At first he thought the bullet hole was bird droppings, and that the blood was from the victim hitting her head on the windshield.

(Supp. Exhibit L, R.T. 10/4/00 at 92-116.)

Kenneth Kowalski -- Mr. Kowalski, a criminalist with the Arizona Department of Public Safety, testified that he examined shoeprints found on the rear door panel of the vehicle with tennis shoes provided by Detective Rock. He determined that the shoeprints could have been made by the shoes.

He examined a spent shell casing from a .380 auto cartridge case. He also examined fragments from a spent, jacketed bullet, that could have been from a .380 or 9mm bullet. The casing was from an auto-ejecting pistol, and had an ejector mark. (Supp. Exhibit L, R.T. 10/4/00 at 117-133.)

Colin Head -- Mr. Head testified that in 1997 he lives in Wittmann, and worked for Petitioner at his store for seven or eight years. He was not paid a regular wage, but would as for money if he needed it or get food or drink from the store. He stocked, swept, and mopped. He had met the victim at the store.

Head denied telling police or defense counsel that Petitioner had approached him about killing someone, and that he was afraid of

Petitioner. He had told Petitioner he thought his girlfriend was cheating on him and that he would hurt her if he found it was true. Petitioner told him that was not right.

He had known Isidro Falcon for several months as of July 3, 1997. He had seen Falcon talking to Petitioner. He had delivered a white enveloped to Falcon sometime after July 3, 1997, as he had been told to do by Cynthia who had been contacted by Petitioner. He delivered it to Falcon outside the store. He told Falcon it was from Petitioner. The envelope was thin and did not feel like it had a wad of money in it.

He had purchased two vehicles from Petitioner, one in 1996 and one in 1997. Petitioner would give him money to go to the doctor or for gas. Head continued working for Petitioner's father at the store until it closed in 1998 or 1999 when the highway was widened. He was at the store when Petitioner was arrested on December 15.

He did not know an El Gato or an Alfonso Munoz.

Petitioner did not come into the store until a month and a half after the murder. Head was taken into custody at the same time as Petitioner.

His statements to the police were while he was in custody, had been threatened with prison, and was scared. While he was being questioned, Falcon came in and told him that Petitioner had paid him to kill his wife, and that Head should tell the police what he knew. He told police that Petitioner had asked him to kill his wife. At first Head asserted he lied to police, but eventually claimed he told the police the truth.

(Supp. Exhibit M, R.T. 10/5/00 at 3-43.)

<u>Don Mecham</u> -- Don Mecham testified that he suffered from cerebral palsy, had relocated from Wittmann to Oregon, and knew Petitioner from the Wittmann Grocery store. He had been working for Petitioner for about three years stocking shelves and backing, and was paid hourly wages.

He saw the victim at least once when she brought Petitioner lunch. He had known Indio Falcon for several months before the murder. He saw Falcon speaking with Petitioner.

He recognized the brown Toyota car that Falcon got from Petitioner. After July 3, 1997, Petitioner asked him to take Falcon to get the car because it had run out of gas. Petitioner and Mecham were both at the store at the time. He took Falcon to Peoria to get the car on a residential street. He did not know whether it was close to Petitioner's residence. Falcon showed him the way. Falcon started the car and drove away. He did not see Falcon use or have a key to start the car. He had taken Falcon other places.

He did not see Falcon come to the store any more after the murder.

He had seen a chrome pistol in the draw of Petitioner's desk at the store. He did not remember seeing it after the murder. After the murder, Petitioner told him to drive around town and tell him if he saw any undercover police officers or detectives. He told Petitioner that he saw new cars in town, but didn't think they were undercover cops.

After the murder, Falcon showed him a lot near Wittmann that he had purchased.

He didn't know an "El Gato." Petitioner told him he married his wife to keep his store.

He knew William Moore ("Tony") who he had visited in prison in California and Nevada. Tony had a daughter who died. He liked Tony.

Later, he took an officer to show him where the picked up the car, and then identified the car at an impound yard. When he spoke with the officer he took to where the car had been parked, he knew Petitioner and Colin had been arrested. He didn't remember the officer telling him anything about Tony.

(Supp. Exhibit M, R.T. 10/5/00 at 43-79.)

<u>Ruby Maribella</u> -- Ruby Maribella testified that her sister Grace was married to Petitioner's brother Ume Gohel. She was friends with Petitioner since 1990, prior to his marriage to the victim, and for at least a little while after the murder. Petitioner visited Maribella almost every weekend. She would help him buy food for his store in Wittman. They would eat together. He would come to her apartment. He had sold her cars and loaned the money for the cars to her. She paid Petitioner back on the car loans and had borrowed several hundred dollars for her mom.

In May, 1997, Petitioner called her while she was in Colorado and said he had received a letter saying his wife was having an affair. She would reach Petitioner by paging him. She would call him at the grocery store but not at home. She paged and called him daily.

Petitioner told her that the victim said that if he wouldn't sleep with her, that she would find someone else to sleep with and there was a guy named Jose at work who was interested in her. He told Maribella this after the phone call in Colorado.

(Supp. Exhibit M, R.T. 10/5/00 at 79-91.)

Aiche Jasser -- Aiche Jasser testified that she was a clinical pharmacist at Del Webb hospital, where she worked with the victim who was a staff pharmacist. They would eat lunch together. She liked her, and they would discuss personal matters. She saw Petitioner come to the hospital once. The victim introduced him to her.

She visited the victim at home in Peoria after she was in an accident in California, which made the victim miss more than a month of work.

There was a pharmacy technician named Jose Munoz who worked at the hospital. He would walk her to her car after work.

The victim had been distraught, but just prior to the murder, the victim seemed in good spirits. She was going traveling with her husband, and seemed in good spirits in conversations about purchasing a new home. (Supp. Exhibit M, R.T. 10/5/00 at 92-104.)

Lupe Gonzales -- Lupe Gonzales testified that she worked as a pharmacy technician at Del Webb Hospital in 1997, and knew the victim and Jose Munoz, an IV technician. The victim and Munoz were inseparable, would follow each other around the pharmacy, he would wait for her after work, and when she returned from lunch they would be sitting talking. She saw them giving each other a good bye kiss in the parking lot.

In May, 1997, she wrote a letter to Petitioner at his store telling him that his wife was seeing someone in the hospital. She didn't sign the letter or put a return address on it. She didn't think what the victim and Munoz were doing was right. She didn't write a letter to Munoz's wife because a friend spoke to Munoz.

She had met Petitioner at the hospital when he could visit the victim. He and the victim would have lunch together. The victim treated him nicely. They seemed glad to see each other. He had visited there once or twice.

She liked the victim and went and talked to her and said she should be careful about what she was doing at the hospital. (Supp. Exhibit M, R.T. 10/5/00 at 104-123.)

Tammy Maurer-Goad -- Tammy Maurer testified that she was formerly Tammy Goad. She knows Doug Maurer and is married to his brother Dan. In 1997 she lived in Wittman, and new Doug Maurer for about two years prior to the murder. She knew Petitioner, who ran the Wittman Grocery, where she traded a lot. Doug Maurer was often in the store and would talk to Petitioner.

Indio or Isidro Falcon was her next door neighbor. He normally drove a truck, but in June of 1997 had an additional vehicle. She talked more with his wife, Catalina. Indio drank a lot.

If they didn't have money for food, Petitioner would let them get food and pay him later. They would always pay him back.

She saw Doug Maurer with a gun. He had it for about a week.

A week after she saw Doug Maurer with the gun, Petitioner told her that Doug had stolen his gun that day. She knew it wasn't that day because she had seen Maurer with the gun. She and her boyfriend Danny told Petitioner to call the police, but he said he couldn't because the gun was not registered. Petitioner seemed nervous, and had brought up the subject of the gun.

About two to four months prior to the murder, she and her husband confronted Petitioner and told him that Doug Maurer was telling people that Petitioner was trying to get his wife killed. Petitioner denied it and smiled.

At that period of time, Doug Maurer was doing drugs, but didn't have problems with his memory. He gave her a tape recorder and told her to listen to it. It was inaudible, but she is deaf in one ear. She could hear male voices but couldn't tell who they were or what they were saying. She gave it to Danny who took it to work and recorded over the tape. Doug was angry when he found out.

She applied for a job at a mobile home park on July 3, 1997. She was with Doug Maurer on that day. He also applied for a job there. They went shopping on that day, and Doug bought some shoes. It may also have been the day she got a tattoo.

She was seeing both Doug and Danny in 1997. She was addicted to crystal methamphetamine at the time. She and Doug would do drugs together. Doug had gotten out of jail in June, 1997, and they were doing a lot of drugs together. (Supp. Exhibit M, R.T. 10/5/00 at 123-147.)

Robert Tavernaro -- Robert Tavernaro, a latent print examiner for Arizona Department of Public Safety, testified that he examined fingerprints in a black pickup truck at the scene and a blue Toyota Camry vehicle at the DPS facility, including objects in the vehicles. He also assisted with photographs, including shoeprints.

He compared the latent prints to prints of the victim, Petitioner, Babula Gohel, Doug Maurer, and Isidro Falcon. On Falcon, he had comparison prints of his entire hand, including fingertips and edges of the hand. No prints of Falcon or any other known person were found in the Camry. Some prints possibly from gloves were found on the outside driver's door.

He also examined a car alarm remote, and there were no identifiable prints on it. There were no identifiable prints on any of the door handles. No prints of Falcon or Maurer were found anywhere in or on the vehicle. The failure to find a person's prints does not mean they were not in the vehicle.

He only examined the exterior of the black pickup, because that is all Detective Lopez asked him to examine. Though the comparison prints he had for Maurer were not "major case prints" he did have good enough prints to not need additional prints to eliminate Maurer.

The only identification made on the black pickup was Petitioner's print. (Supp. Exhibit N, R.T. 10/10/00 at 3-25.)

Jose Munoz -- Jose Munoz testified that he was employed as an IV technician at Del Webb Hospital in 1997. He worked in the same department and same hours as the victim, who was a pharmacist. He also worked with Aiche Jasser, a pharmacist, and Lupe Gonzales a technician. He became friends with the victim, but only at work. They would talk about her marriage. They would talk about the pharmacy and problems she had at home. He would hold her hand when she was upset, and perhaps when he walked her to her car. They would meet when she was on her way to the parking lot and he was on break. He never kissed her, but she kissed him once on the cheek. Perhaps they touched cheek to cheek in the parking lot.

The Peoria police asked if he was having an affair with the victim. He was not and never got close to it. He met the Petitioner in the Pharmacy two or three months before the murder. The victim was upbeat about trips to California with her husband over July 4th and to Tanzania to her family. The victim and Petitioner appeared to be getting closer to each other in the time shortly before her death, and sent flowers to each other.

He knew Lupe Gonzales prior to becoming friends with the victim. After he became friends with the victim, Lupe Gonzales became more quiet toward both of them.

The victim and Aiche Jasser were friends. He was aware of the victim's car accident in California in November, 1996.

(Supp. Exhibit N, R.T. 10/10/00 at 26-39.)

Ella McKinney -- Ella McKinney testified that she has lived in Wittmann for 20 years, and knew Petitioner who ran the grocery store. Around June 26, 1997, she sold a 1984 brown Toyota Camry to Petitioner because she needed the money. She cancelled the insurance two days after she sold the car. She sold it for 500 in cash and 200 in credit for groceries. Petitioner had given her credit at the store before, and she had paid it off.

Petitioner told her to leave the title open because he did not want it in his name. She had a door key and a gas key. Petitioner said he was buying the car for Don, and planned to sell it. She talked about it with Petitioner for about a week before selling it.

(Supp. Exhibit N, R.T. 10/10/00 at 39-46.)

Bobby Garcia -- Bobby Garcia testified that he lives in Wittmann in July of 1997, and worked at Trail Ridge Golf Course in Sun City West. He knew Isidro Falcon, but never met Alfonso Munoz or El Gato.

He bought a brown 1984 Toyota from Falcon for $1700 at the end of July, 1997. The title was in the name of Ella McKinney. He paid the full price in payments to Falcon at work or at his house, with $500 down and $200 per month. He got only one key to the vehicle. Eventually the police seized the vehicle for three days. He got it back and sold it in 1998. It was running when he sold it.

(Supp. Exhibit N, R.T. 10/10/00 at 46-53.)

William Laing -- Officer William Laing, of the Peoria Police Department, testified that he responded to the vicinity of the scene of the murder and conducted a canvas of the neighbors and interviewed Benny Hays. When he canvased the neighborhood of the scene, he was looking for someone based on a description from Benny Hays of a Hispanic male, 20 to 25 years of age. Five seven, five eight, 160 to 170 pounds. Black hair. Wearing a pale olive green army jacket with a white T-shirt underneath, and white tennis shoes. Neat looking and possibly clean shaven. The person was in a dead run. No description of any pants was given by Hays.

He then went to the hospital to talk to Petitioner. Petitioner related that he was awake but in bed as the victim was leaving that morning. She gave him a kiss on the cheek before she left. Their normal routine was to set the alarm for 4:00 a.m. for the victim, but he usually remained in bed and left for work or the gym between 6:30 and 7:00 a.m. The victim was the primary user of the Toyota Camry vehicle she was murdered in. Her normal work days were Wednesdays off and rotating weekends.

Petitioner and the victim had gone out Wednesday night, July 2, 1997, celebrating their second wedding anniversary. The victim's sister, Bijal, went with them. The victim cooked dinner at the house and they went out to see a movie. They went in the Toyota Camry. In anticipation of a trip to California that weekend, they had the tires on the car rotated and it had been washed at a car wash.

Petitioner related that he found out about the murder when he heard the doorbell ring and answered the door to find two men who asked him if it was his vehicle and to tell him that there was a woman inside that was hurt. Petitioner said they had no children, that the victim had been hurt in a serious accident, but they planned to try to have a child within the next year.

Petitioner denied any problems with vandalism around the house. He said he was away from home most of the time.

Petitioner described the car as having an automatic transmission, and the doors automatically locked once the vehicle was started. They had an after-market alarm installed on the vehicle. The victim usually kept the doors of the car locked. The day before they had used Petitioner's keys, but the victim had driven the car the prior day, and he didn't know if the doors were locked or not at the time she got in the vehicle.

On December 15, and December 16, 1997, Laing interviewed Don Mecham. His interview with Don Mecham was to find out the route he had taken. Mecham told him he had given Indio a ride only one time and that was to go get Indio's car. Mecham never mentioned Petitioner being part of the arrangements to take Indio to his car. But Laing never asked him about any involvement by Petitioner. On the 15th, they went for a ride and Mecham showed him a route from Wittmann to near Petitioner's home, on Palo Verde. He took Mecham to the impound yard, and Mecham identified a brown car as the one that had been on Palo Verde.

Laing went to the morgue on July 3, 1997 to view the body of the victim. He examined the wounds, including a laceration on the side of her head, and an entrance wound at the back of the head. He impounded her clothing and jewelry.

Laing admitted that his report did not reflect Petitioner saying the men at his door told him about the victim being hurt. Petitioner told him that their alarm system on the car was not the most reliable, and sometimes did not work.

There was a tape recording of the interview with Petitioner that was misplaced. His written report was based on his notes during the conversation.

Laing interviewed Ruby Garcia with Sergeant Stall on about July 9, 1997. The initial interview with Ruby Garcia was at her employment, but they went to her residence.

He participated in the execution of a search warrant at the residence of Ethel Maurer in Glendale. She was the mother of Doug Maurer. They found a pair of army camouflage pants and other items that appeared to belong to a younger man rather than an older woman.

Detective Lopez was the primary investigating officer, but task assignments were made by Sergeant Stall.

(Supp. Exhibit N, R.T. 10/10/00 at 53-79.)

Eric Stall -- Sergeant Eric Stall, of the Peoria Police Department, testified that he responded to the scene of the murder at 6:30 in the morning, and took charge of the scene. He interviewed Petitioner.

Petitioner said the victim normally left for work at 5:30 a.m., except on Wednesdays, and was employed as a pharmacist at Del Webb Hospital. He said they had a good relationship. He couldn't understand how this could happen and had no idea who did it. Petitioner showed him his truck and it was locked. Petitioner opened it to show him something.

There was nothing to suggest that the victim's car had been broken into or that a car-jacking had been attempted.

He interviewed Lupe Gonzales, Ruby Garcia, and Colin Head. He contacted Colin Head on December 15, 1997, and took him to the Peoria Police Department to be interviewed. Head did not want to answer questions, and he was very direct with him to elicit responses, but was not rude or abrasive. Indio Falcon was brought into confront Head. At that point, Head put his head down and cried. He then answered Stall's questions. The interview was videotaped, but only the audio actually recorded.

Detective Lopez was the lead investigator on the case. Lopez looked to Stall as the sergeant for assistance and advice.

When he interviewed Petitioner, he asked about guns. Petitioner gave him a 9mm gun from his truck.

When he interviewed Lupe Gonzalez, the interview lasted 90 minutes and was not entirely amicable and he was direct with her. When he interviewed Ruby Garcia, it was first at her employment, then at the police station, and then at her apartment. Those interviews occurred on July 9, 1997.

On November 22, 1997, they received an anonymous phone call concerning the case which resulted in him checking into an organization called the Fourth Reich Skin Heads, and three individuals, but that information lead to nothing.

Colin Head was arrested and taken to the Peoria Police Department. Stall wanted to have Head corroborate statements from Falcon that Petitioner had approached Head about killing the victim, and Petitioner had Head deliver an envelope to Falcon. Head initially denied any involvement. Stall asked him to be truthful and got confrontational with Head, including screaming at him, cursing at the subject matter but not at Head, and raising his voice. He called Head a liar and told him he thought he was involved in the murder, even though Stall had no information that Head was directly involved. He told Heat that he could do eight years in prison

No recording was made of his pre-Miranda discussions with Head, which included the confrontation by Indio Falcon, Stall getting confrontational, and Head crying. Those discussions occurred over a half hour period and took a total of about 15 minutes, all prior to the Miranda warnings and tape recordings.

In that time period, he left to confirm with Indio Falcon his story. He asked Falcon to repeat his claims to Head. Falcon did so, and Head put his head down and appeared to cry. Stall then turned the recorder on, and gave Head his Miranda rights. Head then told him that Petitioner had asked him to murder his wife, and Petitioner had him deliver an envelope to Falcon.

He brought Falcon in to Head so Head would know Stall was not speculating or making up the story about Head's involvement.

He didn't record the pre-Miranda conversation because it would not be admissible. Although Head was a suspect, Stall was not certain whether Head would be a witness or a defendant. Head was released later that night. Stall had concluded there was not significant evidence of Head's involvement with the conspiracy to commit homicide. (Supp. Exhibit N, R.T. 10/10/00 at 80-98; and Supp. Exhibit O, R.T. 10/11/00 at 3- 36.)

William Sparpana -- Officer William Sparpana, of the Peoria Police Department, testified that he was asked to assist with surveillance via electronic listening device of conversations between Isidro Falcon and a confidential informant. Detective Lopez was interacting with Falcon. A recording was made of the conversation between Falcon and a confidential informant while they were in a trailer, and later that day in an abandoned old house. This occurred on December 11th.

On December 15th, Sparpana participated in the arrest of Petitioner at the Wittman Grocery. (Supp. Exhibit O, R.T. 10/11/00 at 36-43.)

Thomas Stewart -- Detective Stewart, of the Peoria Police Department, testified that in this case he collected evidence, interviewed witnesses, assisted in searches and seizures, and attended the autopsy. He did not interview Petitioner.

He arrived at the scene of the murder at about 7:45. He collected evidence from the Camry, including a purse from the right front passenger seat. Some items in the purse were removed and separately impounded. The purse did not appear to have been disturbed.

He seized out of the back of the car an Excalibur car remote, a black sweater, and a Winchester 380 caliber auto shell casing. A 380 is a 9mm short round. He seized the key from the car.

He seized shoes from the property of Doug Maurer at the Maricopa County Jail. He had the treads compared at DPS and went to a Payless Shoe Store in Glendale where Doug Maurer claimed he purchased the shoes in the morning hours of July 3, 1997. He got a receipt signed by the store manager, reflecting purchase on July 3, 1997 at 10:24 a.m. He did not take the shoes to the store, but the manager was able to confirm the shoes from a four-digit code on the shoes.

When he got to the scene, the Camry was backed up to a wall across the street from the victim's house, and the doors were opened. There was a bullet hole through the front windshield. There was broken glass on the driveway. He did not examine the glass to determine whether it was windshield glass.

At the autopsy, he impounded projectile fragments removed from the victim's head.

He participated in the search of Petitioner's home on July 17, 1997 pursuant to a search warrant. They seized various items, including a bag with brochures from Caesar's Palace in Las Vegas. There were two Excalibur car remotes that had been seized from the victim's car, one in the back and one on her key chain.

He interviewed the manager of the Payless Shoe Store and Ella McKinney. He went to Three Fountains Mobile Home Park and got a job application submitted by Doug Maurer dated July 3, 1997.

He and Detective Lopez interviewed Doug Maurer on July 9, 1997. They had a discussion for about 30 to 45 minutes, and then began recording the interview. They returned on July 23, 1997, but Mr. Maurer refused to talk to them. They executed the warrant on the shoes the next day, July 24, 1997.

A brown Toyota Camry was seized from Bob Garcia and was taken to the impound lot, perhaps to see if certain keys worked in it.

The receipt from Payless Shoe Store was timed from 10:24 a.m. through 10:46 and the job application was dated 10:30 a.m. The Payless Shoe Store was approximately a quarter mile from the trailer park where Maurer had applied.

(Supp. Exhibit O, R.T. 10/11/00 at 43-82.)

Juan Lopez -- Detective Juan Lopez, of the Peoria Police Department, testified that he was assigned as the case agent, and arrived at the scene at 7:00 a.m. He participated in the investigation of the scene with Officer Stewart. He observed the bullet hole in the windshield, and blood spatter, and residual particles of glass in the driveway of the home.

He observed a weapon in Petitioner's truck. It was a black, semi-automatic handgun, either 9mm or .380 calibers.

The victim had been shot in the back of the head, the car left running, keys in the car, radio on, purse undisturbed with nothing appearing to have been taken, and no indication the car had been broken into, either the doors or the trunk. There was minimal scraping damage to the car from running into the little wall. All four doors were open.

The day before his testimony he tested the remote found in the back seat of the victim's car, and the one found in the ignition, and found that they both would unlock the car. The remote found in the house would not unlock the car.

On December 16, 1997, he tested the key found in the back of the victim's car and it operated the ignition in the brown Toyota Camry sold by Isidro Falcon to Bobby Garcia, as well as opening the passenger door and hatchback door. It did not open the driver's door which appeared to be faulty.

On July 8, 1997, he received a phone message from Deputy Baker. They arranged to meet at the substation and Baker told him information about something Doug Maurer had previously told him. He then went and interviewed Doug Maurer with Detective Stewart on July 9, 1997.

He also received information on December 8, 1997 from Detective Baker about a man named Ron Wallace. He contacted Wallace and set him up with a body wire and monitored conversations he had on December 11, 1997 with Isidro Falcon. The conversations occurred at two separate locations, and concerned the murder and Petitioner. Tapes of the conversations were made.

Wallace picked up Falcon and took him to an old mobile home that had a hard wire installed.

Wallace told Lopez where the brown Toyota Camry could be found. Lopez went to find it, but couldn't see the license plate. He went back later and confirmed the license number. It was at the home of Bob Garcia.

He interviewed Isidro Falcon on December 15, 1997. The interview was audio and video taped.

He interviewed Paula Hernandez at her home in Wittmann, Arizona on December 15, 1997, to attempt to locate her brother-in-law, Alfonso Munoz, otherwise known as El Gato. She provided a phone number in Juarez, Mexico. He tried the number then and a week before trial, and never got an answer at the number. An address was given to the U.S. Customs Service and the Border Patrol, provided photographs to them, to try to locate Munoz in Juarez, Mexico or around El Paso, Texas. Lopez did not try going to the address. They had information that Munoz might be returning to the northwest Phoenix area. The information has not panned out. No one has reported seeing Munoz around Hernandez's residence.

Paula Hernandez also provided an address for her mother, the mother-in-law to Alfonso Munoz. He could not have gotten permission to go look for Munoz in Mexico, from his department, the government of Mexico, or the United States government.

Lopez spoke with Cattie Falcon, wife of Isidro, outside her apartment in Wittmann.

He spoke with Doug Maurer with Detective Stewart. He met with him on July 9th and 23rd. After the meeting on the 9th, he got a warrant to get Maurer's shoes. Maurer was at one point considered a suspect because of shoe impressions found in the victim's car.

Although Maurer had originally waived his Miranda rights and agreed to talk with them, when Maurer expressed fear of Petitioner, started getting upset and asked why they weren't investigating Petitioner and if they were going to book him, Maurer refused to answer more questions.

Lopez later obtained information from Detective Stewart about Maurer's purchase of the shoes, and no longer considered Maurer a suspect. He believed Maurer had thrown his old shoes away.

He interviewed William Moore, Aiche Jasser, Tammy Goad Maurer, and Richard Tan, concerning the investigation. He was present for the search of Petitioner's residence. He spoke with other people as well, took inked prints from Falcon, and spoke with Petitioner.

He spoke with Petitioner on July 3, 1997. Petitioner was not arrested or in custody prior to December 15, 1997. In between those dates, Petitioner wanted to talk to him and would call. Three phone conversations were transcribed, two on July 4th and one on July 9th or 10th. The conversations were discussions. Petitioner was seeking information about what may have happened to his wife, and about her remains.

In a phone conversation on July 4, 1997, Petitioner said the doors in the victim's car did not automatically lock when you put the car in gear. There were two alarms on the car, one installed by the manufacturer, and one installed after market by someone named Joe. He said it didn't always work. There was a kill switch that would cause the engine to die a short time after someone tampered with the car. Petitioner said the victim had been in a car accident in California about a year before. Petitioner said he opened the store only one day per week, but he would arrive between 7:00 and 8:00. Unless he closed, he would leave between five and six p.m. for the 45-minute drive home. When he closed, he would not leave until 10:00 p.m. Petitioner said he worked a lot of hours at the store, and gave credit to people there.

He interviewed Petitioner once at the police station on July 3, 1997. They met at Petitioner's home and they rode together in the police car. Petitioner was not in custody and was not even particularly a suspect at that time. Petitioner answered his questions voluntarily. Video and audio recordings were made of the interview. Petitioner was given his Miranda warnings.

Petitioner told him the victim left around 5:30 a.m. every morning except Wednesdays and weekends. She worked as a pharmacist at Del Webb Hospital. They had been married about two years. He said he and his wife had a near perfect marriage. He said he had no idea who might have harmed his wife.

He drove Petitioner back home and they talked about Petitioner contacting him and about dealing with the media.

He spoke with Petitioner by phone on July 7, 1997, and Petitioner said services for the victim had been dealt with and said that a good friend of the victims from her work, Jose, might have some information. Detective Helen Rock interviewed Jose later that day.

Lopez and Petitioner continued to have conversations until July 11, when Petitioner retained counsel.

Lopez did a search of the Wittmann Grocery Store on December 17, 1997, finding papers reflecting the extension of credit by the store, primarily to store employees. Some just reflected first names.

Petitioner denied hearing any rumors about his wife, other than that he heard around town that people said he had a hit on his wife. He didn't inquire further, and didn't remember who told him that.

Petitioner told him he met the victim at a function at the East Indian dance festival. He had a prior, brief, arranged marriage. His marriage to the victim was not arranged. The victim was of a higher caste than Petitioner, and that caused problems on both sides. They had eloped and married in Las Vegas, Nevada, and then she returned to California, and he to Arizona. Only later did they tell their families and have a marriage in their culture. The second marriage ceremony was a year later. They then moved in with Petitioner's parents. Petitioner was devoted to his father, and as the eldest son was responsible for taking care of his parents in their culture.

Petitioner mentioned to Lopez that he had noticed that when he would ride in the victim's vehicle that the passenger seat would be pushed all the way back and sometimes reclined back. It seemed to bother him. The discussed the possibility that the victim was going out on him, and Petitioner said it crossed his mind, but he didn't believe she would do that. He said his heart also told him maybe, but he threw that feeling away, and he didn't want to talk about it.

Petitioner had heard rumors that someone wanted to car jack his truck. He had a hard time in the business at first because of his skin color, but eventually got to know everybody in town and made a lot of friends. Some got angry when he wouldn't sell to them on credit.

Based on Lopez's reconstruction of the scene and the autopsy, he believed the shooter was behind the victim, in the backseat compartment of the car, close to the center console. A second 380 casing was found in the car when it was at the impound lot, on December 15, 1997, when the driver's seat was removed. It was impounded by Detective Rock. It was found under the driver's seat, closer to the rear floorboard, on the same side of the car as the other casing.

There were TV station vans at Petitioner's home on July 3, 1997, and there was newspaper and television coverage of the murder. Channel 12 did a silent witness re-enactment. There was print coverage when Petitioner was arrested. And Silent Witness circulated flyers, using the victim's driver's license photo. When Lopez handed three of the flyers to Petitioner on November 20, 1997, Petitioner laid them face down on his desk. Petitioner put some of the flyers up in his store. The police department did some media releases through their Public Information Officer.

Lopez interviewed different people about potential motives. It was suggested that there was an inability to divorce in Petitioner's culture. Lopez did not know if Petitioner had obtained a religious divorce to end his religious marriage to his first wife. There was information that the victim was a spendthrift, but Lopez could not corroborate that claim. There was information that there was some insurance policy, but the only one located was the one through the victim's employer in a relatively small amount. There was information about a prenuptial agreement, but the existence of such an agreement could not be substantiated. Although Falcon had told defense counsel that the victim having an affair was a motive, Falcon did not relate such a claim to Lopez. In the interim, police reports had been read to Falcon.

The taped interviews of witnesses did not contain discussions of the criminal or substance abuse histories of the witnesses.

The day before Lopez interviewed Donnie Mecham, he had talked with his close family friend, William Moore, who he referred to as his uncle. During the pre-taping discussions with Donne Mecham, Lopez did not suggest that Mecham helping in the investigation could benefit Moore. They discussed Petitioner agreeing to Mecham taking Falcon to get his car. That was different from what Mecham had previously told Detective Lang, and Lopez.

He also had pre-taping conversations with Catalina Falcon, Cynthia Gragg, Ron Wallace, and Ron Moore. On the tape, he recapped what Gragg had told him and she assented to it. Lopez disagreed that it would be better to tape all but the introductions, because witnesses are reluctant to talk on a recording until they know what they are going to be asked. He always asks witnesses to let him know if they remember anything else. Most people don't.

He was aware that Petitioner and the victim had assets which included three pieces of property in Maricopa County, her car, her insurance policy, and jewelry seized from a Bank of America vault in a search. Property settlements are commonly parts of divorces.

(Supp. Exhibit O, R.T. 10/11/00 at 83-133; Supp. Exhibit P, R.T. 10/12/00 at 3-42.)

Catalina Falcon -- A video deposition of Catalina Falcon was played for the jury on stipulation of the parties. A transcript has not been provided. (Supp. Exhibit P, R.T. 10/12/00 at 42-44.) In the prosecution's closing argument, the testimony was described as relating that Catalina had been called by El Gato to pick him up the morning of the murder, after he left the car. (Supp. Exhibit S, R.T. 10/18/00 at 29.)

Bijal Chollera -- The victim's sister, Bijal Chollera, testified that she was around the victim and Petitioner in July, 1997. Their family is in Mwanza, Tanzania, where they were born. Their ethnic origin is East Indian. They both came to the United States in September, 1986, settled in Phoenix and went to Phoenix College. The victim had a doctor of pharmacy degree from the University of Southern California.

Chollera had known Petitioner as an acquaintance since 1991, four years before he married the victim. She met him at a religious cultural function, his wedding reception with his first wife. She, the victim and Petitioner were Hindu, and of Indian ethnic origin. Petitioner's first wife was Indian as well.

She was aware the Petitioner and the victim had eloped and gotten married after Petitioner left his first wife. In their tradition, a divorce was integrated with western culture, and involved signing papers. If there is no civil marriage, then the parties call their families together, tell them it's not working out and they can take their daughter and her possessions back. They might do it in front of someone within the hierarchy of the society, or the cultural organization to be a witness. In the Hindu tradition, it is disfavored. It was disfavored for a woman to go with a man who left his first wife, as the victim did.

After they eloped in May, 1994, they announced their engagement. The victim was finishing her degree in California, and a year later on July 2, 1995 they got married under Hindu rituals. They then started living together. There were 6 to 8 years' difference in age between Petitioner and the victim.

Petitioner and the victim lived with his parents, consistent with Indian traditions that the eldest son take care of the parents.

Chollera was in their home many times. There was one whole room of the house dedicated to Hindu rituals.

In early 1996, the victim was in an accident on Grand Avenue with a drunk driver. She injured her knee, had trouble walking, and needed therapy. She was working in Phoenix at the Veterans Hospital in a pharmacy internship and residency at the time. She recovered and was physically fine. She did not have seizures.

She obtained a settlement that she used to pay off some credit card debts she had accumulated. She then began paying for most things by cash. She was not a spendthrift, but continued to shop, buy jewelry, go to California and buy things. She loved shopping and if she liked something she got it. She had good taste, and if it cost a lot she would buy it. She especially liked Indian jewelry, which was usually 22 carat gold. She had traditional Indian jewelry when she got married.

In the summer of 1996, Petitioner presented the victim with a Lincoln Mark V. Chollera didn't know how the car was paid for or who bought it. The victim didn't want a vehicle that large. So they bought the Camry involved in this case, using the victim's credit.

In July, 1996, the victim went to work at Del Webb Hospital, and was in an accident in November, 1996 in Los Angeles. She was hit head on, had a head injury, lost her memory for three or four days, and was having seizures. She was hospitalized for a few days. Petitioner was the first person from Arizona to get to the hospital, and rented a car to driver her and Chollera back to Arizona.

Afterwards, the victim would lose her balance, needed support to walk, and had seizures. Chollera saw her have one of these seizures at home. She would have spit coming out of her mouth and her muscles were pulling. She was disabled from the accident for about three months. She took seizure medications. She improved with therapy that lasted about a month. But, she lost weight, lost energy, and was easily angered and seemed dazed. She was off work for three months. She had full medical coverage, and may have had paid time off.

During this time, Petitioner stopped paying as much attention to her and stopped spending time with her. He stopped taking her to therapy, and relied on his parents to take her. He was always at the store in Wittman. The victim preferred to have Chollera take her to therapy.

By March and April, the victim was back to work, and released to drive. The victim was back to her normal self, energetic, positive, active, pleasant and nice to Petitioner. She and Petitioner began doing things more on weekend nights. Chollera would sometimes join them. The victim went to work at 5:30 or 6:00 in the morning and would get home in the middle of the afternoon. But Petitioner was gone on the weekdays and weekday evenings and weekend days. The store was open from about 7:00 a.m. to 10:00 p.m., but Petitioner only worked a few evenings. They would go out in the evenings to dinner or the movies. The last month or two before she was killed, the victim was lively and vibrant.

The victim would help her mother in law in the afternoons with her catering business.

In June, 1997, Chollera noticed some kind of tenseness. They would still go out, but Petitioner would have Chollera drive and would sit in the back of her two-door car by himself. Petitioner would come home tense, and said he was stressed from work.

On July 2, 1997, Chollera had taken the victim to get her car from Discount Tire that afternoon so Petitioner and the victim could take it on a trip. The victim had prepared dinner. Then the three of them went out to go to the movies. Petitioner asked the victim to drive her car, the blue Toyota Camry. The victim seemed surprised and happy to get to drive and had to go back in to get her keys. Chollera asked him about it because it was their anniversary. Petitioner said he was tired and just wanted to sit in the back. He rode in the back seat by himself, behind Chollera.

When they returned, the victim parked the car on the left side, in front of the car port, which was filled with two cars. A truck was parked to the right. Chollera mistakenly took the victim's sunglasses, and the victim kiddingly scolded her and asked her to put them back in the car. The victim had given Petitioner the keys and remote and he unlocked the car for Chollera. She opened the door, put the glasses back in the car, and closed the door. Petitioner clicked again and she heard the doors lock. The sounds of the car locking and unlocking were different. The remote did not make any sound Petitioner went in and put the keys that the victim had been using to drive with on the kitchen dining cabinet. When interviewed by defense counsel, she did not mention Petitioner locking the car. Petitioner and the victim each had their own sets of keys. Chollera didn't know if Petitioner had a set of keys to the car that evening. She did not recall Petitioner mentioning before the murder having problems with the remote, but he did mention it after the murder. She did not remember seeing both sets of keys the day before the murder.

The victim asked her to spend the night that evening, July 2nd, but Chollera wasn't able to.

The victim was anticipating a trip Petitioner had planned to Mexico via San Diego for their anniversary. It was to start on July 4th.

The victim was planning on a trip to Africa around August. It was the first time she had gone back home. Chollera had helped her with her passport. Her passport and ticket arrived the day she passed away. Chollera handled getting a refund.

Their Indian tradition calls for 13 days of hymns and mourning. Chollera only saw Petitioner cry on two occasions. Otherwise, his reaction to her death seemed to be quiet, deep thinking, dazed. On the ritual days, Petitioner would sit for a little bit where the victim's picture and a candle were.

Petitioner went through the victim's things and found a box of pictures. He only wanted the picture on the dresser from when they eloped. That disturbed Chollera. Petitioner left the picture on the dresser. The mother-in-law wanted to keep their wedding pictures. The Hindu tradition was to put a single picture of the deceased in the prayer room. The father-in-law put in the shrine a large picture of the victim from her wedding day. The picture had arrived the night before her death.

After Petitioner and the victim were married in 1994, they sent to Las Vegas from time to time for the weekend. Petitioner said they stayed at Circus Circus.

Chollera had nothing against Petitioner, but objected to the victim seeing him, and to their eloping without discussing it with her family. She responded to the news of their marriage by saying "you're so stupid, how could you." She objected because Petitioner had been married before, the victim was five years younger, the victim had a higher education, and Petitioner's family was from a lower caste in India. No one in the victim's family had ever married outside of their caste.

Chollera spent a lot of time at the Petitioner and victim's house, but did not live there. She was usually there three to four days a week, sometimes for more than several hours. Some of the time Petitioner was gone, but she would have dinner with them. Petitioner and his family had a sense of humor and were fun. In the week or ten days prior to the murder, she was there almost all of the time, but not constantly. She would spend some nights there.

She was aware that Petitioner and the victim had purchased some investment land in the spring and early summer of 1997, and were looking at buying a home for themselves.

Chollera graduated from Western International in June of 1997, and Petitioner and the victim had a graduation party at their home. She planned to move to Los Angeles.

(Supp. Exhibit P, R.T. 10/12/00 at 45-111.)

Joyot Paul Chaudhuri -- Dr. Chaudhuri, professor of political science at Arizona State University, testified that he was born and educated in India until 1952, was from a Hindu background, and wrote articles and functioned as an expert in issues of Hindu and Indian culture and heritage.

Chaudhuri testified that although there is associated regret, and family pressure against it, Hindus do get divorced. There is no religious objection, but the wife usually returns to her family with different settlements being made. The caste system was used to divide people into different social functions, and eventually developed a hierarchy. It is not a legal distinction, but one of family and inter-family relationships.

Oldest sons have ritual obligations, such as cremation of the father. They have special obligations to both parents by custom. Oldest sons of oldest sons have great expectations placed on them.

Hindu families often have shrines in their homes, with different features dependent upon their sect. The rituals for different sects and castes would vary.

Marriage ceremonies may include a ceremony at the bride's home, a parade to the husband's home, and a ceremony at the husband's. Usually the bride will go to live with the husband's family. Arranged marriages are common, although increasingly the husband and wife will have met each other before the marriage.

Indian's often take their customs and Hinduism with them and continue them in a foreign country.

Daily prayer is a common tradition, but it is not ostentatious.

It is common when a death occurs to keep just a few pictures of the deceased out. The notion of death is that life goes on.

(Supp. Exhibit Q, R.T. 10/16/00 at 24-35.)

Stipulation re Reward -- The parties stipulated that the $11,000 reward offered consisted of $10,000 from the Chollera family, and $1,000 from the Silent Witness program.

Conclusion - Petitioner was convicted by the jury of first degree murder and conspiracy to commit first degree murder. (Pet. Exhibit 3, Mem. Dec. 3/27/03 at 3-4.)

After an aggravation/mitigation hearing (Pet. Exhibit 27, M.E. 10/11/01; Pet. Exhibit 29, R.T. 10/11/01), the trial court found the existence of an aggravating factor but declined to impose the death penalty, instead sentencing Petitioner to life in prison without possibility of parole on the murder charge, and life with possibility of parole after 25 years on the conspiracy charge. (*Id.* at 3-4.)

C. PROCEEDINGS ON DIRECT APPEAL
Petitioner filed a notice of direct appeal.

During, Petitioner's trial, the Maricopa County Superior Court was operating under an experimental rule providing for "rapid transcripts" in all but death penalty cases. (Pet. Exhibit 3, Mem. Dec. 3/27/03 at 17.) Under the rule, trial transcripts in criminal appeals were computer generated, and not certified. Counsel could request and the Arizona Court of Appeals could order a certified transcript of any portion. (Pet. Exhibit 17, Order 4.17.) Rapid transcripts were provided for Petitioner's appeal.

Petitioner asserted arguments on appeal that:

(1) the use of the case detective as a bailiff violated Petitioner's right to due process and an impartial jury;

(2) the trial judge erred in denying the motion for mistrial;

(3) the rapid transcript rule was unconstitutional;

(4) the sentencing statute, *Ariz. Rev. Stat. § 13-703*, as applied to non-capital cases, was unconstitutional under *Apprendi v. New Jersey, 530 U.S. 466, 120 S. Ct. 2348, 147 L. Ed. 2d 435 (2000)*, etc.; and

(5) a discrepancy in the sentencing minute entry required remand.

(Pet. Exhibit 1A, Opening Brief at i.)

In a Memorandum Decision filed March 27, 2003 (Pet. Exhibit 3), the Arizona Court of Appeals affirmed Petitioner's convictions and sentences, but modified the sentencing minute entry to remove "clearly excessive" language and orders relating to executive clemency. (*Id.* at 22-23.)

Petitioner filed a Petition for Review (Pet. Exhibit 4), arguing: (1) that the sentencing statute, *Ariz. Rev. Stat. § 13-703*, was unconstitutionally vague as applied to natural life sentences; and (3) and that under *Apprendi* he had a right to jury determination on the aggravating factors even if the sentence ultimately imposed did not exceed the statutory maximum. The Arizona Supreme Court summarily denied review. (Pet. Exhibit 5, Order 10/29/03.)

D. PROCEEDINGS ON POST-CONVICTION RELIEF

On February 11, 2004, Petitioner filed an Application for Leave to File Delayed Notice of Post conviction Relief (Pet. Exhibit 7), noting that his PCR notice was due by December 31, 2003, and seeking leave to filed a delayed notice. Petitioner eventually filed, on May 13, 2005, a

PCR Petition (Pet. Exhibit 8A), arguing that trial counsel was ineffective for failing to conduct an adequate investigation, and that newly discovered evidence indicated Petitioner's innocence. The State argued the petition was untimely, and failed to qualify for consideration under the exceptions to the timeliness rules. (Pet. Exhibit 8B, Response.)

The PCR Court denied Petitioner's ineffective assistance of counsel claim as delinquent, and deferred ruling on the remaining claims until completion of discovery and a motion to amend to clarify the claims. (Pet. Exhibit 9, M.E. 11/7/05.)

Petitioner then filed an Application to Amend (Pet. Exhibit 10B) and an Amended Memorandum (Pet. Exhibit 10A). The Amended Memorandum argued that the events of the shooting as related by Falcon based on Munoz's statements were inconsistent with the evidence at the scene as demonstrated by subsequent experiments by crime scene investigators, including the inability of Munoz to conceal himself in the small backseat, and to exit through the passenger front door without creating more of a blood trail. The State argued in response that the experiments were not newly discovered evidence, could have been developed with reasonable diligence, were merely impeachment and would not have altered the outcome of trial. (Pet. Exhibit 10C.)

On October 24, 2007, the PCR court adopted the State's arguments and dismissed the Petition. (Pet. Exhibit 11, M.E. 10/24/07.)

Petitioner then sought review by the Arizona Court of Appeals, challenging both the dismissal of the ineffective assistance of counsel claim and the rejection of the newly discovery evidence claims. (Pet. Exhibit 12A, PFR.) The State responded (Pet. Exhibit 12C), arguing that the PCR petition had been untimely, and Petitioner had failed to assert a claim within the exceptions to the rule. On September 26, 2008, the Arizona Court of Appeals summarily denied review. (Pet. Exhibit 13.)

Petitioner sought review by the Arizona Supreme Court (Pet. Exhibit 15A), which was summarily denied on March 17, 2009. (Pet. Exhibit 24.)

E. OMITTED TRANSCRIPT PROCEEDINGS

On January 7, 2010, Petitioner filed with the trial court a Motion for Preparation of Omitted Transcript (Pet. Exhibit 25) arguing that the transcript of the aggravation/mitigation had not been prepared and submitted on appeal. The motion was granted. (Pet. Exhibit 26, M.E. 2/18/10.)

F. PRESENT FEDERAL HABEAS PROCEEDINGS

<u>Petition</u> - Petitioner commenced the current case by filing his original *pro se* Petition for Writ of Habeas Corpus pursuant to *28 U.S.C. § 2254* on January 4, 2010. On January 5, 2010, counsel for Petitioner appeared and filed a series of Exhibits (Doc. 4) and a Memorandum in Support (Doc. 5). Service was ordered on January 27, 2010 (Doc. 6).

Prior to an answer being filed, Petitioner filed on March 3, 2010 his Amended Petition (Doc. 12) and Additional Exhibits (Doc. 13), incorporating by reference the earlier filed Exhibits (Doc. 4).

Petitioner's Amended Petition asserts the following seven grounds for relief:

(1) Vagueness - "On its face and as applied to Petitioner, the Arizona statute under which Petitioner received a natural life sentence, the 1997 version of *A.R.S. § 13-703*, violates Petitioner's right to due process under the *Fourteenth Amendment* because the statute is unconstitutionally vague by providing no standards for sentencing and allows for an arbitrary application by Arizona trial and appellate judges."

(2) *Apprendi* - "Petitioner's right to a jury trial under the *Sixth Amendment* and the *Fourteenth Amendments* was violated because the aggravating factor that supported Petitioner's Natural Life sentence was not found by a jury as required by *Apprendi v. New Jersey*."

(3) Rapid Transcripts - "The refusal of the Arizona Court of Appeals to remand the case back to the trial court for transcripts certified to be accurate, edited and corrected and instead relying upon uncertified 'rapid transcripts' violated the *Fourteenth Amendment's equal protection* and *due process clauses*."

(4) Hearsay - "Admission of hearsay and the refusal to grant a new trial violated the rights to confrontation and the right to due process and a fair trial protected by the *Sixth* and *Fourteenth Amendments*."

(5) Actual Innocence - "Newly-discovered evidence exists that would have changed the verdicts and shows the Petitioner is actually innocent of the crimes. The Petitioner is being held in custody in violation of the *Fourteenth Amendment*."

(6) Ineffective Assistance - "Petitioner's right to the effective assistance of trial counsel was denied. Petitioner's trial counsel failed to adequately investigate the case, the Petitioner was prejudiced and the *Strickland v. Washington* standard was violated."

(7) Omitted Transcript - "For the direct appeal, the clerk of the state trial court falsely certified as 'true and complete' an incomplete record of the trial proceedings resulting in important court filings and at least one transcript being omitted from the appellate record. The failure to submit a complete and accurate record to the state appellate court denied this indigent Petitioner a full and fair hearing on direct appeal and in post-conviction proceedings, denied him meaningful and effective direct appellate review and post conviction review, and denied him the right to properly litigate all the issues in the case in violation of the *Due Process* and *Equal Protection Clauses of the Fourteenth Amendment*. The Rapid Transcript Experiment and selection of Petitioner's case to be included in the experimental process violated the *Fourteenth Amendment's equal protection* and *due process clauses*. Moreover, although the Superior Court Clerk was responsible for the erroneous record preparation, Petitioner alternatively argues that if the Clerk's errors alone do not warrant relief that he has in addition been subject to the ineffective assistance of counsel by the failure of his attorneys to have discovered the Clerk's omissions."

A response was ordered. (Order 4/14/10, Doc. 14.)

Response - On May 17, 2010, Respondents filed their Response ("Answer") (Doc. 15). Respondents concede the Petition is timely, but argue that: (a) the equal protection claims in Ground 3, and the claims in Grounds 4 (Hearsay), 5 (Actual Innocence), and 7 (Omitted Transcript) were never fairly presented to the state courts and are procedurally defaulted; (b) the claims in Ground 6 (Ineffective Assistance) are procedurally barred; and (c) the claims in Grounds 1 (Vagueness), 2 (*Apprendi*), and the due process claim in Ground 3 are without merit.

Reply - On August 5, 2010, Petitioner filed a Reply (Doc. 20) and Exhibits (Doc. 21). Petitioner argues that presentation to the Arizona Supreme Court is not necessary for exhaustion because Petitioner received a life sentence, and that other than Ground 7, his claims were properly exhausted and are meritorious. As to Ground 7, Petitioner requests a stay to exhaust those claims.

Request for Stay - On July 6, 2011, the Court noted Petitioner's request to stay these proceedings to assert additional claims in the state court. Consequently, Respondents were ordered to supplement the record to provide any subsequent state court proceedings. (Order 7/6/11 (Doc. 22). On July 7, 2011, Respondents file their Notice (Doc. 23), advising that there have been no intervening state filings.

On September 15, 2011, the undersigned issued a Report and Recommendation (Doc. 24) recommending that Petitioner's Motion to Stay (Doc. 20) be denied. That recommendation was adopted without objection on November 4, 2011 (Doc. 30).

Supplements re Actual Innocence -- In the meantime, on September 15, 2011, the Court ordered the parties to supplement their briefs and the record to address Petitioner's assertion of actual innocence as a means to avoid his procedural defaults or procedural bars. (Order, Doc. 25.) Respondents filed their Supplemental Answer and attachments on October 6, 2011 (Docs. 26, 27, and 28). On October 26, 2011, Petitioner filed his Supplemental Reply (Doc. 29).

III. APPLICATION OF LAW TO FACTS

A. EXHAUSTION & PROCEDURAL DEFAULT: Grounds 3 (part), 4, 5, and 7

Respondents argue that Petitioner's equal protection claims in Ground 3, and the claims in Grounds 4 (Hearsay), 5 (Actual Innocence), and 7 (Omitted Transcript) were never fairly presented to the state courts, his state remedies were not properly exhausted and are now procedurally defaulted, and thus these claims are barred from habeas review.

c. Application to Petitioner's Claims

(1) Ground 3: Equal Protection Claim - Petitioner's Ground 3 challenges the refusal of the Arizona Court of Appeals to remand the case back to the trial court for transcripts certified to be accurate, edited and corrected and instead relying upon the uncertified "rapid transcripts." Petitioner contends that this violated both his equal protection and due process rights under the *Fourteenth Amendment*. Respondents concede that the due process claim was fairly presented on direct appeal, but contend that Petitioner never asserted an equal protection claim to the Arizona Courts. (Answer, Doc. 15 at 8-9.) Petitioner replies that the factual basis is part and parcel of the due process claim, and that the equal protection portion was fairly presented in his Opening Brief on direct appeal by quoting a portion of the Arizona case, *Matter of Hendrix, 145 Ariz. 345, 349, 701 P.2d 841 (1985)*, which in turn cited *Griffin v. Illinois, 351 U.S. 12, 76 S. Ct. 585, 100 L. Ed. 891 (1956)*. Petitioner contends *Griffin* is an equal protection case, and quoting the Arizona Supreme Court's citation of it was sufficient to raise the equal protection claim. Petitioner also contends that in the area of indigent appeals, the two clauses of the *Fourteenth Amendment* are interconnected. (Reply, Doc. 20 at 16-17.)

The fact that the factual basis for Petitioner's due process and equal protection claims is the same is inapposite. A claim has been fairly presented to the state's highest court only if petitioner has described *both* the operative facts *and* the federal legal theory on which the claim is based. *Kelly v. Small, 315 F.3d 1063, 1066 (9th Cir. 2003)*.

Nor was Petitioner's incidental quotation of *Griffith* sufficient to raise an equal protection claim. Petitioner's brief was explicitly limited to asserting a due process right under the Federal constitution.

The specific constitutional problems with *rule 4.17* are that it violates a defendant's right to due process under the *Arizona (art. 2, sec. 4)* and Federal (*5th* and *14th amendments*)

Constitution. Furthermore, it violates a defendant's right to appeal, based on *art. 2, sec. 24, of the Arizona Constitution*.

* * *

This experimental rule allowing quick inaccurate transcripts in felony appeals violates numerous constitutional provisions, the due process guarantees for starters. Defendants are entitled to due process of law pursuant to *art. 2, sec. 4 of the Arizona Constitution*, and the *Fifth Amendment of the US Constitution*.

In addition, the rule violates the Arizona Constitutional right to a criminal appeal, guaranteed by *Art. 2, sec. 24*. What good are hard-working appellate lawyers and conscientious panels of appellate judges when the briefs are based on transcripts which are "not finally edited, corrected, or certified to be accurate."

(Pet. Exhibit 1A, Opening Brief at 13, 15.)
It is true that Petitioner included the following quotation:

Mr. Strange [a defendant] had a constitutional right to a complete and accurate transcript of the sentencing proceedings. *See Griffin v. Illinois, 351 U.S. 12, 76 S. Ct. 585, 100 L. Ed. 891 ... (1956)*.
Matter of Hendrix, 145 Ariz. 345, 349, 701 P.2d 841, 845 (1985).

(*Id.* at 12.) It is also true that "for purposes of exhaustion, a citation to a state case analyzing a federal constitutional issue serves the same purpose as a citation to a federal case analyzing such an issue." *Peterson v. Lampert, 319 F.3d 1153, 1158 (9th Cir. 2003)*.

However, as observed in Petitioner's Opening Brief, this was not a legal conclusion by the *Hendrix* court, but a quotation of the record below of the Arizona Commission on Judicial Qualifications. *Hendrix* involved the censure of a Superior Court judge, in part based upon "indecorous" post-sentencing comments to a defendant. In preparing the transcript for appeal, the court reporter inquired of the judge whether to include the comments in the transcript, and the judge responded it was the court reporter's decision. Ultimately, the comments were not included in the transcript. In finding the judge's conduct (both the court room comment and the instructions to the court reporter) to be violations of the Code of Judicial Conduct, the Court quoted from the Commission's findings, including the foregoing statement. The *Hendrix* court engaged in no analysis of the nature of the federal constitutional rights at play, nor did it discuss any right to the transcript. It simply held: "By allowing these items to be omitted from the reporter's transcript, Judge Hendrix gave the appearance of trying to hide something." *145 Ariz. at 349, 701 P.2d at 845.*

Moreover, *Griffin*, the federal case cited in Petitioner's quotation from *Hendrix* was not uniquely an equal protection case. To the contrary, *Griffin* repeatedly noted that it was proceeding on both equal protection and due process grounds.

> In this tradition, our own constitutional guaranties of due process and equal protection both call for procedures in criminal trials which allow no invidious discriminations between persons and different groups of persons. Both equal protection and due process emphasize the central aim of our entire judicial system-all people charged with crime must, so far as the law is concerned, 'stand on an equality before the bar of justice in every American court.'

Griffin, 351 U.S. 12, 17, 76 S. Ct. 585, 100 L. Ed. 891 (1956) (citations omitted).

> Consequently, at all stages of the proceedings the *Due Process* and *Equal Protection Clauses* protect persons like petitioners from invidious discriminations.

Id. at 18. Even Justice Frankfurter's concurrence separately discussed the due process and equal protection issues at play. *Id. at 20-21.* "The [Supreme] Court also has emphasized that the holdings in the line of cases that began with *Griffin*, involving a criminal defendant's right of access to a transcript, are rooted firmly in both the *due process* and *equal protection clauses of the fourteenth amendment." Bundy v. Wilson, 815 F.2d 125, 131 (1st Cir. 1987).*

Had Petitioner been proceeding *pro se*, it might be tempting to conclude that the Arizona courts should have read past the plain language of his limited due process claim, and have presumed from his indirect citation of *Griffith* that he intended to assert an equal protection claim as well. However, Petitioner was represented by counsel in that brief. "When a document has been written by counsel, a court should be able to attach ordinary legal significance to the words used in that document." *Peterson, 319 F.3d at 1159.* Here, counsel plainly and explicitly asserted only a due process claim under the Federal Constitution. In *Lounsbury v. Thompson, 374 F.3d 785 (9th Cir. 2004)*, the court concluded that a procedural and substantive attack on a competency determination were so intertwined that the explicit presentation [*83] of one necessarily included the other. In light of the intertwined nature of the analysis in *Griffith*, the same might be said of equal protection and due process attacks on denial of appellate transcripts. However, the *Lounsbury* court distinguished *Peterson's* finding of strategic choice in explicit limitations by counsel, because the state appellate rules in *Lounsbury* placed counsel in a "dilemma" of identifying every claim for exhaustion while asserting only novel claims to meet the requirements for state appellate review. *374 F.3d at 788-789.* There is no indication that Petitioner's counsel faced a similar limitation here.

Accordingly, the undersigned finds that an equal protection claim was not fairly presented in Petitioner's direct appeal, nor otherwise. Therefore, this claim was not properly exhausted.

(2) Ground 4: Hearsay - For his Ground 4, Petitioner argues that the admission of out of court statements by "El Gato" (Munoz) through Falcon violated his confrontation and due process rights. Petitioner asserts this claim was presented on direct appeal. (Amend. Pet. Doc. 12 at 9.) Respondents argue that these facts were asserted in connection with a state law claim asserting an abuse of discretion in failing to grant a mistrial after the subject testimony, but it was never asserted as a federal law claim. (Answer, Doc. 15 at 9.) Petitioner replies

that the claim was fairly presented because it was asserted at trial as a *Sixth Amendment* claim.

Petitioner's reliance upon federal law before the trial court is inadequate to exhaust his state remedies. "[O]rdinarily a state prisoner does not 'fairly present' a claim to a state court if that court must read beyond a petition or a brief (or a similar document) that does not alert it to the presence of a federal claim in order to find material, such as a lower court opinion in the case, that does so." *Baldwin v. Reese, 541 U.S. 27, 32, 124 S. Ct. 1347, 158 L. Ed. 2d 64 (2004)*. The Arizona habeas petitioner "must have presented his federal, constitutional issue before the Arizona Court of Appeals within the four corners of his appellate briefing." *Castillo v. McFadden, 370 F.3d 882, 887 (9th Cir. 2004)*.

Accordingly, the undersigned finds that the claim in Ground 4 was not fairly presented in Petitioner's direct appeal, nor otherwise. Therefore, this claim was not properly exhausted.

 (3) Ground 5: Actual Innocence - In his Ground 5, Petitioner argues that he has newly discovered evidence of his actual innocence and therefore is held in violation of the *Fourteenth Amendment*. Respondents concede that Petitioner asserted a newly discovered evidence claim to the trial court in his first PCR proceeding, but argue he did not assert it as a federal claim. (Answer, Doc. 15 at 9-10.) In his Reply, Petitioner argues that Grounds 5 and 6 (Ineffective Assistance for failure to investigate and discover the evidence) should be construed together and Ground 5 should thus not be deemed unexhausted. (Reply, Doc. 20 at 26.) Even if this claim were properly exhausted, "[c]laims of actual innocence based on newly discovered evidence have never been held to state a ground for federal habeas relief absent an independent constitutional violation occurring in the underlying state criminal proceeding...This rule is grounded in the principle that federal habeas courts sit to ensure that individuals are not imprisoned in violation of the Constitution- not to correct errors of fact." *Herrera v. Collins, 506 U.S. 390, 400-401, 113 S. Ct. 853, 122 L. Ed. 2d 203 (1993)*.

The Ninth Circuit rejected a similar argument in *Rose v. Palmateer, 395 F.3d 1108 (9th Cir. 2005)*, where the court found that the petitioner did not fairly present a *Fifth Amendment* claim to the state courts when the claim was merely discussed as one of several issues handled ineffectively by counsel. "While [the ineffective assistance and underlying constitutional claim are] admittedly related, they are distinct claims with separate elements of proof, and each claim should have been separately and specifically presented to the state courts." *395 F.3d at 1112.* The *Rose* court noted that ineffective assistance of counsel claims could be disposed of without reaching the merits of the underlying constitutional claim, if, for example, the court found no prejudice because the outcome of the trial was not affected, or that counsel had made a reasonable tactical decision to not pursue the claim. *Id.*

Here, Petitioner's ineffective assistance of counsel claim was disposed of by the state courts as untimely. (Pet. Exhibit 9, M.E. 11/7/05 at 2.) Thus, the state courts had no cause to examine either the merits of the ineffective assistance claim itself, nor any constitutional claim underlying it.

Moreover, Petitioner did not assert the failure to raise a Federal Due Process due process/actual innocence claim in connection with his ineffective assistance claim. Rather, he simply argued that counsel was ineffective in not discovering the evidence on which he now relies to assert an actual innocence claim. Thus, even if the Arizona courts had reached the merits of the ineffective assistance claim, they would not have thus reached the instant due process claim.

Accordingly, the undersigned finds that the claim in Ground 5 was not fairly presented in Petitioner's PCR proceeding, nor otherwise. Therefore, this claim was not properly exhausted.

(4) Ground 7: Omitted Transcript - In his Ground 7, Petitioner argues that his due process and equal protection rights were violated by the omission on appeal of various documents and transcripts and that appellate counsel was ineffective for failing to correct the omissions. (Amend. Pet., Doc. 12 at 12-13.) Respondents argue these claims are unexhausted and procedurally defaulted. (Answer, Doc. 15 at

11.) Petitioner concedes his state remedies were not exhausted on this claim, asserts they are not procedurally defaulted, and seeks a stay to exhaust the claims. (Reply, Doc. 20 at 29.)

Accordingly, the undersigned finds that the claims in Ground 7 are not properly exhausted.

Summary - Based on the foregoing, the undersigned concludes that Petitioner's equal protection claims in Ground 3 (Rapid Transcript), and the claims in Grounds 4 (Hearsay), 5 (Actual Innocence), and 7 (Omitted Transcript) were never fairly presented to the state courts, and his state remedies were not properly exhausted.

2. Procedural Default

Ordinarily, unexhausted claims are dismissed *without prejudice. Johnson v. Lewis, 929 F.2d 460, 463 (9th Cir. 1991).* However, where a petitioner has failed to properly exhaust his available administrative or judicial remedies, and those remedies are now no longer available because of some procedural bar, the petitioner has "procedurally defaulted" and is generally barred from seeking habeas relief. Dismissal *with prejudice* of a procedurally barred or procedurally defaulted habeas claim is generally proper absent a "miscarriage of justice" which would excuse the default. *Reed v. Ross, 468 U.S. 1, 11, 104 S. Ct. 2901, 82 L. Ed. 2d 1 (1984).*

Respondents argue that Petitioner may no longer present his unexhausted claims to the state courts, and thus they are procedurally defaulted. Respondents generally rely upon Arizona's preclusion bar, set out in *Ariz. R. Crim. Proc. 32.2(a)* and time bar, set out in *Ariz. R. Crim. Proc. 32.4(a).* (Answer, Doc. 15 at 7.)

Remedies by Direct Appeal - Under *Ariz.R.Crim.P. 31.3,* the time for filing a direct appeal expires twenty days after entry of the judgment and sentence. The Arizona Rules of Criminal Procedure do not provide for a successive direct appeal. *See generally* Ariz.R.Crim.P. 31. Accordingly, direct appeal is no longer available for review of Petitioner's unexhausted claims.

Remedies by Post-Conviction Relief - Petitioner can no longer seek review by a subsequent PCR Petition. Under the rules applicable to Arizona's post-conviction process, a claim may not ordinarily be brought in a petition for post-conviction relief that "has been waived at trial, on appeal, or in any previous collateral proceeding." *Ariz.R.Crim.P. 32.2(a)(3)*. Under this rule, some claims may be deemed waived if the State simply shows "that the defendant did not raise the error at trial, on appeal, or in a previous collateral proceeding." *Stewart v. Smith, 202 Ariz. 446, 449, 46 P.3d 1067, 1070 (2002)* (quoting *Ariz.R.Crim.P. 32.2*, Comments). For others of "sufficient constitutional magnitude," the State "must show that the defendant personally, "knowingly, voluntarily and intelligently' [did] not raise' the ground or denial of a right." *Id.* That requirement is limited to those constitutional rights "that can only be waived by a defendant personally." *State v. Swoopes 216 Ariz. 390, 399, 166 P.3d 945, 954 (App.Div. 2, 2007)*. Indeed, in coming to its prescription in *Stewart v. Smith*, the Arizona Supreme Court identified: (1) waiver of the right to counsel, (2) waiver of the right to a jury trial, and (3) waiver of the right to a twelve-person jury under the Arizona Constitution, as among those rights which require a personal waiver. *202 Ariz. at 450, 46 P.3d at 1071*. Some types of claims addressed by the Arizona Courts in resolving the type of waiver required include: ineffective assistance (waived by omission), *Stewart, 202 Ariz. at 450, 46 P.3d at 1071*; right to be present at non-critical stages (waived by omission), *Swoopes, 216 Ariz. at 403, 166 P.3d at 958*; improper withdrawal of plea offer (waived by omission), *State v. Espinosa, 200 Ariz. 503, 29 P.3d 278 (App. 2001)*; double jeopardy (waived by omission), *State v. Stokes*, 2007 WL 5596552 (App. 10/16/07); illegal sentence (waived by omission), *State v. Brashier, 2009 Ariz. App. LEXIS 809, 2009 WL 794501 (App. 2009)*; judge conflict of interest (waived by omission), *State v. Westmiller, 2008 Ariz. App. Unpub. LEXIS 18, 2008 WL 2651659 (App. 2008)*.

Here, Petitioner's unexhausted claims do not fit within the list of claims identified as requiring a personal waiver. Nor are they of the same character. Therefore, it appears that Petitioner's claims would be precluded by his failure to raise them in an earlier proceeding.

Timeliness Bar - Even if not barred by preclusion, Petitioner would now be barred from raising his claims by Arizona's time bars. *Ariz.R.Crim.P. 32.4* requires that petitions for post-conviction relief (other than those which are "of-right") be filed "within ninety days after the entry of judgment and sentence or within thirty days after the issuance of the order and mandate in the direct appeal, whichever is the later." *See State v. Pruett, 185 Ariz. 128, 912 P.2d 1357 (App. 1995)* (applying 32.4 to successive petition, and noting that first petition of pleading defendant deemed direct appeal for purposes of the rule). That time has long since passed.

Exceptions - *Rules 32.2* and *32.4(a)* do not bar dilatory claims if they fall within the category of claims specified in *Ariz.R.Crim.P. 32.1(d) through (h). See Ariz. R. Crim. P. 32.2(b)* (exceptions to preclusion bar); *Ariz.R.Crim.P. 32.4(a)* (exceptions to timeliness bar). Petitioner has not asserted that any of these exceptions are applicable to his claims. Nor does it appear that such exceptions would apply. The rule defines the excepted claims as follows:

d. The person is being held in custody after the sentence imposed has expired;

e. Newly discovered material facts probably exist and such facts probably would have changed the verdict or sentence. Newly discovered material facts exist if:

(1) The newly discovered material facts were discovered after the trial.

(2) The defendant exercised due diligence in securing the newly discovered material facts.

(3) The newly discovered material facts are not merely cumulative or used solely for impeachment, unless the impeachment evidence substantially undermines testimony which was of critical significance at trial such that the evidence probably would have changed the verdict or sentence.

f. The defendant's failure to file a notice of post-conviction relief of-right or notice of appeal within the prescribed time was without fault on the defendant's part; or

g. There has been a significant change in the law that if determined to apply to defendant's case would probably overturn the defendant's conviction or sentence; or

h. The defendant demonstrates by clear and convincing evidence that the facts underlying the claim would be sufficient to establish that no reasonable fact-finder would have found defendant guilty of the underlying offense beyond a reasonable doubt, or that the court would not have imposed the death penalty.

Ariz.R.Crim.P. 32.1.

Paragraph 32.1(d) (expired sentence) generally has no application to an Arizona prisoner who is simply attacking the validity of his conviction or sentence. Here, Petitioner challenges the legality of the sentence imposed by the state court, but does not argue he is simply being held beyond the sentence actually imposed.

Petitioner contends that with regard to his claims in Ground 7 (missing transcripts), the missing records constitute "newly discovered evidence" within the meaning of *paragraph (e)*. The plain import of this provision is not to provide post-conviction relief for any new discovery, but simply discovery of new trial "evidence." In *State v. Sanchez*, the Arizona Court of Appeals rejected a defendant's attempt to rely on *paragraph (e)* where a police crime lab had changed their procedures after trial. *200 Ariz. 163, 166, 24 P.3d 610, 613 (Ariz. App. 2001).* The court observed: "One of the requirements for newly discovered evidence pursuant to *Rule 32.1, Ariz.R.Crim.P.,* is that the evidence have been in existence at the time of trial but not discovered until after trial." *Id. at 166-167, 24 P.3d at 613-614.*

Here, the omission of records did not occur until after trial, did not constitute evidence admissible at trial, and while arguably their absence might have changed the outcome of the appeal, the post-trial omission could not have "changed the verdict or sentence" *Ariz. R. Crim. Proc. 32.1(e).*

Moreover, the underlying records and transcripts were themselves not "discovered after the trial." At best, they were discovered by habeas counsel after the trial. But as part of the record at trial, they were known to the defense.

As to Petitioner's other unexhausted claims, where a claim is based on "newly discovered evidence" that has previously been presented to the state courts, the evidence is no longer "newly discovered" and *paragraph (e)* has no application.

Paragraph (f) has no application because Petitioner filed a timely notice of appeal, and as a defendant convicted at trial, was not entitled to file a "post-conviction relief of-right." *See Ariz. R. Crim. Proc. 32.1.*

Paragraph (g) has no application because Petitioner has not asserted a change in the law since his last PCR proceeding. Finally, *paragraph (h)*, concerning claims of actual innocence, has no application to Petitioner's procedural claims. *See State v. Swoopes, 216 Ariz. 390, 404, 166 P.3d 945, 959 (App. 2007)* (32.1(h) did not apply where petitioner had " not established that trial error ...amounts to a claim of actual innocence").

Summary - Accordingly, the undersigned must conclude that review through Arizona's direct appeal and post-conviction relief process is no longer possible for Petitioner's unexhausted claims, and that the unexhausted claims are now procedurally defaulted.

Remedies Through Recall of the Mandate - Finally, Petitioner argues that he may have available a remedy through a recall of the appellate mandate. That indeed may be the case. However, Petitioner's presentation of his claim in that context would not be "fair presentation." "[W]here the claim has been presented for the first and only time in a procedural context in which its merits will not be considered unless "there are special and important reasons therefor,". . .that "does not, for the relevant purpose, constitute 'fair presentation.' " *Castille v. Peoples, 489 U.S. 346, 351, 109 S. Ct. 1056, 103 L. Ed. 2d 380 (1989).*

It is true that actual consideration of the merits of a federal claim by the state courts, even if the claim were not fairly presented, would result in exhaustion. *See Sandstrom v. Butterworth, 738 F.2d 1200, 1206 (11th Cir.1984)* ("[t]here is no better evidence of exhaustion than a state court's actual consideration of the relevant constitutional issue"). However, this Court is not faced with such actual exhaustion. The mere possibility for such a review of the merits does not avoid the effect of Petitioner's current technical exhaustion and procedural default.

Summary re Procedural Default - Petitioner failed to properly exhaust his state remedies on the federal claims in Petitioner's equal protection claims in Ground 3 (Rapid Transcript), and the claims in Grounds 4 (Hearsay), 5 (Actual Innocence), and 7 (Omitted Transcript), and is now procedurally barred from doing so. Accordingly, these claims are procedurally defaulted, and absent a showing of cause and prejudice or actual innocence, must be dismissed with prejudice.

B. INDEPENDENT AND ADEQUATE STATE GROUNDS: Ground 6

In his Ground 6, Petitioner argues that he received ineffective assistance of counsel at trial, when counsel failed to adequately investigate so as to discover the physical impossibility of the crime as described by Falcon (as suggested in the expert testimony submitted by Plaintiff in support of his claims of actual innocence). Respondents argue this claim was presented in Petitioner's first PCR petition and was found to be precluded because untimely under *Ariz. R. Crim. Proc. 32.4*. Accordingly, Respondents argue that it was disposed of on an independent and adequate state ground and is barred from habeas review.

Petitioner replies that Arizona's time bar is not adequate to bar federal habeas review because it is not regularly applied. Petitioner argues that the rule is not regularly applied because the rule is discretionary, and Arizona courts "consistently use discretion and either grant or deny permission to file late." (Reply, Doc. 20 at 28.) In support of his argument, Petitioner cites *State v. Pope, 130 Ariz. 253, 635 P.2d 846 (1981)*. In that case, the Arizona Court determined that the time limits for a motion for rehearing under *Ariz. R. Crim. Proc. 32.9* is not jurisdictional, and a court may allow a late filing. Petitioner points to no Arizona authority extending *Pope* to late PCR notices under *Rule 32.4(a)*. The undersigned has found no cases extending *Pope* to *Rule 32.4(a)*. Petitioner does cite the unpublished decision in *Barrandez v. Hallahan, 1999 U.S. App. LEXIS 11391, 1999 WL 426403 (9th Cir. June 3, 1999)* for the proposition that *Pope* has been generally extended to all time limits under Arizona's Rule 32. (Reply, Doc. 20 at 28.) However, *Barrandez* did not apply *Pope* to a PCR notice under *Rule 32.4(a)*, but to a motion for rehearing under *Rule 32.9* In the unpublished decision in *State v. Bann, 2010 Ariz. App. Unpub. LEXIS 265, 2010 WL 1493109, *2 (Ariz.App. 2010)*, the court relied on *Pope* to permit a late PCR *petition.*

Nor did Petitioner provide any authority other than *Pope* in the PCR proceeding. (*See* Pet. Exhibit 7, Mot. Delayed Notice at 3; Pet. Exhibit 12A, Pet. Rev. at 9-12; Pet. Exhibit 15A, Pet. Rev. at 6-9.) The PCR Court concluded that *Pope* did not extend to subsequently enacted time limits in *Rule 32.4(a)*, and found that in *Moreno v. Gonzalez, 192 Ariz. 131, 962 P.2d 205 (1998)* the Arizona Supreme Court "implicitly confirmed that the time limits in *Rule 32.4* are mandatory and may not be waived by the trial court." (Pet. Exhibit 9, M.E. 11/7/05 at 2.) The Arizona Court of Appeals and Arizona Supreme Court summarily denied review. (Pet. Exhibit 13, Order 9/26/08; and Pet. Exhibit 14, Order 10/29/03.)

At best, Petitioner now points to *State v. Aaron*, 2008 WL 2623946 (Ariz. App. 2008) where the Arizona Court of Appeals faced a PCR petition filed 17 months after the appeal was denied. The court observed in a footnote: "As the record before us contains no notice, only Aaron's petition, we cannot determine whether Aaron did or did not file a timely notice." *Id.* at *1, n 1. Nonetheless, the Court proceeded to address the merits. "Because the trial court considered his claims on their merits, however, we exercise our discretion to do likewise in considering his petition for review." *Id.* Thus the court in *Aaron* did not conclude that the Arizona courts have discretion to ignore *Rule 32.4(a)*'s time limit, but they had the discretion to address the merits of a petition review where the potential for a violation of *Rule 32.4(a)* appeared from the bare record, but it had not been argued or addressed. That is a far different thing from finding a violation, and then finding the discretion to ignore it.

The plain language of *Rule 32.4(a)* belies any such discretion. The rule provides: "Any notice not timely filed may only raise claims pursuant to *Rule 32.1(d), (e), (f), (g)* or *(h)*." While *Rule 32.4(c)* permits extensions to the time for filing petitions, no similar authority is granted for PCR notices. Petitioner points to not a single instance in which an extension of the time line under *Rule 32.4(a)* has been granted, or the failure to comply with it waived. *Ariz. Rev. Stat. § 13-4234*, which is the statutory authority for PCR proceedings, and contains its own recitation of the 30-day time limit explicitly provides: "The time limits are jurisdictional, and an untimely filed notice or petition shall be dismissed with prejudice." *Ariz. Rev. Stat. § 13-4234(G)*. But see *State v. Fowler, 156 Ariz. 408, 752 P.2d 497 (App. 1987)* (finding prior version of *§13-4234* unconstitutional as an invasion of court's rule making power.

Moreover, even if *Pope* extends to *Rule 32.4(a)*, and the rule permitted discretionary exceptions, that does not render the rule inadequate.

> The mere fact that a state's procedural rule includes an element of discretion does not render it inadequate...So long as standards governing the exercise of discretion are firmly established and are consistently applied, a state's procedural rule will be adequate to bar federal claims.

Fields v. Calderon, 125 F.3d 757, 762 (9th Cir. 1997). The *Pope* rule includes standards to govern the state court's exercise of discretion.

> In so holding, we would remind the bench and bar that the party asserting a valid reason for non-compliance with the time requirements has a heavy burden in showing the court why the non-compliance should be excused. Mere inadvertence or neglect on the part of a party will not be considered a valid reason for allowing a party to avoid the strict time limits of Rule 32.

Pope, 130 Ariz. at 256, 635 P.2d at 849.

In *Bennett v. Mueller, 322 F.3d 573 (9th Cir.2003)*, the Ninth Circuit specifically addressed the burden of proving the adequacy of a state procedural bar.

> Once the state has adequately pled the existence of an independent and adequate state procedural ground as an affirmative defense, the burden to place that defense in issue shifts to the petitioner. The petitioner may satisfy this burden by asserting specific factual allegations that demonstrate the inadequacy of the state procedure, including citation to authority demonstrating inconsistent application of the rule. Once having done so, however, the ultimate burden is the state's.

Bennett, 322 F.3d at 584, 585.

Petitioner has failed to cite any authorities demonstrating inconsistent application of *Rule 32.4(a)*, or to assert factual allegations showing the rules inadequacy. Accordingly, Petitioner has failed to meet his threshold burden, and the undersigned concludes that *Rule 32.4(a)* is adequate to bar federal habeas relief.

C. CAUSE AND PREJUDICE

Here, Petitioner does not show any good cause to excuse his failures to exhaust.

To be sure, Petitioner argues that appellate and/or PCR counsel should have asserted various claims. However, to constitute cause to excuse a procedural default, deficient performance by counsel must constitute an independent constitutional violation. *Ortiz v. Stewart, 149 F.3d 923, 932, (9th Cir. 1998)*. In *Patrick Poland v. Stewart, 169 F.3d 573 (9th Cir. 1999)*, the Ninth Circuit held that "[b]ecause there is no right to an attorney in state post-conviction proceedings, there cannot be constitutionally ineffective assistance of counsel in such proceedings." *Id. at 588* (quoting *Coleman v. Thompson, 501 U.S. 722, 752, 111 S. Ct. 2546, 115 L. Ed. 2d 640 (1991)*).

Moreover, a claim of ineffective assistance of counsel showing "cause" is itself subject to the exhaustion requirements. *Murray v. Carrier, 477 U.S. 478, 492, 106 S. Ct. 2639, 91 L. Ed. 2d 397 (1986)*; *Edwards v. Carpenter, 529 U.S. 446, 120 S. Ct. 1587, 146 L. Ed. 2d 518 (2000)*. Accordingly, "[t]o the extent that petitioner is alleging ineffective assistance of appellate counsel as cause for the default, the exhaustion doctrine requires him to first raise this ineffectiveness claim as a separate claim in state court." *Tacho v. Martinez, 862 F.2d 1376, 1381 (9th Cir. 1988)*. Petitioner has not exhausted a claim of ineffective assistance of appellate counsel or PCR counsel.

It is true that in *Maples v. Thomas, U.S., 132 S. Ct. 912, 181 L. Ed. 2d 807, 2012 WL 125438 (2012)*, the Supreme Court held that cause could be shown when post-conviction counsel was not merely negligent (and under the law of agency that negligence being chargeable to the petitioner) but had abandoned the representation without notice to the petitioner, resulting in the loss of his state remedies. Here, however, Petitioner does not suggest that counsel abandoned the representation, merely that counsel was deficient. Thus, any such deficiency was not external to the defense, and is chargeable to Petitioner.

Petitioner also complains about the omission of records and transcripts on appeal. However, Petitioner also alleges that those omissions should have been discovered by effective appellate counsel. Again, no such claim has been exhausted.

Finally, Petitioner asserts cause to excuse his late PCR filing by arguing that the 30-day time limit applied to PCR proceedings "is very short and was triggered by the mandate of the appellate court that was never sent to Petitioner." (Reply, Doc. 20 at 28.) Petitioner further argues that appellate counsel rendered ineffective assistance when he misinformed Petitioner's family that a 90-day time limit applied, not a 30-day time limit. (*Id.*) All of this except the shortness of the time period amounts to another assertion that Petitioner's claim is procedurally barred because of the ineffective assistance of appellate counsel. However, Petitioner's state remedies on his claims of ineffective assistance of appellate counsel have not been exhausted.

As to the shortness of the time period, Petitioner does not assert that this was the cause of his delinquency, but rather it was his reliance on appellate counsel's misinformation. Petitioner does not allege, for example, that he diligently sought to file within the 30 days but was unable to meet the time period. Moreover, even if this Court were inclined to find 30 days to institute a PCR proceeding too short (a conclusion potentially disruptive of countless comparable time limits in federal and state jurisprudence) the time limit is only for the filing of a PCR notice, which requires little more than basic procedural information, with the PCR petition not due for at least 60 days thereafter. *See Ariz. R. Crim. Proc. 32.4*; and *Isley v. Arizona Dept. of Corrections, 383 F.3d 1054 (9th Cir. 2004)*.

Accordingly, the undersigned finds no basis for a finding of "cause."

<u>Miscarriage of Justice / Actual Innocence</u> -

However, in *Dretke v. Haley, 541 U.S. 386, 124 S. Ct. 1847, 158 L. Ed. 2d 659 (2004)*, the Court held that "a federal court faced with allegations of actual innocence, whether of the sentence or of the crime charged, must first address all non-defaulted claims for comparable relief and other grounds for cause to excuse the procedural default." *Id.*

at 393-394. Accordingly, the undersigned defers addressing the actual innocence claim until the merits of the remaining undefaulted claims are addressed.

D. GROUND 1: VAGUENESS

In his Ground 1, Petitioner argues that on its face and as applied to Petitioner, the Arizona statute under which Petitioner received a natural life sentence, the 1997 version of *A.R.S. § 13-703*, violates Petitioner's right to due process under the *Fourteenth Amendment* because the statute is unconstitutionally vague by providing no standards for sentencing and allows for an arbitrary application by Arizona trial and appellate judges.

Respondents argue that the Arizona Court of Appeals rejection of this claim on direct appeal was not contrary to nor an unreasonable application of applicable federal law, but was a reasonable application of the decision in *Harmelin v. Michigan, 501 U.S. 957, 994, 111 S. Ct. 2680, 115 L. Ed. 2d 836 (1991)*. (Answer, Doc. 15 at 12-13.)

Petitioner replies that the Arizona Court of Appeals wrongly focused on the "fair warning" flavor of vagueness, and ignored his sole argument based upon the "arbitrary application" flavor and thus misapplied federal law.

Limits of Habeas Relief - While the purpose of a federal habeas proceeding is to search for violations of federal law, not every error justifies relief. "[A] federal habeas court may not issue the writ simply because that court concludes in its independent judgment that the state-court decision applied [the law] incorrectly." *Woodford v. Visciotti, 537 U. S. 19, 24- 25, 123 S. Ct. 357, 154 L. Ed. 2d 279 (2002)* (*per curiam*). To justify habeas relief, a state court's decision must be "contrary to, or an unreasonable application of, clearly established Federal law, as determined by the Supreme Court of the United States" before relief may be granted. *28 U.S.C. §2254(d)(1)*.

Arizona Court's Decision - On direct appeal, Petitioner argued:

> In 1993, [*Ariz. Rev. Stat. §]* 13-703 was amended to its current form. It states that a defendant convicted of first degree murder will receive one of three specified sentences: death,

natural1ife in prison, or 25 years in prison. The death sentencing provisions of *13-703* are not at issue in this appeal.

The problem with *ARS 13-703* is that it gives the trial judge no standards to use in determining whether to impose the 25-year sentence or natural life.

* * *

A previous vagueness challenge to *ARS 13-703* argued the general vagueness argument, that *ARS 13-703* cannot be understood.

* * *

The appellant is making a different vagueness argument...

* * *

Instead, we have a criminal law which states two different punishments, one far more severe than the other, with no standards to guide the trial judge in determining which sentence is appropriate.

(Pet. Exhibit 1A, Opening Brief at 16, 18-19.)

In disposing of this claim, the Arizona Court of Appeals observed that in *State v. Wagner, 194 Ariz. 310, 311, 982 P.2d 270, 271 (1999)* the Arizona Supreme Court had disposed of a challenge to the statute based on a lack of fair notice. The appellate court went on to observe, however, that *Wagner* had also rejected a claim that the Constitution required sentencing guidelines to assist judges in selecting among sentencing options (with the exception of the death penalty). Appellate counsel had conceded at oral argument that *Wagner* was controlling law on the issue, and the appellate court relied upon it to dispose of the claim.

<u>Mandate for Sentencing Guidelines</u> - Petition argues that the Arizona court's decision was an unreasonable application of federal law because: (1) it relied on *Harmelin*, which is a cruel and unusual

punishment case not concerned with vagueness; and (2) the court incorrectly applied the "fair warning" standards to an "arbitrary application" claim.

Applicability of *Harmelin* - In *Harmelin*, the Supreme Court rejected a cruel and unusual punishment challenge to a mandatory natural life sentence which was based upon the disproportionality of the sentence and the lack of consideration of mitigating factors. With regard to the latter, the Court refused to extend its "individualized capital sentencing doctrine" to a mandatory natural life sentence. *501 U.S. at 995-996.*

In Petitioner's case, the Arizona Court of Appeals did not directly rely upon *Harmelin*, but simply acknowledged that the Arizona Supreme Court's opinion in *Wagner* had relied on *Harmelin*. (Pet. Exhibit 1A, Mem. Dec. 3/27/03 at 5.) The appellate court found itself bound by the holding of *Wagner* and in reliance on it disposed of Petitioner's claim. *Wagner*, in turn, addressed the substance of the due process challenge to a standard-less imposition of a life sentence:

> Because appellant has no constitutional right to sentencing guidelines in a non-capital proceeding, the lack of guidelines for imposing a sentence of life or natural life does not violate appellant's right to due process or equal protection under the law. *See Harmelin, 501 U.S. at 994, 111 S.Ct. at 2701* (rejecting a claim that the Constitution requires a state "to create a sentencing scheme whereby life in prison without possibility of parole [*112] is simply the most severe of a range of available penalties that the sentence may impose after hearing evidence in mitigation and aggravation"); *United States v. LaFleur, 971 F.2d 200, 211-12 (9th Cir.1991)*(holding that the Constitution does not require an individual assessment of the appropriateness of a life sentence).

Wagner, 194 Ariz. at 313-314, 982 P.2d at 273-274.

Thus, *Wagner*, and consequently the Arizona Court in this case, improperly relied upon the *Eighth Amendment* decision in *Harmelin* to reject a due process/vagueness challenge to a sentencing statute.

However, the Arizona Courts' erroneous application of *Harmelin* does not automatically justify relief. Rather, Petitioner is entitled to relief only if the Court's decision is "contrary to or an unreasonable application of" Supreme Court law.

Contrary To - The Arizona Court of Appeals' decision was not contrary to Supreme Court law.

The Supreme Court has instructed that a state court decision is "contrary to" clearly established federal law "if the state court applies a rule that contradicts the governing law set forth in [Supreme Court] cases or if the state court confronts a set of facts that are materially indistinguishable from a decision of [the Supreme] Court and nevertheless arrives at a result different from [its] precedent." *Lockyer v. Andrade, 538 U.S. 63, 73, 123 S. Ct. 1166, 155 L. Ed. 2d 144 (2003)* (internal quotation marks omitted).

Here, the rule applied did not contradict Supreme Court law. Petitioner points to no Supreme Court law which holds that the vagueness doctrine of due process precludes unguided judicial selection between various non-death penalty sentences. The last time the Supreme Court addressed any similar due process claim was in *McGautha v. California, 402 U.S. 183, 91 S. Ct. 1454, 28 L. Ed. 2d 711 (1971)*.

In *McGautha*, the Supreme Court addressed sentencing statutes, not under the *Eight Amendment*'s ban on cruel and unusual punishment, but under the vagueness mandate of the *Due Process Clause*.

> We consider first McGautha's and Crampton's common claim: that the absence of standards to guide the jury's discretion on the punishment issue is constitutionally intolerable. To fit their arguments within a constitutional frame of reference petitioners contend that to leave the jury completely at large to impose or withhold the death penalty as it sees fit is fundamentally lawless and therefore violates the basic command of the *Fourteenth Amendment* that no State shall deprive a person of his life without due process of law.

402 U.S. at 208. The Court ultimately rejected the claim:

> In light of history, experience, and the present limitations of human knowledge, we find it quite impossible to say that

committing to the untrammeled discretion of the jury the power to pronounce life or death in capital cases is offensive to anything in the Constitution.

Id. "The Court refused to find constitutional dimensions in the argument that those who exercise their discretion to send a person to death should be given standards by which that discretion should be exercised." *Furman v. Georgia, 408 U.S. 238, 247, 92 S. Ct. 2726, 33 L. Ed. 2d 346 (1972).*

Just one year after *McGautha,* the Court decided in *Furman* that a standards-less imposition of the death penalty was a violation of the *Eight Amendment.* In reliance on *Furman,* the Court vacated the judgment in *McGautha,* and remanded it for consideration under *Furman. Crampton v. Ohio, 408 U.S. 941, 92 S. Ct. 2873, 33 L. Ed. 2d 765 (1972).* "Thus, what had been approved under the *Due Process Clause of the Fourteenth Amendment* in *McGautha* became impermissible under the *Eighth* and *Fourteenth Amendments* by virtue of the judgment in *Furman.*" *Lockett v. Ohio, 438 U.S. 586, 599, 98 S. Ct. 2954, 57 L. Ed. 2d 973 (1978).* [*115] *See also Ford v. Wainwright, 752 F.2d 526, 534, n. 7 (1985),* overruled on other grounds, *477 U.S. 399, 106 S. Ct. 2595, 91 L. Ed. 2d 335 (1986)* ("*McGautha* ...was decided on the basis of the *Fourteenth Amendment* and not on *Eighth Amendment* grounds. In *Furman*...the Court recognized and began to explicate the *Eighth Amendment* parameters of capital sentencing."). Here, not only does Petitioner not assert an *Eight Amendment* claim, but he was not subjected to a death penalty.

Petitioner points to no Supreme Court decision since *McGautha* which adopts a contrary conclusion under due process, either as to death penalty cases or in the less formidable context of less-than-death sentences. The undersigned has found none.

Nor has Petitioner shown that the Arizona Court confronted "a set of facts that are materially indistinguishable from a decision of [the Supreme] Court and nevertheless arrive[d] at a result different from [its] precedent." *Lockyer, 538 U.S. at 73.* Indeed, *McGautha* is the closest due process case, and the Arizona decision arrived at the same result.

Unreasonable Application - Nor has Petitioner shown that the Arizona decision was an unreasonable application of Supreme Court law.

Distinguishing between an unreasonable and an incorrect application of federal law, the Court in *Williams v. Taylor, 529 U.S. 362, 120 S. Ct. 1495, 146 L. Ed. 2d 389 (2000)* clarified that an incorrect application is insufficient to justify relief. Distinguishing between an unreasonable and an incorrect application of federal law, the *Williams* Court clarified that even if the federal habeas court concludes that the state court decision applied clearly established federal law incorrectly, relief is appropriate only if that application is also objectively unreasonable. *Id. at 410-411.* "A state court's decision can involve an "unreasonable application" of federal law if it either (1) correctly identifies the governing rule but then applies it to a new set of facts in a way that is objectively unreasonable, or (2) extends or fails to extend a clearly established legal principle to a new context in a way that is objectively unreasonable." *Anthony v. Cambra, 236 F.3d 568, 578 (9th Cir. 2000).*

The first branch - correct rule, unreasonable application - -doesn't apply. The Arizona Court simply selected the wrong rule.

The second branch - unreasonable failure to apply rule in new context - - doesn't apply either. In this regard, it is important to remember that "it is the state court's decision, as opposed to its reasoning, that is judged under the 'unreasonable application' standard." *Merced v. McGrath, 426 F3d 1076, 1081 (9th Cir. 2005).* Here, the Arizona court's reasoning was flawed - - it chose the wrong precedent - - but there is no clearly established Federal law that was applicable and called for a decision different from that reached by the Arizona court. Indeed, *McGautha* mandated the very decision they reached.

Thus, despite the erroneous reliance on *Harmelin*, the Arizona court's decision was neither contrary to nor an unreasonable application of Supreme Court law.

"Fair Warning" v. "Arbitrary Application" - Finally, Petitioner argues that *§ 2254*'s limitation on habeas relief is met because the Arizona court improperly applied a "fair warning" analysis to Petitioner's "arbitrary application" claim.

As recognized in *Anderson v. Morrow, 371 F.3d 1027 (9th Cir. 2004),* the due process proscription of vague statues encompasses both a "notice test" and an "arbitrary enforcement test." The "notice test" is concerned with whether "the statutory language is 'sufficiently precise to provide comprehensible notice' of the prohibited conduct." *Id. at 1032.* The "arbitrary enforcement test" is concerned with the kind of statute that "does not provide explicit standards to those who apply them, so as to avoid arbitrary and discriminatory enforcement." *Id.*

Here, the Arizona Court of Appeals' decision quoted those portions of *Wagner* that focused on notice, *i.e.* that "a person of ordinary intelligence can easily determine the range of punishment he or she faces for committing first degree murder." (Pet. Exhibit 3, Mem. Dec. 3/27/03 at 5 (quoting *Wagner, 194 Ariz. at 313, 982 P.2d at 273*).)

To the extent that the Arizona court failed to address the issue raised by Petitioner (e.g. arbitrary enforcement), it's decision could be considered erroneous or even unreasonable.

However, Petitioner fails to offer any Supreme Court precedent which extends the vagueness prohibition against arbitrary enforcement to the sentencing context.

Petitioner points to *Grayned v. City of Rockford, 408 U.S. 104, 108, 92 S. Ct. 2294, 33 L. Ed. 2d 222 (1972)* for the proposition that the vagueness doctrine prohibits statutes that lack "explicit standards for those who apply them." (Reply, Doc. 20 at 10.) However, *Grayned* was not concerned with discretion in sentencing, but in prosecution decisions under a disturbing-the-peace statute. Petitioner points to no cases extending the vagueness doctrine past the prosecution stage to sentencing.

Ninth Circuit jurisprudence indicates that the Supreme Court has never done so. For example, in *Bradway v. Cate, 588 F.3d 990 (9th Cir. 2009),* the Court noted the inapplicability of the *Eighth Amendment* vagueness jurisprudence to a life sentence, and concluded that no Supreme Court cases had addressed due process vagueness claims based upon a failure to narrow offenses subject to more severe penalties, where the penalties were less than the death penalty. *Id. at 992-993.* In *U.S. v. Johnson,* the Ninth Circuit observed that "[u]nconstitutional vagueness challenges to the Sentencing Guidelines have been questioned as theoretically unsound." *130 F.3d 1352, 1354 (9th Cir. 1997)* (citing *U.S. v. Wivell, 893 F.2d 156, 159-60 (8th Cir. 1990)* (vagueness doctrine does not mandate sentencing guidelines). As recently as 2006, the Ninth Circuit was required to simply assume "that a vagueness argument focused exclusively on sentencing, rather than on criminal conduct giving rise to the sentence, is cognizable." *U.S. v. Hungerford, 465 F.3d 1113 (9th Cir. 2006).*

Again, because Petitioner fails to show that there is Supreme Court law that mandates relief, this Court cannot find that the Arizona court's decision to deny relief was "contrary to or an unreasonable application of" such law.

Therefore, Petitioner's Ground 1 is without merit and must be denied.

E. *APPRENDI*: Ground 2

In his Ground 2, Petitioner argues that his right to a jury trial under the *Sixth Amendment* and the *Fourteenth Amendments* was violated because the aggravating factor that supported Petitioner's natural life sentence was not found by a jury as required by *Apprendi v. New Jersey.* (Amend Pet., Doc. 12 at 7.) Respondents argue that no fact was necessary to be found to justify the judge's choice between a natural life sentence and a life sentence with possibility for parole. (Answer, Doc. 15 at 13-14.) Petitioner responds that to avoid being unconstitutionally arbitrary, the judge's choice must be supported by an aggravating factor, and that the only ones authorized are those in *Ariz. Rev. Stat. § 13-703(F).*

Petitioner's claim is without merit.

Apprendi mandated that: "Other than the fact of a prior conviction, any fact that increases the penalty for a crime beyond the prescribed statutory maximum must be submitted to a jury, and proved beyond a reasonable doubt." *530 U.S. 466 at 490, 120 S. Ct. 2348, 147 L. Ed. 2d 435.*

The applicable statute provided:

> A. A person guilty of first degree murder as defined in *§ 13-1105* shall suffer death or imprisonment in the custody of the

state department of corrections for life as determined and in accordance with the procedures provided in subsections B through G of this section. If the court imposes a life sentence, the court may order that the defendant not be released on any basis for the remainder of the defendant's natural life. An order sentencing the defendant to natural life is not subject to commutation or parole, work furlough or work release. If the court does not sentence the defendant to natural life, the defendant shall not be released on any basis until the completion of the service of twenty-five calendar years if the victim was fifteen or more years of age and thirty-five years if the victim was under fifteen years of age.

Ariz. Rev. Stat. § 13-703(A) (1999). The plain import of this statute is that outside a death penalty (which did require fact finding on aggravating factors) the judge was required to sentence the first degree murder to life in prison, but had discretion to designate it as with or without parole. The statute provided no prerequisites to exercising that discretion. "In *Ariz. Rev. Stat. § 13-703(A)*, the Arizona legislature explicitly authorizes a sentence of natural life upon a conviction for first degree murder without the need for any further factual findings." (Pet. Exhibit 3, Mem. Dec. 3/2703 at 11.)

"The *Sixth Amendment* does not prevent judges from 'exercis[ing] discretion-taking into consideration various factors relating both to offense and offender-in imposing a judgment within the range prescribed by statute.' " *Butler v. Curry, 528 F.3d 624, 643 (9th Cir. 2008)* (quoting *Apprendi, 530 U.S. at 481*).

> We have never doubted the authority of a judge to exercise broad discretion in imposing a sentence within a statutory range. ...For when a trial judge exercises his discretion to select a specific sentence within a defined range, the defendant has no right to a jury determination of the facts that the judge deems relevant.

U.S. v. Booker, 543 U.S. 220, 233, 125 S. Ct. 738, 160 L. Ed. 2d 621 (2005).

Petitioner attempts to bring the statute within the ambit of *Apprendi* jurisprudence by arguing that the statute would be unconstitutional if some limits on discretion were not read into the statute. This claim has been rejected in connection with Petitioner's Ground 1 (vagueness).

Moreover, even if Petitioner could make out such a claim, it would not permit a bootstrapping of an *Apprendi* claim. The sentencing statute would simply be void for vagueness.

Even if the statute were not simply void for vagueness, Petitioner proffers no rationale for his assumption that the limits that would be inscribed would be those that required specific factual findings, let alone the factors in *§ 13-703(F)*, which are referenced in the subsection solely as those which the sentencing court "shall consider." The only mandate for a finding of such an aggravating factor is as a condition of imposing "a sentence of death." *Ariz. Rev. Stat. § 13-703(E)* (1999).

This claim is without merit.

G. ACTUAL INNOCENCE

1. Standard for Actual Innocence

The undersigned has concluded that absent a showing of actual innocence, the equal protection claim in Ground 3, and the claims in Grounds 4, 5, 6, and 7 must be dismissed with prejudice as procedurally defaulted or procedurally barred. All other claims have been deemed to be without merit.

The standard for "cause and prejudice" is one of discretion intended to be flexible and yielding to exceptional circumstances. *Hughes v. Idaho State Board of Corrections, 800 F.2d 905, 909 (9th Cir. 1986)*. Failure to establish cause may be excused under exceptional circumstances. For instance:

.... in an extraordinary case, where a constitutional violation has probably resulted in the conviction of one who is actually innocent, a federal habeas court may grant the writ even in the absence of showing cause for the procedural default.

Murray v. Carrier, 477 U.S. 478, 496, 106 S. Ct. 2639, 91 L. Ed. 2d 397 (1986) (emphasis added).

"[P]risoners asserting innocence as a gateway to defaulted claims must establish that, in light of new evidence, 'it is more likely than not that no reasonable juror would have found petitioner guilty beyond a reasonable doubt.' " *House v. Bell, 547 U.S. 518, 537, 126 S. Ct. 2064, 165 L. Ed. 2d 1 (2006)* (quoting *Schlup v. Delo, 513 U.S. 298, 327, 115 S. Ct. 851, 130 L. Ed. 2d 808 (1995))*. "[T]he habeas court must consider all the evidence, old and new, incriminating and exculpatory, without regard to whether it would necessarily be admitted under rules of admissibility that would govern at trial. *Id. at 538* (internal quotations omitted).

2. Avoidance of Actual Innocence Determination

Congress has recognized that denying a habeas petition on its merits may, at times, be more efficient that fully resolving the exhaustion issues. Thus, *28 U.S.C. § 2254(b)(2)* provides: "An application for a writ of habeas corpus may be denied on the merits, notwithstanding the failure of the applicant to exhaust the remedies available in the courts of the State." Accordingly, the court is free to side step the exhaustion issue when it is more efficient or easier to dispose of a claim on its merits. *Cassett v. Stewart, 406 F.3d 614, 623-624 (9th Cir. 2005)*. The same approach is appropriate where the state has asserted that the claim is procedurally defaulted or procedurally barred.

> We do not mean to suggest that the procedural-bar issue must invariably be resolved first; only that it ordinarily should be. Judicial economy might counsel giving the *Teague* question priority, for example, if it were easily resolvable against the habeas petitioner, whereas the procedural-bar issue involved complicated issues of state law. Cf. *28 U.S.C. § 2254(b)(2)* (permitting a federal court to deny a habeas petition on the merits notwithstanding the applicant's failure to exhaust state remedies).

Lambrix v. Singletary, 520 U.S. 518, 525, 117 S. Ct. 1517, 137 L. Ed. 2d 771 (1997). See also Clark v. Ricketts, 958 F.2d 851, 857 (9th Cir.

1991) (considering merits of claims arguably barred under Arizona procedural bars).

In taking this approach, the habeas court does not simply address the merits of the unexhausted, procedurally defaulted, or procedurally barred claim. Rather, in furtherance of the interests of federalism and comity underlying the procedural default and procedural bar rules, the "federal court may deny an unexhausted petition on the merits only when it is perfectly clear that the applicant does not raise even a colorable federal claim." *Cassett, 406 F.3d at 624.*

Here, the undersigned might be able to conclude that some of Petitioner's procedurally defaulted and procedurally barred claims are plainly without merit, and fail to assert a colorable federal claim.

For example, Ground 3 asserts an equal protection claims but Petitioner fails to allege in prejudice.

In Ground 4, Petitioner asserts a confrontation claim based upon the admission of various hearsay, but in *Crawford v. Washington, 541 U.S. 36, 124 S. Ct. 1354, 158 L. Ed. 2d 177 (2004)*, the Supreme Court analyzed the history of the *Confrontation Clause* and concluded that its "core concerns" were not with simple hearsay, but with out-of-court *testimony*, whether in a separate judicial proceeding or a police investigation. *Id. at 51.* Two years later, in *Davis v. Washington, 547 U.S. 813, 126 S. Ct. 2266, 165 L. Ed. 2d 224 (2006)*, the Court revisited the scope of the *Confrontation Clause*, and held that its focus on testimonial evidence was a "limitation so clearly reflected in the text of the constitutional provision [that it] must fairly be said to mark out not merely its 'core,' but its perimeter." *Id. at 824.* Just this past year, the Court again addressed the issue and held that non-testimonial evidence "is the concern of state and federal rules of evidence, not the *Confrontation Clause.*" *Michigan v. Bryant, U.S., 131 S.Ct. 1143, 1155, 179 L. Ed. 2d 93 (2011).*

In Ground 7, Petitioner complains of omitted transcripts, but fails to assert any prejudice.

On the other hand, although not convinced of their merits, the undersigned cannot say that Petitioner's Grounds 5 (actual innocence) and 6 (ineffective assistance) fail to "raise even a colorable claim." The merits of both turn upon the evaluation of the impact of Petitioner's new evidence, and neither is plainly without merit. "Claims of actual innocence based on newly discovered evidence have never been held to state a ground for federal habeas relief absent an independent constitutional violation occurring in the underlying state criminal proceeding...This rule is grounded in the principle that federal habeas courts sit to ensure that individuals are not imprisoned in violation of the Constitution-not to correct errors of fact." *Herrera v. Collins, 506 U.S. 390, 400-401, 113 S. Ct. 853, 122 L. Ed. 2d 203 (1993)*. However, the Ninth Circuit has concluded that *Herrera* does not foreclose the potential for a free-standing claim of actual innocence, but has also concluded that any such claim would have to be based upon "affirmative proof of actual innocence based on newly discovered evidence." *Turner v. Calderon, 281 F.3d 851, 872 (9th Cir. 2002)*

Accordingly, this Court must evaluate whether Petitioner's new evidence will permit him to pass through the *Schlup* gateway for actual innocence.

3. New Evidence of Actual Innocence

Petitioner argues his actual innocence, relying upon evidence from his experts that, contrary to the prosecution's evidence at trial, a "single assailant could not have hid in the back seat, shot the deceased in the front seat, then climbed over the seat and exited through the passenger door without leaving blood smears or other evidence." (Amend Pet., Doc. 12 at 10.) Petitioner argues that this amounts to a showing of actual innocence and excuses his procedural defaults. (Reply, Doc. 20 at 27.)

Petitioner relies upon Isidro (Indio) Falcon's recounting to police of Alfonso Munoz's (El Gato) purported description of the murder.

> Indio told me that a day or two later Gato again contacted him at his apartment. On this occasion, Indio told me that Gato told him how the murder occurred. Indio said Gato told him that he drove to the area in the brown car. Using the keyless remote he entered the victims [sic] car. Once inside, Gato lay on the rear floorboard and covered himself with a coat.
>
> The victim entered the car and started it. The victim began backing out of the driveway, and in doing so looked behind her

at which time she observed Gato. The victim begins screaming and it is at this point that Gato shoots her twice in the head. According to Indio, Gato told him that one shot grazed the victim and the other struck her in the head. The car continues in reverse at which time Gato tries to get out of the car. The car which has automatic locks prevents him from getting out. Gato tries to kick out a window without success, then reaches to the ignition switch and presses the keyless remote control device on the victims [sic] key ring which unlocks the doors. Gato then runs from the area.

(Supp. Exhibit A, PCR Memo, Exhibit 9, Incident Report Supplement at "49".)

In contrast, Petitioner presented parallel affidavits of criminal reconstructionist Frank Rodgers, forensic scientist William Collier, and forensic consultant Dr. Thomas Streed that based upon personal examination of the vehicle, and the photographs and other information supplied that:

> any person who exited the vehicle from the rear passenger compartment though the front passenger door would have necessarily created blood smears and blood transfer patterns. The blood transfer on the rear door panel demonstrates that the shooter did have blood deposited on his hand or gloved hand. That hand would have had to be used to maneuver out through the front passenger compartment and a transfer such as the one seen on the rear door panel created. The absence of transfer or smear pattern makes it extremely unlikely that any person exited the rear passenger compartment area through the front door after the victim had been shot.

(Supp. Exhibit A, PCR Memo, Common Declarations.)

Petitioner's experts noted that Frank Rodgers unsuccessfully attempted to conceal himself in the backseat of the vehicle. But, they also noted that Rodgers was 5' 10" tall, 180 pounds. (Supp. Exhibit A, PCR Memo, Common

Declarations.) In contrast, testimony at trial by neighbor Benny Hays indicated that the person seen running from the scene was "five seven to five nine," and "looked like he weighed about maybe 150 to 170." (Supp. Exhibit I, R.T. 9/27/00 at 59.) The description given to police was "five-six, 160 pounds". (Supp. Exhibit L, R.T. 10/4/00 at 96.) The width of the back seat was 59 inches. (Supp. Exhibit A, PCR Memo, Common Declarations.) Petitioner's experts offer no opinion that the difference in size was not sufficient to permit Falcon to conceal himself in the manner related by Falcon.

Respondents point out that Falcon was prohibited from relating Munoz's description of the murder under hearsay rules. The parties argue whether the lack of trial testimony by Falcon about the description given by Munoz renders the purported discrepancy in that description irrelevant. However, actual innocence determinations are not limited by the niceties of evidentiary law nor some hypothetical trial scenario. Rather, the question is whether, armed with the new evidence, Petitioner has made a sufficient showing that a reasonable juror armed with all the evidence would have failed to convict. Even if the prosecution would have been prohibited from introducing Falcon's recitation, and thus no impeachment made possible, Respondents have not foreclosed the possibility that the defense could have nonetheless impeached Falcon by introducing his statements to the police on the recitation, and contrasting it with the new evidence.

Concealment - Petitioner's experts noted that Frank Rodgers unsuccessfully attempted to conceal himself in the backseat of the vehicle. But, they also noted that Rodgers was 5' 10" tall, 180 pounds. (Supp. Exhibit A, PCR Memo, Common Declarations.) In contrast, testimony at trial by neighbor Benny Hays indicated that the person seen running from the scene was "five seven to five nine," and "looked like he weighed about maybe 150 to 170." (Supp. Exhibit I, R.T. 9/27/00 at 59.) The description given to police was "five-six, 160 pounds". (Supp. Exhibit L, R.T. 10/4/00 at 96.) The width of the back seat was 59 inches. (Supp. Exhibit A, PCR Memo, Common Declarations.) Petitioner's experts offer no opinion that the difference in size was not sufficient to permit Falcon to conceal himself in the manner related by Falcon.

Exit Path -- Petitioner's experts also suggest that the gunman could not have exited through the front passenger door. Petitioner's experts' opinions would make it "more likely than not that no reasonable juror would have found petitioner guilty beyond a reasonable doubt" if: (1) the jury were required to believe Isidro Falcon on this point to convict; and (2) the jury were required to assume that the shooter had exited through the front passenger door of the car to believe Isidro Falcon.

With regard to the credibility of Isidro Falcon, his testimony was a key part of the prosecution's case. However, there was other evidence that Petitioner had obtained the death of the victim, *i.e.* the evidence that Petitioner had attempted to purchase her death from Doug Maurer, Colin Head, and had attempted to hire William Moore to kill Falcon to cover it up.

Doug Maurer testified that Petitioner had discussions with him about ways Petitioner could kill his wife, offered to hire Maurer to kill his wife with a knife in Las Vegas, and offered to hire Maurer to kill her with a gun at their home, going so far as to give the gun to Maurer. (Supp. Exhibit J, R.T. 10/2/00 at 15-26.)

Maurer's testimony was corroborated by testimony from Tammy Goad-Maurer that: she had seen Doug Maurer with a gun (Supp. Exhibit M, R.T. 10/15/00 at 128-129); that she and Danny Maurer had told Petitioner prior to the murder that Doug Maurer was claiming that Petitioner was trying to get his wife killed (*id.* at 130-132); and Petitioner had complained to her that Maurer had stolen his gun, but Petitioner declined to report it (*id.* at 135-136). This testimony about the conversation between Goad and Petitioner was not presented to the jury, but was taken as part of an offer of proof. Nonetheless, this Court must consider it in making its actual innocence determination. *House, 547 U.S. at 538.*

Further, Deputy Baker's contact of Detective Lopez and their subsequent interview of Maurer, corroborated Maurer's testimony that he had approached Baker about the murder plot.

Colin Head testified that Petitioner had asked him to murder the victim while she was in California, and had related that story to the police. (Supp. Exhibit M, R.T. 10/5/00 at 38-39.)

William Moore testified that in February, 1997, Petitioner had asked Moore about having somebody "disappear." (Supp. Exhibit L, R.T. 10/4/00 at 26-27.) He testified that in December, 1997 Petitioner told him about rumors of him hiring Falcon to kill the victim, and when asked Petitioner said he couldn't have just divorced her because he would have lost everything. Petitioner expressed concern that he was going to be arrested if Falcon was arrested, and asked Moore if he knew someone from Nevada who would kill Falcon, for $10,000 to be split between Moore and the killer. (Id. at 37, 43-45.)

The nature of the murder as a "hit," rather than a robbery, sexual assault, car-jacking or similarly motivated killing, is reflected by the fact that the victim's purse was not taken, evidence that the shooter was in the back seat and lying in wait, that the car was not taken, that lack of evidence of a forced entry, and the limited time elapsed between the victim entering the car and the murder.

Thus, a reasonable juror could have concluded that, even without any belief in Falcon's testimony, Petitioner had finally succeeded in procuring the victim's death.

Further, the evidence does not require an assumption that a reasonable juror would have had to disbelieve Falcon's accusations in the face of the new evidence provided by Petitioner's experts.

Agreement on the open door is not necessary to Falcon's credibility.

Falcon never claimed Munoz exited from the front passenger door. (See Supp. Exhibit A, PCR Memo, Exhibit 9, Incident Report Supplement at "49".)

To be sure, neighbor Benny Hays testified that when he approached the scene, the only door of the car open was the front passenger door.

Q And was the engine on or off?

A There was not - - no engine running when I got there.

Q And you saw a woman slumped over in the driver's seat?

A I seen a lady in there, yes, uh-huh.

Q Did you see any doors open?

A The passenger side door was open. That was the only door that was.

Q Front or rear?

A The front.

Q Is that the only door open?

A Yes, sir.

(Supp. Exhibit I, R.T. 9/27/00 at 61-61.) (*See also id.* at 73.)

Similarly, Officer Stephaniak testified that she was the first responding officer, and when she arrived the front passenger door was open. (Supp. Exhibit I, R.T. 9/27/00 at 89, 91, and 93.)

However, Hayes also testified that he was summoned to the scene by a neighbor, Henry or Hank Watson, who reported "there's a lady down here in the car that went through a short block fence and she's hurt." (Supp. Exhibit I, R.T. 9/27/00 at 58. *See also id.* at 69) Mr. Watson did not testify.

A reasonable juror could easily reconcile the accounts by concluding that Munoz had closed the rear door after exiting, and that Mr. Watson had opened the passenger door in order to determine that the victim was hurt, before Watson went to summon Hays. Or even that Munoz had exited from and closed the rear door, and then opened the passenger door for some other reason (*e.g.* in a moment's hesitation of whether to take the purse, to assure himself the victim was dying or dead, etc.).

Indeed, all of the physical evidence suggested that the shooter had been in the back seat, e.g. the victim's injuries, the bullet hole in the windshield, the casings and car remote in the backseat, the key to Falcon's car being in the floorboard, and the shoe prints in the back seat. Because Petitioner's experts establish that climbing through to the front seat was impossible, in order to discount Falcon's recitation of events, a juror would have to reconstruct the position of the shooter as being in the front passenger seat, solely to explain the open door, and thereby ignoring the other evidence that the shooter he was in the back seat.

Alternatively, a reasonable juror could simply conclude that the facts between Munoz and Falcon had simply gotten convoluted, and that Falcon was faithfully recounting all of his experiences, including Munoz's recitation of his actions, and thus any deficit in credibility did not lie with Falcon.

A reasonable juror could even adopt the argument posited by Petitioner in his PCR proceedings that there were two assailants, one in the front and one in the back, and reconcile it with the other evidence by concluding that Munoz had an accomplice of whom Falcon was unaware.

Thus, the door discrepancy would not have precluded belief in Falcon's core accusations of Petitioner having paid him (and he Munoz) to kill the victim, and their combined accomplishment of the task.

Moreover, there was substantial corroboration of Falcon's story, including the recovery of the jacket, car remote, and key to Falcon's car from the back seat of the victim's vehicle, the bullet hole in the windshield, the description of the man running from the scene, the victim's injuries, Colin Head's delivery of an envelope to Falcon after the murder, Munoz's existence and disappearance after the murder, Catalina's picking Munoz up after the murder, and Mecham's having taken Falcon to get the vehicle after the murder. With all of that corroboration, a reasonable jury could conclude that the essentials of Falcon's story were true, even if his recitation of the murder scene was inaccurate or even fabricated.

Thus, a reasonable juror could have still convicted Petitioner in the face of a discrepancy over the particulars of the execution of the killing.

In sum, even with Petitioner's new evidence, the undersigned cannot find it more likely than not that no reasonable juror could have found Petitioner guilty beyond a reasonable doubt.

3. Conclusion re Actual Innocence
Based upon the foregoing, the undersigned concludes that Petitioner has failed to establish his actual innocence, and thus may not be relieved of the consequences of his procedural defaults and procedural bars.

ERIC MICHAEL CLARK, PETITIONER -VS- CHARLES L. RYAN, ET AL., RESPONDENTS

CV-09-8006-PCT-JAT (JRI) UNITED STATES DISTRICT COURT FOR THE DISTRICT OF ARIZONA

(Text added/modified for emphasis) In Arizona it is very common for lawyers and the state not to disclose to the court all relevant facts in order to convict thereby convicting the incompetent. By so doing the state is able to obtain convictions. Lawyers fail to present federal claims fairly to state courts, thereby preventing federal review. The Attorney General by failing to disclose this practice to the court perpetrates fraud upon the court.

COUNSEL: For Eric Michael Clark, By and Through His Mother, Teresa M. Clark, Petitioner: Carla G Ryan, Law Office of Carla G Ryan, Tucson, AZ. For James Arnold, Warden of the Arizona State Prison Complex-Phoenix, Terry L Goddard, The Attorney General of the State of Arizona, Charles L Ryan, Interim Director of the ADOC, Respondents: Michael Tighe O'Toole, Office of the Attorney General, Phoenix, AZ.

A. FACTUAL BACKGROUND

In disposing of Petitioner's petition for writ of certiorari, the United States Supreme Court summarized the facts of the case as follows:

In the early hours of June 21, 2000, Officer Jeffrey Moritz of the Flagstaff Police responded in uniform to complaints that a pickup truck with loud music blaring was circling a residential block. When he located the truck, the officer turned on the emergency lights and siren of his marked patrol car, which prompted petitioner Eric Clark, the truck's driver (then 17), to pull over. Officer Moritz got out of the patrol car and told Clark to stay where he was. Less than a minute later, Clark shot the officer, who died soon after but not before calling the police dispatcher for help. Clark ran away on foot but was arrested later that day with gunpowder residue on his hands; the gun that killed the officer was found nearby, stuffed into a knit cap.

Clark v. Arizona, 548 U.S. 735, 743, 126 S. Ct. 2709, 165 L. Ed. 2d 842 (2006).

B. PROCEEDINGS AT TRIAL

"The state charged [Petitioner] with one count of first degree murder, for intentionally or knowingly killing a law enforcement officer who is in the line of duty. *A.R.S. § 13-1105(A)(3)*. The state did not seek the death penalty." (Exhibit RR, Mem. Dec. 1/25/05 at 5.) (Exhibits to the Answer, Docs. 32, 33, 34, 35, 36 and 39, are referenced herein as "Exhibit.")

The issue of Petitioner's competency was raised, and on March 28, 2001, the parties entered into a Stipulation (Exhibit D) that Petitioner was incompetent to stand trial. Petitioner was admitted to the Arizona State Hospital for restoration to competency. His competency was revisited in the summer and fall of 2002, and again in the spring of 2003. (Exhibit H, M.E. 7/11/02; Exhibit K, M.E. 9/16/02; and Exhibit O, M.E. 4/25/03.) Petitioner eventually moved to submit the issue of his competency to stand trial on the basis of the submitted reports. (Exhibit P, Motion.) On May 8, 2003, Petitioner was found competent to stand trial. (Exhibit Q, M.E. 5/8/03.)

On July 8, 2003, Petitioner appeared and entered a waiver of his right to a jury trial, which the trial court accepted. (Exhibit T. R.T. 7/8/03 at 3-11.) In exchange for that waiver, the state stipulated that the maximum possible sentence was life, with the possibility for parole after 25 years. (*Id.* at 9.) Without that stipulation, Petitioner faced the potential of a sentence for "natural life," e.g. life without the possibility of parole or commutation. *Ariz. Rev. Stat. § 13-703(A)* (2002). (*See also* Exhibit YY-1, R.T. 2/9/07 at 63 (def. Counsel Goldberg testifying waiver of jury guaranteed no natural life sentence).)

Petitioner proceeded to a bench trial on August 5, 2003. "At trial, Clark did not contest the shooting and death, but relied on his undisputed paranoid schizophrenia at the time of the incident in denying that he had the specific intent to shoot a law enforcement officer or knowledge that he was doing so, as required by the statute." *Clark, 548 U.S. at 742.* The trial court ruled that it could not consider such evidence for that purposes, relying on the Arizona Supreme Court's decision in *State v. Mott 187 Ariz. 536, 931 P.2d 1046 (1997).* Petitioner relied upon the same evidence, as well as testimony of an expert, to assert that he was guilty except insane. *Mott* held that evidence of a mental defect could not be admitted to refute intent. In *Mott v. Stewart, 2002 U.S. Dist. LEXIS 23165, 2002 WL 31017646*

(D.Ariz. Aug 30, 2002), Judge Collins ruled that this restriction on the evidence was a violation of due process, and granted habeas relief. As discussed hereinafter, the U.S. Supreme Court ruled that the *Mott* restriction only excluded expert testimony, and not "observation evidence" by lay and expert witnesses.

After eleven days of trial, Petitioner was found guilty, with the court specifically rejecting Petitioner's plea of guilty except insane on the basis that (despite finding he suffered from paranoid schizophrenia and paranoid delusions on the day of the killing) he was not prevented from knowing "his actions were wrong." (Exhibit II, R.T. 9/3/03 at 6.) (*See* Exhibits V, W, X, Y, Z, BB, CC, DD, EE, FF, GG and HH, R.T. 8/5/03 to 8/27/03.)

On October 2, 2003, Petitioner was sentenced to life in prison without possibility of release for 25 years. (Exhibit LL, R.T. 10/2/03 at 73.)

Petitioner filed a Motion to Vacate (Exhibit MM), arguing that: (1) Arizona's version (or lack thereof) of an insanity defense was a violation of federal rights to due process; (2) the trial court's failure to consider the absence of the requisite *mens rea* was violation of federal rights to due process; (3) the clear and convincing evidence standard for proving insanity was a violation of federal rights to equal protection; and (4) incarcerating Petitioner in prison was cruel and unusual punishment, under the *Eighth Amendment*. The motion was summarily denied (Exhibit NN. M.E. 11/19/03).

C. PROCEEDINGS ON DIRECT APPEAL

Petitioner filed a Notice of Appeal (Exhibit LL.) In his Opening Brief, Petitioner argued *inter alia* that: (1) his federal due process rights were violated because his conviction was not supported by substantial evidence; (2) Arizona's insanity statute violated the *Fifth* and *Fourteenth Amendments of the U.S. Constitution*; (3) due process was violated when he was precluded upon relying upon evidence of his mental condition to negate the *mens rea*; and (4) his life sentence was cruel and unusual punishment in violation of the *Eighth Amendment of the U.S. Constitution*. (Exhibit OO, Opening Brief.) The Arizona Court of

Appeals affirmed Petitioner's conviction and sentence. (Exhibit RR, Mem. Dec. 1/25/05.)

Petitioner filed a Petition for Review (Exhibit SS), which the Arizona Supreme Court summarily denied (Exhibit TT, Order 5/25/05).

Petitioner filed a Petition for Writ of Certiorari with the U.S. Supreme Court. The Court granted review to decide: whether due process prohibits Arizona's use of an insanity test stated solely in terms of the capacity to tell whether an act charged as a crime was right or wrong; and whether Arizona violates due process in restricting consideration of defense evidence of mental illness and incapacity to its bearing on a claim of insanity, thus eliminating its significance directly on the issue of the mental element of the crime charged (known in legal shorthand as the *mens rea*, or guilty mind)

Clark, 548 U.S. at 742. The Court held there was "no violation of due process in either instance." *Id.* The Court also found that the *Mott* decision did not preclude consideration of "observation evidence" on the issue of *mens rea*, but counsel had failed to make an offer of proof to preserve the claim that such evidence had been excluded. The judgment of the Arizona Court of Appeals was affirmed. *Id. at 779.*

D. PROCEEDINGS ON POST-CONVICTION RELIEF

On July 29, 2006, Petitioner filed a Notice of Post-Conviction Relief (Exhibit UU). Counsel was appointed and filed a PCR Petition (Exhibit VV), arguing *inter alia* that under the *Sixth Amendment to the U.S. Constitution*, trial counsel was ineffective: (1) in failing to seek a redetermination of Petitioner's competence to stand trial based upon an evaluation by Dr. Parish received after the final competency determination; (2) in failing to seek a separate determination of Petitioner's competency to waive his right to a jury trial; (3) in allowing Petitioner to waive the right to a jury trial; (4) in failing to call Dr. DiBacco as a defense witness; and (5) in failing to preserve for review by the United States Supreme Court the issue of "observation evidence" on Petitioner's *mens rea*.

In the course of the evidentiary hearing, Petitioner moved to amend (Exhibit OOO) his PCR petition to add claims: (1) that Petitioner was incompetent during trial, (2) his competence deteriorated during trial, (3) that trial counsel was ineffective for failing to seek new competency determinations, and (4) that lead trial counsel had a conflict of interest preventing him from testifying at trial about his failures in assisting Petitioner's family to have Petitioner involuntarily committed for mental health treatment just prior to the killing of officer Moritz. The PCR court denied the motion to amend as belatedly asserted. (Exhibit RRR-1 R.T. 2/20/07 at 4-5.)

After completion of the evidentiary hearing, the PCR Court denied the Petition. (Exhibit AAAA, M.E. 3/15/07.)

Petitioner filed a Petition for Review (Exhibit CCCC), arguing *inter alia* Petitioner's competency, counsel's ineffectiveness and conflict of interest. The state filed a cross-petition for review. The Arizona Court of appeals denied both petitions. (Exhibit DDDD, Amended Order 4/2/08.)

Petitioner filed a Petition for Review (Exhibit EEEE) by the Arizona Supreme Court, which was summarily denied. (Exhibit FFFF, Order 8/4/08.)

E. PRESENT FEDERAL HABEAS PROCEEDINGS

Petition - Petitioner commenced the current case by filing, through his mother, Tersa M. Clark, a Petition for Writ of Habeas Corpus pursuant to *28 U.S.C. § 2254* on January 13, 2009 (#1). Counsel was appointed and filed an Amended Petition (Doc. 17) on June 8, 2009. Petitioner's Amended Petition asserts the following seven grounds for relief:

(1) "Substantial evidence did not support the conviction for first degree murder of a police officer";

(2) "The trial court did not correctly apply well established United States Supreme Court case law by holding that Mr. Clark was sane and that decision was an unreasonable determination of the facts in light of the evidence";

(3) "The sentence imposed in this case constitutes cruel and unusual punishment";

(4) "Mr. Clark was not competent to stand trial or to waive his constitutional rights to a jury trial, to present a defense, or to a full and fair hearing";

(5) "Trial counsel was ineffective because he failed to disclose Dr. Parrish's report regarding competency to co-counsel and to the court prior to requesting to waive a jury; counsel failed to request a re-evaluation of Mr. Clark during the trial when Mr. Clark started to deteriorate; when trial counsel waived the jury; when trial counsel limited the use of experts; when trial counsel failed to preserve observational evidence; and because trial counsel had a conflict of interest";

(6) "Prosecutorial misconduct occurred in this case because the prosecutor, just like defense counsel, failed to advise the trial court of the need for a competency hearing regarding waiving a jury and because the prosecutor expressed concerns about defense council's decision"; and

(7) "Appellate counsel was ineffective because he failed to raise the competency and insanity issues on the direct appeal and failed to preserve the observational evidence."

(Order 7/1/09 at 2.)

Response - On September 16, 2009 Respondents filed their Response ("Answer") (Doc. 31), arguing that Petitioner's state remedies on his claims were unexhausted and procedurally defaulted, or the claims are without merit. In addition to the exhibits filed with the Answer (Docs. 32, 33, 34, 35, and 36), Respondents were granted leave to and filed under seal various psychological evaluations as Exhibit GGGG (Doc. 39).

Reply - On February 25, 2010 Petitioner filed a Reply (Doc. 48), arguing that his claims are meritorious and either were properly exhausted, or *Arizona Rule of Criminal Procedure 32.6(d)* (amendment of PCR petitions) was not adequate to bar habeas review.

III. APPLICATION OF LAW TO FACTS

A. EXHAUSTION & PROCEDURAL DEFAULT

Respondents argue that Petitioner failed to properly exhaust his state remedies on the following claims:

(1) the portions of Ground One based upon "observation evidence" which negated the finding of *mens rea* (Answer, Doc. 31 at 11);

(2) the claims in Ground Two (sanity determination) (*id.* at 30);

(3) the portions of Ground Five based upon trial counsel's conflict of interest (*id.* at 85-86);

(4) the claims in Ground Six (prosecutorial misconduct) (*id.* at 96); and

(5) the claims in Ground Seven (ineffectiveness of appellate counsel) (*id.* at 101).

Respondent argues that these claims are now procedurally defaulted, and thus must be dismissed with prejudice.

1. Exhaustion Requirement
....

However, in reaching its decision, the Ninth Circuit was faced with a habeas petitioner whose appeal to the Arizona Court of Appeals was denied in 1988, prior to the 1989 amendments eliminating life-sentences from the exceptions to Arizona Court of Appeals' jurisdiction. *See State v. Swoopes, 155 Ariz. 432, 747 P.2d 593 (App. 1988)*. Similarly, the Ninth Circuit was required to draw on decisions applying the pre-1989 amendments law. In *State v. Sandon, 161 Ariz. 157, 777 P.2d 220 (1989)*, the Arizona Supreme Court considered the review rights of a defendant whose appeal was denied in 1986. *Sandon, 161 Ariz. at 157, 777 P.2d at 220*. Although the Sandon court noted the adoption of the 1989 amendments in a footnote, they were not applying that law. *Id. at 158 n. 1, 777 P.2d at 221 n.1*.

Similarly, the decision in *State v. Shattuck, 140 Ariz. 582, 684 P.2d 154 (1984)*, also relied on in *Swoopes*, predated the 1989 amendments. Indeed, the only Arizona decision relied upon in *Swoopes* and made after the 1989 amendments was *Moreno v. Gonzalez, 192 Ariz. 131, 962 P.2d 205 (1998)*. *Moreno* did not, however rely upon *Ariz. Rev. Stat. §§ 12-120.21* or *13-4031*, or specifically discuss the death/life sentence limitation. Rather, *Moreno*focused on the "nature and scope of discretionary review by petition for review," *Moreno, 192 Ariz. at 134, 962 P.2d at 207*, and was concerned with whether such discretionary review was an "appeal" within the meaning of the exceptions to Arizona's timeliness bar for claims not presented on "appeal" for good cause.

Moreover, the import of *Sandon* was the Arizona Supreme Court's apparent desire to stop the flood of "large numbers of prisoner petitions seeking to exhaust state remedies." *Sandon, 161 Ariz. at 157, 777 P.2d at 220*. The *Sandon* court concluded that "'[o]nce the defendant has been given the appeal to which he has a right, state remedies have been exhausted." *Id. at 158, 777 P.2d at 221*, quoting *Shattuck, 140 Ariz. at 585, 684 P.2d at 157*. Thus, their recitation of the death/life sentence limitation is not properly read as the limit of their holding, but as a reiteration of the pre-1989 holding of *Shattuck.* Thus *Sandon* may only be reasonably read as an attempt by the Arizona Supreme Court to remove their discretionary review from the cycle of review required for exhaustion of Arizona's state remedies. While a given respondent may desire to require its Arizona prisoner to file a petition for review with the Arizona Supreme Court, it is not the respondents' desire, however, but that of the Arizona court that is controlling.

Finally, *Swoopes* itself did not hinge on any reading of *Ariz. Rev. Stat. §§ 12-120.21* or *13-4031* themselves, but upon the question "whether Arizona has identified discretionary Supreme Court review 'as outside the standard review process and has plainly said that it need not be sought for purpose of exhaustion.' " *Swoopes, 196 F.3d at 1010*, quoting *O'Sullivan, 526 U.S. 838, 850, 119 S. Ct. 1728, 144 L. Ed. 2d 1 (1999)*. The only basis for identifying that discretionary review as being tied to death/life sentences was the language of *Shattuck* and *Sandon*, and their reliance upon the then applicable pre-1989 versions of *Ariz. Rev. Stat. § § 12-120.21* and *13-4031.*

Thus, until this issue is resolved by the Ninth Circuit, the Arizona District Courts are faced with either applying the exact language of *Swoopes*, or applying the principle of *Swoopes* to the facts as they exist in this case. The latter holds truer to the function of a trial court in attempting to apply appellate court precedent.

Using the techniques developed at common law, a court confronted with apparently controlling authority must parse the precedent in light of the facts presented and the rule announced. Insofar as there may be factual differences between the current case and the earlier one, the court must determine whether those differences are material to the application of the rule or allow the precedent to be distinguished on a principled basis.

Hart v. Massanari, 266 F.3d 1155, 1172 (9th Cir. 2001).

Applying the rule of *Swoopes*, the undersigned concludes that in light of the 1989 amendments, claims fairly presented by Petitioner to the Arizona Court of Appeals in his are exhausted notwithstanding any failure to fairly present them to the Arizona Supreme Court. Respondents do not argue otherwise.

Effect of Skipping Intermediate Courts - While presentation to the Arizona Supreme Court was not necessary, neither was it sufficient to properly exhaust Petitioner's state remedies.

In *Casey v. Moore, 386 F.3d 896 (9th Cir. 2004)*, the court reiterated that to properly exhaust a claim, "a petitioner must properly raise it on every level of direct review."

Academic treatment accords: The leading treatise on federal habeas corpus states, "Generally, a petitioner satisfies the exhaustion requirement if he properly pursues a claim (1) throughout the entire direct appellate process of the state, or (2) throughout one entire judicial post conviction process available in the state."

Casey, 386 F.3d at 916 (quoting Liebman & Hertz, *Federal Habeas Corpus Practice and Procedure*, § 23.3b (4th ed. 1998).

Similarly, presentation to the Arizona Supreme Court for the first time in a PCR proceeding is not fair presentation. In Arizona, review of a petition for post-conviction relief by the Arizona Court of Appeals is governed by *Rule 32.9*, Arizona Rules of Criminal Procedure, which clarifies that review is available for "issues which were decided by the trial court." *Ariz. R. Crim. P. 32.9(c)(1)(ii). See also State v. Ramirez, 126 Ariz. 464, 468, 616 P.2d 924, 928 (Ariz.App., 1980)* (issues first presented in petition for review and not presented to trial court not subject to review). Accordingly, PCR claims presented for the first time to the Arizona Court of Appeals are not fairly presented.

Similarly, the Arizona Supreme Court does not grant review of claims not raised below, absent special considerations. *See State v. Logan, 200 Ariz. 564, 565, 30 P.3d 631, 632, n.2 (2001).* Presentation to the Arizona Supreme Court for the first time is not sufficient to exhaust an Arizona state prisoner's remedies. "Submitting a new claim to the state's highest court in a procedural context in which its merits will not be considered absent special circumstances does not constitute fair presentation." *Roettgen v. Copeland, 33 F.3d 36, 38 (9th Cir. 1994)* (citing *Castille v. Peoples, 489 U.S. 346, 351, 109 S. Ct. 1056, 103 L. Ed. 2d 380 (1989)).*

On the other hand, in a direct appeal, failure to present to the trial court does not necessarily prevent exhaustion; all that is required is presentation "at all appellate stages." *Casey, 386 F.3d at 916* (emphasis added). "If the petitioner fails to raise a federal claim at trial (or if the claim was not cognizable at all or did not arise until after trial), the petitioner satisfies the exhaustion requirement by raising the claim on appeal, on a motion for rehearing of the appeal, or even in a delayed appeal." Liebman & Hertz, *Federal Habeas Corpus Practice and Procedure*, § 23.3b (5th ed. 2001). However, failure to present a claim to the trial court in a PCR proceeding may result in a finding that the claim has not been fairly presented, *id. at n. 26, i.e.* if the failure to present to the trial court results in the appellate court applying a procedural bar which qualifies as an "independent and adequate state ground." *See Harris v. Reed, 489 U.S. 255, 260, 109 S. Ct. 1038, 103 L. Ed. 2d 308 (1989).* Nonetheless, the failure to present to the trial court might prevent habeas review if it results in the appellate court applying a procedural bar which qualifies as an "independent and adequate state ground".

d. Fair Presentment
....

e. Application to Petitioner's Claims
(1) Ground One (observational evidence) - In his Ground One, Petitioner argues that his due process rights were violated because

substantial evidence did not support the conviction for first degree murder of a police officer. Petitioner incorporates two arguments in this claim for relief. The first is that the affirmative evidence of intent, *i.e.* the prosecution's case in chief, was inadequate. The second is that upon consideration of the defense's case, *i.e.* "observation evidence" about Petitioner's mental condition and ability to form the *mens rea* of the crime, the evidence was insubstantial. (Amend. Petition, Doc. 17 at 8-22.)

Respondents assert that Petitioner's substantial evidence claim to the Arizona Court of Appeals was limited to the first argument, based upon the prosecution's case, *e.g.* the lack of evidence of events at the time of the shooting, and evidence suggesting a struggle and hence that he was guilty of manslaughter rather than a murder. (Answer, Doc. 31 at 11-12.)

In his reply, Petitioner acknowledges this defense (Reply, Doc. 48 at 16), but fails to respond to it (*id.* at 16-17). In his Petition, Petitioner argued that his claims in Ground One were "raised on the direct appeal and re-raised in the Petition for Review to the Arizona Supreme Court." (Doc. 17 at 8.)

Petitioner clearly raised on direct appeal a substantial evidence claim, citing *Jackson v. Virginia, 443 U.S. 307, 319, 99 S. Ct. 2781, 61 L. Ed. 2d 560 (1979).* (Exhibit OO, Opening Brief at 26.) However, in his Opening Brief, the facts argued in support of this theory were limited to arguing about the prosecution's case, *i.e.* that "the evidence showed at most a struggle leading to a gun fight, not that [Petitioner] intentionally or knowingly shot and killed a police officer." (*Id.* at 28.) Petitioner raised no argument in this claim as to the defense's case, *i.e.* his ability to form the requisite *mens rea*, or the mental condition evidence to which he now points. (*See id.* at 26-28.) Petitioner did challenge the exclusion of this mental condition evidence under *Mott*, but did not do so as part of his claim of sufficiency of the evidence claim (Exhibit OO, Opening Brief at 26-28), but as a separate due process challenge to the exclusion (*id.* at 46-52.)

Similarly, Petitioner's Reply Brief focused solely upon arguments that the shooting was not premeditated, but "during a sudden quarrel." (Exhibit QQ at 4-6.)

In disposing of Petitioner's direct appeal, the Arizona Court of Appeals did not *sua sponte* consider the defense case argument, *i.e.* whether the mental condition evidence rendered the evidence insubstantial. Rather it limited its consideration of the sufficiency of the evidence to the prosecution's case argument, *i.e.* whether the circumstances of Petitioner's conduct, and the other evidence surrounding the course of events at the shooting, established that Petitioner intended to kill a police officer. (Exhibit RR, Mem. Dec. 1/25/05 at 6-10.) Thus, Petitioner failed to fairly present to the Arizona Court of Appeals a substantial evidence claim based on the defense's case argument.

In his Petition for Review to the Arizona Supreme Court, Petitioner repeated his same challenges to the evidence, citing evidence showing a "sudden heat of passion exchange." (Exhibit SS, at 3-5) The only reference to Petitioner's mental capacity in the substantial evidence claim was the single remark that the incident was such an exchange "between the officer and delusional Appellant." (*Id.* at 5.) Petitioner did not argue that those delusions led to a conclusion that Petitioner did not understand the facts sufficiently to form the requisite *mens rea.*

Although a federal habeas petitioner may reformulate somewhat the claims made in state court, *Tamapua v. Shimoda, 796 F.2d 261, 262 (9th Cir. 1986), rev'd in part on other grounds by Duncan v. Henry, 513 U.S. 364, 115 S. Ct. 887, 130 L. Ed. 2d 865 (1995),* the substance of the federal claim must have been "fairly presented" in state court. *Id. at 262.* Thus, a petitioner may not broaden the scope of a constitutional claim in the federal courts by asserting additional operative facts that have not yet been fairly presented to the state courts. Expanded claims not presented in the highest state court are not considered in a federal habeas petition. *Brown v. Easter, 68 F.3d 1209 (9th Cir. 1995); see also, Pappageorge v. Sumner, 688 F.2d 1294 (9th Cir. 1982), cert. denied, 459 U.S. 1219, 103 S. Ct. 1223, 75 L. Ed. 2d 459 (1983); Chacon v. Wood, 36 F.3d 1459, 1468 (9th Cir.1994).*

As observed by the Supreme Court in *Clark,* the species of "observation evidence" at the heart of Petitioner's challenge, and its use to refute the existence of *mens rea* is a unique species of evidence. Raising a separate challenge to *mens rea,* based solely upon the lack of affirmative evidence of intent would not provide a fair opportunity for the state court to pass upon an "observation evidence" claim refuting an ability to form the requisite *mens rea.*

Even if the single reference to Petitioner being delusional was somehow a presentation of the instant "observational evidence" claim, Petitioner's brief to the Arizona Supreme Court failed to cite any federal law (or any law) in connection with this claim. (Beyond four corners). While he did so in making the claim to the Arizona Court of Appeals, he "must have presented his federal, constitutional issue before the Arizona Court of Appeals within the four corners of his appellate briefing." *Castillo v. McFadden, 370 F.3d 882, 887 (9th Cir. 2004).* "[O]rdinarily a state prisoner does not 'fairly present' a claim to a state court if that court must read beyond a petition or a brief (or a similar document) that does not alert it to the presence of a federal claim in order to find material, such as a lower court opinion in the case, that does so." *Baldwin v. Reese, 541 U.S. 27, 32, 124 S. Ct. 1347, 158 L. Ed. 2d 64 (2004).*

Further, that would have been Petitioner's first presentation of the claim, Petitioner having failed to assert the claim to the Arizona Court of Appeals, as discussed herein above it would not be considered by the Arizona Supreme Court absent special circumstances, and thus was not fairly presented. Petitioner simply failed to raise his claim "on every level of direct review." *Casey, 386 F.3d at 916.*

Based upon the foregoing, the undersigned finds that Petitioner never fairly presented to the state courts the instant claim of a lack of substantial evidence of the required *mens rea*, based upon a failure to consider the defense's observational evidence on Petitioner's mental condition. Consequently, the undersigned concludes that this portion of Petitioner's Ground One was not properly exhausted.

(2) Ground Two (Sanity Determination)

For his Ground Two, Petitioner argues that the state courts violated his due process rights by making an unreasonable determination of the facts in determining he was sane, and thus criminally culpable. (Amend. Pet. Doc. 17 at 22-29.) Respondents concede that the facts of this claim were asserted under a state law claim on direct appeal, but argue Petitioner's federal claim is unexhausted and procedurally defaulted.

(Answer, Doc. 31 at 30-32.) Petitioner argues in his Petition that this federal claim was fairly presented by arguing state law cases citing to the "*M'Naghten* Case" (Amend. Pet. Doc. 17 at 22), and replies that his "opening brief [on direct appeal] relied on *McNaugten* [sic], clearly established federal law, which relied on a due process argument." (Reply, Co. 48 at 18.)

To the contrary, Petitioner's Opening Brief contains a single reference on page 38 to the English case, *M'Naghten's Case*, 10 Cl. & Fin. 200, 8 Eng. Rep. 718 (1843), addressed by the Supreme Court in Petitioner's case, *Clark, 548 U.S. at 746*. (*See* Exhibit OO, Opening Brief at viii.) That portion of his Opening Brief was dedicated to Petitioner's third issue on appeal, a challenge to the constitutionality of Arizona's insanity statute. (*Id.* at 37 to 51.) Moreover, *M'Naghten* merely established a principal of English common law on the insanity defense. While *M'Naghten* is a landmark common law case, Petitioner's own case before the Supreme Court identifies that *M'Naghten* itself is not a feature of federal or constitutional law. While "[s]eventeen States and the Federal Government have adopted a recognizable version of the *M'Naghten* test with both its cognitive incapacity and moral incapacity components...due process imposes no single canonical formulation of legal insanity." *Clark, 548 U.S. at 753*.

More importantly, Petitioner's challenge to the state court's factual findings, contained in his second issue on appeal (*id.* at 28-37) included no reference to *M'Naghten*, due process, or any federal authorities, but instead uniformly relied upon state authorities addressing when a trial court's determination of failure to prove insanity is an abuse of discretion, or its jury instructions deficient. (*Id.* (citing *State v. Zmich, 160 Ariz. 108, 111, 770 P.2d 776, 779 (1989)* (state law abuse of discretion); *State v. King, 158 Ariz. 419, 426, 763 P.2d 239, 246 (1988)* (1988) (state law on jury instruction); and *State v. Tamplin, 195 Ariz. 246, 986 P.2d 914 (App. 1999)* (state law on jury instruction)).

Accordingly, Petitioner failed to present the federal claims in his Ground Two to the state courts, and the claim was not properly exhausted.

(3) Ground Five (Conflict of Interest of Trial Counsel - As an alternative to asserting an independent and adequate state bar, as discussed hereinafter, Respondents argue that Petitioner's conflict of

interest claim in Ground Five was not fairly presented because it was raised for the first time on the motion to amend, and that motion did not plainly rely upon federal law. (Answer, Doc. 31 at 84-85.) Indeed, the Motion to Amend cited no authority in support of the claim of a conflict of interest. (*See* Exhibit OOO, Motion to Amend at 5.) Petitioner replies that the Motion to Amend raised an "ineffective assistance of counsel" claim, and that "ineffective assistance of counsel" "is a term of art and is sufficient to raise a *6th Amendment* argument." (Reply, Doc, 48 at 28.)

However, a simple reference to ineffective assistance of counsel is not sufficient to fairly present a federal claim under the *Sixth Amendment. Lyons v. Crawford, 232 F.3d 666, 668-69 (9th Cir.2000), as amended, 247 F.3d 904 (9th Cir.2001). See also Baldwin v. Reese, 541 U.S. 27, 33, 124 S. Ct. 1347, 158 L. Ed. 2d 64 (2004)* (discussing sufficiency of mere reference to "ineffective assistance" absent evidence that the state court utilized the term to refer solely to a federal law claim); *Casey, 386 F.3d at 914* (declining to treat claims as identical where petitioner "failed to demonstrate that the [state] courts would apply a federal constitutional analysis to the claims he presented").

Petitioner presents no authority for his proposition that "ineffective assistance" is a term of art within the Arizona courts that refers solely to a claim founded upon federal law. Arizona's own constitution guarantees effective assistance of counsel. *See Ariz. Rev. Stat. Const. Art. 2 § 24.* It is true that Arizona's standards for ineffective assistance of counsel parallel those adopted by the U.S. Supreme Court in *Strickland v. Washington, 466 U.S. 668, 104 S. Ct. 2052, 80 L. Ed. 2d 674 (1984). See State v. Lee, 142 Ariz. 210, 689 P.2d 153 (1984)* (adopting the prejudice prong of Strickland standard); *State v. Nash, 143 Ariz. 392, 397, 694 P.2d 222, 227 (1985)* (adopting the deficient performance of the Strickland standard); *State v. Valdez, 167 Ariz. 328, 330, 806 P.2d 1376, 1378 (1991)* ("This court has adopted the Strickland test."). However, the Arizona right to effective counsel is not equivalent to the federal right. *See e.g. State v. Krum, 182 Ariz. 108, 110, 893 P.2d 759, 761* (.App. Div. 1 1995), *overturned on statutory grounds, 183 Ariz. 288, 903 P.2d 596 (1995)* (finding right to effective counsel in PCR proceeding, notwithstanding federal law's denial of right to PCR counsel). "[R]aising a state claim that is merely similar to a federal claim does not exhaust state remedies." *Fields v. Waddington, 401 F.3d 1018, 1022 (9th Cir. 2005)*.

The burden of proving that the state and federal claims are identical is on the habeas petitioner. *Casey, 386 F.3d at 914* (declining to treat claims as identical where petitioner "failed to demonstrate that the [state] courts would apply a federal constitutional analysis to the claims he presented"). In *Fields*, the Ninth Circuit refused to deem federal claims exhausted when the petitioner's claims appeared to have been asserted as analogous state law claims. "In the absence of an affirmative statement by the Washington Supreme Court that it considers a particular state and federal constitutional claim to be identical, rather than analogous, or an affirmative statement by the Washington Supreme Court that [the circumstances of the claim] serves to raise federal claims for the purposes of exhaustion, Petitioner was required to raise his federal claims affirmatively; we will not infer that federal claims have been exhausted." *Fields, 401 F.3d at 1024*.

According, the undersigned concludes that Petitioner failed to fairly present the federal claim in Ground Five based upon trial counsel's conflict of interest.

(4) Ground Six (Prosecutorial Misconduct) - For his Ground Six, Petitioner argues that the prosecutor committed misconduct by failing to seek a competency hearing prior to Petitioner's waiver of a jury trial, and by failing to express concerns about defense council's decision to waive the jury trial. (Amend. Pet. Doc. 17 at 63-66.) Presumably, Petitioner intends to argue that this resulted in a denial of due process. Petitioner argues this claim "was raised in the Petition for Post-Conviction Relief in an around about way" through references to the state's failure to call for " a special competency determination regarding the waiver of the right to trial by jury." (*Id.* at 63 (quoting Exhibit VV, PCR Pet. at 6).)

Respondents argue that Petitioner failed to fairly present this argument. (Answer, Doc. 31 at 96-98.) Petitioner replies that he "candidly admitted that this claim was not clearly raised in the PCR; however, it was alluded to and all parties were on notice of the competency issue and concerns." (Reply, Doc. 48 at 29.)

Briefing a case is not like writing a poem, where the message may be conveyed entirely through allusions and connotations. Poets may use ambiguity, but lawyers use clarity. If a party wants a state court to decide whether she was deprived of a federal constitutional right, she has to say so. It has to be clear from the petition filed at each level in the state court system that the petitioner is claiming the violation of the federal constitution that the petitioner subsequently claims in the federal habeas petition.

Galvan v. Alaska Dept. of Corrections, 397 F.3d 1198, 1204 (9th Cir. 2005). Petitioner points to no portion of his state briefs in which he said he had been denied his federal due process rights as a result of prosecutorial misconduct of any kind, nor even any portion wherein he asserted a claim of prosecutorial misconduct. The portion of his PCR Petition to which he points made no reference to any misfeasance on the part of the prosecution, and was plainly ensconced in an argument on ineffective assistance of counsel. The PCR court would had to have been clairvoyant to deduce a prosecutorial misconduct claim from that discussion.

Moreover, Petitioner points to no portion of his Petition for Review to the Arizona Court of Appeals to show that the claim was fairly presented to that court.

This claim was not properly exhausted.

(5) Ground Seven (Ineffectiveness of Appellate Counsel) - For his Ground Seven, Petitioner argues that he was denied effective assistance of appellate counsel as a result of counsel's failure to raise the (a) competency, (b) insanity, and (c) observational evidence issues. (Amend. Pet. Doc. 17 at 66-69.) Petitioner contends that these issues were raised in his motions to amend his PCR petition. (*Id.* at 66.) Respondents argue *inter alia* that presenting the claim in a motion to amend was not fair presentation, and Petitioner never presented the factual basis of his claim in the motion to amend. (Answer, Doc. 31 at 101-103.) Petitioner points out that the same counsel was trial and appellate counsel, and replies that he could not bring the claim on direct appeal, and attempted to do so in his PCR proceeding. (Reply, Doc. 48 at 30.) "Competency" generally refers to issues concerning

Petitioner's mental status at the time of trial. "Insanity" generally refers to Petitioner's mental status at the time of commission of the offense. Respondents also argue that the denial of the motion to amend was a procedural bar on independent and adequate state grounds which bars federal habeas relief. (Answer, Doc. 31 at 101.) Assuming the federal claims in Ground Seven were not fairly presented in the motion to amend, the application of a procedural bar to deny the motion to amend would be irrelevant for habeas purposes. The procedural bar issues are addressed hereinafter on the assumption that the claims in Ground Seven were fairly presented.

The undersigned presumes *arguendo* that a federal claim may be fairly presented to an Arizona PCR court by its presentation in a motion to amend the petition. Even with that assumption, Petitioner's Motion to Amend failed to fairly present two of the three claims in his Ground Seven.

The only reference Petitioner made to appellate counsel in his Motion to Amend was his introductory statement that "appellate counsel was ineffective in failing to raise the competency issue on appeal." (Exhibit OOO, Mot. Amend at 1-2.) While the same attorney that was one of Petitioner's attorneys at trial (Goldberg), also represented him on appeal, it is generally a different claim to assert a failure on appeal versus one at trial. Moreover, the facts argued by Petitioner in his Motion to Amend were limited to attorney Middlebrooks's impairment at trial (*id.* at 3-4), Petitioner's competency to stand trial (*id.* at 4-5), counsel Middlebrooks's conflict of interest in presenting his insanity defense as a result of his deficiencies in assisting Petitioner's families attempt to secure involuntary treatment (*id.* at 5). Petitioner's motion did not otherwise discuss any counsel's handling of the insanity defense or discuss at all the "observational evidence" issues. Thus, the only portion of Petitioner's Ground Seven which was discussed in his Motion to Amend was the bald statement that appellate counsel was ineffective for failing to raise the competency issue. The PCR court did address Petitioner's claim that trial counsel was ineffective for failing to assert (or affirmatively hiding) Petitioner's incompetency at trial and on the waiver of a jury. (Exhibit AAAA, M.E. 3/15/07 at 5-10.)

Further, Petitioner's motion to amend makes no reference whatsoever to any federal claim. He cites no federal authority or constitutional provision. He makes unadorned references to counsel being "ineffective" or "deficient" and purports to seek the amendment "to preserve Defendant's constitutional rights." (*Id.* at 1-2.) Petitioner argues that his references to an "IAC claim" was sufficient to invoke federal law on effective assistance of counsel. (Reply, Doc. 48 at 27-28.) However, as discussed above, a simple reference to ineffective assistance of counsel is not sufficient to fairly present a federal claim under the *Sixth Amendment*.

Moreover, Petitioner must also have presented this claim to the Arizona Court of Appeals. Petitioner plainly relied upon federal law in his Petition for Review, citing *Strickland v. Washington, 466 U.S. 668, 104 S. Ct. 2052, 80 L. Ed. 2d 674 (1984)*. (Exhibit CCCC, PCR Pet. Rev. at 10.) However, Petitioner's only reference, explicit or implicit, to appellate processes in his Petition for Review, was the following:

6. The trial court erred in determining that counsel provided ineffective assistance of counsel concerning an issue that was not addressed by the United States Supreme Court on appeal for the reason that the issue was not properly preserved for appellate review.

(Exhibit CCCC, PCR Pet. Rev. at 3.) Petitioner explained that this related to trial counsel's failure to raise the "observational evidence" issue.

On September 15, 2006, Goldberg signed an affidavit in which he stated in part: "I believed at the time of trial and direct appeal in the State system that *State v. Mott, 187 Ariz. 536, 931 P.2d 1046 (1997)* precluded the court's consideration of the observation evidence. However, I never raised this point on the record with the court nor specifically asked the court to consider the lay testimony on the issue of *mens rea.*

(Exhibit CCCC, PCR Pet. Rev. at 5-6.) Even if this claim amounted to an assertion of ineffectiveness of appellate counsel, that claim had not been presented in Petitioner's motion to amend, or his original PCR petition.

Petitioner did argue that counsel was ineffective for failing to pursue the competency issue, but that was limited to events at trial, including the claim of counsel "withholding from the trial judge a doctor's report", failing to "address the competency issue when Defendant's mental condition deteriorated during trial," "having Defendant waive the right to trial by jury," and "limiting the evidence...on the issue of insanity." (*Id.* at 2-3.)

In sum, at best, Petitioner raised to the PCR Court the portion of Ground Seven based on appellate counsel's failure to raise the competency issues, and raised to the Arizona Court of Appeals the portion based on appellate counsel's failure to raise the observation evidence issue. Neither was, alone, sufficient. *Casey, 386 F.3d at 916.*

Accordingly, the undersigned concludes that Petitioner's Ground Seven was not fairly presented to the state courts, and was not properly exhausted.

(6) Summary Re Presentation of Claims - Based upon the foregoing, the undersigned concludes that Petitioner failed to fairly present the following claims:

(a) the portions of Ground One based upon "observation evidence" which negated the finding of *mens rea*;

(b) the claims in Ground Two (sanity determination);

(c) the portions of Ground Five based upon trial counsel's conflict of interest;

(d) the claims in Ground Six (prosecutorial misconduct); and

(e) the claims in Ground Seven (ineffectiveness of appellate counsel).

2. Procedural Default

....

Respondents argue that Petitioner may no longer present his unexhausted claims [*42] to the state courts. Respondents rely upon Arizona's preclusion bar, set out in *Ariz. R. Crim. Proc. 32.2(a)*, and its timeliness bar in *Ariz. R. Crim. P. 32.4*. (Answer, Doc. 16 at 14-15.)

....

Remedies by Post-Conviction Relief - Petitioner can no longer seek review by a subsequent PCR Petition.

Waiver Bar - Under the rules applicable to Arizona's post-conviction process, a claim may not ordinarily be brought in a petition for post-conviction relief that "has been waived at trial, on appeal, or in any previous collateral proceeding." *Ariz.R.Crim.P. 32.2(a)(3)*. Under this rule, some claims may be deemed waived if the State simply shows "that the defendant did not raise the error at trial, on appeal, or in a previous collateral proceeding." *Stewart v. Smith, 202 Ariz. 446, 449, 46 P.3d 1067, 1070 (2002)* (quoting *Ariz.R.Crim.P. 32.2*, Comments). For others of "sufficient constitutional magnitude," the State "must show that the defendant personally, "knowingly, voluntarily and intelligently' [did] not raise' the ground or denial of a right." *Id.* That requirement is limited to those constitutional rights "that can only be waived by a defendant personally." *State v. Swoopes 216 Ariz. 390, 399, 166 P.3d 945, 954 (App.Div. 2, 2007)*. Indeed, in coming to its prescription in *Stewart v. Smith*, the Arizona Supreme Court identified: (1) waiver of the right to counsel, (2) waiver of the right to a jury trial, and (3) waiver of the right to a twelve-person jury under the Arizona Constitution, as among those rights which require a personal waiver. *202 Ariz. at 450, 46 P.3d at 1071*. None of Petitioner's unexhausted claims fit within those categories. Some other types of claims addressed by the Arizona Courts in resolving the type of waiver required include: ineffective assistance (waived by omission), *Stewart, 202 Ariz. at 450, 46 P.3d at 1071*; right to be present at non-critical stages (waived by omission), *Swoopes, 216 Ariz. at 403, 166 P.3d at 958*; improper withdrawal of plea offer (waived by omission), *State v. Espinosa, 200 Ariz. 503, 29 P.3d 278 (App. 2001)*; double jeopardy (waived by omission), *State v. Stokes*, 2007 WL 5596552 (App. 10/16/07); illegal sentence (waived by omission), *State v. Brashier, 2009 Ariz. App. LEXIS 809, 2009 WL 794501 (App. 2009)*; judge conflict of interest (waived by omission), *State v. Westmiller, 2008 Ariz. App. Unpub. LEXIS 18, 2008 WL 2651659 (App. 2008)*. Petitioner concedes that his claim of ineffectiveness of appellate counsel is now procedurally barred under *Rule 32.2(a)*. (Reply, Doc. 48 at 30.)

Timeliness Bar

....

Accordingly, the undersigned must conclude that review through Arizona's direct appeal and post-conviction relief process is no longer possible for Petitioner's unexhausted claims.

Summary re Procedural Default - Petitioner failed to exhaust his federal claims in part of his Ground One ("observation evidence"), part of his Ground Five (conflict of interest) and in all of Grounds Two, Six and Seven, and is now procedurally barred from doing so. Accordingly, these unexhausted claims are procedurally defaulted, and absent a showing of cause and prejudice or actual innocence, must be dismissed with prejudice.

D. INDEPENDENT AND ADEQUATE STATE GROUNDS

Respondents argue that the following claims were procedurally barred in the state courts upon an independent and adequate state ground, and thus are not subject to habeas review:

(1) the claims in Ground Four (Competence) (Answer, Doc. 31 at 44);

(2) the claims in Ground Five that trial counsel was ineffective for failing to seek a competency redetermination during trial (*id.* at 65), and had a conflict of interest that prevented him from testifying and compromised his performance (*id.* at 84); and

(3) the claims in Ground Seven (ineffective assistance of appellate counsel (*id.* at 101).

"[A]bsent showings of 'cause' and 'prejudice,' federal habeas relief will be unavailable when (1) 'a state court [has] declined to address a prisoner's federal claims because the prisoner had failed to meet a state procedural requirement,' and (2) 'the state judgment rests on independent and adequate state procedural grounds.' " *Walker v. Martin, U.S., 131 S. Ct. 1120, 179 L. Ed. 2d 62, 2011 WL 611627, 6 (2011).*

Ground Four (Competency) - In his Ground Four, Petitioner argues that he was not competent to stand trial, or to waive his rights to a jury trial. (Amend. Pet. Doc. 17 at 33.) Petitioner contends that as a result of the acceptance of his waiver and the prosecution of his trial his due process rights were denied. (*Id.* at 40.) See e.g. *Maxwell v. Roe, 606 F.3d 561, 568 (9th Cir. 2010)* ("undisputed" that conviction of an accused person while he is legally incompetent violates due process.) Petitioner adds that he was not competent to "present a defense, or to a full and fair hearing." (Amend. Pet. Doc. 17 at 33.) Petitioner does not explain how these are different from his claim that he was incompetent to stand trial. Accordingly, the Court treats them as surplusage to Petitioner's claim of incompetence to stand trial.

Petitioner argues he raised these claims in his Ground Four "in the Petition for Post-Conviction Relief and in the Motion to Amend the Petition." (*Id.* at 33-34.) He also argues they were raised in his PCR Reply. (*Id.* at 34-35.) Respondents argue that Petitioner raised these claims in his unsuccessful motion to amend, but the PCR court found them waived under *Ariz. R. Crim. P. 32.2(d)* by failure to present them on direct appeal. (Answer, Doc. 31 at 45.)

These claims were raised in Petitioner's PCR Petition. "Defendant submits that he was not competent to stand trial nor competent to waive constitutional rights... [in violation of] Defendant's rights as guaranteed by the *Sixth* and *Fourteenth Amendments to the Constitution of the United States.*" (Exhibit VV, PCR Pet. At 2.) The claims were addressed in the PCR Court's order. The PCR court noted that it had addressed the substance of the claims in addressing Petitioner's related ineffective assistance claims. The court concluded:

In order to assist appellate review, this Court finds that Arizona Rules of Criminal Procedure *Rule 32.2* does not allow these claims as set forth above as they could have been raised on direct appeal. Finally, this Court finds that even if the competency claims were reviewable on their own, the entire record of this case...show defendant was competent to stand trial and waive his right to a jury trial.

(Exhibit AAAA, M.E. 3/15/07 at 14.) Accordingly, the undersigned finds that this claim was disposed of by the PCR Court as waived under *Rule 32.2*.

On the other hand, before the Arizona Court of Appeals, Petitioner merely contended that the "trial court erred in determining that Defendant was competent to stand trial and waive constitutional rights including the right to trial by jury." (Exhibit EEEE, PFR at 2.) This claim was submitted as a sub issue of an ineffective of assistance of counsel claim. Petitioner never asserted or discussed any authority on competency to stand trial, beyond a state court case (*Bishop v. Superior Court, 150 Ariz. 404, 724 P.2d 23 (1986)*) in connection with arguments that trial counsel was ineffective with regard to Petitioner's competency. *See Rose v. Palmateer, 395 F.3d 1108, 1110-11 (9th Cir. 2005)* (holding that a petitioner does not fairly present a *Fifth Amendment* claim to the state courts when it is merely discussed as one of several issues handled ineffectively by counsel). Thus, if not procedurally barred, the undersigned would find that this claim was procedurally defaulted by failure to fairly present it to the Arizona Court of Appeals.

Petitioner replies that: (1) appellate counsel admitted he should have raised the claim, but believed it to be without merit; (2) he attempted to raise the claim in his motion to amend his PCR petition; (3) it would have been futile to raise because the Arizona Court of Appeals had already rejected the claim; (4) the opinions of the United States Supreme Court differed on whether the claim had been preserved; and (5) in any event, the PCR Court went on to consider the claims. (Reply, Doc. 48 at 20-21.)

To the extent that Petitioner contends that ineffective assistance of appellate counsel shows cause to excuse the procedural bar, that will be addressed in the section on Cause and Prejudice hereinafter. It is irrelevant that Petitioner's Ground Four claims were also presented in his Motion to Amend his PCR petition. The PCR Court addressed them though as raised in the Petition.

Petitioner asserts it would have been futile to present the claims because they had already been rejected by the Arizona Court of Appeals by its decision "that *Mott* did not allow this evidence to be considered." (Reply, Doc. 48 at 20.) Petitioner seems to be confusing his insanity and/or lack of *mens rea* defenses with his competency to stand trial claim. Petitioner's direct appeal dealt solely with his insanity defense, and did not address his competency to stand trial. The referenced case, *State v. Mott, 187 Ariz. 536, 931 P.2d 1046 (1997)* dealt not with a defendant's competency to stand trial, but with diminished capacity in the context of a battered woman defense. *See Clark, 548 U.S. at 756* (discussing *Mott*).

Petitioner argues that the U.S. Supreme Court justices differed on whether the competency claim had been preserved. (Reply Doc. 48 at 20.) Petitioner does not elaborate. Again, however, this appears to refer to Petitioner's lack of *mens rea* claim rather than his competency claim. *See Clark, 548 U.S. at 761-765* (discussing dispute between the majority and dissent as to preservation of claims concerning exclusion of observation evidence on *mens rea*).

Finally, Petitioner's contention that the merits were nonetheless reached is true but inapposite. The state court may reach "the merits of a federal claim in an alternative holding" and still avoid habeas review, "as long as the state court explicitly invokes a state procedural bar rule." *Harris v. Reed, 489 U.S. 255, 264 n. 10, 109 S. Ct. 1038, 103 L. Ed. 2d 308 (1989)*. The PCR Court clearly invoked *Rule 32.2* to dispose of Petitioner's competency claims. Accordingly, the undersigned concludes that the claims in Petitioner's Ground Four were disposed on the basis of *Rule 32.2*'s waiver rule, which Respondents plead is an independent and adequate procedural ground.

Although, as discussed hereinafter, Petitioner challenges the adequacy of Arizona's amendment rule (*Rule 32.6(d)*) (Amend. Pet. Doc. 17 at 37), Petitioner does not argue that the waiver rule of *Rule 32.2* is not independent and adequate.

Petitioner does argue that a competency claim can never be waived (given the potential that the defendant was incompetent when the claim was allegedly waived), citing *Adams v. Wainwright, 764 F.2d 1356, 1359 (11th Cir. 1985)*, and *Commonwealth v. Santiago, 579 Pa. 46, 855 A.2d 682, 692, n. 9 (Pa. 2004)*. (Amend Pet. Doc. 17 at 35.) However, neither of these cases concern the application of Arizona's *Rule 32.2*. Further, what was at issue in the PCR Court was not Petitioner's competence to waive at trial a claim of incompetency, but the effectiveness of his waiver of the claim on direct appeal.

Moreover, Petitioner's argument ignores the holding of the Ninth Circuit in *Martinez-Villareal v. Lewis, 80 F.3d 1301 (9th Cir. 1996)*, which explicitly rejected the Eleventh Circuit's analysis in *Adams* as "untenable when applied to a case in which the State has raised the defense of procedural default, rather than waiver." *Id. at 1307*. Whatever logic this Court might find in Petitioner's arguments and the reasoning of the Eleventh Circuit, the decision in *Martinez-Villareal* is controlling in this circuit.

Finally, the undersigned notes that *Rule 32.2* does require for some types of claims of "sufficient constitutional magnitude" an intentional "personal waiver", rather than a mere waiver by failure to raise it in an earlier proceeding. However, Petitioner points to no Arizona case applying this to appellate claims of incompetency. Nor does Petitioner point to any other case doing so. The parties do discuss *Pate v. Robinson, 383 U.S. 375, 86 S. Ct. 836, 15 L. Ed. 2d 815 (1966)*, in which the Supreme Court found that the defendant had not waived a claim of incompetency at trial by failing to raise the claim at trial. The Court did observe that "it is contradictory to argue that a defendant may be incompetent, and yet knowingly or intelligently 'waive' his right to have the court determine his capacity to stand trial." *Id. at 384*. However, the Court did not hold that such a waiver could not be made, and it explicitly found that the defendant's counsel had put his present competency at issue. In *Drope v. Missouri*, the Court characterized *Pate* as simply "express[ing]" doubt that the right to further inquiry upon the question [of incompetency] can be waived." *420 U.S. 162, 176, 95 S. Ct. 896, 43 L. Ed. 2d 103 (1975)*.

Based upon the foregoing, the undersigned finds Petitioner's competency claims to be procedurally barred from habeas review, absent a showing of a cognizable excuse.

Ground Five (Ineffective Assistance of Trial Counsel - In his Ground Five, Petitioner argues that trial counsel was ineffective for, *inter alia*, failing to seek a competency redetermination during trial, and because trial counsel Middlebrooks had a conflict of interest that prevented him from testifying and compromised his performance. Respondents argue that these claims were not raised in the original PCR Petition, and that the Motion to Amend which sought to assert them was denied pursuant to *Arizona Rule of Criminal Procedure 32.6(d)* on the basis of Petitioner's failure to show good cause to amend. (Answer, Doc. 31 at 65, 84.) Petitioner replies that *Rule 32.6(d)*is not "adequate" because it is not consistently applied in Arizona. (Reply, Doc. 48 at 12.) (*See also* Amend. Pet., Doc. 17 at 44 (citing *Scott v. Schriro, 567 F.3d 573 (9th Cir. 2009)*).

Petitioner argues without explanation that Respondents concede the exhaustion of all portions of Ground 5 other than the conflict of interest issue. (Reply, Doc. 48 at 21.) Respondents clearly assert a procedural bar as to the competency during trial issue. (Answer, Doc. 31 at 65.)

Application of Procedural Bar - The PCR court did deny Petitioner's Motion to Amend. (Exhibit SSS, M.E. 2/20/07.) In doing so, however, the court went to some lengths to identify related claims that it found had been adequately raised in the PCR Petition, distinguishing the ineffectiveness claims based upon failure to raise competency to stand trial as compared to a loss of competency during trial:

THE COURT: All right. I'm going to stand by my ruling to not allow the Motion to Amend. I will allow Mr. Gerhardt to bring the claim as set forth in the - - that on the basis of Dr. Parrish's report, Mr. Middlebrooks was ineffective because he did not raise the issue of competency to Judge Coker with respect to his right to his ability to waive constitutional rights which includes the right to waive a jury trial, and that he was not competent to stand trial.

Now, to the extent that you can tie in his competency during trial to the issue that he was not competent to stand trial, I'll give you that leeway, but I see the competency during trial, that he was not competent during trial - - while it is somewhat related, I still see that as somewhat of a separate issue, because I don't have anything in front of me that says during this phase of the trial there was an evaluation that was done and Mr. Clark was determined not be competent.

* * *

THE COURT: I'm going to deny the Motion to Amend, but I will find that in your initial Petition you did raise the issue, and that issue has been raised as to whether or not Mr. Clark was competent to waive his Constitutional rights, competent to stand trial, and that relates to the issue of Dr. Parrish's report and her findings and whether or not Mr. Middlebrooks was ineffective for failing to bring this to [the trial judge's] attention.

(Exhibit RRR-1, R.T. 2/20/07 at 28-29, 33.)

Notwithstanding that ruling, the PCR Court nonetheless reached at least portions of the competency-during-trial issue, considering whether trial counsel was ineffective for "failing to raise another competency claim during trial due to petitioner's falling asleep during trial." (Exhibit AAAA M.E. 3/15/07 at 10.) Petitioner's current claim concerning a reassertion of incompetency during trial does not appear to extend beyond that claim.

Thus, it appears that despite denying the motion to amend, the PCR court did address the portion of Petitioner's Ground Five based upon trial counsel's failure to urge Petitioner's incompetency during trial. It is true that a state court may reach "the merits of a federal claim in an alternative holding" and still avoid habeas review, "as long as the state court explicitly invokes a state procedural bar rule." *Harris v. Reed, 489 U.S. 255, 264 n. 10, 109 S. Ct. 1038, 103 L. Ed. 2d 308 (1989)*. Here, however, the state court did not address the merits as an alternative holding in the same order in which it applied a procedural bar, but in ruling on a motion to amend prior to the hearing. Rather, the state court appears to have either reversed or clarified its earlier decision that the ineffectiveness-on-competency-during-trial issue was not properly raised. Thus, in its final order on the PCR petition, the merits of this claim were explicitly addressed without reference to any procedural bar. In contrast, when addressing the direct challenges to competency, the PCR Court explicitly found the claims precluded under *Ariz. R. Crim. P. 32.2*, but alternatively held "that even if the competency claims were reviewable on their own, the entire record...show defendant was competent to stand trial and waive his right opt a jury trial." (Exhibit AAAA, M.E. 3/15/07 at 13.)

Accordingly, the undersigned finds that only that portion of Ground Five related to trial counsel's conflict of interest was barred by denial of the motion to amend.

Claim Actually Barred - Alternatively to their procedural bar argument, Respondents argue that Petitioner's conflict of interest claim was not fairly presented because it was raised for the first time on the motion to amend, and that motion did not plainly rely upon federal law. (Answer, Doc. 31 at 84-85.) Because the undersigned has herein above agreed with that proposition, the lack of presentation of the present federal claim in the motion to amend mandates a conclusion that the ruling on that motion could not be a procedural bar to the federal claim.

Nonetheless, the undersigned will assume *arguendo* that the Motion to Amend did adequately assert the federal claim, and will address whether the denial of the motion was on an independent and adequate state ground sufficient to bar habeas review.

Adequacy of Amendment Rule - As last amended in 2000, *Rule 32.6(d)* provides: "After the filing of a post-conviction relief petition, no amendments shall be permitted except by leave of court upon a showing of good cause." Petitioner contends that Arizona's rule on amendments to PCR petitions, *Ariz. R. Crim. P. 32.6(d)*, is not adequate because the PCR court engrafted novel time limitations on amendments.

Federal habeas review of a defaulted federal claim is precluded only when the state court has disposed of the claim on a procedural ground "that is both 'independent' of the merits of the federal claim and an 'adequate' basis for the court's decision." *Harris v. Reed, 489 U.S. 255, 260, 109 S. Ct. 1038, 103 L. Ed. 2d 308 (1989). But see Stewart v. Smith, 536 U.S. 856, 860, 122 S. Ct. 2578, 153 L. Ed. 2d 762 (2002)* ("assum[ing]" independence standard applies on habeas). A state's application of the bar is not adequate unless it is " 'strictly or regularly followed.' " *Johnson v. Mississippi, 486 U.S. 578, 108 S. Ct. 1981, 100 L. Ed. 2d 575 (1988)* (citation omitted) (quoting *Hathorn v. Lovorn, 457 U.S. 255, 262-63, 102 S. Ct. 2421, 72 L. Ed. 2d 824 (1982)).* Further, to be "adequate," the state law or rule upon which the state court's ruling rests must be "firmly established" and "regularly applied" at the time of its application. *Harris v. Reed, 489 U.S. 255, 109 S. Ct. 1038, 103 L. Ed. 2d 308 (1989). See also Poland v. Stewart, 169 F.3d 573, 577 (9th Cir. 1999)* ("firmly established and regularly followed at the time it was applied by the state court").

To qualify as an adequate procedural ground, a state rule must be "firmly established and regularly followed. A discretionary state procedural rule...can serve as an adequate ground to bar federal habeas review." A rule can be "firmly established" and "regularly followed,"

...even if the appropriate exercise of discretion may permit consideration of a federal claim in some cases but not others.

> *Walker v. Martin, U.S., 131 S. Ct. 1120, 179 L. Ed. 2d 62, 2011 WL 611627, 7 (2011).*

Petitioner cites *Insyxiengmay v. Morgan, 403 F.3d 657, 665 (9th Cir. 2005)* for the proposition that Respondents, rather than he, have the burden of showing the state bar is an adequate and independent ground. (Reply, Doc. 48 at 13) While Respondents may bear the "ultimate burden," *Insyxiengmay, 403 F.3d at 666*, Petitioner must first make a *prima facie* showing that the rule is not adequate. In *Bennett v. Mueller, 322 F.3d 573 (9th Cir.2003)*, the Ninth Circuit specifically addressed the burden of proving the adequacy of a state procedural bar.

Once the state has adequately pled the existence of an independent and adequate state procedural ground as an affirmative defense, the burden to place that defense in issue shifts to the petitioner. The petitioner may satisfy this burden by asserting specific factual allegations that demonstrate the inadequacy of the state procedure, including citation to authority demonstrating inconsistent application of the rule. Once having done so, however, the ultimate burden is the state's.

> *Bennett, 322 F.3d at 584, 585.*

Petitioner has met his initial burden here. Petitioner argues that *Rule 32.6(d)* is inadequate because the PCR court in this case ignored the good cause standard within the rule and instead engrafted into that standard a novel timeliness requirement. (Reply, Doc. 48 at 12-13.) Nothing in *Rule 32.6(d)* explicitly imposes a timeliness limitation.

Respondents argue that the PCR court did not apply a timeliness requirement, but simply considered delay as part of its finding of an absence of good cause. The PCR judge opined:

THE COURT: You know, I was here over the weekend, and as I reviewed the Motion to Amend and the cases cited by both counsel, as well as going back over what I could glean from the trial, as well as the interviews, I'm going to deny the Motion to Amend the petition.

I think these issues were apparent and known prior to the hearing, and certainly some of them were known during trial and are apparent from the record in this case, and I understand Mr. Gerhardt's [Petitioner's PCR counsel] position that litigation is a search for the truth and that the issues in this case are great and very, very significant and very serious, but even under our system of criminal justice, there is an end that has to be contemplated in this case, and I find that the Defendant's failed to show good cause for amending the petition.

We're in the middle of the evidentiary hearing, and I think these issues were known prior to - - at least with Mr. Middlebrooks's interview, January 7th or January 8th. I think they were at the very latest apparent at that time and could have been - - could have been the subject of an amendment at that time.

So it is the decision of this Court that the Motion to Amend the petition for post-conviction relief is denied.

(Exhibit RRR-1, R.T. 2/20/07 at 4-5.)

Respondents point to no state authority recognizing that the rule incorporates a timeliness limitation such as that applied to Petitioner. The Arizona Supreme Court has continuously maintained that amendments are to be liberally allowed:

Rule 32.6(d), which permits a defendant to amend his petition "upon a showing of good cause," adopts a liberal policy toward amendment of PCR pleadings. If [the petitioner] uncovers new evidence or exculpatory evidence as a result of his [post-petition] discovery requests, the trial court may allow amendment of the petition.

Canion v. Cole, 210 Ariz. 598, 601, 115 P.3d 1261, 1264 (2005) (citations omitted). The only explicit time limitation on amendments recognized prior to the rulings on Petitioner's PCR petition was under the pre-1992 amendment version of the rule which only directed liberal amendments "prior to the entry of judgment." *See Scott v. Schriro, 567 F.3d 573, 586 (9th Cir. 1009)* (reviewing amendments to *Rule 32.6(d)*); *Ariz. R. Crim. P. 32.6(d)*(1991) ("prior to entry of judgment"); *State v. Ramirez, 126 Ariz. 464, 468, 616 P.2d 924, 928 (Ariz.App., 1980)* ("We hold that *Rule 32.6(d)* requires that amendments to the pleadings be made prior to the trial court's ruling dismissing the petition or prior to the trial court's order granting or denying relief on the merits after a hearing on the petition pursuant to *Rule 32.8(d)*."); *State v. Rogers, 113 Ariz. 6, 8, 545 P.2d 930, 932 (1976)* ("*Rule 32.6(d)*adopts a liberal policy toward amendments of post-conviction pleadings at all stages prior to the entry of judgment.").

In *Scott v. Schriro*, the Ninth Circuit found that the PCR court had incorrectly relied on authorities under the pre-1992 version of *Rule 32.6(d)* to enforce a time limit on amendments, and that the post-1992 version contained no such limits.

Thus, given that neither the text of the 1992 version of *Rule 32.6(d)* nor any case construing that version of the rule state that a post-conviction court cannot grant a motion to amend the petition after the original petition has been dismissed, the state has not met its burden of proving *Rule 32.6(d)* is consistently interpreted as it was interpreted here. Accordingly, the district court erred in holding that *Rule 32.6(d)* constitutes an adequate and independent state procedural bar to federal review on the merits and failing to rule on the merits of the proposed claims.

Scott, 567 F.3d at 582.

However, Respondents argue that *Scott* is inapposite because there the PCR court relied upon an explicit (though non-existent) time limitation, while here, the PCR Court simply made a finding that Petitioner had failed to show good cause, and considered in the course of finding a lack of good cause the timeliness of the request to amend. However, Respondents point to no pre-existing authority which engrafted a timeliness determination into good cause.

That is not to suggest that timeliness is irrelevant to good cause determinations. For example, in the context of amendments to civil pleadings, delay is a consideration. However, the requirement of liberality in amendments is overcome only where delay has resulted in prejudice. In the federal courts, "[d]elay alone does not provide sufficient grounds for denying leave to amend: 'Where there is lack of prejudice to the opposing party and the amended complaint is obviously not frivolous, or made as a dilatory maneuver in bad faith, it is an abuse of discretion to deny such a motion.' " *Hurn v. Retirement Fund Trust of Plumbing, Heating and Piping Industry of Southern California, 648 F.2d 1252, 1254 (9th Cir. 1981)*. Similarly, in the Arizona courts " '[m]ere delay'-the mere fact that the attempt to amend comes late-is not justification for denial of leave to amend." *Owen v. Superior Court of State of Ariz., In and For Maricopa County, 133 Ariz. 75, 79, 649 P.2d 278, 282 (1982)* (quoting *Hageman v. Signal L. P. Gas, Inc., 486 F.2d 479, 484 (6th Cir. 1973)*).

In *Greenway v. Schriro, 653 F.3d 790, 2011 WL 3195310 (9th Cir. 2011)*, the Ninth Circuit again considered the adequacy of Arizona law on amendments, in that case the bar on amendments where there has been a prior PCR proceeding, pursuant to *Ariz. R. Crim. Proc. 32.2(a)(3)*. The court found the rule inadequate to bar a habeas claim because "the state court held that the new claims were brought too late without considering whether there was good cause to amend the petition." *653 F.3d 790, 2011 WL 3195310, *8.*

Here, the PCR court made no finding of any prejudice to the State, nor any bad faith on the part of Petitioner. The Motion to Amend argued that the amendment was necessary only because the PCR court had made a ruling, surprising to Petitioner, that the newly asserted claims were not sufficiently raised in the original PCR petition. (Exhibit OOO, Mot. Amend at 2.) Rather, the court simply found that the amendments could have been made at an earlier time, rather than during the hearing. Similarly, the State did not argue any prejudice, but simply argued delay, at best pointing to the victim's family's right to a "prompt and final conclusion." (Exhibit PPP, Resp. M. Amend at 4; Exhibit YY, R.T. 2/9/07 at 56-57; Exhibit RRR-1, R.T. 2/20/07 at 3.)

Further, the PCR court pointed to no circumstance or factor other than the presence of delay upon which it found a lack of good cause.

That is not to suggest that the PCR court's decision was wrong under Arizona law. Indeed, Respondents correctly note that this federal habeas Court is not free to second guess the state courts upon the application of state law. (Answer, Doc. 31 at 66, n. 35.) *See Bains v.*

Cambra, 204 F.3d 964, 971 (9th Cir. 2000) ("federal court is bound by the state court's interpretations of state law").

But the adequacy of a state procedural rule is not established by the mere fact that it was properly applied under state law, but whether the rule as applied was sufficiently established at the time of its application to permit it to defeat a defendant's federal rights.

A state ground, no doubt, may be found inadequate when "discretion has been exercised to impose novel and unforeseeable requirements without fair or substantial support in prior state law ... ." 16B C. Wright, A. Miller, & E. Cooper, *Federal Practice and Procedure* § 4026, p. 386 (2d ed.1996) (hereinafter Wright & Miller; *see Prihoda, 910 F.2d at 1383* (state ground "applied infrequently, unexpectedly, or freakishly" may "discriminat[e] against the federal rights asserted" and therefore rank as "inadequate").

Walker, 131 S. Ct. 1120, 2011 WL 611627, 9 (citing *Prihoda v. McCaughtry, 910 F.2d 1379 (7th Cir. 1990)).*

Given the complete absence of any Arizona authority upholding a denial of an amendment prior to judgment based solely upon a finding of delay, this Court must conclude that *Rule 32.6(d)*, as applied to Petitioner, was not firmly established. *See Richey v. Mitchell, 395 F.3d 660, 679-680 (6th Cir. 2005)* (finding Ohio's "good cause" exception to timeliness rule inadequate because the state court had not achieved consensus on what constituted "good cause"), *overruled on other grounds sub nom Bradshaw v. Richey, 546 U.S. 74, 126 S. Ct. 602, 163 L. Ed. 2d 407 (2005).*

Ground Seven (Ineffectiveness of Appellate Counsel) - Finally, Respondents argue that Petitioner's claims of ineffective assistance of appellate counsel, asserted in his Ground Seven, were first presented in his Motion to Amend his PCR Petition, and that the denial of his Motion to Amend for lack of good cause constitutes a procedural bar. As with Petitioner's claim of a conflict of interest in Ground Five, the undersigned has determined herein above that Petitioner's federal claim in Ground Seven was not fairly presented to the state courts as a federal claim, and thus could not be procedurally barred.

However, if deemed fairly presented by the Motion to Amend, the undersigned would also conclude (as with the conflict of interest claim) that the "good cause" standard of *Rule 32.6(d)*, as applied to Petitioner, was not adequate to bar federal habeas review.

Summary re Procedural Bar - Based upon the foregoing, the undersigned concludes that only Petitioner's claims in Ground Four were disposed of on an independent and adequate state procedural bar sufficient to bar habeas review.

E. CAUSE AND PREJUDICE

The undersigned has determined herein above that Petitioner has procedurally defaulted part of his Ground One ("observation evidence"), the portion of Ground Five founded on trial counsel's conflict of interest, and all of Grounds Two, Six and Seven. In addition, the undersigned has concluded that Petitioner's claims in Ground Four (Competence) were disposed of on independent and adequate state grounds. Further, Respondents argue (but the undersigned has rejected the argument) that Petitioner's claims in Ground Five (ineffectiveness of trial counsel concerning competency during trial and conflict of interest) and Ground Seven (ineffective assistance of appellate counsel) were disposed of on independent and adequate grounds.

If a habeas petitioner has procedurally defaulted on a claim, or it has been procedurally barred on independent and adequate state grounds, he may not obtain federal habeas review of that claim absent a showing of "cause and prejudice" sufficient to excuse the default. *Reed v. Ross, 468 U.S. 1, 11, 104 S. Ct. 2901, 82 L. Ed. 2d 1 (1984)*. Although both "cause" and "prejudice" must be shown to excuse a procedural default, a court need not examine the existence of prejudice if the petitioner fails to establish cause. *Engle v. Isaac, 456 U.S. 107, 134 n. 43, 102 S. Ct. 1558, 71 L. Ed. 2d 783 (1982); Thomas v. Lewis, 945 F.2d 1119, 1123 n. 10 (9th Cir.1991)*.

Cause - "Cause" is the legitimate excuse for the default. *Thomas, 945 F.2d at 1123*. "Because of the wide variety of contexts in which a procedural default can occur, the Supreme Court 'has not given the term "cause" precise content.'" *Harmon v. Barton, 894 F.2d 1268, 1274 (11th Cir. 1990)* (quoting *Reed, 468 U.S. at 13*), *cert. denied, 498 U.S.*

832, 111 S. Ct. 96, 112 L. Ed. 2d 68 (1990). The Supreme Court has suggested, however, that cause should ordinarily turn on some objective factor external to petitioner, for instance:

... a showing that the factual or legal basis for a claim was not reasonably available to counsel, or that "some interference by officials", made compliance impracticable, would constitute cause under this standard.

Murray v. Carrier, 477 U.S. 478, 488, 106 S. Ct. 2639, 91 L. Ed. 2d 397 (1986) (citations omitted).

Here, Petitioner argues a miscarriage of justice will result if the denial of his Motion to Amend results in the barring of his claims, because of the disparity of resources between appointed counsel and the State. (Reply, Doc. 48 at 4, 15.)

The mere loss of a claim cannot constitute cause. To permit it to do so would at best subsume cause into prejudice, and at worst effectively vitiate the exhaustion requirement and the independent and adequate state grounds rule.

The fact that there are disparate resources between the state and a defendant similarly cannot constitute cause, at least not without vitiating these principals for all but defendant with privately retained counsel and legal budgets that at least extended beyond the budget of the prosecutor's office.

Moreover, in arguing on the basis of resources, Petitioner focuses on the time pressure on counsel to file the PCR petition, and thus the unfairness of the denial of the motion to amend. (Reply, Doc. 48 at 4, 15.) That would be relevant only if this Court relies upon the procedural bar from that denial as urged by Respondents. However, as discussed herein above, the undersigned has not found Petitioner's claims barred because of the denial of the motion to amend, but because Petitioner's appellate brief, PCR petition and motion to amend that petition all failed to fairly present his procedurally defaulted federal claims.

Further, such matters are not "external" to Petitioner's defense. Rather, they are tantamount to arguing that Petitioner was denied effective assistance of PCR counsel (either through counsel's misfeasance or the state's failure to adequately fund PCR counsel).

Ineffective assistance of counsel may constitute cause for failing to properly exhaust claims in state courts and excuse procedural default. *Ortiz v. Stewart, 149 F.3d 923, 932, (9th Cir. 1998).* However, to meet the "cause" requirement, the ineffective assistance of counsel must amount to an independent constitutional violation. *Id.* Accordingly, where no constitutional right to an attorney exists, ineffective assistance will not amount to cause excusing the state procedural default. *Id.* In *Patrick Poland v. Stewart, 169 F. 3d 573 (9th Cir. 1999)*, the Ninth Circuit held that "[b]ecause there is no right to an attorney in state post-conviction proceedings, there cannot be constitutionally ineffective assistance of counsel in such proceedings." *Id. at 588* (quoting *Coleman v. Thompson, 501 U.S. 722, 752, 111 S. Ct. 2546, 115 L. Ed. 2d 640 (1991)*).

Moreover, a claim of ineffective assistance of counsel showing "cause" is itself subject to the exhaustion requirements. *Murray v. Carrier, 477 U.S. 478, 492, 106 S. Ct. 2639, 91 L. Ed. 2d 397 (1986); Edwards v. Carpenter, 529 U.S. 446, 120 S. Ct. 1587, 146 L. Ed. 2d 518 (2000).* Accordingly, "[to the extent that petitioner is alleging ineffective assistance of appellate counsel as cause for the default, the exhaustion doctrine requires him to first raise this ineffectiveness claim as a separate claim in state court." *Tacho v. Martinez, 862 F.2d 1376, 1381 (9th Cir. 1988).* Petitioner has not raised a claim of ineffective assistance of PCR counsel in the state courts.

Accordingly, the undersigned concludes that Petitioner has failed to show "cause" to excuse his procedural default.

Actual Innocence - The standard for "cause and prejudice" is one of discretion intended to be flexible and yielding to exceptional circumstances. *Hughes v. Idaho State Board of Corrections, 800 F.2d 905, 909 (9th Cir. 1986).* Accordingly, failure to establish cause may be excused "in an extraordinary case, where a constitutional violation has probably resulted in the conviction of one who is actually innocent." *Murray v. Carrier, 477 U.S. 478, 496, 106 S. Ct. 2639, 91 L. Ed. 2d 397 (1986)* (emphasis added).

This standard for "actual innocence" is the same as that applied in evaluating whether to allow successive habeas petitions. *Sawyer v. Whitley, 505 U.S. 333, 338, 112 S. Ct. 2514, 120 L. Ed. 2d 269 (1992).*

That standard was articulated in *Kuhlmann v. Wilson, 477 U.S. 436, 106 S. Ct. 2616, 91 L. Ed. 2d 364 (1986)* as follows:

[T]he prisoner must "show a fair probability that, in the light of all the evidence, including that alleged to have been illegally admitted (but with due regard to any unreliability of it) and evidence tenably claimed to have been wrongly excluded or to have become available only after the trial, the trier of the facts would have entertained a reasonable doubt of his guilt."

Id., 477 U.S., at 455, n. 17, quoting Friendly, *Is Innocence Irrelevant? Collateral Attack on Criminal Judgments*, 38 U.Chi.L.Rev. 142, 160 (1970).

Petitioner makes no pretension of establishing his actual innocence. Petitioner does argue in Ground One that there was insubstantial evidence to support his conviction because of the lack of evidence on the requisite *mens rea*, and that the trial court wrongly excluded observational evidence that would tend to show a lack of the *mens rea*, (Amend. Pet. Doc. 17 at 11-22.) For the reasons discussed hereinafter in disposing of Ground One, the undersigned cannot find that a reasonable trier of fact must have entertained a reasonable doubt of Petitioner's guilt on the basis of the evidence other than the "observation evidence." The "observation evidence" is not considered in connection with Petitioner's Ground One based upon Petitioner's procedural default of that portion of Ground One.

Even when considering that observation evidence, the undersigned cannot find that Petitioner has affirmatively shown his actual innocence. Petitioner asserts the state courts failed to consider evidence from family members and other witnesses such as: (1) threats against family members; (2) angry and aggressive behavior; (3) admissions of mental instability; (4) bizarre behavior when confronted by police after the crime; (5) obsessive behaviors, emotional regression; (6) paranoid behaviors; (7) violent outbursts (8) rambling diatribes against the police; (9) fear of aliens and a belief that his parents were aliens, (Amend. Pet., Doc. 17 at 14-20.)

In contrast, as noted by the Arizona Court of Appeals there was significant evidence indicating Petitioner did possess the requisite *mens rea*, including evidence of: (1) Petitioner's professed anger with police officers, and fantasies of retaliating; (2) Petitioner's efforts to attract a police officer the night of the killing; (3) the use of a weapon at close range; (4) the victim's evasive movements as shown by the bullet trajectory and witness statements; (5) obvious indications of the victim's status as a police officer, including his uniform and marked patrol car and Petitioner having pulled over in response to the emergency lights and siren; and (6) Petitioner's flight from the scene. (Exhibit RR, Mem. Dec. 1/25/05 at 8-10.) Thus, if faced with these two sets of conflicting circumstantial evidence, a reasonable factfinder could have rejected all of Petitioner's "observation evidence," and relied instead upon the evidence indicating Petitioner's intent to kill a police officer.

Therefore, the undersigned concludes that Petitioner has failed to establish his actual innocence.

Summary re Procedurally Defaulted Claims - Respondents have shown that Plaintiff failed to properly exhaust, and has procedurally defaulted on part of his Ground One ("observation evidence"), the portion of Ground Five based upon trial counsel's conflict of interest, and all of Grounds Two, Six and Seven. Moreover, Respondents have shown that Petitioner's Ground Four was procedurally barred under an independent and adequate state ground. Petitioner has failed to show cause to excuse his procedural default and/or the procedural bar, and has failed to show his actual innocence to avoid them Accordingly, these claims must be dismissed with prejudice.

H. GROUND THREE: CRUEL AND UNUSUAL PUNISHMENT

For his Ground Three for relief, Petitioner argues that the sentence imposed in this case constitutes cruel and unusual punishment in violation of the *Eight Amendment*, because he is confined in the mental health unit of ADOC, rather than in the state hospital where he can be provided "the proper and necessary medical attention that he requires, and the *Eighth Amendment* mandates consideration of Petitioner's unique characteristics, e.g. his serious mental illness, necessary in evaluating such disproportionality. (*Id.* at 30, 32-33.)

Respondents counter that the Arizona Court of Appeals properly determined that Petitioner's life sentence, with parole available in 25 years, is not disproportionate to his crime of first degree murder. (Answer, Doc, 31 at 40-41.) Respondents argue that consideration of individual characteristics has only been mandated by the U.S. Supreme Court in death penalty cases. (*Id.* at 42-43.) Respondents spend some time analyzing the proportionality of a life sentence without parole for 25 years for the murder of a police officer. (Answer, Doc. 31 at 41.) The undersigned does not understand Petitioner to present such a bare assault on proportionality, but to instead to suggest that his mental illness should have been the determining factor.

Petitioner replies that the cases relied upon by Respondents do not address cases involving serious mental illness. (Reply, Doc. 48 at 19.)

In rejecting Petitioner's *Eighth Amendment* claim, the Arizona Court of Appeals concluded that "even given Clark's mental condition" they could not find there was "an inference of gross disproportionality between Clark's crime and his sentence." (Exhibit RR, Mem. Dec. 1/25/05 at 20.)

The *Eighth Amendment* provides that "[e]xcessive bail shall not be required, nor excessive fines imposed, nor cruel and unusual punishments inflicted." *U.S. Const. amend. XIII.* The *Eighth Amendment* "forbids...extreme sentences that are 'grossly disproportionate' to the crime." *Harmelin v. Michigan, 501 U.S. 957, 1001, 111 S. Ct. 2680, 115 L. Ed. 2d 836 (1991)* (Kennedy, J., concurring in part and concurring in the judgment). This narrow proportionality principle applies to noncapital sentences. *Id. at 997. See also Lockyer v. Andrade, 538 U.S. 63, 72, 123 S. Ct. 1166, 155 L. Ed. 2d 144 (2003)* ("A gross disproportionality principle is applicable to sentences for terms of years.").

Nonetheless, outside the context of capital punishment, successful challenges to the proportionality of particular sentences have been exceedingly rare. *See Ewing v. California, 538 U.S. 11, 123 S. Ct. 1179, 155 L. Ed. 2d 108(2003)* (quoting *Rummel v. Estelle, 445 U.S. 263, 272, 100 S. Ct. 1133, 63 L. Ed. 2d 382 (1980)).*

And, the Court's jurisprudence is conflicting. Indeed, in *Ewing,* Justices Scalia and Thomas both concurred in the judgment of the Court, but both separately wrote that the *Eighth Amendment* was limited to prohibiting certain modes of punishment, and did not encompass a proportionality test. *Id. at 31-32.* In *Harmelin v. Michigan, 501 U.S. 957, 111 S. Ct. 2680, 115 L. Ed. 2d 836 (1991),* the controlling proportionality case, the only opinion to attract a majority of the justices was a portion of Justice Kennedy's concurrence in the judgment. Justice Kennedy observed: "Though our decisions recognize a proportionality principle, its precise contours are unclear." *501 U.S. at 998.* In *Lockyer,* decided in 2003, the Court described its jurisprudence in this area as a "thicket," and admitted that "in determining whether a particular sentence for a term of years can violate the *Eighth Amendment,* we have not established a clear or consistent path for courts to follow." *Lockyer, 538 U.S. at 72.*

Our cases exhibit a lack of clarity regarding what factors may indicate gross disproportionality.

* * *

Thus, in this [AEDPA governed] case, the only relevant clearly established law amenable to the "contrary to" or "unreasonable application of" framework is the gross disproportionality principle, the precise contours of which are unclear, applicable only in the "exceedingly rare" and "extreme" case.

Id. at 72-73.

Petitioner points to no Supreme Court decision which mandates consideration of the health care services available to an inmate in prison in applying a disproportionality review. The undersigned has found none.

Petitioner complains that his seriously mentally ill condition should have been considered. Assuming *arguendo* that Supreme Court jurisprudence mandates consideration of such factors, the Arizona Court of Appeals expressly considered Petitioner's "mental condition." (Exhibit RR, Mem. Dec. 1/25/05 at 20.) Petitioner fails to suggest how the state court's analysis on this point was inadequate.

Although for purposes of applying the limitations of *28 U.S.C. § 2254(d),* the pertinent legal landscape is that which existed when the

Arizona Supreme Court denied review of the Arizona Court of Appeals' decision, *Williams v. Taylor 529 U.S. 362, 412, 120 S. Ct. 1495, 146 L. Ed. 2d 389 (2000)* ("decisions as of the time of the relevant state-court decision"), a recent U.S. Supreme Court case is instructive on that historical landscape. In *Graham v. Florida, U.S., 130 S.Ct. 2011, 176 L. Ed. 2d 825 (2010)*, the Court reviewed the history of *Eight Amendment* jurisprudence. The Court noted that its proportionality cases fell into two categories.

The first category involves sentences for a term of years, in which the Court considered "all of the circumstances *of the case* to determine whether the sentence is unconstitutionally excessive." *Id. at 2021* (emphasis added). The Court denoted *Harmelin v. Michigan, 501 U.S. 957, 111 S. Ct. 2680, 115 L. Ed. 2d 836 (1991)* as the "controlling opinion," and described its two-step process of "comparing the gravity of the offense and the severity of the sentence," and then comparing the sentence to other offenders and other jurisdictions. *Graham, 130 S.C.t. at 2022.*

The second category of cases involved "categorical rules" based upon the "nature of the offense" and the "characteristics *of the offender*." *Graham, 130 S.C.t. at 2022* (emphasis added). The Court observed that the "previous cases in this classification involved the death penalty." *Id.* Indeed, the Supreme Court cases to which Petitioner points (as mandating consideration of his mental illness) are limited to death penalty cases, including *Atkins v. Virginia, 536 U.S. 304, 122 S. Ct. 2242, 153 L. Ed. 2d 335 (2002)* (categorical rejection of death penalty for mentally retarded criminals), *Thompson v. Oklahoma, 487 U.S. 815, 838, 108 S. Ct. 2687, 101 L. Ed. 2d 702 (1988)* (categorical rejection of death penalty for juveniles under 16 at time of offense), and *Stanford v. Kentucky, 492 U.S. 361, 393, 109 S. Ct. 2969, 106 L. Ed. 2d 306 (1983)* (categorical approval of death penalty for juveniles 16 or 17 at time of offense). Although the Court in *Graham* extended this categorical approach outside the death penalty arena, it did so for the first time, noting that the "case involve an issue the Court has not considered previously: a categorical challenge to term-of-years sentence." *Graham, 130 S.Ct. at 2022.* Thus, in 2005, this second category had no application to Petitioner's term-of-years sentence.

Nonetheless, Petitioner argues, in essence, that a *Harmelin* analysis of a non-death penalty sentence requires consideration of the unique characteristics of a defendant. Justice Kennedy's controlling concurrence in that case rejected such an approach in non-capital cases.

Petitioner would have us hold that any severe penalty scheme requires individualized sentencing so that a judicial official may consider mitigating circumstances. Our precedents do not support this proposition, and petitioner presents no convincing reason to fashion an exception or adopt a new rule in the case before us. The Court demonstrates that our *Eighth Amendment* capital decisions reject any requirement of individualized sentencing in noncapital cases.

501 U.S. 957, 1006, 111 S. Ct. 2680, 115 L. Ed. 2d 836 (Kennedy, J. concurring). In *Solem v. Helm, 463 U.S. 277, 103 S. Ct. 3001, 77 L. Ed. 2d 637 (1983)*, the Court counseled that "[w]hen sentences are reviewed under the *Eighth Amendment*, courts should be guided by *objective* factors that our cases have recognized." *Id. at 290* (emphasis added). *See also Harmelin, 501 U.S. at 1000* (Kennedy, J. concurring) ("The fourth principle at work in our cases is that proportionality review by federal courts should be informed by *objective factors* to the maximum possible extent." emphasis added) Those factors, as identified in *Graham*, consist of "the gravity of the offense and the severity of the sentence," and a comparison to other sentences. *Graham, 130 S.C.t. at 2022*. No provision is made for a full blown resentencing by consideration of all the factors relevant to formulating a sentence in the first place. Indeed, significant discourse of the Court has been committed to insuring that disproportionality claims would not require such expansive determinations. *See e.g. Harmelin, 501 U.S. at 1015-1016* (White, J. dissenting).

Where the Court has been willing to look to such individual characteristics, it has done so only under the "categorical rules" which *Graham* for the first time in 2010 extended to non-death penalty cases. Petitioner points to no pre-2006 Supreme Court case where individual characteristics were made relevant considerations in performing a disproportionality determination.

Petitioner does point to the decision in *Solem*, where the Court indicated that consideration of the offense (for purposes of comparing it to the sentence) required consideration of the harm from the crime "and the culpability of the offender." *463 U.S. at 292*. However, the types of culpability characteristics identified by the Court all focused on the general nature of the defendant's crime, e.g. negligent versus intentional acts, motive such as for pecuniary gain, etc. *Id. at 293-294*. There was no suggestion in *Solem* that this would extend to consideration of the individual characteristics of the defendant himself which might be considered at a trial court's sentencing, such as mental or physical illness, troubled or disadvantaged up-bringing, etc.

Petitioner also argues that the Court's decision in *Ewing v. California* rendered "the facts of the crime and the background of the offender" relevant to a proportionality determination. (Amend. Pet. Doc. 17 at 33.) While the *Ewing* Court certainly went to some lengths to review the defendant's criminal history, *538 U.S. at 18-20*, in applying the *Harmelin* analysis it looked only to the objective nature of the offense and his recidivist record.

We first address the gravity of the offense compared to the harshness of the penalty. At the threshold, we note that Ewing incorrectly frames the issue. The gravity of his offense was not merely "shoplifting three golf clubs." Rather, Ewing was convicted of felony grand theft for stealing nearly $1,200 worth of merchandise after previously having been convicted of at least two "violent" or "serious" felonies.

538 U.S. at 28. Moreover, the defendant's recidivist record was only relevant because the sentence he attacked was under a "three strikes" law. Nothing in the Court's opinion in *Ewing* suggests that the Court intended to impose an obligation on reviewing courts to consider the individual characteristics of defendants claiming disproportionality.

Given the absence of any pre-existent Supreme Court holding calling for consideration of a defendant's mental illness (or any other individual characteristic), the undersigned cannot find that the Arizona Court of Appeals' decision was contrary to nor an unreasonable application of federal law, as required by *28 U.S.C. § 2254(d)(1)*. Therefore, Petitioner 's Ground Three must be denied.

J. GROUND FIVE: INEFFECTIVE ASSISTANCE OF TRIAL COUNSEL

In the properly exhausted portions of his Ground Five, Petitioner argues that his trial counsel was ineffective because he: (1) failed to disclose Dr. Parrish's report regarding competency to co-counsel and to the court prior to requesting to waive a jury; (2) failed to request a re-evaluation of Petitioner during the trial when Petitioner started to deteriorate; (3) waived the jury; (4) limited the use of experts; and (5) failed to preserve the observational evidence claim.

1. Standards for Ineffective Assistance of Counsel Claims

Generally, claims of ineffective assistance of counsel are analyzed pursuant to *Strickland v. Washington, 466 U.S. 668, 104 S. Ct. 2052, 80 L. Ed. 2d 674 (1984)*. In order to prevail on such a claim, petitioner must show: (1) deficient performance - counsel's representation fell below the objective standard for reasonableness; and (2) prejudice - there is a reasonable probability that, but for counsel's unprofessional errors, the result of the proceeding would have been different. *Id. at 687-88, 694*. Although the petitioner must prove both elements, a court may reject his claim upon finding either that counsel's performance was reasonable or that the claimed error was not prejudicial. *Id. at 697*.

2. Failure to Disclose Parrish Report

Background on Parrish Report on Competency - On March 28, 2001, Petitioner and the prosecution entered into a stipulation that Petitioner was incompetent to stand trial. (Exhibit D.) Petitioner was committed to the Arizona State Hospital for restoration to competency.

Some 15 months later, the trial court conducted a competency hearing at which testimony was presented by Dr. Di'Bacco that Petitioner understood the proceedings and that the ability to assist in his own defense was a matter of Petitioner's volition, and thus that he was competent to stand trial. (Exhibit E-1, R.T. 6/26/02 at 28-30.) Testimony was also presented from Dr. Kassell and Dr. Jasinski, both of whom opined that Petitioner was competent and that any troubles in communication that he faced were volitional. (Exhibit F-1, R.T.7/10/02 at 28, 31 (Kassell), 70 (Jasinksi).) In contrast Dr. Parrish testified that Petitioner was incompetent, and that his failure to participate in his defense was the result of his schizophrenia, not a volitional choice. (Exhibit F-2, R.T. 7/10/02 at 177, 180-181.) Petitioner's treating psychiatrist, Dr. Franzetti was precluded from opining on Petitioner's competence to stand trial, but testified that Petitioner's refusal to cooperate was not volitional, but as a result of his schizophrenia. (Exhibit G-2, R.T. 7/11/02 at 117-118.) Petitioner's treating psychologist, Dr. Perry, testified that Petitioner was not competent to stand trial because of his inability to appreciate the consequences of his decisions. (Exhibit G-2, R.T. 7/11/02 at 182-183.) The counselor at the jail testified that Petitioner's mental condition deteriorated after he transferred from the Arizona State Hospital to the jail. (Exhibit G-2, R.T. 7/11/02 at 222-233.)

When interviewed during PCR proceedings, attorney Middlebrooks described his working relationship with Petitioner: " He would talk to me about certain things but I could never, ever, ever talk to him about anything meaningful beyond this is the trial, this is the judge, this is the prosecutor, yes, they are out to - -- I mean, you know, there was never any discussions with Eric that I could ever get him to open up with me, even when Dr. Morenz was present, Dr. Parrish was present." (Exhibit OOO, Exhibit A, Interview 1/8/07 at 48-49. *See also id.* at 68-69.) (*See also* Exhibit RRR-2, R.T. 2/20/07 at 102-103 ("That's why we had nothing to present in the case in chief, because there was nothing for us to discuss because Eric never talked to me about the case.").)

The trial court postponed ruling on Petitioner's competency, and in September, 2002, returned him to the Arizona State Hospital. (Exhibit K, M.E. 9/16/02.) The matter was eventually set for a new hearing in April, 2003. On April 25, 2003, Petitioner's trial counsel filed a Motion to Submit (Exhibit O), asking to submit Petitioner's competency determination to the Court on the basis of the reports of Dr. Kassell, Dr. DiBacco, and Dr. Morenz. Dr. Kassell and Dr. Dibacco's reports continued to opine that Petitioner was competent, and his difficulties were volitional. Dr. Morenz, who had been retained by the defense, opined that it was unclear whether Petitioner was incompetent or malingering, and thus recommended alternative therapies and with the hope of thereby clarifying his competence. (Exhibit O, Motion to Submit at Attachments.)

On May 8, 2003, the trial court noted that the State had concurred in the defenses' Motion to Submit, and based upon the "records submitted of Dr. Kassel [sic], Dr. DiBacco, Dr. Morenz, and Dr. Jazinksi, and all other information filed in his matter" the court found Petitioner competent to stand trial. (Exhibit Q, M.E. 5/8/03 at 1.) The court found that Petitioner's "status at this point is one of volition; in other words, he is choosing not to cooperate with his attorney at this time as opposed to being unable to do so." (Exhibit R, R.T. 5/8/03 at 4.)

On July 7, 2003, Dr. Parrish issued a report (Exhibit LLL), based upon evaluations done June 19, 2003 and July 7, 2003, again finding that Petitioner was not competent to stand trial. (*Id.* at 10.) Dr. Parrish reviewed the other reports and their conclusions that Petitioner was malingering. (*Id.* at 4-7.) Rather than focusing on Petitioner's ability to assist in his defense, and whether that was volitional, her findings focused upon a determination that Petitioner's reasoning and appreciation skills were indicative of his incompetence. (*Id.* at 10-11).

On July 8, 2003, Petitioner appeared and waived his right to a jury trial. (Exhibit T, R.T. 7/8/03.) Attorney Middlebrooks specifically advised the Court at that hearing that he had just received a report from Dr. Parrish. (*Id.* at 16.)

On July 17, 2003, Dr. Parrish issued an addendum (Exhibit MMM) based upon intervening interviews of Petitioner, and opining that these served to "strengthen" her prior conclusions. (*Id.* at 2.) In addition, defense counsel had reports from other professionals in July, 2003, opining that Petitioner was competent to stand trial, including Dr. DiBacco's July 25, 2003 report (Exhibit FFF at 3) and Dr. LaWall's July 7, 2003 report (Exhibit KKK at 11.) Dr. DiBacco has previously opined that Petitioner was incompetent. (Exhibit D, Stip. Re Competency.)

On July 25, 2003, the prosecution conducted a transcribed interview of Dr. Parrish, which included questioning about her July 2003 report and addendum. (Exhibit NNN, Interview 7/25/03.) Defendant attorney Middlebrooks was present during that interview. (*Id.* at 3.) The report had been disclosed to the prosecution at the time of her interview on July 25, 2003. (Exhibit NNN, R.T. 7/25/03 at 34.)

Claims and Defenses - Petitioner argues that trial counsel Middlebrooks performed deficiently when, after receiving Dr. Parrish's July 7, 2003 report, he did not seek a subsequent redetermination of Petitioner's competency and did not disclose the report to counsel. (Amend Pet. Doc. 17 at 47-48.) Respondents argue that the PCR correctly rejected this claim because Dr. Parrish's report did not counter the determinative factual finding: *i.e.* that Petitioner's failure to cooperate with counsel was volitional and not the result of his mental illness. Respondents argue that: (1) Dr. Parrish did not evaluate the volitional issue, (2) her evaluations of Petitioner's testing responses was highly subjective and many answers reflected Petitioner's competence; and (3) the trial court had other substantial evidence upon which to make its determination both before and after Dr. Parrish's report. (Answer, Doc. 31 at 48-65.) Petitioner replies that: (1) the expert opinions finding Petitioner competent were marginal enough that Parrish's report could have made the difference; (2) not only Parrish's evaluation of Petitioner's responses to the testing, but the actual answers, demonstrated Petitioner's incompetence. (Reply, Doc. 48 at 22-23.) Petitioner suggests that attorney Middlebrooks actively hid the report from the court and co-counsel. Petitioner points to no portion of the record to support that contention.

Analysis re Failure to Disclose to Court - The PCR court rejected the claim concerning the waiver of the jury trial based upon the conclusions that the evidence failed to show prejudice, *i.e.* that "had Mr. Middlebrooks disclosed Dr. Parrish's opinion regarding petitioner's competency to the trial court, Judge Coker would have vacated the finding of competency and/or granting of the waiver of a jury trial, and ordered petitioner back into restorative treatment." (Exhibit AAAA, M.E. 3/15/07 at 5-6.) The PCR court further found no deficient performance:

The Court does not find that Mr. Middlebrooks' performance failed to meet minimal competence standards by not raising a competency claim at or shortly after the trial court accepted petitioner's waiver of jury trial on the basis of Dr. Parrish's July report. Mr. Middlebrooks testified as to his concerns over the reliability of the methodology and testing conducted by Dr. Parrish. The July 7th written report was based on tests that were not widely recognized or generally accepted by the scientific community.

(*Id.* at 6-7.) The PCR court observed that Mr. Middlebrooks "relied on the expert's opinions even though personally he disagreed with them and proceeded to trial." (*Id.* at 7.)

To succeed on his claim concerning seeking a redetermination of competency based upon the Parrish report, Petitioner bears an extremely heavy burden. He must establish both that the state court got it wrong on prejudice and that it got it wrong on deficient performance. Further, Petitioner must show that both of these determinations were contrary to or an unreasonable application of federal law. *28 U.S.C. § 2254(d)(1)*. Petitioner fails to do so.

As to prejudice, there was substantial evidence in the record that Petitioner was competent, including multiple expert opinions. Moreover, the trial court had heard Dr. Parrish's earlier opinion that Petitioner was incompetent, and her latest reports and evaluations were subject to impeachment as being based on testing which was not generally accepted. (*See* Exhibit RRR-2, R.T. 2/20/07 at 164-165.) This was not some huge new revelation that Petitioner had been discovered to be incompetent. Rather, it was incremental evidence that was not without its problems.

The parties discuss at length their opposing views upon how reliable or persuasive Dr. Parrish and her report could have been. The undersigned might be inclined to find that there was a possibility that the Parrish report could have made a difference in the outcome. But, the undersigned would find it far more difficult to conclude that it is more likely than not that the trial judge would have been swayed. The undersigned finds it impossible to conclude that the PCR Court unreasonably applied *Strickland* and its progeny when it concluded that the evidence failed to show that the outcome would have been different.

As to deficient performance, the undersigned finds it even harder to imagine how the PCR court's decision was unreasonable. Trial counsel was certainly faced with a difficult, albeit common quandary: whether to pursue problematic evidence. Moreover, the issue of Petitioner's competence had been determined by the court and trial counsel made a tactical decision to refocus Dr. Parrish from challenging that decided issue and to focus instead on the insanity defense. Trial counsel testified:

Q. How about raising the issue of competency after you got Dr. Parrish's report?

A. You know, after the interview I thought about that as to why that happened, and I can tell you that I think what happened -- and I'm giving you an intellectual version, as opposed to something that I consciously went through, but I believe at that time we had established his competency in May -- May or June, and we had submitted the reports, and shortly after that, I had contacted Dr. Parrish and the other doctors to look at, again, all of the medical evidence, because by then we had new records from the Arizona State Hospital, we had additional records from the Maricopa County Jail, and we had other observational evidence from various health care providers, et cetera.

So I wanted my expert in particular to go back and look at everything one more time, and so when that occurred with Dr. Parrish and she wrote the July 7th report . . . I got that and I started thinking about what happened with that report, and I think what happened in my mind was that issue is past as far as competency and that now the issue is insanity, and so I -- I know I must have had some kind of discussion with her about, "No, I need you to focus on insanity at this time because he's already been determined to be competent," and like I said, he was deteriorating, but at the time we started trial, and I'm talking day one, day two, I thought he was competent to stand trial.

And so, again I was exercising my - - I don't want to say discretion, but it was discretion, I suppose, looking back, about whether it should be raised again simply because Dr. Parrish had authored that report. I didn't think it should at that point. Later in trial, obviously, I should have, and that's that transcript part of it I talked about.

(Exhibit RRR-2, R.T. 2/20/07 at 98-100.) Under these circumstances, the undersigned cannot conclude that any reasonable attorney must have sought a new competency hearing on the basis of Dr. Parrish's July 7, 2003 report.

Analysis as to Disclosure to Co-Counsel - The PCR Court rejected the claim concerning disclosure to co-counsel based upon a finding that the report had in fact been disclosed to the trial court and prosecution, and as a result there was no prejudice. (*Id.* at 10.)

Co-counsel for the defense, David Goldberg, testified that generally attorney Middlebrooks sent him everything he received in the case, but he had never seen Dr. Parrish's July 7, 2003 report prior to his deposition. (Exhibit YY, R.T. 2/9/07 at 46.) Middlebrooks testified that he routinely sent everything to Goldberg. (Exhibit RRR-1, R.T. 2/20/07 at 91-92.) However, Goldberg testified that as trial approached, due to the press of time and volume, things were not being regularly forwarded. (*Id.* at 67.) He also admitted that he had discussed the Parrish report with Middlebrooks, and that it had been a competency evaluation rather than a mental state evaluation. (*Id.* at 68-69.) He asserted, however, that he was certain he had not seen the report prior to the waiver of the jury trial. (*Id.* at 69-70.) Middlebrooks claimed in his interview that he and Goldberg discussed the testing done by Parrish (Exhibit OOO, R.T. 1/8/07 at 58), which was reflected in the July 7, 2003 report by Parrish.

Attorney Middlebrooks specifically advised the Court on July 8, 2003 that he had just received a report from Dr. Parrish. (Exhibit T, R.T. 7/8/03 at 16.) Attorney Goldberg was present at that hearing. (*Id.* at 2, 31.)

Moreover, the report was disclosed to the prosecution at the time of Dr. Parrish's interview on July 25, 2003. (Exhibit NNN, R.T. 7/25/03 at 34.)

Finally, Middlebrooks and Goldberg testified that Middlebrooks was the lead attorney and that the mental health issues were Middlebrooks's responsibility. (Exhibit RRR-1, R.T. 2/20/07 at 84; Exhibit YY R.T. 2/9/07 at 16-17.) Nonetheless, Goldberg testified that had he seen the Parrish report at the time it was authored he would have insisted on submitting the report to the Court, renewing a request for competency evaluation, and reevaluated various trial strategies including the waiver of jury trial and calling Parrish as a witness. (Exhibit YY R.T. 2/9/07 at 46-47.)

Based upon the foregoing, the undersigned cannot find deficient performance. There is no basis for the assertion that Middlebrooks hid the report. It was provided to the trial court and the prosecution. Moreover, the undersigned finds that it was also made available to Goldberg.

Even if the Parrish report was not provided to Goldberg, the undersigned cannot find that the failure to do so was deficient performance. As between counsel, Middlebrooks had been assigned responsibility for mental health issues and was lead counsel. Under those circumstances, failing to separately forward the report to Goldberg would not be "outside the wide range of professionally competent assistance." *United States v. Houtchens, 926 F.2d 824, 828 (9th Cir. 1991)* (citing *Strickland, 466 U.S. at 687-90*)).

Moreover, the undersigned concludes that, assuming the report was not disclosed, there was no prejudice because Goldberg admitted eventually learning the contents of the report, and took none of the actions he asserts he would have taken had he received the report immediately.

Finally, for the reasons discussed above, the undersigned cannot find that a request for redetermination of competency based upon the Parrish report would have been successful.

Accordingly, the undersigned finds this portion of the claim to be without merit.

3. Competency Re-Determination

Petitioner also argues that trial counsel was ineffective for failing to seek a renewed determination of competency based upon deterioration of his condition at trial. (Amend. Pet. Doc. 17 at 41.) Respondents argue that Middlebrooks did raise the issue during trial, expressing concern to the trial court about Petitioner's mental condition and medication, Petitioner's participation at various points indicated his continuing competence, trial counsel's misgivings about Petitioner's condition do not establish his incompetence, and a request for a redetermination would have been unsuccessful and futile. (Answer, Doc. 31 at 68-72.) In reply, Petitioner points to counsel's own misgivings about Petitioner's competency and inability to justify his failure to seek a redetermination. (Reply, Doc. 48 at 24-25.)

The PCR Court rejected as biased and thus not "legally credible" attorney Middlebrooks' self-admissions of deficient performance. It found counsel "competently represented and undertook to ensure petitioner's competency claims and mental health were protected at all stages of the proceedings including raising petitioner's mental health on at least two significant occasions resulting in petitioner's commitment and re-commitment to the Arizona State Hospital." (Exhibit AAAA M.E. 3/15/07 at 8.) The court specifically found counsel's representation to have been adequate on the competency issue during the competency proceedings, at the waiver of a jury trial, and during trial. (*Id.* at 9.)

The undersigned finds nothing unreasonable about the PCR court's determination. Attorney Middlebrooks made it clear that he believed Petitioner never fully understood what was occurring. While the PCR court observed that Middlebrooks alternatively stated that he did or did not believe Petitioner was ever credible, the undersigned finds Middlebrooks to have simply been wrestling with the dichotomy between his client's legal competence as found by the trial court and the degree of competence that counsel would hope for in a client or even that counsel personally believed was necessary to assure a fair trial.

As pointed out by Respondents, the degree of competence mandated by due process does not dictate that a defendant's mental state leave them acting in what would seem objectively to be their best interest. "To the extent that Williams's dazed or inattentive demeanor was before the trial judge, we agree with the Eleventh Circuit that 'there is no constitutional prohibition against the trial and conviction of a defendant who fails to pay attention in court-whether out of indifference, fear, confusion, boredom, or sleepiness-unless that defendant cannot understand the nature of the proceedings against him or adequately assist counsel in conducting a defense.' " *Williams v. Woodford, 384 F.3d 567, 606 (9th Cir. 2004)* (quoting *Watts v. Singletary, 87 F.3d 1282, 1287 (11th Cir.1996)*). Rather, the competency requirement of due process has the more modest aim of "ascertaining whether a criminal defendant 'has sufficient present ability to consult with his lawyer with a reasonable degree of rational understanding-and whether he has a rational as well as factual understanding of the proceedings against him.' " *Drope v. Missouri, 420 U.S. 162, 172, 95 S. Ct. 896, 43 L. Ed. 2d 103 (1975)* (quoting *Dusky v. United States, 362 U.S. 402, 80 S. Ct. 788, 4 L. Ed. 2d 824 (1960)).*

The fact that Petitioner was persistently unwilling to discuss the events of the crime with counsel, remained detached from much of the proceedings, doodled, laid his head on the table, or even slept, do not of themselves establish his incompetence. Moreover, Petitioner points to nothing (other than the Parrish report discussed herein above) between the trial court's final competency determination and the conclusion of trial that would suggest success would have come from efforts by trial counsel to re-urge incompetency.

The trial court had been made well aware of Petitioner's detachment and refusal to fully participate in his defense, and yet had found Petitioner's competent. There was nothing significantly different in character or degree between Petitioner's lack of participation at trial, and his conduct reflected in the mental health evaluations already before the trial court. Dr. Kassall had observed in March, 2003 that Petitioner "talks with his attorney only when he has to" and that he "continues to be very selective about what he will do, with whom he will interact, and what he will discuss." (Exhibit P, Mot. Submit, Exhibit 1.) Dr. DiBacco observed that Petitioner "selectively chooses not to respond when anyone else broaches legal or quasi legal issues with him." (*Id.* at Exhibit 2 at 4.) Dr. Morenz observed Petitioner "has yet to discuss his case in a meaningful fashion with his attorney." (*Id.* at Exhibit 3 at 6.)

The only new factor during trial pointed to by Petitioner is the issue concerning his medications. Attorney Middlebrooks testified:

A. So the question I though you asked me was, was my professional judgment impaired as to me recognizing his incompetency, and my answer would have been no, it wasn't but was my professional judgment impaired because I did not raise that issue, my answer is yes, it was because - -

MR. O'TOOLE [Prosecution]: Judge, could we have a time frame, please. I'm sorry.

THE WITNESS: And that would have been in trial. At that time when we were in the middle of the trial, and I think you're the one that told me during the interview -- it was either right before Dr. Morenz testified -- I can't remember who testified at that point, but during the trial transcript -- someone showed me something during my interview that indicated that there was an issue where I indicated that Eric had slipped or that we had let something slip and he wasn't getting the proper medication and that I should have raised his competency at that point.

There is no doubt in my mind that I should have done it. I knew better. I knew the facts. There is no doubt -- I have no doubt, zero doubt, that a reasonable attorney under the circumstances should have raised that issue at that moment in time, and the moment I'm talking about is the one in trial where we -- I believe we were in a conference with Judge Coker, and we're telling him - or, I'm telling him that we've let Eric's condition slip, because I can tell you, to even the extent that I know I should have done something, because I thought about it.

I thought about bringing -- having Dr. Morenz reevaluate Eric and look at him at the Coconino County Jail. I thought about talking to Dr. Linsky about the medications. I mean, there is no doubt in my mind that that should have been done at that moment in time, and the moment I'm talking about is the one in trial.

(Exhibit RRR-1, R.T. 2/20/07 at 96-97.)

However, on day seven of the trial, Middlebrooks raised his concerns about Petitioner's medications and mental condition to the trial court:

MR. MIDDLEBROOK: Judge, Dave Goldberg and I have some concerns that Eric may not be following what's occurring in court. And I know that last week or week before, I'm a little unclear now, but there was some concern about making sure that Eric gets medicated and stuff. And I will be the first to admit that we have kind of let that drop off. But I think that -- and I think that Mr. Goldberg agrees with me, we need we probably need to get him medicated. We're getting a little concerned that he's not following, he's starting to kind of go back, and we've explained things to him three or four times. And I'm not sure that he's following everything that's occurring.

THE COURT: Would you check with his doctor at lunch hour and/or the nurse at the jail and find out, and I will try to do the same thing.

MR. MIDDLEBROOK: I can tell you now we're going to need a court order because after he got released from the Arizona State Hospital, there is no present court order that requires him to be medicated.

THE COURT: I ordered that he -- when he returned, that he continue his medications. Yeah.

MR. MIDDLEBROOK: Is there a court order?

THE COURT: Yeah. Absolutely.

MR. MIDDLEBROOK: Then if there is, then we're in good shape. Then I will get probably call Chris Linsky, Dr. Linsky, and make sure he's aware.

THE COURT: If you will, and I'll have Lucy call the jail.

MR. GOLDBERG: That should have already happened, though.

MR. MIDDLEBROOK: Thank you.

THE COURT: I will have her call the jail and get a report from the nurse as to whether he is taking it. I'm concerned he might be cheeking it. Any indication?

MR. MIDDLEBROOK: No. No. The Haldol is an injection.

THE COURT: That's what I thought. Okay.

(Exhibit DD, R.T. 8/20/03 at 68-69.) There is no other indication in the record to suggest that Petitioner's medications actually had been stopped or otherwise had been altered to significantly reduce his level of mental functioning.

Petitioner complains that the PCR court failed to allow the presentation of evidence on this claim. (Amend. Pet. Doc. 17 at 58.) Petitioner fails to point, however, to any additional evidence available then or now to support the claim that Petitioner's condition had deteriorated.

In sum, the record indicates that Petitioner's condition at trial was not significantly different that it had been since his competency determination six months earlier. Thus, despite counsel's protestations to the contrary, the undersigned cannot find that counsel performed deficiently in failing to again raise Petitioner's competency at trial.

Doubtless, any good attorney with a bad result will, with hindsight, find matters that they believe they would and should have done differently. Hindsight is not the proper vantage point for deciding ineffective assistance of counsel. "A fair assessment of attorney performance requires that every effort be made to eliminate the distorting effects of hindsight, to reconstruct the circumstances of counsel's challenged conduct, and to evaluate the conduct from counsel's perspective at the time." *Strickland, 466 U.S. at 690.*

Nor can the undersigned find a significant likelihood, had counsel done so, that the trial court would have retreated from its earlier finding and found Petitioner incompetent to stand trial.

Therefore, neither can the undersigned find that the PCR court's rejection of this claim was contrary to or an unreasonable application of federal law.

4. Waiver of Jury

Petitioner argues that trial counsel was ineffective in waiving the jury trial. Petitioner argues that he was not competent to waive his jury trial rights. (Amend. Pet. Co. 17 at 51.) Petitioner also argues that Attorney Goldberg admits he did not consider the implication of waiving a trial by jury on the issue of *mens rea. (Id.* at 62.)

Respondents argue that the PCR court properly concluded that the decision to waive a jury was a reasonable trial strategy, given the limited likelihood of success before a jury, the agreement for a possibility of parole in exchange, the bad publicity on the trial and denial of a change of venue, the time already spent educating the judge on Petitioner's mental health condition, the other "bad act" evidence, the likely jury sympathy towards a police officer victim, and counsel's faith in the impartiality of the judge. Respondents also argue that Plaintiff cannot show prejudice because a jury would likely have rendered the same verdict as the judge. (Answer, Doc. 31 at 72-76.)

Petitioner replies that Attorney Goldberg would have reconsidered waiving a jury trial if he had known of the Parrish report. (Reply, Doc. 48 at 23.) Petitioner argues that the decision to waive was made without all the facts (e.g. the Parrish report and the deterioration in Petitioner's mental condition experienced at trial). (*Id.* at 26.) Petitioner argues that his personal waiver of the jury does not eliminate counsel's ineffectiveness. (*Id.*)

Several red herrings should be dismissed. It is irrelevant that Petitioner participated in the waiver. He did so upon the advice of counsel, and if that counsel was ineffective, then Petitioner's claim is made out.

It is also irrelevant that attorney Goldberg *might* have reconsidered waiving the jury had he known of the Parrish report. Goldberg's hindsight is not controlling, and unexplained it is not helpful in evaluating what reasonable counsel would have done. As discussed above, the Parrish report, while favorable, was not a game changer. It was cumulative and problematic evidence.

It is also irrelevant that Petitioner's mental condition deteriorated at trial. First, at the time that the waiver was given, those conditions had not yet occurred. Second, even if anticipated, Petitioner's decline at trial would not indicate that a jury was a better choice. A jury would have been without the benefit of the expansive background that the trial judge had in understanding the extent and nature of Petitioner's mental condition. That suggests that the judge may have, in fact, been more favorably impacted by a deterioration at trial than a jury. Moreover, if the deterioration reached a point that the trial court would alter its competency finding, it would seem to have little bearing whether the matter was before a judge or a jury.

It is also irrelevant that attorney Goldberg did not consider the impact of the waiver upon the *mens rea* portion of the case. First, that does not suggest that attorney Middlebrooks, who bore responsibility for that portion of the case, did not consider its impact. Second, it is not controlling whether counsel actually considered a strategic reason for proceeding in a certain manner. It is sufficient that the approach would have been a reasonable strategic decision given the information available to counsel; this court "need not determine the actual explanation [for the attorney's actions], so long as the [action] falls within the range of reasonable representation. *Morris v. California, 966 F.2d 448, 456-457 (9th Cir. 1991), cert. denied, 506 U.S. 831, 113 S. Ct. 96, 121 L. Ed. 2d 57 (1992)*. Third, Petitioner offers no reason to believe that a jury, in fact, would have been more sympathetic to a *mens rea* defense. Indeed, it seems likely that a jury may have been a poor choice for such a defense for all the same reasons that a jury may have been a poor choice to resolve the insanity defense.

Finally, it is also irrelevant that Petitioner now contends that he was incompetent to waive his jury trial rights. In support of his argument, Petitioner cites *Miller v. Dormire, 310 F.3d 600 (8th Cir. 2002)*. (Amend. Pet. Doc. 17 at 45.) In *Miller*, the trial judge "did not address [the defendant] directly," and the defendant was under the mistaken belief that counsel had the unilateral right to waive a jury trial. *310 F.3d at 602*. In contrast, here the trial court conducted an extensive examination of Petitioner at the waiver hearing, including explicitly advising Petitioner of his right to insist on a jury. (Exhibit T, R.T. 7/8/03 at 4-11.) Moreover, counsel had diligently pursued the assertion that Petitioner was not competent to stand trial and the trial court had ruled against Petitioner on the issue. Faced with that reality, trial counsel could not fail to pursue sound trial strategy based upon his personal belief that the trial court had decided incorrectly, and thus Petitioner was not actually competent to waive a jury. Taken to its logical extreme, such a catch 22 would have required counsel to decline an offer for Petitioner to plead to a misdemeanor, had one been extended. While counsel may not be free to ignore his client's mental condition, neither is he free to ignore the court's ruling on the issue.

What is left is that trial counsel made a reasonable strategic calculation that a trial to the bench was more likely to have a favorable result than a jury trial, and obtained in exchange for the waiver a significant concession on sentencing. Doing so was not deficient performance.

Moreover, Petitioner fails to proffer any prejudice. Petitioner provides no reason to believe that a jury would have rendered a different result from the verdict reached by the trial judge. *See Green v. Lynaugh, 868 F.2d 176, 178 (5th Cir. 1989)* (no prejudice absent showing jury trial would have different result). Nor does Petitioner show that with different advice from counsel he would have spurned the sentencing stipulation obtained in exchange for his waiver and proceeded to a jury trial instead. *See Nelson v. Hvass, 392 F.3d 320, 324 (8th Cir. 2004)* (no prejudice in bargained for waiver of jury trial without showing defendant would have insisted on jury trial). *But see Miller v.*

Dormire, 310 F.3d 600, 603 (8th Cir. 2002) ("When a defendant's right to a jury trial is denied as a result of his attorney's deficient performance, this circuit has determined that on the basis of Supreme Court precedent, *Strickland* prejudice is presumed because such misconduct is tantamount to a structural error."); and *U.S. v. Withers, 638 F.3d 1055, 2011 WL 6184, 8 (9th Cir. 2011)* ("The Ninth Circuit has not yet decided whether a trial counsel's failure to object to a structural error is presumptively prejudicial for purposes of the *Strickland* ineffective assistance of counsel inquiry.")

In sum, Petitioner points to nothing relevant which indicates that the PCR court made an unreasonable application of federal law when it rejected this claim.

....

(3) Conclusions re Deficient Performance - Apart from the trial court's admonishment, making an offer of proof on excluded evidence is a plain prerequisite to appealing the exclusion of evidence. "One of the most fundamental principles in the law of evidence is that in order to challenge a trial court's exclusion of evidence, an attorney must preserve the issue for appeal by making an offer of proof." *Holst v. Countryside Enterprises, Inc., 14 F.3d 1319, 1323 (8th Cir. 1994)*. Indeed, the Arizona Rules of Evidence provide:

Error may not be predicated upon a ruling which admits or excludes evidence unless a substantial right of the party is affected, and... (2) *Offer of Proof.* In case the ruling is one excluding evidence, the substance of the evidence was made known to the court by offer or was apparent from the context within which questions were asked.

Ariz. R. Evid. 103(a) (2002). *Cf. Fed.R. Evid 103(a). See also State v. Dickens, 187 Ariz. 1, 13, 926 P.2d 468, 480 (1996)* (evidentiary claim lost without "specific offer of proof"). *Cf. State v. Treadaway, 116 Ariz. 163, 168, 568 P.2d 1061, 1066 (1977)* ("formal offer of proof was not necessary because there is no doubt what response Dr. Tuchler would have made to the defense counsel's questions").

Moreover, long before Petitioner's trial, Arizona had specifically applied the requirement for an offer of proof to psychiatric history, albeit with regard to a witness. "Nonetheless, a trial judge does not abuse his discretion when he excludes testimony about a witness' psychiatric history when the defendant fails to make an offer of proof that the witness' perception or memory was affected by his illness." *State v. Walton, 159 Ariz. 571, 581-582, 769 P.2d 1017, 1027-1028 (1989). See also State v. Zuck,134 Ariz. 509, 513, 658 P.2d 162, 166 (1982)* (same).

In Petitioner's case, there were only two defenses presented: insanity and the absence of the requisite intent. Counsel had all but stipulated that Petitioner had killed the officer. The only evidence available to rebut intent was Petitioner's mental condition. Counsel was aware of and pursued the introduction of evidence to demonstrate that Petitioner lacked that intent because of his mental illness. However, despite being informed that the trial court was going to effectively exclude the evidence by refusing to consider it, and despite being invited to make on offer of proof, and despite the clear necessity of such an offer to preserve the issue for appeal, counsel failed to do so. There has been no strategic reason for that failure ever proposed, and the undersigned can conceive of none. At best, attorney Middlebrooks attributed the failure to a belief that an offer of proof would have been ineffective with the trial judge.

A. . . . So it wasn't an issue of -- I know what the argument is: Well, you could have made a specific offer of proof. But it was kind of like, well, the evidence was there. It wasn't like we left out a piece of evidence. It was, it was there; it was just our, at least my feeling was Judge Coker was not going to let me argue, nor was he going to seriously consider that any. Of this evidence was going to impact or allow us to --

Q. Sure.

A. -- create the defense.

(Exhibit OOO, Mot. Amend., Exh. A, Middlebrooks Interv. at 52.) The belief that it would not make a difference with the trial court would not justify a failure to make the offer of proof to preserve the issue for appeal.

In failing to make an offer of proof, trial counsel acted "outside the wide range of professionally competent assistance." *Strickland, 466 U.S. at 690. See Collier v. Turpin, 177 F.3d 1184, 1202 (11th Cir. 1999)* (counsel ineffective for failing to make an offer of proof).

(d) Analysis re Prejudice

(1) Required Showing - "An error by counsel, even if professionally unreasonable, does not warrant setting aside the judgment of a criminal proceeding if the error had no effect on the judgment." *Strickland, 466 U.S. at 691.* In assessing prejudice, the reviewing court must apply "hindsight," and assess the prejudicial effect of counsel's deficient performance in light of subsequent events. *Lockhart v. Fretwell, 506 U.S. 364, 372, 113 S. Ct. 838, 122 L. Ed. 2d 180 (1993).*

In assessing prejudice from deficient performance of counsel in preserving an issue for appeal (as opposed to raising the issue to the trial court in the first instance), the prejudice inquiry must focus on whether the outcome of the appeal would have been different. "Accordingly, when a defendant raises the unusual claim that trial counsel, while efficacious in raising an issue, nonetheless failed to preserve it for appeal, the appropriate prejudice inquiry asks whether there is a reasonable likelihood of a more favorable outcome on appeal had the claim been preserved." *Davis v. Secretary for Dept. of Corrections, 341 F.3d 1310, 1316 (11th Cir. 2003). Cf. Smith v. Robbins, 528 U.S. 259, 285-286, 120 S. Ct. 746, 145 L. Ed. 2d 756 (2000)* (prejudice from failure on appeal judged by whether defendant "would have prevailed on his appeal"); *Cockett v. Ray, 333 F.3d 938, 944 (9th Cir. 2003)*(same).

It should be noted that the PCR court did not reach the issue of prejudice on this claim. Consequently, there is no state court decision on the merits on this issue to which deference may be extended, and this Court applies *de novo* review. *Lewis v. Mayle, 391 F.3d 989, 996 (9th Cir. 2004)* (no AEDPA deference where pertinent portion of the claim not reached by state court).

And, it should be noted that in assessing prejudice (as in everything else pertaining to this case) this Court is, at a minimum, guided by the Supreme Court's analysis of the trial proceedings.

Based upon the foregoing, the undersigned concludes that to establish the requisite prejudice, Petitioner must show a reasonable probability that the outcome of his appeal would have been different had trial counsel made an offer of proof. That requires Petitioner to show that, had the claim been properly preserved, the Arizona Court of Appeals would have reversed his conviction. That requires Petitioner to show a reasonable probability that the Arizona Court of Appeals would have concluded that: (1) the trial court actually excluded consideration of the "observation evidence;" (2) that such exclusion was legal error; and (3) that such error justified reversal under state law.

(2) Trial Court's Exclusion of Evidence - Although disclaiming the ability to "be sure," the majority in *Clark* observed that "the trial court seems to have applied the *Mott* restriction to all evidence offered by Clark for the purpose of showing what he called his inability to form the required *mens rea.*" *Clark, 548 U.S. at 760.* The dissent was far more assertive, finding that the language of the trial court's ruling and the terms of its verdict led to the conclusion that the "most reasonable assumption, then, would seem to be that the trial court did not consider it, and the Court does not hold otherwise." *Id. at 785* (Kennedy, J. dissenting).

In his article *The Supreme Court's Bout with Insanity: Clark v. Arizona*, Mr. Westen asserts that "Clark was allowed to introduce all of the evidence he offered to show that he did not knowingly kill a policeman, and the trial judge fully considered Clark's evidence for its weight." *4 Ohio St. J. Crim. L. 143, 151 (2006).* However, Mr. Westen's purported explication for that proposition makes no specific reference to the record, but simply argues that the courts have misunderstood the relationship between *mens rea* and the insanity defense. *Id. at 152-156.* In contrast, in her article *Rehabilitating Mental Disorder Evidence after Clark v. Arizona*, Ms. Klein opines that "it is quite clear that the trial judge in *Clark* interpreted Arizona state law as prohibiting Clark from presenting any kind of mental disorder evidence for the purpose of raising reasonable doubt about mens rea." *60 Case W. Res. L. Rev. 645, 665 (2010).* In support, Ms. Klein argues the language of the trial court's ruling and the absence of the distinction in observational evidence from then existing jurisprudence. *Cf. id. at 654* (rejecting Westen's correlation between *mens rea* and insanity defenses because of the disparity of the burdens of proof - - reasonable doubt of no *mens rea* versus clear and convincing evidence of insanity). The undersigned certainly has no greater clairvoyance than the Supreme Court, but this Court is equipped with the record from the PCR proceedings, which were not available to the U.S. Supreme Court. Moreover, in determining prejudice from deficient performance of counsel, a reviewing court is not obligated to "be sure," but to determine matters to a "reasonable degree of probability." For the following reasons, the undersigned finds, to a reasonable degree of probability, that the Arizona Court of Appeals would have found that the trial court in fact did exclude consideration of any of the "observational evidence."

Unlike the PCR court's improper reliance on the Supreme Court decision in this case to find no deficient performance, there is no problem in relying on the post-state-appeal record, because prejudice (as opposed to deficient performance) is determined with the benefit of hindsight. *Lockhart, 506 U.S. at 372*. Indeed, the prejudice determination is based upon a fictitious past in which trial counsel did adequately preserve the issue for appeal (which would erase the need for the future PCR proceeding). First, the record from the trial court was sufficient to conclude to a reasonable probability that the Arizona Court of Appeals would have found the trial court excluded the observational evidence. The defense's stated strategy from opening statements on was to show that the prosecution could not "prove that [Petitioner] knew that the officer was a police officer and knowingly and intentionally shot him." (Exhibit V, R.T. 8/5/03 at 22-23 (Def. Opening Statement.)

MR. GOLDBERG: . . . Overall, your Honor, I'd ask you to consider this evidence over the next four days from not just the perspective of whether the state's proven what it's saying it's going to set out to prove here, but also in light of the fact that whether they can prove specifically that Eric knew that he was involved with a police officer at the time of this offense, because if he did not know that Officer Moritz was, in fact, a police officer but was acting under delusional or otherwise nonintentional thinking at that time, then he is not guilty of first degree murder. And the Court can find him guilty of a lesser offense, such as second degree murder or manslaughter.

(*Id.* at 17-18.)

The trial then proceeded with the state presenting its litany of prosecution witnesses, including:

(1) officers Cooper, Mead, and Wright, who were the first responders at the scene (Exhibit V, R.T.8/5/03 at 24-140);

(2) Randy and Tammy Cupp who had reported to police that someone was driving through their neighborhood with loud music the night of the shooting (*id.* at 141-167);

(3) Cupp neighbor Michael Greenway who observed Petitioner driving with loud music (*id.* at 168-175);

(4) Cupp neighbor Deborah Hill who heard the vehicle driving with loud music, the siren, and gunshots and saw the officer collapsing (*id.* at 176-199);

(5) Gene Waldrip who discovered Petitioner's hat with the gun it (Exhibit W, R.T. 8/6/03 at 3-7);

(6) officer Dale Young who investigated the scene of the shooting, the gun location and Petitioner's residence and took DNA from Petitioner (*id.* at 8-45);

(7) Cupp neighbor Jaime Nyala who heard the exchange between Petitioner and the officer and the gunshots, and saw the scene afterward (*id.* at 4-64);

(8) Cupp neighbor Mary Hartman who heard Petitioner driving with loud music, a siren, and gunshots (*id.* at 65-70);

(9) Cupp neighbor Diana Wittenbreder who heard the siren, saw the police vehicle and another vehicle stopping, heard gunshots and saw the officer at the back of his vehicle, and saw someone walking away quickly (*id.* at 71-90);

(10) Detective Mike Gray who investigated the scene and vehicles (*id.* at 91-112);

(11) Officer Jeff James who searched the neighborhood and participated in apprehending Petitioner (*id.* at 113-129);

(12) medical examiner Philip Keen (Exhibit X, R.T. 8/6/03 at 2-35);

(13) Petitioner's school acquaintance Jason Hackett, a recovering drug addict, who was in a park with friends when Petitioner walked up and announced he wanted to shoot a police officer, and that some months before Petitioner had complained about the police arresting someone, and described Petitioner's unusual behavior at school (Exhibit Y, R.T. 8/7/03 at 5-38);

(14) Mark Fields, a drug addict and homeless person at the time, who was at the park with Hackett, smoking marijuana, and claimed that Petitioner's threat against police stemmed from friends' objections to Petitioner having beer in a public park, that Petitioner appeared to be under the influence and Jason described him as crazy (*id.* at 39-59);

(15) Detective Dale Eske who staked out Petitioner's residence, saw Petitioner coming to the home, chased him and participated in the apprehension (*id.* at 60-71);

(16) Detective Thomas Boughner who responded to the scene and canvassed the neighborhood, and participated in apprehending Petitioner (*id.* at 71-81);

(17) forensic scientist David Spence who performed gunshot residue tests (*id.* at 81-100);

(18) Detective Frank Higgins who responded to the scene and participated in the search for Petitioner, his apprehension, recovery of the hat and weapon (*id.* at 100-121);

(19) Detective Paul Langston who responded to the scene, investigated the location where the weapon was found, and fingerprinted Petitioner (*id.* at 121-133);

(20) criminalist Terry Weaver who investigated the scene and the firearm evidence (Exhibit Z, R.T. 8/8/03 at 4-59); and

(21) criminalist Benito Bock who did DNA testing on the hat found with the weapon (*id.* at 59-71).

The only portions of all this testimony with any significant bearing on the *Mott* issue was the testimony from Hackett and Fields, and Detective Higgins depiction of Petitioner's responses upon being apprehended as "sarcastic...wasn't spontaneous, it seemed almost forced" (Exhibit Y, R.T. 8/7/03 at 120.)

At the conclusion of the prosecution's case, the defense moved for a directed verdict and "reserve[d] the right...to resurge this motion at the completion of the defense case based on the evidence you hear on whether there is sufficient evidence that Eric Clark in his state of mind at that moment knew that this was a police officer and intended to kill a police officer." (Exhibit Z, R.T. 8/8/03 at 78.) The trial court denied the motion. (Exhibit BB R.T. 8/12/03.)

The defense then presented the testimony of lay witnesses Victor Meza and Hillary Engelke, schoolmates of Petitioner, about Petitioner's history and behavior. (Exhibit CC, R.T. 8/12/03.) An off the record discussion was held between the court and counsel concerning the *Mott* issues, and the court directed counsel to brief the matter so the Court could issue a ruling after a recess. (*Id.* at 73-74.) When court reconvened the following week, the court issued its ruling on the *Mott* case, indicating that it had read the parties' memorandum. (Exhibit CC, R.T. 8/19/03 at 5-6.)

The defense then proceeded with the balance of its witnesses, including a host of lay witnesses (Exhibit CC, R.T. 8/19/30; Exhibit DD, R.T. 8/20/03; Exhibit EE, R.T. 8/21/03) and its expert witnesses (Exhibit FF R.T. 8/22/03). The state then presented its expert witness (Exhibit GG, R.T. 8/26/03). Petitioner declined to testify, the defense reasserted its motion for directed verdict relying "on the arguments that Mr. Goldberg had made previously but now *in consideration of all the evidence that's been presented.*" (Exhibit HH, R.T. 8/27/03 at 4 (emphasis added).) The state simply relied "upon the earlier arguments and our memorandum of law." (*Id.* at 5.) The trial court summarily denied the motion, with no indication that it would consider any portion of the evidence submitted during the insanity portion of the case. (*Id.*)

Perhaps most telling is counsel's closing argument. Counsel does not argue insanity plus a lack of intent based upon lay testimony of Petitioner's mental condition. There is absolutely no argument on Petitioner's intent. The words "intent" or "*mens rea*" are not even mentioned. Despite counsel's promises at the commencement of the trial that the mental status evidence would refute intent, no mention of it is made in closing. (*See* Exhibit HH, R.T. 8/27/03 at 7-29.) Indeed, counsel concluded by arguing "there is only one verdict, and it's an unfortunate one, he was guilty but insane because there's no other way to analyze the evidence." (*Id.* at 29.) Thus, defense counsel was either completely deficient in failing to argue the sole defense to the prosecution's case in chief, or counsel believed that the trial judge had already ruled that all the available evidence (lay or expert) would not be considered and thus there was no evidence on which he could argue a lack of *mens rea.* Given the overall fervency and competence demonstrated by defense counsel, the latter is far more probable.

Similarly, the trial court's pronouncement of the verdict on the prosecution's case suggests that the trial court made no consideration of any evidence refuting intent:

The court finds beyond a reasonable doubt that the defendant, Eric Clark, shot and caused the death of police officer, Jeff Moritz.

(Exhibit II, R.T. 9/3/03 at 4.) The court's only discussion of the six days of mental status evidence was solely in connection with the verdict on the insanity defense, where the court went into depth to detail [*160] the evidence and its findings. (*Id.* at 4-6.)

As recognized by the majority in *Clark*, appellate counsel argued in his "brief in the Arizona Court of Appeals...that it was not inconsistent with *Mott* to consider non expert evidence indicating mental illness on the issue of mens rea, and argued that the trial judge had failed to do so." *Clark, 548 U.S. at 763.* (*See* Exhibit OO, Opening Brief at 47-49.) The State, on the other hand, argued that *Mott* was not limited to its facts and thus rejected Petitioner's argument that *Mott* should not be read to bar "'*any evidence* reflecting upon a mentally ill criminal defendant's ability to form the necessary *mens rea*'". (Exhibit PP, Ans. Brief at 36-37 (quoting Opening Brief at 47) (emphasis in original).) The State argued that the such testimony by lay witnesses "was not relevant to the issue of whether [Petitioner] knew Officer Moritz was a police officer." (*Id.* at 37.) The Arizona Court of Appeals complained that trial counsel had failed to specify evidence in an offer of proof to support his *mens rea* defense, but concluded that "[e]ven assuming such evidence was sufficient, the trial court was bound by the supreme court's decision in *Mott*." (Exhibit RR, Mem. Dec. At 19.)

The PCR proceeding goes even further to establish that the trial court had excluded all evidence on Petitioner's mental condition on intent. The state did not argue to the PCR court that the trial court had actually considered the observational evidence. Instead, the state argued that the record was not clear and, given the presumption that judges know and apply the law, the ruling in *Clark* that *Mott* did not extend to observational evidence should create a presumption that the trial court did not exclude the observational evidence. (Exhibit WW, PCR Resp. at 19-20.) Likewise, Respondents argue that this court must, under the *Strickland* standard, presume that the trial court acted within the law. (Answer, Doc. 31 at 83-84.)

However, the presumption relied upon by the State (e.g. that the trial judge knew and applied the law, particularly as subsequently explicated in *Clark*) is rebuttable. *See Townsend v. Sain, 372 U.S. 293, 83 S. Ct. 745, 9 L. Ed. 2d 770 (1963)* (presumption applicable on habeas review rebuttable). As strongly argued by Respondents in asserting counsel's effectiveness, prior to *Clark* there was no case law differentiating between these types of evidence. Either *Clark* charted new territory, or it did not. Indeed, prior to *Clark* there was no jurisprudence holding that *Mott* was limited to expert testimony and did not include "observational evidence." The majority opinion in *Clark* concluded that it was "clear that *Mott* itself imposed no restriction on considering evidence of the first sort, the observation evidence," *Clark, 548 U.S. at 760*, However, Justice Breyer found in his partial concurrence that it was necessary to "remand this case so that Arizona's courts can determine whether Arizona law, as set forth in *Mott* and other cases, is consistent with the distinction the Court draws" *id. at 780*. Justices Kennedy, Stevens and Ginsberg agreed that "*Mott*'s holding was not restricted to mental-disease evidence." *Id. at 786*. For the reasons discussed herein, the undersigned finds that the presumption that the trial judge divined the law according to *Clark* and applied it has been overcome.

It is important to remember that because it is the decision of the PCR court being considered, the AEDPA presumptions and limitations do not apply to the trial court's ruling on the *Mott* issue. Moreover, the

PCR Court made no ruling on whether the trial court had actually excluded the observational evidence.

In opening statements at the PCR proceeding, the State's attorney made no argument that the trial court considered the observational evidence, and instead simply raised the hindsight assisted argument ultimately adopted by the PCR court:

MR. O'TOOLE: Attorney Gerhardt said that first issue, the observational evidence issue, that was initially kind of thought about when this petition was being filed, was an easy issue. The state agrees. It's a very easy issue. Just because you don't win in the United States Supreme Court does not mean you're ineffective. You don't have to create new law and bring it all the way up to the United States Supreme Court to be effective. That's not the standard.

(Exhibit YY-1, R.T. 2/9/07 at 10-11). The state made no assertion that the trial court did not exclude consideration of the observational evidence.

Attorney Goldberg testified that he believed, based upon the contents of the special verdict, that the trial judge did not consider the observational evidence in deciding "whether there was a reasonable doubt of whether [Petitioner] intentionally and knowingly killed a police officer." (Exhibit YY-1, R.T. at 23.) Cross examination [*164] of Goldberg on the issue was limited to the novelty argument:

Q. You never heard the word - - - the praise "observational evidence" before the United States Supreme Court issued their decision in the Clark case?

A. Neither me nor Justice Kennedy and several of the other justices.

(*Id.* at 66.) In its written Closing Argument (Exhibit ZZZ), the state made no assertion that the trial court had actually considered the observational evidence. (*Id.* at 19-24.)

Finally, in his unsworn interview, attorney Middlebrooks related his understanding that the trial judge had precluded the observational evidence:

A. . . . The reason I brought those motions in liming with me is because it occurred to me under the State versus Bay case that a layperson's opinions and observations as to insanity was relevant. In all honesty, I thought I had preserved the issue as far as being able to bring in lay people to discuss mens rea and, in effect, to negate Eric's ability to premeditate and/or perceive that Officer Moritz was in fact a police officer versus an alien.

I'll tell you, when Judge Coker ruled, the effect of Judge Coker's ruling on the Mott issue for me was that I could no longer make that argument. So I don't know if that directly answers your question or not. But I thought by filing the pretrial motions I had preserved the observational evidence issue. But when he ruled that we could not bring in or discuss Matt from the standpoint

Q. Right.

A. -- of negating premeditation -

(Exhibit OOO, Mot. Amend, Exh. A, Middlebrooks Int. at 50.)

Thus, with the exception of the limited post-trial arguments by the state that the failure of counsel to make a record precluded knowing whether the trial court excluded the observational evidence, the balance of the record indicates that the trial court did exclude it. The post-appeal record adds to the information available to the Supreme Court, and thus bolster's the majority's observation that "the trial court seems to have applied the *Mott* restriction to all evidence offered by Clark for the purposes of showing his inability to from the required *mens rea*." *Clark, 548 U.S. at 760.*

Accordingly, the undersigned finds at a minimum a reasonable probability that the trial court excluded consideration of the observational evidence under a mistaken belief that *Mott* precluded its consideration.

(3) Appellate Determination Exclusion Was Error - Because the relevant question is whether the outcome of the appeal would have been different, Petitioner must also show that the Arizona Court of Appeals would have found that the trial court's exclusion of the observation evidence was error.

The majority opinion in *Clark* observed: "It is clear that *Mott* itself imposed no restriction on considering evidence of the first sort, the observation evidence." *Clark, 548 U.S. at 760.* Respondents make no suggestion that if presented with a properly preserved claim the Arizona Court of Appeals would not have deduced the correct application of *Mott.* The majority in *Clark* believed they would have.

We therefore have no reason to believe that the courts of Arizona would have failed to restrict their application of *Mott* to the professional testimony the *Mott* opinion was stated to cover, if Clark's counsel had specified any observation evidence he claimed to be generally admissible and relevant to mens rea.

Id. at 765, n. 34. Thus, by relying on *Mott* to exclude the observational evidence, the trial court acted contrary to Arizona law, and the undersigned finds at the minimum a reasonable probability that but for trial counsel's deficient performance the Arizona Court of Appeals would have found the error.

Respondents argue that although it noted the concerns, *Clark* did not hold that states could not exclude observational evidence. (Answer, Doc. 31 at 83.) That would be relevant only to disposing of a direct due process attack on the exclusion of the observational evidence. Petitioner does not depend upon such an attack in this claim. Rather, Petitioner simply argues that trial counsel was ineffective in failing to properly preserve for appeal his argument that the trial court improperly applied *Mott* to lay testimony. That the application may (or may not) have also been a violation of due process is not necessary to a finding that the Arizona Court of Appeals would have found it to be error under Arizona law.

(4) Appellate Determination Error Justified Reversal - Finally, Petitioner must show that the Arizona Court of Appeals would not only have found error, but would have granted relief. Under Arizona law, evidentiary error does not call for reversal if the court can find that the error was harmless. "Error is harmless or non-prejudicial when it can be said beyond a reasonable doubt that the error did not affect the verdict." *State v. Lundstrom, 161 Ariz. 141, 150, 776 P.2d 1067, 1076 (1989).* For the following reasons, the undersigned finds, to a

reasonable degree of probability, that the Arizona Court of Appeals would have determined that it could not find beyond a reasonable doubt that the exclusion of the "observation evidence" did not affect the verdict.

First, Petitioner's contention has been that the state failed to show the requisite *mens rea* of intending to kill a police officer because Petitioner was acting under a paranoid delusion which caused him to believe that members of the community, and police officers in particular, were a danger to him. To sustain its burden on this point, the state was required to provide "proof beyond a reasonable doubt that a defendant's state of mind was in fact what the charge states." *Clark, 548 U.S. at 766.*

Second, there was substantial lay testimony, to indicate that Petitioner was indeed acting under his paranoid delusions at the time of the shooting.

Jason Tackett (a prosecution witness on the Thorpe Park incident) testified that Petitioner regularly talked to himself, that at school Petitioner wouldn't keep eye contact, always looked at his desk and twirled his pencil, and looked around paranoid. He seemed unusually fidgety and stressed out, and appeared scared, and yet seemed to be trying to intimidate others. He though Petitioner was creepy and that there was something wrong with him. (Exhibit Y, R.T. 8/7/03 at 18, 26-28.) Petitioner seemed calmer and happier when he was using marijuana. (*Id.* at 29.)

Victor Meza testified that he and Petitioner had been best friends through middle school until their junior year in high school, but at the beginning of their junior year, Petitioner began to undergo changes. (Exhibit BB, R.T. 8/12/03 at 32-42.) In January, he began keeping a bird in his car and arranging string throughout the car because he was afraid someone would break into the car and put something in it. (*Id.* at 43-44.) His relationship with his parents declined, and he rented a storage locker and filled it with water, canned food etc. because he was afraid something was going to happen. (*Id.* at 45-47.) Meza described an incident where Petitioner became angry because Meza had taken the front seat in a friend's car, making Petitioner sit in the back. As they drove down the road, Petitioner began choking Meza. The driver stopped and Meza got out to fight Petitioner. Petitioner got out and did not seem to remember choking Meza. (*Id.* at 49-51.)

Hillary Engelke testified that she had been friends with Petitioner since the seventh grade, and noticed that his personality and appearance changed in his junior year, and he became a "loner." (Exhibit BB, R.T. 8/12/03 at 62-72.)

Nancy Edmondson testified that she had been friends with Petitioner since junior high, and she noticed changes in him in January, 2000. (Exhibit CC, R.T. 8/19/03 at 7-13.) In April, 2000, when she was six and a half months pregnant, she was at Petitioner's house. After Petitioner's sister left, she went with Petitioner to his room and he asked her a series of strange and uncharacteristic questions about death, having sex with a pregnant woman, etc. which scared her. She told him she needed to go home and he got angry. Before they left he began running string around his room which he described as his "security system for his parents." When they got to his car, he was acting normal again. (*Id.* at 13-16.) He had his bird in his car. (*Id.* at 21-22.)

Stephen Carrillo testified that he had known Petitioner in high school and played football against him, and Petitioner was popular. He noticed that in January, 2000 Petitioner had become distant from people and they didn't want to be around him. (Exhibit CC, R.T. 8/19/03 at 23-26.) Petitioner kept a bird in his car. (*Id.* at 29-30.)

Adam Lozano testified that he knew Petitioner through Petitioner's older brother, and was helping Petitioner work out to play college football. In 2000, Petitioner had stopped lifting weights, and his appearance and voice changed. The day before the shooting, Petitioner called and asked to lift weights with Lozano. Lozano did not recognize his voice, and asked what was wrong. Petitioner said he was having mental problems. (Exhibit CC, R.T. 8/19/03 at 41-50.)

Anthony Nelson testified that he had known Petitioner since junior high, and noticed changes in him in their junior year in high school. Petitioner stopped socializing, let his appearance go, lost weight, began keeping strings in his car. (Exhibit CC, R.T. 8/19/03 at 64-73.)

Shane Palmer testified that he had known Petitioner since 5th grade, and noticed changes in him between their sophomore and junior years, including his dress and withdrawal from people. Petitioner would string fishing line around his car and kept a bird in the car and a stack of quarters balanced on the seat of the car. (Exhibit CC, R.T. 8/19/03 at 79-87.)

Arthur Salazar testified that he had been friends with Petitioner since junior high, and played sports with him. He noticed changes in Petitioner in their junior year, including a loss of interest in sports, change in appearance, change in his voice, always wearing a backpack, constantly playing with a pen, withdrawal from people, laughing and smiling inappropriately, etc. (Exhibit CC, R.T. 8/19/03 at 88- 105.)

Eric Escobedo testified that he played football at the high school at the same time as Petitioner. He noticed changes in Petitioner including becoming withdrawn. He saw a bird and strings in the back of Petitioner's car. (Exhibit CC, R.T. 8/19/03 at 110-122.)

Rosalind Trillo testified that she knew Petitioner in high school. Petitioner was withdrawn from other people. He would ask Trillo and her boyfriend to go to lunch with them. He would sit in the back seat without talking, and would not eat lunch. She saw his car with strings strung inside and asked Petitioner about it. He said it was not his car. He would talk to her in high pitched tone, but would talk to her boyfriend in a normal voice. (Exhibit CC, R.T. 8/19/03 at 123-143.)

Lois Wells testified that she was Petitioner's 5th grade teacher and high school counselor and her son was on the football team with Petitioner. In the fall of Petitioner's sophomore year, the football coach reported that Petitioner was "crazy." In the spring of that year, she confronted Petitioner about skipping class and going home and he "went ballistic" which she found unusual. In the summer of 1999, Petitioner's mother called and asked for a referral to a counselor for Petitioner. Petitioner had "went ballistic" when he couldn't get the car he wanted, got arrested, and when taken home had "went ballistic" with his dad. In the fall of 2000, Petitioner came to request a schedule change, and uncharacteristically and inappropriately argued with her repeatedly when told it couldn't be done. Petitioner came to get a schedule change for the spring semester, and was loud and demanding and then left when told to wait.

In the spring of 2000, the weight training teacher complained that Petitioner refused to go swimming, and Petitioner's mother reported that the teacher had humiliated Petitioner and Petitioner was afraid of germs in the pool.

Petitioner had gone to her office and to the district office to take the final for a correspondence course, but just left when sent to get his book, or to put his backpack in his car and never took the final.

Petitioner's history teacher reported that Petitioner was behaving bizarrely, that he would sit in class flipping his pencil and zone out. The nurse reported to her that Petitioner had come in with a cut lip but refused to let her touch it because he was afraid she had germs.

After spring break, Petitioner's mother called her and reported that Petitioner had been in her office sobbing saying the voices would not leave him alone and he couldn't take it anymore and he was ready to go to heaven. Wells volunteered to locate Petitioner, and found him in class. He told her he was fine. His parents tried to take him for treatment, but he refused.

Petitioner's mother reported to her that Petitioner was extremely paranoid, tied string all over his room, she would buy him new shoes and he would put them in the trash because they had germs on them, he couldn't eat in the same place because they were going to poison him, and that he thought they had taken his mom and replaced her with an alien. Petitioner's mother denied that Petitioner was taking drugs, and claimed she had been testing him for drugs. Petitioner's behavior was extremely odd but he did not act like other emotionally disturbed students. (Exhibit DD, R.T. 8/20/03 at 4-53.)

Gentry Clark testified that he is Petitioner's older brother and helped coach Petitioner's football teams. He left and went to UofA the fall of 1999. Petitioner's emotions began to vacillate quickly and unpredictably. His clothes and hair appearance changed, and he became reclusive, and his conversation regressed and he was unable to carry a conversation. Three or four months before the shooting, they got in an argument and Petitioner threatened to kill him and didn't seem to be himself. On May 16, 2000, he came home at 1:00 a.m. to find his parents in their front yard with flashlights looking for a gun that Petitioner had hidden. (Exhibit DD, R.T. 8/20/03 at 54-85.)

David Clark testified that he is Petitioner's father, that he observed changes in Petitioner in 1999. In June of 1999, Petitioner had purchased a motorcycle and when his mother objected Petitioner got a wild-eyed look and told her "maybe you've just threatened yourself." When they went to Prescott to buy him a car, Petitioner became agitated on the way, acted inappropriately with the sales person and insisted on a car over their price limit. Petitioner later told him he felt like he could go crazy.

That night Petitioner had abandoned his car in the road. The police officer came to the house. Petitioner saw the police officer and said "I'm not talking to you anymore. I will see you in court." Petitioner then jumped out of his window and began walking away. When David got outside, the officer had Petitioner in the patrol car. When Petitioner got out of the patrol car, he led David to the side to tell him something and began whispering gibberish. Petitioner then laid down on the lawn saying he was going to take a nap. The police officer told David that while he talked to Petitioner, Petitioner had gone from upset to angry to crying. When David and Petitioner began walking into the house, Petitioner began to cuss at David and act in a scary way. David asked the police officer to take Petitioner to juvenile detention. They then decided to admit Petitioner to Aspen Hill. While he was there they searched his room and found marijuana and an anarchist book. He was drug tested and was positive for marijuana. David and Petitioner's mother disagreed about whether Petitioner should stay in Aspen Hill and after four days they took him out.

Petitioner's behavior became more bizarre after he came home. He began sleeping in a sleeping bag in the computer room and rigged the room with fishing line with beads and wind chimes, and asked for a baby monitor so he could monitor his bedroom from the computer room. Eventually he began sleeping in his bedroom and booby trapped it every night. Petitioner told him that it was because "they" were after him. He began fearing being poisoned and started drinking bottled water. He became reclusive, and wouldn't return calls from his friends. Petitioner dropped out of sports and did not return to school but began taking correspondence courses. His paranoia stayed constant through the end of the year. Then he began telling his mother that he was going to be elected president.

He became paranoid about Y2K and surreptitiously used David's debit card to buy survival things, which when confronted he admitted to be for Y2K. He had put them in a storage locker he had. After New Year's, Petitioner was happy that the world had not ended and became more normal for several weeks, and then went back into his severe paranoia.

He would not eat food at home, but insisted on bottled water and food from gas stations and convenience stores and at the Sizzler buffet so he wouldn't be poisoned. He would laugh inexplicably, began wearing multiple layers of clothes, playing the TV loudly and would get a strange look in his eyes.

In April Petitioner had called his mother an alien, then called David an alien, and told him if he would got get some tools he would show him. He said he had special powers and keys to doors that "they" wanted.

On April 24, 2000, Petitioner was arrested for DUI. David went to the police station and Petitioner's eyes were dilated and he was acting very wildly and had alcohol on his breath, and he could or would not perform the breathalyzer test. The DPS officer who had arrested Petitioner later asked to meet with David and told him he thought Petitioner was violent and a danger to the family and wanted to make sure that they slept with their bedroom locked, and removed any guns from the house, because they had found ammunition on Petitioner. David took his guns to his parents' house in Prescott.

In May, he and Petitioner's mother had gone to a movie. When they came home, Petitioner was laying on his bed with a large caliber pistol lying next to him. David grabbed the gun, ran upstairs and gave it to his wife and told her to hide it. Petitioner came upstairs and found the gun in the closet where she had hidden it. David demanded the gun. Petitioner said the gun belonged to someone else and they couldn't have it. He took it outside and hid it. They told him he could not keep a gun. Hours later, David was searching for the gun outside and Petitioner agreed to take it back to its owner. He rode off on his bicycle, and came back without the gun.

They later tried to have Petitioner prosecuted on the DUI so that he could get help. They pursued having him admitted various places and to see a counselor but Petitioner would not go. They considered provoking an incident with him so they could have him committed to juvenile detention.

The day before the shooting he took Petitioner to shower at the athletic club. Petitioner had stopped showering at home because he was didn't feel safe showering at home. They went to the movies with his mother. As usual, Petitioner did not really watch the movie, but appeared to be peering around him out of the corner of his eyes or staring at his hands. He seemed to be in his own world. Afterwards, Petitioner asked to stay and watch another movie. David waited up for him to call for a ride, but eventually went to bed, and was awoken early the next morning by the police.

On August 20th, while Petitioner was in jail, he told his parents that "Aaron" lives in a mirage, it was Flagstaff and it was a platinum city. 50,000 people in Flagstaff were aliens. A thousand people were not aliens. They were after him because he had the keys to the doors and he knew things that they didn't know. He was being tortured and electrocuted. And the only thing that will stop aliens is bullets. Petitioner "slipped up" and supplanted his name for "Aaron" in telling the story. The psychiatric evaluations indicate that Petitioner was still at the Coconino County Jail, and untreated, on this date. (*See e.g.* Exhibit GGGG, DiBacco Report 12/23/00 at 9; [ILLEGIBLE TEXT]

Although Petitioner had not shown a particular fear of police officers, he had a fear of everybody because anybody could be the "they" or the aliens. (Exhibit DD, R.T. 8/20/03 at 86-163.)

Lisa Oedekerk testified that she had known Petitioner since the 4th grade, and noticed changes in him in their junior year of high school, including his withdrawal from people, and unwillingness to look people in the eye. He began rigging his car to see if it was disturbed. (Exhibit DD, R.T. 8/20/03 at 164-178.)

Lauren Beach testified that she had been friends with Petitioner since junior high, and noted that after his sophomore year he became withdrawn. At a party in the summer of 2000, he behaved strangely, unable to focus his eyes on things, repeatedly played with things from his pockets or playing with a pen, acting disconnected and asking people why they were talking to him. Petitioner then got in a fight and hit the other person in the nose, and threatened to kill him if he told anyone. Petitioner appeared to have a gun which he put in his waistband. (Exhibit DD, R.T. 8/20/03 at 179-190.)

Terry Clark [Petitioner's mother] testified that she was a school nurse, that Petitioner had been a loving child, good student, and good athlete. In November, 1988 they moved into an apartment because of a house fire, and Petitioner began to refuse to drink tap water because of a fear of lead poisoning, even though told the pipes were made of PVC. In the spring of 1999, he began to experience wide and rapid mood swings, and began to withdraw from interaction with the family. He started referring to her as "Terry" rather than "mom." She was uncertain at the time whether this resulted from normal teenage rebellion or illegal drug use.

In June of 1999, Petitioner came home and said he wanted to buy a motorcycle and asked her to cosign the loan. She refused, Petitioner got a blank look and said "you may have just threatened yourself," walked away, and never brought up the motorcycle again. Later that month they went to Prescott to buy Petitioner a car. She came separately, and when she arrived Petitioner was gone. She was told that when told he couldn't get the car he wanted, Petitioner had gotten a blank look, started shaking and told his father he thought he could go crazy.

The next evening, a police officer came to their home because he had found their car abandoned in the middle of the road. The officer had gone to another scene, and when he came back the car was gone. He traced the plates to them. When she came to the door, Petitioner was talking to the officer. He said the officer was being rude and would have to talk to him in court, and slammed the door. Petitioner then went down to his room and climbed out the window. Petitioner's father went out to talk to the policeman. When he got back he said he had had Petitioner arrested and understood what she had been telling him about Petitioner's changes in demeanor.

They searched his room and found marijuana seeds. They told the people at juvenile detention to tell him they would not agree to bring him home until he gave them the combination to the safe in his room. He gave it to them and inside they found marijuana seeds and paraphernalia, a copy of "An Anarchists Cookbook," and a notebook with illogical writings in it.

They decided to have Petitioner committed to Aspen Hill. She was unhappy with the care he was receiving, so they took him home against medical advice. He had tested positive for marijuana and promised not to use it anymore and to go to counseling. She saw some improvement in him during the three days he was in Aspen Hill, and for 24 hours after coming home. Then he became more paranoid than ever.

Petitioner began closing all the blinds in the house, turning all the lights on, and locking the doors. If she went to get the mail, he would lock the door behind her. He kept saying "they" were after him and tried to poison him, but wouldn't tell her who "they" were or she would be in danger too.

Petitioner got a cat, but kept its food and box locked up in his room where the cat couldn't get to them. She bought the cat toys and he told her she could have the cat because she made it love her more than him.

He began putting Neosporin and bandages on his fingers, saying that he could tell he had been poisoned because his cuticles were messed up. He would go through many tubes of Neosporin and boxes of 500 bandages. He complained he coughed up brown stuff and it was proof he was being poisoned.

He stopped sleeping in his own room, and put a sleeping bag in their computer room. He put 3 or 4 floor length mirrors around the room, strung fishing line with wind chimes on the door, and set cardboard up around the sleeping bag. When asked, he would explain that "they" were after him.

He did not want to return to his high school for his junior year and wouldn't play football because another player was going to get a jersey with his number on it. She met with the school and they decide to have him take correspondence courses.

In November, 1999, he became obsessed with Y2K, and that the world was going to end. He took a debit card from his father and purchased $1700 of survival gear. They never knew where he kept it. The discovered the missing money and asked him about it. He said he would pay them back if he survived Y2K.

On New Year's Day, 2000, he was ecstatic he had survived and said he was ready to go back to school. He seemed to get better for a short time. Then he would return to bizarre behavior, like wearing shower caps on his head, wearing rubber gloves around the house or when he worked in the yard, with work gloves over them. He would wear little knit gloves, and knee high stockings. And then he would stop for a while.

He had always been very popular, had been voted home coming royalty his freshmen and sophomore years, but by March of 1999 had stopped taking calls from friends, and stayed home. He had become childlike and clung to his mother. He would only watch cartoons or the comedy channel. He changed the posters in his room from rap stars to Disney or cartoon characters. He began writing symbols in the ceiling of his room. That began in November, 1999 but had become more so by April thru June, 2000.

He began washing his clothes over and over, using a box of detergent for 30 or 40 loads in three days for his own clothes.

In December, 1999, he told her some rap stars were going to nominate him to be president of the United States and asked her if she would vote for him. He did not seem to understand what he was talking about.

By February, 2000, she had decided that his behaviors were mental illness. In March and April, she began to get calls from the school, with teachers complaining that he was laughing inappropriately in class, sitting staring at people with a blank look on his face, flicking a pen at them and wouldn't stop when asked.

He would come to her office and start sobbing. She came to his office on April 19, 2000, and began sobbing, saying he couldn't take it anymore, he was ready to go to heaven, and "they" were after him. She was worried he was going to commit suicide. She made an appointment with a psychologist, but Petitioner said he didn't need to go, but needed to take a test at school. They tried numerous times over the next months to get him to go in. She tried to arrange a home visit by the psychologist, but the psychologist cancelled because her malpractice insurance wouldn't let her go to the home.

Petitioner was arrested on April 24 for DUI and possession of drugs. They begged the juvenile people to keep him because of his mental health issues, but they released him. They had hired attorney Middlebrooks to try to get the authorities to keep him and press charges.

Petitioner's condition vacillated between June of 1999 and June of 2000. After his arrest in April, 2000, his condition began to snowball.

Around the time of his fight at the party, she was trying to have him committed at places in Cottonwood and Tucson, and afterwards contacted attorney Middlebrooks to see if Petitioner could be prosecuted over the fight.

By June, Petitioner was filthy. He claimed to be showering at the athletic club, but did not appear to be using soap or shampoo. He had begun wearing layers of clothes and would wear the same ones for a week at a time.

The Monday before the shooting, Petitioner came to her to complaining about warts on his hands. She said she would take him in if he changed his clothes. Instead of taking off the layers of dirty clothes, he put a clean shirt over the top of them. She told him she was still trying to find a place to take him. He said he didn't believe her, and he knew what she was doing because he had a third eye in the back of his head. He began calling her by her middle name, Maria, and he referred to her as an alien. He began sobbing and said how would you like to be me and never know who your real mother is? He said, I know that you love me because you raised me, but I wish I knew who my real mother was. She followed him to his room and said she was his real mother. He got the blank look on his face and said whatever. She believed he truly thought she was an alien and not his mother. She did not believe Eric could distinguish between what was real and what was not.

He had stopped being able to complete tasks like cleaning chores. He was unable to get good grades, even though he was working at his [*189] school work. He had begun throwing his clothes away. At the end of May or beginning of June, she had bought him new shoes. He threw them away, asked for new shoes, and refused to wear the old ones she had taken out of the garbage, but instead began wearing a pair of his father's shoes. He wouldn't eat food served at the house, and would buy prepackaged foods from a gas station. He wouldn't be able to think or plan ahead. He would ask her to take him to the gas station for food, and then 30 minutes later ask to be taken back to get water, and then later to get something else. He kept his clothes in his backpack or a garbage bag. If he was going to leave without the bag, he would make her promise to stay home and watch the bag.

When his license was taken after the DUI, Petitioner told her he was thankful because he felt he could no longer concentrate to drive, and had almost been in a couple of accidents. He had gotten to where he could not concentrate to read, but could only look at pictures in magazines. Near the beginning of May, he signed up for soccer, but didn't seem able to perform the drills or keep up with the other players, and quit.

The day before the shooting, as she left for work, Petitioner was up, having watched the movie The Matrix all night. He said he believed The Matrix was real, and would not believe it when she told him it was just a movie. They later went to the movie theater, and left him there to call for a ride later if he needed one. (Exhibit DD, R.T. 8/20/03 at 192-243.)

In late April, she met with his teachers and told them she thought he was mentally ill. They talked about his bizarre behaviors. People seemed to assume they resulted from drugs. She tried to explain to the teachers that it was from mental illness, and asked for help getting him through the school year. Some of them cried and they said they were willing to help.

Prior to his arrest in April, he had screwed eye hooks into the walls of his room, strung them with fishing line with craft beads and wind chimes on them, and would arrange glasses of water behind the door after it was shut so the beads would move, the wind chimes would ring, and the glasses would fall if the door was opened. Sometime in February he started urinating and defecating with the bathroom door open. His sister complained, but it didn't seem to matter to him. He eventually stopped flushing the toilet.

In the fall of 1999, she noticed that his CDs were skipping. He had scratched his name into the back of them. He didn't seem to notice that they skipped, and continued to listen to them.

About a month before Petitioner was arrested, he had said he wanted a heater for his room and she took him to Walmart, but told him she thought the heaters were seasonal and wouldn't be in stock. An employee confirmed that they didn't have any heaters. Petitioner still walked up and down the aisles looking, cussed her out as they left and tried to take the car keys from her. She called her husband who confronted Petitioner about it when Petitioner got home. Petitioner got a blank look on his face and didn't remember what had happened at the Walmart.

After his arrest, he called and said he had been walking down the street and the police started chasing him and he didn't know why. While Petitioner was in custody, he made references to the CIA and the government and that they could release him if they wanted to. His condition seemed to get worse. He would not shower, and when forced to would just stand under the water. He inexplicably poured water over his papers and pictures. When she would call to talk to him he was very suspicious. During one call he started yelling through the phone as though he thought someone were telling her what to say and he wanted them to stop.

On August 20, 2000, Petitioner called home and was frantic to tell them a story, but wanted to tell each of them separately. He kept calling back for a period of an hour and a half. He told them a story about Aaron. He had never told stories like that before. He said it was Aaron's story, but would occasionally say "Eric" instead of Aaron. He said Flagstaff was a mirage and a platinum city for aliens. There were 50,000 aliens and only about 1,000 real people in the city. Aaron was a real person being held hostage because he knows too many things and has the keys to the doors, and they keep saying they will release him, but they don't do it because they are afraid of his powers. They torture and electrocute him to get the answers. Aliens live forever and they can be destroyed only by bullets. As he kept calling back, he kept embellishing on the story, but sometimes they couldn't understand what he was saying.

A couple of days later, Petitioner called back and all he said was Teresa, I don't have anything to say to you but if I get released today will you come pick me up. They got no more phone calls from him and he refused to see them until November, after he had been medicated with anti-psychotic medication.

The night of the shooting, while they were at the movies, Petitioner's behavior was normal for him. (Exhibit EE, R.T. 8/21/03 at 4-60.)

Carden Hakes testified that he met Petitioner through Petitioner's sister. He saw Petitioner at the Harkins theater on June 20th. Petitioner was slumped on a bench, his eyes appeared half closed, and he seemed intoxicated. Petitioner's parents were with him and walked up and said hello. (Exhibit EE, R.T. 8/21/03 at 61-67.)

Aaron Fitzhugh testified that he had known Petitioner since they were in the 4th grade. Up to March and April 2000, he noted that Petitioner had become withdrawn, and his appearance and dress had changed. On June 16 or 17, 2000, he hosted a party, where they were drinking beer. Petitioner arrived and began smoking marijuana. They were in the back yard, and Petitioner went inside and locked them out. He though it odd that Petitioner had come because he had not been invited. His friend Brandon began talking to him about how much Petitioner had changed since junior high. Petitioner was behind Brandon and started yelling at Brandon and then punched Brandon. He pulled Petitioner off of Brandon, and his nose was bleeding. Petitioner then threw Brandon to the ground again, and Aaron pulled him off again. At that point, Petitioner had a blank stare on his face like he didn't know what he was doing. Petitioner seemed confused and went to the side of the house. He came back and fumbled with his ankle and waistband and a dark object, then went through the house, sprayed beer around, yelled to not call the cops, and then ran off. (Exhibit EE, R.T. 8/21/03 at 67-80.)

Carlos Perez testified he met Petitioner when Petitioner was playing freshman football. In the summer of 1999, he began smoking marijuana with Petitioner, and Petitioner seemed to be paranoid. (Exhibit EE, R.T. 8/21/03 at 81.)

Summary re Defense's Lay Witness Evidence of Mental Condition - The foregoing evidence presents the picture of a teenager who became increasingly delusional and paranoid, to the point that he had become convinced that he was surrounded by those intent upon killing him and that even those closest to him, his parents, were aliens. Those delusions and paranoia had, by the time of the shooting, progressed to the point that every aspect of Petitioner's mental and external life were permeated by his irrational fears. And, the evidence suggested that Petitioner had developed sudden, violent outbursts, which were marked by irrationality.

Third, there was additional "observation evidence" from the experts from which an inference could be made that Petitioner lacked the requisite *mens rea.* As recognized by the Court in *Clark, Mott* did not preclude the consideration of observation testimony by an expert witness that did not go "to mental defect or disease, and its effect on the cognitive or moral capacities on which sanity depends under the Arizona rule. *548 U.S. at 760.* Thus, the Arizona Court of Appeals would have found that the trial court should have considered itself free to consider testimony by the experts "such as descriptions of a defendant's tendency to think in a certain way or his behavioral characteristics." *Id.*

In evaluating this testimony, the undersigned does not look through to the various hearsay records, statements, etc. and other non-admissible evidence upon which an expert may normally rely in reaching an expert opinion. *See e.g. Ariz. R. Evid. 703.* The *Clark* court provided no guidance on the handing of testimony which might be impacted by such information, or how to parse out the purely observation based testimony. Where in doubt, the undersigned has shied away from testimony by the experts which had the appearance of deriving from such non-admissible sources rather than from the expert's own personal observations or statements by Petitioner. With regard to statements by Petitioner, where the relation of those statements was not offered to prove the truth of the matter asserted by Petitioner, but to reflect his demeanor or thought processes, the undersigned does include them. *See Ariz. R. Evid. 801(c)* (defining hearsay as statements "offered in evidence to prove the truth of the matter asserted"). Likewise, where the statements were elicited by the prosecution, they are considered as an admission by a party-opponent, and thus not hearsay. *See Ariz. R. Evid. 801(d)(2).*

Finally, in evaluating this evidence, the undersigned considers it comparatively less weighty than testimony concerning Petitioner's conduct and statements prior to his arrest, in light of the potential for Petitioner to be manipulative in an attempt to exonerate himself.

Defense Expert - The defense's expert witness, Dr. Morenz, testified that in his conversation with Petitioner the morning of Morenz's testimony, Petitioner's comments were fairly bizarre and made no sense. Petitioner continued to profess a belief that his mother was an alien and there were 50,000 aliens in Flagstaff, although he didn't believe they were as malevolent as they used to be. Petitioner continued to profess a belief that he was not mentally ill, and that the medicines being given to him were poisoning him. He continued to profess his innocence of the crime, but proffered no means to prove it. (Exhibit FF, R.T. 8/22/03 at 28-32, 45.) Petitioner never volunteered his belief in aliens, but when questioned directly about it he would at least admit his belief that people are sometimes aliens. (*Id.* at 43.)

He met with Petitioner four times, including an attempt to interview him to determine his competency. Petitioner refused to communicate with him. When he met with Petitioner and defense counsel, Petitioner again refused to communicate. (*Id.* at 63-64.) The third time he met with Petitioner, Petitioner denied any involvement with the shooting. Petitioner claimed he had gone to the movies with his parents, met a girl named Sarah, and went to Lake Powell with her, spent some time there and came back, and shortly after he was arrested. (*Id.* at 65-66.) Petitioner admitted to smoking marijuana most evenings and drinking most weekends in the months leading up to the shooting. (*Id.* at 67-68.) Petitioner admitted to using marijuana and alcohol since the 8th or 9th grade. (*Id.* at 79.) Petitioner claimed that in the weeks or months before the shooting, he had gone to a party and a dance. (*Id.* at 71.) Petitioner denied use of LSD and other drugs. (*Id.* at 72.) Petitioner professed that his family were his best friends but his parents may be aliens. Petitioner denied having hallucinations, mind control or telepathic communications. (*Id.* at 73.) Petitioner never defined what an alien was nor did he refer to the police as aliens. (*Id.* at 75.)

In cross examining Dr. Morenz, the prosecution elicited testimony drawn from his reading of medical records where Petitioner was recorded as referring to the guards at the Coconino County Jail as "aliens." (*Id.* at 77.)

Prosecution Expert - The prosecution's expert, Dr. Moran, testified that during his first interview with Petitioner on June 27, 2003, Petitioner reported that he was not present at the time of the shooting, but had spent a day in Page, Arizona with a girl by the name of Sarah that he had met. When asked about the fishing line in his car and room, Petitioner explained that he didn't want anyone messing with them. When asked who he thought would mess with them, Petitioner said aliens, and that he thinks aliens look like people, terrestrial sophisticated people. He first had the idea of aliens was when he decided to get home schooled and prepared for Y2K. He thought one of the reasons he was put in jail was because the aliens hated him. He thought Flagstaff was full of aliens, and that his mother, father, sister and brother were aliens. He thought the aliens were from a different planet, and look like human beings. He doesn't know why they are here, and didn't know whether the doctors in the room were aliens. The aliens live like human beings and were possibly expanding to trade for stuff like sugar and broccoli. He used to think they were trying to kill him, but he didn't think they were any more. He thought they wanted him dead and were trying to poison him through his clothes and food, and they poisoned him badly at the Coconino County Jail, but he wasn't sure whether they were aliens or humans. He was very sick for three months and was peeing on himself and going to the infirmary. He was a little sick for an entire year. (Exhibit GG, R.T. 8/26/03 at 16-21.)

Petitioner told him that the night of the shooting, his parents had left him at the movie theater and he had gone back in to watch a movie and met a girl there by herself by the name of Sarah. She asked if he wanted to go to Page for the day. She left to go home to get her bathing suit. He went to the Walmart bus stop to wait for her. She picked him up at 1:30 and they drove to Page and spent the day on the beach and went to McDonald's for lunch. He didn't know her last name but had her phone number on a piece of paper in his pants when he was arrested, but the police lost it. The left Page as the sun was going down and she dropped him off around 8:30. He walked home and then the police arrested him and he didn't know why. (*Id.* at 21-22.)

In the second interview on July 11, 2003, Petitioner told him that he first experimented with drugs in the 7th grade, and for three months would smoke marijuana on the weekends. In the summer of 9th grade, he began smoking marijuana on a daily basis and to drink to intoxication on the weekends. His marijuana use increased when he got his car in September of 1998, and he began smoking three or four times per day, sometimes at school, during lunch and after school. On weekends he of the drank to intoxication, sometimes to the point of vomiting. (*Id.* at 23-24.)

Dr. Moran testified that during questioning, Petitioner provided answers showing his thought patterns were unrealistically virtuous, *i.e.* that he would not admit common foibles, he was extremely angry and suspicious that others were taking advantage of him. He was sensitive to criticism, aloof, detached, and "regularly moralistic." (*Id.* at 24-25.) He reacted to threats by projecting and rationalizing, and took little responsibility for his problems, blaming others and holding grudges. He endorsed a number of bizarre thoughts, such as that he has special mystical powers or a special mission in life that others don't understand. He was rigid in relationships and had a closed attitude towards others' viewpoints. (*Id.* at 25-26.)

On cross-examination, Dr. Moran testified that when he interviewed Petitioner he was cooperative, but under the influence of Haldol, an antipsychotic medication. Petitioner told him that he shook his pen because it was a laser that only aliens could see. He believed one of the reasons he was put in jail was because the aliens hated him. He though Flagstaff was full of aliens, and his family were aliens. Petitioner continued to believe that aliens inhabit the planet to expand their territory and trade for broccoli and sugar. Prior to the shooting the aliens were constantly trying to poison him through his food, his clothes, his food at the jail, and in his car. He had the bird in his car like a coal miner's bird to test for poisoned air. He believed the aliens had at some point replaced the bird with a robotic one so he couldn't tell if he was being poisoned. He believed his parents were aliens, and that they were keeping their identities secret from him. When he decided not to play football in his junior year, he believed the aliens had poisoned him. (*Id.* at 103-109.)

Petitioner never attempted to use his belief in aliens as an excuse for his behaviors. (*Id.* at 135.) Petitioner said when he met Sarah at the movie theater he already has his bathing suit on. (*Id.* at 146.) He thought someone was out to get him because his clothes didn't feel clean and he thought they were poisoned. When he opened the door to his car, the air inside seemed poisoned, so he thought the aliens were trying to get to him. He believed the aliens could read your thoughts, and know whether you were moving from the right side of your brain to the left side. He believed they were doing research on Jupiter and Mars and could put thoughts in people's heads, but they have not done it to him. (*Id.* at 168-169.)

Fourth, there was no direct evidence and little circumstantial evidence to controvert Petitioner's evidence suggesting that he was responding to a paranoid delusion at the time that he shot Officer Moritz. As summarized by the Arizona Court of Appeals the evidence of Petitioner's *mens rea*, included: (1) Petitioner's pre-existing anger at police; (2) actions that indicated an intention to attract a police officer (e.g. repeatedly driving in circles with music blaring); (3) the anti-police music played by Petitioner at the time; (4) the close range of the shot; (5) the angle of the shot (from behind the victim); (6) witness statements indicating the victim's attempt to evade Petitioner's shots; (7) Petitioner's flight from the scene; (8) and the uniform worn by the victim and his marked patrol car, and engaged siren and emergency lights. (Exhibit RR, Mem. Dec. 1/25/05 at 8-10.)

The Arizona Court of Appeals did not seem to rely upon the efforts by the prosecution at trial to suggest that Petitioner's behavior was the result of drug usage. The defense made great headway in showing that none of the witnesses ever saw Petitioner using drugs other than marijuana and alcohol. Indeed, Officer Schmidt could not recall having any witness tell him they had actually observed Plaintiff dealing or doing drugs [beyond marijuana]. (Exhibit EE, R.T. 8/21/03 at 110.) Aside from the speculation of heavy drug use by those observing Petitioner's bizarre behaviors, the only connection of Petitioner with drugs other than marijuana was his possession of LSD tablets at the time of his DUI arrest.

Much of that evidence was not contradictory to evidence of Petitioner's paranoid delusions.

For example, (2) driving in circles in the middle of the night with music blaring was as much indicative of a paranoid and delusional teenager, as it was of one plotting to assassinate a police officer. Petitioner had a track record of irrational behavior while driving, such as leaving his car unattended in the middle of the road in the middle of the night. (Exhibit DD, R.T. 8/20/03 at 202-203.) Moreover, there was testimony that Petitioner had begun to turning up the volume on the TV and on music, and leaving it on. Petitioner's brother testified that Petitioner "[left the TVs on all the time." (Exhibit DD, R.T. 8/20/03 at 65.) Petitioner's father testified that Petitioner would "leave water running, lights on, TV on loud." (Exhibit DD, R.T. 8/20/03 at 124.)

Moreover, the testimony showed that Officer Moritz radioed prior to stopping and leaving his vehicle, that Petitioner had started "running from me." (Exhibit V, R.T. 8/5/03 at 63.) Running from the police officer seems not to indicate a plan to trap the officer, as much as surprise and dismay at being pulled over.

Similarly, Petitioner's shooting of the officer, (4) from a close range and (5) behind the officer, (6) even as the officer attempted to evade him, and (7) subsequent flight from the scene are not inconsistent with a paranoid delusion that the officer was an alien intent on killing him.

Nor would Petitioner's having hidden the weapon near his home necessarily be indicative of a plan to shoot a police officer. Petitioner's parents testified that upon finding Petitioner with a gun prior to the date of the shooting, they had directed Petitioner to keep it out of the house, and he purported to have returned it to its owner. (Exhibit EE, R.T. 8/21/03 at 46-47.) Assuming Petitioner was acting in fear of perceived threats to his life, it is reasonable to infer that he had simply hidden the weapon away, somewhere accessible to him, and on the day of the shooting would have again hidden it prior to returning home. Indeed, the fact that he hid the weapon in such an easily discovered manner (e.g. in his hat laying along a fence next to a shed (Exhibit W, R.T. 8/6/03 at 3-6) is more indicative of someone seeking to preserve a source of protection than someone seeking to dispose of incriminating evidence.

Nor would (8) the clear identification of Officer Moritz as a police officer be inconsistent with paranoid delusions. A malevolent alien in a police uniform, driving a squad car with lights and sirens, is still a malevolent alien. Petitioner's delusions did not sway toward little green men, but instead saw aliens in seemingly ordinary people such as his parents.

For the same reason, Petitioner's antipathy to the police in general would not be inconsistent with the evidence of his paranoid delusions. The prosecution pointed to essentially two things to suggest that

Petitioner had such antipathy: (1) his pre-existent anger towards police; and (3) his playing of a CD with anti-police lyrics.

To show Petitioner's anger towards police, the prosecution elicited evidence of: (a) anti-police statements by Petitioner; and (b) the occurrence at Thorpe Park when Petitioner indicated he would shoot a police officer.

Anti-Police Statements - Jason Tackett (one of the drug addicts present in the Thorpe Park incident) was a school mate of Petitioner's, testified that one day a month or more prior to the shooting, as Petitioner passed by Tackett heard him mumbling to himself about being upset about how "someone had been arrested unjustly and that he ... wanted to prove his point to the police." (Exhibit Y, R.T. 8/7/03 at 17.)

On the other hand, Petitioner's friend Victor Meza testified that Petitioner was defensive of the police, although he complained that when arrested at his father's insistence Petitioner felt like the police had used "extra force" on him. (Exhibit BB, R.T. 8/12/03 at 38.) Meza explained that Petitioner had always been incredulous at his friends' claims of police brutality, until after his arrest when he became "more open-minded to that they could be - - they could be guilty for things, too." (Exhibit BB, R.T. 8/12/03 at 54.)

Thorpe Park Incident - In his argument on the motion for directed verdict, the prosecution argued that Petitioner had made comments at Thorpe Park about "a plan he had, about how he was going to fire his .22, he was going to go up on a hill and fire his .22 rifle - - I'm sorry - - handgun, and when the police came, he was going to lure them out of their cars and he was going to shoot them in the head with his .22." (Exhibit BB, R.T. 8/12/03 at 26-27.) The closest testimony to this was that by Jason Tackett, when he adopted his original statement to police:

Q. And just for clarity's sake, this is the statement that was attributed to you, and this interview was on July 1st of 2000, and on page 3 you were asked, and this is again what Mr. Middlebrooks read to you, " Do you remember his exact words? What was said?" And your answer was "'If I came up here with my .22 caliber hand pistol - - hand pistol - - hand gun and started firing off, when the police come I will get them out of their cars and start - - I have rifles and I'll start shooting them in the head,' that's what he said." Then you go on, talk about Don telling him to take off. Now is that as accurately as you recall exactly what he said to you on that day?

A. Yes, sir, it is.

(Exhibit Y, R.T. 8/7/03 at 16-17.) In contrast, his unaided testimony was quite different:

Q. Tell me what happened when [the defendant] first approached. Did he talk to anyone in particular?

A. I initiated a conversation with him, I said, "Hey, Eric, how you doing?", and he kind of went off about he wanted to shoot Officer Moritz to get the emergency response out there, and he was going to hide up in the hills with a rifle and start picking them off like a sniper would.

(Exhibit Y, R.T. 8/7/03 at 11.)

Moreover, Mr. Tackett reported that he had suffered a five year void in his memory as a result of his use of drugs including crystal meth and cocaine, which surrounded the time span of the Thorpe Park incident. (*See* Exhibit Y, R.T. 8/7/03 at 14-15, 21-24.) In addition, Tackett was a two time convicted felon on probation at the time of his testimony. (*Id.* at 22-23.)

Further, Tackett testified that Petitioner's threats against the police were almost instantaneous upon joining the group and were unprovoked. (*Id.* at 31.) In contrast, Mark Fields testified that Petitioner's comments were in response to demands that he put away his beer. (Exhibit Y, R.T. 8/7/03 at 43-44.)

Fields was himself a 20-year marijuana user, four-year cocaine user, and admitted to smoking marijuana just prior to the Petitioner's arrival at the park. He was also a convicted felon. (*Id.* at 47,51.)

Even if Tackett and Fields' story is wholly believed, the testimony indicated that Petitioner was behaving in an erratic manner consistent with his increasingly paranoid and delusional state, albeit attributed by the witnesses to drug usage. Tackett testified:

Q. . . . . You were with him for five or ten minutes that day, and you had seen him stoned, I guess, when you smoked marijuana together. Did you feel he was under the influence of any type of substance at the time?

A. I believe he was, but there's no way of telling for certain. He had the facial expressions and the eyes that kind of stated that he was a little strung out on something.

Q. Well, you had seen him stoned on marijuana?

A. Yes.

Q. Did he have that look?

A. No, he did not. He had the look of either cocaine or methamphetamine in his system.

Q. Now, had you seen him under the influence of coke or meth in the past?

A. No. I'm a recovering drug addict myself, and I used both of those, so I know what it looks like on myself and people that I used to use with, and it's the same look that he had that day, that paranoid look. Eyes kind of shrunk in, black rings around, looking around like he was paranoid.

(Exhibit Y, R.T. 8/7/03 at 13-14.)

Fields testified:

Q. Well, what was his - - what was he like when he first came up before he pulled out the beer?

A. Kind of staggering, looked like he had been under the influence already. I smelled some alcohol on him. I was talking to a young lady at the time.

Q. How would you characterize the smell of alcohol?

A. Heavy.

Q. Did you also suspect that he was on something other than alcohol?

A. Yes, sir. Some kind of narcotic, it wasn't your street marijuana or something, it was - - could have been more hallucinogenic or even cocaine. Didn't seem like it was cocaine, though.

THE COURT: It did not or did? Did you say it did or did not seem like--?

THE WITNESS: It didn't seem like he was on cocaine at the time, it was just like, you know, he was, I don't know, in and out, so I came to the conclusion it could have been a hallucinogenic of some sort.

(Exhibit Y, R.T. 8/7/03 at 45 (Fields).)

Anti-Police Lyrics - The Arizona Court relied upon evidence that "Clark was playing a 'rap CD' at the time that contained 'many antisocial attitudes' and included lyrics expressing violent attitudes toward police officers." (Exhibit RR, Mem. Dec. 1/25/05 at 8.) This apparently came from testimony by the state's expert, Dr. Moran, that he had reviewed a CD by "Dr. Dre" identified to him as the one confiscated from the truck driven by Petitioner, and that it "contained many antisocial attitudes" and included "something to the effect of fuck the cops." (Exhibit GG, R.T. 8/26/03 at 15.) The only other located testimony on the contents of Petitioner's music came from officer Dale Young who simply characterized the lyrics of the CD in the truck as "strange music with strange lyrics." Young testified that he later searched Petitioner's bedroom for "Satanic music or something that might refer to the homicides of a police officer" (Exhibit W, R.T. 8/6/03 at 12-13.) But, the officer testified that no CDs with "lyrics about killing a police officer" was found. (*Id.* at 35.)

In 1988, the musical artist "Dr. Dre" released an album with the "gangsta" hip hop group "N.W.A." entitled "Straight Out of Compton" which included the track "Fuck the Police." In the March 28, 1995 obituary of the album's executive producer, Eric "Eazy-E" Wright, the New York Times described a "song that is a fantasy of violent revenge against racist police officers" and reported that "the Federal Bureau of Investigation wrote to N.W.A.'s label, Ruthless Records, protesting it would incite violence against law enforcement personnel." *See* http://query.nytimes.com/gst/fullpage.html?res=990CE 6DB1F3EF93BA15750C0A963958260, last accessed 4/14/11.

The undersigned is not inclined to assign significant weight to Petitioner's possession of a popular rap CD containing anti-police lyrics. The fact that such lyrics were an isolated instance in Petitioner's music library makes it even harder to assign meaning to it. While it certainly has some meaning that it was the CD that was in the vehicle with Petitioner, there was no testimony that the CD actually belonged to Petitioner, or that he had otherwise chosen it as the CD to be in the vehicle, or even that it was actually the music he was playing (let alone the particular song), as opposed to (for example) a radio station. Indeed, Petitioner's mother had testified that in the fall of 1999, Petitioner had ruined all his CDs by scratching his name on them, but continued to play them even though they repeatedly skipped. (Exhibit EE, R.T. 8/21/03 at 7-8.) This would suggest that Petitioner's music listening was not a rational endeavor by one seeking to absorb lyrics or appreciate musical ability as much as simply fill the air with noise.

While the anti-police statements and the Thorpe Park incident (and to whatever extent the Dr. Dre CD might be deemed meaningful) show a growing distrust of and antipathy towards the police, Petitioner's attitudes were consistent with a paranoid delusion of a town full of aliens some of whom were out to get Petitioner. Indeed, who more likely to be a malevolent alien than those who demonstrated forceful, invasive and coercive behavior against him?

Fifth, although the trial judge determined that Petitioner was not legally insane at the time of the shooting, based upon the conclusion that he knew his actions were wrong, that finding would not preclude a determination that Petitioner lacked the requisite *mens rea*, for at least two reasons.

First, the burdens of proof are different in degree and direction. The defense bore the burden of proof of insanity, by clear and convincing evidence. *Ariz. Rev. Stat. § 13-502(C)*. (Exhibit II, R.T. 9/3/03 at 4.). The prosecution bore the burden of proof of intent beyond a reasonable doubt. Thus a mere reasonable doubt that Petitioner's actions were the result of an intent to kill a police officer, as opposed to his delusions, would have been sufficient for a not guilty verdict, but not sufficient to establish legal insanity.

Second, the insanity determination hinges upon a finding whether the defendant could comprehend that his actions would be deemed morally wrong by the community. Under *Ariz. Rev. Stat. § 13-502*, "the term 'wrong' for purposes of the insanity defense should be defined by a community standard of morality and not the defendant's personal beliefs." *State v. Tamplin, 195 Ariz. 246, 248-249, 986 P.2d 914, 917 (Ariz.App. 1999)*. As noted by the trial court in rendering judgment, there was evidence that suggested Petitioner knew his actions would be considered wrong by the community, *e.g.* his running, hiding, etc. (Exhibit II, R.T. 9/3/03 at 5-6.)

Conversely, however, the prosecution was required to prove not merely that when Petitioner pulled the trigger he knew his conduct to be morally unacceptable to the community, but that Petitioner's subjective belief at that moment was that he was killing a police officer. The trial court could (with benefit of the observation evidence) have concluded that Petitioner believed the officer to be an alien (and thus not a police officer) and yet have simultaneously believed the community would not have accepted that knowledge and would have found his actions morally wrong. Had the trial court done so, it could have rejected the insanity plea, but still have found Petitioner not guilty.

(5) Summary re Appellate Court's Grant of Relief - The Arizona Court of Appeals would have been faced with substantial observation evidence that Petitioner was delusional and paranoid at the time of the shooting, and that in his delusions and paranoia he believed himself to be in mortal danger of aliens who appeared to be normal people. A reasonable juror could have readily concluded that rather than laying a trap to catch a police officer, and then shooting the captured police officer to act out some rational anger towards the police, Petitioner instead found himself driving in circles, music blaring in an effort to escape the delusions that tormented him, and then when faced with a very real embodiment of his paranoia, he acted to protect himself from what he believed to be an alien impostor. As such, there is at least a reasonable probability that the Arizona Court would have found itself unable to say that, beyond a reasonable doubt, the exclusion of that observation evidence had not affected the verdict.

Even if the undersigned were to consider only the "observation evidence" provided through lay witnesses (as opposed to the defense's and state's experts), the undersigned would reach the same conclusion.

(e) Conclusion re Ineffectiveness re Preservation of Claim

For the foregoing reasons, the undersigned concludes that Petitioner was prejudiced as a result of trial counsel's defective performance in failing to make an offer of proof of evidence excluded by the trial court under *Mott.*

Petitioner having established deficient performance, and the Arizona court's rejection of the claim on the lack thereof having been contrary to the holding of *Strickland*, and having established prejudice, this Court must conclude that Petitioner received ineffective assistance of counsel and is entitled to issuance of the writ as a result thereof.

7. Summary re Ineffective Assistance of Counsel

Based upon the foregoing, the undersigned concludes that all of Petitioner's properly exhausted claims of ineffective assistance are without merit, except that based upon counsel's failure to properly preserve the "observational evidence" claim for appellate review.

K. SUMMARY RE PETITION

Petitioner has asserted seven grounds for relief. As to Ground One (Substantial Evidence), the portion based upon the defense's "observation evidence" is procedurally defaulted, and the portion based upon the prosecution's evidence is without merit. Ground Two (Sanity Determination) is procedurally defaulted. Ground Three (Cruel and Unusual Punishment) is without merit. Ground Four (Competency) is procedurally barred. As to Ground Five (Ineffective Assistance), the portion based on trial counsel's conflict of interest is procedurally defaulted. The portions related to (1) the Parrish report; (2) competency during trial; (3) waiver of the jury; and (4) limited use of experts are without merit. The portion related to failure to preserve the observational evidence claim has merit. Ground Six (Prosecutorial Misconduct) and Ground Seven (Ineffectiveness of Appellate Counsel) are procedurally defaulted. Petitioner has failed to excuse his procedural defaults and procedural bar, and those claims should be dismissed with prejudice. The Petition should be granted as to that portion of Ground Five based on trial counsel's failure to preserve the observations evidence claim, and denied as to the balance of the Petition.

Accordingly, the undersigned will recommend that the Court's Writ of Habeas Corpus be granted.

L. PROPER REMEDY

The undersigned has concluded that Petitioner is held in violation of the United States Constitution, and is entitled to relief under *28 U.S.C. § 2254. Section 2243* of the Judicial Code directs that the Court "dispose of the [petition]...as law and justice require." *28 U.S.C. § 2243.*

Habeas remedies generally consist of unconditional release or conditional release, the former being reserved for those situations where the fact of the prosecution and not the manner of the prosecution was illegal, *e.g.*double jeopardy, absence of jurisdiction, etc., or where the violation was egregious, the consequences grave and the term already served makes a retrial unjust. Hertz & Liebman, *Federal Habeas Corpus Pract. & Proced* § 33.1, 33.2 (6th ed.).

"The typical relief granted in federal habeas corpus is a conditional order of release unless the State elects to retry the successful habeas petitioner." *Herrera v. Collins, 506 U.S. 390, 403, 113 S. Ct. 853, 122 L. Ed. 2d 203 (1993).* The undersigned finds no reason to depart from the general rule for the instant grant of relief founded upon ineffective assistance of counsel.

Accordingly, the undersigned will recommend that Petitioner be unconditionally released from all custody as a result of his conviction within 30 days of the issuance of the Court's judgment, unless the State of Arizona sooner elects to retry him on the charges, and within a reasonable time thereafter commences retrial.

STEVEN MICHAEL FERNANDEZ, PETITIONER, VS. CHARLES L. RYAN, ET AL., RESPONDENTS. NO. CV 08-358-TUC-FRZ (BPV) UNITED STATES DISTRICT COURT FOR THE DISTRICT OF ARIZONA

(Text added and modified for emphasis) As a matter of regular practice the Attorney General's Office consistently fails to advise the federal courts that in Arizona counsel fail to advise inmates the time frames for filing federal habeas and paralegals do not assist inmates by policy. There are too many such incidents which constitute a pattern. As this is a pattern with the Arizona Attorney General's Office this should constitute fraud upon the court, because, they are concealing facts on a systemic basis, to defeat valid claims.

COUNSEL: Steven Michael Fernandez, Petitioner, Pro se, TUCSON, AZ. For D Schriro, Respondent: Amy Pignatella Cain, Office of the Attorney General, Tucson, AZ.

I. Factual and Procedural Background

A. Plea Agreement

Petitioner was charged in Graham County Superior Court with one count each of: administration of a narcotic drug, a class 2 felony; possession of a narcotic drug, a class 4 felony; endangerment, a class 6 felony; possession of drug paraphernalia, a class 6 felony; and transfer of a narcotic drug, a class 2 felony, in CR2004-268 ("'268"). (Answer, Ex. A) On October 15, 2004, Petitioner was charged in CR2004-301 ("'301") with one count each of: attempt to obtain or procure the administration of a narcotic drug by fraud, deceit, misrepresentation or subterfuge, a class 4 felony; attempted fraudulent schemes and artifices, a class 4 felony; and three counts of forgery, class 4 felonies. (*Id.*) In both cases allegations of four prior felony convictions and four possessory convictions, as well as the aggravating factors of prior felony history and physical, emotional or financial harm caused to the victim or if the victim died as a result of the conduct of defendant, the emotional and financial harm caused to the victim's immediate family were filed. (*Id.*)

On March 28, 2005, Petitioner pled guilty in '268 to Count 1, attempted administration of a narcotic drug as a class 3 felony (amended), and Count 3, endangerment, a class 6 felony. (Answer, Ex. C, Reporter's Transcript ("R.T."), 3/28/05, at 3-4, 19-20.) As part of the plea agreement, Petitioner admitted a prior conviction for aggravated driving under the influence. (*Id.* at 3, 16-19.) That same date, Petitioner pled guilty in '301 to Count 4, forgery, a class 4 felony. (*Id.* at 7, 21-22.) All other allegations, as well as another case, CR 2004-307, were dismissed as part of the plea agreement. (*Id.*, and Answer, Ex. A at 2.) As part of the plea agreement, Petitioner agreed to give up the right to plead not guilty and the right to a jury trial, as well as "the right to a jury determination of any factor [the court] may use as an aggravator" beyond the presumptive term of 6.5 years, up to the cap of 10.5 years in '268. (Answer, Ex. C, R.T. 3/28/05 at 9.) The court stated that "we're waiving basically *Blakely* rights of a jury determination and empowering the judge to consider aggravating factors." (*Id.*) Counsel explained that he had "outlined that new change in the law" to his client by letter, and confirmed, on the record, that Petitioner understood that "there's been a change in the law," that Petitioner had "a right to have a jury determination of aggravating factors ... proven beyond a reasonable doubt." (*Id.* at 9-10) Counsel explained that if Petitioner accepted the plea agreement, he was "giving up that right and [the trial court] will make that determination by a much lower standard of proof, what is called preponderance of the evidence." (*Id.* at 10.) Petitioner advised that he understood, and agreed to give up that right. (*Id.*) Petitioner admitted the prior felony conviction of aggravated DUI. (*Id.* at 16.)

B. Sentencing

On May 19, 2005, the trial court sentenced Petitioner in '268 to the slightly aggravated term of 10.5 years' imprisonment for attempted administration of a narcotic drug and 1.5 years' imprisonment for endangerment, each with a prior conviction, to run concurrently. (Answer, Ex. D. R.T. 5/19/05 at 44-46.) The state produced certified copy of Petitioner's aggravated DUI conviction from 1991 in Pima County cause number CR 32171, and his conviction for aggravated assault in 1993, also out of Pima County, at the time of sentencing. (*Id.* at 21-22.) Petitioner did not object to the admission of these two priors for sentencing purposes. (*Id.* at 22.) The state also produced a certified copy of Petitioner's conviction for possession of drug paraphernalia, in Graham County cause number 2004-047. (*Id.* at 23.) Additional certified copies of convictions occurring more than ten years' prior in Pima County Superior Court were admitted, over Petitioner's objection, as "background information." (*Id.* at 24.) The trial court found Petitioner's "felony history" and "the emotional harm caused to the family of [his] victim" as aggravating factors. (*Id.* at 44.)

C. First Petition for Post-Conviction Relief

On July 15, 2005, Petitioner filed a *pro se* Notice of Post-Conviction Relief pursuant to Rule 32 of the Arizona Rules of Criminal Procedure. (Answer, Ex. E.) Appointed counsel informed the trial court that she was unable to raise any colorable claim and moved to withdraw and allow Petitioner to file a *pro se* petition. (Answer, Ex. F.) Petitioner filed a *pro se* petition for post-conviction relief on February 9, 2006, raising the following grounds for relief:

> (A) Petitioner's sentence violated his due process rights guaranteed by the *14th Amendment to the United States Constitution* because the trial court failed to comply with the mandates of *A.R.S. § 13-709(B)* by failing to credit Petitioner for his presentence incarceration; and
>
> (B) Petitioner's sentence violated his due process rights guaranteed by the *14th Amendment to the United States Constitution* because the trial court considered an improper aggravating factor of emotional harm caused to the family of the victim to increase the penalty for the offense in violation of *A.R.S. § 13-709(C)(9)*.

((Ex. G, at 3, 6.)

The trial court found Petitioner in error when he cited *A.R.S. § 137-09(C)(9)* when the correct reference is *A.R.S. § 13-702(C)(9)*. (Answer, Ex. A.)

On May 16, 2006, the trial court dismissed the petition for post-conviction relief finding that there are no claims that present a material issue of fact or law that would entitle Petitioner to a hearing or relief and that no purpose would be served by any further proceedings. (Answer, Ex. A.) Specifically, the trial court: (1) found under Arizona law that the trial court did not err in denying credit for time served in CR 2004-047 to be credited against the new time ordered in cause numbers '268, and '301; and (2) rejected Petitioner's claim that his sentence was unconstitutionally aggravated, finding that while the finding that there was significant harm to the victim's family that resulted from the death of the victim and that Petitioner's acts were clearly causal links in the victim's death were supported by Petitioner's statements and

Petitioner's plea to endangerment. (*Id.*) The trial court also found that, "[s]tanding alone, the substantial aggravator of felony history would still result in the slightly aggravated 10.5 years, even if the Court found that consideration of § 13-702(C)(9) "harm to the victim's family" was inappropriate. (*Id.*)

D. Motion for Reconsideration And Motion For The Appointment Of Advisory Counsel and Second Petition for Post-Conviction Relief

Petitioner filed a *pro se* motion for the appointment of advisory council. (Answer, Ex. K.) The trial court received the motion on November 29, 2006, although Petitioner signed and dated the motion May 25, 2006. (*Id.*) Petitioner requested advisory council to assist him in filing his motion to amend his Rule 32 to include claims of ineffective assistance of counsel, abuse of discretion by the trial court, and breach of the plea agreement by the state. (*Id.*)

Petitioner filed a motion for reconsideration and to amend pleadings. (Answer, Ex. L.) The trial court received the motion on November 29, 2006, although the document again reflected a signature and date of May 25, 2006. (Id. at 1,14.) Petitioner raised the following arguments in his motion:

(A) "Access to the courts;"
(B) "Court's abuse of discretion" related to Officer Orr's use of a polygraph test, a discussion that occurred before the tape recording of the Petitioner, and the classification of Count 1 as a class 3 felony instead of a class 4 after the count was amended to "attempt" and the imposition of an aggravated sentence which involved an issue "of *Blakely* character;" and
(C) "Ineffective assistance of counsel."
(*Id.* at 8-12.)

Petitioner filed a second petition for post-conviction relief. (Answer, Ex. M.) Again, the trial court received the motion on November 29, 2006, although the document reflected a signature and date of May 25, 2006. (*Id.*) Petitioner raised the following arguments in his petition:

(A) Petitioner is denied access to adequately trained legal assistance, and access to the tools required to adequately and effectively produce documents;

(B) Petitioner was sentenced in violation of the *Due Process Clause of the Fourteenth Amendment* and notice requirements of the *Sixth Amendment* because his plea agreement failed to put him on notice that he would be facing anything other than the presumptive sentence of 6.5 years for the attempted administration of a narcotic drug; and

C) The trial court sentenced Petitioner to slightly aggravated terms of imprisonment in violation of both *Apprendi*[3] and *Blakely.*

(*Id.*)

On December 7, 2006, the trial court summarily denied all three motions, finding that they were "nothing more than a rehash of his previous Petition for Post Convection Relief." (Answer, Ex. O at 1.) The trial court also reviewed Petitioner's complaints about the investigation, his complaints about his arrest, and his concerns about the lack of access to research facilities in the Department of Corrections and found "no error in the record" (Id. at 2.)

E. Second Motion for Appointment of Counsel

Petitioner filed a second motion for the appointment of counsel, dated May 25, 2006, and received by the court on January 17, 2007. (Answer, Ex. Q.)

The trial court held a hearing on the motion and issued a ruling on April 10, 2007. (Answer, Ex. N.) The trial court found that, for purposes of considering the timeliness of the motions, the time line started on May 16, 2006, when the trial court dismissed the first petition for post-conviction relief. (*Id.* at 1.) The trial court stated that the "record remained silent for six months with regards to an appeal, until the second petition was received on November 29, 2006," the same date that the court received a motion for appointment of advisory council and motion for reconsideration, and to amend the pleadings. (*Id.* at 2.)

The court inquired of the Petitioner why he did not submit originals, and why they were signed in May, 2006, when the court did not receive them until November. (*Id.* at 3.) The trial court found that it had "no reason to believe that the defendant mailed these in May, when the Court received them in November, it appears as though the documents may have backdated six months." (*Id.* at 3.) The trial court further found there was "no reason to give credibility, and say that the DOC is at fault, and defendant is not at fault for missing the deadlines for the filing of a Rule 32." (*Id.*) The trial court concluded that the most recent request for advisory council, the motion for reconsideration, and the second petition for post-conviction relief were untimely. The court ruled that Petitioner "did not appeal within the appropriate time, nor did he file anything with the State." (*Id.*) Petitioner "did not file either one of his petitions on time, which precludes him from filing anything else, unless there was new evidence the defendant was not aware of." (*Id.*) The trial court denied the motion for appointment of advisory council, motion for reconsideration, and second petition for post-conviction relief. (*Id.* at 4.)

F. Petition for Review

Petitioner filed a notice of appeal, dated December 21, 2006, received by the court on January 17, 2007. (Answer, Ex. P.) Petitioner argued that the trial court erred in refusing to appoint him advisory council. (*Id.*) Petitioner filed a petition for review to the Arizona Court of Appeals, dated June 13, 2007. (Ex. T.) Petitioner raised the following issues:

(A) Prosecutorial misconduct;

(B) The trial court erred by: (1) allowing Detective Orr to testify about the lie detector test; (2) not holding a hearing on the ineffective assistance of counsel claim to make a record; (3) regarding statutes used at sentencing time; (4) accepting the plea when there was no proof that defendant had committed any crime; (5) removing appointed counsel prior to a final decision by the court; and (6) using an unusable prior for aggravated DUI; and

(C) Ineffective assistance of counsel before, during and after the plea.

(Answer, Ex. T at iii.)

On October 31, 2007, the Arizona Court of Appeals issued a memorandum decision denying review. (Answer, Ex. U.) The court of appeals held that the motion for reconsideration was untimely, citing *Ariz.R.Crim.P. 32.9(a)*(motion for rehearing must be filed "within fifteen days after the ruling of the court"). (Answer Ex. U at 2.) The court of appeals further held that the petition for review, filed more than one year after the trial court ruled in May 2006, and six months after it ruled in December 2006, was untimely, and denied review, citing *Ariz.R.Crim.P. 32.9(c)*) (petition for review must be filed "[w]ithin thirty days after the final decision of the trial court on the petition for post-conviction relief or the motion for rehearing"). (Answer, Ex. U at 3.) The court of appeals found that it did not appear that the trial court granted Petitioner leave to file a delayed petition for review, nor did Petitioner claim he was granted such leave. (*Id.*) Neither did Petitioner present the trial court with any ground to justify his late filing. (*Id.*) The court of appeals further declined to address issues raised in Petitioner's two "objections" to the state's response to the petition for review, stating that, pursuant to *Rule 32.9(c)(2)*, "a reply to a petition for review 'shall be limited to matters addressed in the response,'" and the second objection was untimely (Answer, Ex. U at 4.) Petitioner's petition for review of the Arizona Court of Appeals decision was denied by the Arizona Supreme Court, without comment, on March 4, 2008. (Answer, Ex. V.)

G. Federal Habeas Petition

On June 18, 2008, Petitioner filed the instant habeas petition. In Ground One, Petitioner alleges a violation of the *Sixth* and *Eighth Amendments* because the "sentence exceeds the statutory maximum allowed by law" because it exceeds the presumptive 6.5-year sentence. In Ground Two, Petitioner asserts a violation of the *Sixth* and *Fourteenth Amendments* because the sentencing court abused its discretion by imposing a "sentence contrary to the legislative intent . . . enacted by

[the] Arizona legislature." In Ground Three, Petitioner claims "to conform with sentencing under Arizona Legislature laws as it pertains to Blak[e]ly and Apprendi violates the *6th*, *8th*, and *14th Amendment[s] of the U.S. Const.*, especially when the method of using priors to conform with Blak[e]ly is contrary to Arizona Legislative intent." In Ground Four, Petitioner claims a violation of his *Sixth Amendment* right to the effective assistance of counsel. (Doc. No. 1.)

II. Discussion

A. Standard of Review
Because Petitioner filed his petition after April 24, 1996, this case is governed by the Antiterrorism and Effective Death Penalty Act of 1996, *28 U.S.C. § 2254(d)* ("AEDPA").

B. Timeliness
A one-year period of limitation shall apply to an application for writ of habeas corpus by a person in custody pursuant to the judgment of a State court. *28 U.S.C. § 2244(d)(1)*. Under the AEDPA, a state prisoner must generally file a petition for writ of habeas corpus within one year from "the date on which the judgment became final by the conclusion of direct review or the expiration of time for seeking such review [.]" *28 U.S.C. § 2244(d)(1)(A)*.

The running of this one-year statute of limitations on habeas petitions for state convictions is tolled during any period when "a properly filed application for state post-conviction or other collateral review with respect to the pertinent judgment or claim is pending" in any state court. *See 28 U.S.C. § 2244(d)(2)*. Thus, the statute of limitations is tolled during the pendency of a state court action for post-conviction relief. *28 U.S.C. § 2244(d)(2)*.

......

This Court rejects Respondents argument that equitable tolling of the Congressionally mandated limitations period cannot survive in the face of *Bowles v. Russell, 551 U.S. 205, 127 S. Ct. 2360, 168 L. Ed. 2d 96 (2007)*. Respondents argue that the United States Supreme Court opinion in *Bowles,* established that the AEDPA limitations period is jurisdictional, and therefore equitable tolling does not apply. This Court disagrees. Prior to *Bowles,* the Supreme Court assumed, without deciding, that equitable tolling is available under *28 U.S.C. § 2244(d). See Lawrence v. Florida, 549 U.S. 327, 336, 127 S. Ct. 1079, 166 L. Ed. 2d 924 (2007).* The Ninth Circuit continues to apply equitable tolling to the AEDPA's statute of limitations *post-Bowles. Harris v. Carter, 515 F.3d 1051, 1054, n.3 (9th Cir. 2008).* Accordingly, this Court rejects Respondents arguments and finds that Petitioner is entitled to equitable tolling.

C. Analysis

The Magistrate Judge finds that, pursuant to the AEDPA, the Petition filed in this Court is untimely. Fernandez had until one year after his conviction and sentence became final to file his federal petition.

1. Limitation Period Under § 2244(d)(1)(A)

Petitioner's conviction and sentence became final on June 15, 2006, thirty (30) days after his petition for post-conviction relief was denied by the trial court on May 16, 2006, when the time for filing a petition for review to the court of appeals expired *See 28 U.S.C. § 2244(d)(1)(A); Summers v. Schriro, 481 F.3d 710, 716-17 (9th Cir. 2007)*("Arizona's Rule 32 of-right proceeding for plea-convicted defendants is a form of direct review within the meaning of *28 U.S.C. § 2244(d)(1)(A)"); Wixom v. Washington, 264 F.3d 894, 897 (9th Cir. 2001)*(Judgment becomes final either by the conclusion of direct review by the highest court, including the United States Supreme Court, or by the expiration of the time to seek such review); *Ariz.R.Crim.P., Rule 32.9(a)*(providing for the filing of a petition for post-conviction review "[w]ithin thirty days after the final decision of the trial court on the petition for post-conviction relief or the motion for rehearing") . Accordingly, Petitioner was required to file his petition for writ of habeas corpus within 1 year of the date his convictions became final, *i.e.,* June 15, 2007, absent statutory tolling.

2. Statutory Tolling

a. Second Petition, Motion to Reconsider, Motions for Appointment of Counsel, and Petition for Review.

Neither the second petition for post-conviction relief, the petition for review, or the motion to reconsider or appoint advisory council could toll the limitations period in this case. All of the petitions and motions were held to be untimely, rendering them not "properly filed" for tolling purposes under § 2244(d)(2). Untimely pleadings summarily dismissed by the state courts are not "properly filed" and do not result in statutory tolling of the 1-year statute of limitations. *See Pace, 544 U.S. at 417* (holding that "[b]ecause the state court rejected petitioner's PCR petition as untimely, it was not 'properly filed,' and he was not entitled to statutory tolling under § 2244(d)(2)"); *Allen v. Siebert, 552 U.S. 3, 4, 128 S. Ct. 2, 169 L. Ed. 2d 329 (2007)* ("[w]hether a time limit is jurisdictional, an affirmative defense, or something in between, it is a 'condition to filing,") (citation omitted).

Petitioner was required to file his petition for writ of habeas corpus within the 1-year period of limitations, excluding time where the statute of limitations was properly tolled. See *28 U.S.C. § 2244(d)(1)(A) & (d)(2)*. Petitioner did not file his federal petition for writ of habeas corpus within the 1-year statute of limitations. Unless there is a basis for equitably tolling the limitations period, Petitioner's habeas petition, filed on June 18, 2008, is untimely. This Court must recommend denial of Petitioner's petition for writ of habeas corpus as untimely filed.

3. Newly Discovered Constitutional Right Or Factual Predicate

Respondents assert that Grounds One and Three of the Petition stem from the United States' Supreme Court decision in *Apprendi* and *Blakely,* but that Petitioner cannot avoid the statute of limitation bar with respect to these claims pursuant to *28 U.S.C. § 2244(d)(1)(C). Section 2244(d)(1)(C))* renews the AEDPA's one-year statute of limitations from "the date on which the constitutional right asserted was initially recognized by the Supreme Court, fi the right has been newly recognized by the Supreme Court and made retroactively applicable to cases on collateral review." *28 U.S.C. § 2244(d)(1)(C)).* Respondents argue that although *Blakely* recognized a new constitutional rule of criminal procedure, the Supreme Court has not made the rule retroactively applicable to cases on collateral review. The

Court need not decide if *Blakely* should be retroactively applied, however, because, at the time *Blakely* was decided, Petitioner had not yet been convicted or sentenced as reflected in the discussion of the holding in *Blakely* at the time Petitioner entered his guilty plea. Thus, for purposes of Petitioner's collateral proceedings, *Blakely* is not a "new constitutional rule."

Neither does the Petition demonstrate any new factual predicate underlying his claims that would allow for an alternative statute of limitations under *28 U.S.C. § 2244(d)(1)(D)*.

4. Equitable tolling

"A *pro se* petitioner's lack of legal sophistication is not, by itself, an extraordinary circumstance warranting equitable tolling." *Rasberry v. Garcia, 448 F.3d 1150, 1154 (9th Cir. 2006)*. Petitioner asserts, in response to Respondents' contention that his Petition is untimely, that "Petitioner was not advised by post-conviction relief counsel [...] that he had [to] file a petition for review which counsel was obligated to advise Petitioner of his next step in the Rule 32 proceeding." (Doc. No. 17, Reply at 8.) Neither a failure to perfect an appeal nor counsel's negligence in calculating the limitations period for a habeas petition constitutes an "extraordinary circumstance" warranting equitable tolling. *Randle v. Crawford, 578 F.3d 1177, 1186 (9th Cir. 2009)* (citing *Miranda v. Castro, 292 F.3d 1063, 1066-67 (9th Cir. 2002),* citing *Frye v. Hickman, 273 F.3d 1144 (9th Cir. 2001))*. As in *Randle,* the alleged negligence of counsel in this case has little to no bearing on the ability of a petitioner to file a timely federal habeas petition. *578 U.S. at 1186.*

Petitioner has also asserted in his state court pleadings, although not directly in response to Respondents' equitable tolling argument, that he lacked access to "a law library or people trained in law." (Answer, Ex. K at 2, Ex. L at 8, Ex. Q at 2.) The Ninth Circuit has indicated that a petitioner's inability to access information about the statute of limitations deadline may warrant equitable tolling. *See Whalem/Hunt, 233 F.3d 1146, 1148 (9th Cir.2000) (en banc)* (remanding case to district court for development of facts concerning whether AEDPA materials were unavailable in the prison law library and the legal significance of such a finding). The record as submitted in this case, however, does not demonstrate that Petitioner's ability to access the relevant limitations provisions of the AEDPA or other necessary legal material was eliminated, rather, Petitioner seems to be asserting that he was not capable of researching an issue about polygraph evidence, or to have a speedy way to get copies made. (*See* Ex. K at 2.) Petitioner does not allege that he did not have access to the provisions of the AEDPA, or that he was denied such material after requesting it. Petitioner has not, at this time, sufficiently alleged that, due to circumstances beyond his control it was impossible to file a petition on time. Accordingly, this Court finds no cause for equitably tolling the limitations period in this case.

TRISTAN DESMOND ROSSUM, PETITIONER, V. CHARLES L RYAN, ET AL., RESPONDENTS.

NO. CV-12-00391-TUC-CKJ UNITED STATES DISTRICT COURT FOR THE DISTRICT OF ARIZONA

(Text added and modified for emphasis) As a matter of regular practice the Attorney General's Office consistently fails to advise the federal courts that in Arizona counsel fail to advise inmates the time frames for filing federal habeas and paralegals do not assist inmates by policy. There are too many such incidents which constitute a pattern. As this is a pattern with the Arizona Attorney General's Office this should constitute fraud upon the court, because, they are concealing facts on a systemic basis, to defeat valid claims.

COUNSEL: Tristan Desmond Rossum, Petitioner, Pro se, TUCSON, AZ. For Charles L Ryan, Attorney General of the State of Arizona, Respondents: Alan Liardon Amann, LEAD ATTORNEY, Office of the Attorney General, Criminal Appeals Section, Tucson, AZ.

………..

III. Statute of Limitations

The AEDPA mandates that a one-year statute of limitations applies to applications for a writ of habeas corpus by a person in state custody. *28 U.S.C. § 2244(d)(1)*. Generally, the limitation period begins to run from "the date on which the judgment became final by the conclusion of direct review or the expiration of the time for seeking such review." *28 U.S.C. § 2244(d)(1)(A)*. "The time during which a properly filed application for State post-conviction or other collateral review with respect to the pertinent judgment or claim is pending shall not be counted toward any period of limitation under this subsection." *28 U.S.C. § 2244(d)(2)*. The AEDPA mandates that the limitation period begins to run from the latest of four possible dates; however, none of these are applicable to the instant case, and are therefore not considered here.

Petitioner's Petition is untimely. Petitioner's initial Rule 32 Petition proceedings ceased to be pending on December 16, 2004 after the Arizona Court of Appeals denied relief. Petitioner did not file his second Rule 32 Petition until June 23, 2008 over three years later. His second Rule 32 Petition ceased to be pending thirty (30) days after the trial court's May 22, 2009 denial of relief. Petitioner then took no action for nearly three years until May 21, 2012. Additionally, Petitioner does not argue in his objections that his Petition for habeas relief was timely filed. As such, after an independent review of the record, the Court finds that Petitioner's Petition Pursuant to *28 U.S.C. §2254* is untimely. *See Pace v. Diguglielmo, 544 U.S. 408, 412-413, 125 S. Ct. 1807, 161 L. Ed. 2d 669 (2005)*.

IV. Equitable Tolling

In his Objection, Petitioner argues that he is entitled to equitable tolling due to a severe mental impairment. "Generally, a litigant seeking equitable tolling bears the burden of establishing two elements: (1) that he has been pursuing his rights diligently, and (2) that some extraordinary circumstance stood in his way." *Pace v. DiGuglielmo, 544 U.S. 408, 418, 125 S. Ct. 1807, 161 L. Ed. 2d 669 (2005)*. Mental incompetency may be an extraordinary circumstance that justifies equitable tolling of the AEDPA statute of limitations. *Laws v. Lamarque, 351 F.3d 919, 923 (9th Cir. 2003)*. A determination of whether the limitations period should be tolled due to Petitioner's alleged [*7] mental illness is dependent on whether he was prevented from making a timely filing due to the severity of his mental illness. *Laws v. Lamarque, 351 F.3d 919, 922-923 (9th Cir. 2003)*.

Eligibility for equitable tolling due to mental impairment requires the petitioner to:

> (1) ... show his mental impairment was an 'extraordinary circumstance' beyond his control, by demonstrating the impairment was so severe that either (a) petitioner was unable rationally or factually to personally understand the need to timely file, or (b) petitioner's mental state rendered him unable personally to prepare a habeas petition and effectuate its filing.
>
> (2) Second, the petitioner must show diligence in pursuing the claims to the extent he could understand them, but that the mental impairment made it impossible to meet the filing deadline under the totality of the circumstances, including reasonably available access to assistance.

Bills v. Clark, 628 F.3d 1092, 1100 (9th Cir. 2010) (internal citations omitted). "The relevant question is: Did the mental impairment cause an untimely filing?" *Bills, 628 F.3d at 1100 n.3* citing *Spitsyn v. Moore, 345 F.3d 796, 799 (9th Cir. 2003)*. In evaluating whether a petitioner is entitled to equitable tolling, the court must

> (1) find the petitioner has made a non-frivolous showing that he had a severe mental impairment during the filing period that would entitle him to an evidentiary hearing; (2) determine, after considering the record, whether the petitioner satisfied his burden that he was in fact mentally impaired; (3) determine whether the petitioner's mental impairment made it impossible to timely file on his own; and (4) consider whether the circumstances demonstrate the petitioner was otherwise diligent in attempting to comply with the filing requirements.

Bills v. Clark, 628 F.3d 1092, 1100-1101 (9th Cir. 2010). The mere allegation of mental incompetency by Petitioner in a verified pleading or affidavit may be enough to satisfy the "non-frivolous showing." *See Laws v. Lamarque, 351 F.3d 919, 924 (9th Cir. 2003)*. However, an allegation of mental incompetency does not require the court to hold evidentiary hearings or permit discovery if the record was amply developed with evidence to indicate that Petitioner's alleged mental incompetence was not so severe as to cause his untimely filing. *Roberts v. Marshall, 627 F.3d 768, 773 (9th Cir. 2010).*

The record in this case establishes that Petitioner's alleged mental impairment was not so severe as to cause his untimely filing. Petitioner asserts that he has been in special education all his life. However, being in special education while in school does not sufficiently demonstrate a non-frivolous showing that Petitioner had a severe mental impairment during the filing period that would entitle him to an evidentiary hearing.

Petitioner also argues for the first time in his Request for a New Writ of Habeas Corpus that his prior appellate counsel indicated that seizures in Petitioner's brain may be caused by different neurological or medical problems including head injury, infection or some other reason and that his counsel attempted to have a physician examine Petitioner for the purpose of an *Atkins* hearing. However, Petitioner does not argue that he actually suffers from a mental impairment or that any alleged mental impairment caused his untimely filing. Petitioner only argues that if he was examined, a physician may have found that Petitioner had a mental and developmental disability. As such, Plaintiff has failed to make a non-frivolous showing that he suffered from a mental impairment or satisfy his burden that he was mentally impaired during the filing period. Petitioner's reference to *Atkins*, likely implies the Supreme Court case, which held that capital punishment for the mentally retarded violates the *Eighth Amendment. Atkins v. Virginia, 536 U.S. 304, 122 S. Ct. 2242, 153 L. Ed. 2d 335 (2002)*

Moreover, the record demonstrates that Petitioner understood the need to timely file his petition. The State record reveals that after Petitioner's direct appeal concluded, Petitioner timely filed a *pro se* Notice of Post-Conviction Relief. Petitioner then filed a *pro se* Motion for Appointment of Counsel, which was granted by the court. (Doc. 15-1, p. 2-9). After Petitioner's appointed counsel was unable to find any meritorious claims to raise in a post-conviction proceeding, Petitioner filed a *pro se* Motion requesting an extension of time to file a *pro se* petition for post-conviction relief. In his Motion, Petitioner noted that he had filed two prior *pro se* motions for extensions of time and requested a ruling on his prior motions so that he could have a clear due date for his petition. (Doc. 15-2, p. 7-8).

Subsequently, Petitioner filed 8 *pro se* Motions to extend the time to file his Petition. (Doc. 15-2, p. 11-35). Then, on March 10, 2003, Petitioner filed *a pro se* Rule 32 Petition raising 5 claims for relief. After his *pro se* Rule 32 Petition was denied, Petitioner filed a *pro se* Motion to extend his time to file a Motion for Reconsideration. (Doc. 15-2, p. 51-52). Later Petitioner timely filed *a pro se* Motion for Reconsideration on January 9, 2004. After his *pro se* Motion for Reconsideration was denied, Petitioner filed a Motion to extend the time to file a petition for review of his Rule 32 Petition. (Doc. 15-2, p. 59-60).

Accordingly, the record demonstrates that throughout Petitioner's post-conviction relief proceedings, he was aware of and understood the impending deadlines and made efforts to comply with those deadlines. In those instances, where he could not comply with the deadline, Petitioner filed motions seeking to extend the deadline. Further, the Court notes that in Petitioner's numerous motions for extensions of various deadlines in state court, Petitioner never once asserted that he suffered from any mental impairment. His requests for extensions primarily relied on his limited access to the prison's law library and his failure to timely receive necessary documentation.

DENNIS SCHILINSKI, PETITIONER, VS. CHARLES L. RYAN, RESPONDENT. CIV 13-8278-PCT-JAT (MHB) UNITED STATES DISTRICT COURT FOR THE DISTRICT OF ARIZONA

(Text added and modified for emphasis) As a matter of regular practice the Attorney General's Office consistently fails to advise the federal courts that in Arizona counsel fail to advise inmates the time frames for filing federal habeas and paralegals do not assist inmates by policy. There are too many such incidents which constitute a pattern. As this is a pattern with the Arizona Attorney General's Office this should constitute fraud upon the court, because, they are concealing facts on a systemic basis, to defeat valid claims.

COUNSEL: Dennis Charles Schilinski, also named as: Dennis C. Schilinski, Petitioner, Pro se, FLORENCE, AZ.For Charles L Ryan, named as: Charles Ryan, Respondent: Andrew Stuart Reilly, LEAD ATTORNEY, Office of the Attorney General - Phoenix, Phoenix, AZ.

BACKGROUND

The presentence report provides the following factual background:

On August 3, 2008 about 5:15 pm, Deputy Giralde was dispatched to 3825 Neal Avenue, Kingman regarding a weapons offense which occurred next door at 3815 Neal Avenue. On arrival the deputy noticed the body of a female, later identified as Carol Bunn, lying on the ground with blood foaming from her mouth. Dispatch was notified to send assistance.

No one else was found at the residence and medical responders confirmed Bunn was deceased. Detectives interviewed Sandra Reuter, who lived directly west of the residence, who reported hearing two gunshots and seeing the male resident, known to her as Dennis, later identified as Dennis Charles Schilinski (37), hurriedly going inside. Ms. Reuter also observed the female lying motionless on the ground in front of the residence.

Another neighbor, Tammi Hendrickson, reporting [sic] hearing arguing, two gunshots and a female voice scream, "Oh God, someone help me please." Hendrickson identified Schilinski via photo line-up as the male residing at the scene.

Bobby Shultz informed officers he gave Schilinski a ride to the area of Walgreens, reporting [Schilinski] had said, when he got into his vehicle, "Man I just shot my old lady." He reported Schilinski said he had shot her twice in the side.

Kingman Police located [] Schilinski in the area of Beverly and Western and [he] was turned over to the Sheriff's Office. Schilinski declined to speak in detail with detectives and requested a [*3] lawyer. He did inquire about Bunn and where they had taken her. A gunshot residue test of Schilinski's hands returned positive.

(Exh. D at 1-2.)

Petitioner was booked into jail, and the State filed an indictment in the Mohave County Superior Court charging him with first degree murder, a class 1 felony (Count 1), and misconduct involving weapons, a class 4 felony (Count 2). (Id. at 2; Exh. A at 3-4.) Petitioner later admitted that he shot and killed Carol during a fight over money that occurred during a weekend binge, where the two consumed a copious amount of drugs and alcohol. (Exh. E.)

On September 8, 2009, Petitioner entered into a stipulated guilty plea, where he pled guilty to second degree murder, a class 1 felony (reduced from the charge in Count 1 of the indictment). (Exh. C at 1-2.) Pursuant to the plea agreement, the State agreed to dismiss Count 2. (Exh. B at 2.) Before entering into the agreement, Petitioner acknowledged that he understood the guilty plea would subject him to a prison term ranging from 10 to 18 years, and that he would also be "sentenced to community supervision upon his release from prison for a period of time equal to 15% of his prison sentence." (Id. at 1-3; Exh. C at 1-2.)

Petitioner then formally pled guilty, pursuant to the agreement, which the superior court accepted. (Exh. C at 2.) Petitioner was sentenced to 18 years in prison and, upon his release from prison, was ordered to serve the term of community supervision that was delineated in the plea agreement. (Exh. F at 2.)

Sometime later, Petitioner apparently "read [a] DOC policy that said [the superior courts] have the power to waive [orders of] community supervision." (Exh. G at 2-3.) So Petitioner wrote a letter to the superior court on February 10, 2010, requesting that it "waive [his] community supervision" because Petitioner believed the 18-year term of imprisonment was "more than enough punishment." (Id.) The superior court acknowledged receipt of Schilinski's letter and noted that the request was "not made in the form of a petition for post-conviction relief." (Id. at 1.) The superior court then denied Petitioner's request but, nonetheless, remarked that Arizona's sentencing laws had been correctly applied in this case. (Id.)

On March 25, 2010 -- approximately 163 days after he was sentenced -- Petitioner attempted to commence an "of right" post-conviction relief (PCR) proceedings by filing a notice of PCR. (Exh. H.)

Petitioner's notice for PCR, however, was untimely. Accordingly, the superior court dismissed Petitioner's untimely PCR petition on April 12, 2010. (Exh. I.) The superior court also rejected Petitioner's claim that he was unaware of the time frame in which to file his notice of PCR because he had been "advised at his Judgment and Sentencing Hearing, both verbally and in writing, that a Notice of PCR must be filed within 90 days." (Id.) Moreover, Petitioner's notice of PCR failed to "specify any justification for his untimely filing, nor does it specify any claims for relief that would survive the expiration of this time frame." (Id.)

More than 3 years later, on June 21, 2013, Petitioner filed a special action with the Arizona Court of Appeals. (Exhs. J, N.) The court of appeals declined jurisdiction. (Exhs. K, N.) Petitioner subsequently petitioned the Arizona Supreme Court to review the court of appeals' decision, but the petition was summarily denied. (Exhs. L, O.)

On November 21, 2013, Petitioner filed the instant habeas petition in this Court. (Doc. 1.) Petitioner raises one ground for relief. Petitioner asserts that the trial court imposed a two-year term of community supervision as part of his sentence pursuant to a state statute that is "vague, overbroad [] and suscep[]t[i]ble to a broad interpretation other than its expressed intention." Petitioner asserts that his sentence violates his *Sixth* and *Eighth Amendment* rights because, under Arizona Revised Statute ("A.R.S.") *§ 13-710*, he is not eligible for parole release, or any early release, prior to completion of his entire sentence and so the imposition of community supervision under *A.R.S. § 13-603* potentially extends the length of his prison sentence (if he violates the terms of his community supervision) beyond the sentence "lawfully imposed."

DISCUSSION

In his Answer, Respondent contends that Petitioner's habeas petition is untimely and, as such, must be denied and dismissed.

The Antiterrorism and Effective Death Penalty Act of 1996 ("AEDPA") imposes a statute of limitations on federal petitions for writ of habeas corpus filed by state prisoners. See *28 U.S.C. § 2244(d)(1)*. The statute provides:

A 1-year period of limitation shall apply to an application for a writ of habeas corpus by a person in custody pursuant to the judgment of a State court. The limitation period shall run from the latest of --

(A) the date on which the judgment became final by the conclusion of direct review or the expiration of the time for seeking such review;

(B) the date on which the impediment to filing an application created by State action in violation of the Constitution or laws of the United States is removed, if the applicant was prevented from filing by such State action;

(C) the date on which the constitutional right asserted was initially recognized by the Supreme Court, if the right has been newly recognized by the Supreme Court and made retroactively applicable to cases on collateral review; or

(D) the date on which the factual predicate of the claim or claims presented could have been discovered through the exercise of due diligence.

An "of-right" petition for post-conviction review under *Arizona Rule of Criminal Procedure 32*, which is available to criminal defendants who plead guilty, is a form of "direct review" within the meaning of *28 U.S.C. § 2244(d)(1)(A)*. See *Summers v. Schriro, 481 F.3d 710, 711 (9th Cir. 2007)*. Therefore, the judgment of conviction becomes final upon the conclusion of the *Rule 32* of-right proceeding, or upon the expiration of the time for seeking such review. *See id.*

Additionally, "[t]he time during which a properly filed application for State post conviction or other collateral review with respect to the pertinent judgment or claim is pending shall not be counted toward" the limitations period. *28 U.S.C. § 2244(d)(2)*; see *Lott v. Mueller, 304 F.3d 918, 921 (9th Cir. 2002)*. A post-conviction petition is "clearly pending after it is filed with a state court, but before that court grants or denies the petition." *Chavis v. Lemarque, 382 F.3d 921, 925 (9th Cir. 2004)*. A state petition that is not filed, however, within the state's required time limit is not "properly filed" and, therefore, the petitioner is not entitled to statutory tolling. See *Pace v. DiGuglielmo, 544 U.S. 408, 413, 125 S. Ct. 1807, 161 L. Ed. 2d 669 (2005)*. "When a post conviction petition is untimely under state law, 'that [is] the end of the matter' for purposes of § 2244(d)(2)." *Id. at 414.*

In Arizona, post-conviction review is pending once a notice of post-conviction relief is filed even though the petition is not filed until later. See *Isley v. Arizona Department of Corrections, 383 F.3d 1054, 1056 (9th Cir. 2004).* An application for post-conviction relief is also pending during the intervals between a lower court decision and a review by a higher court. See *Biggs v. Duncan, 339 F.3d 1045, 1048 (9th Cir. 2003)* (citing *Carey v. Saffold, 536 U.S. 214, 223, 122 S. Ct. 2134, 153 L. Ed. 2d 260 (2002)).* However, the time between a first and second application for post-conviction relief is not tolled because no application is "pending" during that period. See *id.* Moreover, filing a new petition for post-conviction relief does not reinitiate a limitations period that ended before the new petition was filed. See *Ferguson v. Palmateer, 321 F.3d 820, 823 (9th Cir. 2003).*

The statute of limitations under the AEDPA is subject to equitable tolling in appropriate cases. See *Holland v. Florida, 560 U.S. 631, 645-46, 130 S. Ct. 2549, 177 L. Ed. 2d 130 (2010).* However, for equitable tolling to apply, a petitioner must show "'(1) that he has been pursuing his rights diligently and (2) that some extraordinary circumstances stood in his way'" and prevented him from filing a timely petition. *Id. at 2562* (quoting *Pace, 544 U.S. at 418*).

The Court finds that Petitioner's Petition for Writ of Habeas Corpus is untimely. Petitioner was sentenced under the plea agreement on October 13, 2009. (Exhs. C, F.) By pleading guilty, Petitioner waived his right to a direct appeal, and had 90 days to file an "of-right" petition for post-conviction relief under *Rule 32 of the Arizona Rules of Criminal Procedure.* Because Petitioner failed to file such a petition within the prescribed time, the judgment became final for statute of limitations purposes when the 90-day period expired, on January 11, 2010, and the limitations period began to run on that date. See *28 U.S.C. § 2244(d)(1)(A)*; *Summers, 481 F.3d at 711.* The statute of limitations expired one year later on January 11, 2011.

Petitioner is not entitled to statutory tolling. Petitioner filed his untimely notice of post-conviction relief on March 25, 2010 -- which was well after the January 11, 2010 deadline to file an "of-right" petition for post-conviction relief under *Rule 32 of the Arizona Rules of Criminal Procedure*. Consequently, the untimely notice of PCR failed to constitute a "properly filed" petition to the state court and did not toll the limitations period. See *Pace, 544 U.S. at 414-17* (holding that "[b]ecause the state court rejected petitioner's PCR petition as untimely, it was not 'properly filed,' and he was not entitled to statutory tolling under § 2244(d)(2)"). Additionally, Petitioner's subsequent state court pleadings (special action initiated June of 2013) did not toll the limitations period. These pleadings were filed after the statute of limitations ended and could not restart the expired 1-year limitations period. See *Ferguson, 321 F.3d at 823*. Petitioner wrote a letter to the superior court on February 10, 2010, requesting that the court waive the term of community supervision he received. (Exh. G at 2-3.) The letter, however, was merely a "correspondence" to the superior court; it was "not made in the form of a petition for post-conviction relief[.]" (Id. at 1.) Regardless, the correspondence was filed after the January 11, 2010 deadline had passed. (Id. at1-2.)

In sum, Petitioner filed the instant habeas petition almost three years after the 1-year limitations period expired. The Petition is therefore untimely.

The Ninth Circuit recognizes that the AEDPA's limitations period may be equitably tolled because it is a statute of limitations, not a jurisdictional bar. See *Calderon v. United States Dist. Ct. (Beeler), 128 F.3d 1283, 1288 (9th Cir. 1997)*, overruled in part on other grounds by *Calderon v. United States Dist. Ct. (Kelly), 163 F.3d 530, 540 (9th Cir. 1998)*. Tolling is appropriate when "'extraordinary circumstances' beyond a [petitioner's] control make it impossible to file a petition on time." *Id.*; see *Miranda v. Castro, 292 F.3d 1063, 1066 (9th Cir. 2002)* (stating that "the threshold necessary to trigger equitable tolling [under AEDPA] is very high, lest the exceptions swallow the rule") (citations omitted). "When external forces, rather than a petitioner's lack of diligence, account for the failure to file a timely claim, equitable tolling of the statute of limitations may be appropriate." *Miles v. Prunty, 187 F.3d 1104, 1107 (9th Cir. 1999)*. A petitioner seeking equitable tolling must establish two elements: "(1) that he has been pursuing his rights diligently, and (2) that some extraordinary circumstance stood in his way." *Pace, 544 U.S. at 418*. Petitioner must also establish a "causal connection" between the extraordinary circumstance and his failure to file a timely petition. See *Bryant v. Arizona Attorney General, 499 F.3d 1056, 1060 (9th Cir. 2007)*.

Petitioner has not proffered any extraordinary circumstance that would justify equitable tolling or demonstrated that an external impediment hindered the diligent pursuit of his rights. Petitioner's *pro se* status, indigence, limited legal resources, ignorance of the law, or lack of representation during the applicable filing period do not constitute extraordinary circumstances justifying equitable tolling. See, e.g., *Rasberry v. Garcia, 448 F.3d 1150, 1154 (9th Cir. 2006)* ("[A] *pro se* petitioner's lack of legal sophistication is not, by itself, an extraordinary circumstance warranting equitable tolling.").

Accordingly, Petitioner is not entitled to equitable tolling and his habeas petition is untimely.

RICHARD JAMES SKAGGS, PETITIONER, V. CHARLES L. RYAN, ARIZONA ATTORNEY GENERAL, RESPONDENTS. NO. CV 14-00151 PHX JAT MEA UNITED STATES DISTRICT COURT FOR THE DISTRICT OF ARIZONA

(Text added and modified for emphasis) As a matter of regular practice the Attorney General's Office consistently fails to advise the federal courts that in Arizona counsel fail to advise inmates the time frames for filing federal habeas and paralegals do not assist inmates by policy. There are too many such incidents which constitute a pattern. As this is a pattern with the Arizona Attorney General's Office this should constitute fraud upon the court, because, they are concealing facts on a systemic basis, to defeat valid claims.

COUNSEL: Richard James Skaggs, also named as: Richard J Skaggs and Richard Skaggs, Petitioner, Pro se, WINSLOW, AZ. For Charles L Ryan, Attorney General of the State of Arizona, Respondents: Alice Mae Jones, LEAD ATTORNEY, Office of the Attorney General - Phoenix, Phoenix, AZ.

I Procedural History

A Maricopa County grand jury indictment returned November 1, 2004, charged Petitioner with one count of first-degree murder, alleged to have occurred on July 28, 2002. *See* Answer, Exh. A. The Arizona Court of Appeals summarized the facts underlying Petitioner's ultimate conviction: as follows

On July 28, 2002, [Skaggs] and two friends, Patrick H. and Oliver P., shot and killed their acquaintance, Mark B., in Patrick H.'s apartment and subsequently disposed of his body in a dumpster. The victim's body was never found. The motive for the killing was either a disagreement between [Skaggs] and the victim caused by the victim's conduct towards a woman employee of ... a strip club they both frequented, or the fact that [Skaggs] needed money and decided to rob the victim.

***

In mid-August 2002, [Skaggs] and Patrick H. moved to Seattle, Washington, "[t]o get away from the cops." Patrick H. was arrested there in December 2002 on a probation violation for leaving Arizona without permission. On October 1, 2004, Patrick H. eventually entered into a plea agreement in which he pled guilty to the charge of manslaughter, a Class 2 non-dangerous felony, in exchange for his truthful testimony against [Skaggs] and Oliver P.

Id., Exh. I at 2 & 9.

On September 18, 2006, after a thirteen-day trial, a jury found Petitioner guilty of first-degree murder. Id, Exh. B. On January 12, 2007, Petitioner was sentenced to serve a term of life imprisonment without parole pursuant to this conviction. Id, Exh. C.

Petitioner took a timely direct appeal of his conviction and sentence. Petitioner asserted in his direct appeal that: (1) the state wrongfully sequenced or "piecemealed" its prosecution of a criminal episode in order to impeach Petitioner with a conviction for a crime which occurred at the same time as the crime being tried; (2) Arizona should adopt California common law and prohibit long delays between the close of evidence and the start of the jury's deliberations, such as the eleven-day delay in the instant case; (3) the trial judge wrongfully dismissed a deliberating juror for juror misconduct without giving that juror a chance to be heard. Id, Exh. D & Exh. E.

At Petitioner's request, the Arizona Court of Appeals held oral argument on the issues raised in Petitioner's direct appeal. Id, Exh. ZZ at 3. The Arizona Court of Appeals affirmed Petitioner's conviction and sentence in a memorandum decision issued May 27, 2008. Id., Exh. I. Petitioner sought review by the Arizona Supreme Court. Id, Exhs. K & L. In addition to the three issues presented to the Arizona Court of Appeals, Petitioner presented an additional issue to the Arizona Supreme Court, alleging one of the state's witnesses gave false testimony and that the state should have corrected the testimony and the testimony "should have been excluded." Id, Exh. L. The Arizona Supreme Court summarily denied review in Petitioner's direct appeal on December 22, 2008. Id., Exh. M.

On December 28, 2008, Petitioner initiated a timely action for post-conviction relief pursuant to *Rule 32, Arizona Rules of Criminal Procedure*. Id, Exh. O. Petitioner was appointed counsel to represent him in his Rule 32 proceedings. Id, Exh. P. In his Rule 32 action Petitioner alleged several ineffective assistance of trial counsel claims. Id, Exh. R. In a decision entered March 30, 2010, the state trial court considered Petitioner's claims and determined that Petitioner had not established that his trial counsel's performance was deficient or that he was prejudiced by any alleged deficiency and, accordingly, the court found he was not denied his right to the effective assistance of counsel pursuant to the test stated in Strickland v. Washington. Id, Exh. W. Petitioner sought review of this decision by the Arizona Court of Appeals. Id, Exh. BB. The Arizona Court of Appeals denied review in a decision entered November 17, 2011. Id., Exh. FF.

Petitioner initiated a second Rule 32 action on March 24, 2012. Id., Exh. GG. Petitioner asserted he had newly discovered facts establishing his actual innocence. Id., Exh. GG. On April 20, 2012, the trial court dismissed the second Rule 32 action, stating:

> The defendant claims, pursuant to *Ariz. R. Crim. P. 32.1(a)*,
> that his conviction and sentence were obtained in violation of

his constitutional rights. Specifically, the defendant claims that the manner in which the state obtained an indictment against him was in violation of due process. The defendant cannot raise a claim of this nature in an untimely or successive notice of post-conviction relief. See *Ariz. R. Crim. P. 32.4(a)*. Additionally, the defendant could have raised this issue on direct appeal but failed to do so. Therefore, the defendant is now procedurally precluded from raising the issue in *Rule 32* proceedings. See *Ariz. R. Crim. P. 32.2(a)(1)*.

Id., Exh. HH at 1-2. The state trial court concluded Petitioner had "fail[ed] to state a claim for which relief can be granted in an untimely or successive *Rule 32* proceeding," citing *Rule 32.4(a)*, and dismissed the action as untimely and successive. Id., Exh. HH at 2.

Petitioner filed his federal habeas action on January 14, 2014. Petitioner asserts, as construed by Respondents:

Ground 1: Skaggs alleges violations of the *Fourth*, *Fifth*, and *Fourteenth Amendments*, and *Federal Rules of Evidence 403* and *608*. Skaggs generally alleges that he was "wrongfully accused" and "misrepresented by ineffective counselors." Skaggs claims that someone else "openly admitted and confessed" to first-degree murder as part of plea agreements, and states neither the grand jury nor the trial jury was made aware of the confession. He claims he did not receive a fair trial as a result.

Ground 2: Skaggs states his *Fifth* and *Fourteenth Amendment* "rights [to] a speedy trial and due process of the law" were violated. He alleges his right to due process was violated because he was not allowed to be present at the Grand Jury hearing. He asserts that witnesses were "allowed to testify falsely against [him]," and the prosecutor used "perjured testimony." He also seems to claim that his prior convictions were improperly used to "mislead the judge" and to cause "prejudice."

Ground 3: Skaggs asserts his *Sixth*, *Ninth*, and *Fourteenth Amendment* rights were violated. He claims he "did not receive a 'fair trial' when [he] constantly complained about the racial (make-up) of the jury" when there were no jurors of "Puerto Rican, Mexican, and African American" descent and Skaggs "is of Puerto Rican descent," and the jurors "were all 'whites.'" Skaggs also generally claims that his counsel was "solely committed [to] pleasing both the prosecution and the court" and his counsel persuaded him "to make decisions that [were] not in [his] best interest."

Ground 4: Skaggs asserts violations of the *Eighth Amendment* and *Rule 33(a) of the Federal Rules of Criminal Procedure*. Skaggs asserts he is innocent and claims others have confessed to committing the murder for which he was "indicted, tried, and convicted." He claims witnesses "were intimated not to testify openly and honestly" on his behalf.

(Dkt. #1, at 5-9.)

Id. at 10-11.

Respondents contend the petition for federal habeas relief was not timely filed.

II Analysis

The petition seeking a writ of habeas corpus is barred by the applicable statute of limitations found in the Antiterrorism and Effective Death Penalty Act ("AEDPA"). The AEDPA imposed a one-year statute of limitations on state prisoners seeking federal habeas relief from their state convictions. See, e.g., *Espinoza Matthews v. California, 432 F.3d 1021, 1025 (9th Cir. 2005)*; *Lott v. Mueller, 304 F.3d 918, 920 (9th Cir. 2002)*. The one-year statute of limitations on habeas petitions generally begins to run on "the date on which the judgment became final by conclusion of direct review or the expiration of the time for seeking such review." *28 U.S.C. § 2244(d)(1)(A)*. The AEDPA provides that a petitioner is entitled to tolling of the statute of limitations during the pendency of a "properly filed application for state post-conviction or other collateral review with respect to the pertinent judgment or claim." *28 U.S.C. § 2244(d)(2)*. See also, e.g., *Artuz v. Bennett, 531 U.S. 4,*

8, 121 S. Ct. 361, 363-64, 148 L. Ed. 2d 213 (2000); Harris v. Carter, 515 F.3d 1051, 1053 (9th Cir. 2008).

At the conclusion of Petitioner's direct appeal, Petitioner filed a state action for state post-conviction relief, which tolled the running of the one-year statute of limitations. The Arizona Court of Appeals denied review of the trial court's decision denying relief in Petitioner's Rule 32 action in a decision entered November 17, 2011. Petitioner did not seek review of this decision by the Arizona Supreme Court. Therefore, the statute of limitations on Petitioner's federal habeas action began to run on December 17, 2011, when the time expired to seek review, and expired on December 17, 2012. Petitioner's second Rule 32 action for state post-conviction relief did not toll the statute of limitations because this action was not "properly filed. See *Pace v. DiGuglielmo, 544 U.S. 408, 414, 125 S. Ct. 1807, 1812, 161 L. Ed. 2d 669 (2005); Allen v. Siebert, 552 U.S. 3, 5-7, 128 S. Ct. 2, 169 L. Ed. 2d 329 (2007)* (holding that the Pace rule applies even where there are exceptions to the state-court filing deadlines, and reaffirming that a state court's rejection of a petition as untimely is "the end of the matter"); *Zepeda v. Walker, 581 F.3d 1013, 1018 (9th Cir. 2009)* (rejecting contention that state must prove that rules concerning time bars are "firmly established and regularly followed before noncompliance will render a petition improperly filed for AEDPA tolling").

The one-year statute of limitations for filing a habeas petition may be equitably tolled if extraordinary circumstances beyond a prisoner's control prevent the prisoner from filing on time. See *Holland v. Florida, 560 U.S. 631, 130 S. Ct. 2549, 2554, 2562, 177 L. Ed. 2d 130 (2010); Bills v. Clark, 628 F.3d 1092, 1096-97 (9th Cir. 2010).* A petitioner seeking equitable tolling must establish two elements: "(1) that he has been pursuing his rights diligently, and (2) that some extraordinary circumstance stood in his way." *Pace, 544 U.S. at 418, 125 S. Ct. at 1814-15.* See also *Ford v. Gonzalez, 683 F.3d 1230, 1237 (9th Cir. 2012); Porter v. Ollison, 620 F.3d 952, 959 (9th Cir. 2010); Waldron-Ramsey v. Pacholke, 556 F.3d 1008, 1011-14 (9th Cir. 2009).* In Holland the Supreme Court eschewed a "mechanical rule" for determining extraordinary circumstances, while endorsing a flexible, "case-by-case" approach, drawing "upon decisions made in other similar cases for guidance." *Bills, 628 F.3d at 1096-97.*

The Ninth Circuit Court of Appeals has determined equitable tolling of the filing deadline for a federal habeas petition is available only if extraordinary circumstances beyond the petitioner's control make it impossible to file a petition on time. See *Chaffer v. Prosper, 592 F.3d 1046, 1048-49 (9th Cir. 2010)*; *Porter, 620 F.3d at 959*; *Waldron-Ramsey, 556 F.3d at 1011-14 & n.4*; *Harris v. Carter, 515 F.3d 1051, 1054-55 & n.4 (9th Cir. 2008)*. Equitable tolling is only appropriate when external forces, rather than a petitioner's lack of diligence, account for the failure to file a timely habeas action. See *Chaffer, 592 F.3d at 1048-49*; *Waldron-Ramsey, 556 F.3d at 1011*. Equitable tolling is also available if the petitioner establishes their actual innocence of the crimes of conviction. See *Lee v. Lampert, 653 F.3d 929, 933-34 (9th Cir. 2011)*.

Equitable tolling is to be rarely granted. See, e.g., *Waldron-Ramsey, 556 F.3d at 1011*; *Jones v. Hulick, 449 F.3d 784, 789 (7th Cir. 2006)*; *Steed v. Head, 219 F.3d 1298, 1300 (11th Cir. 2000)*. Equitable tolling is inappropriate in most cases and "the threshold necessary to trigger equitable tolling [under AEDPA] is very high, lest the exceptions swallow the rule." *Miranda v. Castro, 292 F.3d 1063, 1066 (9th Cir. 2002)*. Petitioner must show that "the extraordinary circumstances were the cause of his untimeliness and that the extraordinary circumstances made it impossible to file a petition on time." *Porter, 620 F.3d at 959*. It is Petitioner's burden to establish that equitable tolling is warranted in his case. See, e.g., id., *620 F.3d at 959*; *Espinoza Matthews, 432 F.3d at 1026*.

In reply to the answer to his habeas petition, Petitioner re-asserts that he is innocent and that a witness lied to grand jury and at trial. Petitioner states, with regard to the timeliness of his petition: "The instant Petitioner request for Writ of Habeas Corpus should be reconsidered for the seriousness of the matter, that this is an person is currently serving Natural-Life!! for crimes he didn't commit.(sic)" Doc. 15.

Petitioner has not stated an adequate basis for equitable tolling of the statute of limitations. Compare *Holland, 130 S. Ct. at 2564*; *Porter, 620 F.3d at 961* (noting the circumstances of cases determined before and after Holland). A petitioner's pro se status, ignorance of the law, and lack of legal representation during the applicable filing period do not constitute circumstances justifying equitable tolling because such circumstances are not "extraordinary." See, e.g., *Chaffer, 592 F.3d at 1048-49*; *Waldron-Ramsey, 556 F.3d at 1011-14*; *Rasberry v. Garcia, 448 F.3d 1150, 1154 (9th Cir. 2006)*; *Shoemate v. Norris, 390 F.3d 595, 598 (8th Cir. 2004)*. The vicissitudes of prison life are not "extraordinary" circumstances that make it impossible to file a timely habeas petition. See, e.g., *Ramirez v. Yates, 571 F.3d 993, 997 (9th Cir. 2009)*.

The Ninth Circuit Court of Appeals has held that a petitioner is entitled to tolling of the statute of limitations if they can establish that they are actually innocent of the crimes of conviction. See *Lee, 653 F.3d at 934*. The petitioner must show "it is more likely than not that no reasonable juror would have convicted him in the light of the new evidence." *Id. at 938*. Petitioner has not made a showing of any new evidence. Accordingly, Petitioner is not entitled to tolling of the statute of limitations based on the theory of actual innocence.

Because the habeas action was not filed within the statute of limitations and Petitioner has not stated a proper basis for equitable tolling of the statute of limitations, the Court need not consider the merits of his claims.

KHALIL SHAKUR, PETITIONER, V. CHARLES RYAN, ARIZONA ATTORNEY GENERAL, RESPONDENTS. CIV 11-02169 PHX FJM (MEA) UNITED STATES DISTRICT COURT FOR THE DISTRICT OF ARIZONA

(Text added and modified for emphasis) As a matter of regular practice the Attorney General's Office consistently fails to advise the federal courts that in Arizona counsel fail to raise federal issues thereby waiving claims. There are too many such incidents which constitute a pattern. As this is a pattern with the Arizona Attorney General's Office this should constitute fraud upon the court, because, they are concealing facts on a systemic basis, to defeat valid claims.

COUNSEL: Khalil Shakur, Petitioner, Pro se, KINGMAN, AZ. For Charles L Ryan, Director of the Department of Corrections, Attorney General of the State of Arizona, Respondents: Craig William Soland, LEAD ATTORNEY, Office of the Attorney General, Phoenix, AZ.

I Procedural History

In a direct complaint entered August 13, 2007, Petitioner, named as Eric Thomas, was charged by a grand jury indictment with one count of trafficking in the identity of another. See Answer, Exh. A. On September 14, 2007, a preliminary hearing was ordered. See id., Exh. B. Petitioner and a co-defendant were charged with selling a debit card to two undercover police officers for $80.

On September 18, 2007, a grand jury indictment was returned charging Petitioner with one count of trafficking in the identity of another. See id., Exh. C. That same date the state moved to vacate the preliminary hearing, which motion was granted. See id., Exh. C & Exh. D.

On December 12, 2007, the state amended the indictment to allege Petitioner had previously been convicted of seven felonies. See id., Exh. F. Petitioner was tried before a jury, which found him guilty as charged on February 7, 2008. Id., Exh. O. The state initially alleged a 2007 pending charge for possession of marijuana and a 1997 conviction for aggravated assault, in addition to two convictions for possession of narcotics in 1992 and 1988, and four other convictions occurring between 1979 and 1986. Answer, Exh. F. Two pre-trial settlement conferences were conducted with two different commissioners and at both conferences Petitioner indicated he was not interested in a plea agreement regardless of the sentence he faced if found guilty. Answer, Exh. L.

At sentencing, in return for the state recommending a "super-mitigated" sentence, Petitioner stipulated that he had two prior convictions. Id., Exh. OO at Exh. D. The trial court sentenced Petitioner to an "exceptionally mitigated" sentence of 10.5 years in prison. Id., Exh. OO at Exh. Petitioner took a timely direct appeal of his conviction and sentence. On October 23, 2008, Petitioner's appointed appellate counsel informed the Arizona Court of Appeals that counsel had found no legitimate argument to raise on Petitioner's behalf. Id., Exh. V. Counsel averred to the Court of Appeals that he had contacted Petitioner "soliciting suggested issues," and that Petitioner had identified the following issues that he wished to raise on appeal:

1. Petitioner's rights were violated when his preliminary hearing was vacated and his case presented to the grand jury;

2. Petitioner's right to the effective assistance of counsel was violated;

3. Petitioner's constitutional rights were violated by the state's selective and vindictive prosecution; and

4. Petitioner's constitutional rights were violated by prosecutorial misconduct.

Petitioner was given the opportunity to file a supplemental brief in his direct appeal but did not file a pro se brief. Id., Exh. W & Exh. Z at 2.

On June 23, 2009, the Arizona Court of Appeals affirmed Petitioner's conviction and sentence in a memorandum decision addressing each of the issues related by Petitioner's appointed counsel. Id., Exh. Z. The Arizona Court of Appeals also addressed, inter alia, whether there was sufficient evidence to convict Petitioner and whether the jury had been properly empaneled and instructed. Petitioner did not seek review of this decision by the Arizona Supreme Court.

Petitioner initiated an action for state post-conviction relief pursuant to *Rule 32, Arizona Rules of Civil Procedure*, on September 9, 2009. Id., Exh. EE. Petitioner was appointed counsel to represent him in his Rule 32 proceedings. On May 24, 2010, counsel informed the trial court that she could find no colorable claim to present on Petitioner's behalf. Id., Exh. II.

On July 21, 2010, Petitioner filed a supplemental petition. Id., Exh. KK. On August 19, 2010, Petitioner filed a second supplemental petition, which the trial court struck without prejudice because it did not comply with *Rule 32.5, Arizona Rules of Criminal Procedure*. Id., Exh. LL & Exh. NN.

On September 22, 2010, Petitioner filed a third supplemental petition in his Rule 32 action, alleging:

1. The state had "misled" the grand jury by presenting hearsay testimony rather than "first hand" testimony;

2. The state violated Petitioner's rights by depriving him of a preliminary hearing;

3. He was denied his right to the effective assistance of counsel. Petitioner alleged his counsel failed to challenge the grand jury proceedings, failed to adequately present Petitioner's motion for a voluntariness hearing, failed to inform Petitioner of his right to have grand jury transcripts, and failed to object on conflict of interest

grounds to the commissioner who conducted Petitioner's settlement conference and a trial management conference; and

4. Ineffective assistance of counsel, with regard to establishing Petitioner's historical priors. See id., Exh. OO.

On February 16, 2011, the state Superior Court dismissed Petitioner's action for post-conviction relief. The trial court found Petitioner's claims of ineffective assistance of counsel were not colorable and that Petitioner's remaining claims were precluded under *Rule 32.2(a)(2), Arizona Rules of Criminal Procedure*, because they had been finally adjudicated on appeal. Id., Exh. RR.

In his federal habeas action Petitioner asserts that his constitutional rights were violated by prosecutorial misconduct (Ground One), the denial of his right to a preliminary hearing (Ground Two), prosecutorial misconduct and ineffective assistance of counsel with respect to Petitioner's prior convictions (Ground Three), and ineffective assistance of counsel during his trial and appellate proceedings (Ground Four).

Respondents contend that Grounds One, Three, and Four of Petitioner's habeas claims have not been properly exhausted in state court, and therefore, are procedurally barred. Respondents assert habeas relief should not be granted on Ground Two of the petition because the Arizona court's conclusion that Petitioner was not denied his federal constitutional rights by the termination of the preliminary hearing upon Petitioner's indictment was not clearly contrary to nor an unreasonable application of federal law.

II Analysis

....

1. Petitioner contends that his rights were violated by "Prosecutorial Misconduct: misleading the Grand Jury to Indict."

Respondents assert this claim is procedurally barred because Petitioner failed to properly exhaust his claim either on direct appeal or in a properly-filed action for state post-conviction relief. Respondents contend that, although Petitioner's appointed appellate counsel noted in an "Anders" brief that Petitioner believed his "constitutional rights" were violated by "prosecutorial misconduct," Petitioner did not provide the court with any factual basis for this claim because Petitioner did not file a pro per brief in his direct appeal.

A petitioner must present to the state courts the "substantial equivalent" of the claim presented in federal court. *Picard v. Connor, 404 U.S. 270, 278, 92 S. Ct. 509, 513-14, 30 L. Ed. 2d 438 (1971); Libberton v. Ryan, 583 F.3d 1147, 1164 (9th Cir. 2009)*. Full and fair presentation requires a petitioner to present the substance of his claim to the state courts, including a reference to a federal constitutional guarantee and a statement of facts that entitle the petitioner to relief. See *Scott v. Schriro, 567 F.3d 573, 582 (9th Cir. 2009); Lopez v. Schriro, 491 F.3d 1029, 1040 (9th Cir. 2007)*.

Although a habeas petitioner need not recite "book and verse on the federal constitution" to fairly present a claim to the state courts, *Picard, 404 U.S. at 277-78, 92 S. Ct. at 512-13*, they must do more than present the facts necessary to support the federal claim. See *Anderson v. Harless, 459 U.S. 4, 6, 103 S. Ct. 276, 277, 74 L. Ed. 2d 3 (1982)*. Petitioner never even presented the facts necessary to support this claim to the state court in a direct appeal. Accordingly, because the factual and legal predicate for this claim was not fairly presented to the state court in Petitioner's direct appeal, Petitioner has procedurally defaulted this claim. *Rose, 395 F.3d at 1111*.

To the extent Petitioner raised the factual and constitutional basis for this habeas claim in his action for state post-conviction relief, the state court found the issue precluded because it was decided on the merits in Petitioner's direct appeal. The state court concluded that, as a matter of fact, Petitioner was not subjected to either prosecutorial vindictiveness nor was he subjected to prosecutorial misconduct. The state court did not discuss nor cite to federal cases discussing the United States Constitution when denying these claims.

To constitute an adequate and independent state procedural ground sufficient to support a state court's finding of procedural default, "a state rule must be clear, consistently applied, and well-established at the time of [the] petitioner's purported default." *Lambright v. Stewart, 241 F.3d 1201, 1203 (9th Cir. 2001)*. A state rule is considered consistently applied and well-established if the state courts follow it in the "vast majority of cases." *Scott, 567 F.3d at 580*, quoting *Dugger v. Adams, 489 U.S. 401, 417 n.6, 109 S. Ct. 1211*,

1221 n.6, 103 L. Ed. 2d 435 (1989). The Ninth Circuit Court of Appeals has held that "federal courts should not insist upon a petitioner, as a procedural prerequisite to obtaining federal relief, comply [] with a rule the state itself does not consistently enforce." *Id., 567 F.3d at 581-82,* quoting *Siripongs v. Calderon, 35 F.3d 1308, 1318 (9th Cir. 1994).* It is Respondents' burden to prove the rule cited and relied upon by the state court in denying relief was clear, consistently applied, and well-established at the time the rule was applied to Petitioner's case. Id.

As noted supra, the Arizona Rules of Criminal Procedure regarding timeliness, waiver, and the preclusion of claims have been found to be clear, consistently applied, and well-established at the time the rules were applied to Petitioner's state action for post-conviction relief. See *Stewart, 536 U.S. at 860, 122 S. Ct. at 2581* (holding Arizona's state rules regarding the waiver and procedural default of claims raised in attacks on criminal convictions are adequate and independent state grounds for affirming a conviction and denying federal habeas relief on the grounds of a procedural bar). Therefore, to the extent that it can be found that Petitioner properly presented this habeas claim to the state court in his Rule 32 action, the state court found relief on the merits of the claim procedurally barred by operation of the state rules of criminal procedure. Additionally, Petitioner did not seek review of the Superior Court's denial of relief by the Arizona Court of Appeals. Therefore, Petitioner did not fairly present this habeas claim to the state's "highest court" in a procedurally correct manner.

In response to the answer to his habeas petition, Petitioner asserts that he could not properly pursue his habeas claims in the state courts because his appellate counsel's performance was deficient, i.e., counsel failed to raise and properly present the issues in Petitioner's direct appeal. Petitioner also asserts that his transfer to a prison in Colorado prevented him from filing a pro per brief in his direct appeal. Petitioner also contends that he was denied his right to the effective assistance of post-conviction counsel, asserting that his appointed post-conviction counsel had a conflict because all public defendants' counsel is conflicted with regard to their representation of defendants in Rule 32 proceedings.

Petitioner has not established cause for nor prejudice arising from his procedural default of this habeas claim. Nor has Petitioner established that a fundamental miscarriage of justice will occur if the merits of this claim are not considered.

....

3. Petitioner asserts that he was subjected to "prosecutorial misconduct" and denied his right to the effective assistance of counsel because the state alleged prior convictions that Petitioner contends could not properly be used to enhance his sentence.

Respondents argue that Petitioner did not fairly present this claim to the state courts in a procedurally correct manner and that the claim has been defaulted.

Petitioner did not file a pro per brief in his direct appeal. Accordingly, Petitioner did not allege that he was denied his federal constitutional right to a fair trial or due process of law based on the prosecutor alleging prior convictions which Petitioner asserts could not be used to enhance his sentence. Petitioner did not "fairly present" this claim to the state's highest court in a procedurally correct manner.

Additionally, even if Petitioner properly presented this claim in his state action for post-conviction relief, Petitioner did not seek review by the Arizona Court of Appeals of the trial court's decision denying relief pursuant to Rule 32, Arizona Rules of Criminal Procedure. Therefore, the claim was not "fairly presented" to the state's "highest court" in a procedurally correct manner and the claim has been procedurally defaulted.

As noted supra, Petitioner has not shown cause for nor prejudice arising from his procedural default of this claim. Petitioner has not established that a fundamental miscarriage of justice will occur absent a consideration of the merits of the claim. Therefore, the claim does not warrant the granting of relief.

4. Petitioner contends that he was denied his right to the effective assistance of counsel.

Petitioner raised an ineffective assistance of counsel claim in his first Rule 32 proceedings.

....

AN INEXPLICABLE DECEPTION | 255

The state court thoroughly examined Petitioner's claims regarding ineffective assistance of counsel presented in his state Rule 32 action and denied relief on this claim. The state court concluded that no alleged incident of deficient performance was prejudicial with regard to the outcome of Petitioner's criminal proceedings.

This decision was not clearly contrary to nor an unreasonable application of *Strickland*. The Court notes that Petitioner's counsel was prepared to try the issue of his prior felonies. See Answer, Exh. T. Additionally, as noted by the state court, the sentencing agreement to stipulate to two prior historical felony convictions in return for receiving a super-mitigated sentence was extremely beneficial to Petitioner. The state alleged seven prior felony convictions and, if proved, Petitioner faced a considerably longer term of imprisonment.

HANS G. HIGGINS, PETITIONER, V. CHARLES RYAN, ARIZONA ATTORNEY GENERAL, RESPONDENTS. CIV 09-00345 PHX PGR (MEA) UNITED STATES DISTRICT COURT FOR THE DISTRICT OF ARIZONA

(Text added and modified for emphasis) As a matter of regular practice the Attorney General's Office consistently fails to advise the federal courts that in Arizona counsel fail to raise federal issues thereby waiving claims. There are too many such incidents which constitute a pattern. As this is a pattern with the Arizona Attorney General's Office this should constitute fraud upon the court, because, they are concealing facts on a systemic basis, to defeat valid claims.

COUNSEL: Hans G Higgins, Petitioner, Pro se, FLORENCE, AZ. For Charles L Ryan, Interim Director of the ADOC, Respondent: Aaron Jay Moskowitz, Office of the Attorney General, Phoenix, AZ.

I Procedural background

On June 12, 2006, Petitioner was indicted by a grand jury on one count of theft of a means of transportation and one count of unlawful flight from a law-enforcement vehicle. Answer, Exh. C The indictment was later amended to allege Petitioner had six prior felony convictions, in 1984, 1987, 1990, and 1992.

The state filed an amended allegation of historical priors on December 12, 2006. Traverse, Exh. B. On December 18, 2006, Petitioner's counsel filed a motion to strike this pleading because it was not timely. Id., Exh. C & Exh. D. The state trial court held a hearing on the motion on December 20, 2006. Id., Exh. D. The court took the motion under advisement at that time and set a trial date for January 2, 2006. Id., Exh. D. It would appear from the record in this matter that the motion was denied but it is unclear from the record before the Court when the motion was denied.

Petitioner's first trial on the 2006 charges, in January of 2007, ended in a mistrial resulting from a hung jury. Id., Exh. C. Petitioner filed a special action in the Arizona Court of Appeals and the Arizona Supreme Court asserting the trial judge erred by denying his motion for a directed verdict and that there was insufficient evidence to find he had driven the allegedly stolen vehicle. The Arizona Court of Appeals and the Arizona Supreme Court declined jurisdiction over the special action.

Petitioner's second trial in March of 2007 resulted in a twelve-member jury finding Petitioner guilty on both counts charged in the indictment. Id., Exh. C. At a sentencing hearing conducted December 7, 2007, the trial court denied Petitioner's motion for a new trial. The trial court found Petitioner had three prior felony convictions for aggravated driving under the influence. At the hearing Petitioner's counsel argued for the mitigation of Petitioner's sentence based on his history of substance abuse, mental illness, and physical ill-health. Counsel noted that Petitioner's prior felony convictions occurred in 1994, which was relatively remote in time to the crimes of conviction.

After consideration of the evidence and the statements made at the hearing, the state trial court sentenced Petitioner to a mitigated term of 7.5 years' imprisonment pursuant to his conviction for theft of means of transportation. Petitioner was also sentenced to a concurrent super-mitigated term of three years' imprisonment pursuant to his conviction for unlawful flight from a law-enforcement vehicle.

Petitioner filed a timely notice of appeal with regard to his convictions and sentences. On May 23, 2008, Petitioner's appointed counsel filed a brief pursuant to Anders v. California and Arizona v. Clark, asserting they could find no meritorious issues to raise on Petitioner's behalf. Id., Exh. N. Petitioner's counsel also filed a motion for an extension of the time allowed for Petitioner to file a *pro se* brief in his direct appeal. See id., Exh. O. On May 28, 2008, the Arizona Court of Appeals granted the motion and set a deadline of July 7, 2008, for Petitioner to file a brief in his direct appeal. Id., Exh. P. The premise of Petitioner's special action after his first trial was that the state had produced no evidence that Petitioner had driven the allegedly stolen vehicle. After his conviction, Petitioner's appointed appellate counsel's statement of facts in his Anders brief notes that, during the second trial, a witness "pointed out defendant in court as the man he saw driving the victim's vehicle on the date in question." Answer, Exh. N at 5.

In his pro se brief in his direct appeal Petitioner made arguments with regard to errors which occurred in his first trial. Petitioner asserted the trial court erred by denying his motion to strike the state's amended allegation of historical prior felony convictions. See Answer, Exh. A at 1-4. Petitioner also argued that the prosecutor misled the jury during closing argument by misstating the law, and further argued that the trial court should have granted a judgment of acquittal under *Arizona Rule of Criminal Procedure 20.* Id., Exh. A at 4-5.

The Arizona Court of Appeals affirmed Petitioner's conviction in a memorandum decision. The court rejected Petitioner's arguments regarding errors in his first trial as moot:

> Appellant alleges in his supplemental brief that the trial court erred at multiple points during the first trial. Appellant argues that the State's allegation of historical priors was untimely and violated *Rule 16.1(b)* of the Arizona Rules of Criminal Procedure. Appellant also argues that misstatements of law to the jury by the State during the first trial prejudiced the jury, leading to the hung jury that resulted in a mistrial. Appellant's first trial ended in a mistrial, and thus, resulted in no conviction or sentence, which has the limited procedural effect of a vacated conviction. Because Appellant only raises issues from the first trial, such issues are moot. See *State v. Fritz, 157 Ariz. 139, 141, 755 P.2d 444, 446 (App. 1988)* (noting that any issue concerning a vacated conviction and sentence is moot).

Petition, Exh. A at 6-7.

Petitioner sought review of the Court of Appeals' decision by the Arizona Supreme Court. Id., Exh. B. On January 13, 2009, the Arizona Supreme Court summarily denied review. Id., Exh. C.

On September 3, 2008, Petitioner filed a notice of post conviction relief pursuant to Arizona Rule of Criminal Procedure 32. Id., Exh. D. The trial court appointed counsel. Id., Exh. E. Appointed counsel filed a motion for extension of time and a request for the reporter's transcript of the proceeding that occurred on December 20, 2006. Thereafter Petitioner's appointed post-conviction counsel filed a notice stating she could find no meritorious issues to raise on Petitioner's behalf. Id., Exhs. F-H.

Petitioner filed a pro se petition. See Arizona v. Hans Higgins, S-0700-CR-2006131161 (docket available through public access to case information). The public docket indicates the state trial court denied post-conviction relief on or about November 24, 2009. Id. Petitioner evidently asserted in his post-conviction action that his federal constitutional rights were violated because three prior felony convictions were improperly "allowed." The state court found that Petitioner's federal claims were precluded by *Rule 32.2* because they were not raised in Petitioner's direct appeal. There is no indication in the public docket, nor does Petitioner assert, that he appealed the decision denying Rule 32 relief to the Arizona Court of Appeals.

On February 18, 2009, Petitioner filed the pending federal habeas petition in which he raises one "count" for relief which encompasses several allegations of constitutional error. Petitioner's "count" for relief asserts the violation of his rights pursuant to the "*5th, 8th*, and *14th Amendments to the United States Constitution*."

Petitioner contends he has been subjected to a miscarriage of justice and double jeopardy. Petitioner contends that, therefore, his detention is improper. Petitioner asserts that, on the opening date of his first trial the prosecutor filed an untimely amended allegation of Petitioner's historical prior felonies. Petitioner argues that this constituted procedural error and violated the Arizona Rules of Criminal Procedure. Petitioner further alleges that the filing of the amended allegation of prior felonies was done out of spite for Petitioner's decision not to plead guilty. Petitioner asserts the untimely amendment exposed him to a lengthier sentence and resulted in a jury of twelve, rather than eight individuals, pursuant to Arizona law. Petitioner maintains that, had his first trial not been marred by these errors, he would have been tried before eight jurors and he would have been acquitted. Petitioner further alleges the Arizona Court of Appeals erred by concluding that these claims were moot because his first trial resulted in a mistrial.

In his federal habeas petition Petitioner also alleges that he was deprived of due process because, during his second trial, a witness made a mistaken identification of Petitioner as the perpetrator of the charged crimes.

In response to the habeas petition, Respondents maintain that Petitioner did not properly exhaust his claims in the state courts. Respondents also argue:

> ...Petitioner has alleged only a violation of state law surrounding the timeliness of the State's disclosure that Petitioner had prior felony convictions that the State would use to seek an enhanced sentence. (Doc. 1 at 6.) Although Petitioner strongly believes that the prosecutor lied to the trial judge when she defended the late disclosure, no attribute of Petitioner's claim--the timing of the disclosure, the reasons for the timing of the disclosure, or the actual sentence imposed-- concerns federal law, rendering the allegations noncognizable in this Court.

II Analysis

A. Exhaustion and procedural default
....
D. Petitioner's claims for relief

Petitioner did not properly exhaust any of his federal habeas claims in the state courts. In his action for post conviction relief Petitioner did assert that his right to due process was violated by an improper witness identification. However, Petitioner did not present this claim to the Arizona Court of Appeals. The record before the Court does not indicate that Petitioner appealed the state Superior Court's decision denying post-conviction relief to the Arizona Court of Appeals. Because the time for doing so has expired, this claim is procedurally defaulted.

In his direct appeal Petitioner argued that the state trial court erred during his first trial. Petitioner alleged claims factually similar to those stated in his habeas petition, asserting the trial court's mistakes constituted "fundamental error." In his direct appeal Petitioner emphasized that the improper acts violated state law, rather than his federal constitutional rights. A petitioner's "general appeal to a constitutional guarantee," such as due process, is insufficient to achieve fair presentation. See *Shumway v. Payne, 223 F.3d 982, 987 (9th Cir. 2000)*. Similarly, a federal claim is not exhausted merely because its factual basis was presented to the state courts on state law grounds-a "mere similarity between a claim of state and federal error is insufficient to establish exhaustion." *Id., 223 F.3d at 988*. A claim is not "fairly presented" if the state court must read beyond a brief to find material that alerts it to the presence of a federal claim. See *Wooten v. Kirkland, 540 F.3d 1019, 1025 (9th Cir. 2008)*. Accordingly, as federal constitutional claims the habeas claims were not exhausted in Petitioner's direct appeal.

Petitioner arguably raised his federal claims regarding errors in the first trial in his action for post-conviction relief. However, in his action for post-conviction relief Petitioner did not pursue the claims to the Arizona Court of Appeals, i.e., he did not provide the opportunity for the state's "highest court" to evaluate the merits of his federal constitutional claims.

Petitioner has not shown cause for, nor prejudice arising from his procedural default of all of his claims stating violation of his federal constitutional rights. Accordingly, relief may not be granted on these claims.

Additionally, to the extent Petitioner might have asserted the violation of a federal constitutional right in his direct appeal, those claims were denied based on the Arizona Court of Appeals' conclusion that the claims were moot pursuant to Arizona law. The District Courts are not to review habeas claims presented to a state court if the decision of that state court denying rests on a state ground that is both independent of the federal claim and adequate to support that judgment. See, e.g., *Cook v. Schriro, 538 F.3d 1000, 1028-29 (9th Cir.*

2008); Amos v. Scott, 61 F.3d 333, 338 (5th Cir. 1995). The procedural bar doctrine proscribes federal habeas review of a claim when the state court declined to address the petitioner's federal constitutional claim because the petitioner failed to meet a state procedural requirement with regard to the proper exhaustion of the claim in the state courts. See *Coleman, 501 U.S. at 729-30, 111 S. Ct. at 2553-54; Pitts v. Anderson, 122 F.3d 275, 278 (5th Cir. 1997)*. If the Court finds an independent and adequate state procedural ground, "federal habeas review is barred unless the prisoner can demonstrate cause for the procedural default and actual prejudice, or demonstrate that the failure to consider the claims will result in a fundamental miscarriage of justice." *Noltie v. Peterson, 9 F.3d 802, 804-05 (9th Cir. 1993)*. Petitioner has not established cause and prejudice nor has he established that a fundamental miscarriage of justice has occurred.

The undersigned further concludes that Petitioner's double jeopardy claim may be denied on the merits notwithstanding any failure to properly procedurally exhaust this claim in the state courts. See, e.g., *Arizona v. Washington, 434 U.S. 497, 505, 98 S. Ct. 824, 830, 54 L. Ed. 2d 717 (1978)* (explaining that while a prosecutor is generally entitled to only one opportunity to require an accused to stand trial, a retrial after a mistrial due to manifest necessity does not violate the protections of constitutional double jeopardy). "It is well-established that retrial following a hung jury does not constitute double jeopardy." *Wilson v. Belleque, 554 F.3d 816, 830 (9th Cir. 2009)*.

Furthermore, as noted by Respondents, a state prisoner may obtain a writ of habeas corpus only upon a showing that he is being held in violation of the Constitution, laws, or treaties of the United States. See *28 U.S.C. § 2254(a) (1994 & Supp. 2009); Engle v. Isaac, 456 U.S. 107, 119, 102 S. Ct. 1558, 1567, 71 L. Ed. 2d 783 (1982)*. Federal habeas relief is not available for alleged errors in the interpretation or application of state law, including a state's rules of criminal procedure See *Estelle v. McGuire, 502 U.S. 62, 67-68, 112 S. Ct. 475, 480, 116 L. Ed. 2d 385 (1991); Middleton v. Cupp, 768 F.2d 1083, 1085 (9th Cir. 1985)*.

To the extent that Petitioner asserts his convictions were obtained in violation of his right to due process because his first trial was improper conducted pursuant to Arizona statutory law or rules of criminal procedure, Petitioner has not stated a claim for federal habeas relief. See *Souch v. Schaivo, 289 F.3d 616, 623 (9th Cir. 2002)*. Although Petitioner asserts that his right to due process was violated because the state engaged in misconduct resulting in a hung jury rather than an acquittal, the characterization of this claim in this fashion does not render it cognizable on federal habeas review. See *Cacoperdo v. Demosthenes, 37 F.3d 504, 507 (9th Cir. 1994)*; *Dellinger v. Bowen, 301 F.3d 758, 765 (7th Cir. 2002)*.

RICKY NAPIER, PETITIONER, V. CHARLES L. RYAN AND ARIZONA ATTORNEY GENERAL, RESPONDENTS. CIV 09-02386 PHX ROS (MEA) UNITED STATES DISTRICT COURT FOR THE DISTRICT OF ARIZONA

(Text added and modified for emphasis) As a matter of regular practice the Attorney General's Office fails to advise federal courts that lawyers appointed to represent inmates in state courts do not traditionally fairly present federal claims to state courts preventing federal review. As this is a pattern with the Arizona Attorney General's Office this should constitute fraud upon the court, because, they are misrepresenting facts on a systemic basis, to defeat valid claims.

COUNSEL: Ricky Napier, also named Rick Napier in original complaint, Petitioner, Pro se, TUCSON, AZ. For Charles L Ryan, Director, Attorney General of the State of Arizona, Respondents: Aaron Jay Moskowitz, Office of the Attorney General, Criminal Appeals Section, Phoenix, AZ.

....

D. Petitioner's claims for relief

1. Petitioner's first claim for relief is "involuntariness of incriminative statements (sic)".

In the section of his habeas petition specifying facts in support of his first claim for relief, Petitioner asserts that he was not competent during his interrogation because he was in extreme pain and because he is mentally deficient. Petitioner contends that he was not competent to assist in his own defense during his interrogation. Petitioner does not cite to any provision of the United States Constitution that he believes was violated by these actions.

In his direct appeal Petitioner raised a claim similar to his first habeas claim, regarding the alleged involuntariness of Petitioner's statements to police officers investigating the crimes of conviction. However, when raising this claim in his direct appeal Petitioner did not cite to any provision of the federal constitution.

Petitioner did not "fairly present" his first federal habeas claim to the state courts as alleging the violation of a federal constitutional right. Arizona's rules regarding timeliness and the presentation of claims bar Petitioner from properly exhausting this claim at this time. Accordingly, the Court should not consider the merits of this claim absent a showing of cause and prejudice.

Petitioner has not filed a traverse to the response to his petition. Petitioner has not shown cause for, nor prejudice arising from his procedural default of this claim. Accordingly, habeas relief may not be awarded on this claim.

MICHAEL A. RIVERA, Petitioner - Appellant, v. STATE OF ARIZONA ATTORNEY GENERAL and CHARLES L.

RYAN, RESPONDENTS - APPELLEES. NO. 09-16119 UNITED STATES COURT OF APPEALS FOR THE NINTH CIRCUIT

(Text added and modified for emphasis) As a matter of regular practice the Attorney General's Office fails to advise federal courts that lawyers appointed to represent inmates in state courts do not traditionally timely transmit files to inmates thereby preventing them from timely filing federal petitions. There are too many such incidents. They also fail to advise the court that Arizona prisons do not have law books and materials which inmates may use to present these claims., that they have a system of paralegals which is a sham. These paralegals are not allowed to assist inmates in presenting claims, ADOC Policy DO 902. As this is a pattern with the Arizona Attorney General's Office this should constitute fraud upon the court, because, they are misrepresenting facts on a systemic basis, to defeat valid claims.

COUNSEL: For MICHAEL A. RIVERA, Petitioner - Appellant: Anders V. Rosenquist, Jr., Esquire, Attorney, ROSENQUIST & ASSOCIATES, Anthem, AZ; Florence Bruemmer, Attorney, LAW OFFICES OF FLORENCE M. BRUEMMER, PC, Anthem, AZ. MICHAEL A. RIVERA, Petitioner - Appellant, Pro se, Buckeye, AZ. For STATE OF ARIZONA ATTORNEY GENERAL, CHARLES L. RYAN, Respondents - Appellees: Katia Mehu, Assistant Attorney General, ARIZONA ATTORNEY GENERAL'S OFFICE, Phoenix, AZ.

Petitioner Michael A. Rivera appeals the denial of his habeas corpus petition, filed pursuant to *28 U.S.C. § 2254*. In denying Petitioner's petition, the district judge accepted and adopted a magistrate judge's report that recommended denying the petition as untimely. That report also contained an alternative ruling that, even if the petition were timely, Petitioner would not be entitled to relief, because all of his claims were either procedurally barred, not exhausted, or substantively not cognizable on federal habeas. On appeal, Petitioner challenges only the untimeliness portion of the district court's decision.

Having failed to raise, in his opening brief, a challenge to any part of the alternative holding, Petitioner has now waived the opportunity to do so. See *Smith v. Marsh, 194 F.3d 1045, 1052 (9th Cir. 1999)* ("[A]rguments not raised by a party in its opening brief are deemed waived."). Even though the certificate of appealability did not encompass any issue relating to the merits holding, our rules permit briefing of uncertified issues. See *9th Cir. R. 22-1(e)* ("[I]f a petitioner concludes during the course of preparing the opening brief, that an uncertified issue should be discussed in the brief, the petitioner shall first brief all certified issues under the heading, 'Certified Issues,' and then, in the same brief, shall discuss any uncertified issues under the heading, 'Uncertified Issues.'"). Because the unchallenged alternative holding is independently sufficient to decide the case, we need not and do not decide the timeliness-related issues.

MARQUIS LEE JOHNSON, PETITIONER - APPELLANT, V. ARIZONA ATTORNEY GENERAL; ET AL., RESPONDENTS - APPELLEES. NO. 07-16849 UNITED STATES COURT OF APPEALS FOR THE NINTH CIRCUIT

COUNSEL: MARQUIS LEE JOHNSON (State Prisoner: 149257), Petitioner - Appellant, Pro se, Tucson, AZ. For ARIZONA ATTORNEY GENERAL, DORA B. SCHRIRO, Respondent - Appellees: Alan L. Amann, Assistant Attorney General, AGAZ - OFFICE OF THE ARIZONA ATTORNEY GENERAL (TUCSON), Tucson, AZ.

(Text added and modified for emphasis) As a matter of regular practice the Attorney General's Office fails to advise federal courts that lawyers appointed to represent inmates in state courts do not traditionally advise inmates of the time frames to file habeas petitions. There are too many such incidents. They also fail to advise the court that Arizona prisons do not have law books and materials which inmates may use to present these claims., that they have a system of paralegals which is a sham. These paralegals are not allowed to assist inmates in presenting claims, ADOC Policy DO 902. As this is a pattern with the Arizona Attorney General's Office this should constitute fraud upon the court, because, they are misrepresenting facts on a systemic basis, to defeat valid claims.

Johnson contends that his appellate counsel was ineffective for failing to raise on direct appeal the various claims of prosecutorial misconduct and trial court error that he raises in his *§ 2254* petition. Johnson admits in his petition that counsel told him she had reviewed his suggested claims and found them to be without merit, and Johnson has not demonstrated that any of these claims were viable on direct appeal. Accordingly, Johnson has failed to meet his burden of showing that appellate counsel was deficient for declining to raise his suggested claims on direct appeal, or that he suffered prejudice as a result. *See Strickland v. Washington, 466 U.S. 668, 688, 694, 104 S. Ct. 2052, 80 L. Ed. 2d 674 (1984); see also Smith v. Robbins, 528 U.S. 259, 288, 120 S. Ct. 746, 145 L. Ed. 2d 756 (2000)* (noting that the presumption that appellate counsel acted reasonably will generally be overcome only when claims not raised are clearly stronger than those presented). The state court's decision rejecting Johnson's ineffective assistance of counsel claim was therefore not contrary to, nor an unreasonable application of, clearly established federal law. *See 28 U.S.C. § 2254(d); see also Strickland, 466 U.S. at 694.*

Because Johnson has not set forth any specific facts that, if proven, would entitle him to relief, he has not shown that he is entitled to an evidentiary hearing. *See Gonzalez v. Pliler, 341 F.3d 897, 903 (9th Cir. 2003).*

WILLIAM LANDRUM, PETITIONER - APPELLANT, V. LAURA SCHWEITZER; STATE OF ARIZONA ATTORNEY GENERAL, RESPONDENTS - APPELLEES. NO. 08-17771 UNITED STATES COURT OF APPEALS FOR THE NINTH CIRCUIT

(Text added and modified for emphasis) As a matter of regular practice the Attorney General's Office fails to advise federal courts that lawyers appointed to represent inmates in state courts do not traditionally advise inmates of the time frames to file habeas petitions. There are too many such incidents. They also fail to advise the court that Arizona prisons do not have law books and materials which inmates may use to present these claims., that they have a system of paralegals which is a sham. These paralegals are not allowed to assist inmates in presenting claims, ADOC Policy DO 902. As this is a pattern with the Arizona Attorney General's Office this should constitute fraud upon the court, because, they are misrepresenting facts on a systemic basis, to defeat valid claims.

COUNSEL: WILLIAM LANDRUM, Petitioner - Appellant, Pro se, Buckeye, AZ. For LAURA SCHWEITZER, Respondent - Appellee: Robert Anthony Walsh, Assistant Attorney General, ARIZONA ATTORNEY GENERAL'S OFFICE, Phoenix, AZ.

Arizona state prisoner William Landrum appeals pro se from the district court's judgment dismissing his *28 U.S.C. § 2254* habeas petition for untimeliness. We have jurisdiction under *28 U.S.C. § 2253*, and we affirm.

Landrum contends that several extraordinary circumstances prevented the timely filing of his federal habeas petition and that equitable tolling was warranted. This argument is waived because it was not properly raised before the district court. *See United States v. Carlson, 900 F.2d 1346, 1349 (9th Cir. 1990).* Furthermore, Landrum was not entitled to equitable tolling. *See Rasberry v. Garcia, 448 F.3d 1150,*

1154 (9th Cir.2006) ("[A] pro se petitioner's lack of legal sophistication is not, by itself, an extraordinary circumstance warranting equitable tolling.").

MICHAEL DAVID LENDAHL, Petitioner - Appellant, v. PALOSAARI, Warden ASPC Douglas and STATE OF ARIZONA ATTORNEY GENERAL, Respondents - Appellees. No. 09-15496 UNITED STATES COURT OF APPEALS FOR THE NINTH CIRCUIT

(Text added and modified for emphasis) As a matter of regular practice the Attorney General's Office fails to advise federal courts that in Arizona defendants are pressured into pleading guilty and waiving their rights. There are too many such incidents. As this is a pattern with the Arizona Attorney General's Office this should constitute fraud upon the court, because, they are misrepresenting facts on a systemic basis, to defeat valid claims.

COUNSEL: For MICHAEL DAVID LENDAHL, Petitioner - Appellant: Kurt Michael Altman, Attorney, KURT M. ALTMAN, P.L.C., Attorney at Law, Scottsdale, AZ. MICHAEL DAVID LENDAHL, Petitioner - Appellant, Pro se, Douglas, AZ. For PALOSAARI, Warden ASPC Douglas, STATE OF ARIZONA ATTORNEY GENERAL, Respondents - Appellees: Sarah E. Heckathorne, I, Esquire, Acting Assistant Attorney General, OFFICE OF THE ATTORNEY GENERAL, Phoenix, AZ.

Although Lendahl exhausted his claim that his sentence was improperly enhanced because a judge, not a jury, found the facts underlying the enhancement, we affirm the district court's denial of his federal habeas petition. The state court's denial of Lendahl's claim was not an unreasonable application of clearly established Federal law, because no Supreme Court precedent clearly establishes that a prior conviction must be proved to a jury when it is used as a sentencing factor. *See Almendarez-Torres v. United States, 523 U.S. 224, 118 S. Ct. 1219, 140 L. Ed. 2d 350 (1998).* Further, Lendahl's claim that he did not knowingly and intelligently waive his right to a jury determination of any aggravating factors is unavailing, given that Lendahl's plea agreement and colloquy reflect that he knew and understood his jury-sentencing rights, consulted his attorney regarding those rights and the consequences of waiving them, and then agreed, orally and in writing, to give up those jury-sentencing rights.

GREGORY RICHARD TORREZ, PETITIONER - APPELLANT, V. STATE OF ARIZONA ATTORNEY GENERAL AND CHARLES L. RYAN, INTERIM DIRECTOR OF ARIZONA DEPARTMENT OF CORRECTIONS, RESPONDENTS - APPELLEES. NO. 09-16577 UNITED STATES COURT OF APPEALS FOR THE NINTH CIRCUIT

(Text added and modified for emphasis) As a matter of regular practice the Attorney General's Office fails to advise federal courts that lawyers appointed to represent inmates in state courts do not traditionally advise inmates of the time frames to file habeas petitions. There are too many such incidents. They also fail to advise the court that Arizona prisons do not have law books and materials which inmates may use to present these claims., that they have a system of paralegals which is a sham. These paralegals are not allowed to assist inmates in presenting claims, ADOC Policy DO 902. As this is a pattern with the Arizona Attorney General's Office this should constitute fraud upon the court, because, they are misrepresenting facts on a systemic basis, to defeat valid claims.

COUNSEL: GREGORY RICHARD TORREZ, Petitioner - Appellant, Pro se, Buckeye, AZ. For STATE OF ARIZONA ATTORNEY GENERAL, CHARLES L. RYAN, Interim Director of Arizona Department of Corrections, Respondents - Appellees: Sherri Tolar Rollison, Esquire, Assistant Attorney General, OFFICE OF THE ATTORNEY GENERAL, Phoenix, AZ.

Arizona state prisoner Gregory Richard Torrez appeals pro se from the district court's judgment denying and dismissing his *28 U.S.C. § 2254* habeas petition as untimely. We have jurisdiction under *28 U.S.C. § 2253*, and we affirm.

Torrez contends that the district court erred by treating his second state petition for post-conviction relief as a collateral attack on his conviction rather than as an amendment to his original Rule 32 petition for purposes of calculating the timeliness of his petition. The district court did not err. *See Summers v. Schriro, 481 F.3d 710, 715-17 (9th Cir. 2007)*. Accordingly, Torrez's federal petition was properly dismissed as untimely.

DANIEL ELOY ROMERO, PLAINTIFF - APPELLANT, V. GAY; ARIZONA ATTORNEY GENERAL, RESPONDENTS - APPELLEES. NO. 07-16353 UNITED STATES COURT OF APPEALS FOR THE NINTH CIRCUIT

(Text added and modified for emphasis) As a matter of regular practice the Attorney General's Office fails to advise federal courts that lawyers appointed to represent inmates in state courts do not traditionally advise inmates of the time frames to file habeas petitions. There are too many such incidents. They also fail to advise the court that Arizona prisons do not have law books and materials which inmates may use to present these claims., that they have a system of paralegals which is a sham. These paralegals are not allowed to assist inmates in presenting claims, ADOC Policy DO 902. As this is a pattern with the Arizona Attorney General's Office this should constitute fraud upon the court, because, they are misrepresenting facts on a systemic basis, to defeat valid claims.

COUNSEL: For DANIEL ELOY ROMERO, Plaintiff - Appellant: Patrick Edward McGillicuddy, I, Esquire, Attorney, LAW OFFICES OF PATRICK E. McGILLICUDDY, Phoenix, AZ. DANIEL ELOY ROMERO, Plaintiff - Appellant, Pro se, Florence, AZ. For GAY, ARIZONA ATTORNEY GENERAL, Respondents - Appellees: A.J. Rogers, Esquire, Assistant Attorney General, ARIZONA ATTORNEY GENERAL'S OFFICE, Phoenix, AZ.

Arizona state prisoner Daniel Eloy Romero appeals from the district court's judgment dismissing his *28 U.S.C. § 2254* habeas petition as untimely. We have jurisdiction pursuant to *28 U.S.C. § 2253*, and we affirm.

The district court did not err by finding that Romero's federal habeas petition is barred by the one-year statute of limitations of *28 U.S.C. § 2244(d)(1)*. Romero is not entitled to statutory tolling under *28 U.S.C. § 2244(d)(2)*because his February 2003 letter requesting sentence clarification cannot be construed as a "properly filed application for

State post-conviction relief or other collateral review . . .." *28 U.S.C. § 2244(d)(2).* Furthermore, Romero is not entitled to equitable tolling because he has failed to demonstrate the existence of extraordinary circumstances beyond his control that made it impossible for him to file a petition on time. *Spitsyn v. Moore, 345 F.3d 796, 799 (9th Cir. 2003).*

DEWEY DERALD GULLICK, PETITIONER - APPELLANT, V. BOCK, DEPUTY WARDEN; STATE OF ARIZONA ATTORNEY GENERAL, RESPONDENTS - APPELLEES. NO. 10-15409 UNITED STATES COURT OF APPEALS FOR THE NINTH CIRCUIT

(Text added and modified for emphasis) As a matter of regular practice the Attorney General's Office fails to advise federal courts that lawyers appointed to represent inmates in state courts do not traditionally advise inmates of the time frames to file habeas petitions. There are too many such incidents. They also fail to advise the court that Arizona prisons do not have law books and materials which inmates may use to present these claims., that they have a system of paralegals which is a sham. These paralegals are not allowed to assist inmates in presenting claims, ADOC Policy DO 902. As this is a pattern with the Arizona Attorney General's Office this should constitute fraud upon the court, because, they are misrepresenting facts on a systemic basis, to defeat valid claims.

COUNSEL: DEWEY DERALD GULLICK, Petitioner - Appellant, Pro se, Tucson, AZ. For BOCK, Deputy Warden, STATE OF ARIZONA ATTORNEY GENERAL, Respondent - Appellees: Kent Ernest Cattani, Chief Counsel, Robert Anthony Walsh, Assistant Attorney General, ARIZONA ATTORNEY GENERAL'S OFFICE, Phoenix, AZ.

Gullick contends that the district court erred by denying equitable tolling of AEDPA's one-year statute of limitations. In light of Gullick's ability to file other petitions, represent himself at a hearing, and the reports on his mental condition during the relevant time period, Gullick has failed to demonstrate that his mental condition caused his untimely filing. *See Gaston v. Palmer, 417 F.3d 1030, 1034-35 (9th Cir.*

2005), modified on other grounds, 447 F.3d 1165 (9th Cir. 2006). Further, any inadequate assistance Gullick received from other inmates is not an extraordinary circumstance that warrants equitable tolling. *See Chaffer v. Prosper, 592 F.3d 1046, 1049 (9th Cir. 2010)* (per curiam).

Finally, Gullick contends that, because the state courts incorrectly denied his state petitions as untimely, statutory tolling renders his federal petition timely. When a post-conviction petition is untimely under state law, that is the end of the matter for statutory tolling purposes. *See Pace v. DiGuglielmo, 544 U.S. 408, 414, 417, 125 S. Ct. 1807, 161 L. Ed. 2d 669 (2005).*

ARTIS GIPSON, PETITIONER - APPELLANT, V. CHARLES RYAN AND STATE OF ARIZONA ATTORNEY GENERAL, RESPONDENTS - APPELLEES.NO. 10-15792 UNITED STATES COURT OF APPEALS FOR THE NINTH CIRCUIT

(Text added and modified for emphasis) As a matter of regular practice the Attorney General's Office fails to advise federal courts that lawyers appointed to represent inmates in state courts do not traditionally timely transmit files to inmates thereby preventing them from timely filing federal petitions. There are too many such incidents. They also fail to advise the court that Arizona prisons do not have law books and materials which inmates may use to present these claims., that they have a system of paralegals which is a sham. These paralegals are not allowed to assist inmates in presenting claims, ADOC Policy DO 902. As this is a pattern with the Arizona Attorney General's Office this should constitute fraud upon the court, because, they are misrepresenting facts on a systemic basis, to defeat valid claims.

COUNSEL: ARTIS GIPSON, Petitioner - Appellant, Pro se, Buckeye, AZ. For ARTIS GIPSON, Petitioner - Appellant: Thomas James Phalen, Attorney, Thomas J. Phalen, Phoenix, AZ. For CHARLES RYAN, STATE OF ARIZONA ATTORNEY GENERAL, Respondents - Appellees: Robert Anthony Walsh, Assistant Attorney General, ARIZONA ATTORNEY GENERAL'S OFFICE, Phoenix, AZ.

Artis Gipson appeals the district court's dismissal of his *28 U.S.C. § 2254* petition as untimely under the Antiterrorism and Effective Death Penalty Act of 1996. Reviewing de novo, *see Mendoza v. Carey, 449 F.3d 1065, 1068 (9th Cir. 2006)*, we affirm.

The parties agree that AEDPA's one-year statute of limitations began to run on July 13, 2006, when Gipson's 90-day window for petitioning the U.S. Supreme Court for certiorari expired. *See 28 U.S.C. § 2244(d)(1).* Gipson is correct that he is entitled to statutory tolling while he pursued timely state post-conviction relief -- that is, from when Gipson's conviction became final on July 13, 2006 until October 25, 2007, when the time for Gipson to file a petition for review for post-conviction relief (after receiving one extension of time) expired. *See id. § 2244(d)(2).* Gipson filed his federal habeas petition one year and 122 days later, on February 23, 2009.

Gipson argues that he is entitled to equitable tolling of that one year and 122 days based on (1) the state trial court's inexplicable decision to forward Gipson's pro se transcript request to his appointed counsel, with whom Gipson allegedly could not communicate, and (2) the state trial court's miscalculation of his filing deadline and concomitant denial of his second request for an extension of time to file a petition for review for post-conviction relief.

A petitioner is entitled to equitable tolling only when he shows "'(1) that he has been pursuing his rights diligently, and (2) that some extraordinary circumstance stood in his way' and prevented timely filing." *Holland v. Florida, 130 S. Ct. 2549, 2562, 177 L. Ed. 2d 130 (2010)* (citation omitted).

Here, even if Gipson had pursued his rights diligently, the state trial court's errors did not prevent him from filing a timely federal habeas petition. First, with respect to the miscommunication about Gipson's transcript request, Gipson has failed to identify anything in the transcript that was necessary for him to be able to file his federal habeas petition. Furthermore, Gipson received the transcript on October 3, 2008, more than three weeks before AEDPA's limitations period ran, but has failed to show that it was impossible for him to file his petition within those three weeks. And second, with respect to the denial of the extension of time as a result of the miscalculated filing deadline, even after Gipson exhausted his state appeals of that denial, he still had five months left on AEDPA's limitations period to timely file his petition. Alternatively, as the Supreme Court has noted, Gipson could have filed a "protective" petition with the district court and asked it to "stay and obey the federal habeas proceedings until state remedies are exhausted." *Pace v. DiGuglielmo, 544 U.S. 408, 416, 125 S. Ct. 1807, 161 L. Ed. 2d 669 (2005)*. Accordingly, Gipson has not met his burden to show that extraordinary circumstances made it impossible for him to file a timely habeas petition.

Thus, because Gipson filed his *§ 2254* petition 122 days after AEDPA's one-year limitations period expired, and because he is not entitled to equitable tolling, we affirm the district court's dismissal of his petition as untimely. We therefore need not address Gipson's argument that the state court's denial of his motion for a second extension of time amounted to an inadequate state procedural bar.

MICHAEL MARTIN SANDERS, PETITIONER - APPELLANT, V. CHARLES L. RYAN; DORA B. SCHRIRO; ARIZONA ATTORNEY GENERAL, RESPONDENTS - APPELLEES.NO. 09-17088 UNITED STATES COURT OF APPEALS FOR THE NINTH CIRCUIT

(Text added and modified for emphasis) As a matter of regular practice the Attorney General's Office fails to advise federal courts that lawyers appointed to represent inmates in state courts ail to meaningfully present federal claims as a matter of practice. They fail to disclose the fact that lawyers representing the defendants and appointed by the state refuse to preserve and present federal issues. There are too many such incidents. They also fail to advise the court that Arizona prisons do not have law books and materials which inmates may use to present these claims., that they have a system of paralegals which is a sham. These paralegals are not allowed to assist inmates in presenting claims, ADOC Policy DO 902. As this is a pattern with the Arizona Attorney General's Office this should constitute fraud upon the court, because, they are misrepresenting facts on a systemic basis, to defeat valid claims.

COUNSEL: For MICHAEL MARTIN SANDERS, Petitioner - Appellant: Thomas James Phalen, Attorney, Thomas J. Phalen, Phoenix, AZ. MICHAEL MARTIN SANDERS, Petitioner - Appellant, Pro se, Buckeye, AZ.

Sanders's primary contention is that trial counsel was ineffective for not arguing at trial and in post-trial proceedings that Sanders's entry into the house was justified under *Arizona Revised Statutes § 13-3892*, which provides that a private person may enter a building to arrest someone who commits a felony in the private person's presence. *See Ariz. Rev. Stat. § 13-3892*. The state court concluded in post-conviction proceedings that counsel was not ineffective, and this conclusion was not an unreasonable application of the facts. The person Sanders claimed committed a felony in his presence was not in the house during the invasion, and the *§ 13-3892*defense was thus inapplicable. *See Juan H. v. Allen, 408 F.3d 1262, 1273 (9th Cir. 2005)* ("[T]rial counsel cannot have been ineffective for failing to raise a meritless objection."). The state court's alternative finding that the verdict would not have been different had trial counsel presented the *§ 13-3892* defense was also not unreasonable, because the jury rejected Sanders's argument that the invasion was for legitimate bail enforcement purposes. *See Strickland v. Washington, 466 U.S. 668, 694, 104 S. Ct. 2052, 80 L. Ed. 2d 674 (1984)*.

Sanders further maintains that trial counsel was ineffective for not offering expert testimony concerning the tactics that bail enforcement agents employ when entering a house to apprehend a bail absconder. The state court's rejection of this claim of ineffective assistance was not unreasonable. Sanders does not identify the exculpatory evidence that any purported expert would have provided. *See Grisby v. Blodgett, 130 F.3d 365, 373 (9th Cir. 1997)*. Moreover, the state court's finding that the verdict would have been the same had counsel proffered expert testimony on bail enforcement tactics was not unreasonable, because evidence that Sanders complied with the standards governing bail enforcement agents would have been irrelevant. Such evidence would have been irrelevant since Sanders could have entered the house with the sole intent to commit a robbery, yet executed the robbery using tactics that were consistent with bail enforcement standards.

Sanders also contends that appellate counsel was ineffective for not asserting on direct appeal that the jury instructions constituted fundamental error under *Sullivan v. Louisiana, 508 U.S. 275, 113 S. Ct. 2078, 124 L. Ed. 2d 182 (1993)*. An examination of the record reveals, however, that appellate counsel did raise this argument on direct appeal, and, in any event, the substance of the claim is meritless. The state court's conclusion that appellate counsel was not ineffective was thus not unreasonable.

....

Sanders further contends that the State violated his right to counsel by interfering with the attorney-client relationship. The state courts rejected these claims in Sanders's motion to vacate the judgment and in post-conviction relief proceedings. The state courts' rejection of these claims was not unreasonable. Sanders has not established that the State's alleged interferences with the attorney-client relationship were prejudicial. *See Williams v. Woodford, 384 F.3d 567, 584-85 (9th Cir. 2004)* (noting that government interference "with the confidential relationship between a criminal defendant and defense counsel . . . violates the *Sixth Amendment* right to counsel if it substantially prejudices the criminal defendant").

STATE OF ARIZONA, APPELLEE, V. EDDIE JESUS MELENDEZ, APPELLANT.
NO. 1 CA-CR 14-0593

(Text added/modified for emphasis) These same lawyers as a matter of routine practice file briefs asserting there are no appealable issues. The appellate courts refuse to take judicial notice of their own records which records show that lawyers who represented the defendants in the trial court as a matter of routine fail to make the necessary record and do not subject the state's case to a meaningful testing. These same lawyers surface again and again engaging in exactly the same conduct. As it was never their intent to subject the state's case to a meaningful adversarial process, when viewed in the totality, and not in isolation, this should constitute fraud upon the court by these lawyers.

COUNSEL: Arizona Attorney General's Office, Phoenix, By Joseph T. Maziarz, Counsel for Appellee. Droban & Company PC, Anthem, By Kerrie M. Droban, Counsel for Appellant.

This appeal is filed in accordance with *Anders v. California, 386 U.S. 738, 87 S. Ct. 1396, 18 L. Ed. 2d 493 (1967)* and *State v. Leon, 104 Ariz. 297, 451 P.2d 878 (1969)*. Counsel for Eddie Jesus Melendez asks this Court to search the record for fundamental error. Melendez was given an opportunity to file a supplemental brief in propria persona. He has not done so. After reviewing the record, we affirm Melendez's convictions and sentences.

In April 2012, a Phoenix police officer responded to a citizen's complaint about marijuana growing on the roof of a backyard shed where Melendez lived. Melendez had admitted to the citizen that the plants were marijuana, but stated that he had a valid Arizona Medical Marijuana Card authorizing him to cultivate them. When the officer arrived at the reported address, he could not see anything on the roof from the front of the main house so he went to the rear alley. There, over a six-foot fence which surrounded the backyard, he saw several potted plants organized in rows on the top of the shed. Using binoculars, the officer looked at the plants' pointed leaves and serrated edges and suspected that the plants were marijuana.

For the following month, the officer frequently returned to the house and noted that the plants remained on the shed's roof and appeared taken care of. On one occasion, the officer saw Melendez on the roof watering the plants. Based on these observations, the officer sought and received a search warrant for the exterior of the shed. When the officer knocked and announced to execute the warrant, Melendez exited the shed and showed officers his valid medical marijuana card. Police began their investigation and impounded the plants for testing, which later confirmed that the plants were indeed marijuana. In total, police collected from the shed's roof 19 marijuana plants, each in its own pot and supported by a stake, and eight marijuana sprouts, each in its own plastic cup. The State subsequently charged Melendez with one count of production of marijuana.

Before trial, the trial court transferred Melendez's case to the *Arizona Rule of Criminal Procedure 11* Commissioner's Court. The Commissioner's Court appointed two mental examination experts to conduct an evaluation on Melendez's competency to stand trial pursuant to *A.R.S. § 13-4509*, which requires experts to submit written reports of their evaluations to the court, and *Arizona Rule of Criminal Procedure 11.3*, which requires that the court appoint these experts to evaluate the defendant if reasonable grounds to do so exist. The experts conducted the examinations and subsequently submitted their reports to the court. Based on the reports, the State and Melendez entered into a stipulation for determination of his competency. The Commissioner's Court accepted the stipulation, found Melendez competent to stand trial, and transferred the case back to the trial court.

Two months later, Melendez moved for an evaluation of his competency pursuant to *Arizona Rule of Criminal Procedure 11.2*, which provides that a party may make such a request in writing to determine the defendant's competency to stand trial. Counsel argued that Melendez was unable to understand the nature of the charges and that his mental state prevented him from focusing and otherwise assisting counsel in preparing a viable defense. The trial court conducted an evidentiary hearing and denied the motion, noting that Melendez "presented what he believed to be his defense in the clear logical fashion."

Before trial, the State moved to preclude evidence of Melendez's medical marijuana card citing *State v. Fields ex rel. Cty. of Pima, 232 Ariz. 265, 269 ¶ 14, 304 P.3d 1088, 1092 (App. 2013)*, which provides that if a cardholder does not comply with the Arizona Medical Marijuana Act ("AMMA"), he may be prosecuted for marijuana-related offenses. The State argued that because Melendez possessed more than an "allowable amount of marijuana," under the AMMA, the law did not protect Melendez from prosecution and the card was therefore irrelevant. The trial court conducted an evidentiary hearing and granted the motion, finding that Melendez failed to comply with the AMMA by possessing more than 12 marijuana plants and not containing them in an enclosed, locked facility.

The AMMA defines an "allowable amount of marijuana" for a card holder authorized to cultivate as "twelve marijuana plants contained in an enclosed, locked facility." *A.R.S. § 36-2801(1)(a)(ii)*. An "enclosed area" for purposes of the AMMA means an "outdoor space surrounded by solid, 10-foot walls . . . and a 1-inch thick metal gate." *Ariz. Admin. Code R9-17-101(16)*.

Melendez was then tried by a jury. After deliberating, the jurors notified the trial court that they could not reach a decision. The trial court instructed the jurors to deliberate again and that if they could not reach a decision by the end of the morning that the trial court would "make a decision what you're going to do from there." The jury returned later that morning and convicted Melendez as charged.

STATE OF ARIZONA, APPELLEE, V. CHELSEA NICHOLE EATON, APPELLANT.
NO. 1 CA-CR 15-0218

(Text added/modified for emphasis) These same lawyers as a matter of routine practice file briefs asserting there are no appealable issues. The appellate courts refuse to take judicial notice of their own records which records show that lawyers who represented the defendants in the trial court as a matter of routine fail to make the necessary record and do not subject the state's case to a meaningful testing. These same lawyers surface again and again engaging in exactly the same conduct. As it was never their intent to subject the state's case to a meaningful adversarial process, when viewed in the totality, and not in isolation, this should constitute fraud upon the court by these lawyers.

COUNSEL: Arizona Attorney General's Office, Phoenix, By Joseph T. Maziarz, Counsel for Appellee. Maricopa County Public Defender's Office, Phoenix, By Kathryn L. Petroff, Counsel for Appellant.

Chelsea Nichole Eaton ("Appellant") appeals her convictions and subsequent placement on probation for two counts of aggravated driving while under the influence of drugs ("DUI"), each a class six undesignated felony. Appellant's counsel has filed a brief in accordance with *Smith v. Robbins, 528 U.S. 259, 120 S. Ct. 746, 145 L. Ed. 2d 756 (2000); Anders v. California, 386 U.S. 738, 87 S. Ct. 1396, 18 L. Ed. 2d 493 (1967);* and *State v. Leon, 104 Ariz. 297, 451 P.2d 878 (1969),* stating that she has searched the record on appeal and found no arguable question of law that is not frivolous. Appellant's counsel therefore requests that we review the record for fundamental error. *See State v. Clark, 196 Ariz. 530, 537, ¶ 30, 2 P.3d 89, 96 (App. 1999)* (stating that this court reviews the entire record for reversible error). Although this court allowed Appellant to file a supplemental brief *in propria persona,* she has not done so.

On October 15, 2013, a grand jury issued an indictment, charging Appellant with two counts of aggravated DUI. The State alleged that on June 8, 2012, Appellant drove or was in actual physical control of a vehicle (1) while under the influence of any drug and impaired to the slightest degree, and (2) while a drug defined in *A.R.S. § 13-3401* or its metabolite was in her body. *See A.R.S. § 28-1381(A)(1),* (3). The State further alleged that, as to both counts, Appellant's daughter, who was under fifteen years of age, was in the vehicle at the time. *See A.R.S. § 28-1383(A)(3)(a).*

At trial, the State presented the following evidence: At approximately 7:00 p.m. on June 8, 2012, a witness travelling on a two-lane road in Mesa observed a vehicle, later identified as a white Scion, ahead of him moving erratically into oncoming traffic, swerving in and out of lanes, spinning into the dirt on both sides of the road, and travelling at erratic speeds, which the witness estimated reached more than sixty miles per hour in a forty-five mile-per-hour zone. The witness called "911," and a police dispatcher directed him to stay in sight of the Scion from a safe distance. While following the Scion, the witness observed it bump against the curb and the barrier of an overhead freeway, and drive through a four-way stop without slowing, before police arrived and pulled it over near another intersection.

The dispatcher instructed the witness to drive to a nearby grocery store parking lot, where he provided police with a written statement. As the witness drove away, he saw the Scion's driver, later identified as Appellant, sitting with an infant in her lap.

Officer Dyas of the Gilbert Police Department responded to the 911 call and located the Scion by its description and license plate. He activated the lights of his unmarked police car and pulled the Scion over near a grocery store lot. The officer noticed that when he confronted the driver (Appellant), she seemed slumped over and relaxed, with her speech slightly slurred. While speaking with Appellant, the officer observed Appellant's two-year-old child crawling around in the rear seat of the Scion.

Appellant told the officer she had been trying to buckle the child into the safety seat while she drove the vehicle. She denied having consumed any alcohol, but admitted having taken Zoloft, a prescription medication, three hours earlier. The officer, concerned Appellant might be impaired, asked Appellant to perform DUI field tests, and she agreed to do so. As Appellant stepped away from her vehicle, she was swaying and caught hold of the side of the car once to regain her balance and avoid falling to the ground.

The officer administered horizontal gaze nystagmus ("HGN") and walk-and-turn tests. During the HGN test, Appellant exhibited two of six "clues" of impairment, including having her eye "bounce" while following a moving object. During the walk-and-turn test, Appellant exhibited six of eight clues of impairment, including losing her balance three times, keeping her hands up while walking, failing to touch her heel to her toe, taking the wrong number of steps, and pivoting in the wrong direction upon returning. The officer then stopped the testing out of concern that Appellant might fall and injure herself.

Officer Dyas placed Appellant under arrest and advised her of her rights pursuant to *Miranda*. At that time, Appellant advised him she had taken Xanax, rather than Zoloft. Appellant's daughter was placed in the custody of her grandmother, who had been called to the scene, and Appellant's car--which by that time had a flat rear tire on the driver's side--was towed, per departmental policy.

Appellant was transported to the police station, and Officer Dyas, a qualified phlebotomist, drew two vials of her blood at 8:36 p.m. At approximately this time, Appellant advised the officer that she was also taking an anti-depressant drug, which he heard to be "A Surgeline." On a scale of one to ten, with one being completely sober and ten being completely "intoxicated" by medication, Appellant gave herself a "two."

Officer Dyas asked Appellant to submit to an additional voluntary forty-five-minute drug recognition exam, but she declined and was released. Based on the record, it appears Appellant stated she was taking Sertraline.

Two criminalists testified for the State. Each had tested a sample of Appellant's blood and detected the presence of Benzodiazepine, a central nervous system depressant or sedative, typically found in anti-anxiety drugs. The first criminalist, Kimberly Guerra, noted the specific Benzodiazepine derivatives detected were Diazapam, Lorazepam, and Nordiazapam. The second criminalist, Giang Phan, analyzed Appellant's blood sample to confirm the presence of Benzodiazepine and found twenty-one nanograms per milliliter of Diazepam, also known as Xanax; forty-one nanograms per milliliter of Lorazepam, also known as Ativan; and forty-five nanograms per milliliter of Nordiazepam, a metabolite of Diazepam. Phan conceded the levels of the drugs detected in Appellant's blood were within or below the therapeutic range, but opined that even when used in the correct therapeutic range, the drugs could be similar in effect to alcohol, producing drowsiness, poor coordination, slurring of speech, and lack of divided attention, which could be manifested as an inability to both control speed and stay within a given lane at the same time. Phan could not say with certainty what effect the active chemicals would have had on Appellant on the day she was arrested. Diazepam, Lorazepam, and Nordiazepam are included as dangerous drugs under A.R.S. § 13-3401(6)(d)(xvi), (xxxiv), and (l), respectively.

Appellant presented two witnesses whose testimony indicated she may have been using prescription medications on the date she was arrested. A records custodian at Banner Health Hospital testified that on June 5, 2012, Appellant was seen as an emergency room patient and given Ativan and Bactrim by the pharmacy. A family nurse practitioner, Mary Quihuis, testified that on March 24, 2012, she wrote Appellant a prescription for Sertraline, the generic equivalent of Zoloft, which is often prescribed for anxiety, obsessive compulsive disorder, depression, or other psychological problems. Although Sertraline may cause dizziness, nausea, headaches, wakefulness, drowsiness, or anxiousness, Quihuis said there are typically no warnings to avoid driving associated with Sertraline/Zoloft because the medicine is not a controlled substance known to cause undue drowsiness in everyone. She conceded, however, that she did not regularly review the caution labels on prescription bottles because she had not learned of any new warnings coming out regarding Zoloft.

Quihuis also stated somebody who suffers from anxiety might be prescribed both Zoloft and Ativan. Quihuis agreed she did not know what drugs Appellant had taken on the evening in question, and although there was no expected interaction between Zoloft and Ativan and they were commonly used together, it was possible a person taking them in combination could experience dizziness, drowsiness, and blurred vision.

THE STATE OF ARIZONA, APPELLEE, V. LAWRIS DOUGLAS STATEN II, APPELLANT.
NO. 2 CA-CR 2015-0197

(Text added/modified for emphasis) These same lawyers as a matter of routine practice file briefs asserting there are no appealable issues. The appellate courts refuse to take judicial notice of their own records which records show that lawyers who represented the defendants in the trial court as a matter of routine fail to make the necessary record and do not subject the state's case to a meaningful testing. These same lawyers surface again and again engaging in exactly the same conduct. As it was never their intent to subject the state's case to a meaningful adversarial process, when viewed in the totality, and not in isolation, this should constitute fraud upon the court by these lawyers.

COUNSEL: Flores & Clark, LLC, Globe, By Daisy Flores, for Appellant.

Counsel has filed a brief in compliance with *Anders v. California, 386 U.S. 738, 744, 87 S. Ct. 1396, 18 L. Ed. 2d 493 (1967)*, and *State v. Clark, 196 Ariz. 530, ¶ 30, 2 P.3d 89, 96 (App. 1999)*, asserting she has reviewed the record but found no arguable issue to raise on appeal. Consistent with *Clark, 196 Ariz. 530, ¶ 32, 2 P.3d at 97*, she has provided "a detailed factual and procedural history of the case with citations to the record" and asks this court to search the record for error. Staten has not filed a supplemental brief.

STATE OF ARIZONA, APPELLEE, V. ERIK GABRIEL BENALLY, APPELLANT.
NO. 1 CA-CR 15-0022

(Text added/modified for emphasis) These same lawyers as a matter of routine practice file briefs asserting there are no appealable issues. The appellate courts refuse to take judicial notice of their own records which records show that lawyers who represented the defendants in the trial court as a matter of routine fail to make the necessary record and do not subject the state's case to a meaningful testing. These same lawyers surface again and again engaging in exactly the same conduct. As it was never their intent to subject the state's case to a meaningful adversarial process, when viewed in the totality, and not in isolation, this should constitute fraud upon the court by these lawyers.

COUNSEL: Arizona Attorney General's Office, Phoenix, By Joseph T. Maziarz, Counsel for Appellee. Coconino County Public Defender's Office, Flagstaff, By Brad Bransky, Counsel for Appellant.

This appeal was timely filed in accordance with *Anders v. California, 386 U.S. 738, 87 S. Ct. 1396, 18 L. Ed. 2d 493 (1967)*, and *State v. Leon, 104 Ariz. 297, 451 P.2d 878 (1969)*, following Erik Gabriel Benally's conviction of aggravated assault, a Class 3 felony; shoplifting, a Class 1 misdemeanor; and refusal to provide name, a Class 2 misdemeanor. Benally's counsel has searched the record on appeal and found no arguable question of law that is not frivolous. *See Smith v. Robbins, 528 U.S. 259, 120 S. Ct. 746, 145 L. Ed. 2d 756 (2000); Anders, 386 U.S. 738, 87 S. Ct. 1396, 18 L. Ed. 2d 493; State v. Clark, 196 Ariz. 530, 2 P.3d 89 (App. 1999)*. Benally has filed a supplemental brief identifying various issues, which we address below. After reviewing the entire record, we affirm Benally's convictions and sentences.

FACTS AND PROCEDURAL HISTORY

Benally entered a department store, selected a pair of sweatpants and two sweatshirts and removed their price tags. He continued to another area of the store, where he took two energy drinks and concealed them in the sweatshirt he had picked up. Without paying for the items, Benally then walked to the store exit, where he was stopped by store asset protection employees. The employees asked Benally if he had paid for the items, and Benally offered to give the items back. Benally then accompanied the employees to an office at the back of the store. While the employees were questioning Benally, he suddenly stood and rushed toward the door, where one of them was standing. After a brief physical altercation, Benally pulled out a knife, flipped it open and moved toward the employee standing at the door. The employee felt the tip of the knife against his abdomen, but was not injured. He moved aside and Benally exited the office and the store and ran toward a nearby hotel.

Two police officers who were called to the scene apprehended Benally, handcuffed him and placed him under arrest. One officer repeatedly asked Benally for his name, but Benally refused to respond.

A jury convicted Benally of aggravated assault, shoplifting, and refusal to give name. The jury also found the aggravated assault to be a dangerous offense. After finding Benally was convicted of two prior felonies, the superior court sentenced him to an aggravated term of nine years' incarceration for aggravated assault and time served for the other convictions. The court granted Benally 325 days of presentence incarceration credit.

STATE OF ARIZONA, APPELLEE, V. NICHOLAS PUMA, APPELLANT.
NO. 1 CA-CR 15-0010

(Text added/modified for emphasis) These same lawyers as a matter of routine practice file briefs asserting there are no appealable issues. The appellate courts refuse to take judicial notice of their own records which records show that lawyers who represented the defendants in the trial court as a matter of routine fail to make the necessary record and do not subject the state's case to a meaningful testing. These same lawyers surface again and again engaging in exactly the same conduct. As it was never their intent to subject the state's case to a meaningful adversarial process, when viewed in the totality, and not in isolation, this should constitute fraud upon the court by these lawyers.

COUNSEL: Arizona Attorney General's Office, Phoenix, By Joseph T. Maziarz, Counsel for Appellee. Maricopa County Public Defender's Office, Phoenix, By Terry J. Adams, Counsel for Appellant.

Nicholas Puma appeals from his convictions and sentences for one count of armed robbery, a class two dangerous felony, one count of theft, a class one misdemeanor, and two counts of theft of credit card, class five felonies. Puma's counsel filed a brief in compliance with *Anders v. California, 386 U.S. 738, 87 S. Ct. 1396, 18 L. Ed. 2d 493 (1967)*, and *State v. Leon, 104 Ariz. 297, 451 P.2d 878 (1969)*, stating that he has searched the record and found no arguable question of law and requesting that this court examine the record for reversible error. Puma was afforded the opportunity to file a *pro se* supplemental brief and did so. *See State v. Clark, 196 Ariz. 530, 537, ¶ 30, 2 P.3d 89 (App. 1999)*. For the following reasons, we affirm with one modification.

On September 1, 2013, a man robbed a Pizza Hut in Scottsdale Arizona. The store manager ("A.B.") testified that the man slid over the counter and demanded she give him the money in the drawer and vault. The man was wearing all dark clothing, had his face covered, and was wearing a backpack in front of him with a crowbar sticking out of it. The man had one hand in the backpack. A.B. was frightened for her safety and turned over approximately $200 in cash from the drawer, but she told the man she could not open the vault. The man told A.B. to leave the store.

The intruder was not apprehended at the scene. After the police arrived, A.B. and another employee, B.S., realized that their purses had been removed from the restaurant. Their purses collectively contained cash and several credit and debit cards. B.S. also had an iPad in her purse. Following the incident at Pizza Hut, A.B. and B.S.'s cards were used at several gas stations and a Best Buy. Video footage from one gas station showed a man wearing a shirt with distinct lettering on it attempting to use the cards. Although most of the transactions were denied, B.S.'s card was used to purchase a laptop for $895.63 at Best Buy.

The Best Buy transaction also involved use of a Reward Zone card, and investigators were able to identify Nicholas Puma as the owner of the rewards card used. Investigators learned a possible address for Puma, obtained a search warrant, and executed a search of the residence and a vehicle at the residence. Detectives found a laptop and box that matched the sale from Best Buy, an iPad matching the one B.S. had in her purse, a shirt matching the one worn by the subject in the gas station surveillance video, B.S.'s voter registration card from her wallet, a purse matching one taken from Pizza Hut, clothing and a backpack matching those worn by the intruder at Pizza Hut, and several crowbars.

After a four day trial, a jury returned a verdict of guilty on Count 1 for armed robbery, Count 3 for theft, and Counts 4 and 5 for theft of a credit card. The jury acquitted Puma of Count 2, aggravated assault. The trial court then held a hearing in which the State presented evidence of Puma's criminal history. The trial court found that Puma had at least two qualifying prior armed robbery convictions, requiring sentencing under *Arizona Revised Statutes ("A.R.S.") section 13-706*. Specifically, Puma had convictions in 1995, arising from offenses on separate dates in 1994 and prior convictions in 1980, resulting from offenses in 1979.

On Count 1, armed robbery, the trial court sentenced Puma to life in prison with no possibility of release for 35 years, with 434 days of presentence incarceration credit. On Count 3, theft, the trial court ordered six months in jail with credit for time served. On Counts 4 and 5, theft of credit card, the trial court ordered prison for the presumptive term of five years with 434 days of presentence credit for each conviction. The sentences were ordered to be served concurrently.

STATE OF ARIZONA, APPELLEE, V. STEVE ALLEN BAKER, JR., APPELLANT.
NO. 1 CA-CR 14-0398

(Text added/modified for emphasis) These same lawyers as a matter of routine practice file briefs asserting there are no appealable issues. The appellate courts refuse to take judicial notice of their own records which records show that lawyers who represented the defendants in the trial court as a matter of routine fail to make the necessary record and do not subject the state's case to a meaningful testing. These same lawyers surface again and again engaging in exactly the same conduct. As it was never their intent to subject the state's case to a meaningful adversarial process, when viewed in the totality, and not in isolation, this should constitute fraud upon the court by these lawyers.

COUNSEL: Arizona Attorney General's Office, Phoenix, By Joseph T. Maziarz, Counsel for Appellee. Maricopa County Public Defender's Office, Phoenix, By Carlos Daniel Carrion, Counsel for Appellant.

This appeal is filed in accordance with *Anders v. California, 386 U.S. 738, 87 S. Ct. 1396, 18 L. Ed. 2d 493 (1967)* and *State v. Leon, 104 Ariz. 297, 451 P.2d 878 (1969)*. Counsel for Steve Allen Baker, Jr. asks this Court to search the record for fundamental error. Baker was given an opportunity to file a supplemental brief in propria persona. He has not done so. After reviewing the record, we affirm Baker's convictions and probation order.

Two police officers were on patrol one night when the car in front of them immediately made a left-hand turn on a red light. The officers pulled the car over. One officer spoke with the driver--later identified as Baker. The officer asked Baker for his driver's license and car registration and insurance, but Baker responded that he did not have to give the officer anything. The officer told Baker that to operate a "vehicle" in Arizona, he needed a driver's license. Baker said that he was not operating a "vehicle," but rather an "automobile." The officer again asked Baker for his driver's license; Baker instead gave a "sovereign national ID card."

Meanwhile, the other officer was talking with Baker's passenger. Because it was dark, the officer directed a flashlight inside Baker's car. Baker yelled at the officer and told him that he did not have to have the flashlight on and pointing inside the car. Baker then insisted that a sergeant come to the scene. Because of Baker's request and his being "[v]ery resistant to any of the questions" the officers posed, an officer radioed for a sergeant, who soon arrived with two additional officers. One of these officers took over the conversation with Baker, asking him if the "vehicle" was his. Baker responded that "this was not a vehicle," but an "automobile mobile transportation device."

Standing 6 inches from the car window, the officer smelled fresh marijuana from inside the car. The officer asked Baker whether he had any marijuana, but Baker responded that he did not have to answer. Baker then demanded that the police release his passenger. Meanwhile, another officer was checking Baker's records and found that he had a suspended license. He told the other officers to arrest Baker.

The police arrested Baker, transported him and his passenger to the station, and impounded his car. Before leaving for the station, however, the police told Baker his *Miranda* rights. Baker said he did not understand them, so the police stopped questioning him. On the way to the station, Baker blurted out that the passenger "was only a guest inside his automobile and that all items inside that automobile were his."

Because of the smell of marijuana, the police searched the car and found two backpacks. One of the backpacks belonged to Baker's passenger and was given to him when he was released. The other backpack had individually packaged bags of marijuana, a purple prescription bottle with marijuana, and documents regarding the "sovereign citizen" movement. A forensic analyst concluded that the bags had usable quality and conditioned marijuana.

During booking, the police impounded hydroponic cards found inside Baker's wallet. The cards detailed instructions for indoor watering and lighting for marijuana plants. The police also impounded a booklet with a daily checklist for hydroponic plants--marijuana plants--and other documents, including a "Sovereign National Automobile Title" with Baker as the car's registered owner and five photocopied sovereign national ID cards, three of them had Baker's picture.

The State charged Baker with felony possession or use of marijuana, felony possession of drug paraphernalia, and a misdemeanor resisting arrest. The resisting arrest charge was subsequently dismissed without prejudice, and the two remaining charges were designated as misdemeanors.

During the bench trial, three officers testified about the incident and identified Baker as the person they interacted with. After the State rested, defense counsel moved for an Arizona Rule of Criminal Procedure 20 judgment of acquittal, but the trial court denied the motion. The court found Baker guilty of possession or use of marijuana and possession of drug paraphernalia.

STATE OF ARIZONA, APPELLEE, V. TRAVIS ADAM SANTO, APPELLANT.
NO. 1 CA-CR 15-0108

(Text added/modified for emphasis) These same lawyers as a matter of routine practice file briefs asserting there are no appealable issues. The appellate courts refuse to take judicial notice of their own records which records show that lawyers who represented the defendants in the trial court as a matter of routine fail to make the necessary record and do not subject the state's case to a meaningful testing. These same lawyers surface again and again engaging in exactly the same conduct. As it was never their intent to subject the state's case to a meaningful adversarial process, when viewed in the totality, and not in isolation, this should constitute fraud upon the court by these lawyers.

COUNSEL: Arizona Attorney General's Office, Phoenix, By Joseph T. Maziarz, Counsel for Appellee. Maricopa County Public Defender's Office, Phoenix, By Joel M. Glynn, Counsel for Appellant.

Travis Adam Santo ("Defendant") appeals from his conviction and sentence for two counts of Aggravated Driving Under the Influence (DUI) pursuant to *Arizona Revised Statues ("A.R.S.") sections 28-1381(A)(1) and (A)(2)*. Defendant's counsel filed a brief in accordance with *Anders v. California, 386 U.S. 738, 87 S. Ct. 1396, 18 L. Ed. 2d 493 (1967)*, and *State v. Leon, 104 Ariz. 297, 451 P.2d 878 (1969)*, advising this Court that after a search of the entire appellate record, no arguable ground exists for reversal. Defendant was granted leave to file a supplemental brief *in propria persona*, and did not do so.

Facts and Procedural History

During the early morning hours of August 12, 2012, an officer saw a car driving erratically on both the State Route 101 and the U.S. 60. The officer initiated a traffic stop, and the vehicle pulled over in a parking lot. Defendant, the driver of the vehicle, gave the officer his December 29, 2008 driver's license.

The officer noticed Defendant's eyes were bloodshot and watery, his face was flushed, and he exhibited slow and deliberate movements. When asked to get out of the car, Defendant lost his balance and fell against it. The officer also noticed a strong odor of alcohol coming from Defendant.

The officer performed a Horizontal Gaze Nystagmus ("HGN") test on Defendant at the scene. The officer observed six of six HGN cues, indicating Defendant was alcohol impaired. The officer arrested Defendant, checked the status of his driver's license, and learned that it had been suspended.

The officer then drove Defendant to a mobile DUI van where Defendant agreed to submit to breathalyzer and blood tests. Defendant's breath tests showed a BAC of .211 and .212; his blood test showed a BAC of .204.

A review of Defendant's MVD Records showed that he was issued two driver's licenses. The first license was issued on December 29, 2008, and the second was issued, after a change of address request, on August 20, 2011. Defendant did not surrender his December 29, 2008 driver's license when the MVD issued his August 20, 2011 license.

MVD records also showed that a written affidavit and suspension order was served to him on July 21, 2012, and submitted to the MVD with Defendant's driver's license attached to it. Defendant signed the affidavit/suspension order, thereby confirming personal service. The suspension order stated that the MVD had destroyed Defendant's driver's license, and that his suspension commenced on August 5, 2012.

At the conclusion of trial, the jury found Defendant guilty on both counts of Aggravated DUI.

STATE OF ARIZONA, APPELLEE V. MARSHALL EDWARD LEEDS, APPELLANT.
NO. 1 CA-CR 14-0709

(Text added/modified for emphasis) These same lawyers as a matter of routine practice file briefs asserting there are no appealable issues. The appellate courts refuse to take judicial notice of their own records which records show that lawyers who represented the defendants in the trial court as a matter of routine fail to make the necessary record and do not subject the state's case to a meaningful testing. These same lawyers surface again and again engaging in exactly the same conduct. As it was never their intent to subject the state's case to a meaningful adversarial process, when viewed in the totality, and not in isolation, this should constitute fraud upon the court by these lawyers.

COUNSEL: Arizona Attorney General's Office, Phoenix, By Joseph T. Maziarz, Counsel for Appellee. Maricopa County Public Defender, Phoenix, By Joel M. Glynn, Counsel for Appellant.

Marshall Edward Leeds timely appeals from his conviction and sentence for one count of misconduct involving weapons, a class 4 felony. After searching the record on appeal and finding no arguable question of law that was not frivolous, Leeds' counsel filed a brief in accordance with *Anders v. California, 386 U.S. 738, 87 S. Ct. 1396, 18 L. Ed. 2d 493 (1967)*, and *State v. Leon, 104 Ariz. 297, 451 P.2d 878 (1969)*, asking this court to search the record for fundamental error. This court granted counsel's motion to allow Leeds to file a supplemental brief *in propria persona*, and Leeds did so. We reject the arguments raised in Leeds' supplemental brief and, after reviewing the entire record, find no fundamental error. Therefore, we affirm Leeds' conviction and sentence as corrected.

FACTS AND PROCEDURAL BACKGROUND

On October 18, 2013, D.P., Leeds' probation officer, joined by other officers, visited Leeds' home and conducted a "probation search" for a weapon. After answering the door, Leeds was handcuffed and then asked for the weapon. Leeds initially said his father's guns were in storage, but eventually admitted the gun was on a table in the bedroom. After a quick search, the officers located the gun in the bedroom. Officers arrested Leeds, and, subsequently, at the police station, read Leeds his *Miranda* rights. Leeds admitted to carrying the gun while walking the family dog around the neighborhood because he was worried about his safety. He also acknowledged he knew carrying a gun was illegal.

Based on the foregoing evidence, a jury found Leeds guilty of one count of misconduct involving weapons. Leeds admitted to being on probation at the time of the offense. At the combined "priors trial" and sentencing hearing, the court found Leeds had committed two historical priors. The court sentenced Leeds to a presumptive term of ten years as a category three repetitive offender and awarded Leeds 329 days of presentence incarceration credit.

STATE OF ARIZONA, APPELLEE, V. RAFAEL ALLEN ZAMORANO, APPELLANT.
NO. 1 CA-CR 15-0040

(Text added/modified for emphasis) These same lawyers as a matter of routine practice file briefs asserting there are no appealable issues. The appellate courts refuse to take judicial notice of their own records which records show that lawyers who represented the defendants in the trial court as a matter of routine fail to make the necessary record and do not subject the state's case to a meaningful testing. These same lawyers surface again and again engaging in exactly the same conduct. As it was never their intent to subject the state's case to a meaningful adversarial process, when viewed in the totality, and not in isolation, this should constitute fraud upon the court by these lawyers.

COUNSEL: For Appellee: Joseph T. Maziarz, Arizona Attorney General's Office, Phoenix. For Appellant: Paul J. Prato, Maricopa County Public Defender's Office, Phoenix.

Rafael Zamorano appeals his convictions for aggravated assault and disorderly conduct. Pursuant to *Anders v. California, 386 U.S. 738, 87 S.*

Ct. 1396, 18 L. Ed. 2d 493 (1967), and *State v. Leon, 104 Ariz. 297, 451 P.2d 878 (1969)*, defense counsel has searched the record, found no arguable question of law, and asked us to review the record for reversible error. *See State v. Richardson, 175 Ariz. 336, 339, 857 P.2d 388 (App. 1993)*. Zamorano was given the opportunity to file a supplemental brief *in propria persona*, but he has not done so. For the following reasons, we affirm.

FACTS AND PROCEDURAL HISTORY

T.H. drove her daughter, M.H., and cousin, E.J., to a restaurant. The restaurant's small parking lot was full, so T.H. parked at an angle behind other parked cars and waited in the car with E.J. while M.H. went inside to order food to go.

Zamorano and two other men walked out of the restaurant to their Chevy. Zamorano yelled, "[B] , move out the way," and he and T.H. began yelling at each other. By then, T.H. had opened the driver's side door and was standing up, facing Zamorano. M.H. returned from the restaurant and stood near the passenger's side door, facing Zamorano. Zamorano stated, "I bet you'll move fast now, b " and pointed a gun towards the women. T.H. and M.H. got into their car and drove away. They noticed the Chevy behind them, so they pulled over and called the police. Officers found an empty holster on Zamorano's person and a gun in the backseat of the Chevy.

Zamorano was charged with aggravated assault against T.H., a class three felony, in violation of *Arizona Revised Statutes ("A.R.S.") § 13-1203(A)(2) and -1204(A)(2)*, and disorderly conduct against T.H., M.H., and/or E.J., a class six felony, in violation of *A.R.S. § 13-2904(A)(6)*. A jury found Zamorano guilty of the charged offenses and found that both counts were dangerous offenses. The court sentenced Zamorano to 6.25 years' imprisonment for count one and a concurrent term of 2 years' imprisonment for count two. Zamorano timely appealed.

STATE OF ARIZONA, APPELLEE, V. MARQUISE JA MONTE JOHNSON, APPELLANT.
NO. 1 CA-CR 14-0867

COUNSEL: Arizona Attorney General's Office, Phoenix, By Joseph T. Maziarz, Counsel for Appellee. Maricopa County Public Defender's Office, Phoenix, By Paul J. Prato, Counsel for Appellant.

(Text added/modified for emphasis) These same lawyers as a matter of routine practice file briefs asserting there are no appealable issues. The appellate courts refuse to take judicial notice of their own records which records show that lawyers who represented the defendants in the trial court as a matter of routine fail to make the necessary record and do not subject the state's case to a meaningful testing. These same lawyers surface again and again engaging in exactly the same conduct. As it was never their intent to subject the state's case to a meaningful adversarial process, when viewed in the totality, and not in isolation, this should constitute fraud upon the court by these lawyers.

Marquise Ja Monte Johnson appeals his convictions and sentences for one count of aggravated assault, a class 3 felony, and one count of misconduct involving weapons, a class 4 felony. Johnson's counsel filed a brief in compliance with *Anders v. California, 386 U.S. 738, 87 S. Ct. 1396, 18 L. Ed. 2d 493 (1967),* and *State v. Leon, 104 Ariz. 297, 451 P.2d 878 (1969),* stating that he has searched the record and found no arguable question of law and requesting that this court examine the record for reversible error. Johnson was afforded the opportunity to file a *pro se* supplemental brief but did not do so. *See State v. Clark, 196 Ariz. 530, 537, ¶ 30, 2 P.3d 89 (App. 1999).* For the following reasons, we affirm.

STATE OF ARIZONA, APPELLEE, V. ALAN SCOTT MCBRIDE, APPELLANT.
NO. 1 CA-CR 15-0146

COUNSEL: Arizona Attorney General's Office, Phoenix, By Joseph T. Maziarz, Counsel for Appellee. Maricopa County Legal Defender's Office, Phoenix, By Cynthia D. Beck, Counsel for Appellant.

(Text added/modified for emphasis) These same lawyers as a matter of routine practice file briefs asserting there are no appealable issues. The appellate courts refuse to take judicial notice of their own records which records show that lawyers who represented the defendants in the trial court as a matter of routine fail to make the necessary record and do not subject the state's case to a meaningful testing. These same lawyers surface again and again engaging in exactly the same conduct. As it was never their intent to subject the state's case to a meaningful adversarial process, when viewed in the totality, and not in isolation, this should constitute fraud upon the court by these lawyers.

Alan Scott McBride ("Defendant") appeals from his conviction and sentence for one count of aggravated assault. Defendant's counsel filed a brief in accordance with *Anders v. California, 386 U.S. 738, 87 S. Ct. 1396, 18 L. Ed. 2d 493 (1967)*, and *State v. Leon, 104 Ariz. 297, 451 P.2d 878 (1969)*, advising this Court that after a search of the entire appellate record, no arguable ground exists for reversal. Defendant was granted leave to file a supplemental brief *in propria persona*, and did not do so.

Facts and Procedural History

Defendant, the victim and two women were gathered in a Carl's Junior restaurant in Phoenix. At one point during the meeting, Defendant left his debit card on the table and momentarily walked away. The victim allegedly picked up the debit card and walked outside with the two women, leaving Defendant in the restaurant. Defendant followed the group outside and yelled at them to return his debit card. Defendant then ran up behind the victim and stabbed him in the back with a knife. At trial, a witness testified that he was standing next to the victim and saw Defendant stab him.

Defendant retreated to a Motel 6 and proceeded to tell the clerk that he "just stabbed a black guy for pimping out a white girl." When the police officers located Defendant, they found the knife in his front pocket. While in police custody, Defendant repeatedly told the police he had stabbed a black male for "pimping out a white girl" and stealing his debit card.

During a pretrial hearing Defendant told the court he wanted to "fire" his attorney. The court advised Defendant it would consider the request but that Defendant needed to file his request in writing. However, Defendant never filed a written request for new counsel, and Defendant did not raise the issue again.

The case went to trial and the jury found Defendant guilty of aggravated assault. Following the verdict, the jury made a finding that the offense was a dangerous nature offense.

STATE OF ARIZONA, APPELLEE, V. BURL LAWRENCE ROBINSON, APPELLANT. NO. 1 CA-CR 14-0783

(Text added/modified for emphasis) These same lawyers as a matter of routine practice file briefs asserting there are no appealable issues. The appellate courts refuse to take judicial notice of their own records which records show that lawyers who represented the defendants in the trial court as a matter of routine fail to make the necessary record and do not subject the state's case to a meaningful testing. These same lawyers surface again and again engaging in exactly the same conduct. As it was never their intent to subject the state's case to a meaningful adversarial process, when viewed in the totality, and not in isolation, this should constitute fraud upon the court by these lawyers.

COUNSEL: Arizona Attorney General's Office, Phoenix, By Joseph T. Maziarz, Counsel for Appellee. Maricopa County Legal Advocate's Office, Phoenix, By Colin F. Stearns, Counsel for Appellant.

Instead of treating mental health conditions the state prosecutes and incarcerates them and courts refuse to do anything they are aware.

Two women were standing in a front yard on March 2, 2012, when they saw a gold-colored pickup truck driving slowly down the street. One, A.T., noticed that the driver's head was tilted forward and his eyes were closed. She watched the truck crash into her husband's parked pickup truck. Fearing that the driver, who was later identified as Robinson, had experienced a heart attack, the two witnesses went to help. The two women, with others, approached the truck and someone opened the door and tried to wake Robinson, who appeared to be sleeping. When he did not respond, someone called 9-1-1.

When Robinson finally woke up, he stood next to the driver's door, was unresponsive, and stared into the distance for several minutes. He then began acting erratically, jumping in and out of the bed of the pickup truck, and running around. He pointed at vehicles driving by saying, "I got you," or "You guys can't catch me," before trying to run away.

When the Phoenix Fire Department arrived, Robinson ran in front of the fire truck, attempting to stop it. He was uncooperative and unwilling to allow emergency personnel to assess him for injuries. Fearing that Robinson would get injured in traffic, Captain Caskey submitted an emergency request for police assistance. Officers Miller and Francetic responded, and were able to identify Robinson when he provided his Arizona identification card. A subsequent records check revealed that Robinson's driver's license had been suspended.

Officer Francetic noticed that Robinson had a glazed look on his face, his eyes were bloodshot, and that he was experiencing extreme mood changes. Robinson, however, told Officer Miller that he had not been driving the truck, and refused to submit to a field sobriety test. After being taken to and admitted into the hospital, Robinson's blood was drawn and given to the police for testing. The laboratory results revealed that his blood tested positive for Phencyclidine ("PCP"), a prohibited drug as defined in *Arizona Revised Statutes ("A.R.S.") section 13-3401* (2014).

Robinson was indicted for aggravated driving or actual physical control of a vehicle while under the influence of alcohol or any drug while his privilege of driving was suspended, cancelled or revoked, a class 4 felony, and with aggravated driving or actual physical control of a vehicle while there was any drug defined in Arizona law in his body while his driver's license or privilege to drive was suspended, cancelled, or revoked, a class four felony. He pled not guilty, and subsequently was evaluated pursuant to *Arizona Rule of Criminal Procedure ("Rule") 11* to determine whether he was competent to stand trial. After he was determined to be competent, the case proceeded to trial.

In addition to Captain Caskey, the police officers, and the two witnesses to the slow-speed accident, the jury heard from Gayle Swanson, a forensic scientist, about the results of Robinson's blood test and the impact of PCP on the body, including impairing the mental process, speech, and vision, and causing delusions and hallucinations. The jury also heard testimony from an investigator from the Motor Vehicle Department that Robinson's driving privileges had been suspended and had not been reinstated by the time of the accident. After the State rested, Robinson unsuccessfully moved for a Rule 20 judgment of acquittal.

After the defense rested, the jury was instructed and heard closing arguments, and found Robinson guilty on both counts. The case moved to an aggravation hearing, and after the presentation of evidence and arguments, the jury found that Robinson had been on pretrial release in CR 2011-006914 at the time of the offense.

Before sentencing, Robinson asked for a Rule 26.5 mental health examination. The court granted the request, and Dr. Drake evaluated Robinson and provided the court with a mental health evaluation to assist with sentencing. At sentencing, the court considered Robinson's five historical felony convictions, the mental health evaluation, and the fact that he had been on a pretrial services release when he committed the offenses. The court also considered Robinson's expressed remorse for his actions and that his family needed his support. Robinson was then sentenced to prison for twelve years, and was given credit for 461 days of presentence incarceration on both counts.

STATE OF ARIZONA, APPELLEE, V. HUMBERTO MARTIN SANCHEZ, APPELLANT.
NO. 1 CA-CR 14-0796

(Text added/modified for emphasis) These same lawyers as a matter of routine practice file briefs asserting there are no appealable issues. The appellate courts refuse to take judicial notice of their own records which records show that lawyers who represented the defendants in the trial court as a matter of routine fail to make the necessary record and do not subject the state's case to a meaningful testing. These same lawyers surface again and again engaging in exactly the same conduct. As it was never their intent to subject the state's case to a meaningful adversarial process, when viewed in the totality, and not in isolation, this should constitute fraud upon the court by these lawyers.

COUNSEL: For Appellee: Arizona Attorney General's Office, Phoenix, By Joseph T. Maziarz. For Appellant: Office of the Legal Advocate, Phoenix, By Xochitl Orozco.

Humberto Martin Sanchez appeals the trial court's order resentencing him for the following convictions: one count of attempted first-degree murder, three counts of aggravated assault with a knife, one count of burglary in the second degree, and one count of threatening or intimidating. Counsel for Sanchez filed a brief in accordance with *Anders v. California, 386 U.S. 738, 87 S. Ct. 1396, 18 L. Ed. 2d 493 (1967)*, and *State v. Leon, 104 Ariz. 297, 451 P.2d 878 (1969)*, advising that after searching the record on appeal, she was unable to find any arguable grounds for reversal. Sanchez was granted the opportunity to file a supplemental brief *in propria persona*, but he has not done so.

....

A jury convicted Sanchez of attempted first-degree murder (Count 1); aggravated assault with a knife, a deadly weapon or dangerous instrument (Count 2); aggravated assault with a rock, a deadly weapon or dangerous instrument (Count 3); aggravated assault by means of force (Count 4); burglary in the second degree (Count 5); and threat or intimidation (Count 7). The jury also found that Counts 1-4 were domestic violence offenses, and the trial court found that Sanchez had one prior felony conviction. The trial court sentenced Sanchez to twenty-two years' imprisonment for Count 1, eighteen years for Count 2 and for Count 3, six years for Count 4, seven years for Count 5, and a six-month jail term for Count 7 with a terminal disposition based on time served.

STATE OF ARIZONA, APPELLEE, V. JAIME SOTO JACOTT, APPELLANT.

NO. 1 CA-CR 14-0307

(Text added/modified for emphasis) These same lawyers as a matter of routine practice file briefs asserting there are no appealable issues. The appellate courts refuse to take judicial notice of their own records which records show that lawyers who represented the defendants in the trial court as a matter of routine fail to make the necessary record and do not subject the state's case to a meaningful testing. These same lawyers surface again and again engaging in exactly the same conduct. As it was never their intent to subject the state's case to a meaningful adversarial process, when viewed in the totality, and not in isolation, this should constitute fraud upon the court by these lawyers.

COUNSEL: For Appellee: Arizona Attorney General's Office, Phoenix By Joseph T. Maziarz. For Appellant: Maricopa County Public Defender's Office, Phoenix By Carlos Daniel Carrion.

This case comes to us as an appeal under *Anders v. California, 386 U.S. 738, 87 S. Ct. 1396, 18 L. Ed. 2d 493 (1967)*, and *State v. Leon, 104 Ariz. 297, 451 P.2d 878 (1969)*. Defendant's appellate counsel has searched the record on appeal and found no arguable nonfrivolous question of law; he now asks us to review the record for fundamental error. *See Anders, 386 U.S. 738, 87 S. Ct. 1396, 18 L. Ed. 2d 493; Smith v. Robbins, 528 U.S. 259, 120 S. Ct. 746, 145 L. Ed. 2d 756 (2000); State v. Clark, 196 Ariz. 530, 2 P.3d 89 (App. 1999)*. Defendant has filed a supplemental brief *in propria persona* in which he raises several issues for appeal.

FACTS AND PROCEDURAL HISTORY

The state charged Defendant with sale or transportation of dangerous drugs under *A.R.S. § 13-3407(A)(7)*. Defendant pled not guilty, and the court set the matter for a jury trial. Defendant, who was out of custody on a surety bond, failed to appear at several hearings immediately before trial. He then failed to appear at trial. His counsel informed the court that he had spoken with Defendant after each missed pretrial hearing, that Defendant was aware of the hearings and the trial, and that counsel was unaware of any legal excuse for Defendant's absence. The court found that Defendant had voluntarily chosen not to be present and ordered that trial proceed in his absence.

After jury selection, but before the presentation of any evidence, defense counsel made two oral motions in limine. First, counsel moved to preclude evidence that Defendant was seen storing a firearm in his vehicle after conducting the transaction at issue. The court granted this motion. Counsel next moved to preclude evidence that the "buy house" at which the relevant acts occurred had been set up by law enforcement because of a drug problem in the neighborhood. Counsel argued that such evidence was unduly prejudicial because it implied that Defendant was a contributor to the problem. The court disagreed, concluding that any potential prejudice could be cured by the introduction of evidence that Defendant was not known to live in the neighborhood.

The state presented to the jury evidence of the following facts. In July 2010, police officers were using an audio- and video-surveilled residence to conduct undercover operations in a Phoenix neighborhood. On July 7, Detective David Mendez, working undercover, encountered an individual named Charlie Martinez at a gas station. Mendez spoke with Martinez, and Martinez asked him if he was interested in purchasing "some G" -- a slang term for methamphetamine. Mendez told Martinez that he would check with a friend. After telephoning Det. Kevin Chadwick, who was waiting at the undercover residence, Mendez made arrangements with Martinez for Martinez to bring methamphetamine to the residence.

Following Martinez's instructions, Mendez returned to the area of the residence and waited outside. Martinez arrived with Defendant, introducing Defendant by his first name and stating that Defendant would be "taking care" of them. The three men then entered the residence together. Inside, Chadwick asked Defendant if he was going to be "taking care" of him, and Defendant said yes. Chadwick then informed Defendant that he wanted 0.5 grams of methamphetamine. Defendant removed a substance from his bag and used Chadwick's scale and (for calibration) a coin to measure out an amount. Chadwick paid Defendant $40, placed the substance in a plastic bag, and put it in his pocket. Testing later revealed that the substance was 0.67 grams of methamphetamine.

Mendez accompanied Defendant and Martinez out of the residence. Defendant asked whether Mendez would be receiving some of the methamphetamine as payment for brokering the deal, and Mendez said no. Defendant removed additional substance from his bag, wrapped it in a plastic bag, and gave it to Mendez. Testing later revealed that the substance was 0.096 grams of methamphetamine.

At the close of the state's evidence, Defendant moved for a judgment of acquittal under *Ariz. R. Crim. P. 20*. The court denied the motion. After considering the evidence and counsels' arguments, the jury returned a guilty verdict.

Five months later, Defendant was taken into custody for a new offense. A trial on Defendant's prior felony convictions soon followed. At the trial on priors, Defendant objected to the admission of imprisonment and court records, arguing that they were not self-authenticating documents. The court overruled Defendant's objections and found that the state had proved eight prior Arizona felony convictions: (1) aggravated assault, a class 3 felony, committed in February 1994; (2) possession of drug paraphernalia, a class 6 felony, committed in June 1994; (3) attempted possession of narcotic drugs for sale, a class 3 felony, committed in July 1994; (4) aggravated assault, a class 2 felony, committed in January 2000; (5) possession of dangerous drugs (specifically, methamphetamine) for sale, a class 2 felony, committed in January 2000; (6) unlawful flight from a law enforcement vehicle, a class 5 felony, committed in August 2006; (7) criminal trespass in the first degree, a class 6 felony, committed in December 2007; and (8) possession or use of marijuana, a class 6 felony, committed in August 2010.

Sentencing was delayed so that the proceedings for Defendant's latest offenses could be c2ombined. At the sentencing hearing, the court entered judgment on the jury's verdict [*6] and, as relevant to this appeal, sentenced Defendant to a minimum prison term of 10 years of flat time, with credit for 611 days of presentence incarceration. Defendant timely filed a notice of appeal from the conviction and sentence.

THE STATE OF ARIZONA, APPELLEE, V. ARNOLD MILLS GRANILLO, APPELLANT.
NO. 2 CA-CR 2014-0399

(Text added/modified for emphasis) These same lawyers as a matter of routine practice file briefs asserting there are no appealable issues. The appellate courts refuse to take judicial notice of their own records which records show that lawyers who represented the defendants in the trial court as a matter of routine fail to make the necessary record and do not subject the state's case to a meaningful testing. These same lawyers surface again and again engaging in exactly the same conduct. As it was never their intent to subject the state's case to a meaningful adversarial process, when viewed in the totality, and not in isolation, this should constitute fraud upon the court by these lawyers.

COUNSEL: For Appellant: Steven R. Sonenberg, Pima County Public Defender By Abigail Jensen, Assistant Public Defender, Tucson.

After a jury trial, Arnold Granillo was convicted of second-degree murder and sentenced to a sixteen-year prison term. Counsel has filed a brief in compliance with *Anders v. California, 386 U.S. 738, 87 S. Ct. 1396, 18 L. Ed. 2d 493 (1967)*, and *State v. Clark, 196 Ariz. 530, 2 P.3d 89 (App. 1999)*, asserting she has reviewed the record but found no arguable issue to raise on appeal. Consistent with *Clark, 196 Ariz. 530, ¶ 32, 2 P.3d at 97*, she has provided "a detailed factual and procedural history of the case with citations to the record" and asks this court to search the record for error. Granillo has not filed a supplemental brief.

STATE OF ARIZONA, APPELLEE, V. LAISDEL VIERAS CARDENAS, APPELLANT.
NOS. 1 CA-CR 14-0316, 1 CA-CR 14-0382 (CONSOLIDATED)

(Text added/modified for emphasis) These same lawyers as a matter of routine practice file briefs asserting there are no appealable issues. The appellate courts refuse to take judicial notice of their own records which records show that lawyers who represented the defendants in the trial court as a matter of routine fail to make the necessary record and do not subject the state's case to a meaningful testing. These same lawyers surface again and again engaging in exactly the same conduct. As it was never their intent to subject the state's case to a meaningful adversarial process, when viewed in the totality, and not in isolation, this should constitute fraud upon the court by these lawyers.

COUNSEL: For Appellee; Arizona Attorney General's Office, Phoenix By Joseph T. Maziarz.For Appellant: Maricopa County Public Defender's Office, Phoenix By Tennie B. Martin.

Defendant Laisdel Vieras Cardenas appeals his conviction and sentence for possession or use of a dangerous drug, and the revocation of his probation for an earlier felony offense.

This case comes to us as an appeal under *Anders v. California, 386 U.S. 738, 87 S. Ct. 1396, 18 L. Ed. 2d 493 (1967)*, and *State v. Leon, 104 Ariz. 297, 451 P.2d 878 (1969)*. Defendant's appellate counsel searched the record on appeal, found no arguable nonfrivolous question of law, and asks us to review the record for fundamental error. *See Anders, 386 U.S. 738, 87 S. Ct. 1396, 18 L. Ed. 2d 493*; *Smith v. Robbins, 528 U.S. 259, 120 S. Ct. 746, 145 L. Ed. 2d 756 (2000)*; *State v. Clark, 196 Ariz. 530, 2 P.3d 89 (App. 1999)*. Defendant has filed a supplemental brief *in propria persona* in which he raises several issues for appeal.

FACTS AND PROCEDURAL HISTORY
The state charged Defendant with possession or use of a dangerous drug and misconduct involving weapons, and alleged that Defendant committed the offenses while on probation and had two prior felony convictions.

Before trial, Defendant twice moved to change his court- appointed counsel, and the court granted both requests. The court also granted Defendant's motion to withdraw from a plea agreement, and thereafter assigned Defendant a fourth new attorney after his counsel moved to withdraw. The court denied Defendant's subsequent motions to change counsel.

The matter proceeded to a jury trial, at which the jury found Defendant guilty of possession or use of a dangerous drug but was unable to decide whether he was guilty of misconduct involving weapons. The state presented evidence of the following relevant facts. As of June 5, 2012, Defendant was on probation for a felony offense. On that date, police contacted him at a retail establishment, arrested him, and searched him incident to the arrest. The officers found a large amount of cash in Defendant's pants pocket, including a dollar bill that was folded into a triangle. One of the officers unfolded the bill and discovered a white crystallized substance. Later tests revealed that the substance was 87 milligrams of methamphetamine.

The jury found that Defendant committed the methamphetamine offense while on felony probation, and the court found that Defendant had two prior felony convictions. The court further found that Defendant was in violation of his probation, and entered judgment on the jury's verdict. The court revoked Defendant's probation and sentenced him to 3.5 years in prison in that matter, with credit for 887 days of presentence incarceration. The court sentenced Defendant to a consecutive term of 10 years for the methamphetamine offense.

STATE OF ARIZONA, APPELLEE, V. DAVID RAY LOW, APPELLANT.
NO. 1 CA-CR 14-0798

(Text added/modified for emphasis) These same lawyers as a matter of routine practice file briefs asserting there are no appealable issues. The appellate courts refuse to take judicial notice of their own records which records show that lawyers who represented the defendants in the trial court as a matter of routine fail to make the necessary record and do not subject the state's case to a meaningful testing. These same lawyers surface again and again engaging in exactly the same conduct. As it was never their intent to subject the state's case to a meaningful adversarial process, when viewed in the totality, and not in isolation, this should constitute fraud upon the court by these lawyers.

COUNSEL: Arizona Attorney General's Office, Phoenix, By Joseph T. Maziarz, for Appellee. Maricopa County Public Defender's Office, Phoenix, By Terry J. Adams, for Appellant.

David Ray Low appeals his conviction and sentence for possession or use of narcotic drugs. Counsel for Low filed a brief in accordance with *Anders v. California, 386 U.S. 738, 87 S. Ct. 1396, 18 L. Ed. 2d 493 (1967)*, and *State v. Leon, 104 Ariz. 297, 451 P.2d 878 (1969)*, advising that after searching the record on appeal, he was unable to find any arguable grounds for reversal. Low was granted the opportunity to file a supplemental brief *in propria persona*, but he has not done so.

On July 14, 2012, at approximately 8:15 p.m., Officer Petker and Officer Ramirez were on patrol in the area of 67th Avenue and Heatherbrae in Phoenix. The officers observed Low riding a bicycle with no rear reflector, a violation of *A.R.S. § 28-817*. The officers initiated a traffic stop and asked Low if he had "any guns, bombs, drugs, knives, weapons [or] anything . . . that's going to hurt . . . or injure [either officer]." Low stated he did not have anything, but Petker observed Low move "his left hand into his pocket." Petker removed Low's hand from the pocket and placed Low in handcuffs. Low told Petker he had a pocket-knife in the pocket and was trying to remove it.

At that point, Low complained he was having chest pains, so the officers contacted the Phoenix Fire Department to respond and check Low's medical condition. While Low was being examined by paramedics, Petker noticed a small plastic baggie on the ground near where Low had been standing. Petker believed that the baggie contained heroin.

Low needed further medical attention so the officers transported Low to a hospital. When they arrived, Low informed Officer Ramirez "he wanted to talk." After Ramirez advised Low of his rights pursuant to *Miranda v. Arizona, 384 U.S. 436, 86 S. Ct. 1602, 16 L. Ed. 2d 694 (1966)*, Low stated that "the heroin that [they] found on the ground . . . belonged to him." A forensic scientist with the Phoenix crime laboratory identified the substance as 960 mg of heroin.

Low was tried in absentia and the jury found him guilty as charged. At sentencing, Low stipulated he had prior convictions and the trial court sentenced him to eight years' imprisonment, with 50 days of presentence incarceration credit. This timely appeal followed.

STATE OF ARIZONA, APPELLEE, V. BRIAN JAMEL MATTHEWS, APPELLANT.
NO. 1 CA-CV 14-0698

COUNSEL: Arizona Attorney General's Office, Phoenix, By Joseph T. Maziarz, Counsel for Appellee. Maricopa County Public Defender's Office, Phoenix, By Jeffrey L. Force, Counsel for Appellant.

(Text added/modified for emphasis) These same lawyers as a matter of routine practice file briefs asserting there are no appealable issues. The appellate courts refuse to take judicial notice of their own records which records show that lawyers who represented the defendants in the trial court as a matter of routine fail to make the necessary record and do not subject the state's case to a meaningful testing. These same lawyers surface again and again engaging in exactly the same conduct. As it was never their intent to subject the state's case to a meaningful adversarial process, when viewed in the totality, and not in isolation, this should constitute fraud upon the court by these lawyers. The state has the tendency to release/destroy evidence and again the same police/prosecutors are involved. Courts consistently sanction this systematic practice refusing to find bad faith thereby condoning this misconduct which is on the rise.

Brian Jamel Matthews appeals his conviction for one count of theft, a class one misdemeanor, and the resulting sentence. Matthews's counsel filed a brief in accordance with *Smith v. Robbins, 528 U.S. 259, 120 S. Ct. 746, 145 L. Ed. 2d 756 (2000); Anders v. California, 386 U.S. 738, 87 S. Ct. 1396, 18 L. Ed. 2d 493 (1967)*; and *State v. Leon, 104 Ariz. 297, 451 P.2d 878 (1969)*, indicating he has searched the entire record on appeal and has found no arguable question of law that was not frivolous, and has requested this court review the entire record for fundamental error. *See State v. Clark, 196 Ariz. 530, 537, ¶ 30, 2 P.3d 89 (App. 1999)*. Matthews was afforded the opportunity to file a supplemental brief in propria persona, but did not do so.

....

FACTS AND PROCEDURAL HISTORY

In September 2013, I.J., the victim, encountered Matthews near a pawn shop where I.J. had gone to reclaim his laptop. I.J. invited Matthews to come to his apartment because Matthews said his phone was dead and needed a charge. While at the apartment, I.J. let Matthews take a shower and shave in his bathroom. I.J. also let Matthews use his laptop to play games. Matthews stayed in I.J.'s apartment for about three hours and left around 4:00 p.m.

I.J. went to work around 9:30 p.m. that day. He returned home around 3:00 a.m. and found the bathroom window open, footprints in the bathtub, and his laptop, debit card, brother's cell phone, motor scooter, backpack, lamp, and a case of CDs missing. He called the police and they came to his apartment. I.J. told the police that he suspected it was Matthews who had broken into his apartment.

Approximately one month later, police came into contact with Matthews, who had a laptop, cell phone, and backpack on his person. During the search of the laptop, police discovered I.J.'s W-2. Based on the information in the W-2, police ran I.J.'s name through the police database and discovered I.J. had been the victim of a residential burglary. Although officers took photos of the seized items, they did not take a picture of I.J.'s W-2 before they returned the laptop to him.

The police called I.J. to the station and he identified the items as his property. I.J. did not recall if he powered up the laptop at the station or at home, but when he did, he recognized his W-2, some pictures and music. Although I.J. initially reported that the stolen laptop was a Dell, the laptop was actually a Hewlett-Packard. I.J. also noticed new items saved on the laptop including pictures, music and a different screen saver. At least one of those pictures was of Matthews. I.J. was shown a photo lineup and asked if he recognized anyone as the person who he believed stole his property, and I.J. identified Matthews, saying he was "a hundred percent sure" it was Matthews.

Matthews was charged with one count of burglary in the second degree, a class three felony, and one count of theft, a class one misdemeanor. The trial court held evidentiary hearings on Matthews's motion to suppress the search of the laptop and denied the motion.

Matthews was originally charged with a class six felony; however, during trial, the court granted the State's oral motion to amend the

Indictment to reflect the true value of the stolen property as being less than $1,000.00, making the offense a misdemeanor.

On the first day of trial, Matthews's counsel filed a motion asking the trial court to either dismiss the charges against Matthews or give the jury a *Willits* instruction *See State v. Willits, 96 Ariz. 184, 393 P.2d 274 (1964)* based on the State having released the laptop to I.J. The laptop contained I.J.'s W-2, and neither the laptop nor the W-2 were available for trial. After hearing counsels' arguments, the court denied the motion to dismiss, found no showing of bad faith on the part of the police, but agreed a *Willits* instruction was appropriate.

The jury acquitted Matthews on count one (Burglary) and found him guilty on the amended count two (Theft). The trial court sentenced Matthews to 180 days' incarceration, with a presentence incarceration credit of 330 days. The trial court retained jurisdiction over the issue of restitution for sixty days.

THE STATE OF ARIZONA, APPELLEE, V. LEONARD TURNER, APPELLANT.
NO. 2 CA-CR 2015-0126

COUNSEL: The Hopkins Law Office, P.C., Tucson, By Cedric Martin Hopkins, Counsel for Appellant.

(Text added/modified for emphasis) These same lawyers as a matter of routine practice file briefs asserting there are no appealable issues. The appellate courts refuse to take judicial notice of their own records which records show that lawyers who represented the defendants in the trial court as a matter of routine fail to make the necessary record and do not subject the state's case to a meaningful testing. These same lawyers surface again and again engaging in exactly the same conduct. As it was never their intent to subject the state's case to a meaningful adversarial process, when viewed in the totality, and not in isolation, this should constitute fraud upon the court by these lawyers...............

After a jury trial, Leonard Turner was convicted of criminal damage and four counts of aggravated driving under the influence of an intoxicant (DUI), specifically: DUI with a suspended or revoked license and driving with an alcohol concentration (BAC) at or above .08 with a suspended or revoked license, DUI having two or more DUI violations in the preceding eighty-four months, and driving with a BAC of .08 or greater having two or more DUI violations in the previous eighty-four months. The trial court sentenced him to concurrent prison terms, the longest of which were ten years.

Counsel has filed a brief in compliance with *Anders v. California, 386 U.S. 738, 87 S. Ct. 1396, 18 L. Ed. 2d 493 (1967)*, and *State v. Clark, 196 Ariz. 530, 2 P.3d 89 (App. 1999)*, asserting he has reviewed the record but found no arguable issue to raise on appeal. Consistent with *Clark, 196 Ariz. 530, ¶ 32, 2 P.3d at 97*, he has provided "a detailed factual and procedural history of the case with citations to the record" and asks this court to search the record for error. Turner has not filed a supplemental brief.

Viewing the evidence in the light most favorable to sustaining the verdicts, *see State v. Tamplin, 195 Ariz. 246, ¶ 2, 986 P.2d 914, 914 (App. 1999)*, sufficient evidence supports the jury's verdicts here. In July 2013, a law enforcement officer responding to a 9-1-1 call found Turner trapped in the driver's seat of a crashed vehicle; the vehicle had struck a traffic camera, causing approximately $4,000 in damage. Turner had an odor of intoxicants and showed signs of intoxication, and analysis of his blood drawn less than two hours after the accident showed his BAC to be .263. Turner's driver's license was suspended and revoked at the time of the incident, and he previously had been convicted of DUI offenses committed in 2010 and 2013. *See A.R.S. §§ 13-1602(A)(1); 28-1381(A)(1), (2); 28-1383(A)(1), (2)*. The evidence also supports the trial court's decision to sentence Turner as a category-two repetitive offender. *A.R.S. §§ 13-105(22)(a)(iv); 13-703(C)*. The prison terms imposed for his convictions are within the statutory limit and were imposed properly. *See A.R.S. §§ 13-703(J); 13-1602(B)(3); 28-1383(L)(1)*.

Pursuant to our obligation under *Anders*, we have searched the record for fundamental error and found none. *See State v. Fuller, 143 Ariz. 571, 575, 694 P.2d 1185, 1189 (1985)* (*Anders* requires court to search record for fundamental error). Accordingly, we affirm Turner's convictions and sentences.

STATE OF ARIZONA, APPELLEE V. STEPHEN EUGENE EATON, APPELLANT.
NO. 1 CA-CR 15-0163

COUNSEL: Arizona Attorney General's Office, Phoenix, By Joseph T. Maziarz, Counsel for Appellee. Yavapai County Public Defender's Office, Prescott, By John David Napper, Counsel for Appellant.

(Text added/modified for emphasis) These same lawyers as a matter of routine practice file briefs asserting there are no appealable issues. The appellate courts refuse to take judicial notice of their own records which records show that lawyers who represented the defendants in the trial court as a matter of routine fail to make the necessary record and do not subject the state's case to a meaningful testing. These same lawyers surface again and again engaging in exactly the same conduct. As it was never their intent to subject the state's case to a meaningful adversarial process, when viewed in the totality, and not in isolation, this should constitute fraud upon the court by these lawyers.

....

Stephen Eugene Eaton timely appeals from his probation revocation and disposition sentence. After searching the record on appeal and finding no arguable question of law that was not frivolous, Eaton's counsel filed a brief in accordance with *Anders v. California, 386 U.S. 738, 87 S. Ct. 1396, 18 L. Ed. 2d 493 (1967)*, and *State v. Leon, 104 Ariz. 297, 451 P.2d 878 (1969)*, asking this court to search the record for fundamental error. This court granted counsel's motion to allow Eaton to file a supplemental brief *in propria persona*, but he did not do so. After reviewing all relevant portions of the record concerning Eaton's probation revocation proceedings, we find no fundamental error and, therefore, affirm Eaton's probation revocation and disposition sentences.

SEARCH AND SEIZURES

THE STATE OF ARIZONA, APPELLEE, V. STEVEN RICHARD WEISNER JR., APPELLANT. NO. 2 CA-CR 2015-0055

(Text added/modified for emphasis) The appellate courts refuse to take judicial notice of their own records which records show that the same law enforcement officers and prosecutors consistently engage in warrantless searches, Officers often manufacture their pretext to stop such as "meandering" rather than walking and courts consistently condone this conduct, continuing to find the conduct harmless. When viewed in the totality, and not in isolation, this should constitute fraud upon the court by these lawyers.

COUNSEL: Mark Brnovich, Arizona Attorney General, Joseph T. Maziarz, Section Chief Counsel, Phoenix, By Tanja K. Kelly, Assistant Attorney General, Tucson, Counsel for Appellee. Steven R. Sonenberg, Pima County Public Defender, By David J. Euchner, Assistant Public Defender, Tucson, Counsel for Appellant.

Factual and Procedural Background

In January 2014, Sergeant G.E. of the University of Arizona Police Department was patrolling the campus in the hours after a basketball game. At "about ten minutes before midnight," when the area "had pretty much cleared out," the sergeant observed a person acting suspiciously. He followed the man and saw him enter the back seat of a car that had two other occupants. The sergeant talked to Weisner, who was in the driver's seat, identified the passenger as a woman named Wendy, identified the man he had been following as Wendy's son Mark, and asked for consent to search the car. Weisner consented. Because the two passengers in the car happen to have identical initials, we have identified them by pseudonyms for ease of reference.

During the search, the sergeant located a "glass smoking pipe" wrapped in a jacket in the back seat. He also found "a small container of a white crystalline substance" in the console between the driver's seat and the passenger's seat, along with "paperwork indicating that those papers belonged to Mr. Weisner." He field tested the white substance, and it was "presumptive positive" for methamphetamine. Wendy admitted to owning the jacket and the glass pipe, but denied ownership of the methamphetamine.

....

Reasonable Suspicion

Weisner challenges the trial court's denial of his motion to suppress the drugs and the pipe, arguing Sergeant G.E. did not have reasonable suspicion to stop his vehicle.

> In reviewing a trial court's decision on a motion to suppress evidence based on an alleged *Fourth Amendment* violation, we defer to the trial court's factual findings . . . but we review de novo . . . the trial court's ultimate legal conclusions as to whether the totality of the circumstances warranted an investigative detention.

State v. Teagle, 217 Ariz. 17, ¶ 19, 170 P.3d 266, 271 (App. 2007) (footnote omitted). We consider only the evidence presented at the suppression hearing, and we view that evidence in the light most favorable to upholding the trial court's ruling. *State v. Gay, 214 Ariz. 214, ¶ 4, 150 P.3d 787, 790 (App. 2007).*

The sergeant stopped Weisner's car based on Mark's suspicious actions. *See State v. Richcreek, 187 Ariz. 501, 505, 930 P.2d 1304, 1308 (1997)* (stop of automobile may be based on reasonable suspicion that passenger was engaged in criminal activity). The sergeant initially observed Mark late at night in an area of the university where no buildings were open. Mark appeared to be "meandering" rather than walking to a particular destination. When Mark saw the sergeant, he turned and walked in the other direction. The sergeant made a U-turn to follow Mark. Mark again reversed his direction to avoid the sergeant. Throughout this time, Mark was "[c]onstantly looking back to see where [the sergeant] was."

The sergeant continued to watch Mark as he entered a parking lot. Mark walked between two vehicles and looked inside one of them. After seeing the sergeant's car enter the parking lot, Mark immediately headed toward Weisner's car.

Flight from police officers in a high-crime area may constitute reasonable suspicion. *See Illinois v. Wardlow, 528 U.S. 119, 124-25, 120 S. Ct. 673, 145 L. Ed. 2d 570 (2000); State v. Ramsey, 223 Ariz. 480, ¶¶ 21, 26, 224 P.3d 977, 981-82 (App. 2010)*. State courts have come to differing conclusions on the issue of whether, standing alone, flight from police officers can justify a finding of reasonable suspicion. *See* Keven Jay Kercher, Case Comment, *Criminal Law--Search and Seizure: The Investigative Stop: What Happens When We Run?* Illinois v. Wardlow, *528 U.S. 119 (2000), 77 N.D. L. Rev. 123, 133-34 (2001)*. Neither Weisner nor the state has presented us with any Arizona authority governing this issue, and we have found none.

Weisner cites *State v. Rogers, 186 Ariz. 508, 924 P.2d 1027 (1996)*, and *State v. Stricklin, 191 Ariz. 245, 955 P.2d 1 (App. 1996)*, in support of the proposition that a person's presence in a deserted area late at night is insufficient to support reasonable suspicion. We agree with this proposition, but, as noted below, conclude these were not the only circumstances supporting the sergeant's decision to stop Mark.

But we need not decide whether Mark's behavior constituted flight and whether flight from police, standing alone, may constitute reasonable suspicion. In addition to his evasive behavior, Mark stopped to peer into the window of a parked car. The sergeant testified that this behavior is typical of people "looking for items of property that they may be able to take." *See State v. Sweeney, 224 Ariz. 107, ¶ 22, 227 P.3d 868, 873 (App. 2010)* (court considers "officer's relevant knowledge, experience, and training"). The time of day likewise is relevant to reasonable suspicion considerations. *State v. Fornof, 218 Ariz. 74, ¶ 6, 179 P.3d 954, 956 (App. 2008)*. And while evasive behavior may or may not be sufficient to justify a stop, in and of itself, it is a relevant factor in the determination. *Ramsey, 223 Ariz. 480, ¶ 20, 224 P.3d at 981*. Given the late hour of the evening, Mark's evasion of the sergeant, and his peering into parked vehicles, we conclude the trial court did not err in finding the officer had reasonable cause to conduct a brief investigative detention.

STATE OF ARIZONA, APPELLEE, V. JOHNATHON BERNARD SERNA, APPELLANT.
NO. CR-13-0306-PR

(Text added/modified for emphasis) Law enforcement officers consistently engage in warrantless searches, Officers often manufacture their pretext to stop. When viewed in the totality, and not in isolation, this should constitute fraud upon the court by these lawyers.

COUNSEL: Maricopa County Public Defender, Mikel Steinfeld (argued), Deputy Public Defender, Phoenix, for Johnathon Bernard Serna. Thomas C. Horne, Arizona Attorney General; Robert L. Ellman, Solicitor General; Joseph T. Maziarz (argued), Chief Counsel, Criminal Appeals Section, Phoenix, for State of Arizona.

At approximately 10:00 at night, two officers patrolling a "gang neighborhood" in Phoenix observed Johnathon Serna and a woman standing in the middle of the street. As they turned their patrol car toward the pair, Serna and the woman separated, walking in opposite directions. The officers stopped the patrol car and Officer Richey called to Serna, who, in response, turned and walked toward them; the officers described Serna as "very cooperative and polite." While speaking with Serna, Officer Richey observed a bulge on Serna's waistband and asked if he had any firearms. Serna replied that he had a gun. The officer then ordered Serna to put his hands on his head and removed the gun from Serna's waistband. When, in response to follow-up questions, Serna admitted that he had a felony conviction, the officers arrested him as a prohibited possessor of the firearm.

Before trial, Serna moved to suppress the gun as the fruit of a search that violated his Fourth Amendment rights. The trial court denied the motion, finding that the entire encounter was consensual and that "[o]nce the officers became aware [that Serna] had a gun, they were allowed to remove the gun and conduct a pat down for safety purposes." A jury convicted Serna of misconduct involving weapons, and Serna appealed.

A divided panel of the court of appeals affirmed, finding the frisk justified for officer safety reasons. *State v. Serna, 232 Ariz. 515, 519 ¶ 19, 521 ¶ 25, 307 P.3d 82, 86, 88 (App. 2013)*. Rejecting the majority's assessment that the entire encounter was consensual, the dissenting opinion concluded that the officers were not entitled to frisk Serna absent reasonable suspicion that criminal activity was afoot. *Id. at 522 ¶ 33, 307 P.3d at 89* (Norris, J., dissenting).

III. DISCUSSION

Whether an officer must possess reasonable suspicion that criminal activity is afoot in order to frisk an individual is a question of law, which we review de novo. *See State v. Moody, 208 Ariz. 424, 445 ¶ 62, 94 P.3d 1119, 1140 (2004)*. The *Fourth Amendment* protects the right of people to be free from "unreasonable searches and seizures." *U.S. Const. amend. IV*. Of course, not all encounters between law enforcement and citizens constitute seizures, *Florida v. Bostick, 501 U.S. 429, 434, 111 S. Ct. 2382, 115 L. Ed. 2d 389 (1991)*, and not all seizures are constitutionally unreasonable, *see Elkins v. United States, 364 U.S. 206, 222, 80 S. Ct. 1437, 4 L. Ed. 2d 1669 (1960)*. Encounters that are entirely consensual do not implicate the *Fourth Amendment*. *Bostick, 501 U.S. at 434*; *see also Terry v. Ohio, 392 U.S. 1, 19 n.16, 88 S. Ct. 1868, 20 L. Ed. 2d 889 (1968)*. A police officer may approach an individual and ask questions without running afoul of the *Fourth Amendment*: "So long as a reasonable person would feel free 'to disregard the police and go about his business,' the encounter is consensual and no reasonable suspicion is required." *Bostick, 501 U.S. at 434* (quoting *California v. Hodari D., 499 U.S. 621, 628, 111 S. Ct. 1547, 113 L. Ed. 2d 690 (1991)*). "The encounter will not trigger Fourth Amendment scrutiny unless it loses its consensual nature." *Id*. Police officers are thus free to ask questions of persons they encounter "as long as the police do not convey a message that compliance with their requests is required." *Id. at 435*.

At the outset, the encounter between Serna and the officers was consensual. When addressed, Serna walked toward the officers and voluntarily answered their questions. He was "very cooperative" and demonstrated no ambivalence about conversing with them. But police interactions with members of the public are inherently fluid, and what begins as a consensual encounter can evolve into a seizure that prompts Fourth Amendment scrutiny. *See id.; see also State v. Wyman, 197 Ariz. 10, 14 ¶ 12, 3 P.3d 392, 396 (App. 2000)* (consensual encounter became seizure when juvenile complied with several requests from officer to return); *Commonwealth v. Narcisse, 457 Mass. 1, 927 N.E.2d 439, 443 (Mass. 2010)* (consensual stop became a Fourth Amendment seizure "once the officers told the defendant that they intended to pat frisk him"). Thus, the relevant question is not simply whether the encounter was consensual at the start, but whether at some point it became non-consensual, thus triggering Fourth Amendment protections. *See Terry, 392 U.S. at 16.*

The State argues that when an encounter begins consensually, an officer's order, given for safety reasons, does not alter the consensual nature of the interaction. At the suppression hearing, the State's counsel maintained that if Serna, after putting his hands up, had simply said, "I don't want to talk to you . . ., [he] could have walked away." But the record belies this assertion. Earlier at that hearing, Officer Richey had testified that his direction to Serna to put his hands on his head was an order, not a request. A reasonable person would not have felt free to disregard such a command from a law enforcement officer. *See State v. Rogers, 186 Ariz. 508, 509-10, 924 P.2d 1027, 1028-29 (1996)* (finding that a reasonable person would not feel free to leave when the officer held out his badge and stated, "police officers, we need to talk to you"); *see also Gentry v. Sevier, 597 F.3d 838, 844-45 (7th Cir. 2010)* (concluding that a *Terry* stop occurred when the "officer exited the [patrol] car and told Gentry to 'keep [his] hands up'" (second alteration in original)). The Supreme Court has said that "whenever a police officer . . . restrains [a person's] freedom to walk away, he has 'seized' that person," and such a seizure implicates the *Fourth Amendment. Terry, 392 U.S. at 16.* Officers may not involuntarily detain individuals "even momentarily without reasonable, objective grounds for doing so." *Florida v. Royer, 460 U.S. 491, 498, 103 S. Ct. 1319, 75 L. Ed. 2d 229 (1983).*

The order and frisk at issue here "restrain [ed Serna's] freedom to walk away" and thus constituted a seizure for Fourth Amendment purposes. *See Terry, 392 U.S. at 16; see also id. at 19* (finding it beyond question that the officer seized Terry when he "took hold of him and patted down the outer surfaces of his clothing"). Such a seizure requires constitutional justification. *See Royer, 460 U.S. at 498.* In *Terry*, the Court stated that an officer is justified in frisking individuals for weapons if the officer can reasonably conclude "[1] that criminal activity may be afoot *and* [2] that the persons with whom he is dealing may be armed and presently dangerous." *392 U.S. at 30*(emphasis added). The question before us now is whether a frisk must be supported by both of these conditions, or whether satisfying just one will suffice. The Supreme Court's opinions are instructive. Just three years after *Terry*, the Court suggested that both conditions must be met, stating that officers may conduct weapons searches if the "officer is entitled to make a forcible stop, and has reason to believe that the suspect is armed and dangerous." *Adams v. Williams, 407 U.S. 143, 146, 92 S. Ct. 1921, 32 L. Ed. 2d 612 (1972)* (internal footnote omitted). In 2009, the Supreme Court again reiterated this two-part [***7] analysis, explaining that in *Terry*, it

> upheld "stop and frisk" as constitutionally permissible *if two conditions are met*. First, the investigatory stop must be lawful. That requirement is met in an on-the-street encounter, *Terry* determined, when the police officer reasonably suspects that the person apprehended is committing or has committed a criminal offense. Second, to proceed from a stop to a frisk, the police officer must reasonably suspect that the person stopped is armed and dangerous.

Arizona v. Johnson, 555 U.S. 323, 326-27, 129 S. Ct. 781, 172 L. Ed. 2d 694 (2009) (emphasis added).

Justice Harlan's concurrence in *Terry* provides the clearest explanation of the rationale for requiring that both conditions be met:

[I]f the frisk is justified in order to protect the officer during an encounter with a citizen, the officer must first have constitutional grounds to insist on an encounter, to make a forcible stop. Any person, including a policeman, is at liberty to avoid a person he considers dangerous. If and when a policeman has a right instead to disarm such a person for his own protection, he must first have a right not to avoid him but to be in his presence. That right must be more than the liberty (again, possessed by every citizen) to address questions to other [***8] persons, for ordinarily the person addressed has an equal right to ignore his interrogator and walk away; he certainly need not submit to a frisk for the questioner's protection. I would make it perfectly clear that the right to frisk . . . depends upon the reasonableness of a forcible stop to investigate a suspected crime.

Terry, 392 U.S. at 32-33 (Harlan, J., concurring). The Court expressly acknowledged Justice Harlan's concurrence in *United States v. Place,* 462 U.S. 696, 702 n.4, 103 S. Ct. 2637, 77 L. Ed. 2d 110 (1983). And a prominent Fourth Amendment commentator has endorsed this analysis as "eminently sound." *See* Wayne R. LaFave, 4 Search & Seizure § 9.6(a), at 839 (5th ed. 2012). So while the dual justification required for a frisk was not explicitly recognized in *Terry,* the Court's evolving Fourth Amendment jurisprudence supports the conclusion that both conditions must be met to justify a frisk of an individual. *See Johnson,* 555 U.S. at 326-27; *Williams,* 407 U.S. at 146.

Our conclusion is buttressed by the decisions of other state and federal courts that have considered the issue. *See, e.g., United States v. Massenburg,* 654 F.3d 480, 485 (4th Cir. 2011) (noting that reasonable suspicion is "required prior to a frisk when the officer's initial encounter with the citizen is voluntary"); *United States v. Burton,* 228 F.3d 524, 527 (4th Cir. 2000) (stating that a "police officer may elevate a police-citizen encounter into an investigatory detention only if the officer has 'a reasonable suspicion [***9] supported by articulable facts that criminal activity may be afoot'" (quoting *United States v. Sokolow,* 490

U.S. 1, 7, 109 S. Ct. 1581, 104 L. Ed. 2d 1 (1989)); United States v. Ubiles, 224 F.3d 213, 214 (3d Cir. 2000) (finding stop and search based on possession of gun unjustified because carrying firearms was not illegal and thus could not alone provide reasonable suspicion of criminal activity); *United States v. Gray, 213 F.3d 998, 1000-01 (8th Cir. 2000)* (finding protective frisk violated *Fourth Amendment* because officers had no reasonable suspicion that a man who willingly stopped and answered questions was engaged in criminal activity); *accord In re Ilono H., 210 Ariz. 473, 477 ¶ 12, 113 P.3d 696, 700 (App. 2005)* (observing that "an officer's right to conduct a pat-down search should be predicated on the officer's right to initiate an investigatory stop in the first instance"); *Gomez v. United States, 597 A.2d 884, 890-91 (D.C. 1991)* (noting that, without reasonable suspicion, police could not justify a frisk based on officer safety concerns alone); *Narcisse, 927 N.E.2d at 445* (stating that "police officers may not escalate a consensual encounter into a protective frisk absent reasonable suspicion that an individual has committed, is committing, or is about to commit a criminal offense *and* is armed and dangerous"); *Speten v. State, 2008 WY 63, 185 P.3d 25, 33 (Wyo. 2008)* (observing that "there is neither a 'freestanding' right to search based solely upon officer safety concerns, nor is there a 'freestanding' right to search based solely upon reasonable suspicion of the presence of weapons").

Nonetheless, the State argues that a frisk satisfies the *Fourth Amendment* when the officer has reason to believe that the individual to be frisked is armed and dangerous, even if the officer has no reasonable suspicion of criminal activity. But many of the cases on which the State relies for this proposition are unhelpful because the courts there found reasonable suspicion of criminal activity. *See, e.g., United States v. Ellis, 501 F.3d 958, 962 (8th Cir. 2007)* (finding "there was reasonable suspicion [of criminal activity] to justify a pat-down search"); *United States v. Romain, 393 F.3d 63, 71-72 (1st Cir. 2004)* (evaluating whether pat-down was appropriate "following a valid *Terry* stop" and determining that defendant's behavior "gave rise to a reasonable suspicion . . . [of] criminal wrongdoing"); *United States v. Davis, 202 F.3d 1060, 1062 (8th Cir. 2000)* (stating that "[t]o be constitutionally reasonable, a protective frisk must also be based upon reasonable suspicion that criminal activity is afoot"); *United States v. $84,000 U.S. Currency, 717 F.2d 1090, 1098-99 (7th Cir. 1983)* (upholding pat down, but finding reasonable suspicion of criminal activity).

Another case on which the State relies, *United States v. Bonds*, considered the frisk of a drug dealer who arrived at an associate's apartment while police were executing a search warrant. *829 F.2d 1072, 1073-74 (11th Cir. 1987)*. The court found it unnecessary to establish reasonable suspicion of criminal activity by the defendant, [***11] instead focusing on the inherent dangerousness of the circumstances: the officer was executing a search warrant for drugs, knew Bonds dealt drugs, and "had reason to believe that Bonds was a person to be feared and . . . was carrying a gun." *See id. at 1074-75.* Thus, while *Bonds* provides some support for the State's argument, it is distinguishable from the case at hand. The State urges us to follow *United States v. Orman, 486 F.3d 1170, 1173 (9th Cir. 2007)*, in which the Ninth Circuit determined that "*Terry* did not cabin the use of officer safety patdowns to lawful investigatory detentions." In *Orman*, an off-duty officer, having heard that Orman was carrying a gun in the mall, stopped him and asked if he was armed. *Id. at 1171-72*. Orman acknowledged that he had a gun in his waistband. *Id. at 1172*. The officer retrieved the weapon, and Orman was later charged with unlawfully possessing the firearm. *Id*. The district court denied Orman's motion to suppress the gun. *Id. at 1173*. The Ninth Circuit affirmed, reasoning that "a *Terry* stop-and-frisk 'constitutes two independent actions.'" *Id. at 1174* (quoting *United States v. Flippin, 924 F.2d 163, 165 n.2 (9th Cir. 1991)*). The court held that the encounter was consensual, but the seizure was nonetheless justified "for safety purposes." *Id. at 1176-77*. It concluded that "reasonable suspicion that [a person is] carrying a gun . . . is all that is required for a protective search under *Terry*." *Id. at 1176*.

We disagree and conclude that *Terry* allows a frisk only if two conditions are met: officers must reasonably suspect both that criminal activity is afoot and that the suspect is armed and dangerous. *See, e.g.,*

Johnson, 555 U.S. at 326. Because the analysis in *Orman* ignores one prong of *Terry*, we disagree with the Ninth Circuit's reasoning. We also disagree with the Ninth Circuit's determination that mere knowledge or suspicion that a person is carrying a firearm satisfies the second prong of *Terry*, which itself involves a dual inquiry; it requires that a suspect be "armed *and* presently dangerous." *See Terry, 392 U.S. at 30* (emphasis added); *see also Johnson, 555 U.S. at 326-27* (observing that "to proceed from a stop to a frisk, the police officer must reasonably suspect that the person stopped is armed and dangerous"). In a state such as Arizona that freely permits citizens to carry weapons, both visible and concealed, the mere presence of a gun cannot provide reasonable and articulable suspicion that the gun carrier is presently dangerous.

Here, the initial stop was based on consent, not on any asserted suspicion of criminal activity. Had reasonable suspicion of criminal activity existed before the encounter or developed during the encounter, given that Serna was armed, the officer may have had grounds to frisk Serna. *See Narcisse, 927 N.E.2d at 446.* But when officers consensually engage citizens on the street without having any evidence of wrongdoing, the mere presence of a weapon does not afford officers constitutional permission to search weapons-carrying individuals. To conclude otherwise would potentially subject countless law-abiding persons to patdowns solely for exercising their right to carry a firearm. We recognize, as did the Massachusetts Supreme Judicial Court in *Narcisse*, that "consensual encounters between police officers and citizens frequently escalate to the point of a search without being preceded by an analytically distinct stop." *927 N.E.2d at 444.* These fast-developing situations may "blur the tidiness of the two-pronged *Terry* analysis." *Id.* In such cases, the facts that may support reasonable suspicion of criminal activity may develop as the officer is determining whether the individual is dangerous or appears ready to commit violence. *See id. at 446.* As the *Narcisse* court explained, "[w]hen an individual appears to be ready to commit violence, either against police officers or bystanders, it is reasonable to believe [both] that he is 'about to commit a crime,'" and "that he is armed and dangerous," *id.*, and thus a frisk would be justified. But without the additional justification provided by such facts, officers may not conduct protective searches of persons they engage in consensual conversations.

We also find inapposite *Pennsylvania v. Mimms, 434 U.S. 106, 107, 98 S. Ct. 330, 54 L. Ed. 2d 331 (1977)*, on which the court of appeals relied. *Serna, 232 Ariz. at 520-21 ¶¶ 20, 24, 307 P.3d at 87-88*. In *Mimms*, when examining a search that occurred in the course of a lawful traffic stop, the Supreme Court stated that a "bulge in the [individual's] jacket permitted the officer to conclude that Mimms was armed and thus posed a serious and present danger to the safety of the officer." *434 U.S. at 112. Mimms* is distinguishable because there, the police already had probable cause to believe that Mimms had committed at least one offense. *See 434 U.S. at 109*. The Court also noted that "approximately 30% of police shootings occurred when a police officer approached a suspect seated in an automobile." *Id. at 110* (citing Bristow, Police Officer Shootings -- A Tactical Evaluation, 54 J. Crim. L.C. & P.S. 93 (1963)). Finally, carrying a concealed weapon was itself a criminal act in Pennsylvania. *Id. at 106*. Here, the State presented no evidence that the police had either probable cause or reasonable suspicion that Serna was engaged in criminal activity when Officer Richey ordered him to put his hands on his head.

We instead follow cases from the Supreme Court requiring compliance with both parts of the *Terry* analysis. *See Johnson, 555 U.S. at 326-27; Williams, 407 U.S. at 146*. In applying the two-part analysis here, we conclude that while the initial encounter was consensual, that consent ended when the officer ordered Serna to put his hands on his head. At that point, because the officer had no reasonable suspicion that Serna had committed or was about to commit a crime, the officer had no justification for frisking Serna, and the frisk violated the *Fourth Amendment*.

The court of appeals observed that requiring an officer to suspect criminal activity before permitting a *Terry* frisk "would hinder the officer's ability to investigate suspicious behavior" or to assist individuals in need. *Serna, 232 Ariz. at 519 ¶ 17, 307 P.3d at 86*. But such reasons cannot justify unwarranted infringements on Fourth Amendment rights. There are appropriate ways for officers to protect themselves once they become aware that a person is armed. An officer can, for example, ask for consent to remove a gun for the duration of the encounter. But absent consent, to seize a weapon the officer must justify a frisk with facts sufficient to establish a reasonable suspicion of criminal activity -- a low standard, readily established in many search settings. *See Navarette v. California, 134 S. Ct. 1683, 1687, 188 L. Ed. 2d 680 (2014)* ("Although a mere 'hunch' does not create reasonable suspicion, the level of suspicion the standard requires is 'considerably less than proof of wrongdoing by a preponderance of the evidence,' and 'obviously less' than is necessary for probable cause." (internal citations omitted)). Our holding governs only those circumstances in which the police wish to search a person with whom they are engaged in a consensual encounter. In such cases, absent consent, an officer may frisk an individual only when the officer possesses both a reasonable suspicion that the person to be searched has engaged or is about to engage in criminal activity and a reasonable belief that the person is armed and dangerous.

While we understand the need for officers to protect themselves in the course of their duties, we must balance that weighty interest against the "inestimable right" of citizens to be free from unreasonable governmental searches and seizures. *See Terry, 392 U.S. at 8-9.* That officers must have a constitutional justification to search an individual has been firmly established by *Terry* and its progeny. *See id. at 30; see also Johnson, 555 U.S. at 326-27; Williams, 407 U.S. at 146.*

STATE OF ARIZONA, APPELLEE, V. JIMMY EDWARD ESTELL, JR., APPELLANT.
NO. 1 CA-CR 11-0846

(Text added/modified for emphasis) Law enforcement officers consistently manufacture consent and courts allow this. The appellate courts refuse to take judicial notice of their own records which records show that the same law enforcement officers and prosecutors consistently engage in warrantless searches, continuing to find the conduct harmless. When viewed in the totality, and not in isolation, this should constitute fraud upon the court by these lawyers.

COUNSEL: Thomas C. Horne, Arizona Attorney General, By Kent E. Cattani, Chief Counsel, Criminal Appeals/Capital Litigation Division And Angela Corinne Kebric, Assistant Attorney General, Phoenix, Attorneys for Appellee. James J. Haas, Maricopa County Public Defender, By Mikel P. Steinfeld, Deputy Public Defender, Phoenix, Attorneys for Appellant.

Motion to Suppress

Estell argues that the trial court erred when it denied his motion to suppress the firearm. He contends that police conducted an illegal search when they used their authority to compel him to open the apartment door and later obtained a search warrant based in part on the smell of marijuana emanating from the open door.

The *Fourth Amendment* bars unreasonable searches and seizures. *U.S. Const. amend. IV*. A warrantless search is presumptively unreasonable under the *Fourth Amendment*, "subject only to a few specifically established, 'jealously and carefully drawn' exceptions." *Rodriguez v. Arellano, 194 Ariz. 211, 214, ¶ 9, 979 P.2d 539, 542 (App. 1999)* (citations omitted). Consent and exigent circumstances are among the recognized exceptions to the requirement that officers obtain a warrant before entering a home. *State v. Canez, 202 Ariz. 133, 151-52, ¶¶ 52-56, 42 P.3d 564, 582-83 (2002)*. In reviewing a trial court's ruling on a motion to suppress, we restrict our review to consideration of the facts the trial court heard at the suppression hearing. *State v. Blackmore, 186 Ariz. 630, 631, 925 P.2d 1347, 1348 (1996)*. We review the facts in the light most favorable to sustaining the trial court's ruling. *State v. Hyde, 186 Ariz. 252, 265, 921 P.2d 655, 668 (App. 1996)*.

At the suppression hearing, a police detective testified that the manager of an apartment complex informed police that Estell, who had outstanding warrants for his arrest, lived in one of the apartments. He also stated that Estell was home most of the day babysitting the children and was seen there the morning of the incident. The detective also testified that he repeatedly knocked on the apartment door and announced that he was with the El Mirage Police and was looking for Estell. When Estell finally came to the door, he opened it about four inches secured by a chain, identified himself, and said he knew he had outstanding warrants. Estell told the detective, however, that he was not going to come out until his girlfriend returned and closed the door.

The detective testified that when Estell cracked the door open, he saw children in the house, and he "believe[d] it was at that point when [he] smelled some burning marijuana." He later testified, however, that the smell of marijuana "was strong from the first time I smelled it. I smelled it from standing on the sidewalk out - 20 feet away from the front door I could smell it."

Etsell's girlfriend arrived at the apartment within fifteen minutes and yelled to Estell to open the door and come out. After Estell exited the apartment and was handcuffed, he walked by his girlfriend and asked her, "Are you going to tell them about that?" When the detective asked, "What?", Estell responded, "The Glock."

After police cleared the house, Etsell's girlfriend gave consent to the detective, allowing him into the apartment to secure the firearm. She told the detective that the Glock was in the downstairs master bathroom under some clothes in a basket. Police secured the firearm and subsequently obtained a warrant. The warrant was based on the smell of marijuana emanating from the apartment and the presence of the firearm.

Relying on United States v. Connor, 127 F.3d 663 (8th Cir. 1997), Estell argues that the police illegally gained "olfactory access" to the apartment when they used their authority to compel him to open the door. In Connor, the court held that "an unconstitutional search occurs when officers gain visual or physical access to a motel room after an occupant opens the door not voluntarily, but in response to a demand under color of authority." Id. at 666. Estell argued that the gun found during the subsequent consensual search, and seized after police obtained a search warrant based in part on the marijuana smell, was the fruit of the initial illegal search. The trial court denied the motion to suppress, finding that Connor was neither persuasive nor applicable and that the gun was "not the fruit of an illegal search." The court found that defendant's girlfriend, "a resident of the home, consented to the search and told the officers where the gun was located. The items were found during a valid protective sweep for safety based on knowledge of a weapon and at least one other adult male inside the residence."

We review the court's ruling for abuse of discretion if it involves a discretionary issue but review constitutional issues and purely legal issues de novo. *State v. Moody, 208 Ariz. 424, 445, ¶ 62, 94 P.3d 1119, 1140 (2004)*. We find no error in the court's denial of the motion to suppress.

The holding in *Connor* is inapplicable under the facts of this case. In *Connor*, acting on an anonymous tip that the suspects in a burglary were hiding out in a motel room, police knocked loudly and repeatedly on the door of a room they believed might contain the burglars. The officers identified themselves as police and, with at least one weapon drawn, ordered the occupants to "Open Up." *Connor, 127 F.3d at 665*. The court held that under those circumstances, when the suspects opened the door in response to the police command that they do so, the police conducted an illegal search when they observed the contraband in plain sight. *Id. at 666*. Here, the detective, who was in plain clothes and had his gun holstered, did not command Estell to open the door but simply announced that he was a police officer looking for Estell. We find that when Estell voluntarily opened the front door, albeit only a crack and only momentarily, the "olfactory access" the detective had to the apartment did not constitute a search within the meaning of the *Fourth Amendment. See United States v. Cephas, 254 F.3d 488, 494 (4th Cir. 2001)* (holding that when defendant opened the door without knowing who was on the other side, "he voluntarily exposed to the public any odors and such a view as one standing at the door could perceive," and no search occurred); *cf. United States v. Perea-Rey, 680 F.3d 1179, 1188 (9th Cir. 2012)* (noting that it is permissible to initiate consensual contact with the occupants of a home. Once such an attempt fails, however, "the officers should end the knock and talk and change their strategy by retreating cautiously, seeking a search warrant, or conducting further surveillance."). Although Estell cracked the door momentarily, he refused to exit the apartment for another fifteen minutes, indicating that he felt under no compulsion to respond to the detective's authority. Therefore, we find *Connor* is distinguishable, and its holding that police conduct an illegal search when they view items in plain sight after compelling occupants to open a door has no applicability.

Even assuming arguendo that police conducted an illegal search by implicitly demanding that Estell open the door, we find that Etsell's girlfriend's subsequent consent to a search for, and seizure of, the weapon was voluntary and was prompted by intervening circumstances that purged any taint of illegality. Whether the taint of an illegal search has dissipated is analyzed by evaluating the temporal proximity between the police illegality and the consent to search, the presence of intervening circumstances, and the purpose and flagrancy of the police misconduct. *State v. Blakley, 226 Ariz. 25, 31, ¶ 20, 243 P.3d 628, 634 (App. 2010)*. Although the record indicates that the girlfriend consented to a search for the gun within fifteen minutes of the alleged illegal search, we give little weight to this temporal proximity in light of the intervening circumstances. *See State v. Guillen, 223 Ariz. 314, 318, ¶ 16, 223 P.3d 658, 662 (2010)*.

First, the record gives no indication that the girlfriend was even aware of the pertinent details of the initial interaction between the detective and Estell. This constituted a break in causation that placed her "in the same posture . . . as a person not previously subject to an illegal entry." *See United States v. Furrow, 229 F.3d 805, 814 (9th Cir. 2000)*. Second, the spontaneous reference by Estell to the presence of a firearm in the apartment constituted another intervening circumstance, breaking the chain of causation between the initial alleged illegality and the girlfriend's consent to search the apartment for the weapon. *See Guillen, 223 Ariz. at 318, ¶¶ 17-18, 223 P.3d at 662*. Finally, we find that the alleged illegality in this case was not flagrant misconduct, further weighing in favor of finding that the taint had dissipated.

We find that the girlfriend's consent supplied an independent source for the seizure of the gun, notwithstanding any alleged initial illegality. We find no error in the court's denial of Etsell's motion to suppress the gun.

STATE OF ARIZONA, APPELLANT, V. ASKIA MUHAMMAD SHAHEED, APPELLEE.

NO. 1 CA-CR 12-0736

(Text added/modified for emphasis) Law enforcement officers consistently manufacture consent and courts allow this. The same officers consistently manufacture probable cause and courts allow this. The appellate courts refuse to take judicial notice of their own records which records show that the same law enforcement officers and prosecutors consistently engage in warrantless searches, continuing to find the conduct harmless. When viewed in the totality, and not in isolation, this should constitute fraud upon the court by these lawyers.

COUNSEL: Maricopa County Attorney Office, Phoenix, By Arthur G. Hazelton, Jr., Counsel for Appellant. The Law Office of David Jameson Kephart, PLLC, Tempe, By David J. Kephart, Counsel for Appellee.

The events that led to Shaheed's arrest began shortly after 1:00 a.m. on December 17, 2011. Sergeant Alan Phohl was dispatched to a call at the Alaska Bush Company for a physical altercation in the parking lot involving gunfire. The dispatch calls described the suspect group as six to ten African American males. When Sergeant Phohl arrived at the scene, he saw a pickup truck with gunshot damage to it and spent shotgun shell casings in the parking lot. Three or four other officers had already arrived at the scene and were speaking with witnesses.

Sergeant Phohl was present when a witness described a person involved in the shooting as a tall, thin, black male wearing a dark hat, white shirt and jeans, with his hair tied in two ponytails, one on each side of his head, and possessing a handgun. The witness stated that the suspect was on his way to Teasers, a strip club down the road. Sergeant Phohl conveyed this information to Officer Michael Raines and asked him to go to Teasers to see if the suspect was there. Sergeant Phohl did not take down the witness's name, but remembered that he was male, that they spoke face-to-face, and that he looked like a "bouncer type."

Officer Raines arrived at Teasers at approximately 1:30 a.m. and saw a man standing in the middle of the parking lot who was "a very strong match" to the description given by Sergeant Phohl. Officer Raines approached Shaheed and asked him to stop and if he had been at the

Alaska Bush Company. Shaheed turned and walked away from Officer Raines without responding. Officer Raines then asked Shaheed if he had any weapons in his possession, and Shaheed said "no." When Officer Raines asked if he could conduct a *Terry* pat-down because he was investigating a shooting, Shaheed said he "didn't do anything," and proceeded to walk away towards the entrance of Teasers. Officer Raines testified that he was concerned for his own safety and those at Teasers because of Shaheed's strong resemblance to the suspect description, and decided to detain Shaheed and perform a pat-down to make sure he did not have any weapons. Officer Raines found an Intratec Tec-9 handgun on Shaheed's right hip and then detained him for misconduct involving weapons.

The state charged Shaheed with one count of misconduct involving weapons (prohibited possessor), a class 4 felony. Shaheed filed a motion to suppress the evidence seized pursuant to the pat-down, challenging the reasonableness of his stop and frisk because of the unreliability of the face-to-face tip. Following the state's response and an evidentiary hearing, the trial court suppressed the evidence seized during the stop.

DISCUSSION

The state argues that the trial court erred by exclusively examining the witness's reliability rather than the totality of the circumstances because the crime was already confirmed by police and the central issue was the identity and whereabouts of the suspects. We agree, and hold that the stop and resulting seizure of evidence was reasonable. Whether the police have reasonable suspicion to make an investigative stop is a mixed question of law and fact which we review de novo. *State v. Rogers, 186 Ariz. 508, 510, 924 P.2d 1027, 1029 (1996).*

The *Fourth Amendment* prohibits "unreasonable searches and seizures." *U.S. Const. amend. IV.* An investigatory stop does not violate the *Fourth Amendment* and is permissible where police have "reasonable suspicion, grounded in specific and articulable facts" that the person was involved in or is wanted in connection with a completed felony. *United States v. Hensley, 469 U.S. 221, 229, 105 S. Ct. 675, 83 L. Ed. 2d 604 (1985).* The reasonableness of the search involves "all the circumstances of the particular governmental invasion of a citizen's personal security," balanced alongside legitimate government interest. *Terry v. Ohio, 392 U.S. 1, 19, 88 S. Ct. 1868, 20 L. Ed. 2d 889*

(1968); Wyoming v. Houghton, 526 U.S. 295, 300, 119 S. Ct. 1297, 143 L. Ed. 2d 408 (1999). The totality of the circumstances takes into account "the whole picture." *United States v. Cortez, 449 U.S. 411, 417, 101 S. Ct. 690, 66 L. Ed. 2d 621 (1981).*

Face-to-face encounters with informants, even where they are unidentified, are considered to be some of the more reliable tips. *United States v. Palos-Marquez, 591 F.3d 1272, 1275 (9th Cir. 2010); see State v. Anderson, 204 Neb. 186, 281 N.W.2d 743, 746 (Neb. 1979)* (victims or witnesses of a crime are not to be viewed in the same way as the usual police informant). In *United States v. Sierra-Hernandez, 581 F.2d 760, 762 (9th Cir. 1978)*, the Ninth Circuit upheld a stop by a border patrol agent based on an unidentified man pointing to a nearby pickup truck and saying, "[t]he black pickup truck just loaded with weed at the cane break." *Id.* Factors considered by the court were that the tip was not vague as to the time of the criminal activity, it was not imprecise as to the kind of crime being committed, and the suspect was clearly indicated and his criminal actions were described with some particularity. *Id. at 763; see also* W. LaFave, Search & Seizure: A Treatise on the Fourth Amendment, § 9.5(h) (5th ed.) (2012) (factors appropriately taken into account to determine whether reasonable suspicion exists to justify an investigatory stop for a completed offense based on a physical description given by a witness at the scene include: (1) the particularity of the description of the offender; (2) the size of the area in which the offender might be found; (3) the number of persons about in that area; (4) the known or probable direction of the offender's flight; (5) observed activity by the particular person stopped; and (6) knowledge or suspicion that the person stopped has been involved in other criminality of the type presently under investigation.). The court was not concerned that the agent failed to converse further with the informant and get his name or note the license of his car, because the suspect was in a vehicle moving away from the agent when the tip came and the agent needed to take quick action or risk losing the suspect. *Sierra-Hernandez, 581 F.2d at 763.*

Other courts have made similar holdings. In a *Terry* stop and frisk case dealing with an anonymous tip of a man with a gun, the police were dispatched to a luncheonette to investigate "a black individual wearing a black hat, black leather coat and checkered pants . . . with a gun in his possession." *State in Interest of H.B., 75 N.J. 243, 248, 381 A.2d 759 (1977)*. The court upheld the patdown after balancing the constitutional imperatives enunciated in *Terry,* despite the tip coming from an anonymous source and that that the defendant was not acting suspiciously. *Id. at 252; see also State v. Satter, 2009 SD 35, 766 N.W.2d 153, 154, 156-58 (2009)* (where a "concerned citizen" approached an officer face-to-face, making "no effort to hide or conceal his identity," and informed him that he had seen two men drinking beer in a van, the officer had a reasonable suspicion to pull the van over even though he did not witness any erratic driving); *Mitchell v. State, 187 S.W.3d 113, 117-18 (Tex. App. 2006)* (unidentified citizen-informant's report of an intoxicated driver could support a reasonable suspicion because it contained "sufficient indicia of reliability," including, "most importantly," the fact that his face-to-face encounter with the officer "placed him [] in a position to be easily identified by [the officer] and held accountable for his report"); *People v. Lucero, 182 Colo. 39, 42, 511 P.2d 468, 470 (1973)* (police officers reasonably relied on unidentified citizen informants at the scene of the crime to pull over a robbery suspect based on their description of the getaway vehicle); *cf. People v. Tooks, 403 Mich. 568, 271 N.W.2d 503, 504, 508 (1978)* (holding that information about a suspect with a concealed weapon, received from a citizen who approached police face-to-face but refused to identify himself for fear of "gangs in the area," supported a reasonable suspicion for a weapons frisk); *but see State v. Tibbet, 96 Or.App. 116, 771 P.2d 654, 654-55 (1989)* (in banc) (holding that an unidentified driver who pulled off the road to inform a police officer of "a vehicle [that] had been 'driving all over the road' in front of him" was "just as anonymous" as an unidentified telephone informant).

Here, it was imperative that police officers move quickly in order to apprehend any suspects after the shooting at the Alaska Bush Company. Although the police knew the kind of crime and the criminal actions involved, they needed to quickly ascertain the identity and direction of travel of any suspects before a substantial amount of time passed. The witness here provided a detailed physical description shortly after the incident, and not only gave the direction of travel, but the exact location the suspect was headed. *See United States v. Valentine, 232 F.3d 350,*

354 (3d Cir. 2000) (the fact that "the officers in our case knew that the informant was reporting what he had observed moments ago, not what he learned from stale or second-hand sources" weighed in favor of a tip's reliability). When Officer Raines arrived at Teasers, he encountered Shaheed who very closely matched the detailed description. Although the witness in *Sierra-Hernandez* may have been more identifiable because he was in a car, the court stated that the point was not that the police could necessarily track him down, but rather that the informant himself may believe he could be tracked down and held accountable by the police if the information proved false. *581 F.2d at 763*. We have no reason to think that the witness here was not also under the impression that he could be tracked down and held accountable for his story after giving the information in the presence of more than one officer.

Shaheed asserts that the state "totally fails to appreciate" that at the completion of the investigation Shaheed was not listed nor described as a suspect by the investigating officers. However, police officers are not required "to be all-knowing, only to be prudent and reasonable." *State v. Vasquez, 167 Ariz. 352, 355, 807 P.2d 520, 523 (1991)*. They "must make immediate decisions on how to protect themselves and others from possible danger." *State v. Sinclair, 159 Ariz. 493, 496, 768 P.2d 655, 658 (App. 1988)*. As with all *Terry* stops, the police officer's conduct must be reasonable under the circumstances known to the officer at the time he initiated the stop. *Terry, 392 U.S. at 21-22*. We cannot judge the reasonability of the stop based on facts found out later. The United States Supreme Court permits investigative stops because:

> In allowing such detentions, *Terry* accepts the risk that officers may stop innocent people. Indeed, the *Fourth Amendment* accepts that risk in connection with more drastic police action; persons arrested and detained on probable cause to believe they have committed a crime may turn out to be innocent. The *Terry* stop is a far more minimal intrusion, simply allowing the officer to briefly investigate further. If the officer does not learn facts rising to the level of probable cause, the individual must be allowed to go on his way.

Illinois v. Wardlow, 528 U.S. 119, 126, 120 S. Ct. 673, 145 L. Ed. 2d 570 (2000).

Shaheed's strong resemblance to the suspect description, and the officer's knowledge that the suspect possessed a firearm, could justify a reasonably prudent police officer in believing that Shaheed could be the suspect and that the officer's safety and the safety of others was in danger. *See State v. Nichols, 26 Ariz. App. 455, 458, 549 P.2d 235, 238 (1976), citing Terry, 392 U.S. 1, 88 S. Ct. 1868, 20 L. Ed. 2d 889* (police need not be absolutely certain that the individual is armed; the issue is whether a reasonably prudent man in the circumstances, would be warranted in the belief that his safety or that of others was in danger). "[A]ny reasonable fear for safety is enough to warrant a search under Terry . . .." *State v. Garcia Garcia, 169 Ariz. 530, 532, 821 P.2d 191, 193 (App. 1991)*. "The *Fourth Amendment* does not require that a police officer 'simply shrug his shoulders and allow a crime to occur or a criminal to escape' [*12] even in the absence of sufficient information to establish probable cause." *State v. Romero, 178 Ariz. 45, 48, 870 P.2d 1141, 1144 (App. 1993), citing Adams v. Williams, 407 U.S. 143, 145, 92 S. Ct. 1921, 32 L. Ed. 2d 612 (1972)*. "If an officer has a reasonable suspicion, based upon specific and articulable facts, that a suspect is involved or wanted in connection with a crime, then a brief stop to investigate that suspicion in fact may be the best and most sensible response." *Romero, 178 Ariz. at 49, 870 P.2d at 1145, citing Terry, 392 U.S. at 21-24.*

THE STATE OF ARIZONA, APPELLEE, V. FELICIANO ONTIVEROS-LOYA, APPELLANT.
NO. 2 CA-CR 2014-0159

(Text added/modified for emphasis) Law enforcement officers and prosecutors consistently engage in warrantless searches, and search without consent. When viewed in the totality, and not in isolation, this should constitute fraud upon the court by these lawyers.

COUNSEL: Mark Brnovich, Arizona Attorney General, Joseph T. Maziarz, Section Chief Counsel, Phoenix, By David A. Sullivan, Assistant

Attorney General, Tucson, Counsel for Appellee. Lori J. Lefferts, Pima County Public Defender, By Erin K. Sutherland, Assistant Public Defender, Tucson, Counsel for Appellant.

JUDGES: Presiding Judge Miller authored the opinion of the Court, in which Chief Judge Eckerstrom and Judge Espinosa concurred.

Factual and Procedural Background

On an evening in May 2013, Ontiveros-Loya approached S.R. outside a motel in Tucson and told her if she did not go back to his motel room with him, he would shoot her. S.R. saw a gun tucked into Ontiveros-Loya's pants. He grabbed her arm, but she pushed away and fled.

A detective with the Pima County Sheriff's Department responded to a market near the motel after S.R. called 9-1-1. Detectives later found Ontiveros-Loya in his motel room. He initially identified himself as Oscar Lopez, but at some unspecified later time he provided his true name. The detectives asked for consent to search the room, which they testified Ontiveros-Loya gave. The detectives found a firearm magazine and a cell phone in the room. The cell phone included photographs of a silver handgun.

Ontiveros-Loya was charged with one count of possession of a weapon by a prohibited possessor, one count of attempted kidnapping, and one count of aggravated assault. He filed several suppression motions, including a motion to suppress the evidence found on the cell phone, which the trial court denied. The jury found him guilty of the prohibited possessor charge, and the court sentenced him as described above. Ontiveros-Loya timely appealed. We have jurisdiction pursuant to A.R.S. §§ 12-120.21(A)(1) and 13-4033(A)(1).

Discussion

Ontiveros-Loya argues the trial court abused its discretion by denying his motion to suppress the photographs found on his cell phone. We review the denial of a motion to suppress for an abuse of discretion. State v. Jacot, 235 Ariz. 224, ¶ 9, 330 P.3d 981, 984 (App. 2014). We consider only the evidence presented at the suppression hearing, and we view that evidence in the light most favorable to sustaining the court's rulings. *State v. Kinney, 225 Ariz. 550, ¶ 2, 241 P.3d 914, 917 (App. 2010).*

In his motion, Ontiveros-Loya argued that, because he had no access to the cell phone at the time of his arrest, the "search incident to arrest" exception to the warrant requirement did not apply. He further contended that the search "exceeded the scope of any reasonable search incident to arrest." The state argued that officers were permitted to search Ontiveros-Loya's cell phone incident to his arrest because "[i]t is more than reasonable that deputies believed that [the] cell phone could contain evidence of the incident involving [S.R.]." The state also contended that Ontiveros-Loya knowingly and voluntarily consented to a search of his motel room, where the phone was found, so its search "was permissibly within the scope of the search of [the] motel room." The state also suggested the detectives could search the cell phone because it was in plain view but did not pursue that argument at the suppression hearing and has not raised it on appeal.

The trial court denied the motion to suppress, stating "the search incident to arrest in large part could be justified in the fact that [Ontiveros-Loya] gave conflicting information regarding his ID" and "one of the reasons given eventually for the search of the cellphone data in the warrant was for identification purposes." The court concluded, "[T]hat was a legitimate use of the phone as a search incident to arrest where having access to the phone would have assisted [detectives] in getting correct information to verify who [Ontiveros-Loya] was." The court also found "it was inevitable that [detectives] would discover the photographs" of the gun.

After the trial court denied his motion to suppress, Ontiveros-Loya interviewed Detectives Garrick Carey and Rogelio Moreno. In his interview, Moreno stated the detectives only had consent to search for a gun, and Carey confirmed they were "[l]ooking for a firearm." Moreno also stated Ontiveros-Loya was not under arrest when they searched the cell phone, but he was seated in the back of a patrol car, and Carey stated the decision to arrest him was made at the end of the investigation. Moreno stated the detectives were looking for "anything that . . . was pertinent to the investigation," such as "[p]ictures of a female, pictures of the gun that was in question, pictures of . . . [Ontiveros-Loya] holding the gun," and Carey stated the detectives were looking for evidence that would otherwise possibly be lost or destroyed if they did not keep the phone.

Based on the interviews, Ontiveros-Loya filed a motion for reconsideration of the trial court's denial of his motion to suppress. He argued "the search of the cell phone was not incident to or contemporaneous with an actual arrest." Ontiveros-Loya also asserted the detectives were not looking for information about his identity and instead were "trying to figure out whether they could find additional evidence of the crimes alleged." The court denied the motion.

The *Fourth Amendment of the United States Constitution* and *Article II, § 8, of the Arizona Constitution* protect against unreasonable searches and seizures. Warrantless searches of homes are presumptively invalid, *Jacot, 235 Ariz. 224, ¶ 10, 330 P.3d at 984*, and motel rooms have been afforded the same protections as homes, *see, e.g., State v. Davolt, 207 Ariz. 191, ¶ 23, 84 P.3d 456, 467 (2004)* ("Hotel guests are entitled to full constitutional protection against unreasonable searches and seizures."). The state carries the burden of proving that a warrantless search is constitutionally valid under an exception to the warrant requirement. *See State v. Olm, 223 Ariz. 429, ¶ 5, 224 P.3d 245, 247 (App. 2010)*. In its ruling on the motion to suppress, the trial court concluded that the warrantless search of Ontiveros-Loya's cell phone was justified as a search incident to arrest.

In *Chimel v. California*, the United States Supreme Court considered "the permissible scope under the *Fourth Amendment* of a search incident to a lawful arrest." *395 U.S. 752, 753, 89 S. Ct. 2034, 23 L. Ed. 2d 685 (1969)*. There, officers executing an arrest warrant searched the defendant's entire house incident to his arrest. *Id. at 753-54*. The Court offered two justifications for permitting searches of an arrestee's person incident to arrest--officer safety and the prevention of concealment or destruction of evidence. *Id. at 763*. The Court reasoned that "[w]hen an arrest is made; it is reasonable for the arresting officer to search the person arrested in order to remove any weapons that the latter might seek to use in order to resist arrest or effect his escape." *Id. at 762-63*. In addition, "the area into which an arrestee might reach in order to grab a weapon or evidentiary items must, of course, be governed by a like rule" because a weapon within the reach of an arrestee "can be as dangerous to the arresting officer as one concealed in the clothing of the person arrested." *Id. at 763*. Thus, the Court concluded, officers may search "the arrestee's person and the area 'within his immediate control'--construing that phrase to mean the area from within which he might gain possession of a weapon or destructible evidence." *Id.*

The Court declined, however, to extend the exception to searches of an entire house. *Id.* The Court explained, "There is no comparable justification . . . for routinely searching any room other than that in which an arrest occurs--or, for that matter, for searching through all the desk drawers or other closed or concealed areas in that room itself." *Id.* Such searches must be made pursuant to a warrant, unless another exception applies. *Id.*

In *Riley v. California*, the Court considered "whether the police may, without a warrant, search digital information on a cell phone seized from an individual who has been arrested." *U.S., , 134 S. Ct. 2473, 2480, 189 L. Ed. 2d 430 (2014)*. There, officers searched each arrestee's person incident to arrest and found cell phones, which the officers also searched. *Id. at , 134 S. Ct. at 2480-81*. The Court observed that the two risks identified in *Chimel*--harm to officers and destruction of evidence--do not exist when the search is of digital data. *Id. at , 134 S. Ct. at 2484-85*. The Court also reasoned that "[a] search of the information on a cell phone bears little resemblance to [a] brief physical search" because "[c]ell phones . . . place vast quantities of personal information literally in the hands of individuals." *Id. at , 134 S. Ct. at 2485*. Thus, the Court held that "officers must generally secure a warrant before conducting" a search of a phone found on the person of an arrestee. *Id.* Ontiveros-Loya was sentenced before *Riley* was decided. However, "newly announced rules of constitutional criminal procedure must apply 'retroactively to all cases, state or federal, pending on direct review or not yet final, with no exception.'" *Davis v. United States, U.S. , , 131 S. Ct. 2419, 2430, 180 L. Ed. 2d 285 (2011), quoting Griffith v. Kentucky, 479 U.S. 314, 328, 107 S. Ct. 708, 93 L. Ed. 2d 649 (1987); see also United States v. Spears, 31 F. Supp. 3d 869, 874 (N.D. Tex. 2014)* (treating *Riley* as new rule of constitutional criminal procedure); *State v. Henderson, 289 Neb. 271, 854 N.W.2d 616, 630 (Neb. 2014)* (same).

The Court further observed that "[d]igital data stored on a cell phone cannot itself be used as a weapon to harm an arresting officer or to effectuate the arrestee's escape." *Id.* Officers may seize and secure cell phones to prevent destruction of evidence while they seek a warrant, but "once law enforcement officers have secured a cell phone, there is no longer any risk that the arrestee himself will be able to delete incriminating data from the phone." *Id. at , 134 S. Ct. at 2486.* The Court rejected the argument that concerns about "remote wiping and data encryption" justified searches of cell phones incident to arrest, stating, "[T]hese broader concerns about the loss of evidence are distinct from *Chimel*'s focus on a defendant who responds to arrest by trying to conceal or destroy evidence within his reach." *Id.*

In response to the argument that an arrestee's reduced privacy interests justify the search of a cell phone incident to arrest, the Court stated, "The fact that an arrestee has diminished privacy interests does not mean that the *Fourth Amendment* falls out of the picture entirely." *Id. at , 134 S. Ct. at 2488.* Rather, the Court observed that "[m]odern cell phones, as a category, implicate privacy concerns far beyond those implicated by the search of a cigarette pack, a wallet, or a purse." *Id. at , 134 S. Ct. at 2488-89.* Thus, the Court's "answer to the question of what police must do before searching a cell phone seized incident to an arrest is accordingly simple--get a warrant." *Id. at , 134 S. Ct. at 2495.*

We have found no Arizona case that applies *Riley* to the warrantless search of a cell phone located in the room where a person has been arrested, but not within the arrestee's reach. We conclude *Chimel* and *Riley* prohibit such a search. First, neither of the justifications identified in *Chimel* applies here. The cell phone was not within Ontiveros-Loya's reach because he was seated in the back of a patrol car during the search of the motel room, so he could not have used it to endanger the officers or destroy evidence. In addition, the detectives searched Ontiveros-Loya's photographs, implicating the privacy interests described by the Court in *Riley*. As the Court observed, "The sum of an individual's private life can be reconstructed through a thousand photographs labeled with dates, locations, and descriptions; the same cannot be said of a photograph or two of loved ones tucked into a wallet." *Id. at , 134 S. Ct. at 2489*. Thus, we conclude the warrantless search of the cell phone was invalid under *Chimel* and *Riley*.

The trial court also found the warrantless search justified because Ontiveros-Loya had given "conflicting information" regarding his identity. The state cites no authority, and we have found none, that permits a search of a cell phone incident to arrest for the purpose of verifying the arrestee's identity. Even if such a search came within an exception to the warrant requirement, the evidence produced at the suppression hearing established only that Ontiveros-Loya initially gave a false name and at some unspecified time later provided his true name. There is no indication from the testimony presented at the hearing that the detectives had any reason to doubt Ontiveros-Loya's identity before they searched the cell phone. Thus, we conclude its search was not incident to his arrest and the court abused its discretion in denying the motion to suppress on that basis. Indeed, the state does not argue the trial court's rationale was correct.

The trial court also found the detectives inevitably would have discovered the photographs on Ontiveros-Loya's cell phone. Pursuant to the inevitable discovery doctrine, illegally obtained evidence is admissible if "'the prosecution can establish by a preponderance of the evidence that the illegally seized items or information would have inevitably been seized by lawful means.'" *State v. Rojers, 216 Ariz. 555, ¶ 18, 169 P.3d 651, 655 (App. 2007), quoting State v. Jones, 185 Ariz. 471, 481, 917 P.2d 200, 210 (1996)*.

The detectives eventually obtained a warrant to search the cell phone.[5] But Ontiveros-Loya argues the application for the warrant was based on the photographs found during the initial search of the cell phone. He states "it appears that the evidence found during the unlawful search is what prompted the officers to subsequently seek the warrant." The state responds, "[T]here is nothing in the record demonstrating that information was used to later obtain the search warrant" and Ontiveros-Loya "fails to overcome the presumption that the search warrant was valid." But it was the state's burden at the suppression hearing to prove inevitable discovery applied, *see id.*, so it was the state's responsibility to produce the affidavit to demonstrate it was not based on the photographs found during the initial search. The warrant permitted the officers to search Ontiveros-Loya's cell phone for digital photographs, text messages, emails, telephone numbers and contacts, and owner identification.

Because the affidavit supporting the search warrant was not proffered at the suppression hearing, the trial court could not determine on what basis the police sought the warrant or whether it was supported by probable cause after omitting any unlawfully obtained information. There was no testimony that would allow the court to conclude the officers could have obtained the warrant to search the cell phone without the photographs found during the initial search. *See Davolt, 207 Ariz. 191, ¶ 36, 84 P.3d at 469* (refusing to apply inevitable discovery doctrine where "no information was adduced that the evidence discovered . . . might ever have been obtained lawfully"). Thus, we conclude the court abused its discretion in denying Ontiveros-Loya's motion to suppress based on the inevitable discovery doctrine.

Although the trial court erred by denying Ontiveros-Loya's motion to suppress, we will not reverse a conviction if the error was harmless. *Id. ¶ 39.* "Error is harmless if we can conclude beyond a reasonable doubt that it did not contribute to or affect the verdict." *State v. Towery, 186 Ariz. 168, 185, 920 P.2d 290, 307 (1996).* Under that standard, the question "'is not whether, in a trial that occurred without the error, a guilty verdict would surely have been rendered, but whether the guilty verdict actually rendered in this trial was surely unattributable to the error.'" *State v. Valverde, 220 Ariz. 582, ¶ 11, 208 P.3d 233, 236 (2009), quoting State v. Anthony, 218 Ariz. 439, ¶ 39, 189 P.3d 366, 373 (2008).* "We can find error harmless when the evidence against a defendant is so overwhelming that any reasonable jury could only have reached one conclusion." *Anthony, 218 Ariz. 439, ¶ 41, 189 P.3d at 373.*

The strongest evidence produced at trial that Ontiveros-Loya had possessed a deadly weapon was the photographs of him holding a gun. The only other such evidence was S.R.'s testimony that she saw a gun in Ontiveros-Loya's waistband and the magazine found in the motel room. Despite an "extensive" search of the motel room and the surrounding area, police never found a gun. In addition, another person had rented the motel room, and the jury could have believed that the magazine belonged to that individual. S.R. testified that the incident took place late at night in an area that was not well-lit. She also had difficulty remembering the sequence of events, stating she could not remember at what point Ontiveros-Loya told her he would shoot her if she did not come back to his room with him. S.R. also testified that the incident happened "really fast" and that Ontiveros-Loya never pulled out the gun, showed it to her, pointed it at her, or "made any indication . . . of using the gun or having the gun." We cannot eliminate the possibility that the error contributed to the guilty verdict or conclude the other evidence was so overwhelming that any reasonable jury was bound to reach one conclusion. *Id. ¶¶ 39, 41*. Thus, the error was not harmless.

Although the trial court did not rely on Ontiveros-Loya's purported consent to search the motel room in denying his motion to suppress the evidence found on the cell phone, the state raised the consent question in its response to the motion to suppress, and both parties addressed consent at the suppression hearing. Specifically, the state argued that Ontiveros-Loya gave the detectives his consent to search the motel room, and that consent also allowed them to search the cell phone, which was located in the room. Ontiveros-Loya responded that "the idea that his consent to search a hotel room means that he also consented to search everything that was on a phone that happened to be in the hotel room . . . goes way too far." The state argues Ontiveros-Loya waived all but fundamental error review of the question of his consent to search the cell phone because he did not argue in his suppression motion that the search exceeded the scope of his consent to search the motel room. But the state argued at the hearing that Ontiveros-Loya consented to the search of the cell phone, and Ontiveros-Loya responded to the argument. The trial court therefore was given the opportunity to rule on the issue. *See State v. Deschamps, 105 Ariz. 530, 533, 468 P.2d 383, 386 (1970)*. We conclude the issue is preserved for our review.

Consent is another "long recognized exception to the warrant requirement." *State v. Guillen, 223 Ariz. 314, ¶ 11, 223 P.3d 658, 661 (2010)*. It was the state's burden to show Ontiveros-Loya consented to the search of the motel room, *State v. Lucero, 143 Ariz. 108, 110, 692 P.2d 287, 289 (1984)*, and that the search was conducted within the scope of consent, *State v. Ahumada, 225 Ariz. 544, ¶ 14, 241 P.3d 908, 912 (App. 2010)*. The scope of consent "is a question of fact to be determined from the totality of the circumstances," *State v. Swanson, 172 Ariz. 579, 583, 838 P.2d 1340, 1344 (App. 1992)*, based on an objective standard of what a reasonable person would understand from the exchange between the officer and the suspect, *Florida v. Jimeno, 500 U.S. 248, 251, 111 S. Ct. 1801, 114 L. Ed. 2d 297 (1991)*. "[T]he scope of a consensual search is defined by the scope of the consent given," *State v. Flores, 195 Ariz. 199, ¶ 26, 986 P.2d 232, 238 (App. 1999)*, and "is limited by the items about which the officer inquired as a predicate to the search." *Swanson, 172 Ariz. at 583, 838 P.2d at 1344*.

The testimony at the suppression hearing did not establish which items the detectives inquired about as a predicate to the search. In addition, there was no evidence that Ontiveros-Loya's consent to search the motel room extended to a search of the contents of his cell phone. The consent form he signed was not admitted into evidence at the suppression hearing. Because the parties raised this issue below, but the trial court did not rule on it and the record is insufficient for us to rule on the issue as a matter of law, we remand this matter to the court for the limited purpose of considering the issue of consent to search the cell phone. "Taking into consideration 'the goals of timely administering justice and searching for the truth,' we believe a remand for limited proceedings most efficiently resolves the issues at hand and preserves [Ontiveros-Loya's] right to seek relief from the court's ruling on remand." *State v. Peterson, 228 Ariz. 405, ¶ 19, 267 P.3d 1197, 1203 (App. 2011)* (citation omitted).

STATE OF ARIZONA, APPELLANT, V. DONALD EUGENE REED, JR., APPELLEE.
1 CA-CR 09-0591

(Text added/modified for emphasis) The appellate courts refuse to take judicial notice of their own records which records show that the same law enforcement officers and prosecutors consistently engage in warrantless searches, continuing to condone this practice. When viewed in the totality, and not in isolation, this should constitute fraud upon the court by these lawyers.

COUNSEL: Terry Goddard, Attorney General, By Kent E. Cattani, Chief Counsel, Criminal Appeals/Capital Litigation Section and Andrea L. Kever, Deputy County Attorney, Appeals and Westside Juvenile Division, Phoenix, Attorneys for Appellant. James J. Haas, Maricopa County Public Defender, By Paul J. Prato, Deputy Public Defender, Phoenix, Attorneys for Appellee.

A grand jury indicted Reed on one count of sale or transportation of narcotic drugs ("crack" cocaine), one count of possession or use of dangerous drugs (methamphetamine) and one count of possession or use of marijuana. Reed moved to suppress "all evidence" seized following a traffic stop in which police recovered "crack" cocaine, methamphetamine, and marijuana from his car.

At the suppression hearing, Officer A. testified he pulled Reed over for speeding. As the officer approached Reed's car, the "window was rolled down [and] [w]hen I contacted him I could smell an odor of marijuana emitting from inside the vehicle." The officer also testified Reed had "red, watery, bloodshot eyes, and when he was looking for his driver's license he was fumbling through the wallet and having difficulty with his dexterity and faculties, and appearing to be very nervous."

Officer A. stated he "pulled" Reed out of the car to "detain [] [him] for a DUI investigation" and saw, from outside the car, "a plastic baggie with a rock substance that appeared to be rock cocaine" located in the "center console cup holder between the two front seats." Officer A. handcuffed Reed, placed Reed in his patrol car, removed the plastic baggie, and had Reed's car towed to a nearby convenience store. At this convenience store parking lot, while other officers investigated Reed for DUI, Officer A. searched Reed's car, performed a field test of the cocaine-like substance, and determined it was cocaine. Officer A. found two pill bottles, one containing what he believed to be ecstasy and the other containing what he believed to be "meth" in a covered part of the center console, and marijuana in the trunk. It is not clear from the record whether the officer field tested the cocaine-like substance before or after searching Reed's car.

Relying on *Arizona v. Gant, 556 U.S. 332, , 129 S. Ct. 1710, 1723, 173 L. Ed. 2d 485 (2009)*, the superior court determined "there was no longer an issue of officer safety, and no longer an issue of concealment, destruction, or spoliation of evidence in the Defendant's vehicle" and granted Reed's motion.

DISCUSSION

I. Offense of Arrest Exception

Also relying on *Gant,* the State first asserts the superior court did not address its argument Officer A. had a reasonable belief Reed's car contained evidence of his offense of arrest, and thus argues we should reverse the court's ruling. Because we agree with the State, we vacate and remand to the court for consideration of this argument.

The State may not conduct "unreasonable searches and seizures." *U.S. Const. amend. IV.* Warrantless searches and seizures are per se unreasonable unless a recognized exception to the warrant requirement exists. *Katz v. United States, 389 U.S. 347, 357, 88 S. Ct. 507, 514, 19 L. Ed. 2d 576 (1967).* One such exception is the search incident to arrest, which permits police to search within an arrestee's "immediate control,' meaning 'the area from within which [the arrestee] might gain possession of a weapon or destructible evidence.'" *Gant, 556 U.S. at , 129 S. Ct. at 1714* (quoting *Chimel v. California, 395 U.S. 752, 763, 89 S. Ct. 2034, 2040, 23 L. Ed. 2d 685 (1969)). Gant*explained this "officer safety" or "evidence preservation" exception does not "authorize a vehicle search incident to a recent occupant's arrest after the arrestee has been secured and cannot access the interior of the vehicle." *Id. at , , 129 S. Ct. at 1714, 1716. Gant* also recognized an "offense of arrest" exception, where "circumstances unique to the automobile context justify a search incident to arrest when it is reasonable to believe that evidence of the offense of arrest might be found in the vehicle." *Id. at , 129 S. Ct. at 1714.*

Here, based on the evidence presented at the suppression hearing, the superior court correctly concluded Officer A.'s search of Reed's car was not authorized under *Gant's* officer safety or evidence preservation exception. The court did not, however, address the State's argument "the search actually d[id] relate to the cause for arrest," and thus, the search was permissible under *Gant's* offense of arrest exception. Because the court did not address the State's argument the search was authorized under that exception, we remand to the superior court to consider whether Officer A.'s search of Reed's car was permissible on that basis. We decline to decide whether, based on the evidence presented at the suppression hearing, Officer A.'s search was justified by this exception. The superior court is in the best position to determine the credibility of witnesses. *See, e.g., State v. Ossana, 199 Ariz. 459, 461, ¶ 7, 18 P.3d 1258, 1260 (App. 2001)* (superior court determines the credibility of witnesses). On remand, the court may exercise its discretion to consider the applicability of the offense of arrest exception based on the existing record or as supplemented by the parties. The superior court found Officer A.'s testimony unreliable on an issue unrelated to this appeal, but contemporaneous with Reed's traffic stop. *See supra* note i. Although the superior court made no such finding *concerning* Officer A.'s memory of the traffic stop and recovery/testing of the contraband, the record demonstrates conflicts between his recollection of events and his police report.

II. Automobile Exception

Also on appeal, as it did in the superior court, the State argues Officer A.'s search was authorized under another exception to the warrant requirement, the "automobile exception." *See State v. Reyna, 205 Ariz. 374, 375, ¶ 5, 71 P.3d 366, 367 (App. 2003)* (citing *California v. Carney, 471 U.S. 386, 390, 392-93, 105 S. Ct. 2066, 2068, 2070, 85 L. Ed. 2d 406 (1985)*). This exception permits a warrantless search when probable cause exists "to search a readily mobile vehicle that is stopped on the roadway or parked on a public street or in a parking lot." *Id.* The superior court did not address this argument in granting the motion to suppress. Thus, on remand, the superior court may also evaluate the reasonableness of the search under the automobile exception. In *Reyna*, we held police could conduct a warrantless search following a traffic stop of a truck when the officer "smelled the odor of marijuana coming from a support column in the bed of the truck" and "noticed that a compartment area had been welded to the truck, making its contents inaccessible." *205 Ariz. at 374-75, ¶ 2, 378, ¶ 16, 71 P.3d at 366-67, 370.*

STATE OF ARIZONA, Appellee, v. LAQUINN ANTHONY FISHER, Appellant.

Arizona Supreme Court No. CR-10-0315-PR
SUPREME COURT OF ARIZONA

(Text added/modified for emphasis) It is a very common practice for officers to manufacture reasons for a protective sweep. There are too many such instances and prosecutors by concealing this perpetrate fraud upon the court.

COUNSEL: For State of Arizona: Kent E. Cattani, Chief Counsel, Criminal Appeals/Capital Litigation Section, Joseph T. Maziarz, Assistant Attorney General, THOMAS C. HORNE, ARIZONA ATTORNEY GENERAL, Phoenix.

For Laquinn Anthony Fisher: Margaret M. Green, Deputy Public Defender, JAMES J. HAAS, MARICOPA COUNTY PUBLIC DEFENDER, Phoenix.

I. FACTS AND PROCEDURAL BACKGROUND

In May 2006, Mesa police responded to a call alleging an aggravated assault. The victim, who was bleeding from a cut on his head, told police he had been pistol-whipped by a man known as "Taz." The victim described Taz and directed police to an apartment complex where he believed Taz lived.

Other officers went to that apartment complex, where Laquinn Anthony Fisher lived. After officers knocked and announced their presence, Fisher and two others came out. None had a weapon and all three were cooperative. Fisher, whose appearance matched the description given by the victim, identified himself to officers as "TA." The responding officer testified that the police dispatch broadcast said the suspect went by both "TA" and "Taz."

Despite having this information, officers thought further investigation was necessary because the gun allegedly used in the assault was still "unaccounted for." Apparently without asking whether anyone was still inside, police entered the apartment to see if anyone else was present. Inside, officers smelled marijuana and observed open duffle bags containing marijuana. They did not find anyone in the apartment. After the sweep, officers obtained written consent from Fisher's roommate to search the apartment and seized the marijuana.

Officers later brought the assault victim to the apartment, and he identified Fisher as his attacker.

Charged with various crimes, including possession of marijuana for sale, Fisher moved to suppress any evidence of the marijuana found in the apartment. The trial court denied the motion, and a jury subsequently found Fisher guilty of the possession charge. The court of appeals affirmed, reasoning as follows: "Because the weapon used in the assault in this case was unaccounted for and the police articulated sufficient reasons for performing the sweep, . . . the trial court did not err in determining that the protective sweep was supported by reasonable suspicion." *State v. Fisher, 225 Ariz. 258, 260 P 7, 236 P.3d 1205, 1207 (App. 2010)*. Before trial, the State dismissed the other charges, including the aggravated assault charge.

....

II. DISCUSSION

The *Fourth Amendment to the United States Constitution* protects "[t]he right of the people to be secure in their persons, houses, papers, and effects, against unreasonable searches and seizures." "Unlawful entry into a home is the 'chief evil' against which the provision protects." *State v. Guillen, 223 Ariz. 314, 316 P 10, 223 P.3d 658, 660 (2010)*. Typically, police officers must obtain a warrant to enter a home, but because the "touchstone of the *Fourth Amendment* . . . is reasonableness," the Supreme Court has recognized several exceptions to the warrant requirement. *Michigan v. Fisher, 130 S. Ct. 546, 548, 175 L. Ed. 2d 410 (2009)* (internal quotation omitted). Although Fisher's petition cites *Article 2, Section 8 of the Arizona Constitution*, he does not develop any separate argument based on that provision or explain how any analysis under it should differ from Fourth Amendment analysis; nor did the court of appeals address this issue. Because a single reference to the Arizona Constitution is insufficient to preserve a claim, we do not address whether the protective sweep violated the Arizona Constitution. *State v. Dean, 206 Ariz. 158, 161 P 8 n.1, 76 P.3d 429, 432 n.1 (2003)*.

One such exception is the protective sweep, first recognized in *Maryland v. Buie, 494 U.S. 325, 110 S. Ct. 1093, 108 L. Ed. 2d 276 (1990)*. Relying heavily on *Terry v. Ohio, 392 U.S. 1, 88 S. Ct. 1868, 20 L. Ed. 2d 889 (1968)*, and *Michigan v. Long, 463 U.S. 1032, 103 S. Ct. 3469,*

77 L. Ed. 2d 1201 (1983), Buie held that "incident to [an] arrest the officers [can], as a precautionary matter and without probable cause or reasonable suspicion, look in closets and other spaces immediately adjoining the place of arrest from which an attack could be immediately launched." *Buie, 494 U.S. at 334.* But to justify a broader sweep, "there must be articulable facts which, taken together with the rational inferences from those facts, would warrant a reasonably prudent officer in believing that the area to be swept harbors an individual posing danger to those on the arrest scene." *Id.*

Buie thus authorizes two types of limited warrantless searches. The first involves the area immediately adjacent to the place of arrest. *Id.* The second allows a search of adjoining areas where persons posing a danger might be found. *Id.; see also United States v. Archibald, 589 F.3d 289, 295 (6th Cir. 2009)* (explaining two types of searches approved by *Buie); United States v. Lemus, 582 F.3d 958, 963 n.2 (9th Cir. 2009)* (describing difference between searches authorized by *Buie*). This case concerns the second type of *Buie* search.

In *Buie,* officers conducted the protective sweep after arresting the defendant inside his residence. Here, in contrast, Fisher was detained outside his apartment and not arrested until after the protective sweep. We assume, but do not decide, that a protective sweep is not forbidden when a suspect is detained and questioned but not yet arrested outside of a residence. The State concedes in its supplemental brief that Fisher was not under arrest when the protective sweep occurred.

Although we have upheld protective sweeps based on exigent circumstances, *see, e.g., State v. DeWitt, 184 Ariz. 464, 467, 910 P.2d 9, 12 (1996)* (finding warrantless entry of home justified by burglary in progress); *State v. Greene, 162 Ariz. 431, 433, 784 P.2d 257, 259 (1989)* (upholding "protective walk-through" of residence when initial entry was based on an exigency), we have never specifically applied the *Buie* test.

Buie teaches that a protective sweep of a residence is permissible only if the officers have a reasonable belief supported by "specific and articulable facts" that a home "harbored an individual posing a danger to the officers or others." *Buie, 494 U.S. at 327.* Conversely, if officers act purely on speculation, a protective sweep is unreasonable. *See, e.g.,*

Archibald, 589 F.3d at 300 ("Clearly, *Buie* requires more than ignorance or a constant assumption that more than one person is present in a residence."); *United States v. Gandia, 424 F.3d 255, 264 (2d Cir. 2005)* (requiring more than lack of information to justify a protective sweep).

The common thread among cases interpreting *Buie* is that officers must have specific articulable facts that someone who could pose a safety threat is inside a residence. *See, e.g., United States v. Murphy, 516 F.3d 1117, 1120-21 (9th Cir. 2008)* (determining fact that owner of storage unit who had outstanding arrest warrant was not accounted for justified officer's reasonable belief that another person could be present); *United States v. Lawlor, 406 F.3d 37, 42 (1st Cir. 2005)* (finding quick protective sweep justified when officers arrived at residence where gunshot had been reported, shooter had not been identified, and defendant "shrugged" when asked about the gun); *United States v. Gould, 364 F.3d 578, 592 (5th Cir. 2004)* (en banc) (upholding protective sweep of mobile home when officers have consent to enter bedroom and a known dangerous suspect was not in bed, as previously reported) ; *United States v. Taylor, 248 F.3d 506, 514 (6th Cir. 2001)* (approving protective sweep when officers heard scuffling noises from inside before being admitted into apartment and suspect's demeanor indicated he was hiding something). The more specific facts supporting a reasonable belief that an area contains a potentially dangerous individual, the more likely the protective sweep is valid. *See, e.g., United States v. Tapia, 610 F.3d 505, 511 (7th Cir. 2010)* (protective sweep proper when officers had six separate valid articulable facts); *United States v. Davis, 471 F.3d 938, 945 (8th Cir. 2006)* (listing several articulable facts).

We find particularly persuasive the Second Circuit's decision in *Gandia*. There, officers responded to a reported dispute between a building superintendent and a tenant. *424 F.3d at 258*. Officers were given a description of a suspect who might be carrying a gun. *Id*. Upon arrival, they saw Gandia, who matched the description of the suspect, but determined that he was unarmed. *Id*. Officers escorted him to his apartment and asked if anyone else was there. *Id*. He said "no" and allowed the officers to enter his apartment, but not to search it. *Id*. Once inside, they nonetheless conducted a protective sweep and discovered a bullet. *Id. at 259*. The Second Circuit held that the sweep was invalid because the officers had no reason to believe that a person might be hiding in Gandia's apartment. *Id. at 264*. Although there was an unaccounted-for weapon, nothing indicated that "there was a person hiding in the apartment who might use it." *Id.* The court emphasized that "'lack of information cannot provide an articulable basis upon which to justify a protective sweep.'" *Id.* (quoting *United States v. Moran Vargas, 376 F.3d 112, 117 (2d Cir. 2004)).*

Similarly, the officers in this case could not articulate specific facts indicating that another person was inside Fisher's apartment. The record does not reflect any attempt by the officers to find out how many people lived with Taz. Three people, including Fisher, exited the apartment. Fisher identified himself and matched the victim's detailed description of the assailant. Although there was still an unaccounted-for weapon, as in *Gandia*, nothing indicated that anyone else was inside the apartment. Officers cannot conduct protective sweeps based on mere speculation or the general risk inherent in all police work. Because the officers here did not articulate specific facts to establish a reasonable belief that someone might be in the apartment, the protective sweep was invalid.

We are mindful that:

> [P]olice officers have an incredibly difficult and dangerous task and are placed in life threatening situations on a regular basis. It would perhaps reduce the danger inherent in the job if we allowed the police to do whatever they felt necessary, whenever they needed to do it, in whatever manner required, in every situation in which they must act. However, there is a *Fourth Amendment* to the Constitution which necessarily forecloses this possibility.

United States v. Colbert, 76 F.3d 773, 778 (6th Cir. 1996). We likewise are aware of the high price of suppressing evidence. *See State v. Bolt, 142 Ariz. 260, 266-67, 689 P.2d 519, 525-26 (1984); cf. Herring v. United States, 555 U.S. 135, 129 S. Ct. 695, 700-01, 172 L. Ed. 2d 496 (2009)* ("The principal cost of applying the [exclusionary] rule is, of course, letting guilty and possibly dangerous defendants go free -

something that 'offends basic concepts of the criminal justice system.'" (quoting *United States v. Leon, 468 U.S. 897, 908, 104 S. Ct. 3405, 82 L. Ed. 2d 677 (1984)*). But the right to privacy in one's home is "'basic to a free society.'" *Mapp v. Ohio, 367 U.S. 643, 656, 81 S. Ct. 1684, 6 L. Ed. 2d 1081, 86 Ohio Law Abs. 513 (1961)* (quoting *Wolf v. Colorado, 338 U.S. 25, 27, 69 S. Ct. 1359, 93 L. Ed. 1782 (1949)*). Thus, specific facts, and not mere conjecture, are required to justify a protective sweep of a residence based on concerns for officer safety.

STATE OF ARIZONA, APPELLEE, V. KURT ANDREW GOETTL, APPELLANT.
NO. 1 CA-CR 14-0040

COUNSEL: Arizona Attorney General's Office, Phoenix, By William Scott Simon, Counsel for Appellee.

Maricopa County Public Defender's Office, Phoenix, By Terry Reid, Counsel for Appellant.

(Text added/modified for emphasis) The appellate courts refuse to take judicial notice of their own records which records show that the same law enforcement officers and prosecutors consistently engage in warrantless searches, continuing to find the conduct harmless. When viewed in the totality, and not in isolation, this should constitute fraud upon the court by these lawyers.

....

Appellant Kurt Andrew Goettl appeals his convictions and sentences for possession of dangerous drugs for sale (methamphetamine), possession of drug paraphernalia (plastic baggies), and possession or use of narcotic drugs (hydrocodone). Goettl argues that the superior court abused its discretion by failing to suppress and admitting text message evidence obtained from his cell phone during a warrantless search in violation of the *Fourth Amendment*. Goettl argues his convictions should be reversed, and admission of the text messages was not harmless error because such evidence was "the only *direct* evidence supporting [his] *confession*" that he possessed methamphetamine for sale and "absent the text messages . . . the jury would give less weight to [his] confession . . .." (Emphases added.) Because we determine any error in admitting the text message evidence was harmless beyond a reasonable doubt, we affirm his convictions and sentences.

FACTUAL AND PROCEDURAL HISTORY

Detective G observed Goettl run a red light on his bicycle. Thereafter, Detective G surveilled Goettl and watched as he met a woman on a bicycle. As Goettl and the woman walked together with their bicycles Goettl opened a saddle bag on the back of his bicycle and then made a "hand-to-hand transaction" with the woman. Goettl and the woman then rode away from each other. Observing the hand-to-hand transaction was significant to Detective G because such a transaction "is when typically, a drug item is transferred from one person to the other" for drugs or payment. Detective G followed Goettl, arrested him, and searched him.[1] During the search, Detective G found a bag of pills later determined to contain hydrocodone, $480 in cash, and a bag containing a crystal substance later determined to be one gram of methamphetamine. In Goettl's saddle bag, Detective G found more bags containing a substance later determined to total two grams of methamphetamine as well as small clear plastic bags that were empty.

A different officer followed the woman, but no drugs were found when she was searched. Detective G also viewed and later photographed text messages on Goettl's phone purportedly reflecting that the purpose of meeting the woman was to sell her drugs. Goettl was taken to the city jail where he was given *Miranda* warnings and interviewed by Detective G.

Goettl moved to suppress the text messages arguing they were obtained in violation of his Fourth Amendment rights. The superior court refused to suppress the text messages after determining that cell phones are "containers" which may be searched incident to arrest.

The superior court made this ruling before the United States Supreme Court decided *Riley v. California, 134 S. Ct. 2473, 189 L. Ed. 2d 430 (2014)*. At trial Detective G testified that during the police interview Goettl stated that the woman wanted to buy drugs from him, but he talked her out of that and gave her some money. Although Goettl did not tell Detective G that he was selling drugs that day, Goettl stated he did not have a job, his only source of income was selling methamphetamine, and that the $480 was cash he made from selling methamphetamine. Goettl said that he got the methamphetamine with which he was found earlier that day from his supplier and stated that he typically bought one half ounce to one ounce from his supplier. Detective G also testified that Goettl admitted that he used methamphetamine earlier that day. Goettl told Detective G that he believed the pills he had were Vicodin and he had traded methamphetamine for them because sometimes people asked for pills. After Goettl's hearsay objection was overruled, Detective G read into evidence the text message conversation that took place between Goettl and the woman before their encounter. In addition, the photographs of the messages were admitted into evidence.

Detective M testified about his training and experience for eighteen years as a patrol officer and narcotics detective and opined that based on the totality of the circumstances the methamphetamine Goettl possessed was for the purpose of sale. Detective M testified about what he takes into account when forming such opinions and stated that he formed his opinion in Goettl's case after reviewing the police reports, evidence, and police interview of Goettl. Detective M explained that when forming his opinions about whether drugs are for sale as opposed to personal use, a person's statements to police are the most important factor. According to Detective M, his opinion was largely based on the statements provided by Goettl during the police interview including that Goettl traded a bag of methamphetamine for Vicodin, that he did not have a regular job, and that Goettl told police that the $480 in cash with which he was found was drug sale proceeds. Detective M explained that selling drugs is a "cash business" and people selling drugs typically carry "bulk cash." He also thought that Goettl's statement about trading methamphetamine for Vicodin because sometimes people asked for Vicodin indicated that Goettl was a person who sells drugs and wanted to have product on hand if someone asked for it.

Apart from Goettl's statements, Detective M's opinion that Goettl possessed the methamphetamine for sale was based on Goettl possessing multiple small plastic bags, typical of those used by drug dealers, which contained methamphetamine, as well as other unused small plastic bags. Detective M explained that in his experience, drug sellers tend to buy a quantity of drugs and then repackage the drugs in smaller quantities for resale using small plastic baggies like the ones Goettl had. According to Detective M if a person intended the drugs for personal use, there would be no reason to have multiple small bags of drugs. In addition, Detective M noted that Goettl was not found with any tools to use drugs, such as a syringe or pipe that a typical drug user carries. Detective M also testified about the current approximate value of methamphetamine and stated that a gram was worth $50 to $60.

Detective M testified about how in general drug dealers set up drug deals including that drug users usually contact the dealer via cell phone, or some type of electronic communication, or in person, or through another party. Later in his testimony, Detective M was asked about the relevance of the text message conversation between Goettl and the woman. Detective M indicated that when he worked undercover he would order drugs in a similar fashion to the text message conversation by concealing the true nature of his request through the use of certain code words to communicate the desire for drugs and the quantity requested. This was the only testimony Detective M provided with respect to the text message conversation.

In closing arguments, the State twice referred to the text message conversation:

> When the case began back on March 20, 2012, the defendant was out engaging in his illegal business of selling methamphetamine and he received a text message from [a woman]. And we talked about those. And [the woman] wanted to get a dime. She wanted to get high. And eventually the defendant told her through the conversation, Okay. I'm at the McDonalds.
>
> . . . .
>
> The text messages are in evidence. You'll be able to review them if you'd like. The text messaging pretty clearly shows that [the woman] wanted to buy drugs off the defendant and the defendant admitted, Yeah, she wanted to buy drugs off of me and that's why I met her. And later he did deny selling drugs to

her, but nevertheless, [the woman] wanted to buy drugs off of him and that was the purpose of the meeting.

....

DISCUSSION

Relying upon *Riley v. California, 134 S. Ct. 2473, 2495, 189 L. Ed. 2d 430 (2014)*, Goettl argues it was reversible error to admit the text message evidence. *Riley* held that the contents of cell phones cannot be searched pursuant to the "incident to arrest" exception to the warrant requirement. *134 S. Ct. at 2493-94* (leaving open the possibility that "other case-specific exceptions may still justify a warrantless search of a particular phone" such as exigent circumstances). The State argues that even if the search was unlawful under *Riley*, the good faith exception applies which would allow the evidence to be admitted and that even if admission was erroneous, it was harmless error given the other evidence.

For purposes of resolving Goettl's appeal, we assume without deciding that the cell phone search was unconstitutional and the good faith exception did not apply because "[e]rror, be it constitutional or otherwise, is harmless [and does not require reversal] if we can say, beyond a reasonable doubt, that the error did not contribute to or affect the verdict." *State v. Bible, 175 Ariz. 549, 588, 858 P.2d 1152, 1191 (1993)*. Thus, "we consider the error in light of all of the evidence," to determine whether the State has met its burden to prove that "'the guilty verdict actually rendered in *this* trial was surely unattributable to the error.'" *Id.* (quoting *Sullivan v. Louisiana, 508 U.S. 275, 279, 113 S. Ct. 2078, 124 L. Ed. 2d 182 (1993)*); accord *State v. Valverde, 220 Ariz. 582, 585, ¶ 11, 208 P.3d 233, 236 (2009)*.

Goettl maintains that because the State "referred repeatedly" to the text messages during closing arguments, and Detective M based his opinion in part on the text messages, "it is likely, absent the text messages, that the jury would give less weight to [Goettl's] confession" that he possessed the methamphetamine for sale. Goettl directs us to Detective M's testimony that a drug dealer's clients normally make contact by cell phone, and his opinion that Goettl possessed the drugs for sale as opposed to personal use.

To support this contention, Goettl claims that his "confession was not commensurate with the facts of the case," because: (1) although police observed Goettl's hand-to-hand transaction with a woman, when police stopped the woman she did not possess any drugs; and (2) Detective M testified that a typical amount of methamphetamine sold to a user is about one gram and the total weight of the methamphetamine Goettl possessed was only three grams. We disagree that Goettl's confession was not commensurate with the facts of the case. His confession that the woman wanted to buy drugs he had for sale, but Goettl convinced her not to, is not inconsistent with the fact that the woman did not have drugs when the police searched her. In addition, that Goettl had a total of three grams of methamphetamine including one gram in one bag and the remainder in multiple other bags is not inconsistent with Detective M's opinion that a typical amount of methamphetamine sold to a methamphetamine user is one gram.

We disagree that the text message evidence contributed to the guilty verdict here. *See Bible, 175 Ariz. at 588, 858 P.2d at 1191.* First, Detective M emphasized that although he considered the totality of the evidence, Goettl's statements to police were the most important factor in forming his opinion that Goettl possessed the methamphetamine for sale. Goettl's statements to police established the elements of the offense independent of the other circumstantial evidence or Detective M's opinion about the evidence. *See A.R.S. §§ 13-3407(A)(2)* (Supp. 2015), *-3401(6)(c)(xxxviii)* (Supp. 2015). Goettl does not dispute that he was in possession of methamphetamine when he was arrested and that he told police the woman he met with wanted to buy drugs from him but he talked her out of it. It is also undisputed that Goettl told police the $480 he had was from methamphetamine sales, that his only source of income was selling methamphetamine, and that he had met with his supplier earlier that day.

In addition, Detective M stated that his opinion was based on other circumstantial evidence that the methamphetamine Goettl had was for sale including that the quantity of methamphetamine Goettl possessed was enough to be sold, the drugs were packaged in a way typical to drugs for sale, Goettl was in possession of multiple small bags like those typically used to repackage and sell methamphetamine, Goettl had a bulk cash on him and no utensils to use drugs that are often carried by users.

Regardless of whether we agree with Goettl that the text message evidence was the only "direct" evidence supporting his *confession*, there was a wealth of circumstantial evidence supporting not only his confession, but also the elements of the offense. *See State v. Harvill, 106 Ariz. 386, 391, 476 P.2d 841, 846 (1970)* (stating the probative value of direct and circumstantial evidence carry the same evidentiary weight).

For these same reasons we also disagree that the State's reference in closing argument that the purpose of meeting the woman was to sell methamphetamine contributed to the guilty verdict. Goettl's confession and the wealth of circumstantial evidence that Goettl possessed the methamphetamine for sale convinces us that any error in admitting the text messages was harmless beyond a reasonable doubt. *See Bible, 175 Ariz. at 588, 858 P.2d at 1191*.

STATE OF ARIZONA, APPELLEE, V. DON JACOB HAVATONE, APPELLANT.
NO. 1 CA-CR 14-0223

(Text added/modified for emphasis) The appellate courts refuse to take judicial notice of their own records which records show that the same law enforcement officers and prosecutors consistently engage in warrantless searches, continuing to find the conduct under the good faith exception and harmless. When viewed in the totality, and not in isolation, this should constitute fraud upon the court by these lawyers.

COUNSEL: Arizona Attorney General's Office, Phoenix, By Colby Mills, Counsel for Appellee. David Goldberg, Fort Collins, CO, Counsel for Appellant.

FACTS AND PROCEDURAL HISTORY

On September 17, 2012, Havatone drove his red SUV head on into the path of an oncoming vehicle driving westbound on Route 66 between Kingman and Valle Vista, Arizona. A witness driving behind

Havatone saw Havatone's SUV drive "erratically" and cross over the center line "four or five times" over the space of several miles prior to the collision. Havatone had four passengers in his vehicle. The other vehicle was occupied by the driver, L.S., only. Shortly after the collision, L.S. saw a male with his foot caught in the SUV's windshield crawl out over the hood and lie down on the ground in front of the vehicle; he saw a second male occupant exit the driver's side of the vehicle and lie down behind the SUV. L.S. recognized the man behind the SUV as Havatone, his acquaintance.

Department of Public Safety Officer M.P. was among the first to respond to the scene. He contacted Havatone, who was still lying on the ground behind the SUV being attended by medics. When M.P. asked Havatone "[w]ho was driving," Havatone replied, "I was." When M.P. asked him "what happened," M.P. "got no response." M.P. smelled a "heavy odor" of alcohol coming from all occupants of the SUV, including Havatone. M.P. looked inside the SUV and observed numerous beer cans and an open bottle of liquor in the vehicle. Havatone was air-evacuated to a hospital in Las Vegas for treatment. A blood sample taken at the hospital indicated he had a blood alcohol concentration ("BAC") of 0.212.

The State charged Havatone with Count 1, aggravated driving under the influence of intoxicating liquor while his license was suspended or revoked, a Class 4 felony; Count 2, aggravated driving under the extreme influence of intoxicating liquor with a BAC of .20 or more while his license was suspended or revoked, a Class 4 felony; Count 3, aggravated assault of L.S. with a deadly weapon or dangerous instrument, a Class 3 felony; Count 4, recklessly endangering L.S. with a substantial risk of imminent death, a Class 6 felony; and Counts 5, 6, 7 and 8, aggravated assault with a deadly weapon or dangerous instrument of the occupants of his vehicle. A jury found Havatone guilty of Counts 1 through 4 as charged. Furthermore, the jury found Counts 3 and 4 to be dangerous offenses along with three additional aggravators: 1) Havatone's BAC was greater than .15 at the time of his DUI offenses; 2) Havatone had committed at least two DUIs in the ten years prior to the current DUI offenses; and 3) Havatone had previously been convicted of involuntary manslaughter while driving impaired. As to

Counts 5 through 8, involving the passengers/victims in Havatone's vehicle, the jury found him guilty of the lesser included offenses of assault, each a Class 2 misdemeanor. The parties stipulated that Havatone's "privilege to drive was suspended and cancelled, and that he knew it was suspended and cancelled."

I. Motion to Suppress Blood Test Results

As Havatone was being helicoptered to a hospital in Las Vegas, Officer M.P. asked dispatch to contact Nevada law enforcement to obtain a blood sample from Havatone. Nevada authorities obtained a sample of Havatone's blood from medical personnel at the hospital. Prior to trial, Havatone moved to suppress the blood test results, arguing that the blood sample was obtained without a search warrant in violation of his *Fourth Amendment* rights. Havatone argued that no exceptions applied to the failure to obtain a warrant for the draw.

Following a hearing, the trial court denied the motion, finding the evidence admissible under both Nevada and Arizona law. In reaching its decision, the trial court found, among other things, that the "officers involved in this case collectively had probable cause to believe that [Havatone] had been driving a vehicle while under the influence of intoxicating liquor." Because Havatone was unconscious when the blood draw occurred, the court determined that Arizona implied consent law applied and no warrant was necessary. The trial court also found that the blood draw was objectively reasonable and that, even if the implied consent statute is unconstitutional, the good-faith exception to the exclusionary rule applied:

> Finally, the Court finds that the officers acted with a reasonable good faith reliance on statutes and cases in effect at the time the blood was seized. Even if *McNeely* applies, the Court finds that no legitimate purpose would be served by suppression of the blood evidence in this case.

(Internal citations omitted.)

Havatone does not assert Nevada law applies; on appeal, he expressly maintains that Arizona law controls.

We review a trial court's denial of a motion to suppress based solely on the evidence presented at the suppression hearing, *State v. Spears, 184 Ariz. 277, 284, 908 P.2d 1062 (1996)*, and we view that evidence in the light most favorable to sustaining the trial court's ruling, *State v. Gay, 214 Ariz. 214, 217, ¶ 4, 150 P.3d 787 (App. 2007)*. We review the factual findings underlying the determination for abuse of discretion but review the court's legal conclusions *de novo. See State v. Moody, 208 Ariz. 424, 445, ¶ 62, 94 P.3d 1119 (2004)*. We will not disturb a trial court's ruling on a motion to suppress absent a clear abuse of discretion, *Spears, 184 Ariz. at 284*, and will affirm the court's ruling if it is legally correct for any reason, *State v. Perez, 141 Ariz. 459, 464, 687 P.2d 1214 (1984)*.

"Under Arizona law, police may obtain a DUI suspect's blood sample only pursuant to a valid search warrant, Arizona's implied consent law, *A.R.S. § 28-1321*, or the medical blood draw exception in *A.R.S. § 28-1388(E)*." *State v. Aleman, 210 Ariz. 232, 236, ¶ 11, 109 P.3d 571 (App. 2005)*. The trial court found that *A.R.S. § 28-1321(A)* authorized the blood draw in this case without a warrant. That statute states the following:

> A person who operates a motor vehicle in [Arizona] gives consent . . . to a test or tests of the person's blood, breath, urine or other bodily substance for the purpose of determining alcohol concentration or drug content if the person is arrested for any offense arising out of acts alleged to have been committed in violation of this chapter . . . while the person was driving or in actual physical control of a motor vehicle while under the influence of intoxicating liquor or drugs.

A.R.S. § 28-1321(A). Further, the "unconscious clause" of the same statute provides:

A person who is dead, unconscious, or otherwise in a condition rendering the person incapable of refusal is deemed not to have withdrawn the consent provided by subsection A of this section and the test or tests may be administered.

A.R.S. 28-1321(C).

For purposes of *A.R.S. § 28-1321(C)*, it is not necessary that there be an actual arrest prior to the blood draw. *See State v. Huffman, 137 Ariz. 300, 302-03, 670 P.2d 405 (App. 1983)*. An officer must, however, have probable cause to believe a defendant was driving while under the influence. *Campbell v. Super. Ct., 106 Ariz. 542, 553-54, 479 P.2d 685 (1971); Aleman, 210 Ariz. at 236-37, ¶¶ 11-12*.

Nevada has a similar statutory mandate requiring the blood draw of an unconscious DUI suspect:

> Except as otherwise provided in subsections 4 and 5, any person who drives or is in actual physical control of a vehicle on a highway or on premises to which the public has access shall be deemed to have given his or her consent to an evidentiary test of his or her blood, urine, breath or other bodily substance to determine the concentration of alcohol in his or her blood or breath . . . .
>
> If the person to be tested pursuant to subsection 1 is dead or unconscious, the officer *shall direct* that samples of blood from the person be tested.

Nev. Rev. Stat. ("N.R.S.") § 484C.160(1), (3) (emphasis added).

The Nevada Supreme Court recently held *N.R.S. § 484C.160(7)* unconstitutional because it does not allow a driver to withdraw consent, though the court avoided interpreting the "unconscious" provision of *§ 484C.160*. See *Byars v. State, 336 P.3d 939, 946 (Nev. 2014)*.

A. Application of the Good-Faith Exception

We agree with the trial court that the unconscious clause applies under these facts. The officers had probable cause to believe Havatone drove while impaired. At the suppression hearing, M.P. testified that, when he asked Havatone "if he'd been driving [the SUV]," Havatone "advised he was driving the vehicle." As M.P. spoke with Havatone at the scene, M.P. could smell a "strong odor" of alcohol. When M.P. looked inside the SUV, he saw an open liquor bottle that was partly consumed and open and unopened cans of beer. M.P. also learned from L.S. that immediately prior to the collision, the SUV had crossed into L.S.'s lane of traffic and driven straight at his vehicle. This evidence is sufficient to sustain the trial court's finding that M.P. had probable cause to believe Havatone was driving under the influence.

Havatone argues that even if there was probable cause to suspect that he was driving while impaired, the blood draw violated his *Fourth Amendment* rights under the United States Constitution. He points to the U.S. Supreme Court's ruling in *Missouri v. McNeely, 133 S. Ct. 1552, 185 L. Ed. 2d 696 (2013)*, to argue that Arizona's unconscious clause violates the *Fourth Amendment*.

Even if the unconscious clause is unconstitutional, however, we may still affirm the trial court's decision declining to suppress the blood evidence if we find the good-faith exception to the exclusionary rule applies. We therefore turn to application of the good-faith exception, which requires determining whether suppression of evidence in this case serves the rule's sole purpose--deterring deliberate, reckless, or grossly negligent law enforcement violations of the *Fourth Amendment. See Davis v. United States, 131 S. Ct. 2419, 2426-28, 180 L. Ed. 2d 285 (2011).*

In deciding whether to seek and execute a search warrant, officers M.P. and S.R. were the relevant law enforcement personnel for their respective public safety agencies in Arizona and Nevada. Both officers testified they made no effort to obtain a search warrant and that it was standard police practice at the time to automatically draw the blood of an unconscious DUI suspect. S.R. explicitly commented that the practice was based on Nevada's implied consent statute.

In *Davis*, the Supreme Court addressed whether the exclusionary rule applies "when the police conduct a search in compliance with binding precedent that is later overruled." *Davis, 131 S. Ct. at 2423.* The Court emphasized that suppression of evidence is a judicially created prudential doctrine, not a constitutionally granted right. *Id. at 2426.* As such, every police violation of the *Fourth Amendment's* prohibition against unreasonable searches and seizures does not mandate automatic application of the exclusionary rule. *See United States v. Leon, 468 U.S. 897, 906-07, 104 S. Ct. 3405, 82 L. Ed. 2d 677 (1984).*

Rather, possible *Fourth Amendment* violations by police must be assessed case by case, and the exclusionary rule is only appropriate in those cases when police culpability outweighs the "substantial social costs" generated by the rule. *Davis, 131 S. Ct. at 2427* (quoting *Leon, 468 U.S. at 907*).

The primary social cost of the exclusionary rule is the suppression of what is often reliable evidence, and "an officer who conducts a search in reliance on binding appellate precedent does no more than 'act as a reasonable officer would and should act' under the circumstances." *Id. at 2427, 2429* (quoting *Leon, 468 U.S. at 920*). In other words, suppression of evidence acquired by an officer relying on then-existing binding common law precedent would have no deterrent effect. Accordingly, the Supreme Court has applied the good-faith exception to situations in which law enforcement relied on an objectively constitutional and valid statute. *See Illinois v. Krull, 480 U.S. 340, 349, 107 S. Ct. 1160, 94 L. Ed. 2d 364 (1987)* (explaining that the "application of the exclusionary rule to suppress evidence obtained by an officer acting in objectively reasonable reliance on a statute would have [] little deterrent effect").

To determine whether the good-faith exception to the exclusionary rule applies, we follow the two-part test recently articulated by this court in *State v. Mitchell, 234 Ariz. 410, 419, ¶ 31, 323 P.3d 69 (App. 2014)*. First, we ask whether binding Arizona or Supreme Court authority explicitly authorized the particular police conduct in question at the time. Second, we determine whether "application of the exclusionary rule would provide meaningful deterrence" of future police conduct. *Id.*

Initially, the trial court considered the legal issue of which jurisdiction's law applies. Regardless of whether we assess Arizona or Nevada law, statutes in both states "explicitly authorized the particular police conduct" at issue here. *See id.* Arizona's unconscious clause states, "A person who is dead, unconscious or otherwise in a condition rendering the person incapable of refusal is deemed not to have withdrawn the consent provided by subsection A of this section and the test or tests may be administered." *A.R.S. § 28-1321(C)*. Nevada's unconscious provision is an outright statutory command: "If the person to be tested pursuant to subsection 1 is dead or unconscious, the officer *shall* direct that samples of blood from the person be tested." N.R.S. § 484C.160(3) (emphasis added). Both of these statutes were in effect at the time of Havatone's blood draw. Although the search at issue here involved officers from both jurisdictions, the search was objectively reasonable in either state, so we--like the trial court--need not decide whether Arizona or Nevada law applies.

Havatone cites several Arizona cases that he contends disallowed the police conduct in the present case. None of these cases can be read as declaring the unconscious clause to be unconstitutional for purposes of the good-faith exception. The strongest is *Carrillo v. Houser, 224 Ariz. 463, 232 P.3d 1245 (2010).* In that case, our supreme court held *A.R.S. § 28-1321* requires an arrestee to "unequivocally manifest assent to the testing by words or conduct" before a warrantless blood draw is conducted. *Id. at 467, ¶ 19.* Havatone argues that *Carrillo,* which was decided in 2010, as well as other Arizona precedent stretching as far back as 1998, condemned the police action here. *See State v. Flannigan, 194 Ariz. 150, 153, ¶ 17, 978 P.2d 127 (App. 1998)* ("Absent express consent to the blood draw, the police would have been entitled to conduct the warrantless seizure of [defendant's] blood only if (1) they had probable cause . . . and (2) exigent circumstances justified dispensing with the warrant requirement.").

Nevada case law explicitly rejected a *Fourth Amendment* attack on the warrantless drawing of an unconscious suspect's blood. *See Galvan v. State, 98 Nev. 550, 655 P.2d 155, 157 (Nev. 1982)* ("The officer, faced with the inevitable and rapid destruction of the evidence *and [the defendant's] unconsciousness,* could reasonably have believed that he was confronted with an emergency, so that he could not delay by obtaining a warrant *or waiting until [the defendant] regained consciousness.*") (emphasis added). We need not decide whether *McNeely* casts doubt on that holding since *McNeely* was decided after the events in this case.

Neither *Carrillo* nor *Flannigan,* however, explicitly invalidated (or even addressed) the unconscious clause of the implied consent statute. In fact, the *Carrillo* court emphasized, "We also do not consider here circumstances in which subsection (C) of the implied consent law . . . may allow warrantless testing of persons incapable of refusing a test." *224 Ariz. at 467, ¶ 21*. And the *Flannigan* opinion, though it discussed exigent circumstances and exceptions to the warrant requirement, noted "that this case does not involve an application of the Arizona implied consent statute in effect at the time of the arrest. . .. [The defendant] was arrested for violating provisions of Title 13 of the Arizona Revised Statutes, not Title 28." *194 Ariz. at 152-53, ¶ 13*.

Similarly, at the time of the accident, no directly applicable United States Supreme Court authority held the unconscious clause unconstitutional. All relevant events occurred in September of 2012, prior to the Supreme Court's 2013 decision in *McNeely*. The reasoning of the United States Supreme Court in *Krull* applies here. As the Court stated,

> Unless a statute is clearly unconstitutional, an officer cannot be expected to question the judgment of the legislature that passed the law. If the statute is subsequently declared unconstitutional, excluding evidence obtained pursuant to its prior to such a judicial declaration will not deter future *Fourth Amendment* violations by an officer who has simply fulfilled his responsibility to enforce the statute as written.

Krull, 480 U.S at 350. While that good-faith exception does not apply if we conclude a law enforcement officer relied upon a statute and "its provisions are such that a reasonable officer should have known that the statute was unconstitutional," *id. at 355*, this caveat does not apply here when no court has expressly found the unconscious clause unconstitutional and the cases at the time of the underlying event cannot be said to have led a reasonable officer to know that the clause was unconstitutional. We do not expect police officers to be legal scholars so long as the overarching police practices on which they relied are not examples of "recurring or systemic negligence" on the part of law enforcement. *Davis, 131 S. Ct. at 2428* (quoting *Herring v. United States, 555 U.S. 135, 144, 129 S. Ct. 695, 172 L. Ed. 2d 496 (2009)*).

We agree with the trial court that given the presumptively constitutional unconscious clauses, the Arizona and Nevada officers in this case objectively relied in good-faith on statutory mandates allowing the blood draw of unconscious DUI suspects absent express consent.

Under the circumstances, including the then-existing statutes and case authorities, they did not act culpably or in any way that society should seek to deter. Instead, the officers acted with a reasonable, good-faith reliance on statutes and cases in effect at the time. We find no abuse of discretion in the trial court's assessment, and therefore affirm its application of the good-faith exception to the warrant requirement. The exclusionary rule is a "bitter pill" that must be used as a "last resort" only when it outweighs its "substantial social costs." *Davis, 131 S. Ct. at 2427* (citations omitted). The rule serves no purpose when, as here, police actions were consistent with an existing statute which had not been declared unconstitutional at the time of the blood draw.

Because we affirm the trial court's finding that the good-faith exception to the exclusionary rule applies, we need not reach the issue of whether the unconscious clause, *A.R.S. § 28-1321(C)*, is constitutional. Accordingly, we decline to do so. *See Fragoso v. Fell, 210 Ariz. 427, 430, ¶ 6, 111 P.3d 1027 (App. 2005)* (explaining that courts should avoid constitutional issues "when other principles of law are [*17] controlling and the case can be decided without ruling on the constitutional questions" (quoting *In re United States Currency of $315,900.00, 183 Ariz. 208, 211, 902 P.2d 351 (App. 1995)*)).

B. No Waiver of Good-Faith Exception

Havatone also argues the State waived its argument for application of the good-faith exception to the exclusionary rule when it failed to address the issue in its answering brief. Havatone quotes *Arizona Rule of Criminal Procedure 31.13(c)(1)*, which he argues mandates that appellate briefs contain the parties' "contentions . . . with respect to the issues presented, and the reasons therefor, with citations to the authorities, statutes and parts of the record relied on." The State maintains the overarching "implied-consent argument presented by the State on appeal is sufficient to dispose of the ultimate issue at hand-- whether the search was valid and admissible." According to the State, because it argued that this court should uphold the trial court's ruling, which included a ruling on the good-faith exception to the warrant requirement, the application of the good-faith exception is encompassed within its arguments.

Waiver is most often invoked on appeal when an appellant raises an issue for the first time in the reply brief. *See, e.g., State v. Carver, 160 Ariz. 167, 175, 771 P.2d 1382 (1989); State v. Rodriguez, 160 Ariz. 381, 384, 773 P.2d 486 (App. 1989).* In that context, the doctrine of waiver helps avoid the possibility of substantial prejudice to the appellee, who, not on notice of a possible issue on appeal, does not address the issue in the answering brief. More generally, application of the waiver doctrine also prevents the court from "surprising the parties" by deciding issues not raised in the briefing. *See Meiners v. Indus. Comm'n, 213 Ariz. 536, 538-39 n.2, ¶ 8, 145 P.3d 633 (App. 2006)* (explaining that waiver is intended "to prevent the court from deciding cases with no research assistance or analytical input from the parties" (internal quotations omitted)). Furthermore, waiver is a procedural, rather than a jurisdictional, concept. *Id.* As such, we do not apply waiver rigidly or mechanically. *State v. Boteo-Flores, 230 Ariz. 551, 553, ¶ 7, 288 P.3d 111 (App. 2012).* In our discretion, we may choose to address issues one or more of the parties failed to properly address in the briefs. *See State v. Lopez, 217 Ariz. 433, 438 n.4, ¶ 17, 175 P.3d 682 (App. 2008)* ("Generally, issues raised for the first time in a reply brief are waived. . . [i]n our discretion, however, we address [defendant's] arguments.").

Exercising our discretion here, we conclude that applying the waiver doctrine is not appropriate in this case. First, the good-faith exception was expressly argued and ruled on by the trial court. As we note above, we have an obligation to avoid deciding constitutional issues "when other principles of law are controlling and the case can be decided without ruling on the constitutional questions." *Fragoso, 210 Ariz. at 430, ¶ 6* (citations omitted). Addressing the good-faith exception in this context is consistent with that obligation. Second, the policy of waiver in the opening brief does not apply in equal force when an issue is omitted or not clearly raised in an *answering*brief. This is especially true here. The trial court's application of the good-faith exception to the exclusionary rule was an independent basis for its decision to decline to suppress the evidence. For that reason, Havatone properly addressed the issue in his opening brief. He was not prejudiced by any lack of notice. Under these circumstances, we decline to decide this case based on the procedural mechanism of waiver, and we exercise our discretion to rule on the merits of whether the trial court abused its discretion in declining to apply the exclusionary rule.

The doctrine of confession of error may also be applicable here. When an appellee fails to address a relevant issue in its answering brief or fails altogether to file an answering brief, the court may hold that the appellee's failure to support its position constitutes a confession of reversible error. *Bulova Watch Co. v. Super City Dept. Stores of Ariz., Inc., 4 Ariz. App. 553, 556, 422 P.2d 184 (App. 1967)*. Like waiver, however, application of confession of error is within the reviewing court's discretion. *State v. Greenlee Cnty. J.P. Ct., 157 Ariz. 270, 271, 756 P.2d 939 (App. 1988); State v. Stewart, 3 Ariz. App. 178, 180, 412 P.2d 860 (App. 1966)*. We decline to hold the State confessed error here. Because the application of the good faith exception is factual in nature and the record is sufficient to support a conclusion on that issue, a decision on the merits is appropriate. *See State ex rel. McDougall v. Maricopa Cnty. Super. Ct., 174 Ariz. 450, 452, 850 P.2d 688 (App. 1993)*.

For these reasons, the good-faith exception to the warrant requirement is applicable and the trial court did not err in denying Havatone's motion to suppress the blood test results.

PROSECUTORIAL MISCONDUCT

STATE OF ARIZONA, APPELLEE, V. MICHAEL JENSEN, APPELLANT.
NO. 1 CA-CR 14-0690

(Text added/modified for emphasis) The appellate courts refuse to take judicial notice of their own records which records show that the same law enforcement officers and prosecutors consistently engage in profiling. The state has the tendency to release/destroy evidence. Courts consistently sanction this systematic practice refusing to find bad faith thereby condoning this misconduct which is on the rise . As it was never their intent to subject the state's case to a meaningful adversarial process, when viewed in the totality, and not in isolation, this should constitute fraud upon the court by these lawyers.

COUNSEL: Arizona Attorney General's Office, Phoenix, By Myles A. Braccio, Counsel for Appellee. Coconino County Public Defender's Office, Flagstaff, By Brad Bransky, Counsel for Appellant.

I. Jensen's Motion to Preclude the Breath Test Evidence

Jensen argues the trial court abused its discretion in denying his pretrial motion to preclude evidence that he registered a blood alcohol concentration ("BAC") of .260 and .263 on duplicate breath tests within two hours of driving. He argues on appeal, as he did before trial, that the State offered insufficient evidence that the gas standard used to calibrate the Intoxilyzer 8000 used in his case contained the purported .1 standard alcohol concentration solution, foundation necessary to show the machine "was in proper operating condition" under *A.R.S. § 28-1323(A)(5)*. The court denied the motion following an evidentiary hearing.

In reviewing a trial court's denial of a motion to suppress evidence, this court restricts its review to consideration of the facts the trial court heard at the suppression hearing, *State v. Blackmore, 186 Ariz. 630, 631, 925 P.2d 1347, 1348 (1996)*, viewed in the light most favorable to sustaining its ruling. *State v. Hyde, 186 Ariz. 252, 265, 921 P.2d 655, 668 (1996)*. This court reviews for an abuse of discretion a trial court's decision that sufficient foundation has been laid to admit evidence. *State v. George, 206 Ariz. 436, 446, ¶ 28, 79 P.3d 1050, 1060 (App. 2003)*.

The trial court did not abuse its discretion. Under *A.R.S. § 28-1323(A)(5)*, results of breath tests are admissible on a showing in pertinent part that the device "was in proper operating condition," which can be demonstrated by periodic maintenance records, such as "[c]alibration checks with a standard alcohol concentration solution bracketing each person's duplicate breath test." As Jensen recognizes, the State sought to satisfy *§ 28-1323(A)(5)* by providing calibration checks done before, during, and after the subject tests to show the particular Intoxilyzer 8000 used was in proper operating condition. Jensen argues on appeal, as he did in his pretrial motion, that the State was required to demonstrate the "standard alcohol concentration solution" referenced in *A.R.S. § 28-1323(A)(5)* was "NIST traceable" as required by *Arizona Administrative Code R13-10-104(A)(4)*, meaning that it was certified as a .1 standard alcohol concentration solution by the National Institute of Standards and Technology. Subsection (B) of § 28-1323, however, provides that compliance with subsection (A) "is the only requirement for the admission in evidence of a breath test result." *Section 28-1323(A)(5)* does not require the "standard alcohol concentration solution" be "NIST traceable," and accordingly, "NIST traceability" is not a foundational requirement for the admission of breath-test results. *See State ex rel. McDougall v. Superior Court, 181 Ariz. 202, 204-07, 888 P.2d 1389, 1391-94 (App. 1995)* (holding the State was not required to demonstrate under the predecessor statute full compliance with Department of Health Services regulations).

Moreover, the State offered sufficient evidence that the calibration checks conducted in this case utilized a solution that was not only a .1 "standard alcohol concentration solution," but was "NIST traceable." At the evidentiary hearing on Jensen's motion to suppress, the quality-assurance specialist for the Intoxilyzer 8000 used in Jensen's case testified he checked the attached cylinder containing the alcohol concentration solution, and the cylinder registered a standard gas concentration of .1. He further testified the label on all such cylinders stated they were "certified, traceable by NIST." Although he admitted on cross-examination that he could not specifically say the label on this particular cylinder bore the words "NIST traceable," he had confirmed with the person at the Department of Public Safety ("DPS") crime lab responsible for sending the cylinders that all cylinders DPS sends to police for use with an Intoxilyzer are NIST traceable. On this record, the trial court acted within its discretion in denying Jensen's motion to preclude the breath-test results on the ground the State could not show the Intoxilyzer 8000 was calibrated with a "standard alcohol concentration solution" under *A.R.S. § 28-1323(A)(5)*.

Jensen did not object to this testimony on hearsay or other grounds. In any event, hearsay is generally admissible in a suppression hearing. *See State v. Keener, 110 Ariz. 462, 465, 520 P.2d 510, 513 (1974); see also State v. Riley, 196 Ariz. 40, 43, ¶¶ 6-7, 992 P.2d 1135, 1138 (App. 1999)* (holding that confrontation rights do not apply to the same extent at a pretrial suppression hearing as they do at trial); *Ariz. R.*

Evid. 104(a) (stating a court is not bound by rules of evidence in preliminarily determining the admissibility of evidence).

II. Jensen's Profiling Objection

Jensen next argues the trial court abused its discretion in overruling his "profiling" objection to the investigating officer's testimony that Jensen's minimization of how drunk he was at the scene was a "common practice" among DUI suspects. The officer testified Jensen stated at the scene that, on a scale of "0" (completely sober) to "10" (passed out), he considered himself a "1." However, after the officer arrested Jensen, advised him of his rights pursuant to *Miranda*, and informed him that he had performed poorly on the field sobriety tests and registered a high BAC, Jensen told the officer he believed he ranked a "6" on the same scale. The prosecutor asked the officer if it was a "common practice" for someone to minimize his drinking at the scene of a DUI stop, and the officer answered affirmatively. Defense counsel objected on the ground of "profiling." The trial court overruled the objection. We review the court's ruling for an abuse of discretion. *State v. Ketchner, 236 Ariz. 262, 264, ¶ 13, 339 P.3d 645, 647 (2014).*

This was not an impermissible use of "profile evidence." Profile evidence is evidence that "tends to show that a defendant possesses one or more of an informal compilation of characteristics or an abstract of characteristics typically displayed by persons engaged in a particular kind of activity." *Id. at ¶ 15* (citations and internal quotations omitted). "Although there may be legitimate uses for profile evidence . . . profile evidence may not be used as substantive proof of guilt because of the risk that a defendant will be convicted not for what he did but for what others are doing." *Id. at 264-65, ¶ 15, 339 P.3d at 647-48* (citations and internal quotation omitted). The testimony was not offered to show that because Jensen possessed a characteristic common among DUI suspects, he was guilty of DUI; rather, it was offered to show he initially minimized his level of inebriation, a tactic not uncommon among drivers when first stopped for DUI.

Moreover, even assuming *arguendo* this evidence was improper, any error in admitting it was harmless. To demonstrate an objected-to error was harmless, the State must prove beyond a reasonable doubt the error in admitting the evidence "did not contribute to or affect the verdict or sentence." *State v. Henderson, 210 Ariz. 561, 567, ¶ 18, 115 P.3d 601, 607 (2005)*. The State has met its burden. On this record, in which Jensen ultimately ranked himself a "6" on a scale of "0" to "10" measuring drunkenness, and registered, at a minimum, a .260 BAC within two hours of driving, any error in eliciting testimony that he initially minimized his intoxication neither contributed to nor affected the verdicts of guilt.

III. Jensen's Request for a Willits Instruction

Jensen also argues the trial court abused its discretion in denying his request for a *Willits* instruction, based on the failure of the investigating officer to videotape him performing all of his field sobriety tests. The court denied the request, reasoning that the officer's first priority was safety, not videotaping the field sobriety tests, and noting the officer had recorded in his report and testified how Jensen performed on the tests. The court also concluded that, even if the officer had captured all of the field sobriety tests on the video (which he was not required to do), the evidence was insufficient to show it would have been exculpatory. The *Willits* instruction allows the jury to draw an inference from the State's destruction of material evidence that the lost or destroyed evidence would be unfavorable to the State. *See State v. Fulminante, 193 Ariz. 485, 503, ¶ 62, 975 P.2d 75, 93 (1999)*. Nevertheless, even "[d]estruction or no retention of evidence does not automatically entitle a defendant to a *Willits* instruction." *State v. Murray, 184 Ariz. 9, 33, 906 P.2d 542, 566 (1995)*. "To be entitled to a *Willits* instruction, a defendant must prove that (1) the [S]tate failed to preserve material and reasonably accessible evidence that could have had a tendency to exonerate the accused, and (2) there was resulting prejudice." *State v. Glissendorf, 235 Ariz. 147, 150, ¶ 8, 329 P.3d 1049, 1052 (2014)* (citations omitted).

A defendant is not entitled to a *Willits* instruction in a case like this -- where a law enforcement officer has merely failed "to seek out and gain possession of potentially exculpatory evidence." *State v. Perez, 141 Ariz. 459, 463, 687 P.2d 1214, 1218 (1984); see also Murray, 184 Ariz. at*

33, 906 P.2d at 566 (recognizing a defendant is not entitled to a *Willits* instruction "merely because a more exhaustive investigation could have been made"); *State v. Willcoxson, 156 Ariz. 343, 346, 751 P.2d 1385, 1388 (App. 1987)* (concluding "a failure to pursue every lead or gather every conceivable bit of physical evidence" does not require a *Willits* instruction). Moreover, the evidentiary value of additional video of Jensen's performance of field sobriety tests relies on speculation, an insufficient basis for a *Willits* instruction. *See Glissendorf, 235 Ariz. at 150, ¶ 9, 329 P.3d at 1052.* Jensen suggests only that a videotape *might* have shown the uneven surface of the shoulder of the road was responsible for his poor performance on the "balance [-]based field tests." Jensen performed the walk-and-turn test, however, on the paved road, and one of the patrol vehicle's video cameras captured his performance, albeit only from the waist up. Also, Jensen has failed to explain how uneven ground or a sand and gravel substrate would have impaired his ability to perform the one-leg stand. The trial court did not abuse its discretion in denying Jensen's request for a *Willits* instruction.

ROBERT GONZALEZ, PETITIONER, VS. CHARLES RYAN, ET AL., RESPONDENTS.
NO. CV-08-658-TUC-FRZ-DTF UNITED STATES DISTRICT COURT FOR THE DISTRICT OF ARIZONA

(Text added/modified for emphasis) The state has the tendency to release/destroy evidence, not investigate thoroughly, and again the same police/prosecutors are involved. Courts consistently sanction this systematic practice refusing to find bad faith thereby condoning this misconduct which is on the rise . Courts consistently sanction this systematic practice refusing to find bad faith thereby condoning this misconduct which is on the rise . As it was never their intent to subject the state's case to a meaningful adversarial process, when viewed in the totality, and not in isolation, this should constitute fraud upon the court by these lawyers.

COUNSEL: For Robert Michael Gonzalez, Petitioner: Stanton Bloom, Stanton Bloom PC, Tucson, AZ.

For Dora B Schriro, Director of ADOC, Respondent: Joseph Lanius Parkhurst, III, Office of the Attorney General, Tucson, AZ.

FACTUAL AND PROCEDURAL BACKGROUND

Gonzalez was convicted in two separate jury trials, for shooting at Mark Humo and Officer Lewis, in incidents that occurred two weeks apart. The following factual summary of the crimes is taken from the Arizona Court of Appeals' opinion, construing all facts in favor of the prosecution:

> On the evening of November 3, 2001, the victim, M [ark Humo] was outside of the apartment he shared with his girlfriend, A[lyssa Preciado], and A[lyssa's] three children, one of whom was fathered by Gonzalez. Carrying a firearm, Gonzalez approached M[ark] and asked about his daughter. The two men began to argue and A[lyssa] came outside to help defuse the situation. After a contentious exchange, Gonzalez shot M[ark] four times. Although M[ark] was seriously injured, the injuries were not fatal. Gonzalez then fled.
>
> About two weeks later on November 19, 2001, police attempted to serve Gonzalez with an arrest warrant in connection with the November 3 incident. For the arrest, they initiated a "dynamic takedown," meaning that they would have their weapons drawn. The officers waited in a strategic location, and when the supervising officer spotted Gonzalez, he announced "Tucson Police" and ordered Gonzalez to get on the ground. Gonzalez drew a handgun and fired four shots at one of the other officers, L[ewis], who was not seriously injured. The supervising officer then fired and hit Gonzalez, which subdued him and allowed the officers to arrest him.

(Doc. 18, Ex. D at 2-3.)

As to the first event, Gonzalez was convicted of attempted first degree murder, three counts of aggravated assault and two counts of endangerment. He was convicted of attempted first degree murder, aggravated assault and disorderly conduct as to the second shooting.

(*Id.* at 3.) The longest sentences imposed were two, consecutive eighteen-year terms for the attempted murders. (*Id.* at 2.)

Gonzalez filed a direct appeal challenging his convictions and sentences arising from both trials. (Doc. 18, Ex. B.) The Arizona Court of Appeals affirmed his convictions and sentences. (*Id.*, Ex. D.) Gonzalez sought review at the Arizona Supreme Court, which was summarily denied on October 26, 2004. (*Id.*, Exs. E, F.) Petitioner filed a pro se petition for post-conviction relief (PCR), which he supplemented twice. (*Id.*, Exs. G, H, I.) The PCR court denied relief. (*Id.*, Ex. J.) Petitioner appealed the decision, and the appellate court adopted the decision of the PCR court and affirmed. (*Id.*, Ex. K.) The Arizona Supreme Court denied review on December 17, 2007. (*Id.*, Ex. L.)

DISCUSSION

....

Fair Presentation

....

Claim 15 alleges nine instances of prosecutorial misconduct during the closing argument of Trial II: (a) emphasizing that premeditation can be any length of time; (b) stating that purchasing a gun is a substantial step toward committing first degree murder; (c) vouching for Officers Lewis and Blue; (d) arguing that Gonzalez had been dishonest and had a motive to lie; (e) referencing Gonzalez's prior conviction, which was not yet final; (f) asking the jury not to let Gonzalez "get away with it"; (g) arguing that Gonzalez resisted arrest because he knew he would be imprisoned for a very long time if arrested for his prior crime; (h) arguing that defense counsel did not know what Gonzalez was going to say on the stand and "concocted a story at the last second"; and (i) arguing that Officer Blue needed to move the police car after the shooting due to criminal activity in the area connected to Gonzalez. Respondents argue that only sub claims (e), (h) and (i) were presented on direct appeal. Gonzalez did not argue to the contrary (Doc. 21 at 62), and his appellate brief reveals that sub claims (a) to (d), (f) and (g) were not fairly presented on appeal (Doc. 18, Ex. B at 35-43). Gonzalez's assertion of prosecutorial misconduct on other grounds were not sufficient to exhaust all of the sub claims. *See Kelly v. Small, 315 F.3d*

1063, 1069 (9th Cir. 2002) (satisfying the requirement that "a federal habeas petitioner [must] provide the state courts with a 'fair opportunity' to apply controlling legal precedent to the facts bearing upon his constitutional claim," requires presenting the state courts with the operative facts) (quoting *Harless, 459 U.S. at 6*), *overruled on other grounds by Robbins v. Carey, 481 F.3d 1143 (9th Cir. 2007).*

....

Respondents contend that, although Gonzalez raised the factual basis of Claims 2, 3 and 9 in state court, he did not allege that these claims were based on federal law. With respect to Claim 2, on direct appeal, Gonzalez argued only that denial of a *Willits* instruction deprived him of a fair trial. (Doc. 18, Ex. B at 14-16.) Gonzalez contends the claim was fairly presented because "the factual scenario suggesting bad faith, loss of exculpatory evidence and favorable inferences from the loss of the evidence, all make it clear that Petitioner was alleging violations of his *Sixth* and *Fourteenth Amendment* rights, depriving him of a fair trial." (Doc. 21 at 25.) However, "[i]f a habeas petitioner wishes to claim that an evidentiary ruling at a state court trial denied him the due process of law guaranteed by the *Fourteenth Amendment*, he must say so, not only in federal court, but in state court." *Duncan v. Henry, 513 U.S. 364, 366, 115 S. Ct. 887, 130 L. Ed. 2d 865 (1995).* A general assertion accompanied by factual inferences that a defendant was deprived of a fair trial does not fairly present a federal constitutional claim. *See Casey v. Moore, 386 F.3d at 913; Johnson v. Zenon, 88 F.3d 828, 830 (9th Cir. 1996).*

....

In Claim 14, Gonzalez alleges the police destroyed exculpatory evidence in violation of his right to due process and a fair trial. Respondents concede that Gonzalez fairly presented this claim in a supplemental PCR petition. (Doc. 18, Ex. H.) Respondents argue, however, that the PCR court found this claim waived for failure to raise it on appeal and that it is procedurally defaulted. To the contrary, the PCR court did not mention this claim specifically and did not find any claims waived for failure to raise them on appeal. (*See id.*, Ex. J.) Because Gonzalez fairly presented Claim 14 and it was not barred by the state court, the Court will address it on the merits.

············

MERITS

The Court reviews the exhausted claims on the merits, Claims 1, 4, 5, 6 (as to Duran), 10, 12, 14, 15(e), (h) and (i), 16(A) (4), (7)(a) and (8), 17(A), and 17(B)(1).

Claim 14 (Trial II)

Gonzalez alleges he was denied due process and a fair trial by police destruction of exculpatory evidence. Specifically, Officer Blue moved his car prior to the investigation of the shooting. As discussed in the procedural default section above, Gonzalez fairly presented this claim in a supplemental PCR brief. The PCR court did not address it. Therefore, the Court reviews the claim *de novo*. *See Pirtle v. Morgan, 313 F.3d 1160, 1167 (9th Cir. 2002)*.

In *Arizona v. Youngblood, 488 U.S. 51, 58, 109 S. Ct. 333, 102 L. Ed. 2d 281 (1988)*, the Court held that absent a showing of bad faith on the part of the police, "failure to preserve potentially useful evidence does not constitute a denial of due process of law." The duty to preserve evidence is limited to "evidence that might be expected to play a significant role in the suspect's defense," which requires that the "evidence must both possess an exculpatory value that was apparent before the evidence was destroyed, and be of such a nature that the defendant would be unable to obtain comparable evidence by other reasonably available means." *California v. Trombetta, 467 U.S. 479, 488-89, 104 S. Ct. 2528, 81 L. Ed. 2d 413 (1984)*. The bad faith requirement of *Youngblood* hinges on whether the government had knowledge of the exculpatory value of the evidence before its destruction. *See United States v. Cooper, 983 F.2d 928, 931 (9th Cir. 1993)*.

Gonzalez argues that Officer Blue was very experienced and, therefore, knew his car would be part of the investigation and moving it would amount to destruction of evidence. Petitioner explained that "[t]he location of Officer Blue at the time of the shooting became extremely important when it was the Defendant's and other witnesses' testimony that he was shooting from behind the open door of his vehicle, located in the middle of the road." There was conflicting testimony about whether Officer Blue remained behind his door or immediately stepped into full view as he exited his car. Petitioner fails to explain how the exact location of Officer Blue's car would have helped establish whether he was behind his door when he began shooting.

Although Petitioner does not discuss the significance of Officer Blue's location, presumably the issue was whether Gonzalez had a good view of Officer Blue prior to the shooting, such that he should have known he was a police officer. That point turns out not to be critical, as conceded by defense counsel in closing arguments. She emphasized that even if Officer Blue was not behind his door, that Officer Blue himself stated that he fired his weapon from behind a tall truck, which would have obscured him being fully seen. (RT 10/11/02 at 80.) As counsel stated, the more critical factor was whether Officer Blue identified himself (*id.* at 69) and Gonzalez knew he was a police officer. Similarly, Officer Blue testified that he announces himself because a person might not otherwise know he was a police officer. (RT 10/9/02 at 99.) The jury concluded beyond a reasonable doubt that Gonzalez knew or should have known that the victim, Officer Lewis, was a peace officer on official duty. (*Id.* at 122-23.) Thus, Officer Blue's location did not play a "significant role in the suspect's defense." Further, the exact location of his car is a distinct, irrelevant, matter from Officer Blue's location in relation to the car when he exited his vehicle and when he shot his weapon. Finally, Petitioner has not demonstrated bad faith because, regardless of Officer Blue's experience, he could not have known when he moved his car that there would later be a conflict in the testimony at trial, which could have been resolved if he had not moved his car. Thus, the exact location of his car did not have apparent exculpatory value.

Petitioner has failed to establish that he was denied due process by Officer Blue moving his vehicle prior to investigation of the crime scene.

....

Sub claim i

Gonzalez argues that the prosecutor improperly suggested that Officer Blue needed to move his police car after the shooting because the police had to take some action in relation to the house Gonzalez was heading towards at the time of the shooting. The trial court had precluded admission of evidence regarding why the police raided the house, and Gonzalez argues the prosecutor improperly suggested Petitioner was tied to criminal activity at that house.

In her rebuttal argument, the prosecutor discussed the location of Officer Blue's car (RT 10/11/02 at 102-03), a dispute that defense counsel addressed in her closing argument (*id.* at 79). The prosecutor stated: "You heard the testimony. They wanted to give him a, before he went in there, they wanted -- why they needed to do that is immaterial. They needed to take him down before he went into that house." (*Id.* at 103.) The court of appeals found that this statement was fair rebuttal to the closing argument of Gonzalez's counsel. (Doc. 18, Ex. D at 16.)

The Supreme Court has directed that "a court should not lightly infer that a prosecutor intends an ambiguous remark to have its most damaging meaning or that a jury, sitting through lengthy exhortation, will draw that meaning from the plethora of less damaging interpretations." *DeChristoforo, 416 U.S. at 647.* When looking at the challenged statement, standing alone or in context, it has very little meaning. It does not unambiguously imply that Gonzalez was involved in criminal activity being conducted in that house. The jury could easily have inferred that taking a person down in the open rather than inside a home was standard police procedure. In fact, there was testimony, to which there was no objection, that the officers were instructed to take Gonzalez down outside. (RT 10/9/02 at 54, 121-22, 186, 198.) The prosecutor made the statement in the context of discussing where Officer Blue, his car, and the other officers were located at the time of the shooting, during which she acknowledged that Officer Blue's car was moved prior to the scene being photographed. (RT 10/11/02 at 102-03.) Officer Blue testified without objection that he moved his car because the house at 138 Calle Evelina was going to be cleared after the shooting. (RT 10/9/02 at 77). Those limited references did not prejudice Gonzalez by implying he was involved in criminal activity at the house. In sum, nothing in the brief argument was improper or rendered Gonzalez's trial fundamentally unfair.

Conclusion

A prosecutor "may prosecute with earnestness and vigor - indeed, he should do so. But, while he may strike hard blows, he is not at liberty to strike foul ones." *Berger v. United States, 295 U.S. 78, 88, 55 S. Ct.*

629, 79 L. Ed. 1314 (1935). Here, the prosecutor struck hard blows to Gonzalez's defense, but none were foul blows. Therefore, the Arizona Court of Appeals' denial of these sub claims was not an unreasonable application of Supreme Court law.

STATE OF ARIZONA, APPELLEE, V. ROBERT JEFFREY MORRISON, APPELLANT.
NO. 1 CA-CR 14-0674

COUNSEL: Arizona Attorney General's Office, Phoenix, By David A. Simpson, Counsel for Appellee. The Law Office of Stephen L. Crawford, Phoenix, By Stephen L. Crawford, Counsel for Appellant.

....

(Text added/modified for emphasis) The state has the tendency to release/destroy evidence, not investigate thoroughly, and again the same police/prosecutors are involved. Courts consistently sanction this systematic practice refusing to find bad faith thereby condoning this misconduct which is on the rise . Courts consistently sanction this systematic practice refusing to find bad faith thereby condoning this misconduct which is on the rise . As it was never their intent to subject the state's case to a meaningful adversarial process, when viewed in the totality, and not in isolation, this should constitute fraud upon the court by these lawyers.

On November 25, 2012, Morrison entered a cosmetics and fragrance store (Ulta) in Paradise Valley. The store manager, J.F., became suspicious that Morrison might try to shoplift, so she asked an employee to speak to Morrison in the fragrance department and another employee to watch the store's live security footage. J.F. was then informed that Morrison had placed two bottles of fragrances in his bag. J.F. waited at the store's exit and asked Morrison to return the fragrances as he approached her. Morrison returned the fragrances and pushed his way past J.F. to exit the store.

Officer Montoya was called to the store and detained Morrison as he walked out of the store. After speaking with J.F. and conducting a further investigation, Officer Montoya arrested Morrison.

Morrison called his brother, Rick, from jail. At the beginning of the call, Morrison was informed that the call would be recorded and monitored, and if "the call is in place to legal counsel," to hang up and notify the sheriff's office. While relaying incriminating information, Morrison asked Rick to contact an attorney on his behalf.

At trial, Morrison moved to exclude the entire recording of the conversation from evidence because he disclosed information while attempting to persuade Rick to call an attorney. He further argued that the recording should be excluded pursuant to *Arizona Rules of Evidence 401, 402, 403, and 404(b)*. The following redacted recording was played before the jury:

> Rick: The problem is that you went and shoplifted.
> Morrison: That's true. I know.
> Rick: What is your problem? What is the deal with you?
> Morrison: I didn't have any money, Ricky. I didn't have any money.

* * *

> Morrison: I know. I shoplifted.
> Rick: Where did you commit it?
> Morrison: Where?
> Rick: Yeah.
> Morrison: At the Ulta store across from Paradise Valley Mall next to Sports Authority.

The State initially declined prosecution of the case and the video surveillance recording was destroyed. When charges were later filed, the recording was no longer available and Ulta did not retain a copy of the recording. Because the State destroyed the surveillance recording, the trial court provided a *Willits* instruction *See State v. Willits, 96 Ariz. 184, 393 P.2d 274 (1964)* to the jury.

Morrison was convicted of two counts of felony shoplifting with artifice and was sentenced to ten years' imprisonment for each count, to run concurrently. The trial court further sentenced Morrison to .33 years' imprisonment for a probation violation. Morrison appealed, and we have jurisdiction pursuant to *Article 6, Section 9, of the Arizona Constitution* and *Arizona Revised Statutes (A.R.S.) sections 12-120.21.A.1* and *13-4031* and *-4033.A.1* (West 2015).

....

II. *Willits* Instruction was Sufficient

Morrison next argues that his right to a fair trial was violated because the State destroyed Ulta's surveillance recording. He contends, "[w]hile the *Willits* instruction is normally sufficient unless the state has acted in bad faith, when a piece of evidence is fundamental to a defendant's case, it is not clear that the *Willits* instruction is enough."

"[W]here evidence which might have tended to exonerate the defendant is destroyed while in the state's possession, a defendant is entitled to a *Willits* instruction." *State v. Perez, 141 Ariz. 459, 464, 687 P.2d 1214 (1984)*. The trial court provided the following instruction:

> If you find the State has lost, destroyed, or failed to preserve evidence whose contents or quality are important to the issues in this case, then you should weigh the explanation, if any given, for the loss or unavailability of the evidence. If you find that any such explanation [*7] is inadequate, then you may draw an inference unfavorable to the State, which in itself may create a reasonable doubt as to defendant's guilt.

Quoting Chief Justice Feldman's opinion in *State v. Youngblood, 173 Ariz. 502, 511, 844 P.2d 1152 (1993)*, concurring and dissenting in part, Morrison contends that a *Willits* instruction was insufficient if the defendant did not receive "what the *due process clause* of the constitution requires: a fair trial under fundamentally fair procedures." In *Youngblood*, the Arizona Supreme Court held: "With respect to evidence which *might* be exculpatory, and where there is no bad faith conduct, the *Willits* rule more than adequately complies with the fundamental fairness component of Arizona due process." *173 Ariz. at 506-07.*

Morrison contends that the recording is "critically important to the defense" without further explaining its significance nor claiming that it is exculpatory evidence. Moreover, Morrison does not argue, and we find no evidence in the record suggesting, that the State destroyed the video in bad faith. Thus, we find the trial court's *Willits* instruction comported with the requirements of due process.

STATE OF ARIZONA, APPELLEE, V. FRANCISCO CONTRERAS, APPELLANT
NO. 1 CA-CR 14-0529

(Text added/modified for emphasis) The state has the tendency to release/destroy evidence, not investigate thoroughly, and again the same police/prosecutors are involved. Courts consistently sanction this systematic practice refusing to find bad faith thereby condoning this misconduct which is on the rise . As it was never their intent to subject the state's case to a meaningful adversarial process, when viewed in the totality, and not in isolation, this should constitute fraud upon the court by these lawyers.

COUNSEL: Arizona Attorney General's Office, Tucson, By Tanja K. Kelly, Counsel for Appellee.
Carr Law Office, PLLC, Parker, By Sandra Carr, Counsel for Appellant.

FACTS AND PROCEDURAL HISTORY
In January 2012, Contreras climbed onto a truck's running board at a truck stop in Ehrenberg, told the driver he was going to kill him, and, using a knife, slashed the driver's forearm and stabbed him in the abdomen. Contreras was charged with one count of attempted first-degree murder and two counts of aggravated assault.
At trial, Contreras testified "they" had been after him for years, and the driver had threatened to kill Contreras's son. The driver testified, however, he had never met Contreras and had not threatened him or his son in any way. Contreras admitted to one of the responding officers that he used methamphetamine on the weekends and had used it "recent[ly]." Contreras also admitted on a jail intake form the day of the

stabbing that he had used methamphetamine, cocaine, and marijuana two days prior.

Contreras was initially found incompetent to stand trial and was committed to Yavapai County's Restoration to Competency Program (the Program) in May 2012. In December 2013, the Program reported Contreras was mentally competent to proceed to trial notwithstanding diagnoses of delusional disorder and methamphetamine abuse in sustained remission. In April 2013, after additional Rule 11 evaluations were completed, the trial court found Contreras was competent to stand trial.

At trial, defense counsel raised a guilty except insane defense. The experts agreed Contreras suffered from a delusional disorder; however, the State's witnesses opined Contreras knew his actions were wrongful at the time he engaged in them.

Defense counsel sought a directed verdict on the attempted murder charge, but the trial court found sufficient evidence had been presented by the State for all counts to go to the jury. The jury convicted Contreras as charged, and the court sentenced him to slightly mitigated concurrent prison terms of ten years for attempted murder and seven years for each count of aggravated assault.

DISCUSSION

IV. The Trial Court Did Not Err in Failing to Give a *Willits* Instruction.

Contreras argues the trial court erred in failing to, *sua sponte*, instruct the jury that it could infer from the State's failure to obtain a blood or urine sample following Contreras's arrest that the results would be unfavorable to the State, pursuant to *State v. Willits, 96 Ariz. 184, 393 P.2d 274 (1964)*. Contreras argues the absence of this instruction allowed the State to undermine his insanity defense by asserting without physical evidence that he had recently taken methamphetamine. Because Contreras did not ask for a *Willits* instruction, we review the court's decision for fundamental error. *State v. Henderson, 210 Ariz. 561, 567, ¶ 19, 115 P.3d 601 (2005)*.

A *Willits* instruction may be given when police "negligently fail to preserve potentially exculpatory evidence . . . permit[ting] the jury to infer that the evidence would have been exculpatory." *State v.*

Fulminante, 193 Ariz. 485, 503, ¶ 62, 975 P.2d 75 (1999). A defendant is entitled to a *Willits* instruction upon proving: "(1) the state failed to preserve material and reasonably accessible evidence that could have had a tendency to exonerate the accused, and (2) there was resulting prejudice." *State v. Glissendorf, 235 Ariz. 147, 150, ¶ 8, 329 P.3d 1049 (2014)* (citing *State v. Speer, 221 Ariz. 449, 457, ¶ 40, 212 P.3d 787 (2009)*, and *State v. Smith, 158 Ariz. 222, 227, 762 P.2d 509 (1988)*).

This is not a case where law enforcement officers lost or destroyed evidence; rather, it is a case where law enforcement officers were unsuccessful in collecting evidence which the defendant now desires. Contreras is not entitled to a *Willits* instruction "merely because a more exhaustive investigation could have been made." *See State v. Murray, 184 Ariz. 9, 33, 906 P.2d 542 (1995)*; *see also State v. Willcoxson, 156 Ariz. 343, 346, 751 P.2d 1385 (App. 1987)* (noting "failure to pursue every lead or gather every conceivable bit of physical evidence" does not require a *Willits* instruction). We therefore find no error, fundamental or otherwise.

STATE OF ARIZONA, APPELLEE, V. DANNY WISE, APPELLANT.
NO. 1 CA-CR 13-0888

(Text added/modified for emphasis) The state has the tendency to release/destroy evidence, not investigate thoroughly, and again the same police/prosecutors are involved. Courts consistently sanction this systematic practice refusing to find bad faith thereby condoning this misconduct which is on the rise . As it was never their intent to subject the state's case to a meaningful adversarial process, when viewed in the totality, and not in isolation, this should constitute fraud upon the court by these lawyers.

COUNSEL: Arizona Attorney General's Office, Phoenix, By Joseph T. Maziarz, Counsel for Appellee. The Hopkins Law Office, P.C., Tucson, By Cedric Martin Hopkins, Counsel for Appellant.

Dan Wise appeals his convictions and sentences for eight counts of fraudulent schemes and twenty-two counts of theft. After searching the entire record, Wise's defense counsel has identified no arguable question of law that is not frivolous. Therefore, in accordance with *Anders v. California, 386 U.S. 738, 87 S. Ct. 1396, 18 L. Ed. 2d 493 (1967)*, and *State v. Leon, 104 Ariz. 297, 451 P.2d 878 (1969)*, defense counsel asks this Court to search the record for fundamental error. Wise was afforded the opportunity to file a supplemental brief *in propria persona*, which he elected to do. After reviewing the record, we find no error. Accordingly, Wise's convictions and sentences are affirmed.

Wise was indicted on eight counts of fraud and twenty-two counts of theft based upon events occurring between June 2006 and April 2008 while Wise was engaged as the victims' accountant. At trial, six victims, several of whom were family or close friends of Wise, testified Wise, a certified public accountant, regularly prepared their tax returns, represented he had filed returns or requests for an extension to file returns with the Internal Revenue Service and state tax agencies (collectively, the IRS) between 2006 and 2008, and further represented he had paid estimated taxes on their behalf. Wise advised the victims of the amount he allegedly paid on their behalf, and they "reimbursed" him those sums. However, the IRS was never paid.

Counts 1 through 16 alleged theft and Count 17 alleged fraud against Arthur K. Count 18 alleged fraud and Count 19 alleged theft against Francesco C. Counts 20, 22, and 24 alleged thefts and Counts 21, 23, and 25 alleged frauds against Elissa G. Counts 26 and 27 alleged theft and Count 28 alleged fraud against Carl F. Counts 29 and 30 alleged frauds against Beth S. and Neil B., respectively.

Although amounts varied from victim to victim, the total sum Wise took was nearly $1 million. Each victim testified he or she primarily communicated directly with Wise on all issues but occasionally relayed to or received routine information from Wise's assistant, and none of the victims were aware of any other employees or partners working with Wise.

When confronted by the victims, Wise blamed the IRS for misplacing or misapplying the funds and promised each victim he would resolve the issue. After months of delay, Wise was ultimately unable to document that the checks had ever been sent to or negotiated by the IRS. At trial, a representative from Wise's bank testified that none of the checks he wrote to the IRS for payment of the victims' taxes had ever been presented for payment. Wise ultimately paid the full amount owed to the IRS by Neil B. and Beth S., including interest and penalties, after they reported his conduct to law enforcement; the other victims, however, received nothing.

In mid-2008, three of the victims filed complaints against Wise with the Arizona State Board of Accountancy. Wise failed to respond to the complaints in writing as required by law and, in December 2008, consented to the revocation of his certification.

A fourth victim filed a complaint in February 2009, after Wise's certification had been revoked.

When confronted by the police in early 2009, Wise advised he had been an accountant for twenty-five years, but retired approximately two years prior. He stated he had legal issues with a previous business partner resulting in difficulties with his banking institution.

Wise testified in his defense at trial. He characterized himself as an "absentee owner" of an extremely busy accounting firm who, between 2004 and 2008, delegated more and more responsibility to his assistant to manage both his professional and personal affairs so he could develop his business and spend more time with his family. As a result, Wise's assistant had complete access to his business and personal information, including personal identification information, accounts, passwords, and the company checkbook. But, according to Wise's testimony, as his business continued to grow, he did not have time to monitor what occurred within the office.

Wise admitted receiving funds from the victims as "repayment" for their tax liability and acknowledged being ultimately responsible for what happened within his office, but denied any intent to steal money and denied knowledge of where the funds were. He testified his signature was "a scribble" that could have been signed by anyone, including his assistant, and that he assumed his assistant was performing the ministerial tasks he assigned including forwarding payment to the IRS on behalf of the victims as promised and confirming the IRS later negotiated the checks. Wise testified that only when he closed his business in late 2008 did he realize his files were not well kept and his reliance upon his assistant may have been misplaced, intimating she could have taken the funds and hidden from him that the IRS was never paid. In essence, Wise conceded an error in business judgment amounting only to negligence or malpractice.

A forensic accountant testified that Wise's practice of extending his own funds to pay his clients' estimated taxes was not illegal or unethical but expressed concern that Wise had no readily apparent or effective internal control procedures and placed too much trust in his staff. Although the expert was unable to exclude Wise as having perpetrated the scheme, neither could he exclude the assistant or Wise's partner in a boxing promotion business that operated from the same office.

The jury found Wise guilty on all counts. It also found the State had proven beyond a reasonable doubt that all of the offenses were committed for pecuniary gain and caused emotional and/or financial harm to the victims; all but counts 29 and 30 involved the taking of property in an amount sufficient to be an aggravating circumstance. The trial court classified the offenses as non-repetitive and non-dangerous and sentenced Wise to slightly aggravated terms of 7.5 years' imprisonment on counts 1, 2, and 17 to run concurrently with each other; slightly aggravated terms of 5 years' imprisonment on counts 3 through 16 to run concurrently with each other and with counts 1, 2, and 17; slightly aggravated terms of 7.5 years' imprisonment on counts 18 and 19 to run concurrently with each other and consecutive to counts 1 through 17; slightly aggravated terms of 7.5 years' imprisonment on counts 20 through 25 to run concurrently with each other and consecutive to counts 1 through 19; slightly aggravated terms of 7.5 years' imprisonment on counts 26 and 28 to run concurrently with each other and consecutive to counts 1 through 25; a slightly aggravated term of 5 years' imprisonment on count 27 to run concurrently with counts 26 and 28 and consecutive to counts 1 through 25; and the presumptive term of 5 years' imprisonment on counts 29 and 30 to run concurrently with each other and consecutive to counts 1 through 28.

....

DISCUSSION

I. Disclosure of Evidence

Wise argues the State violated his right to due process and deprived him of a fair trial by losing, destroying, and/or delaying disclosure of exculpatory and impeachment evidence seized by the Scottsdale Police Department pursuant to search warrants executed upon Wise's home, office, and storage unit, and the office of the U.S. Bankruptcy Trustee (the Trustee). He implicitly contends the trial court erred in: (1) denying his request for disclosure of 196 bankers' boxes of documents; and (2) denying his motion to dismiss for failure to preserve material evidence located on computers and servers. Wise preserved these issues for appeal, and we review the trial court's rulings for an abuse of discretion. *State v. Kevil, 111 Ariz. 240, 243, 527 P.2d 285 (1974)* (discovery motion); *State v. Gerhardt, 161 Ariz. 410, 413, 778 P.2d 1306 (App. 1989)* (motion to dismiss).

At the time of his arrest in May 2009, Wise had been forced into an involuntary bankruptcy, and all of his property and assets were seized by the Trustee and placed in receivership for liquidation.

A. Disclosure of Bankers' Boxes

In October 2010, Wise filed a comprehensive request for disclosure seeking, among other things, certain items impounded during the execution of the search warrants including cancelled checks, tax returns, legal and banking documents, client files, bank statements, and hard drives. The trial court directed briefing in regard to Wise's request for materials currently in possession of the Trustee. Instead of providing the relevant brief, Wise submitted another request for disclosure of the contents of various bankers' boxes, which he contended contained bank statements and tax returns that would verify Wise had made payments to the IRS on behalf of the victims and client files containing correspondence to the IRS proving he attempted to rectify discrepancies in payment and lacked a specific intent to defraud. Wise argued that because the State seized the evidence and voluntarily "gave it away" to another agency, the State had an obligation to find the evidence and make it available to the defense.

At an evidentiary hearing in April 2011, the State presented evidence that the Scottsdale Police Department seized 147 bankers' boxes of documents from Wise's storage unit, not knowing the Trustee had taken possession of the premises prior to execution of the search warrant. The next day, an additional 49 bankers' boxes of documents were seized from the Trustee's attorney's office. All 196 boxes were inventoried and, when the State determined their contents were not relevant to the charges, they were placed at an off-site location until the Trustee picked them up about eight months later. The State did not review any of the documents contained in the boxes and did not rely upon them in returning the indictments.

The trial court denied Wise's request for disclosure finding the State was not obligated to provide items not relevant to its investigation and which were no longer in its possession. It further noted that "whatever access the defendant would have had, had [these items] never been seized, is exactly the same access that the defendant has now." The court did, however, order the State to provide Wise with any information it had regarding the location and custodian of those materials.

A trial court has broad discretion in ruling upon disclosure and discovery matters. *See State v. Birdsall, 116 Ariz. 196, 198, 568 P.2d 1094 (App. 1977)* (citing *Kevil, 111 Ariz. at 243*); *see also Ariz. R. Crim. P. 15.1(g)*. In reviewing for an abuse of discretion: "The question is not whether the judges of this court would have made an original like ruling, but whether a judicial mind, in view of the law and circumstances, could have made the ruling without exceeding the bounds of reason." *Associated Indem. Corp. v. Warner, 143 Ariz. 567, 571, 694 P.2d 1181 (1985)* (quoting *Davis v. Davis, 78 Ariz. 174, 179, 277 P.2d 261 (1954)* (Windes, J., specially concurring)).

Here, the trial court correctly noted that the State can only disclose materials in its possession. *Ariz. R. Crim. P. 15.1(a), (b)*. And, the court offered a solution to allow Wise to gain access to the information he requested which was apparently successful given that, as early as August 2011, Wise's attorney reported having "examined most of the needed boxes" being held in the custody of the Trustee. In July 2012, the prosecuting attorney reported receiving a copy, from defense counsel, of all the file materials related to the victims. In September 2012, Wise's counsel admitted having received over 65,000 pages of disclosure, and Wise's December 2012 request for disclosure was nothing more than a form document that did not identify any specific materials believed to have been withheld. Finally, although the trial court specifically advised Wise it would entertain requests for orders needed to obtain items necessary to his defense, Wise did not seek any further assistance from the court, indicating he had, in fact, received the materials sought. We find no abuse of discretion.

Wise relies upon an April 2015 affidavit in arguing "materials were missing, lost, in complete disar[r]ay, [or] clearly never copied or opened." This affidavit is not contained in the record below, and we do not consider it. *See State v. Schackart, 190 Ariz. 238, 247, 947 P.2d 315 (1997)* (citations omitted). Moreover, claims based upon newly discovered evidence are not appropriate for direct appeal. *See Krone v. Hotham, 181 Ariz. 364, 366, 890 P.2d 1149 (1995)* (citing *State v. Scrivner, 132 Ariz. 52, 54, 643 P.2d 1022 (App. 1982)*).

B. Computers and Servers

In May 2012, Wise filed a motion to dismiss the charges against him arguing the State had failed to properly preserve information contained on one of the servers which he believed was "no longer functional." Wise argued the server contained information regarding who had accessed the victims' electronic files and when and what functions were performed -- for example, writing a check, working on tax forms, or corresponding with clients or the IRS -- that would support his defense that he lacked specific intent to defraud, and that this information was impossible to recreate. Additionally, he presented an affidavit of a senior-level technologist averring the server was "in perfect working order" at the time it was seized and opining the "crash" would occur only if the server was improperly shut down, transported, or tampered with.

The record reflects Wise's counsel ultimately admitted receiving the server in September 2012 -- a full year before trial -- and the court deemed Wise's motion moot. Wise's contention within his supplemental brief that he was denied access to this material is not supported by the record and, therefore, provides no basis for relief on appeal.

STATE OF ARIZONA, APPELLEE, V. MULUGETA YEMANE MICAEL, APPELLANT.
NO. 1 CA-CR 14-0098

COUNSEL: Arizona Attorney General's Office, Phoenix, By Andrew Reilly, Counsel for Appellee. Maricopa County Office of the Legal Advocate, Phoenix, By Kerri L. Chamberlin, Counsel for Appellant.

....

(Text added/modified for emphasis) Trial courts with a consistency limit cross-examination of defense witnesses ensuring facts not be elicited that favor the defendant. The state has the tendency to make such requests. Courts consistently sanction this systematic practice refusing to find bad faith thereby condoning this misconduct which is on the rise . As it was never their intent to subject the state's case to a meaningful adversarial process, when viewed in the totality, and not in isolation, this should constitute fraud upon the court by these lawyers.

C. Limitation on Cross-Examination.

The victim failed to appear at the time scheduled by the State at Micael's second trial, and the State requested a bench warrant to ensure his appearance the next day. Before the victim testified the following day, the trial court, without objection, stated that there was to be no comment on how the witness "came here today," ruling it was both irrelevant and subject to preclusion under *Rule 403 of the Rules of Evidence* because any probative value is outweighed by its prejudice. Micael argues this restriction on cross-examination of the victim violated his confrontation rights by improperly precluding him from informing the jury that the only reason the victim appeared to testify is because "he was arrested and forced to attend the trial," asserting that his unwillingness to testify was relevant to his motive, bias and credibility. Because Micael did not object below, our review is limited to fundamental error. *Henderson, 210 Ariz. at 567, ¶ 19.*

The *Confrontation Clause of the Sixth Amendment* protects a defendant's ability to prove a witness's motive or bias. *U.S. Const. amend. VI*; *Davis v. Alaska, 415 U.S. 308, 316-17, 94 S. Ct. 1105, 39 L. Ed. 2d 347 (1974)*. The *Confrontation Clause*, however, does not prevent a trial judge from imposing limits on defense counsel's inquiry into the potential bias of a prosecution witness; courts retain wide latitude to impose reasonable limits on cross-examination based on, among other things, prejudice, confusion of the issues, and interrogation that is only marginally relevant. *Delaware v. Van Arsdall, 475 U.S. 673, 679, 106 S. Ct. 1431, 89 L. Ed. 2d 674 (1986)*. We generally review rulings on the admissibility of evidence for abuse of discretion, but we review rulings that implicate the Confrontation Clause de novo. *State v. Ellison, 213 Ariz. 116, 129, ¶ 42, 140 P.3d 899 (2006)*.

There was no error in the limitation of cross-examination of the victim about the arrest warrant. Although the failure to appear in response to a subpoena may suggest animosity and bias *against* the party serving the subpoena, there is no "bright line rule" on whether the trial court abuses its discretion in ruling on the admissibility of such evidence. *State v. Riggs, 189 Ariz. 327, 334, 942 P.2d 1159 (1997)*. In this case, the record indicates there was no unwillingness by the victim to testify, but rather merely a scheduling conflict. This conclusion finds support in the fact that the victim freely appeared and testified against Micael at his first trial. Under these circumstances, the trial court could reasonably find that the matter of the issuance of the warrant to insure the victim's appearance at the second trial was only marginally relevant at best and that injecting this issue into the trial would only serve to confuse the issues. Thus, there was no abuse of discretion by the trial court in precluding evidence of the bench warrant issued to compel the victim's appearance.

Moreover, to obtain relief under fundamental error review, Micael bears the burden of establishing prejudice from the alleged error. *Henderson, 210 Ariz. at 567, ¶ 20*. On appeal, however, Micael does not even argue that he was prejudiced. Instead, he asserts the burden is on the State to prove beyond a reasonable doubt that he was not prejudiced by the error. Accordingly, even if error occurred, Micael would not be entitled to relief because he has not met his burden of showing prejudice.

STATE OF ARIZONA, APPELLEE, V. JOHN JOSEPH MURPHY, APPELLANT.
NO. 1 CA-CR 14-0273

COUNSEL: Arizona Attorney General Office, Phoenix, By Joseph T. Maziarz, Counsel for Appellee. Maricopa County Public Defender's Office, Phoenix, By Cory Engle, Counsel for Appellant.

(Text added/modified for emphasis) Trial courts with a consistency allow the state to present testimony the defendant is "not stable per se as far as the top educated person" and was "very e[c]centric" e]xtremely prejudicial and irrelevant," testimony to ensure convictions. Courts consistently sanction this systematic practice refusing to find bad faith thereby condoning this misconduct which is on the rise . As it was never their intent to subject the state's case to a meaningful adversarial process, when viewed in the totality, and not in isolation, this should constitute fraud upon the court by these lawyers.

FACTS AND PROCEDURAL BACKGROUND

Murphy and the victim had been neighbors in Mesa. In early 2013, the victim moved into a trailer with her boyfriend approximately a block away. Murphy continued to visit the victim daily or weekly after the move.

In late September 2013, the victim temporarily ran out of funds for food and electricity, and Murphy offered to help by selling a coin collection and lending the victim money. Murphy returned to the victim's house the next day. Over the course of two hours, Murphy drank more than half of a large bottle of whiskey, then became angry when the victim and her boyfriend teased him about a rumor that he had called the police on another neighbor. Agitated, Murphy said that he needed to kill the neighbors who were accusing him or, failing that, he might as well kill himself. Murphy threw a "wad of money" at the victim's boyfriend and left the trailer.

The victim left the trailer for a while, and when she returned, Murphy had returned with a gun. The victim eventually went into the trailer and stood across the room from Murphy, near her boyfriend. She saw Murphy loading a bullet into the gun, waving the gun back and forth, and pointing the gun briefly at her chest.

After the victim's boyfriend left the trailer, she told Murphy to get out, and then she went into the backyard to call 9-1-1. While the victim was on the phone, Murphy left the trailer and walked back toward his neighbor's house. Maricopa County Sheriff's deputies found Murphy standing outside the house with a pistol pointed at a porch window. Murphy was arrested at the scene.

A jury found Murphy guilty of aggravated assault and disorderly conduct, both dangerous offenses, and Murphy timely appealed.

DISCUSSION

Murphy argues the superior court erred by allowing testimony suggesting that he suffered from an unspecified mental illness. During trial, mental illness was overtly or obliquely mentioned on three occasions. First, the victim testified, without objection, that although Murphy was very friendly and open-hearted, he was "not stable per se as far as the top educated person" and was "very e[c]centric." Second, the victim described her motive for calling 9-1-1 as that she "would want [Murphy] to be evaluated for mental illness. . . . That he needed to be evaluated for mental illness and to be medicated if necessary so these situations wouldn't happen any further." Defense counsel objected to this testimony as "[e]xtremely prejudicial and irrelevant," but the court overruled the objection. Finally, a sheriff's deputy testified, without objection, that many of the people living in the community where Murphy lived had methamphetamine, alcohol, and "psychological problems that haven't been addressed properly."

We review evidentiary rulings for an abuse of discretion, deferring to the superior court's assessment of relevance and unfair prejudice. *State v. Smith, 215 Ariz. 221, 232, ¶ 48, 159 P.3d 531, 542 (2007).* Absent a timely objection at trial, however, we review only for fundamental, prejudicial error. *See State v. Henderson, 210 Ariz. 561, 567, ¶¶ 19-20, 115 P.3d 601, 607 (2005).*

Murphy asserts that the victim's and the deputy's statements regarding mental illness were irrelevant to the facts at issue, were unfairly prejudicial, and improperly suggested that an unspecified mental illness equated to violence. But the victim's statements described her motives for calling the police, and Murphy's defense put the victim's motives directly at issue. Beginning in opening statements, defense counsel suggested that Murphy had never pointed a gun at the victim, but rather that the victim had called the police to have Murphy arrested so she could steal his money, characterizing the victim's financial difficulties as her motive to falsely report an aggravated assault. In closing, defense counsel again asserted that Murphy had not committed a crime, but that the victim had a motive to fabricate her story because she wanted Murphy's money and valuables.

The victim's explanation that she had called 9-1-1 because she thought Murphy "needed to be evaluated for mental illness and to be medicated if necessary so these situations wouldn't happen any further" was thus directly relevant to rebut Murphy's defense. *See Ariz. R. Evid. 401* (defining relevant evidence as that which "has any tendency to make a [material] fact more or less probable"). Because this testimony rebutted the cornerstone of his defense, it potentially carried substantial probative value, whereas the danger of unfair prejudice was comparatively slight. *See Ariz. R. Evid. 403* (stating that relevant evidence may be excluded if its probative value is substantially outweighed by the danger of unfair prejudice). Moreover, even as character evidence, the testimony served a valid, non-propensity purpose because it was relevant to the victim's motive. *See Ariz. R. Evid. 404(a)-(b)*. Accordingly, the superior court did not err by allowing this testimony.

Because Murphy did not object to the victim's other comment or to the deputy's description of the neighborhood, we review these statements only for fundamental, prejudicial error. *See Henderson, 210 Ariz. at 567, ¶¶ 19-20, 115 P.3d at 607*. The victim's initial characterization of Murphy as very friendly and open-hearted, but "not stable per se as far as the top educated person" and "very e[c]centric" arguably does not implicate mental illness at all, and to the extent it does, the characterization was permissible as relevant to the victim's motives as described above. And the deputy's testimony was not directed at Murphy individually, but rather stated his perception of general characteristics of the neighborhood. Under the circumstances, Murphy has not shown error, much less reversible error.

THE STATE OF ARIZONA, APPELLEE, V. LUIS RANDULFO PARRADO, APPELLANT.
NO. 2 CA-CR 2015-0075

(Text added/modified for emphasis) Consistently police do not conduct thorough investigations and witnesses are unable to identify the defendants. Courts allow this practice to continue. Courts consistently sanction this systematic practice refusing to find bad faith thereby condoning this misconduct which is on the rise . As it was never their intent to subject the state's case to a meaningful adversarial process, when viewed in the totality, and not in isolation, this should constitute fraud upon the court by these lawyers.

COUNSEL: Mark Brnovich, Arizona Attorney General; Joseph T. Maziarz, Section Chief Counsel, Phoenix, By Kathryn A. Damstra, Assistant Attorney General, Tucson, Counsel for Appellee. Barton & Storts, P.C., Tucson, By Brick P. Storts, III, Counsel for Appellant.

Luis Parrado was convicted after a jury trial of two counts each of kidnapping, armed robbery, aggravated robbery, aggravated assault, and possession of a narcotic drug, and one count each of first-degree burglary, kidnapping a minor under the age of fifteen, aggravated assault of a minor under the age of fifteen, and possession of drug paraphernalia. He was sentenced to consecutive and concurrent prison terms totaling 19.5 years. Parrado argues on appeal that there was insufficient evidence identifying him because the testifying victim was unable to identify him at trial and "was inconsistent in her description" of one of her assailants. We affirm.

We view the facts in the light most favorable to sustaining the jury's verdicts. *State v. Haight-Gyuro, 218 Ariz. 356, ¶ 2, 186 P.3d 33, 34 (App. 2008).* In December 2015, Parrado and another man entered the apartment of K., C., and their three-year-old son. They beat C. repeatedly with pistols and herded the family into the bedroom; while Parrado stayed in the living room, his companion entered the bedroom and pointed a pistol at the family and threatened to kill them. The attackers fled, taking several items from the apartment, when Parrado yelled that police were nearby. Both were arrested a short time later, and K. identified Parrado as one of her attackers just after his arrest. Parrado was carrying oxycodone pills and a baggie containing cocaine base when he was arrested.

Parrado's sole argument on appeal is that the evidence was insufficient to sustain his convictions because K., the only victim who testified, did not identify him at trial and gave a "varied" description of the assailant who had stayed in the living room. We review the sufficiency of the evidence de novo, *State v. Pena, 235 Ariz. 277, ¶ 5, 331 P.3d 412, 414 (2014),* and will affirm if the conviction is supported by "substantial evidence," *State v. Ellison, 213 Ariz. 116, ¶ 65, 140 P.3d 899, 916-17 (2006).* Evidence is substantial if reasonable people could accept it as proving, beyond a reasonable doubt, all the elements of a crime and the defendant's responsibility for it. *See State v. Bearup, 221 Ariz. 163, ¶ 16, 211 P.3d 684, 688 (2009).*

Any variance or weaknesses in K.'s description of Parrado were for the jury to weigh against her identification of him just after his arrest. "'[I]t is not necessary that the identification of the defendant as the perpetrator of the crime be made positively or in a manner free from inconsistencies. It is the function of the jury to pass upon the strength or weakness of the identification.'" *State v. Dutton, 83 Ariz. 193, 198, 318 P.2d 667, 670 (1957),* quoting *People v. Houser, 85 Cal. App. 2d 686, 193 P.2d 937, 941 (Cal. Ct. App. 1948); see also State v. Cox, 217 Ariz. 353, ¶ 27, 174 P.3d 265, 269 (2007)* (jury resolves witness credibility and assigns value to testimony). And, even if K.'s identification were somehow deficient, Parrado ignores that C.'s blood was found on his hands, clearly tying him to the offenses.

Because there was ample evidence that Parrado committed the offenses for which he was convicted, his convictions and sentences are affirmed.

STATE OF ARIZONA, APPELLEE, V. MATTHEW JAY FOGEL, APPELLANT.
NO. 1 CA-CR 14-0784

(Text added/modified for emphasis) . Courts upon the request of the state consistently prevent the defendant from presenting a complete defense so as to ensure a guilty verdict. Trial courts with a consistency limit cross-examination of defense witnesses ensuring facts not be elicited that favor the defendant. The state has the tendency to make such requests. Courts consistently sanction this systematic practice refusing to find bad faith thereby condoning this misconduct which is on the rise . As it was never their intent to subject the state's case to a meaningful adversarial process, when viewed in the totality, and not in isolation, this should constitute fraud upon the court by these lawyers

COUNSEL: Law Office of Nicole Farnum, Phoenix, By Nicole Farnum, Counsel for Appellant. Arizona Attorney General's Office, Phoenix, By Myles A. Braccio, Counsel for Appellee.

Fogel was visiting W.J.'s two roommates, when W.J. arrived after work. The four of them drank beer, played poker, and grilled food. Fogel and W.J. talked and joked during the poker game, but as the evening progressed, their comments escalated to bickering and trash talking. Eventually, the poker game ended and the group started cleaning up.

Believing the tension between W.J. and Fogel was about to escalate into a fight, one of the roommates stepped out of the kitchen to alert the other. While they were alone in the kitchen, Fogel made a derogatory statement and W.J. asked him to leave. Fogel then walked over to the cutting board, picked up the butcher knife, and said, "Why don't you make me leave?" W.J. told Fogel to put the knife down, and again asked him to leave the house. Fogel lunged at W.J., cutting W.J.'s hand and severing the tendons when W.J. tried to block the knife. As W.J. tried to get the knife away from Fogel, Fogel stabbed him in the chest and twice in the abdomen. When the two roommates came into the kitchen, Fogel dropped the butcher knife and ran. And when the roommates realized that W.J.'s intestines were falling out, they helped lie him down and called 9-1-1. A couple of hours later, Fogel surrendered to the police.

Fogel was indicted for aggravated assault, a class three dangerous felony. The case went to trial and after presentation of the prosecution's evidence, Fogel unsuccessfully moved for judgment of acquittal under Arizona Rule of Criminal Procedure ("Rule") 20. After the defense presented its evidence, closing arguments, and jury instructions, the jury deliberated and convicted Fogel as charged. The jury subsequently found beyond a reasonable doubt that the offense involved the infliction or threatened infliction of serious physical injury, and was a dangerous offense involving the use or threatening exhibition of a dangerous weapon. Fogel was later sentenced to six years in prison and given 42 days of presentence incarceration credit.

DISCUSSION

Fogel argues the trial court erred in precluding evidence that W.J. had a fight with his ex-girlfriend because that evidence was relevant and admissible. He also contends the court's ruling violated his due process right to present a complete defense. Although he did not raise the due process argument to the trial court, we may consider a constitutional argument raised for the first time on appeal, *see State v. Gilfillan, 196 Ariz. 396, 401 n.4, 998 P.2d 1069, 1074 n.4 (App. 2000)*, but will only review it for fundamental prejudicial error, *see State v. Abdi, 226 Ariz. 361, 367, ¶ 26, 248 P.3d 209, 215 (App. 2011)* [*4] . We review the ruling excluding evidence for an abuse of discretion. *State v. Vandever, 211 Ariz. 206, 209, ¶ 10, 119 P.3d 473, 476 (App. 2005)* (citation omitted). An abuse of discretion occurs when the court's ruling is "clearly untenable, legally incorrect, or amount[s] to a denial of justice." *State v. Fish, 222 Ariz. 109, 114, ¶ 8, 213 P.3d 258, 263 (App. 2009)* (citation omitted).

The *Due Process Clause of the Fourteenth Amendment to the United States Constitution* provides a criminal defendant the right to "be afforded a meaningful opportunity to present a complete defense." *California v. Trombetta, 467 U.S. 479, 485, 104 S. Ct. 2528, 81 L. Ed. 2d 413 (1984)*. This right is not unlimited, but is subject to evidentiary rules. As a result, the "right to present evidence in one's defense is limited to evidence which is relevant and not unduly prejudicial." *Abdi, 226 Ariz. at 368, ¶ 32, 248 P.3d at 216* (citation omitted).

The State filed a motion in limine to exclude testimony of a specific act of violence between W.J. and his ex-girlfriend that allegedly occurred several days before his altercation with Fogel. The court held a hearing and received offers of proof about the testimony the court would hear. The court concluded that although evidence of the victim's general reputation for violence was admissible, testimony about the victim's fight with his ex-girlfriend was not relevant, and any probative value was substantially outweighed by prejudice. The court explained that the incident was not relevant because Fogel did not have "actual knowledge" of the fight, but only heard about it from W.J.'s two roommates, who were at home when the fight occurred in W.J.'s bedroom.

Generally, evidence to prove that a person acted in conformity with a character trait is not admissible, but a defendant may offer evidence of a victim's pertinent character trait. *Ariz. R. Evid. 404(a)(2).* Character evidence is generally established by reputation and opinion testimony, not through evidence of specific acts. *Ariz. R. Evid. 405(a), (b).* An exception to that general rule exists when (1) the victim's character is an essential element of a defense, *Ariz. R. Evid. 405(b),* or (2) the evidence is otherwise admissible to prove "motive, opportunity, intent, preparation, plan, knowledge, identity, or absence of mistake or accident," *Ariz. R. Evid. 404(b); Fish, 222 Ariz. at 117, ¶ 21, 213 P.3d at 266.*

A defendant asserting self-defense may present evidence to demonstrate that he or she was justified in using physical force against the victim because a reasonable person would have believed that physical force was necessary to protect himself or herself. *A.R.S. § 13-404(A).* We have consistently held that the victim's character is not an essential element of self-defense. *See id.; Fish, 222 Ariz. at 119, ¶ 29, 213 P.3d at 268* (citation omitted); *State v. Williams, 141 Ariz. 127, 130, 685 P.2d 764, 767 (App. 1984).* Thus, the specific incident between W.J. and his ex-girlfriend would not be admissible as a specific element of a defense under *Rule 405(b),* and must otherwise fall within the parameters of *Rule 404(b)* to be admissible.

Under *Rule 404(b),* a defendant may introduce evidence of the victim's prior violent acts to demonstrate that he was apprehensive of the victim, and knew of the victim's violent tendencies. *See State v. Taylor, 169 Ariz. 121, 124, 817 P.2d 488, 491 (1991).* The defendant, however, must have been aware of the victim's prior acts before his altercation with the victim. *Fish, 222 Ariz. at 121, ¶ 37, 213 P.3d at 270; State v. Connor, 215 Ariz. 553, 559, ¶ 13, 161 P.3d 596, 602 (App. 2007)* (citation omitted); *State v. Zamora, 140 Ariz. 338, 341, 681 P.2d 921, 924 (App. 1984)*.

Even though Fogel learned about W.J.'s fight with his ex-girlfriend from W.J.'s roommates five days before he stabbed W.J., the court ruled the evidence was not relevant. The court reasoned that Fogel did not have "actual knowledge" of specific acts between W.J. and his ex-girlfriend that would have led Fogel to believe W.J. would "act aggressively towards him."

"Actual knowledge" of the prior act, however, is not required before evidence may be admitted under *Rule 404(b)*. Actual knowledge requires that a person have "[d]irect and clear knowledge." Black's Law Dictionary (10th ed. 2014). Ordinary knowledge, on the other hand, only requires "[a]n awareness or understanding of a fact or circumstance; a state of mind in which a person has no substantial doubt about the existence of a fact." Black's Law Dictionary (10th ed. 2014). Although a defendant is required to have knowledge of the victim's prior violent act under *Rule 404(b)*, the rule does not require actual knowledge. Instead of personal observations, a defendant can have knowledge of a victim's prior violent act through other information he substantially believes. *See Fish, 222 Ariz. at 121, ¶ 37, 213 P.3d at 270* (applying knowledge analysis used in homicide defense cases to non-homicide case where self-defense defense used); *cf. State v. Young, 109 Ariz. 221, 223, 508 P.2d 51, 53 (1973)* ("accused should be permitted to introduce evidence of specific acts of violence by the deceased, whether observed by the defendant himself or simply known by him prior to the homicide."); *State v. Jackson, 94 Ariz. 117, 121, 382 P.2d 229, 231 (1963)* ("Personal observation by a defendant is not required but only that he be informed of the acts."); *Williams, 141 Ariz. at 130, 685 P.2d at 767* (homicide defendant may "introduce evidence of specific acts of violence by a deceased only when those acts were personally observed by the defendant or made known to him prior to the homicide."). Here, Fogel learned about W.J.'s fight with his ex-girlfriend from W.J.'s roommates, who were present at the time of the fight, and told him the details about what they heard and saw, including W.J. leaving his room with a bloody nose. As a result, Fogel had knowledge of the incident between W.J. and his ex-girlfriend.

Although the trial court mistakenly believed that Fogel needed "actual knowledge" of the incident, the error was not prejudicial because the court continued, and found that any probative value of the evidence was outweighed by its prejudicial effect under *Rule 403*. The rule provides that a court "may exclude relevant evidence if its probative value is substantially outweighed by a danger of . . . unfair prejudice." *Ariz. R. Evid. 403*. A court is granted "considerable discretion in determining whether the probative value of the evidence is substantially outweighed by its unfairly prejudicial effect," *Gilfillan, 196 Ariz. at 405, ¶ 29, 998 P.2d at 1078*, and because "*Rule 403* weighing is best left to the trial court," we will not disturb a trial court's finding absent an abuse of discretion, *State v. Fernane, 185 Ariz. 222, 226, 914 P.2d 1314, 1318 (App. 1995)* (citation omitted).

The trial court explicitly weighed the probative value of the fight against its prejudice, and made a finding based on the specific facts asserted by the attorneys and the circumstances in which the fight arose. *See id. at 227 n.2, 914 P.2d at 1319 n.2*. Although Fogel knew about the incident, there were differences between that incident and Fogel's fight with W.J. For example, there was no suggestion that the domestic incident involved the use of a weapon, nor was there any evidence that suggested that W.J. was likely to [*9] use deadly force. W.J. fought with his ex-girlfriend after he looked at entries on her phone and saw she had been talking with other men. His jealous argument escalated into a fight when he slammed her into the bedroom wall and, in response, she punched him in the nose, causing it to bleed. The court had sufficient information to determine that the facts of the incident were not relevant to demonstrate that Fogel had a reasonable belief that W.J. would attack him with a weapon after asking Fogel to leave the house. And given that Fogel was permitted to present other evidence of W.J.'s reputation for violence in order to present his self-defense theory, which the jury considered, the court did not abuse its discretion by determining the admission of the specific details of the incident were more likely to cause prejudice than prove Fogel's state of mind to justify his actions. Consequently, Fogel was not deprived of his right to present a complete defense, and there was no fundamental prejudicial error.

JOHNNY RAY WASHINGTON, PETITIONER - APPELLANT, V. CHARLES L. RYAN,˙ DIRECTOR, AZ DEPARTMENT OF CORRECTIONS AND STATE OF ARIZONA ATTORNEY GENERAL, RESPONDENTS - APPELLEES. NO. 08-17039 UNITED STATES COURT OF APPEALS FOR THE NINTH CIRCUIT

(TEXT ADDED AND MODIFIED FOR EMPHASIS) AS A MATTER OF REGULAR PRACTICE THE ATTORNEY GENERAL'S OFFICE CONSISTENTLY FAILS TO ADVISE THE FEDERAL COURTS THAT WHEN THE ATTORNEY GENERAL CONCEALED THE FACT THAT ARIZONA PROSECUTORS WHEN THEY REALIZE THEY MAY NOT PREVAIL, ENGAGE IN MISCONDUCT, TO PROVOKE MISTRIALS, AND STATE COURTS DO NOTHING. BECAUSE OF THE FAILURE OF THE ATTORNEY GENERAL TO BE CANDID THERE ARE TOO MANY SUCH INCIDENTS WHICH CONSTITUTE A PATTERN .AS THIS IS A PATTERN WITH THE ARIZONA ATTORNEY GENERAL'S OFFICE THIS SHOULD CONSTITUTE FRAUD UPON THE COURT, BECAUSE, THEY ARE CONCEALING FACTS ON A SYSTEMIC BASIS, TO DEFEAT VALID CLAIMS.

COUNSEL: For JOHNNY RAY WASHINGTON (-: #042919), Petitioner - Appellant: David Eisenberg, I, Esquire, Attorney, David Eisenberg, PLC, Phoenix, AZ. JOHNNY RAY WASHINGTON (-: #042919), Petitioner - Appellant, Pro se, Buckeye, AZ. For DORA SCHRIRO, Director, AZ Department of Corrections, Respondent - Appellee: Joseph Thomas Maziarz, ARIZONA ATTORNEY GENERAL'S OFFICE, Phoenix, AZ.

Arizona state prisoner Johnny Ray Washington appeals from the district court's judgment denying his *28 U.S.C. § 2254* habeas petition. We have jurisdiction under *28 U.S.C. § 2253(c)*, and we affirm.

Washington contends that the prosecutor in his first trial intended to provoke the defense into moving for a mistrial and that, consequently, his retrial violated the *Double Jeopardy Clause of the 5th Amendment*. Washington's contention is not supported by the record. Accordingly, the state court's decision was not contrary to, or an unreasonable application of, clearly established Supreme Court law, or an unreasonable determination of the facts in light of the evidence. *See 28 U.S.C. § 2254(d); see also Oregon v. Kennedy, 456 U.S. 667, 676, 102 S. Ct. 2083, 72 L. Ed. 2d 416 (1982)* ("[o]nly where the governmental conduct in question is intended to 'goad' the defendant into moving for a mistrial may a defendant raise the bar of double jeopardy to a second trial after having succeeded in aborting the first on his own motion").

MARTIN SOTO FONG, PETITIONER, VS. CHARLES RYAN, ET AL., RESPONDENTS.

NO. CV 04-68-TUC-DCB UNITED STATES DISTRICT COURT FOR THE DISTRICT OF ARIZONA

(Text added/modified for emphasis) The Attorney General fails to disclose to the court that in Arizona it is the norm for prosecutors to present false evidence to convict and rarely are they penalized. Failure to disclose this systemic problem is fraud upon the court.

COUNSEL: For Martin Soto Fong, Petitioner: Amy Sara Armstrong, LEAD ATTORNEY, Arizona Capital Representation Project, Tucson, AZ. For Charles L Ryan, Respondent: Aaron Jay Moskowitz, Office of the Attorney General, Criminal Appeals Section, Phoenix, AZ.

…………

FACTUAL BACKGROUND

Investigation and Trial

At 10:15 p.m. on June 24, 1992, police were dispatched to the El Grande Market in response to a 911 call. There, they found the bodies of Fred Gee, Ray Arriola, and Zewan Huang, all employees of the market. Gee had been shot in the head and torso with a .25 caliber handgun. Arriola and Huang had been shot in the head with a .38 caliber weapon and in the torso with a .25 caliber weapon. The facts set forth herein are derived from the Court's review of the state court record as well as the Arizona Supreme Court's opinions in *Soto-Fong, 187 Ariz. at 190-91, 928 P.2d at 614-15*, and *State v. Minnitt, 203 Ariz. 431, 433-34, 55 P.3d 774, 776-77 (2002)*.

Shortly thereafter, police found an abandoned car that was parked out of place several blocks from the market. Tire tracks indicated an abrupt stop, and the engine was still warm. Christopher McCrimmon's fingerprint was found on the driver's side window. The car belonged to David Durbin, who had lent it to his girlfriend, Queen E. Ray. The morning after the shootings Ray initially told Durbin it had been impounded for unpaid parking tickets. She told the lead homicide investigator, Tucson Police Detective Joseph Godoy, that she had driven a friend to some apartments, experienced mechanical problems, and abandoned the car. Months later, on the eve of a preliminary hearing for McCrimmon and Andre Minnitt, Godoy confronted Ray about the truthfulness of her statement and told her she would be charged with perjury if she lied on the witness stand. At the hearing, Ray testified that on the night of the market shooting, she had loaned McCrimmon the car in return for money. She said that McCrimmon, Minnitt, and a third person, whom she knew as Martinez, left McCrimmon's apartment with the car around 10:00 p.m. and that about an hour later the three returned without the car. McCrimmon gave Ray $30 and the car keys. During trial, Ray, who had seen pictures of Petitioner on television following his arrest, identified Petitioner as "Martinez."

At the time of the murders, the market was in the process of closing. Two registers had been cleared, leaving only one open. The body of the manager, Fred Gee, was found at the open register at the liquor counter. The register had a $1.69 sale rung up on it, and nearby on the counter were produce bags containing a cucumber and three lemons. Petitioner's fingerprints were found on each bag. On the floor near Gee's body were two crumpled $1 food stamps, not yet stamped with the market's name. Petitioner's fingerprints were also found on one of these food stamps. At least $175.52 was missing from the store. Testimony at trial indicated that Gee routinely permitted known customers through the iron security gate after the store's 9:00 closing time.

The investigation took a significant turn on August 31, 1992, when Detective Godoy received a tip from an anonymous caller and obtained information from a confidential informant working with Gang Unit Sergeant Zimmerling. From these sources, Godoy gleaned the name "Martin Soto," along with that of Christopher McCrimmon. A background check revealed that Soto and Fong were the same person. Godoy also learned from the Gee Family that Martin Fong was a former market employee.

Around this same time, Tucson Police Detective Fuller began investigating an August 26, 1992, robbery and non-fatal shooting at Mariano's Pizza. McCrimmon became a potential suspect after forensic evidence linked him to the crime scene. Fuller discovered that Minnitt also may have been involved in the robbery and relayed this information to Godoy on September 1. At that point, McCrimmon was already a suspect for the market murders. With the additional information connecting McCrimmon and Minnitt, Godoy considered Minnitt a possible suspect. Moreover, according to Fuller, McCrimmon and Martin Soto Fong were close friends. On September 2, McCrimmon and Minnitt were arrested for the pizzeria robbery and in the days that followed Godoy tried to locate Petitioner.

Also in late August, Keith Woods, a close friend of McCrimmon's, was released from prison. On August 30, Tucson police arrested him on drug charges. Because Woods was already a three-time felon, and possessing drugs was a parole violation subjecting him to a possible twenty-five year prison sentence, he agreed to become an informant in exchange for release and dismissal of the drug charges. On September 8, following an initial 30 to 45-minute untapped conversation, Godoy created a ruse to move Woods into a wired room. While being surreptitiously recorded, Woods told Godoy that on the day he was released from prison McCrimmon and Minnitt told him they committed the El Grande murders along with a third person, Cha-Chi, a Mexican guy, who had worked at the market and set up the robbery. Woods also said they told him Cha-Chi went into the store by himself "masked down or whatever," someone rebelled, and Cha-Chi shot them with a .25 caliber gun. (Doc. 45, Ex. 43 at 5.) McCrimmon and Minnitt then ran in, and the latter shot two of the victims after they were already down. Woods initially denied ever meeting or knowing Cha-Chi but in a later statement to Godoy on November 20 Woods said Cha-Chi was a guy named Martin, who was Betty Christopher's boyfriend. There was no dispute at trial that Petitioner was Betty Christopher's boyfriend.

Using an outstanding juvenile runaway complaint filed by Petitioner's mother, police finally found, arrested, and fingerprinted Petitioner on September 9, the day after Woods made his initial statement. In response to questioning, Petitioner denied any involvement in the crime, claiming that he had last been in the store about two weeks before the murders to buy beer. The next day, Godoy learned of Petitioner's fingerprint match to items found at the crime scene, and Petitioner was re-arrested.

Petitioner's trial took place before that of his co-defendants. The prosecution theorized that Fong was recognized by market employees, permitted to enter the store during closing, filled plastic bags with lemons and a cucumber, and paid Gee at the liquor counter register with two $1 food stamps before the shooting began. The defense theory was one of mistaken identity: Petitioner claimed Cha-Chi was Martin Garza, another acquaintance of McCrimmon's. The defense also maintained that investigators improperly handled the forensic evidence, making the fingerprints inherently unreliable. Further, the defense called Keith Woods as a witness to support the theory that Detective Godoy improperly coerced both Woods and Ray to implicate Fong.

Co-Defendant Retrials

After their convictions were reversed due to juror coercion, the trial court severed the retrials of McCrimmon and Minnitt. Minnitt's initial retrial resulted in a hung jury. *See State v. Minnitt, 203 Ariz. 431, 433, 55 P.3d 774, 777 (2002).* He was tried again in 1999, found guilty of all charges, and resentenced to death for the murders. *Id.*

On appeal, the Arizona Supreme Court determined that Minnitt's third trial should have been barred by principles of double jeopardy resulting from prosecutorial misconduct at the first two trials. *Id.* Specifically, the court found that the prosecutor, Kenneth Peasley, knowingly elicited false testimony from Detective Godoy concerning how and when McCrimmon, Minnitt, and Fong became suspects in the market murders. The court recounted the following relevant facts:

> In all three Minnitt trials and in both McCrimmon trials, the state's case depended heavily on Keith Woods' credibility. Importantly, as of September 2, the police had identified Soto-Fong, McCrimmon, and Minnitt as suspects in the El Grande crimes and had interviewed them. But according to Godoy, police had yet to interview anyone who could provide direct evidence linking any of the three to the crimes. Woods was not interviewed until September 8, six days after the McCrimmon and Minnitt interviews. Godoy claimed to have received his first knowledge of any involvement by McCrimmon and Minnitt from his interview with Woods. This was the information the police were seeking - that McCrimmon and Minnitt had implicated themselves in the murders and that a witness would so testify.
>
> Woods' credibility was tenuous. He was a convicted felon and drug addict who entered into an agreement with the state to provide testimony to avoid a lengthy prison sentence. The state had no plausible explanation why Godoy conducted the untaped interview with Woods. The defense strategy in the Minnitt and McCrimmon trials was to show that Godoy was the source of Woods' information about Minnitt's and McCrimmon's involvement in the case, and that during the untaped interview, he fed that information to Woods. If Godoy was indeed the source, Woods' testimony would not have helped the state. Similarly, without Woods, the state's case would be significantly weakened because no direct or physical evidence connected Minnitt to the crime, and the credibility of the remaining witnesses was questionable.

Id. at 434-35, 55 P.3d at 777-78.

Peasley was aware Godoy had begun investigating McCrimmon, Minnitt, and Fong before Godoy first met with Woods. Nonetheless, during the initial 1993 joint trial, Peasley repeatedly told the jury and elicited from Godoy information to the contrary--that police did not have the suspects' names until after Godoy interviewed Woods on September 8, 1992--thus bolstering Woods's credibility. Peasley repeated this conduct during Minnitt's 1997 retrial, asking the detective "a series of questions designed to erase any doubt that the source of Godoy's information could have been anyone but Woods." *Id. at 436, 55 P.3d at 779.* One week after the jury in Minnitt's initial retrial failed to reach a verdict, McCrimmon's retrial began. By this time McCrimmon's defense counsel had learned of Godoy's false testimony and vigorously pursued the issue. During McCrimmon's trial, Godoy admitted he testified falsely at Minnitt's trial because he feared causing a mistrial by revealing information obtained from a confidential informant. The jury ultimately acquitted McCrimmon on all charges.

Based on his misconduct in the McCrimmon and Minnitt trials, Peasley was later disbarred from the practice of law. *In Re Peasley, 208 Ariz. 27, 90 P.3d 764 (2004).*

Post conviction Proceedings

On direct appeal, Fong was represented by his trial attorney, James Stueringer. After the Arizona Supreme Court denied appellate relief on August 19, 1996, Stueringer sought certiorari in the United States Supreme Court. That petition was denied on May 19, 1997. *Soto-Fong v. Arizona, 520 U.S. 1231, 117 S. Ct. 1826, 137 L. Ed. 2d 1033 (1997).* In February 1998, Stueringer's son was arrested in Ohio for various criminal offenses. (Doc. 46, Ex. 61.) Stueringer asked Peasley, the prosecutor in Fong's case, for assistance, and Peasley ultimately wrote a letter to an Ohio judge in June 1998 urging probation for Stuehringer's son. (Doc. 46, Ex. 60.) Around this same time, Stuehringer, acting *pro bono,* wrote a letter defending Peasley against charges of ethical misconduct lodged with the state bar by McCrimmon's defense lawyer. On December 17, 1998, the Arizona Supreme Court issued its mandate in Petitioner's case and appointed new counsel to represent him in post conviction proceedings. In May 2000, the State Bar of Arizona filed a formal complaint against Peasley and the Pima County Attorney hired Stueringer to defend Peasley in the disciplinary proceeding. (Doc. 46, Exs. 62, 63.)

On August 20, 1999, Petitioner filed his first state PCR petition raising numerous claims, including prosecutorial misconduct based on alleged perjured testimony from Detective Godoy concerning his investigation of Petitioner. He also raised several claims of ineffective assistance of counsel (IAC), challenging *inter alia* Stueringer's failure to retain an identification expert, failure to call Petitioner as a witness, failure to challenge Godoy's testimony both during trial and on appeal, and decision to call Keith Woods as a witness. In supplemental filings dated November 13, 2000, and July 9, 2001, Petitioner added claims alleging conflict of interest arising from Stueringer's representation of Peasley in the state bar proceedings and a violation of *Brady v. Maryland* from the prosecutor's failure to disclose one of Godoy's reports. All told, Petitioner raised 35 claims in his PCR petition.

In August 2000, the State Bar of Arizona sought clarification concerning Stuehringer's representation of Peasley in light of Stuehringer's role as Petitioner's trial counsel. (Doc. 183-1 at 95, Ex. 129.) In January 2001, the state bar hearing officer found no conflict because the allegations in Peasley's disciplinary case arose from his conduct in the trials of McCrimmon and Minnitt, not Petitioner. (Doc. 184-1 at 88-90, Ex. 131 at 4-6.) The officer further ordered that Stuehringer could not be called as a witness and that it was unclear how any confidential communications between Petitioner and Stuehringer could relate to Peasley's conduct in prosecuting McCrimmon and Minnitt. (*Id.*)

In January and August 2001, Pima County Superior Court Judge Gordon Alley, serving in place of the deceased trial judge, held evidentiary hearings on Petitioner's ineffectiveness claims. (Doc. 144-1 at 2, Ex. U; Doc. 144-2 at 2, Ex. V; Doc. 195-1 at 58, Ex. 170.) Because Godoy was under indictment for perjury stemming from the McCrimmon and Minnitt trials, he invoked his rights under the *Fifth Amendment* and refused to testify. Stuehringer testified as to his defense strategy, and the court also heard testimony from several other witnesses, including Peasley, regarding the alleged *Brady* and prosecutorial misconduct violations.

Judge Alley unexpectedly died prior to ruling on Petitioner's claims. Judge Clark Munger was reassigned to the case, and the parties agreed that approximately half of Petitioner's claims could be decided without further evidentiary development. In June 2002 the state court issued a 34-page ruling addressing those claims. (Doc. 144-3 at 120, Ex. X.) At Petitioner's request the court held another evidentiary hearing in August 2002 on the remaining claims. (Doc. 144-3 at 2, Ex. W.) However, Petitioner did not present any new witnesses. Stuehringer, Peasley, and two other witnesses provided testimony substantially similar to that given at the 2001 hearing. Although no longer under indictment, Godoy was not called as a witness. In October 2002, the court issued a 29-page ruling rejecting the remaining claims. (Doc. 144-3 at 152, Ex. Y.)

Following this Court's order staying federal habeas proceedings pending resentencing in light of *Roper* and exhaustion of new claims relating to actual innocence and a Vienna Convention violation, Petitioner's federal habeas counsel were appointed as counsel for Petitioner by the state court and filed a second PCR petition raising (and re-raising) numerous claims. The actual innocence claim was based primarily on a January 2005 article from *The New Yorker* magazine which contained a summary of a statement by an alleged new witness, Carole Grijalva-Figueroa, who claimed she was the "lookout" during the El Grande Market robbery and that Petitioner, McCrimmon, and Minnitt were not involved. (Doc. 47, Ex. 67.) In mid-2005, the state court vacated Petitioner's death sentence, summarily dismissed the majority of Petitioner's successive PCR claims on procedural grounds, and directed Petitioner to obtain an affidavit from Grijalva-Figueroa to substantiate the innocence allegation. (Doc. 146-2 at 126, Ex. PP.) In January 2006, the court denied relief when Petitioner failed to produce any supporting evidence. (Doc. 146-3 at 27, Ex. UU.) The Arizona Court of Appeals affirmed. *State v. Soto-Fong,* No. 2 CA-CR 2006-0091 & No 2 CA-CR 2006-0056-PR (consolidated) (Ariz. App. May 3, 2007) (unpublished memorandum decision). (Doc. 146-3 at 67, Ex. WW.)

Subsequently, Petitioner filed a third PCR petition in state court, again asserting an actual innocence claim and requesting leave to conduct discovery. (Doc. 232-1 at 12, Ex. B.) In May 2009, the PCR court denied discovery and dismissed the petition, finding the claims precluded because they had been addressed previously. (Doc. 232-1 at 57, Ex. E.) Accepting a discretionary petition for review, the court of appeals denied relief. *State v. Soto-Fong, No. 2 CA-CR 2009-0294-PR, 2010 Ariz. App. Unpub. LEXIS 467, 2010 WL 1138956 (Ariz. App. Mar. 25, 2010)* (unpublished memorandum decision). (Doc. 232-1 at 93, Ex. G.)

STANDARD OF REVIEW

Because Petitioner initiated this habeas proceeding after the effective date of the Antiterrorism and Effective Death Penalty Act (AEDPA), relief can be granted on claims denied on the merits only if the state court's adjudication either:

> (1) resulted in a decision that was contrary to, or involved an unreasonable application of, clearly established Federal law, as determined by the Supreme Court of the United States; or
> (2) resulted in a decision that was based on an unreasonable determination of the facts in light of the evidence presented in the State court proceeding.

28 U.S.C. § 2254(d). In conducting review under *§ 2254(d)(1)*, this Court "is limited to the record that was before the state court that adjudicated the claim on the merits." *Cullen v. Pinholster, 131 S. Ct. 1388, 1398, 179 L. Ed. 2d 557 (2011)*.

DISCUSSION

I. CLAIM A: PROSECUTORIAL MISCONDUCT

Petitioner asserts that his rights under the *Fifth*, *Sixth*, *Eighth*, and *Fourteenth Amendments* were violated by prosecutorial misconduct. He divides the specific allegations underlying this claim into three categories: (1) Testimonial Evidence; (2) Physical Evidence; and (3) Confrontation, Abuse of Process & Other Misconduct. Each of these categories contain multiple allegations. Petitioner also asserts deprivation of his rights based on the cumulative effect of the alleged misconduct.

A.Testimonial Evidence

Prosecutorial misconduct will rise to a constitutional violation warranting federal habeas relief only if such conduct "so infected the trial with unfairness as to make the resulting conviction a denial of due process." *Darden v. Wainwright, 477 U.S. 168, 181, 106 S. Ct. 2464, 91 L. Ed. 2d 144 (1986).* In *Napue v. Illinois, 360 U.S. 264, 269, 79 S. Ct. 1173, 3 L. Ed. 2d 1217 (1959),* the Supreme Court held "that a conviction obtained through the use of false evidence, known to be such by representatives of the State, must fall under the *Fourteenth Amendment*." To prevail on a *Napue* claim, Petitioner must show that (1) the testimony was actually false, (2) the prosecution knew or should have known that the testimony was false, and (3) the false testimony was material. *Hayes v. Brown, 399 F.3d 972, 984 (9th Cir. 2005)* (en banc). False testimony is material if there is "any reasonable likelihood that [it] could have affected the judgment of the jury," in which case the conviction must be set aside. *United States v. Agurs, 427 U.S. 97, 103, 96 S. Ct. 2392, 49 L. Ed. 2d 342 (1976).* "Under this materiality standard, [t]he questions is not whether the defendant would more likely than not have received a different verdict with the evidence, but whether in its absence he received a fair trial, understood as a trial resulting in a verdict worthy of confidence." *Hayes, 399 F.3d at 984* (quotation omitted).

1. Keith Woods

Petitioner asserts that the prosecution failed to disclose a report by a Detective Nunez indicating that the prosecutor, Kenneth Peasley, was waiting with Detective Godoy when arresting officers brought Keith Woods into the police station on November 20 and that Peasley was present during the untaped portion of Woods's statement that day. Petitioner next alleges that Peasley and Godoy coached Woods to correct inconsistencies from his earlier September 8 statement, including for the first time linking "Cha-Chi" to Petitioner. From this, Petitioner argues that Peasley committed misconduct by knowingly using Woods's "false" testimony at trial. (Doc. 94 at 84.)

Respondents assert that this aspect of Claim A was not properly exhausted. Because the claim is meritless, the Court declines to reach this issue. *See 28 U.S.C. § 2254(b)(2)* (allowing denial of unexhausted claims on the merits); *Rhines v. Weber, 544 U.S. 269, 277, 125 S. Ct. 1528, 161 L. Ed. 2d 440 (2005).*

Petitioner does not identify or reference the specific parts of Woods's testimony that are allegedly false. Although Petitioner characterizes Woods as the "state's leading witness" (Doc. 94 at 84), Woods was called as a witness at Petitioner's trial by the defense, not, as in the McCrimmon and Minnitt trials, by the prosecution. (Doc. 147-2 at 4, Ex. DDD (RT 10/15/93) at 3.). On cross-examination by Peasley, Woods confirmed his September 8 statement to Godoy that McCrimmon and Minnitt said Cha-Chi, a former market employee, had set up the robbery. (*Id.* at 60, Ex. DDD at 59.) Woods also testified to his November 20 statement, in which he for the first time described Cha-Chi as "Martin" and "Betty Christopher's boyfriend." (*Id.* at 60-61, Ex. DDD at 59-60.) After detailing his conversation with McCrimmon and Minnitt, Peasley asked Woods to confirm a pretrial interview with Stuehringer, during which Woods said he had assumed Cha-Chi wore a mask because it was a robbery, not because McCrimmon and Minnitt actually mentioned a mask. Woods also denied that Godoy ever told him what to say, suggested he lie, or threatened him to provide a particular statement. (*Id.* at 69, Ex. DDD at 68.)

In these proceedings, Petitioner, relying on a declaration signed by Woods on August 11, 2005, asserts summarily that Woods "now admits his testimony was false and coerced." (Doc. 94 at 31.) The declaration states in part that Woods "did not know who Martin Soto Fong or 'Cha-Chi' was until Detective Godoy told me they were the same person," that Godoy met with him "at least 10 times before trial," and that he learned for the first time from Godoy that "Cha-Chi worked at the El Grande Market." (Doc. 93-2 at 205, Ex. 98 at 1.) Woods also states that he met with Peasley, who told him portions of his story "were mixed up or wrong" and that Peasley would "correct" him. (*Id.* at 206, Ex. 98 at 2.)

Although not entirely clear, it appears Petitioner's claim of "false testimony" rests on an allegation that Woods's November 20 statement to police is itself false and thus Peasley's cross-examination of Woods concerning this statement amounted to misconduct. (*See* Doc. 181 at 232 n.72.) Although the November statement does not contradict the September statement in any significant manner, it does include the additional "Martin" and "Betty Christopher's boyfriend" details that more directly implicated Petitioner. In his declaration, Woods now claims, "The person that originally told me about what happened inside the El Grande told me 'Cha-Chi' was involved but did not otherwise identify him in any way.'" (Doc. 93-2 at 206, Ex. 98 at 2.) However, Woods does not assert that Godoy or Peasley coached or coerced him to provide the additional identifying details about Cha-Chi during the November interview. Woods does claim that Peasley said he would "correct" him, but the declaration does not state whether the meeting with Peasley was in regard to Woods's testimony at the McCrimmon and Minnitt preliminary hearing and trial or in preparation for Woods's recorded statement on November 20. Finally, although Woods now says it was Godoy who first told him Cha-Chi was a former market employee, this was not a new detail revealed during the November interview; rather, Woods made that assertion in his initial September statement. Petitioner also provides a transcript of a December 2004 interview with Tanisha Price Woods, who at the time of the murders was Keith Woods's girlfriend. Without elaboration, Price Woods claims Godoy "would just like feed [Keith] information." (Doc. 47, Ex. 88, at 7.) However, Keith Woods's declaration post-dates the interview with Price Woods, and he does not assert therein that Godoy told him to provide the additional identifying details about Cha-Chi, which is the allegation before this Court.

Petitioner's claim is highly speculative. While Woods's declaration implies that the additional identifying information about Cha-Chi provided in the November statement did not come from McCrimmon or Minnitt, it does not directly implicate either Godoy or Peasley. Thus, even assuming Woods's testimony on cross-examination regarding his November 20 statement was false, Petitioner's claim fails because he has not alleged sufficient facts demonstrating that the prosecution knew or should have known of the alleged falsity.

2. Detective Godoy

Petitioner argues that the prosecution knowingly suborned false testimony from Detective Godoy as to when Petitioner, McCrimmon, and Minnitt first became suspects. (Doc. 94 at 85.) Petitioner raised this claim in his first PCR petition. (Doc. 143-2 at 19-30, Ex. J at 16-27.) Petitioner also argues that Peasley improperly vouched for Godoy's credibility in closing argument. That issue is addressed in Section I.C below along with Petitioner's other allegations of misconduct in closing argument.

Background

In a report dated September 15, 1992, Godoy described receiving on August 31 a call from an anonymous tipster, who claimed a black man named "McKinney" and another person nicknamed "Cha-Chi" were involved in the market murders. (Doc. 93-1 at 30, Ex. 26 at 1.) This report further stated that Godoy received a second call on August 31 from Sgt. Zimmerling, who relayed that a reliable confidential informant told him the murders were committed by a young black male named Christopher McCrimmon and a Mexican male named Martin Soto, also known as Cha-Chi. (Id. at 30-31, Ex. 26 at 1-2.) The report then stated Godoy spoke with the Gee family and learned of an ex-employee named Martin Fong, who had worked at the market during the summer of 1991. (Id. at 31, Ex. 26 at 2.)

In a separate report dated September 9, 1992, apparently prepared for the Mariano's Pizza case, Godoy reported that the August 31 anonymous caller told him to look for "Martin Soto and a black guy named McKinney." (Doc. 46, Ex. 54 at 1.) This report then states that Sgt. Zimmerling's confidential informant gave him the names Cha-Chi and McCrimmon, and that Godoy learned from the Gang Unit that Martin Fong went by "Cha-Chi" and was an associate of McCrimmon's. Because the reports are inconsistent, Godoy's source of the name "Martin Soto" is unclear.

Prior to trial, defense counsel Stuehringer interviewed Sgt. Zimmerling as well as Detective Cuestas and Officer Cruze from the Gang Unit. Zimmerling stated that his confidential informant described the perpetrators as Chris McCrimmon and a Mexican kid by the name of Martin or Cha-Chi. (Doc. 93-2 at 160, Ex. 76 at 7.) Cuestas denied knowing Cha-Chi's identity and said Godoy had not asked him whether Cha-Chi was Martin Fong. (Doc. 45, Ex. 46.) In response to Cuestas' inquiry, Cruze said he was not familiar with anyone named Cha-Chi. (Doc. 93-2 at 5, Ex. 71 at 4.)

During Godoy's first day of direct trial testimony, the following exchange occurred:

> Q. What I'm going to do is this: Ask you to focus on the time period of June 24th until the end of August of 1992. During that time period, had you developed any information up to the end of August, had you developed any information that would lead you to believe that either Christopher McCrimmon, Andre Minnitt, or Martin Fong were suspects in the killings of these three men at the El Grande Market?
> A. No, sir.

(Doc. 187-1 at 183, Ex. 147 (RT 10/19/93) at 100.) The next day, during cross-examination, Stuehringer asked Godoy about Keith Woods's September 8 statement:

> Q. In the course of that statement is when you learn about Mr. McCrimmon and Mr. Minnitt?
> A. Yes.
> Q. And this third person named Cha-Chi?
> A. That's correct.

(Doc. 148-1 at 62-63, Ex. FFF (RT 10/20/93) at 61-62.) Stuehringer also elicited from Godoy that sometime between late June and late August Petitioner had been identified by the Gee family as a former employee. (*Id.* at 59, Ex. FFF at 58.)

On re-direct, Peasley asked Godoy about his contacts with the Gee family, and Godoy testified that he spoke to them a couple of times that summer and specifically asked about Petitioner after he became a focus of the case during the first week of September. (*Id.* at 88-89, Ex. FFF at 87-88.) Peasley then sought to question Godoy about how he had first gotten Petitioner's name, which prompted Stuehringer to object to admission of information obtained from an anonymous source. (*Id.* at 91, Ex. FFF at 90.) After the objection was overruled, Peasley continued:

> Q. Sir, I was asking you about your conversation with Sergeant Zimmerling of the Tucson Police Department. When was it that you actually spoke with Sergeant Zimmerling?

A. The exact date I believe was August 31st.

. . . .

Q. Without going into the nature of the information, did Sergeant Zimmerling give you information that you thought was pertinent to this particular case?

MR. STUEHRINGER: Judge, May I just have a continuing objection?

THE COURT: Yes, you may.

THE WITNESS: Yes.

Q. Was it after your conversation with Sergeant Zimmerling that you contacted the Gees and made inquiry about employment records?

A. Yes.

(*Id.* at 92-93, Ex. FFF at 91-92.)

In his first PCR petition, Petitioner asserted that Godoy had committed perjury at trial by claiming Petitioner had not been a suspect until after the September 8 Woods interview. (Doc. 143-2 at 19-20, Ex. J at 16-17.) He later added a claim that Godoy's September 9 report had never been disclosed and thus Stuehringer had been unaware of Godoy's false avowals that Zimmerling and the Gang Unit had identified Cha-Chi as Martin Soto Fong.[6] (Doc. 139, Ex. Q at 8.) After reviewing the trial record and holding an evidentiary hearing, the state court denied relief:

> Petitioner/defendant's argument is premised upon a finding that Detective Godoy perjured himself. The knowing use of perjured testimony on a critical issue is sufficient to require a new trial. *U.S. v. Young, 17 F.3d 1201 (9th Cir. 1994); State v. Razinha, 123 Ariz. 355, 599 P.2d 808 (1979 Div 2).*
>
> Initially, the Petitioner/defendant argues Det. Godoy provided the following perjured testimony:
>
> a) Woods was his initial source for the names of Minnett [sic], McCrimmon and Soto-Fong, and
>
> b) These three men had not been suspects before they were named by Woods on September 8, 1999.

Subsequently, Petitioner/defendant states the perjury consisted of Det. Godoy's testimony:

a) that Soto-Fong had not been a suspect in the El Grande case until Godoy interviewed Keith Woods on September 8, 1992, and

b) that Godoy had conducted no investigation into Soto-Fong until that date.

The perjury analysis of Petitioner/defendant's claim must focus on Det. Godoy's exact testimony rather than Petitioner/defendant's paraphrase or summarization of Det. Godoy's testimony.

Perjury is defined by statute in *Arizona Revised Statutes 13-2702*. Petitioner/defendant also asserts Det. Godoy admitted that he committed perjury as to these two statements. However, no references are given to transcripts of Det. Godoy's admission of perjury in *State v. Soto-Fong*. The State denies Det. Godoy made any such admissions. The court could not find any admission by Det. Godoy that he committed perjury in *State v. Soto-Fong*. The court is unaware of any judicial or administrative proceeding in which Det. Godoy's testimony in this case was determined to be perjury.

1) As to Det. Godoy's testimony on October 19, 1993, on page 100, lines 8 - 16: Petitioner/defendant concedes "This, technically was true (although misleading) . . ." If technically true it is not perjury as it is not false. . . .

2) As to Det. Godoy's testimony on October 20, 1993, starting on page 61: Petitioner/defendant focuses on Det. Godoy's testimony on October 20, 1993, beginning on page 61 at line 22 and continuing through page 62 line 18. Specifically, there appear to be two questions by Mr. Stuehringer concerning what happened at the September 8, 1992 meeting with Keith Woods and Det. Godoy's responses that might be objectionable:

Beginning at page 61, line 22:

"Q. In the course of that statement is when you learn about Mr. McCrimmon and Mr. Minnitt?

A. Yes.

Q. And this third person named Cha-Chi?

A. That's correct.

Q. I think you testified earlier this afternoon that after September 8th, your next contact with Mr. Woods wasn't until November 20th?

A. That's correct.

Q. So whatever information you had that you testified to between September 8th and November 20th came from that September 8th session?

A. Yes."

However, the court must consider Det. Godoy's entire testimony rather than take individual parts out of the context of the whole. Det. Godoy did not state that he had not heard of those three names before the September 8. On cross-examination Det. Godoy testified that somewhere in late June to late August time frame Det. Godoy had contact with members of the Gee family and asked them to supply names of present and former employees, and sooner or later found that Mr. Fong was a former employee. On re-direct, Det. Godoy was asked further about the information from the Gee family. Just as the prosecutor was delving into the very concern Petitioner/defendant now raises, the defense counsel objected to the question. A vigorous exchange took place between the prosecutor and defense counsel as to admissibility of Sgt. Zimmerling's information and other sources that implicated Mr. Soto-Fong. The prosecutor was attempting to elicit the information Petitioner/defendant now says Det. Godoy did not disclose. Det. Godoy could not testify in narrative form but must respond to direct questions. If the questions to elicit the information concerning the contents of the September 9, 1992 and September 15, 1992 reports were not asked, then Det. Godoy as the witnesses [sic] cannot be faulted. Defense counsel did not want to ask the questions and tried to stop the prosecutor when he asked the question. Of particular import as to the timing of the pre-September 8, 1992 information see the

Trial Record for October 20, 1993, at page 91, line 21-25 in which Det. Godoy testified he received the information about Mr. Soto-Fong on August 31, 1992.

Det. Godoy has not been indicted regarding his testimony in *State v. Soto-Fong.* The court finds Det. Godoy did not commit perjury in his testimony.

False impression analysis:

Petitioner/defendant's position does not fail if Det. Godoy's testimony was not technically perjury as defined in *ARS 13-2702* but leaves the jury with a false impression. [HN4] A defendant's due process rights are violated when the State elicits and argues testimony which "taken as a whole" leaves the jury with a "false impression." *Alcorta v. Texas, 355 U.S. 28 (1957), 78 S. Ct. 103, 2 L. Ed. 2d 9.*

If perjured or misleading testimony was given and defense counsel was able to expose the fallacy within the testimony then the testimony will no longer taint the verdict. The jury alone must weigh the testimony and the witnesses' credibility and decide what really happened. The courts will intercede only if the perjured or misleading testimony could not be challenged because it was not known to be perjured or misleading and the defendant could not have exposed the state's error and the jury could not, therefore, have considered that aspect in its deliberations. Even then the court will not automatically grant a new trial where there has been perjury. *State v. Orantez, 183 Ariz. 218, 902 P.2d 824 (1995).* A defendant is not entitled to a new trial every time a witness is impeached by an inconsistent statement at trial, even if it is a critical witness testifying on a critical issue.

Petitioner/defendant's trial counsel interviewed Detectives Cuestas, Zimmerling and Cruze prior to the trial. Defense counsel knew of the inconsistency between Det. Godoy's reports and what he was told by the other officers. It was part of defense counsel's strategy to not have the jury focus on the reports or what Det. Godoy knew before September 8, 1992.

Petitioner/defendant's trial strategy is critical in this issue. Defense counsel knew of Det. Godoy's September 9, 1992 and September 15, 1992 reports but as a reasoned strategy did not want the jury to know of either of those reports. Both reports deal with information Det. Godoy had prior to September 8, 1992 concerning possible perpetrators, including the Petitioner/defendant. The portion of Det. Godoy's testimony that is now alleged to be offensive was in response to defense counsel's artful questioning which attempted to elicit what Keith Woods had told Det. Godoy on September 8, 1992, but avoid an answer that included information Det. Godoy had before September 8, 1992 from other sources. The Petitioner/defendant now attacks Det. Godoy for answering the question in the manner defense counsel wanted him to answer the question. He also attacks the prosecutor, Kenneth Peasley, for not asking questions about Det. Godoy's pre-September 8 knowledge when defense counsel did not want that information to go to the jury. In apparent contradiction, Petitioner/defendant agrees the prosecutor tried to bring in the evidence Det. Godoy had about the suspects prior to September 8, 1992. In fact, the prosecutor did ask questions to elicit that information, see Trial Record October 20, 1993, page 89, line 7-10.

In overly simplified terms defense counsel had two options in his defense strategy:

1) utilize the September 9 and September 15 reports and the initial unrecorded portion of the September 8, 1992 interview with Keith Woods to attempt to show what Det. Godoy knew prior to meeting with Keith Woods and that he first fed the confidential informant information regarding the Petitioner/defendant to Keith Woods in the unrecorded portion of the interview and then elicited that same information back from him in the recorded portion of the interview in return for not prosecuting him on the parole [sic] violation which would have resulted in a twenty-five year prison term for Keith Woods, or

2) try to keep the pre-September 8, 1992 information from the jury (which the defense counsel and the prosecutor felt was not admissible anyway) and emphasize the September 8, 1992 recorded interview with Keith Woods in which Keith Woods referred to the third perpetrator as a Mexican dude named ChaChi who was masked, tie the ChaChi reference to Martin Garza, an Hispanic, who knew one or both of the co-defendants and lived in a referenced neighborhood and went by the nickname ChaChi, and then either exclude the November 20, 1992 interview or attempt to show that the new information in Keith Woods testimony as given in the November 20, 1992 interview was prompted by Det. Godoy and was a tradeoff for non-prosecution for the parol [sic] violation.

Defense counsel chose the second option after considered deliberation. It must be emphasized these were defense options and strategies NOT prosecution options or strategies. Petitioner/defendant now wants to blame the witness, Det. Godoy, and the prosecution for the defense strategy. If the defense counsel sought to keep out the two reports it was not incumbent upon the prosecution to make sure the jury knew of the reports.

New Evidence Analysis:

Petitioner/defendant seeks to expand this claim to include two distinct issues: 1) that perjured or misleading testimony violates due process and requires a new trial, and 2) that a witnesses' testimony or conduct in a subsequent trial of a co-defendant constitutes new evidence for purposes of impeachment. If Det. Godoy's testimony in *State v. Soto-Fong* was not perjury or otherwise constitutionally offensive, then the question shifts to whether his testimony or conduct in the subsequent McCrimmon/Minnett [sic] trials was so offensive or inconsistent with his testimony in this case that it constitutes new evidence sufficient to warrant a new trial. Any such inconsistent evidence or conduct would only be to impeach Det. Godoy.

New impeachment evidence is not evidence that will be remedied by a new trial. *Rule 32.1(e)(3). State v. Cooper, 166 Ariz. 126, 800 P.2d 992 (1990 Div. 1).*

The Petitioner/defendant's Rule 32 motion as to this claim is denied.

(Doc. 144-3 at 158-64, Ex. Y at 7-13 (footnotes omitted).)

Discussion

Petitioner asserts that the state court's ruling is based on both an unreasonable application of controlling federal law and an unreasonable determination of the facts under *28 U.S.C. § 2254(d)*. However, his argument with regard to unreasonable application of the law rests on the assertion that Godoy's testimony was false, Peasley knew it was false, and the testimony was material both substantively and to impeach Godoy's credibility. The Court therefore must first determine whether the state court's factual findings in this regard are objectively unreasonable. The Court concludes they are not.

Petitioner argues that Godoy's direct testimony was misleading because it implied that Godoy did not suspect Petitioner prior to August 31, when in fact Godoy noted in one of his reports that he had requested a list of former employees shortly after the murders and, according to an interview with the author of *The New Yorker* article, had been searching for but kept missing Fong. (Doc. 181 at 71; *see* Doc. 93-1 at 174, Ex. 52 at 16; Doc. 47, Ex. 67 at 57.) Petitioner also argues that Godoy lied during cross-examination when he answered "yes" to Stuehringer's question of whether it was in the course of Woods's September 8 statement that he learned about McCrimmon, Minnitt, and Cha-Chi. (Doc. 181 at 71-72.) The Court disagrees.

The fact that Godoy may have had Fong's name on a list of former employees does not mean that Godoy suspected him of the murders at that point in the investigation. In *The New Yorker* article, Godoy stated only that he had been searching for Fong to either "make him or clear him" as part of his investigation of all the market's employees. (Doc. 47, Ex. 67 at 57.) The question posed at trial by Peasley was whether Godoy had "developed any information" prior to the end of August that led him to believe McCrimmon, Minnitt, or Fong were "suspects." (Doc.

187-1 at 183, Ex. 147 (RT 10/19/93) at 100.) As Petitioner acknowledged in his first PCR petition, Godoy's negative answer was technically correct. (Doc. 143-2 at 20, Ex. J at 17.) The state court's determination that Godoy did not commit perjury when he testified that Petitioner was not a suspect prior to August 31 was not objectively unreasonable.

Similarly, the state court's finding that Godoy "did not state that he had not heard of those three names before the [sic] September 8" also was objectively reasonable. (Doc. 144-3 at 160, Ex. Y at 9.) On cross-examination Godoy acknowledged that he "learn[end] about" McCrimmon, Minnitt, and Cha-Chi in the course of Woods's September 8 statement; however, the question posed by Stuehringer did not specify what Godoy learned--i.e., their identities, their respective roles in the crime, etc.

The thrust of Petitioner's argument is that Godoy's cross-examination testimony left the jury "with the impression that Godoy received Martin Fong's name from Woods" on September 8. (Doc. 181 at 71.) However, Godoy testified on re-direct that Fong became a suspect on August 31, as a result of information obtained from Sgt. Zimmerling, not from any statement by Woods. In addition, Woods himself testified that McCrimmon and Minnitt never identified the third perpetrator as Martin Soto or Martin Fong, only as "Cha-Chi," "Martin," and "Betty Christopher's boyfriend." (Doc. 147-2 at 60, Ex. DDD (RT 10/15/93) at 59.) Therefore, the jury could not have been left with a false impression that Godoy obtained Petitioner's name from Woods.

Petitioner's case stands in sharp contrast to that of his co-defendants. There, Woods testified for the prosecution that McCrimmon and Minnitt had confessed to him their role in the murders, and Godoy testified falsely that he did not have the suspects' names prior to meeting with Woods on September 8 (when in fact both had been questioned the week before). Godoy also testified falsely at McCrimmon's and Minnitt's trial that he did not know a former employee was a participant in the murders until after the Woods interview, and Peasley repeated the falsehoods in both his opening statement and closing argument. Godoy's testimony greatly bolstered Woods's credibility because the jury was left with the impression that Godoy knew nothing about McCrimmon, Minnitt, or Fong prior to meeting with Woods. Given the absence of any other significant evidence implicating either McCrimmon or Minnitt in the market crimes, Woods was a critical prosecution witness. Thus, Godoy's and Peasley's misconduct materially affected the defense's ability to argue that Woods was fed the defendants' names. *See In Re Peasley, 208 Ariz. at 30-31, 90 P.3d at 767-68; Minnitt, 203 Ariz. at 435, 55 P.3d at 778.*

In this case, Woods was not a witness for the prosecution and did not testify to either hearing a confession from Petitioner or hearing Petitioner's name from McCrimmon or Minnitt. Indeed, Woods affirmatively testified that neither of Petitioner's co-defendants used Petitioner's name. Any possible misimpression from the brief exchange between defense counsel and Godoy that Godoy "learned" Petitioner's name from Woods was ameliorated on re-direct when Godoy testified that he had obtained Petitioner's name on August 31, over a week before first interviewing Woods. Although Godoy testified falsely in the subsequent McCrimmon and Minnitt trial, the state court's determination that he did not do so in Petitioner's case was not objectively unreasonable. *28 U.S.C. § 2254(d)(2).* Consequently, the state court's denial of this claim was neither contrary to nor based on an unreasonable application of *Napue. 28 U.S.C. § 2254(d)(1).*

Because Petitioner has failed to satisfy either prong of *§ 2254(d)*, his requests for discovery, expansion of the record, and an evidentiary hearing are denied. *See Pinholster, 131 S. Ct. at 1398.* Petitioner argues he is entitled to develop this claim because the state court's evidentiary hearing was limited to his ineffectiveness claims and thus he never received a hearing on his prosecutorial misconduct allegations. (Doc. 94 at 114-15.) However, Judge Munger ruled in his June 27, 2002 order that an evidentiary hearing would be held with regard to 17 of Petitioner's claims, including prosecutorial misconduct. (Doc. 144-3 at 121, Ex. X at 2.) In addition, Peasley twice was called as a witness during the PCR hearings and questioned with regard to alleged misconduct.

Confrontation, Abuse of Process & Other Misconduct

Petitioner alleges a plethora of additional instances of prosecutorial misconduct. These include limiting defense access to the fingerprint examiner, abusing the grand jury process, failing to investigate exculpatory leads, and making improper remarks in closing argument, including vouching for Godoy, commenting on Petitioner's right to remain silent, and inflaming the jury. (Doc. 94 at 95-108.)

Respondents assert, and Petitioner concedes, that his allegation concerning the fingerprint examiner was never raised in state court. (Doc. 139 at 37; Doc. 181 at 102-03.) Petitioner has no available state remedy to exhaust this claim now. Because, as discussed below, Petitioner has failed to establish cause and prejudice or a fundamental miscarriage of justice to excuse the default, this allegation is barred from merits review.

Respondents also assert that the grand jury allegation was found precluded by the state court in Petitioner's second PCR proceeding and is therefore defaulted. (Doc. 139 at 38.) The Court addresses this misconduct allegation as part of Claim B in Section II below.

Respondents do not allege lack of exhaustion or procedural default for Petitioner's remaining misconduct allegations. Nonetheless, this Court is not precluded from *sua sponte* reaching those issues. *See Vang v. Nevada, 329 F.3d 1069, 1073 (9th Cir. 2003)*. A review of the state record reveals that Petitioner never raised a claim challenging the prosecution's failure to investigate exculpatory leads. Because Petitioner has no available state remedies and is not excused from his procedural default on the grounds of cause and prejudice or a fundamental miscarriage of justice, this allegation is procedurally barred.

Petitioner's remaining allegations concerning Peasley's closing argument were raised in his first PCR petition. Specifically, he argued that Peasley improperly vouched for Godoy, commented on Petitioner's failure to testify or produce witnesses, inflamed the jury, and attacked defense counsel. (Doc. 143-2 at 62-71, Ex. J at 59-68.) In response to the PCR petition, the State argued that Petitioner had waived these issues by failing to object at trial and that they were precluded because the claims could and should have been raised on direct appeal. In its ruling, the PCR court noted that under Arizona's *Rule 32.2(a)(3)*, a defendant is precluded from relief on any claim that has been waived at trial, on appeal, or in a previous collateral proceeding. (Doc. 144-3 at 174, Ex. Y at 23.) The court further noted, however, that under *Stewart v. Smith, 202 Ariz. 446, 46 P.3d 1067 (2002)*, a claim of "sufficient constitutional magnitude" requires a knowing, voluntary, and intelligent waiver by the defendant, and the failure to raise such a claim may constitute ineffective assistance of counsel. (Doc. 144-3 at 174, Ex. Y at 23.) The court then concluded that none of the alleged misconduct, either individually or cumulatively, was of sufficient constitutional magnitude to require a knowing, voluntary, and intelligent waiver and were thus precluded. (*Id.*at 175-76, Ex. Y at 24-25.) The court further found that counsel was not ineffective for failing to previously raise the allegations. (*Id.* at 176, Ex. Y at 25.)

"A federal habeas court will not review a claim rejected by a state court 'if the decision of [the state] court rests on a state law ground that is independent of the federal question and adequate to support the judgment.'" [*51] *Beard v. Kindler, 130 S. Ct. 612, 614, 175 L. Ed. 2d 417 (2009)* (quoting *Coleman, 501 U.S. at 729.*) It is well established that Arizona's preclusion rule is independent of federal law, *see Stewart v. Smith, 536 U.S. 856, 860, 122 S. Ct. 2578, 153 L. Ed. 2d 762 (2002)*, and the Ninth Circuit has repeatedly determined that Arizona regularly and consistently applies its procedural default rules such that they are an adequate bar to federal review of a claim. *See, e.g., Ortiz, 149 F.3d at 932 (Rule 32.2(a)(3)* regularly followed and adequate). Because Petitioner has failed to overcome his procedural default, this aspect of Claim A is procedurally barred. Moreover, as discussed below in Section IV, they lack merit.

Cumulative Effect

Petitioner asserts that even if his individual allegations of misconduct do not warrant relief, cumulatively such misconduct demonstrates that his due process rights were violated. However, because Petitioner has not established any specific instance of misconduct, there can be no cumulative prejudicial effect.

II. CLAIM B: *BRADY* VIOLATIONS

Petitioner asserts that the prosecution failed to disclose the following exculpatory material: (1) Det. Godoy's September 9 report, which contradicts his September 15 report; (2) Det. Nunez's report, which reflects Peasley's presence at the police station on November 20; (3) Det. Fuller's report, which details how Keith Woods came to the attention of authorities; (4) reports indicating police contacts with potentially exculpatory witnesses; (5) Det. Wright's handwritten notes detailing evidence collection; (6) undisclosed benefits to Keith Woods, including permitting him to continue dealing drugs and shielding him from prosecution for his alleged role in the Mariano's Pizza case; and (7) the grand jury transcript from the pizzeria case, which demonstrates alleged misconduct by Peasley. (Doc. 94 at 117-26.)

A. Procedural Defenses

First, Respondents concede that Petitioner properly exhausted in his first PCR petition a claim based on the failure to disclose Godoy's September 9 report. (Doc. 139 at 39.) Accordingly, this aspect of Claim B will be addressed on the merits.

Next, Respondents contend Petitioner never exhausted claims based on a failure to disclose the Fuller report, Wright notes, and reports relevant to alleged exculpatory witnesses. (*Id.* at 39-40.) The Court agrees. Following denial of his first PCR petition, Petitioner filed a motion to reopen the proceedings, alleging that newly-discovered evidence demonstrated the prosecution had failed to disclose Wright's notes as well as other potentially exculpatory material from several witnesses. (Doc. 144-3 at 189-94, Ex. Z at 4-9.) However, the state court denied the motion, finding it procedurally improper and advising Petitioner to file a successive petition based on Rule 32's "newly-discovered evidence" or "actual innocence" exceptions if newly-discovered material facts existed. (Doc. 193-1 at 2, Ex. 156 at 1.) When Petitioner later filed his second PCR petition, the factual background section included references to Fuller's report, Wright's notes, and alternative lead information not investigated by police. (Doc. 146-2 at 25-28, 33, Ex. MM at 3-6, 11.) However, Petitioner did not allege a claim based on the failure to disclose these materials, despite asserting *Brady* violations on several other grounds. (*See id.* at 45-46.) Because Petitioner now has no available state remedies and is not excused from his procedural default on the grounds of cause and prejudice or a fundamental miscarriage of justice, these aspects of Claim B are procedurally barred.

Finally, Respondents acknowledge that the allegations regarding the Nunez report, undisclosed benefits to Woods, and the grand jury proceeding were raised in Petitioner's second PCR petition but argue they are defaulted because the state court found them precluded. (Doc. 139 at 40-42, 46-47.) Petitioner counters that the state court's preclusion ruling was based on successiveness, not waiver; therefore, his allegations are not barred from federal review. (Doc. 181 at 159.)

Petitioner raised a "failure to disclose" claim in his first PCR petition based on the Godoy report. Petitioner re-raised a "failure to disclose" claim in his second PCR petition based on newly-discovered evidence concerning the Nunez report, undisclosed benefits to Woods, and the pizzeria case's grand jury proceeding. The PCR court dismissed the claim as precluded by *Rule 32.2* because Petitioner had raised a similar claim in the first PCR petition. (Doc. 146-2 at 132, Ex. PP at 7.) On petition for review to the Arizona Court of Appeals, Petitioner argued that the superior court's preclusion ruling was erroneous because the claim was based on newly-discovered evidence under *Rule 32.1(e)* and demonstrated actual innocence under *Rule 32.1(h)*, both exceptions to preclusion. (Doc. 146-3 at 114, Ex. VV at 24.) The Court of Appeals disagreed, finding that "none of the claims at issue falls under the exceptions to the preclusion doctrine for claims already raised and ruled upon in prior post conviction proceedings. *See Ariz. R. Crim. P. 32.2(b).*" (Doc. 146-3 at 85, Ex. WW at 19.)

Invoking independent and adequate state grounds, the state court exercised its discretion and declined to address the merits of Petitioner's new allegations. Therefore, these aspects of Petitioner's "failure to disclose" claim are procedurally defaulted. Because as discussed below Petitioner has established neither cause and prejudice nor a fundamental miscarriage of justice, these allegations are procedurally barred. Moreover, as discussed next, they lack merit.

Merits Analysis

Under *Brady v. Maryland, 373 U.S. 83, 83 S. Ct. 1194, 10 L. Ed. 2d 215 (1963)*, the government has a constitutional obligation to disclose information favorable to the defense. A successful *Brady* claim requires three findings: (1) the government willfully or inadvertently suppressed evidence; (2) the evidence was favorable to the accused; and (3) the evidence was material to the issue of guilt or punishment. *Strickler v. Greene, 527 U.S. 263, 281-82, 119 S. Ct. 1936, 144 L. Ed. 2d 286 (1999)*; see *Banks v. Dretke, 540 U.S. 668, 691, 124 S. Ct. 1256, 157 L. Ed. 2d 1166 (2004)*; *Kyles v. Whitley, 514 U.S. 419, 433, 115 S. Ct. 1555, 131 L. Ed. 2d 490 (1995)*. Evidence is material for *Brady* purposes "if there is a reasonable probability that, had the evidence been disclosed to the defense, the result of the proceeding would have been different." *Kyles, 514 U.S. at 433* (quoting *United States v. Bagley, 473 U.S. 667, 682, 105 S. Ct. 3375, 87 L. Ed. 2d 481 (1985)*). This does not require a showing that the defendant would have been acquitted had the suppressed evidence been disclosed. *Id. at 434-35*. Instead, a *Brady* violation occurs if "the favorable evidence could reasonably be taken to put the whole case in such a different light as to undermine confidence in the outcome." *Id. at 435*. The duty to disclose includes impeachment as well as exculpatory material. *Bagley, 473 U.S. at 676*; *Giglio v. United States, 405 U.S. 150, 154, 92 S. Ct. 763, 31 L. Ed. 2d 104 (1972)*.

1. Godoy Report

In his September 15 report Godoy described receiving two phone calls on August 31 with information about possible suspects in the market murders--the first from an anonymous caller claiming a black man named "McKinney" and another person nicknamed "Cha-Chi" were involved, and the other from Sgt. Zimmerling, whose confidential informant identified Christopher McCrimmon and a Mexican male named Martin Soto or Cha-Chi. (Doc. 44, Ex. 26; Doc. 93-1 at 31-32, Ex. 26 at 1-2.) However, in an earlier report dated September 9, Godoy attributed Martin Soto's name to the anonymous caller, not to Sgt. Zimmerling's confidential informant, and said he learned from the Gang Unit that Martin Fong went by Cha-Chi. (Doc. 46, Ex. 54 at 1.)

During his first PCR proceeding, Petitioner alleged that the prosecution had failed to disclose Godoy's September 9 report, which was prepared for the Mariano's Pizza case file. (Doc. 139, Ex. Q.) In denying relief on this claim, the state court ruled:

> Based on the evidence produced at the August 28, 2002 Rule 32 evidentiary hearing the court finds the state did timely disclose the Marianos case report dated 9/9/92 (Exhibit E) to

defense counsel. The court found both Mr. Stuehringer and Ms. Susan Grimes credible witnesses and finds that both were aware of and had seen the report prior to the Petitioner/defendant's trial.

The court also finds that defense counsel intentionally and with good reason did not want Exhibit E produced to the jury. Defense counsel's reasoned strategy was to exclude both the September 9, 1992 report (Exhibit E) and the September 15, 2002 report (Exhibit N). Petitioner/defendant has not shown why the decision not to use Exhibit E revealed ineptitude, inexperience, or lack of preparation. There may be a difference of opinion as to trial strategy but that does not lead to a conclusion of ineffective assistance of counsel. The trial strategy used in the Petitioner/defendant's trial was necessarily different than the strategies used in the trials of the Petitioner/defendant's co-defendants for one clear and compelling reason, the Petitioner/defendant's fingerprints were found at the crime scene in highly incriminating locations. There was no such physical evidence incriminating the co-defendants.

(Doc. 144-3 at 164-65, Ex. Y at 13-14.)

Petitioner argues that the state court's factual finding--that the report had been disclosed--is objectively unreasonable. He asserts that the state court failed to take into account that Stuehringer, and his long-time paralegal Susan Grimes, were operating under a conflict of interest from their work on Peasley's disciplinary case at the time of the Rule 32 evidentiary hearing. (Doc. 181 at 142.) He further contends that the state court's determination is unreasonable because Stuehringer's testimony regarding the report was equivocal and the court failed to consider other evidence suggesting non-disclosure. (*Id.* at 142-45.) Finally, Petitioner argues the finding is flawed because Stuehringer's defense strategy was to undermine Godoy's credibility and it is likely counsel would have emphasized the discrepancies between Godoy's September 9 and 15 reports had he known of them. (*Id.* at 144.)

Under the standard set forth in *§ 2254(d)(2)*, habeas relief is available only if the state court decision was based on an unreasonable determination of the facts. *Miller-El v. Dretke, 545 U.S. 231, 240, 125 S.*

Ct. 2317, 162 L. Ed. 2d 196 (2005). "[A] state-court factual determination is not unreasonable merely because the federal habeas court would have reached a different conclusion in the first instance." *Wood v. Allen, 130 S. Ct. 841, 849, 175 L. Ed. 2d 738 (2010); see also Rice v. Collins, 546 U.S. 333, 341-42, 126 S. Ct. 969, 163 L. Ed. 2d 824 (2006)* ("Reasonable minds reviewing the record might disagree about the prosecutor's credibility, but on habeas review that does not suffice to supersede the trial court's credibility determination.").

At the first Rule 32 hearing, Stuehringer testified that he assumed he was aware of the September 9 report because he and his paralegal reviewed a lot of materials from the Mariano's Pizza case file. (Doc. 144-1 at 108-09, Ex. U (RT 8/27/01) at 107-08.) Billing records documented several trips by Susan Grimes to the prosecutor's office to review disclosure, and she recalled seeing the report even though it was not included in a list of Godoy reports she generated from a case database. (*Id.* at 135-36, Ex. U at 134-35; Doc. 144-2 at 134-36, Ex. V (RT 8/28/01) at 133-35.) In addition, Stuehringer explained that he interviewed members of the Gang Unit before trial because "Godoy, somewhere along the line, had said that he found out from someone in the Gang Unit that Martin Fong had the nickname of Chachi." (Doc. 144-1 at 81, Ex. U (RT 8/27/01) at 80.) It is the September 9 report that references this information from the Gang Unit, not the September 15 report. Based on this record, the Court cannot say that the state court's finding that the September 9 report had been disclosed was objectively unreasonable.

In any event, even if the September 9 report was not disclosed, Petitioner's claim fails because he cannot show that the report was material. He asserts that Godoy's September 9 and 15 reports demonstrate that Godoy was lying about his information concerning Cha-Chi's identity before the September 8 interview with Woods. (Doc. 94 at 117.) This lie, he contends, is itself "highly exculpatory" and would have put Stuehringer "in a far better position to attack Godoy." (*Id.* at 117-18.) However, the record demonstrates that Stuehringer was already aware that Godoy did not get Fong's name from Sgt. Zimmerling or the Gang Unit and thus at least one of Godoy's reports contained false information.

There is no dispute that Stuehringer had the September 15 report, in which Godoy described getting the name "Martin Soto" from Zimmerling. In preparation for trial, Stuehringer interviewed Zimmerling, as well as Detective Cuestas and Officer Cruze from the Gang Unit. Zimmerling told Stuehringer that the informant described the Mexican male only as Martin and Cha-Chi, without an identifying last name, and neither Cuestas nor Cruze were aware of Cha-Chi's identity. In an April 1993 pretrial interview with Godoy, Stuehringer challenged Godoy's assertion that he had gotten the name "Martin Soto" from Zimmerling, and Godoy conceded that Zimmerling had not been the source of Martin's last name. (Doc. 144-1 at 95-96, Ex. U (RT 8/27/01) at 94-95.) Godoy further stated he got the name from the Gee family after asking them if there had been a former employee named Martin. (*Id.* at 96, Ex. U at 95.)

During a pretrial suppression hearing, Stuehringer again questioned Godoy about the source of Fong's name. Godoy testified that he believed Zimmerling had told him Cha-Chi was someone who "used to work at the store by the name of Soto, Martin Soto." (*Id.* at 139, Ex. U at 138.) Stuehringer then impeached Godoy with his earlier pretrial interview, in which he acknowledged Zimmerling had not been the source of Petitioner's name. (*Id.* at 140, Ex. U at 139.) He also cross-examined Godoy about the information the defense had obtained from Cuestas and Cruze, who denied knowing Cha-Chi's identity and thus could not have provided a link between Cha-Chi and Petitioner. (*Id.*)

It is apparent from this record that with or without the September 9 report, Stuehringer was well aware of the discrepancy in the September 15 report concerning Zimmerling and the source of Petitioner's name. Stuehringer testified in the Rule 32 hearing that he had interviewed Zimmerling, Cuestas, and Cruze to disprove Godoy's assertion that Cha-Chi was Martin Fong. (*Id.* at 77-85, Ex. U at 76-84.) He knew before trial that Godoy's September 15 report was not credible and contained the false claim that Zimmerling had identified Cha-Chi as Martin Soto. Nonetheless, Stuehringer chose to forgo presenting this evidence at trial. Given these facts, the Court concludes that the September 9 report would not have affected Stuehringer's chosen trial strategy, the reasonableness of which is discussed below in Section IV. Thus, the report was not material, and Petitioner's claim also fails on this ground.

2. Nunez Report

Petitioner claims that the prosecution failed to disclose a report from Det. Nunez, wherein Nunez indicates that Peasley was waiting with Godoy for the arresting officers to bring Keith Woods to the police station on November 20. (Doc. 94 at 119.) Although the report contains a disclosure stamp, Petitioner asserts that the report is "conspicuously absent" from a disclosure list generated from trial counsel's database. (Doc. 46, Exs. 58, 64.) Because this allegation was not raised in his first PCR petition, during the state evidentiary hearing Petitioner did not question Stuehringer or his paralegal about the report, and there is nothing in the record regarding the breadth of counsel's database (i.e., whether every piece of disclosure was entered into the system). Even assuming the report was never disclosed, it does not provide evidence favorable to the defense and is not material.

The Nunez report documents police efforts to locate Keith Woods, who had gone into hiding apparently in an effort to avoid testifying against McCrimmon and Minnitt at an impending preliminary hearing. The fact that the prosecutor was at the police station and may have spoken with Woods provides neither exculpatory nor impeaching evidence. As discussed with respect to Claim A, Woods did not claim in his declaration that either before or during the November 20 recorded statement Peasley coerced or threatened him to add the additional identifying information about Cha-Chi or to clarify that neither McCrimmon nor Minnitt actually said Cha-Chi wore a mask. The entirety of the declaration with respect to Peasley reads: "When I met with Mr. Peasley at [the Tucson Police Department] he told me that portions of my story were mixed up or wrong and he would correct me." (Doc. 93-2 at 206, Ex. 98 at 2.) Woods does not state when this meeting took place, whether it was in preparation for the November 20 statement or Woods's testimony at the McCrimmon/Minnitt preliminary hearing and subsequent trial, or whether Peasley ever actually corrected any aspects of his "story." In short, there is simply no foundation for Petitioner's conjecture that the Nunez report "corroborates Woods' admission that

Peasley and Godoy conspired together to fabricate his testimony." (Doc. 94 at 120.)

3. Benefits to Keith Woods & Grand Jury Transcript

Petitioner alleges the prosecution failed to disclose that Keith Woods was permitted to continue dealing drugs between his September 8 and November 20 statements and was shielded from prosecution in the Mariano's Pizza case. (Doc. 94 at 124-25.) He further contends the prosecution failed to disclose the entirety of a transcript from the grand jury's investigation into the pizzeria robbery and non-fatal shooting, which would have substantiated the allegation that Peasley abused the grand jury process to protect Woods. (*Id.* at 125-26.)

The only support for the drug-selling allegation is a 2004 interview with Woods's girlfriend, who claims Godoy "probably" said Woods could continue selling drugs. (Doc. 47, Ex. 88, at 16.) In response to the question, "Did Keith ever tell you that Godoy had told him he could continue to sell drugs?", Price Woods responded "probably not in so many words but he didn't tell him to stop or I'll arrest you if you don't, or anything." (*Id.* at 17.) She further offered that Godoy knew Woods had sold drugs before and that he did not have a job. (*Id.*) These statements, even if true, do not establish that Godoy affirmatively told Woods he could continue selling drugs with impunity. Similarly, Petitioner only speculates concerning Peasley's motives during the Mariano's Pizza grand jury proceedings. Nonetheless, even assuming the prosecution was under an obligation to disclose these alleged benefits to Woods and that such disclosure did not occur, they do not constitute material impeachment in light of the information about Woods revealed at trial.

Petitioner insists that conviction in the Mariano case would have made Woods "useless to the state as a witness" and that the disclosure violation obscured the discovery of additional benefits Woods received "by turning state's evidence." (*Id.*) However, the Court reiterates that Woods did not testify on behalf of the prosecution. As discussed in depth below, Stuehringer called Woods as a defense witness as part of his strategy to undermine Godoy's credibility and offer the jury an alternate suspect. During his direct examination of Woods, Stuehringer brought out the following information concerning Woods's character:

he previously was convicted of at least three felonies as well as giving false information to a police officer, served time in prison twice, was arrested for cocaine possession within a week of release from prison in August 1992, and was facing 25 years to life if convicted on the cocaine charge. (Doc. 147-2 at 5-13, Ex. DDD (RT 10/15/93) at 4-12.) Woods testified that he agreed to be an informant for an unrelated case, was released, and then rearrested on September 8 when he failed to contact police with the promised information. (*Id.* at 14-17, Ex. DDD at 13-16.) Woods further testified that police threatened him with the cocaine charge and *told him he was a possible suspect in an armed robbery case.*(*Id.* at 20, Ex. DDD at 19.) It was at this point Woods offered police information about the El Grande murders, and Det. Godoy was called in. (*Id.* at 19, Ex. DDD at 18.)

At Petitioner's trial, the jury was aware that Woods was facing a possible life sentence for cocaine possession and was a suspect in an unrelated armed robbery case when he agreed to provide information concerning the market murders. Consequently, the Court finds there is no reasonable probability the result of the proceeding would have been different had the jury also learned that Det. Godoy chose not to pursue Woods for continuing to sell drugs and that prosecutors chose not to seek indictment against Woods for the armed robbery.

DARREL ESTON LEE, PETITIONER, VS. CHARLES L. RYAN, ET AL., RESPONDENTS.

NO. CV-04-39-PHX-MHM UNITED STATES DISTRICT COURT FOR THE DISTRICT OF ARIZONA

(Text added/modified for emphasis). The Attorney General perpetrated fraud upon the court by failing to disclose that in Arizona it is the norm, a systemic problem, improperly vouch for their witnesses, appealed to the passions of the jury thereby preventing a meaningful defense. Courts consistently sanction this systematic practice refusing to find bad faith thereby condoning this misconduct which is on the rise . As it was never their intent to subject the state's case to a meaningful adversarial process, when viewed in the totality, and not in isolation, this should constitute fraud upon the court by these lawyers. Failure to disclose this systemic problem is fraud upon the court.

COUNSEL: For Darrel Eston Lee, Petitioner: Carmen Lynne Fischer, LEAD ATTORNEY, Law Office of Carmen L Fischer, Phoenix, AZ; Stephen E Eberhardt, LEAD ATTORNEY, Attorney at Law, Tinley Park, IL. For Charles L Ryan, Director, Arizona Department of Corrections, Charles Goldsmith, Warden, Arizona State Prison - Eyman Complex, Dora B Schriro, Director, Arizona Department of Corrections, Respondents: Kent E Cattani, Office of the Attorney General, Criminal Appeals Section, Phoenix, AZ.

FACTUAL AND PROCEDURAL BACKGROUND

The Arizona Supreme Court summarized the facts surrounding the crime and Petitioner's arrest, trial, and conviction as follows:

On December 5, 1991, defendant Darrel E. Lee and a companion, Karen Thompson, approached 57-year-old John Anderson as he was leaving a Phoenix medical clinic and asked him for a ride. When Anderson agreed, they got into his car. Although unarmed, Lee announced that he had a gun and directed Anderson to drive south on the freeway. When they arrived in Chandler, Thompson demanded Anderson's wallet, which contained a small amount of cash, some credit cards, and an automatic teller machine (ATM) card. Thompson, accompanied by defendant, used the ATM and credit cards repeatedly throughout the next five days, both before and after Anderson's murder.

At some point, defendant suggested that they tie up Anderson and dump him alongside the road. After binding his hands and feet and placing him in a ditch, however, the couple decided not to leave him there. Instead, they put him in the trunk of the car. During most of this time, Anderson was pleading for his life.

Defendant and Thompson drove back to Phoenix and then toward California, stopping frequently to use cocaine and alcohol. They eventually decided to kill Anderson to avoid apprehension. Defendant stated that he would asphyxiate Anderson with the car's exhaust fumes and obtained a hose for this purpose. The couple discussed the anticipated killing as they continued their journey. Approximately eight hours after placing Anderson in the trunk, defendant and Thompson turned back toward Phoenix.

Anderson somehow managed to get untied and pry open the trunk of the car. He found a windshield sun screen reading "NEED HELP; CALL POLICE," and held it out of the vehicle. Two men in another car saw the sign and the frightened victim and called the police at the first available telephone. At approximately 11:45 p.m., two officers responded to the call. Because of darkness and rugged terrain in the area, however, they were able to conduct only a rudimentary search.

Meanwhile, defendant had exited the interstate highway and stopped the car at about 10:30 p.m. He and Thompson attempted to suffocate Anderson with car fumes by running the hose from the exhaust pipe into the trunk, but were unsuccessful because Anderson kept pushing up the trunk lid. During a pause in which the couple used more cocaine and discussed the situation, the victim escaped from the trunk and attempted to flee. Defendant chased Anderson and wrestled him to the ground. Thompson then brought defendant a belt, with which he attempted to strangle Anderson. The belt broke, and defendant yelled for Thompson to get a rock. As defendant choked Anderson with his hands, Thompson hit the victim in the head with the rock, fracturing his skull.

Defendant and Thompson placed the body in the trunk of the car. After driving to California, and then back to Phoenix, the couple eventually went to Tucson. There, they purchased a shovel and buried Anderson in a shallow grave outside the city.

The foregoing facts are taken primarily from Thompson's testimony. Defendant initially denied all participation in the crimes, later admitted some involvement with the car and the credit card spending in California, and finally confessed to a defense-requested psychiatrist that he was present during the murder and was holding Anderson down when Thompson struck him. Evidence found at the scene of the crime included the sun shield, pieces of a belt containing blood spatters, defendant's prescription sunglasses, and a rock bearing blood and hair. Anderson's trifocals were found in the trunk of the automobile, along with blood stains matching his type. Information given by Thompson after she entered into a plea agreement in April 1992 led to the discovery of the victim's remains.

On January 28, 1992, a La Paz County grand jury indicted defendant and Thompson on one count each of first-degree murder, kidnapping, theft, armed robbery, and credit card theft. Defendant pleaded not guilty to all charges. Thompson entered a plea of guilty to first-degree murder and armed robbery. A condition of her plea agreement was that she testify against defendant. On November 18, 1992, following a jury trial, defendant was convicted on all counts.

State v. Lee, 185 Ariz. 549, 552-53, 917 P.2d 692, 695-96 (1996).

La Paz County Superior Court Judge Michael Irwin sentenced Petitioner to death for the murder and to terms of imprisonment for the other counts. On direct appeal, the Arizona Supreme Court affirmed. *Id. at 559, 917 P.2d at 702*. Petitioner did not seek certiorari. At the time of Petitioner's trial, Arizona law required trial judges to make all factual findings relevant to capital punishment and to determine sentence. Following the Supreme Court's decision in *Ring v. Arizona, 536 U.S. 584, 122 S. Ct. 2428, 153 L. Ed. 2d 556 (2002)*, which held that a jury must determine the existence of facts rendering a defendant eligible for capital punishment, Arizona's sentencing scheme was amended to provide for jury determination of eligibility factors, mitigating circumstances, and sentence.

Petitioner filed a petition for post-conviction relief ("PCR") pursuant to Rule 32 of the Arizona Rules of Criminal Procedure in June 1999. Following an evidentiary hearing, PCR Judge William Schafer denied relief in May 2003. Subsequently, the Arizona Supreme Court summarily denied a petition for review.

Petitioner then commenced these proceedings and filed an amended habeas petition on November 29, 2004. (Doc. 52.) Petitioner moved for discovery, an evidentiary hearing, and expansion of the record on a number of claims. (Doc. 78.) On September 29, 2006, the Court denied Petitioner's consolidated motion and dismissed Claims 1 (in part), 2, 4 (in part), 5-B, 6, and 9-C as either procedurally defaulted or meritless. (Doc. 87.) The Court now addresses Petitioner's remaining claims.

<u>Claim 4-A</u>

Petitioner contends that he was denied the right to a fundamentally fair trial when the prosecutor vouched for two prosecution witnesses during closing argument. This claim was exhausted on direct appeal and thus entitled to review on the merits.

Background

During closing argument, the prosecutor commented on Karen Thompson's testimony while discussing the evidence linking Petitioner to the crime scene:

> The sheriff's office found the glasses out at the scene, all the things described out here [sic] the shoe was found at the scene; the pool of blood next to the belt. The blood's analyzed, found to be of a type consistent with Mr. Anderson; the drag marks; the other section of the belt just as it was described by Karen; and everything that Karen said about what happened as she talked about getting off the exit is consistent again with what Hornback and Wagner saw, but getting off on that exit, going across the overpass, and she said initially they went on past there about a quarter of a mile and they stopped.
>
> *Now, she's been, I think, honest when she says she wasn't even aware that Hornback and Wagner had seen her and made these observations.*

(RT 11/18/92 at 51-52 (emphasis added).) During rebuttal argument, the prosecutor further stated:

Karen gave us some testimony that he was wearing those glasses that night, but my recollection of the testimony was never that he actually had those things on his face as he attacked Mr. Anderson out there. Maybe he - maybe he did. Maybe he had them in his pocket, you know. Maybe he had them who knows where.

. . . .

Is it critical to the State's case that he had those glasses on his face as he ran over Mr. Anderson? No, it's not, but he had them on his person somewhere because he left them there, and we know he left them there. There's no other evidence. *There's no other reasonable alternative, I believe, of how the glasses got there.*

(*Id.* at 108-10 (emphasis added).)

Regarding Gene Vernoy, the convenience store clerk who saw a man with Thompson shortly after the murder, the prosecutor argued:

So now all of a sudden, Gene Vernoy is being put on the spot, well if the guy that was with this woman was actually taller and he goes along with that and says, "yeah, he was taller," but I think there's a couple things about Gene Vernoy that you have to keep in mind.

First of all, other than they see thousands of people over time and the man could easily make an honest mistake in perception and memory about the man that was with Karen Thompson and to demonstrate that, maybe his memory was a little fuzzy in that regard.

If you recall, he thought the car they were in was a - was a yellow Toyota; thought the car was a yellow Toyota. No. That's not right; and again, this is not the fault of Mr. Vernoy. *I think he was an honest man, certainly an honest man, but I think he made a honest mistake* and that was demonstrated best, I think, in - when - Mr. Lee, Darrel's father, talked to him on the phone there and Mr. Vernoy said that he thought that he, Gene Vernoy, was taller than Karen, so this is how his perception of height operates here.

(*Id.* at 56-57 (emphasis added).)

Defense counsel did not object to any of these comments at trial. Accordingly, the Arizona Supreme Court on appeal reviewed Petitioner's vouching contentions only for fundamental error:

> It is impermissible for a prosecutor to place the prestige of the government behind his witness or suggest that information not presented to the jury supports a witness's testimony. That did not occur here. The prosecutor essentially conceded that Thompson and Vernoy had been mistaken in parts of their testimony (regarding the presence of another car in the area, and the size of the man seen with the woman). Moreover, the remark pertaining to defendant's glasses was more about the physical evidence at the scene than about Thompson's testimony. Defendant had maintained that the glasses were found in a position that would be unexpected if they had fallen off while being worn. The prosecutor's argument, read in context, was that even though Thompson might have been wrong when she said defendant had his glasses on during the struggle, the fact that they were found at the location made it immaterial whether they fell off his face or out of his pocket.
>
> . . . The evidence supporting Karen Thompson's story was compelling. The prosecution corroborated different parts of it with at least five independent witnesses. Moreover, Thompson was willing to implicate herself as the more active participant in the events that took place.

Even apart from Thompson's testimony, however, there was evidence that defendant was with her a few days before the killing, a few minutes before the victim disappeared from the medical center, and a few hours after his death; that Thompson was accompanied by a man less than an hour after the murder and by someone in the car with her minutes before it; that defendant had possession of the victim's car days later; and that defendant's prescription glasses, which he claimed to have lost on or about December 2, were seen on his face December 5, minutes before the victim disappeared, and were found by police at the scene of the homicide.

Vernoy's testimony was relatively tangential and served only to place Thompson with a man, perhaps taller than she, possibly mustached, and maybe Hispanic, in California shortly after the murder. The prosecutor's comments about it were insignificant.

Lee, 185 Ariz. at 554, 917 P.2d at 697 (citation omitted).

Discussion

Federal habeas review for a claim of prosecutorial misconduct is "the narrow one of due process, and not the broad exercise of supervisory power." *Darden v. Wainwright, 477 U.S. 168, 181, 106 S. Ct. 2464, 91 L. Ed. 2d 144 (1986)* (quoting *Donnelly v. DeChristoforo, 416 U.S. at 642*). In order to obtain relief, Petitioner must prove not only that the prosecutor's remarks and other conduct were improper but that they "so infected the trial with unfairness as to make the resulting conviction a denial of due process." *Id.; see also Johnson v. Sublett, 63 F.3d 926, 930 (9th Cir. 1995)* (habeas relief is limited to cases in which the petitioner can establish that prosecutorial misconduct resulted in actual prejudice); *Smith v. Phillips, 455 U.S. 209, 219, 102 S. Ct. 940, 71 L. Ed. 2d 78 (1982)* ("The touchstone of due process analysis in cases of alleged prosecutorial misconduct is the fairness of the trial, not the culpability of the prosecutor.").

In determining if a defendant's due process rights were violated by a prosecutor's remarks during closing argument, a reviewing court "must consider the probable effect [of] the prosecutor's [comments] on the jury's ability to judge the evidence fairly." *United States v. Young, 470 U.S. 1, 12, 105 S. Ct. 1038, 84 L. Ed. 2d 1 (1985)*. To make such an assessment, it is necessary to place the prosecutor's remarks in context. *See Boyde v. California, 494 U.S. 370, 385, 110 S. Ct. 1190, 108 L. Ed. 2d 316 (1990); United States v. Robinson, 485 U.S. 25, 33-34, 108 S. Ct. 864, 99 L. Ed. 2d 23 (1988); Williams v. Borg, 139 F.3d 737, 745 (9th Cir. 1998)*. In *Darden,* for example, the Court assessed the fairness of the trial by considering, among other circumstances, whether the prosecutor's comments manipulated or misstated the evidence; whether the trial court gave a curative instruction; and the weight of the evidence against the accused. *477 U.S. at 181-82*.

As a general rule, a prosecutor may not vouch for the credibility of a witness. *See Young, 470 U.S. at 18-19; Lawn v. United States, 355 U.S. 339, 359-60 n.15, 78 S. Ct. 311, 2 L. Ed. 2d 321, 1958-1 C.B. 540 (1958); Berger v. United States, 295 U.S. 78, 86-88, 55 S. Ct. 629, 79 L. Ed. 1314 (1935).* "Vouching consists of placing the prestige of the government behind a witness through personal assurances of the witness's veracity, or suggesting that information not presented to the jury supports the witness's testimony." *United States v. Necoechea, 986 F.2d 1273, 1276 (9th Cir. 1993)* (citing *United States v. Roberts, 618 F.2d 530, 533 (9th Cir. 1980)).* Vouching constitutes misconduct because it may lead the jury to convict on the basis of evidence not presented; it also carries the imprimatur of the government, which may induce the jury to adopt the government's judgment rather than its own. *See Young, 470 U.S. at 18.*

Based on an assessment of the relevant factors considered in *Darden,* the Court concludes that the prosecutor's comments taken together did not so infect the trial as to render it fundamentally unfair. First, the comments did not manipulate or misstate the evidence presented at trial. Thompson testified that due to the amount of cocaine she had used that night she didn't recall seeing another vehicle approach as they exited the freeway. The prosecutor's comment did not vouch for Thompson's testimony, but explained that, in light of her intoxicated state, it was a distinct possibility she did not see the other vehicle. Nor did the prosecutor vouch when stating that he "believed" Thompson's testimony about Petitioner's prescription sunglasses. Rather, he referred to the lack of any other explanation for how the glasses could have been found at the scene. The prosecutor's comment about Vernoy being an honest man who may have made an honest mistake also did not constitute vouching, but suggested an explanation as to how the witness may have made a mistake regarding the height of the man he saw with Thompson, just as he had made a mistake about the type of car the individuals were driving. Overall, none of these comments misstated or manipulated the evidence presented at trial. Instead, the prosecutor "argue[d] reasonable inferences based on the evidence[.]" *Necoechea, 986 F.2d at 1276.*

Second, the lack of a curative instruction did not infect the trial because Petitioner failed to object or request such an instruction. The trial court instructed the jurors that what the lawyers said in argument was not evidence and that the jurors had to determine the facts only from the evidence. (RT 11/18/92 at 11-12; *see also id. at 25.*) The jury is presumed to follow the court's instructions. *See Weeks v. Angelone, 528 U.S. 225, 234, 120 S. Ct. 727, 145 L. Ed. 2d 727 (2000); Cook v. LaMarque, 593 F.3d 810, 828 (9th Cir. 2010).*

Third, Petitioner had an opportunity to rebut the prosecutor's comments. (RT 11/18/92 at 65-96.) Defense counsel argued that Thompson's testimony lacked credibility and that the man with Thompson was taller than Petitioner. (*Id.* at 65-72, 87-90.)

Finally, the evidence of Petitioner's guilt was substantial. Petitioner admitted being with Thompson on the day of the crimes when they attempted to gain entrance to the home of an individual named Leza McCurty, who lived near the location where the kidnapping took place. (RT 11/17/92 at 132-34, 166.) McCurty said this occurred around noon, positively identified Thompson, and said the man accompanying her wore sunglasses. (RT 11/13/92 at 134-36.) Thompson testified that around noon that same day she and Petitioner were looking for someone to rob and that the victim agreed to give them a ride. (RT 11/17/92 at 23-24; RT 11/13/92 at 35-36.) Thompson also testified that after the victim attempted to escape, Petitioner chased him down, tried to strangle him with a belt, and then held him down while Thompson killed him with a rock. (*Id.*) Subsequently, Petitioner's prescription sunglasses were found at the crime scene. (RT 11/12/92 at 179; RT 11/17/92 at 167-68.) Petitioner also admitted that he was with Thompson as they traveled throughout Southern California using the victim's credit cards. (RT 11/17/92 at 138-42.) Thus, the strength of the evidence against Petitioner supports a determination that he was not prejudiced by the prosecutor's remarks.

Petitioner has not established prosecutorial misconduct. The Arizona Supreme Court's rejection of this claim was not contrary to or based on an unreasonable application of clearly established federal law, nor was it based on an unreasonable determination of the facts.

FRANK ROQUE, PETITIONER, V. CHARLES L. RYAN AND ARIZONA ATTORNEY GENERAL, RESPONDENTS. CIV 08-02154 PHX PGR (MEA) UNITED STATES DISTRICT COURT FOR THE DISTRICT OF ARIZONA

(Text added/modified for emphasis) Courts consistently allow the state prosecutor to engage in misconduct so that convictions be obtained thereby preventing a meaningful defense. Courts consistently sanction this systematic practice refusing to find bad faith thereby condoning this misconduct which is on the rise . As it was never their intent to subject the state's case to a meaningful adversarial process, when viewed in the totality, and not in isolation, this should constitute fraud upon the court by these lawyers.

COUNSEL: Frank Silva Roque, also known as Frank Roque, Petitioner, Pro se, TUCSON, AZ. For Dora B Schriro, Respondent: William Scott Simon, Office of the Attorney General, Phoenix, AZ.

I Procedural History
....
D. Petitioner's claims for relief

1. Petitioner asserts the state violated his right to due process of law by withholding exculpatory evidence regarding his blood alcohol level during the offenses.

Petitioner argues his constitutional rights were violated by the state's failure to disclose evidence regarding his blood alcohol level during the offenses. Petitioner contends the prosecutor did not disclose that a police detective had determined that Petitioner's blood alcohol content would have been below the legal limit for driving while intoxicated after the consumption of two Fosters beers three and one half hours prior to the crime. Petitioner contends the failure to disclose this evidence prior to trial violated his rights pursuant to Brady v. Maryland. Regardless of any failure to fully or properly exhaust this claim, it may be denied on the merits.

In Brady v. Maryland the United States Supreme Court held that a defendant's right to due process of law is violated when the government fails to disclose evidence that is material to the defendant's guilt or innocence, including impeachment evidence. See *373 U.S. 83, 86-87, 83 S. Ct. 1194, 1196-97, 10 L. Ed. 2d 215 (1963); Schad v. Ryan, 595 F.3d 907, 915 (9th Cir. 2010)*. The state violates this obligation and denies a criminal defendant due process of law if "(1) the evidence in question was favorable to the defendant, meaning that it had either exculpatory or impeachment value; (2) the state 'willfully or inadvertently' suppressed the evidence; and (3) the defendant was prejudiced by the suppression." *Schad, 595 F.3d at 915*, quoting *Strickler v. Greene, 527 U.S. 263, 281-82, 119 S. Ct. 1936, 1948, 144 L. Ed. 2d 286 (1999)*. See also *Horton v. Mayle, 408 F.3d 570, 578 (9th Cir. 2005)* (holding the government's failure to disclose a leniency deal with a witness was reversible error).

Petitioner's state of intoxication, or not, at the time of the crimes, and whether Petitioner had a preexisting alcohol consumption issue, were disputed during testimony. The inferences that Petitioner was intoxicated at the time of the crimes was countered by testimony that signs of intoxication could have resulted from allergies or extreme mental agitation. Petitioner's counsel elicited testimony from the employees of the restaurant and sports bar who had contact with Petitioner on the day of the crimes that they regularly called taxis for people who were obviously intoxicated and that they did not think it necessary to call a taxi for Petitioner. *Inter alia*, Petitioner's brother testified he believed Petitioner had a problem with alcohol prior to the events of September 11, 2001. See Answer, Exh. C. Petitioner's brother testified that Petitioner was so incoherent when he spoke with him by telephone on September 15, 2001, that the brother initially surmised Petitioner was intoxicated. Id., Exh. C. The record indicated that Petitioner had purchased two beers and consumed at least one of them at the Wild Hare bar at approximately 11:30 on the morning of September 15, 2001. See, e.g., Answer, Exh. E.

Any undisclosed evidence regarding Petitioner's blood alcohol level at the time of the crimes could not have been exculpatory because evidence that Petitioner's blood alcohol level was below the legal limit for driving while intoxicated would not necessarily prove or disprove Petitioner's affirmative defense of insanity. No prejudice resulted from the alleged "failure" to disclose this evidence because in Arizona a defendant's voluntary intoxication is not a defense to a charge of murder, assault with a deadly weapon, or drive-by shooting. *Arizona v. Kiles, 222 Ariz. 25, 33, 213 P.3d 174* & n.10, *222 Ariz. 25, 213 P.3d 174, 182 & n.10 (2009)* ("The statute unambiguously provides that intoxication is a defense only against the culpable mental state of intentionally."); *Arizona v. Lavers, 168 Ariz. 376, 389, 814 P.2d 333, 346 (1991)* (concluding that voluntary intoxication is not defense to knowing first degree murder). Accordingly, this claim for federal habeas relief may be denied on the merits of the claim. "The legislature amended the statute in 1994 to eliminate intoxication as a defense 'for any criminal act or requisite state of mind.' *A.R.S. § 13-503 (2001)*; 1993 Ariz. Sess. Laws, ch. 256, §§ 2, 3 (1st Reg. Sess.).'"

....

9. Petitioner alleges that he was subjected to prosecutorial misconduct.

Petitioner raised twenty-eight specific claims of prosecutorial misconduct in his direct appeal. The state Supreme Court thoroughly addressed these claims, stating:

> Roque asserts that twenty-eight incidents of prosecutorial misconduct occurring throughout the guilt and sentencing proceedings denied him a fair trial. We have addressed fifteen of the alleged incidents elsewhere in this opinion, and, of those, only the State's failure to disclose the scope of Dr. Ben-Porath's testimony warrants inclusion here. Roque also alleges thirteen additional incidents, which we now address.

213 Ariz. at 228, 141 P.3d at 403. "After reviewing each incident for error," the state court assessed "whether the incident should count toward [Petitioner's] prosecutorial misconduct claim." After the specific incidents contributing to a finding of misconduct were identified, the court went on to "evaluate their cumulative effect on the trial." *213 Ariz. at 230, 141 P.3d at 405*.

The state Supreme Court then concluded:

> Under the Hughes test, we cannot say that the cumulative effect of the misconduct here so permeated the entire

atmosphere of the trial with unfairness that it denied Roque due process. [] We recognize in particular that the prosecutors' failure to disclose the scope of Dr. Ben-Porath's testimony was improper and potentially prejudicial, but the defense did not make a good faith effort to resolve that discovery dispute. As a result, we cannot now assess the prejudice the defendant may ultimately have suffered. The cumulative effect of the incidents of misconduct in this case thus does not warrant reversal.

213 Ariz. at 230, 141 P.3d at 405.

Only those specific acts of the prosecutor alleged to be instances of prosecutorial misconduct that were exhausted in state court would be properly considered in this habeas action. The undersigned concludes the state court's determination that the asserted instances of prosecutorial misconduct did not deprive Petitioner of his right to procedural due process of law was not clearly contrary to federal law. Petitioner contends the prosecutor committed misconduct by introducing the testimony of Dr. Ben Porath; by telling the jury Petitioner had said he had a preexisting conflict with Mr. Sodhi; by calling Petitioner a terrorist and comparing Petitioner to Osama Bin Laden; by discrediting the defense experts with harassment and innuendo; by being insolent and dismissive about Dr. Toma's qualifications; by calling the defense experts "so called medical experts presented by the defense" and calling Dr. Potts a "so called" psychiatrist; by saying he was using the term "doctor" "loosely" with regard to the defense experts; by telling the jury they could not consider Petitioner's IQ or any mental impairment because it did not excuse his conduct. Petitioner further asserts prosecutorial misconduct because, he asserts, the prosecution's statement that he was urging them not to accept the "distorted" story told via the expert witnesses testifying as to what Petitioner had said to them constituted a comment on Petitioner exercising his right to remain silent. Petitioner additionally argues the prosecutor committed misconduct by eliciting testimony from Dr. Scialli that he had previously worked with Petitioner's defense counsel and by repeatedly telling the jury that Petitioner was a drunk, an alcoholic, and a racist. Petitioner notes his defense counsel moved for a mistrial based on the prosecutor's misconduct, which motion was denied.

A habeas petitioner is not entitled to federal habeas relief based on a prosecutor's improper statements unless the statements infected the entire proceeding and rendered it fundamentally unfair in violation of defendant's right to due process of law. See *Darden v. Wainright, 477 U.S. 168, 181, 106 S. Ct. 2464, 2471, 91 L. Ed. 2d 144 (1986),* quoting *Donnelly v. DeChristoforo, 416 U.S. 637, 643, 94 S. Ct. 1868, 1871, 40 L. Ed. 2d 431 (1974); Davis v. Woodford, 384 F.3d 628 (9th Cir. 2004).*

On a petition for a writ of habeas corpus, the standard of review for a claim of prosecutorial misconduct is the narrow one of due process, and not the broad exercise of supervisory power. *Darden v. Wainwright, 477 U.S. 168, 181, 106 S. Ct. 2464, 91 L. Ed. 2d 144, [] (1986)* (quoting *Donnelly v. DeChristoforo, 416 U.S. 637, 642, 94 S. Ct. 1868, 40 L. Ed. 2d 431, [] (1974)).* Thus, to succeed, [the petitioner] must demonstrate that it so infected the trial with unfairness as to make the resulting conviction a denial of due process. *Donnelly, 416 U.S. at 643, 94 S. Ct. 1868.*

Renderos v. Ryan, 469 F.3d 788, 799 (9th Cir. 2006).

Thus, we must examine the entire proceedings to determine whether the prosecutor's remarks so infected the trial with unfairness as to make the resulting conviction a denial of due process. Before granting relief, we must also determine that any constitutional error was not harmless. Specifically, we must find that the error had substantial and injurious effect or influence in determining the jury's verdict. Only if the record demonstrates that the jury's decision was substantially influenced by the error or there is grave doubt about whether an error affected a jury will [the petitioner] be entitled to relief.

Sechrest v. Ignacio, 549 F.3d 789, 807-08 (9th Cir. 2008) (internal citations and quotations omitted).

To be entitled to relief on this claim, Petitioner must demonstrate that the prosecutor's comments "had [a] substantial and injurious effect or influence in determining the jury's verdict." *Brecht v. Abrahamson,*

507 U.S. 619, 623, 113 S. Ct. 1710, 1714, 123 L. Ed. 2d 353 (1993), quoting *Kotteakos v. United States, 328 U.S. 750, 776, 66 S. Ct. 1239, 1253, 90 L. Ed. 1557.* In making this determination, the Court must look at the nature of the prosecutor's comments, the nature and quantum of the evidence before the jury, the arguments of opposing counsel, the judge's charge, and whether the alleged errors were isolated or repeated. See *Billings v. Polk, 441 F.3d 238, 250 (4th Cir. 2006).*

The United States Supreme Court has concluded that habeas relief on this type of claim is not appropriate unless the prosecutor manipulated or misstated the evidence or implicated other specific rights of the defendant, such as his right to counsel or his right to remain silent. See *Darden, 477 U.S. at 181-82, 106 S. Ct. at 2471-72.* A prosecutor's statements might satisfy the standard if they are racially motivated or if they attempt to establish guilt by association. See *United States v. Wolfswinkel, 44 F.3d 782, 787 (9th Cir. 1995).*

The complained of statements were not racially motivated insofar as they did not disparage Petitioner because of his race or his associations. The prosecutor did not manipulate the evidence or wrongfully implicate Petitioner's invocation of his right to counsel. The statement alleged by Petitioner to have implicated his right to remain silent did not explicitly do so, instead it encouraged the jury not to accept the version of events proffered by the defense expert witnesses, based on what Petitioner had told them. Neither did the prosecutor explicitly implicate Petitioner had exercised his right to remain silent after his arrest. Additionally, Petitioner's counsel successfully argued to limit the effect of the improper statements by the prosecutor and to challenge the prosecutor's characterization of factual evidence.

The contested statements made by Petitioner's prosecutor reflected emotional reactions and attempts to elicit emotional responses to the evidence from the jury, which, even if classified as improper, undesirable, or even universally condemned, did not violate Petitioner's right to due process. See *Darden, 477 U.S. at 180-81, 106 S. Ct. at 2470-71; Hovey v. Ayers, 458 F.3d 892, 923 (9th Cir. 2006); Allen v. Woodford, 395 F.3d 979, 997 (9th Cir. 2005).*

The Magistrate Judge concludes the statement of the prosecutor did not so infect the trial with unfairness as to make the resulting conviction a violation of due process. See *Williams v. Borg, 139 F.3d*

737, 745 (9th Cir. 1998); Thompson v. Borg, 74 F.3d 1571, 1576-77 (9th Cir. 1996) (denying habeas relief based on a due process claim regarding a prosecutor's comments in closing argument because, in part, the jury returned a verdict of second degree murder rather than first degree murder). Accordingly, the state courts' decision that Petitioner was not deprived of a constitutional right by the prosecutor's challenged comments was not clearly contrary to federal law and Petitioner is not entitled to federal habeas relief on the merits of this claim.

KEVIN ROCHON BLAISE, PETITIONER, V. CHARLES L. RYAN, ET AL., RESPONDENTS.

NO. CV-13-01483-PHX-NVW (BSB) UNITED STATES DISTRICT COURT FOR THE DISTRICT OF ARIZONA

(Text added/modified for emphasis). The Attorney General failed to disclose that in Arizona it is the norm for prosecutors to use false testimony to convict and that there are too many such incidents. This systemic problem is fraud upon the court.

COUNSEL: Kevin Rochon Blaise, also named as: Kevin Blaise, Petitioner, Pro se, BUCKEYE, AZ. For Charles L Ryan, named as: Charles Ryan, Attorney General of the State of Arizona, Thomas C Horne, named as: Tom Horne, Respondents: Alice Mae Jones, LEAD ATTORNEY, Office of the Attorney General - Phoenix, Phoenix, AZ.

....

E. Federal Petition for Writ of Habeas Corpus
On July 16, 2013, Petitioner filed the pending Petition for Writ of Habeas Corpus, raising the following claims for relief:

....

C. Ground Two
In Ground Two, Petitioner asserts that the "prosecutor knowingly used perjured testimony to obtain a conviction." (Doc. 1 at 8.) Petitioner contends that four of the State's witnesses (TyR, MR, DH, and the investigating detective) committed perjury and that the prosecution

knowingly used that perjured testimony at trial. (*Id.*) A criminal defendant's right to due process is violated when false testimony is used to convict him. *See Napue v. Illinois, 360 U.S. 264, 269, 79 S. Ct. 1173, 3 L. Ed. 2d 1217 (1959)*. To prevail on a false testimony claim, the petitioner must show that: "(1) the testimony (or evidence) was actually false, (2) the prosecution knew or should have known that the testimony was actually false, and (3) the false testimony was material." *Henry v. Ryan, 720 F.3d 1073, 1084 (9th Cir. 2013)* (internal quotation omitted).

On direct appeal, Petitioner argued that the prosecution either knowingly used, or failed to correct, false testimony because the victims testified inconsistently at trial. (Doc. 10-1 at 167-69.) The appellate court rejected Petitioner's claim as "unsubstantiated," and unsupported by the record. (Doc. 10, Ex. AA at 5.) Petitioner has not shown that state court's resolution of this claim was based on an unreasonable determination of the facts, or that it was contrary to, or based on an unreasonable application of, controlling Supreme Court precedent. *See 28 U.S.C. § 2254(d); see also Mitchell, 540 U.S. at 16* ("A state court's decision is not 'contrary to . . . clearly established Federal law' simply because the court did not cite [Supreme Court] opinions." (quoting *Early, 537 U.S. at 8*)).

Petitioner has not presented any support for his assertion that the testimony of the State's witnesses was false -- rather than merely inconsistent -- and that the prosecutor knew the testimony was false. *See Schad v. Ryan, 671 F.3d 708, 717 (9th Cir. 2011)* (finding that even if a state's witnesses' testimony was false, a petitioner's *Napue* claim failed because there was no evidence that the state "knew or should have known that [the witness]'s testimony was false"). Additionally, as the state court found, the state court record does not support Petitioner's claim that his conviction was based on false testimony.

1. Ty.R's Testimony

At trial, Ty.R. testified that she saw S.R. fire a shot in the air, and that she saw Petitioner shoot at the car in which she was a passenger. She testified that "[a]fter the first shot [,] he immediately squatted down and fired towards the car." (Doc. 10, Ex. EEE at 73.) She also described where S.R. and Petitioner were standing in relation to the car. (*Id*. at 73-74.) On cross examination, defense counsel elicited testimony that Ty.R. previously told the police that she "didn't know who fired any shots" and that she "saw the first shot fired" by "a guy squatting by the car" who she had "never seen . . . before." (*Id*. at 82-86.) [*67] Ty.R. explained that she learned S.R.'s and Petitioner's names after the shooting, but she did not know their names at the time of the shooting. (*Id*. at 86.) Petitioner also presented the testimony of the detective who had interviewed Ty.R. (Doc. 10, Ex. GGG at 29-34.) This detective testified that although Ty.R. said that she did not know S.R.'s and Petitioner's names at the time of the shooting, during the investigation, Ty.R. told him that she saw two individuals holding guns, one standing and shooting a gun in the air, and the other squatting and firing a gun at the car. (*Id*. at 43-46.) She said that she later learned these individuals' names.

Petitioner alleges that Ty.R. committed perjury at trial because she "could not have seen anyone shooting" based on her location in the car, she changed her story "after discussing the case with the prosecutor," and she did not actually "see the shooter" and "only heard from a friend it was [Petitioner]." (Doc. 1 at 8.) Petitioner has not cited any evidence to support his assertion that the prosecutor influenced Ty.R.'s testimony. (*Id*.) Additionally, at trial and during her interviews with the police, Ty.R. said she saw Petitioner shooting at the car. (Doc. [*68] 10, Ex. EEE at 72-74.) She explained that although she did not know Petitioner's name until after the shooting, she saw him shooting at the car. (Doc. 10, Ex. EEE at 72-74; Ex. GGG at 43-46.)

Although Ty.R. made some inconsistent statements, which defense counsel pointed out at trial, inconsistent statements are "not enough for a *Napue* violation." *See United States v. Bingham, 653 F.3d 983, 995 (9th Cir. 2011)* ("We cannot presume that the prosecutor knew that the prior [inconsistent] statement was true but elicited perjured testimony anyway.") (internal quotation omitted). The record does not support a finding that Ty.R.'s trial testimony was false or that the prosecutor knew it was false. *See United States v. Sherlock, 962 F.2d 1349, 1364 (9th Cir. 1989)* ("The record does not show and we do not presume that the prosecutor used false testimony.").

2. M.R.'s Testimony

Petitioner also claims that M.R. gave false testimony at trial. (Doc. 1 at 8.) On direct-examination, M.R. testified that she saw S.R. with a gun, heard "gunfire," "brought [her] legs up towards [her] chest area and put [her] head down [on her] chest," and was then shot in the left foot. (Doc. 10, Ex. EEE at 21-22, 24-25.) On cross-examination, M.R. testified that she saw Petitioner fire a gun, and that he was "squatted down at that time." (*Id.* at 37-40.) M.R. also testified that she told detectives that she saw Petitioner with a gun. (*Id.*)

On re-direct examination, M.R. testified that she "probably" saw Petitioner with a gun. (*Id.* at 54-55.) In response to questions from the jury, M.R. testified that she saw Petitioner with a gun, that it was "probably" pointed towards the floor of the car, and that she did not see who fired shots into the car. (*Id.* at 57-58.) The prosecutor then asked follow-up questions and M.R. clarified that although she saw Petitioner with a gun, she did not see anyone shoot at the car but only heard the gunfire. (*Id.* at 62-63.)

Although M.R. gave inconsistent testimony at trial, inconsistent testimony alone does not support a *Napue* violation. *See Bingham, 653 F.3d at 995*. Additionally, M.R.'s testimony that she saw Petitioner shoot at the car was elicited by defense counsel on cross-examination, not by the prosecutor. (Doc. 10, Exhibit EEE at 37-40.) The prosecutor clarified that M.R. did not see who shot at the car. (*Id.* at 62-63.) Thus, the record does not indicate that the prosecutor knowingly presented false testimony.

3. D.H.'s Testimony

Petitioner also claims that D.H. gave inconsistent testimony at trial and that on re-direct examination, the prosecutor "persuade[d] [D.H] into perjured statements by leading her to say that she [saw Petitioner] fire [a] gun" even though she had testified that her eyes were closed. (Doc. 1 at 8.) On direct examination, D.H. testified that she saw that Petitioner "had a gun" and that she saw another "gentlemen shooting in the air." (Doc. 10, Ex. DDD at 101.) She described where Petitioner stood, stated that he had a gun in his hand, that he pointed it at the car, and that she saw "sparks from the gun" "about four or five times." (*Id.* at 103-04, 109-10.) On cross-examination, D.H. testified that she "leaned back" during the shooting, but that she kept her "head up." (*Id.* at 121.) She said she "looked out for a moment," and then "leaned back" and "closed [her] eyes." (*Id.* at 122.) On re-direct examination, D.H. testified that she saw Petitioner shoot at the car and that she closed her eyes "[i]n the middle of the shooting," after she saw the "muzzle flashes" from Petitioner's gun. (*Id.* at 122-23.)

Petitioner has not shown that D.H.'s testimony was false or that the prosecutor knew it was false. Additionally, D.H.'s testimony was consistent. She testified that she saw Petitioner shoot a gun at the car in which she was a passenger. On re-direct examination, D.H. clarified that she closed her eyes and leaned back *after* she saw Petitioner fire the gun.

4. The Investigating Detective's Testimony

Finally, Petitioner claims that the investigating detective testified falsely by stating that Petitioner was standing upright and then moved into a crouching position when he shot at the car. (Doc. 1 at 9.) In response to a jury question, the detective opined that the bullet that hit L.H. above her right eye came through an open car window, which was consistent with the "description being given that . . . the suspect began firing and then continued to slide down the back or the side of the car he was leaning up against." (Doc. 10, Ex. FFF at 133-34.) Petitioner does not cite any evidence to support his assertion that the detective's testimony was false, and the record contains testimony that support the detective's testimony. D.H. testified that she saw Petitioner "standing" and holding a gun. (Doc. 10, Ex. DDD at 10-03.) Ty.R. testified that after Petitioner fired "the first shot [,] he immediately squatted down and fired towards the car." (Doc. 10 Ex. EEE at 73.)

As set forth above, Petitioner has not shown that the prosecutor knowingly presented any false testimony. Accordingly, his false testimony claims fail. Petitioner also has not shown that the state court's rejection of Petitioner's due process claim based on the prosecutor's alleged presentation of false testimony at trial was based on an unreasonable determination of the facts, or that it was contrary to, or based on an unreasonable application of, *Napue*. Accordingly, he is not entitled to habeas corpus relief based on this claim. *See 28 U.S.C. § 2254(d)*.

JOE CLARENCE SMITH, PETITIONER, VS. CHARLES L. RYAN, ET AL., RESPONDENTS.
NO. CV-12-00318-PHX-PGR UNITED STATES DISTRICT COURT FOR THE DISTRICT OF ARIZONA

(Text added/modified for emphasis). The Attorney General failed to disclose that in Arizona it is the norm for appointed PCR counsel not to raise all federal claims. Courts consistently allow the state to prevent defendants from a fair trial. The same prosecutors consistently misstate the evidence, improperly vouch for their witnesses, appealed to the passions of the jury thereby preventing a meaningful defense. Courts consistently sanction this systematic practice refusing to find bad faith thereby condoning this misconduct which is on the rise . As it was never their intent to subject the state's case to a meaningful adversarial process, when viewed in the totality, and not in isolation, this should constitute fraud upon the court by these lawyers. Failure to disclose this systemic problem is fraud upon the court.

COUNSEL: For Joe Clarence Smith, Jr., Petitioner: Jon M Sands, Michael Llewellyn Burke, LEAD ATTORNEYS, Federal Public Defenders Office, Phoenix, AZ; Kelly Leann Culshaw, Federal Public Defenders Office - Phoenix, Phoenix, AZ. For Charles L Ryan, Director, Arizona Department of Corrections, Ron Credio, Warden, Arizona State Prison - Eyman Complex, Respondents: Jon George Anderson, LEAD ATTORNEY, Office of the Attorney General, Phoenix, AZ.

......
Petitioner has raised a series of habeas claims that were never presented in state court. The claims are procedurally defaulted. Petitioner asserts, however, that pursuant to *Martinez v. Ryan, 132 S. Ct. 1309, 182 L. Ed. 2d 272 (2012)*, his default of the claims is excused by the ineffective assistance of his post-conviction counsel. To support this argument Petitioner seeks to expand the record to include, for example, correspondence from trial counsel Sinclair to post-conviction counsel

Dew to show that the latter was aware of various allegations of ineffectiveness of appellate counsel. "A federal court may not grant habeas relief to a state prisoner unless he has properly exhausted his remedies in state court." *Peterson v. Lampert, 319 F.3d 1153, 1155 (9th Cir. 2003)* (en banc). An unexhausted claim will be procedurally defaulted if state procedural rules would now bar the petitioner from bringing the claim in state court. *See Beaty v. Stewart, 303 F.3d 975, 987 (9th Cir. 2002).*

The Ninth Circuit has summarized the holding in *Martinez* as follows:

> a petitioner may establish cause for procedural default of a trial [ineffective assistance of counsel] claim, where the state (like Arizona) required the petitioner to raise that claim in collateral proceedings, by demonstrating two things: (1) "counsel in the initial-review collateral proceeding, where the claim should have been raised, was ineffective under the standards of *Strickland v. Washington, 466 U.S. 668, 104 S. Ct. 2052, 80 L. Ed. 2d 674 (1984)*," and (2) "the underlying ineffective-assistance-of-trial-counsel claim is a substantial one, which is to say that the prisoner must demonstrate that the claim has some merit."

Cook v. Ryan, 688 F.3d 598, 607 (9th Cir. 2012) (quoting *Martinez, 132 S. Ct. at 1318*).

The Ninth Circuit recently extended the holding in *Martinez* to apply to procedurally defaulted claims of ineffective assistance of appellate counsel. *Ha Van Nguyen v. Curry, 736 F.3d 1287, 1294--95 (9th Cir. 2013).*

In order to determine whether post-conviction counsel's performance excused the procedural default of Petitioner's claims of ineffective assistance of appellate counsel, the Court must determine whether those claims are substantial or have some merit. *See Sexton v. Cozner, 679 F.3d 1150, 1159 (9th Cir. 2012)* ("To establish that PCR counsel was ineffective, Sexton must show that trial counsel was likewise ineffective. . . .").

Ineffective assistance of appellate counsel claims is evaluated under the standard set forth in *Strickland v. Washington, 466 U.S. 668, 104 S. Ct. 2052, 80 L. Ed. 2d 674 (1984)*. *Moormann v. Ryan, 628 F.3d 1102, 1106 (9th Cir. 2010)* (citing *Smith v. Robbins, 528 U.S. 259, 285, 120 S. Ct. 746, 145 L. Ed. 2d 756 (2000)*). First, the petitioner must show that counsel's performance was objectively unreasonable, which in the appellate context requires the petitioner to demonstrate that counsel acted unreasonably in failing to discover and brief a merit-worthy issue. *Id.* Second, the petitioner must show prejudice, which in this context means that he must demonstrate a reasonable probability that, but for appellate counsel's failure to raise the issue, he would have prevailed in his appeal. *Id.*

As discussed below, Petitioner cannot demonstrate that his claims of ineffective assistance of appellate counsel are substantial because the claims appellate counsel failed to raise were without merit. Appellate counsel therefore did not perform incompetently by failing to raise the claims, and Petitioner suffered no prejudice from counsel's performance. *See Jones v. Smith, 231 F.3d 1227, 1239 n.8 (9th Cir. 2000)* (finding no prejudice when appellate counsel fails to raise an issue on direct appeal that is not grounds for reversal); *Miller v. Keeney, 882 F.2d 1428, 1434 (9th Cir. 1989)* (explaining that appellate counsel remains above an objective standard of competence and does not cause prejudice when he declines to raise a weak issue on appeal); *Boag v. Raines, 769 F.2d 1341, 1344 (9th Cir. 1985)* ("Failure to raise a meritless argument does not constitute ineffective assistance.").

......

For the same reason, Petitioner is not entitled to an evidentiary hearing. Having reviewed the entire record, including the evidence presented by Petitioner in the PCR proceedings and in his motion to expand the record, the Court concludes that an evidentiary hearing is not warranted. *See Rule 8(a) of the Rules Governing Section 2254 Cases*. Whether Petitioner's allegations of ineffective assistance of trial and appellate counsel are "substantial" under *Martinez* is resolvable on the record. *Cf. Dickens v. Ryan, 740 F.3d 1302, 1321 (9th Cir. 2014)* (en banc) (explaining that "a district court *may take evidence to the extent necessary* to determine whether the petitioner's claim of ineffective assistance of trial counsel is substantial under *Martinez*") (emphasis added).

....

Claims 24 and 25

In Claim 24 Petitioner alleges several instances of prosecutorial misconduct. (Doc. 25 at 100--11.) Claim 25 alleges that appellate counsel rendered ineffective assistance by failing to raise these claims on direct appeal. (*Id.* at 111--12.)

Petitioner contends that the prosecutor committed misconduct during his cross-examination of one of Petitioner's witnesses; by vouching for the medical examiner; and by various comments made during his opening statements and closing arguments, including comments about the burden of proof. None of the alleged instances of misconduct entitles Petitioner to habeas relief.

"A prosecutor's actions constitute misconduct if they 'so infected the trial with unfairness as to make the resulting conviction a denial of due process.'" *Wood v. Ryan, 693 F.3d 1104, 1113 (9th Cir. 2012)* (quoting *Darden v. Wainwright, 477 U.S. 168, 181, 106 S. Ct. 2464, 91 L. Ed. 2d 144 (1986)*). The "appropriate standard of review for such a claim on writ of habeas corpus is 'the narrow one of due process, and not the broad exercise of supervisory power.'" *Darden, 477 U.S. at 181* (quoting *Donnelly v. DeChristoforo, 416 U.S. 637, 642, 94 S. Ct. 1868, 40 L. Ed. 2d 431 (1974)*). "On habeas review, constitutional errors of the 'trial type,' including prosecutorial misconduct, warrant relief only if they 'had substantial and injurious effect or influence in determining the jury's verdict.'" *Wood, 693 F.3d at 1113* (quoting *Brecht, 507 U.S. at 637--38*).

Cross-examination

Petitioner alleges that the prosecutor improperly cross-examined a defense witness. (Doc. 25 at 101--02.) During the mitigation phase of the Spencer resentencing, the defense offered the testimony of James Aiken, a corrections expert who discussed Petitioner's disciplinary record as a death row prisoner, which Aiken characterized as minor. Aiken testified about a March 24, 1978, major violation received by

Petitioner for possessing a toothbrush with a blade attached to it. (RT 4/21/04 at 23.) Aiken characterized the weapon as defensive, noting that it was discovered after Petitioner had been attacked by other inmates earlier that month. (*Id.* at 23--24.)

On cross-examination, Aiken acknowledged that he was unfamiliar with the facts of Petitioner's crimes. (*Id.* at 52.) The prosecutor proceeded to question Aiken about Petitioner's use of a knife in the prior rapes and in the Spencer and Lee murders. (*Id.* at 55--56.) Aiken testified that these details did not change his opinion that the weapon found in Petitioner's cell was defensive in nature. (*Id.* at 56.)

The prosecutor's question was well within the latitude allowed in cross examination. *See Wood, 693 F.3d at 1114.* The prosecutor did nor misstate or manipulate the evidence. *See Darden, 477 U.S. at 182.* There was no misconduct.

Next, Petitioner alleges that the prosecutor improperly vouched for the work of non-testifying medical examiners. (Doc. 25 at 102.) Dr. Phillip Keen testified at the resentencing proceedings after reviewing the work of the medical examiners who performed the Spencer and Lee autopsies, Drs. Karnitschnig and Jarvis, respectively. The prosecutor asked Dr. Keen whether Drs. Karnitschnig and Jarvis were "qualified forensic pathologists." (RT 4/6/04 at 29.) Dr. Keen testified that they were "board certified and qualified and trained and functioned as good, competent pathologists." (*Id.*)

To prove a claim of improper vouching, Petitioner must show the prosecutor placed "the prestige of the government behind a witness through personal assurances of the witness's veracity." *United States v. Younger, 398 F.3d 1179, 1190 (9th Cir. 2005).* This colloquy with Dr. Keen about the professional qualifications of his colleagues did not constitute vouching.

Opening statement and closing argument

Petitioner next alleges that the prosecutor committed misconduct during the aggravation phase of the Spencer resentencing by making derogatory comments about the defense in closing argument. (Doc. 25 at 102--03.) In discussing the concept of reasonable doubt, the prosecutor stated that "[d]efense attorneys for many years make a career arguing reasonable doubt." (RT 4/6/04 at 118.) He then urged the jurors to read the definition of reasonable doubt provided in the court's instructions. (*Id.*) In his rebuttal argument the prosecutor commented, with respect to the issue of whether Spencer was conscious when she was killed, "I guess I am not trying to make light, I guess that the defense wants you to think that the defendant walked up to Sandy, and she passed out. I mean, isn't that what we need to have her, she just passed out?" (*Id.* at 129.)

These comments did not constitute misconduct. Prosecutors and defense lawyers are given "wide latitude" in closing arguments. *United States v. Sayetsitty, 107 F.3d 1405, 1409 (9th Cir. 1997)*; [*47] *see United States v. Wilkes, 662 F.3d 524, 538 (9th Cir. 2011)*. "Prosecutors have considerable leeway to strike 'hard blows' based on the evidence and all reasonable inferences from the evidence." *United States v. Henderson, 241 F.3d 638, 652 (9th Cir. 2000)* (citing *Berger v. United States, 295 U.S. 78, 88, 55 S. Ct. 629, 79 L. Ed. 1314 (1935)*). The prosecutor's comments about reasonable doubt did not amount to an *ad hominem* attack on defense counsel. *See Williams v. Borg, 139 F.3d 737, 744--45 (9th Cir. 1998)* (finding no misconduct when prosecutor referred to defense's closing argument as "trash"); *United States v. Ruiz, 710 F.3d 1077, 1086 (9th Cir. 2013)* (finding that "the prosecutor's characterization of the defense's case as 'smoke and mirrors' was not misconduct"); *Runningeagle v. Ryan, 686 F.3d 758, 781 (9th Cir. 2012)* (finding no due process violation where comments merely characterized evidence).

Petitioner also cites the prosecutor's comment that, "We're not here to solve this crime. This was done by an independent jury" (RT 4/6/04 at 129), noting that, in fact, Petitioner pleaded guilty to the Spencer murder. (Doc. 25 at 110.) Petitioner does not indicate in what manner the prosecutor's misstatement about [*48] how the conviction was reached could be prejudicial in the context of an argument about the existence of aggravating factors. The Court finds the comment harmless.

Petitioner also alleges that the prosecutor engaged in misconduct in his opening statement during the penalty phase of the Spencer resentencing when he commented that a sentence of less than death would amount to a "free murder" for Petitioner. (Doc. 25 at 103.) The comment was made in the context of the prosecutor's preview of testimony from Department of Corrections witnesses, who would explain that Petitioner was already serving a life sentence for other crimes so that if a death sentence were not imposed Petitioner "would do the same time in the same place for the rest of his life, as if he had not murdered anyone." (RT 4/19/04, a.m., at 21.) Defense counsel did not object to the comment, but later cited it in their motion for a new trial. (ROA 991.)[9] "ROA" refers to the record on appeal from resentencing (CR-04-0208-AP). As is the general practice in this District, the original reporter's transcripts, the trial court's presentence report, and certified copies of the trial records were provided to this Court by the Arizona Supreme Court. (*See* Doc. 39.)

Respondents contend that the comment was not prejudicial given the jury instructions provided by the court. (Doc. 30 at 124.) At the close of evidence, the court instructed the jury that what the lawyers say during their opening statements and closing arguments is "not the law and the evidence." (RT 4/21/04 at 167.) The court also explained that Petitioner was serving three consecutive life sentences for three rapes; that he was not eligible for release until he had served 90 years in prison; that "[i]f the jury imposes a life sentence concerning the murder of Sandy Spencer, then the Court will be required to sentence the defendant to life in prison without eligibility for release under any circumstances until not less than 25 years has been served"; and that this information was not aggravating or mitigating but was "being explained to you only to complete the information regarding the defendant's current and future imprisonment." (*Id.* at 171.)

These instructions were sufficient to eliminate any potential prejudice from the prosecutor's comment about a "free murder." In *Runningeagle*, the Ninth Circuit found no due process violation from the prosecutor's statement that "[t]he evil is among us," because "before opening statements and after the close of the trial, the court instructed the jurors that what the attorneys said in opening was not evidence, that they should decide the case only on the evidence, and that they should not be influenced by sympathy or prejudice." *686 F.3d at 781*. In *Darden*, during closing the prosecutor referred to the defendant as an "animal" and said that he should not be allowed out of a cell unless he was on a leash and that he wished he could see Darden "sitting here with no face, blown away by a shotgun." *477 U.S. at 181--83 nn.11 & 12*. The Court found that these improper statements did not deprive Darden of a fair trial, because of the substantial evidence against him and because the trial court instructed the jury that the arguments made by counsel were not evidence. *Id. at 181--83; see Donnelly, 416 U.S. at 645* (holding that an improper statement by a prosecutor during closing argument did not amount to a due process violation in part because the judge instructed the jury that the remark was not evidence).

Petitioner argues that the prosecutor engaged in misconduct by urging the jurors to revisit the photographs of the victims, by emphasizing Petitioner's lack of remorse, and by asking the jurors to put themselves in the victim Lee's place. (Doc. 25 at 108--10.) While the last of these was arguably improper argument, it does not entitle Petitioner to relief. In *Drayden v. White, 232 F.3d 704, 712--14 (9th Cir. 2000)*, the prosecutor's closing argument featured a soliloquy delivered in the murder victim's persona. The court found that the performance, "as deplorable as it was," did not violate the defendant's due process rights given the trial court's instruction to the jury that statements by the attorneys are not evidence and that jurors must not be influenced by sympathy, passion, or prejudice. *Id. at 713*. The trial court here gave similar instructions. (RT 5/27/04 at 6.)

Petitioner makes other allegations of misconduct, including that the prosecutor improperly denigrated the defense, mischaracterized the evidence, and misstated the standard for consideration of Petitioner's mental health evidence. (*See* Doc. 25 at 104--06.) None of these merit relief. Prosecutors are allowed to strike "hard blows" based on reasonable inferences from the evidence, *Henderson, 241 F.3d at 652*, and any improper or erroneous statements by the prosecutor were corrected by the jury instructions.

Burden of proof

Petitioner contends that the prosecution committed misconduct during its closing argument in both the Spencer and Lee resentencing's when he stated that the defendant had the "burden of showing mitigation sufficiently substantial to call for leniency." (RT 5/27/04 at

82; *see, e.g.,* RT 4/22/04 at 6, 7.) The trial court overruled defense objections to the statements. (*See* RT 4/22/04 at 32--33.)

Unlike his other allegations of prosecutorial misconduct, Petitioner raised this claim in his PCR petition, together with a claim of ineffective assistance of appellate counsel. (Doc. 30-2, Ex. B at 20.) The PCR court denied the ineffective assistance claim, finding that Petitioner was not prejudiced by counsel's failure to raise the misconduct claim because the prosecutor's misstatement of the law was harmless. (*Id.*, Ex. C at 4.) The PCR court noted that jurors are presumed to follow the court's instructions, which, in this case, did not place the burden on the defendant to show the mitigating evidence was sufficiently substantial to call for lenience. (*Id.*) Instead, as the PCR court correctly noted, the trial court simply instructed the jurors make an individual determination as to the sufficiency of the mitigating evidence. (*Id.*)

DOMINIQUE MARTINEZ, PETITIONER, VS. CHARLES RYAN, ET AL., RESPONDENT.

NO. CV 12-0254-TUC-JGZ (BPV) UNITED STATES DISTRICT COURT FOR THE DISTRICT OF ARIZONA

(Text added/modified for emphasis). The Attorney General failed to disclose that in Arizona it is the norm for appointed PCR counsel not to raise all federal claims. Courts consistently allow the state to prevent defendants from a fair trial. The same prosecutors consistently misstate the evidence, improperly vouch for their witnesses, appealed to the passions of the jury thereby preventing a meaningful defense. Courts consistently sanction this systematic practice refusing to find bad faith thereby condoning this misconduct which is on the rise . As it was never their intent to subject the state's case to a meaningful adversarial process, when viewed in the totality, and not in isolation, this should constitute fraud upon the court by these lawyers. Failure to disclose this systemic problem is fraud upon the court.

COUNSEL: Dominique Martinez, Petitioner, Pro se, TUCSON, AZ. For Charles L Ryan, Attorney General of the State of Arizona, Respondents: Laura Patrice Chiasson, LEAD ATTORNEY, Office of the Attorney General, Tucson, AZ.

....

E. Timeliness

Petitioner had until one year after his conviction and sentence became final to file his federal petition. Respondents do not contest the timeliness of the Petition. Upon review of the state-court record, the Court finds that, pursuant to the AEDPA, the Petition is timely.

F. Ground One

In Ground One, Petitioner alleges that he was denied due process and a fair trial by prosecutorial misconduct in violation of the *Fifth*, *Sixth*, and *Fourteenth Amendments*. Petitioner notes several instances of prosecutorial misconduct in the Petition which this Court addresses separately as claims (A) through (D) under Ground One: (A) the malicious and deliberate use of improper and prejudicial references during the course of trial relating to evidence the prosecutor knew would not be presented at trial; (B) the prosecutor's violation of disclosure and discovery obligations; (C) the prosecutor's pattern of egregious behavior permeating the entire trial, including a harassing, abusive, unethical pattern of behavior, "constant non-verbal communication with the jury, continual violations of the court's order prohibiting speaking object[ion]s, gesturing and making facial gestures toward defense counsel, and defendant" and "other theatrics"; and (D) the prosecutor's "absolute contradiction of his avowal made to the court that he would not argue that a key defense witness was mistaken." (Petition, at 6.)

1. Ground One (A): The prosecutor's use of improper and prejudicial references during trial.

Pursuant to *Rule 2(c) of the Rules Governing Section 2254 Cases*, a petitioner is obligated to specify in a federal habeas petition all grounds for relief, as well as the facts supporting each of these grounds. *See Mayle v. Felix, 545 U.S. 644, 661, 125 S. Ct. 2562, 162 L. Ed. 2d 582 (2005)* (observing that *Rule 2(c)* requires pleading "separate congeries of facts" in support of each ground for relief); *Blackledge v. Allison, 431 U.S. 63, 75 n. 7, 97 S. Ct. 1621, 52 L. Ed. 2d 136 (1977)* (observing that "notice" pleading in habeas is insufficient and that petition "is expected

to state facts that point to a 'real possibility of constitutional error' ")
(quoting Advisory Committee Note to *Rule 4, Rules Governing Section
2254 Cases*). Martinez's Petition is defective because it does not provide
enough specific facts in support of Ground One (A), to enable a court to
tell from the face of the Petition whether further habeas review is
warranted. *See Shepherd v. Nelson, 432 F.2d 1045, 1046* (allegation that
petitioner was deprived of his rights and cross-examination [*21] was
properly dismissed as a bare conclusion, unsupported by allegations of
underlying fact); *Adams v. Armontrout, 897 F.2d 332, 334 (8th Cir.
1990)* (holding that "in order to substantially comply with the *Section
2254 Rule 2(c)*, a petitioner must state specific, particularized facts
which entitle him or her to habeas corpus relief for each ground
specified. These facts must consist of sufficient detail to enable the
court to determine, from the face of the petition alone, whether the
petition merits further habeas corpus review."); *see also Rules
Governing Section 2254 Cases In The United States District Courts
2(c), 4* (1996). The Petitioner's allegation that the malicious and
deliberate use of improper and prejudicial references during the course
of trial relating to evidence the prosecutor knew would not be
presented at trial lacks the specificity required for this court to analyze
his claim without an exhaustive factual review of the entire state court
record. Petitioner does not identify what statements made by the
prosecutor were improper or constituted misconduct, and how such
statements caused him prejudice. In fact, in order to address this, claim
on the merits, the Respondents considered the allegedly offending
statements that Petitioner had identified in his state appellate-court
brief. Conclusory allegations which are not supported by a statement of
specific facts do not warrant habeas relief. *Boehme v. Maxwell, 423 F.2d
1056, 1058 (9th Cir. 1970)*. Accordingly, the Magistrate Judge
recommends that the District Court dismiss Ground One (A).

2. Ground One (B): Disclosure Obligations

As the undersigned found in Ground One (A), Petitioner's allegation
that the prosecutor "repeatedly violated his disclosure and discovery
obligations" also lacks the specificity required for this court to analyze
his claim without an exhaustive factual review of the entire state court
record. Petitioner does not identify what discovery and disclosure

violations amounted to prosecutorial misconduct in this Petition, or how he was harmed by the State's failure to disclose. As in Ground One (A), in order to address the claim at all, Respondents again were required to ascertain Petitioner's claims by referring to the claims argued in Petitioner's opening brief to the state court of appeals. Conclusory allegations which are not supported by a statement of specific facts do not warrant habeas relief. *Boehme, 423 F.2d at 1058.* Accordingly, the Magistrate Judge recommends that the District Court dismiss Ground One (B).

3. Ground One (C)

Petitioner contends that the prosecutor engaged in a "harassing, [abusive], unethical pattern of behavior, including constant non-verbal communication with the jury, [and] gesturing and making facial gestures toward defense counsel, . . . and other theatrics designed to demean and degrade the defense in the eyes of the jury." (Petition at 6.)

a. Ground One (C): Procedural Default

Respondents argue that Petitioner's citation to the *Fourteenth Amendment* and *Darden v. Wainwright, 477 U.S. 168, 106 S. Ct. 2464, 91 L. Ed. 2d 144 (1986)*, in the final sentence of his argument on direct appeal was insufficient to state a proper federal law basis for this claim in the state courts. (Answer, at 26, citing Ex. D, at 42.)

Petitioner argued in his opening brief to the appellate court that the prosecutor "engaged in a pattern of misconduct so egregious that it permeated the entire trial, from opening statement to closing arguments, depriving Mr. Martinez of a fair trial." (Ex. D), at 29.) Alone, this general appeal to deprivation of a fair trial is insufficient to establish exhaustion of a federal claim. *See Gray, 518 U.S. at 162* ("[I]t is not enough to make a general appeal to a constitutional guarantee as broad as due process to present the 'substance' of such a claim to a state court."). The Court finds, however, that Petitioner's contention, in the last sentence of his argument regarding prosecutorial misconduct, that his "right [] to a fair trial guaranteed him under the *due process clause of the fourteenth amendment to the U.S. Constitution*" and accompanying citation to the applicable clearly established federal law *Darden v. Wainwright, 477 U.S. 168, 106 S. Ct. 2464, 91 L. Ed. 2d 144 (1986)*, suffices to exhaust Petitioner's *Fourteenth Amendment* due process claim. *See Baldwin v. Reese, 541 U.S. 27, 32, 124 S. Ct. 1347, 158 L. Ed. 2d 64 (2004)*(A litigant wishing to raise a federal issue can easily indicate the federal law basis for his claim in a state-court petition or brief, for example, by citing in conjunction with the claim the federal source of law on which he relies or a case deciding such a claim on federal grounds, or by simply labeling the claim "federal.") Petitioner, however, did not exhaust his claims of violations of the *Fifth* and *Sixth Amendments*, and those claims are procedurally defaulted.

b. Ground One (C): Merits

The "clearly established Federal law" relevant to Petitioner's claims regarding prosecutorial misconduct is the Supreme Court's decision in *Darden, 477 U.S. 168, 106 S. Ct. 2464, 91 L. Ed. 2d 144*, which explained that a prosecutor's improper comments will be held to violate the Constitution only if they " 'so infected the trial with unfairness as to make the resulting conviction a denial of due process.' " *Parker v. Matthews, U.S. 132 S.Ct. 2148, 2153, 183 L. Ed. 2d 32 (2012)* (quoting *Darden, 477 U.S. at 181*); *Donnelly v. DeChristoforo, 416 U.S. 637, 643, 94 S. Ct. 1868, 40 L. Ed. 2d 431 (1984)*. Even if prosecutorial misconduct is established, on habeas review a federal court will not disturb a conviction unless the alleged prosecutorial misconduct had a "substantial and injurious effect or influence in determining the jury's verdict." *Brecht v. Abrahamson, 507 U.S. 619, 637-38, 113 S. Ct. 1710, 123 L. Ed. 2d 353 (1993)* (citation and internal quotations omitted); *see Shaw v. Terhune, 380 F.3d 473, 478 (9th Cir. 2004)* (*Brecht* applies to claim of prosecutorial misconduct).

Because the prosecutor's nonverbal conduct described by Petitioner was not captured in the written record, the appellate court resolved this claim by deferring to the trial court's determination that the prosecutor's conduct did not warrant a mistrial or a new trial. (Doc. A, at ¶36.)

Under the AEDPA, state-court findings of fact are given considerable deference. *See 28 U.S.C. § 2254(d)(2)*. Petitioner has not demonstrated that the state court's findings that the prosecutor's conduct at trial did not constitute misconduct was unreasonable in light of the evidence presented to the state court. "A federal court may not second-guess a state court's fact-finding process unless, after review of the state-court record, it determines that the state court was not merely wrong, but actually unreasonable." *Taylor v. Maddox, 366 F.3d 992, 999 (9th Cir. 2004)* (internal citation omitted). The habeas court presumes that the state court's factual determinations are correct, and Petitioner bears the burden of rebutting this presumption by clear and convincing evidence *28 U.S.C. § 2254(e)(1)* (stating that "a determination of factual issues made by a[s]tate court shall be presumed to be correct" and observing that "the applicant shall have the burden of rebutting the presumption of correctness by clear and convincing evidence"); *Williams v. Rhoades, 354 F.3d 1101, 1106 (9th Cir. 2004)*. Petitioner does not indicate which facts from the state-court's order are incorrect, nor does he provide any citations to the record that support another version of the facts; therefore, he fails to carry his burden of demonstrating by clear and convincing evidence that the state court's findings of fact are unreasonable. Accordingly, Petitioner is not entitled to relief on Ground One (C).

4. Ground One (D)

Petitioner claims that the prosecutor acted in contradiction of his avowal made to the court that he would not argue that a key defense witness was mistaken. This claim lacks sufficient specificity to merit federal review. The Court cannot determine from this short statement what "key defense witness" was mistaken, and when, during Petitioner's twenty-three-day trial, the prosecutor made this avowal. Accordingly, for the same reasons stated in Ground One (A) and (B), the Magistrate Judge recommends dismissing Ground One (D).

Alternatively, reviewing Petitioner's appellate brief to determine the factual basis for this claim, Petitioner argued that the prosecutor stated, just prior to the end of trial, that it was not necessary to call Herman Moreno as a witness because the prosecutor would not argue that Maria Alvarez, a waitress who testified she waited on Cornejo after the time that prosecution witnesses testified he was beaten and kidnapped, was mistaken. (Ex. D, at 17-18.) Petitioner argued that contrary to the prosecutor's avowal to the court, the prosecutor told the jury that Alvarez had seen Cornejo on a different night, and that Cornejo was not at the restaurant on the night Cornejo was abducted. (*Id.*) Petitioner failed to exhaust this claim, however, by asserting a federal-law basis for this claim. In fact, while Petitioner recited the facts of this claim in his brief, he did not argue in the "Argument" section of his brief that the prosecutor's argument contrary to his avowal violated any law, state or federal. Petitioner failed to fairly present Ground One (D) as a federal claim in state court. If Petitioner were to return to state court now to litigate this claim it would be found waived and untimely under *Rules 32.2(a)(3)* and *32.4(a)* of the Arizona Rules of Criminal Procedure because it does not fall within an exception to preclusion. *Ariz.R.Crim.P. 32.2(b)*; *32.1(d)-(h)*. The Ninth Circuit has held that Arizona's procedural rules, including its timeliness rule, are "clear" and [*29] "well-established." *Simmons v. Schriro, 187 Fed. Appx. 753, 754 (9th Cir. 2006); see also Ortiz, 149 F.3d at 931-32* (addressing Arizona's waiver rule); *Poland v. Stewart, 117 F.3d 1094, 1106 (9th Cir. 1997)* (same); *Martinez-Villareal v. Lewis, 80 F.3d 1301, 1306 (9th Cir. 1996)* (same); *Carriger v. Lewis, 971 F.2d 329, 333 (9th Cir. 1992)*(same). Therefore, because Petitioner's claim was procedurally defaulted on independent and adequate state law grounds, the Court will not review it. *See Coleman, 501 U.S. at 729*, ("This Court will not review a question of federal law decided by a state court if the decision of that court rests on a state law ground that is independent of the federal question and adequate to support the judgment."). This claim is technically exhausted but procedurally defaulted. Petitioner filed no reply, and presents no cause for the default. Accordingly, Ground One (D) is properly dismissed.

In sum, the Arizona Court of Appeal's rejection of Petitioner's prosecutorial misconduct claim did not contradict or unreasonably apply binding United States Supreme Court precedent and the state appellate court's ruling was not otherwise based on any unreasonable factual determination. [*30] *See, e.g., 28 U.S.C. § 2254(d)*. The Magistrate Judge recommends that the District Court, after its independent review, dismiss Ground One (A) through (D).

STATE OF ARIZONA, APPELLEE, V. JAY CHRISTOPHER GRADY, APPELLANT.
NO. 1 CA-CR 14-0834

COUNSEL: For Appellee: Myles Braccio, Arizona Attorney General's Office, Phoenix. For Appellant: Edward F. McGee, Yuma County Public Defender's Office, Yuma.

(Text added/modified for emphasis) Courts consistently allow the state to vouch for witnesses and amend the charges so that convictions be obtained thereby preventing a meaningful defense. Courts consistently sanction this systematic practice refusing to find bad faith thereby condoning this misconduct which is on the rise . As it was never their intent to subject the state's case to a meaningful adversarial process, when viewed in the totality, and not in isolation, this should constitute fraud upon the court by these lawyers.

FACTS AND PROCEDURAL BACKGROUND

In mid-March 2012, the victim and his father-in-law drove to Martinez Lake in Yuma County to pick up the victim's boat. The victim lived in California but for many years had vacationed at the lake. They arrived around 10:30 p.m. on a Friday night and went to a nearby bar for drinks.

The victim and his father-in-law sat by themselves at a table across the bar from a large group. After about half an hour, the victim bought a second round of drinks, and an inebriated woman named Lisa sat down at the table across from them. Lisa was physically carried out of the bar by her friends a short time later.

Within about a minute, Grady walked up behind the victim, spun him around by the shoulder, and punched him in the throat while saying "you dissed my buddy's wife." When the victim came to, he could not talk, had difficulty breathing, and sought medical attention. His father-in-law also had been knocked out, and the victim stayed with him while waiting for an ambulance to arrive. After an EMT found no immediate life-threatening injuries, the victim declined to go to the hospital.

The victim and his father-in-law drove home the next morning, and the victim sought medical treatment there. According to the victim, medical imaging two days later showed that he had fractured his larynx and that, had the fracture shifted, it could have blocked his airway.

A Yuma County Sheriff's deputy interviewed Grady several weeks after the incident. Grady admitted striking the victim once and seemed apologetic, but stated that he had walked over to talk and the victim had raised his elbow (albeit without striking him), and that he had responded by striking the victim.

The State charged Grady with one count of aggravated assault, and the jury convicted him of the offense. Grady timely appealed after the court imposed 48 months of supervised probation. We have jurisdiction under *Arizona Revised Statutes ("A.R.S.") § 13-4033(A)*.

I. Amending the Indictment to Conform to the Evidence.

Grady argues the superior court erred by granting the State's motion during closing argument to amend the indictment to reflect that the aggravated assault resulted in a "torn larynx" instead of a "fractured thyroid." We review an order amending the indictment for an abuse of discretion. *State v. Johnson, 198 Ariz. 245, 247, ¶ 4, 8 P.3d 1159, 1161 (App. 2000)*.

Arizona Rule of Criminal Procedure 13.5(b) permits amendment of an indictment "to correct mistakes of fact or remedy formal or technical defects," and provides that the indictment "shall be deemed amended to conform to the evidence adduced at any court proceeding." A defect is "formal or technical" if its correction "does not operate to change the nature of the offense charged or to prejudice the defendant in any way." *State v. Freeney, 223 Ariz. 110, 112, ¶ 11, 219 P.3d 1039, 1041 (2009)* (citation omitted).

Here, Grady was charged with one count of aggravated assault "by any means of force which causes . . . temporary but substantial loss or impairment of anybody organ or part, or a fracture of any body part, to-wit: defendant struck victim in the throat causing a fractured thyroid and voice box." At trial, the victim testified that he had suffered a fractured larynx. But he also enumerated several ramifications of the injury, including trouble breathing for a week, trouble speaking for three months, and swelling of his neck for a year.

Defense counsel's closing argument focused primarily on the absence of medical testimony or records to substantiate the victim's claimed injury, but he also pointed out, in reference to the indictment, that he had "not heard anything about a fractured thyroid at all in this whole hearing." The court noted that the indictment could be amended to conform to the evidence, and after defense counsel concluded his closing, the State moved to amend the indictment to reflect that "the victim suffered a torn larynx instead of the other portions." The court allowed the amendment over a defense objection that the amendment would alter the charges. Defense counsel did not ask to reopen the evidence or for an opportunity to supplement his closing argument in the wake of the amendment.

The superior court did not abuse its discretion by permitting what was at most a formal or technical amendment. Although the indictment originally alleged that Grady's punch to the victim's throat caused "a fractured thyroid and voice box," "voice box" is a colloquial term for the larynx. *See American Heritage Dictionary* 1940 (5th ed. 2011) (defining "voice box" as "[t]he larynx"). Thus, the amendment to reflect a "torn larynx" thus only narrowed the indictment by removing the reference to a "fractured thyroid," and substituting a synonym ("larynx") for the originally-alleged "voice box."

The amendment after defense counsel had completed closing argument did not deprive Grady of adequate notice of and opportunity to defend against the newly asserted charges. *See Johnson, 198 Ariz. at 249, ¶ 13, 8 P.3d at 1163*. Grady's counsel in fact defended against the charges as amended, focusing primarily on the lack of medical evidence to establish any substantial injury to the victim, and he did not seek to supplement his closing after the court granted the amendment.

Grady further asserts that the prosecutor's characterization of the injury as a "torn" rather than "fractured" larynx is fatal to the amendment. But an allegation of a torn larynx did not change the conduct alleged or modify the elements of the offense. Grady was still alleged to have punched the victim in the throat, causing "temporary but substantial loss or impairment of anybody organ or part, or a fracture of any body part." *A.R.S. § 13-1204(A)(3)*. Even assuming there is a difference between a torn and a fractured larynx, the victim's testimony that he suffered breathing and speaking difficulties along with neck swelling established a substantial impairment of his larynx, and a "temporary but substantial loss or impairment of anybody organ or part" and "a fracture of any body part" under *§ 13-1204(A)(3)* are not separate offenses but rather alternative manners in which to commit the same offense. *See State v. Manzanedo, 210 Ariz. 292, 294, ¶¶ 8-9, 110 P.3d 1026, 1028 (App. 2005)* (indicating that consistent or connected acts listed in a statute generally create a single offense that may be committed in different ways, and noting that the Legislature can readily indicate an intent to create multiple offenses "by enacting separate statutes or, at least, separate subsections"). Accordingly, the superior court did not abuse its discretion by allowing the amendment.

II. Prosecutorial Misconduct.

Grady argues that, by stating in closing that the victim had suffered a torn larynx, the prosecutor referred to information not presented to the jury and thus impermissibly vouched for evidence of the victim's injury. Because Grady did not object at trial, we review only for fundamental, prejudicial error. *See State v. Henderson, 210 Ariz. 561, 567-68, ¶¶ 19-20, 115 P.3d 601, 607-08 (2005).*

Prosecutorial vouching is a form of misconduct in which the "prosecutor suggests that information not presented to the jury supports the witness's testimony," *State v. Vincent, 159 Ariz. 418, 423, 768 P.2d 150, 155 (1989)*, or the prosecutor asserts personal knowledge of facts in issue. *State v. Bible, 175 Ariz. 549, 601, 858 P.2d 1152, 1204 (1993)* (citation omitted).

Prosecutorial misconduct warrants reversal only if "(1) misconduct is indeed present [,] and (2) a reasonable likelihood exists that the misconduct could have affected the jury's verdict, thereby denying defendant a fair trial." *State v. Moody, 208 Ariz. 424, 459, ¶ 145, 94 P.3d 1119, 1154 (2004)*. We consider all instances of alleged misconduct cumulatively. *State v. Roque, 213 Ariz. 193, 230, ¶ 164, 141 P.3d 368, 405 (2006)*. A defendant is not entitled to relief based on an assertion of prosecutorial misconduct unless the misconduct is "so pronounced and persistent that it permeates the entire atmosphere of the trial," rendering "the resulting conviction a denial of due process." *State v.*

Morris, 215 Ariz. 324, 335, ¶ 46, 160 P.3d 203, 214 (2007) (citations omitted).

During closing, the prosecutor twice referred to the victim's injury as a torn larynx rather than as a fracture (as the victim had testified). Grady argues that these statements in effect constituted testimony by the prosecutor that the victim's medical files referred to a laryngeal tear.

Even assuming something more than a semantic difference between a laryngeal tear and fracture, however, the prosecutor referred to a torn larynx not as an assertion of personal knowledge, but rather in the context of recounting the evidence presented at trial, including the victim's description of his injuries and the victim's characterization of his doctor's diagnosis. *Compare, e.g., State v. Newell, 212 Ariz. 389, 403, ¶¶ 64-65, 132 P.3d 833, 847 (2006)* (concluding that, absent opinion testimony about the primacy of DNA evidence, the prosecutor's comment that "we all know that DNA is . . . the most powerful investigative tool in law enforcement at this time" improperly vouched for the strength of the State's case by suggesting evidence not presented to the jury supported the evidence presented), *and State v. Salcido, 140 Ariz. 342, 343-44, 681 P.2d 925, 926-27 (App. 1984)*(concluding that prosecutor's argument that "I went over with the agents and saw the [evidence]" constituted improper vouching both as an assertion of personal knowledge and by directing the jurors' attention to facts not in evidence to bolster the credibility of State's witnesses). The prosecutor's references to a torn larynx did not "call [] to the jurors' attention matters that they should not consider," *Roque, 213 Ariz. at 224, ¶ 128, 141 P.3d at 399*, and did not constitute prosecutorial misconduct.

STATE OF ARIZONA, APPELLEE, V. FRANCISCO CORNELIO BEJINEZ, APPELLANT. NO. 1 CA-CR 14-0349

(Text added/modified for emphasis) Courts consistently allow the state to prevent defendants from a fair trial. The same prosecutors consistently misstate the evidence, improperly vouch for their witnesses, appealed to the passions of the jury thereby preventing a meaningful defense. Courts consistently sanction this systematic practice refusing to find bad faith thereby condoning this misconduct which is on the rise . As it was never their intent to subject the state's case to a meaningful adversarial process, when viewed in the totality, and not in isolation, this should constitute fraud upon the court by these lawyers.

COUNSEL: Arizona Attorney General's Office, Phoenix, By Joseph T. Maziarz, Counsel for Appellee. Maricopa County Public Defender, Phoenix, By Mikel Steinfeld, Counsel for Appellant.

FACTS AND PROCEDURAL HISTORY

During an unrelated investigation, Officer Jones noticed Bejinez's vehicle exhibiting suspicious behavior by attempting to avoid the area where Officer Jones was located. Officer Jones then had his partner, who was in an unmarked vehicle, follow Bejinez. After his partner informed him that Bejinez committed a civil traffic violation, Officer Jones followed Bejinez into a parking lot. There, Bejinez exited his vehicle, left the door open, and began to walk away. As Officer Jones approached Bejinez's vehicle, he noticed one small bag of methamphetamine on the driver's seat. The officers found ten additional bags of methamphetamine inside the vehicle, $2358.00 on Bejinez, and Arizona and Illinois license plates both registered to Bejinez's vehicle.

The state charged Bejinez with one count of possession of dangerous drugs for sale, a class two felony; one count of transportation of dangerous drugs, a class two felony; and one count of possession of drug paraphernalia, a class six felony. After trial, the jury found Bejinez guilty on all three counts and that Bejinez committed the offenses for pecuniary gain. The trial court sentenced Bejinez to a mitigated, concurrent term of five years for possession of dangerous drugs for sale and transportation of dangerous drugs, with presentence incarceration credit of 208 days. The trial court ordered Bejinez to serve a two-year probation sentence for possession of drug paraphernalia.

DISCUSSION

Bejinez argues that the prosecutor committed misconduct in opening statement and closing argument by stating that Bejinez "made a living selling drugs" and that "Bejinez believed the jury would let him go free because there was no direct evidence." Bejinez contends that these comments fundamentally impacted his right to a fair trial by forcing him to address arguments not drawn from the evidence and urged the jury to convict him based on these assertions.

Because Bejinez did not object to the prosecutor's remarks in the opening statement or closing argument, we review solely for fundamental error. *State v. Roque, 213 Ariz. 193, 228, ¶ 154, 141 P.3d 368, 403 (2006)*. To prevail, Bejinez must establish that fundamental error exists and that the error prejudiced him. *State v. Henderson, 210 Ariz. 561, 567, at ¶ 20, 115 P.3d 601, 607 (2005)*. Fundamental error is error that goes "to the foundation of the case, error that takes from the defendant a right essential to his defense, and error of such magnitude that the defendant could not possible have received a fair trial." *Id. at ¶ 19* (quoting *State v. Hunter, 142 Ariz. 88, 90, 688 P.2d 980, 982 (1984)*). "Reversal on the basis of prosecutorial misconduct requires that the conduct be so pronounced and persistent that it permeates the entire atmosphere of the trial." *State v. Hughes, 193 Ariz. 72, 79, ¶ 26, 969 P.2d 1184, 1191 (1998)* (internal quotation marks omitted) (citations omitted).

During the opening statement, the prosecutor said the following:

> Ladies and gentlemen, this case is about a drug dealer. A small-time drug dealer who is trying to make a profit selling methamphetamine. He thinks because no one saw him sell the methamphetamine, no one saw him in the act of the transaction and receiving money, for methamphetamine, you will let him go free. Your verdict will decide if that is true.

The prosecutor's closing argument repeated the opening statement:

> When I started this morning, I said this case about is about [sic] a drug dealer. It is about a small town drug dealer, a pager dealer making a living selling methamphetamine.
>
> And I said because no one saw him actually sell the methamphetamine, to get the methamphetamine someone

else received money, he thinks you will let him go free. Your verdict will decide if that is true.

Bejinez argues that the prosecutor committed fundamental error by: 1) arguing inferences and conclusions in the opening statement; 2) misstating the evidence; 3) vouching; 4) appealing to the passions of the jury; and 5) commenting on Bejinez's constitutional right to remain silent. Bejinez argues this conduct constituted reversible error. We disagree.

A. Inferences and Conclusions During Opening Statement

Bejinez first argues that the prosecutor's opening statement was argumentative and encouraged the jury to return a verdict to convict him. Bejinez attempts to distinguish *State v. Bible, 175 Ariz. 549, 602, 858 P.2d 1152, 1205 (1993)*, asserting that here, the inferences and conclusions argued by the prosecutor during opening statements were not supported by evidence later admitted during trial. However, as we note hereinafter, even if we assume the prosecutor's opening statement improperly argued inferences and conclusions to be drawn from the evidence, it did not prejudice Bejinez because the statements were supported by evidence at trial. *See id., 175 Ariz. at 602, 858 P.2d at 1205* (holding that there was no reversible error when the inferences and conclusions made during opening statement were permissible during closing argument). Therefore, any alleged error in the prosecutor's opening statement did not amount to reversible error.

B. Misstatement of the Evidence

We also reject Bejinez's argument that the prosecutor misstated the evidence during opening statement and closing argument by asserting that Bejinez was "a pager dealer making a living selling methamphetamine." Officer Jones testified that a "pager dealer" is term used to refer to a "street-level drug dealer" who sells small quantities of drugs. Officer Jones also testified that the quantity and packaging of the methamphetamine, Bejinez's lack of a device for using the methamphetamine, the manner in which Bejinez kept his money, and the fact that Bejinez's cell phone was constantly ringing were consistent with items and characteristics of individuals who sell methamphetamine. Accordingly, the record supports the prosecutor's statement.

The record also supports the prosecutor's assertion during closing argument that Bejinez "believed the jury would let him go free" because no one witnessed Bejinez make a transaction. During his cross-examination, counsel for Bejinez repeatedly asked witnesses whether they actually saw him sell methamphetamine. A reasonable inference from this line of questioning is that Bejinez relied on the lack of direct evidence that he participated in a transaction to sell methamphetamine to establish that he was not guilty. Accordingly, the prosecutor did not misstate the evidence during closing arguments. *See State v. Morris, 215 Ariz. 324, 336, ¶ 51, 160 P.3d 203, 215 (2007)* ("Prosecutors have wide latitude in presenting their arguments to the jury" and may argue "all reasonable inferences from the evidence.") (internal quotations and citations omitted).

C. Vouching During Closing Argument

Bejinez relies on *State v. Leon, 190 Ariz. 159, 945 P.2d 1290 (1997)* to argue that the prosecutor improperly vouched during closing argument by asserting that Bejinez made a living selling drugs and believed the jury would let him go free. Bejinez also bases his vouching argument by again alleging a lack of evidentiary support for the State's assertions. In *Leon*, unlike this case, the court sustained objections to the state's closing argument because the state specifically told the jury that there was inadmissible evidence that they did not get to hear. *Id., 190 Ariz. at 161-62, 945 P.2d at 1292-93*. Here, the prosecutor did not tell the jury that there was evidence outside of the record. Moreover, as previously discussed, the record supports the prosecutor's statements in opening statement and closing argument. We find no error, much less fundamental error.

D. Appealing to the Passions of the Jury

Next, Bejinez argues that the prosecutor improperly appealed to the passions of the jury by ascribing to Bejinez the belief that because there were no observed transactions, the jury would "let him go free" and concluded, "your verdict will decide if that is true." He argues that this statement communicated a message that the jury has a "duty to perform" and they should send Bejinez a message. In support, he relies on *Viereck v. U.S., 318 U.S. 236, 63 S. Ct. 561, 87 L. Ed. 734 (1943).* In *Viereck*, the government alluded to the nation's then-current participation in World War II, stating, "this is war, harsh, cruel, murderous war." *Id. at 247, n.3.* The government told the jury that it had a duty to perform, stating that "the American people are relying upon you ladies and gentlemen for their protection against this sort of crime." *Id.* The Supreme Court found this argument improper because the government "indulged in an appeal wholly irrelevant to any facts or issues in the case, the purpose and effect of which could only have been to arouse passion and prejudice." *Id. at 247-48.*

Here, the prosecutor did not refer to any irrelevant facts or inflame the jurors' passions. Instead, the prosecutor reminded the jurors that their role in the case was to determine whether Bejinez was guilty or innocent regardless of what Bejinez believed. Nor did the prosecutor encourage the jury to send Bejinez a message. Moreover, this statement did not permeate the entire trial. We find no error no less fundamental error.

E. Comments on Bejinez's Refusal to Testify

Lastly, we reject Bejinez's argument that by ascribing a belief to him, the prosecutor "pointed out" that Bejinez did not testify. Here, the prosecutor's assertion that Bejinez "believed the jury would let him go free" does not relate to Bejinez's failure to testify, but rather to Bejinez's position as the defendant contesting the charges against him. Thus, the prosecutor did not comment on Bejinez's failure to testify, and we find no error.

STATE OF ARIZONA, APPELLEE, V. THOMAS LEROY CROM, IV, APPELLANT.
NO. 1 CA-CR 14-0751

(Text added/modified for emphasis) Courts consistently allow the state to prevent defendants from receiving a fair trial. The same prosecutors repeatedly argue in case after case that the defendant failed to present evidence showing he/she is innocent. There are too many such incidents. As it was never their intent to subject the state's case to a meaningful adversarial process, when viewed in the totality, and not in isolation, this should constitute fraud upon the court by these lawyers. The same prosecutors repeatedly do just that.

COUNSEL: Arizona Attorney General's Office, Phoenix, By Robert A. Walsh, Counsel for Appellee.

The Hopkins Law Office PC, Tucson, By Cedric Martin Hopkins, Counsel for Appellant.

FACTS AND PROCEDURAL BACKGROUND

Police arrested Crom and Hans Barkowski in the summer of 2013 after finding Crom driving a stolen car with Hans in the passenger seat. Crom first told police that "he did not own the vehicle," but "had borrowed it from a friend whose name he didn't know and it was actually that friend's brother's whose name he didn't know." He later changed his story, stating that "he got the keys to the car from a guy that he met at a bar in Old Town Scottsdale," but "[h]e didn't remember his name" or "which bar it was."

At trial, Crom testified that the day of his arrest began at his friend Matt's house where Hans arrived in the stolen car, claiming he had located Crom's recently stolen truck. Before leaving to find the truck, Crom retrieved a jiggle key that he intended to use to try to start the truck because he no longer had keys to it. Crom said he saw the stolen car for the first time when he and Hans left in it to find his truck, and although Hans drove the stolen car to Matt's house, Crom asked for and received the car keys from Hans because he knew Hans lacked a valid driver's license. When the prosecutor noted that Crom's testimony as to how he obtained the keys was inconsistent with his prior statements to police, Crom admitted that he previously told police "a bunch of lies" because he did not want to "snitch" on Hans.

Crom further testified that after leaving Matt's apartment, he and Hans drove to the location of the stolen truck and spoke with an unnamed woman about the truck. After failing to locate the person with the keys to his truck, Crom broke into it and tried to start the engine with the jiggle key, damaging the ignition, which, he said, his aunt later paid to repair. After failing to start the truck, Crom and Hans left to find a friend to help hotwire it. The police arrested them shortly thereafter.

Prior to trial, Crom notified the prosecutor and the superior court of his intent to call Hans as a trial witness. The superior court appointed counsel for Hans, who was incarcerated at the time, and had him transported to court on the first day of trial. Counsel for Hans informed the superior court that Hans intended to invoke his Fifth Amendment right to remain silent as to all questions. Crom argued that Hans should be forced to invoke his right to remain silent in front of the jury because he might change his [*5] mind on the stand. Relying on *Arizona Rule of Evidence 403*, the superior court found that calling Hans as a witness simply to have him invoke his right to remain silent would "be a needless use of the jury's time," and excused Hans from testifying.

During cross-examination of Crom, and over the objection of defense counsel, the superior court allowed the prosecutor to ask Crom about Hans' absence from court, suggesting that Crom failed to call Hans because he would not corroborate Crom's story. The superior court denied defense counsel's request on redirect that Crom be permitted to tell the jury that Hans was unavailable because he had invoked his right to remain silent.

The jury found Crom guilty of theft of means of transportation.

DISCUSSION

....

II. Improper Inference

Because Hans invoked his Fifth Amendment right to remain silent and was therefore unavailable to both parties, we find that the prosecutor's questioning about Hans' absence created an improper inference, and the superior court erred in admitting the testimony without any curative instructions.

When a defendant attacks the accuracy of the State's evidence, "elemental fairness" allows the State to comment on the defense's failure to present potentially exculpatory witnesses to which he has access. *McDougall, 153 Ariz. at 160, 735 P.2d at 770*. The defendant's "access" to these witnesses is the foundation of this "elemental fairness," and if a witness is equally available to both sides or not available to either side, no party is permitted to create an inference from any other party's failure to call that witness. *Id.; State v. Condry, 114 Ariz. 499, 500, 562 P.2d 379, 380 (1977)* (citation omitted).

In assessing the propriety of a comment regarding an uncalled witness, the superior court may consider "whether the witness was under the control of the party who failed to call him or her;" "whether the party failed to call a seemingly available witness whose testimony it would naturally be expected to produce if it were favorable;" and "whether the existence or nonexistence of a certain fact is uniquely within the knowledge of the witness." *Gordon v. Liguori, 182 Ariz. 232, 236, 895 P.2d 523, 527 (App. 1995)* (citations omitted).

Despite the superior court having excused Hans as a witness because he invoked his Fifth Amendment right to remain silent, the prosecutor repeatedly questioned Crom about Hans' absence, and, in doing so, created a prejudicial inference that Crom had not called Hans because his testimony would not support Crom's story. This prejudice was compounded by the superior court's limitation on the scope of information that would be provided to the jury on Hans' unavailability. The relevant testimony follows:

> Prosecutor: Where is Hans right now?
> Crom: In jail.
> Prosecutor: And how long has he been in custody, do you know?
> Crom: Nine months, ten months.
> Prosecutor: But you do know exactly where he is?
> Crom: Yes, I do.
> Prosecutor: But yet he's not here to tell the jury and verify what you want the jury to believe; correct?

After the superior court overruled defense counsel's burden-shifting objection, the questioning continued:

> Prosecutor: You were transported today by the Sheriff's Office to court; correct?
> Crom: Yes.

Prosecutor: And Hans . . . is housed in the Sherriff's custody; correct?

Crom: Yes, he is.

Prosecutor: So Hans could have been brought to this court in the same manner you were to tell this jury exactly what you want them to believe after you told the police two different stories and a third story for the jury here in trial; correct?

Crom: Correct.

Prosecutor: And yet he's not here to do that, to back up your story? That's a yes or no question.

Crom: No, he's not.

On redirect, the prosecutor objected to the following question posed by defense counsel: "You don't have any control over how deputies . . . transport [] people; correct?" During a bench conference, the superior court explained that it could not "have the jury believe that [Crom] didn't have the ability to get [Hans to court] if [Crom] wanted him [t]here." Defense counsel responded that the prosecutor told the jury, falsely, that Crom *could* bring Hans to court when in fact he *could not* because he had invoked his Fifth Amendment rights.

Defense counsel: He invoked. He invoked. Can I talk about that?

The Court: No, we're not going into whether [Hans] invoked.

Defense counsel: Judge, Mr. Crom did bring [Hans] here in front of all of us. He did bring him here so that's absolutely--he did bring him here.

. . .

Prosecutor: Well, again, Judge, State's concern, the Court picked up on, is the false impression that's being given to the jury that somehow the defendant could not procure the witness.

Defense counsel: We'll talk about that because he did procure the witness. He did procure him and we all saw him.

. . .

The Court: We will not get into invocations.

Defense counsel: Your Honor, the Court just allowed [the prosecutor] to say to Mr. Crom: You have the power to bring Hans [to court] . . . and you didn't. My client did bring Hans . . . here in front of all of us, Judge, and he should be able to tell the jurors that.

The Court: You can tell the jurors that [Hans] came. You can't tell them whether or not [Hans] invoked or didn't invoke. . . . You want him to invoke in front of the jury, you had the right to ask for that, but you chose not to [do] so.

In short, the superior court ruled that defense counsel could "say that [Hans] came [to court] to talk to [Crom]" but they were "leaving it at that" and "not getting into whether he invoked or didn't invoke."

During his closing, the prosecutor again mentioned the absence of corroborating witnesses stating "the power of subpoena cuts both ways," and "the Defense . . . can subpoena whoever they choose to come in and testify."

Here, because Hans was not available to Crom or to the State due to the invocation of his right to remain silent, the State was not permitted to comment on his absence from trial. *See McDougall, 153 Ariz. at 160, 735 P.2d at 770*. Thus, the superior court erred by admitting this testimony without allowing clarification by defense counsel or providing the jury with curative instructions. *See State v. Payne, 233 Ariz. 484, 513, ¶ 120, 314 P.3d 1239, 1268 (2013)* (no reversible error for improper questioning by prosecutor where the court sustained objections and issued curative instructions); *State v. Leon, 190 Ariz. 159, 163, 945 P.2d 1290, 1294 (1997)* ("because the record does not reflect a ruling or a curative instruction by the court, the potential harm went unmitigated").

We now turn to whether the superior court's error was harmless. *See State v. Ramos, 235 Ariz. 230, 234, ¶ 8, 330 P.3d 987, 991 (App. 2014)* (harmless error review used when objections are raised at trial to a prosecutor's arguments or comments) (citing *State v. Henderson, 210 Ariz. 561, 567, ¶ 18, 115 P.3d 601, 607 (2005)* ("Reviewing courts consider alleged trial error under the harmless error standard when a defendant objects at trial and thereby preserves an issue for appeal.").

The State argues that any conceivable error was harmless because the impeachment was cumulative to other legitimately admitted evidence that undermined Crom's credibility, including his prior felony convictions, his admission to telling detectives "a bunch of lies," and his failure to call four other witnesses mentioned on direct-examination. We disagree.

First, we note that Hans was a key player in the events leading to Crom's arrest, and the State does not suggest otherwise. According to Crom, Hans drove the car to Matt's house; initiated contact [*12] with Crom to tell him about his stolen truck; initially possessed the car keys; gave Crom the car keys; directed Crom to the unnamed woman's house; told Crom not to speed; and was in the car at the time of the arrest.

The centrality of Hans' involvement was also not lost on the jury, who submitted approximately seventeen questions regarding Hans. The superior court refused to ask several of these questions, and answers elicited from others greatly minimized the apparent role of Hans in the events. For instance, jury question 8 asked why a detective who interviewed Crom did not ask him about Hans during the interview. The detective responded that he "honestly [did not] have an answer for that," except that he knew "that when detectives had arrested [Crom and Hans], [Crom] was driving the vehicle and [he] was interested about what [Crom] was doing driving the vehicle and where he got the car," and once Crom "said that he got the car from someone [else], [he] didn't have any reason" to ask about Hans because Crom "wasn't giving a story about Hans." The improper adverse inference therefore greatly downplayed the importance of Hans' involvement in this case.

In addition, detectives on the case provided testimony that was favorable to Crom. For example, one detective testified that unlike most stolen cars, here there were no signs of forced entry, such as a broken window, a jammed ignition, hanging wires, or other damage. Further, police found the actual car key in the ignition at the time of Crom's arrest, and Crom had a reasonable explanation for having a jiggle key in his possession: he intended to use it to try to start his truck.

Given the significance of Hans' role in the events leading to Crom's arrest and the existence of testimony favorable to Crom, we cannot say that the improper adverse inference created by the prosecutor was harmless beyond a reasonable doubt. We therefore reverse Crom's conviction for theft of means of transportation and remand for a new trial. III. Jury Instructions

RODOLFO ROMERO, PETITIONER, V. CHARLES RYAN AND ARIZONA ATTORNEY GENERAL, RESPONDENTS. CIV 08-02020 PHX SRB (MEA) UNITED STATES DISTRICT COURT FOR THE DISTRICT OF ARIZONA

(Text added/modified for emphasis) The state consistently changes the charges to meet its end. Courts consistently sanction this systematic practice refusing to find bad faith thereby condoning this misconduct which is on the rise . As it was never their intent to subject the state's case to a meaningful adversarial process, when viewed in the totality, and not in isolation, this should constitute fraud upon the court by these lawyers.

COUNSEL: Rodolfo Romero, Petitioner, Pro se, TUCSON, AZ. For Dora Schriro, Respondent: Robert Anthony Walsh, Office of the Attorney General, Criminal Appeals Section, Phoenix, AZ.

I Background

A Maricopa County grand jury indictment returned June 21, 1988, charged Petitioner and a co-defendant, Mr. Conde, with one count of first-degree murder, one count of burglary in the first-degree, five counts of armed robbery, one count of attempted armed robbery, and three counts of aggravated assault. See Answer, Exh. A. The charges arose from a bank robbery occurring on May 27, 1988, in Phoenix, Arizona. A police officer was shot and killed as he attempted to stop the fleeing robbers. Id., Exh. C. The following is taken from the Arizona Court of Appeals' decision in Mr. Conde's appeal:

The evidence at trial showed that [Mr. Conde] and an accomplice entered a bank armed with handguns which they pointed at customers and bank personnel. Conde leaped on the top of a counter and ordered a teller to place money in a plastic bag. He then ordered a customer to surrender her car keys so that he and his accomplice could escape. They obtained their getaway vehicle in the bank parking lot by taking it from its driver at gunpoint. At this juncture, the police officer, working off-duty as a bank security guard, opened fire on Conde and his accomplice. In the exchange of shots the officer was killed.

The robbers fled the scene in the stolen car. During the next half-hour, they commandeered two other vehicles at gunpoint. When police located Conde and ordered him to stop, he fired at them. He was wounded and was eventually taken into custody.

Arizona v. Conde, 174 Ariz. 30, 31, 846 P.2d 843, 844 (1992). See also Conde v. Flanagan, CIV 02-2034 PHX SRB GEE (D. Ariz).

At a pretrial conference in Petitioner's case the state indicated its theory of Petitioner's case was that Mr. Conde actually shot the bullet that killed the police officer; the charge of murder against Petitioner was predicated on accomplice liability. See Response, Exh. G at 46-48.

Petitioner's co-defendant was taken into custody the day the crimes occurred. Id., Exh. C at 3. Petitioner left the United States after the crimes occurred. Petitioner's co-defendant was tried and convicted by a jury of the charges stated in the indictment in late 1989, and was sentenced to an aggregate in excess of 200 years' imprisonment. Id., Exh. TT at 2.

In May of 1996, eight years after the indictment was issued, the Arizona Attorney General submitted an extradition request to the United States Department of Justice, asking for Petitioner's extradition in the event that law enforcement authorities could locate Petitioner in Mexico. Id., Exh. CC at 3 & App. A at 1. Approximately four years later, in June of 2000, Petitioner was arrested by Mexican authorities in Mexico. Id., Exh. C at 3.

On February 20, 2001, a Mexican district court approved the United States' request to extradite Petitioner to Arizona. Id., Exh. CC at 34. On March 15, 2001, Mexico's Secretary of Foreign Relations formally granted the extradition request. Id., Exh. CC at 34. Before Petitioner could be brought to the United States, however, on October 2, 2001, the Mexico Supreme Court concluded that the sentence of life imprisonment constituted cruel and unusual punishment and could not be imposed on a Mexican national by any court. Id., Exh. CC at 34. Accordingly, Petitioner subsequently successfully moved a Mexico federal court to set aside the grant of extradition because one of the offenses charged by Arizona, i.e., first degree murder, was punishable by life imprisonment. Id., Exh. CC at 35. The Mexican federal court's opinion setting aside the approval of extradition allowed Mexico's Secretary of Foreign Relations to file a pleading addressing whether Petitioner's extradition was barred by the possible imposition of a life sentence. Id., Exh. CC at 35.

Accordingly, on October 18, 2001, Mexico's Secretary of Foreign Relations requested assurances from the United States that Petitioner "[would] not be subject to imprisonment for life for murder..." if extradited to Arizona. Id., Exh. F, Attach. Referencing the governing extradition treaty between the United States and Mexico, the American ambassador responded *inter alia* that, in the event of Petitioner's conviction, "the State of Arizona [would not] seek or recommend a penalty of 25 years to life imprisonment at the sentencing phase of the judicial proceeding in this case," but that instead the State of Arizona would recommend imposition of a sentence of "50 to 60 years' imprisonment." Id., Exh. F, Attach. Regarding the possibility that the Arizona trial court might impose a life sentence upon Petitioner's conviction, notwithstanding the above-referenced recommendation, the United States ambassador informed Mexico that, should that circumstance arise, "the State of Arizona will take appropriate action to formally request that the court reduce such sentence to a term of years." Id., Exh. F, Attach. The ambassador acknowledged that, nonetheless, "[i]t would then be for the court to decide whether to accept the executive authority's determination." Id., Exh. F, Attach.

On November 28, 2001, Mexico granted the United States' request to extradite Petitioner on every requested charge except the charge of burglary. Id., Exh. CC, App. A at 7. The opinion approving the extradition noted the agreement complied with the relevant treaty in that Petitioner was not facing a death sentence and also noted the exchange of diplomatic notes regarding Mexico's insistence that Petitioner be sentenced to a term of years, rather than an indeterminate sentence, i.e., a sentence of life imprisonment. Id., Exh. CC, App. A at 13-14. On March 21, 2002, Mexico extradited Petitioner to Arizona. Id., Exh. CC at 3. Mexico did not extradite on this charge because the Mexican criminal code lacked an offense equivalent to second degree burglary. See Answer, Exh. DD at 28 & App. A at 7, 14-15

Just prior to trial, Petitioner's counsel moved the court to reduce the charge of first-degree murder to second-degree murder, citing the extradition treaty and agreement between Mexico and the United States. Id., Exh. E & Exh. G. After the matter was fully pled, the trial court heard argument on the motion November 18, 2002. Id., Exh. G. The trial court denied the motion at that time. Id., Exh. G at 15.

Petitioner's jury trial on the 1988 charges began on November 18, 2002. Id., Exh. H. Due to unavailability of witnesses, the trial court granted the state's motion to dismiss one count of armed robbery and one count of aggravated assault. Id., Exh. O at 132-33; Exh. S. Without any objection from the defense, the jury was instructed as to the lesser-included offense of second-degree murder. Id., Exh. EE at 4 & Exh. P at 38. Defense counsel told the jury during closing argument that Petitioner was "only guilty of Second Degree Murder." Id., Exh. P at 94.

The jury found Petitioner guilty of one count of first-degree murder, one count of burglary, four counts of armed robbery, one count of attempted robbery, and three counts of aggravated assault. Id., Exh. P at 112-17.

During the trial, and after Petitioner was convicted but prior to sentencing, his defense counsel notified the Mexican government of Petitioner's trial and conviction on the charge of first degree murder. Id., Exh. DD at 33; Exh. EE at 5. The Mexican government responded that it was not in favor of the imposition of a life sentence. Id., Exh. DD at 33; Exh. EE. A letter from a Mexican diplomat states:

> I reiterate that the government of Mexico is interested in seeing that the aforementioned reassurance of no application of life sentence on the accused, is complied with, this in case he is found guilty in the legal process being pursued against him in the United States of America, he is handed down a sentence of a determined number of years and not a life sentence, without

concern for how these assurances are complied with by the United States government...

Answer, Exh. DD at 33.

Petitioner's trial counsel filed a motion for a new trial asserting Petitioner could not be convicted of murder in the first degree or burglary because the charges were precluded by the extradition agreement. Defense counsel also moved to dismiss both these charges. Id., Exh. CC at 6. At a hearing on February 7, 2003, the parties stipulated to dismissal of the conviction for burglary. Id., Exh. CC at 6.

In response to Petitioner's post-trial motion to dismiss, the state offered to reduce the murder charge; however, Petitioner wanted dismissal of the count on the basis that jurisdiction was not proper. Id., Exh. CC at 6. On March 19, 2003, the state moved the trial court to reduce Petitioner's conviction from guilty of first-degree murder to guilty of second-degree murder, which would allow for a sentence of less than life imprisonment. Id., Exh. UU. The motion states it was "made to satisfy extradition agreement between the governments of the United States and Mexico. Defendant and defense counsel are aware of this motion and have no objection thereto." Id., Exh. UU. The trial court granted the motion on March 21, 2003. Id., Exh. BB & Exh. VV.

The trial court conducted an aggravation and mitigation hearing on March 21, 2003, at which hearing Petitioner spoke on his own behalf. Id., Exh. R & Exh. XX. At that time the court imposed an aggravated term of 20 years' incarceration pursuant to Petitioner's conviction on the charge of second-degree murder. Id., Exh. BB. The trial court found as aggravating circumstances the fact that the victim was a police officer who acted in his official capacity by trying to prevent the bank robbery, and the severe emotional harm to the officer's family. The state court also found as aggravating circumstances the presence of an accomplice, Petitioner's flight from the scene, and Petitioner's failure to self-surrender. The trial court found as other aggravating circumstances the fact that the murder occurred "in the immediate flight from a robbery to prevent detection" and Petitioner's decision to arm himself with assault rifles equipped with "banana-clips" and high-powered ammunition to ensure that he was "not apprehended at all costs." Id., Exh. R at 68-69. Stating that "the aggravating factors far, far outweigh the mitigating factors," the trial court indicated it would have imposed the same sentence even if it had disregarded the victim's status as a police officer and the pecuniary motive of the underlying armed robbery. The trial court also stated the sentence was warranted by the aggravating factors, which outweighed Petitioner's youthfulness and lack of a prior criminal record at the time of the crime. Id., Exh. R at 69.

The trial court imposed aggravated prison terms on the remaining convictions based upon the presence of an accomplice, flight from the scene, and the fact that the murder committed in immediate flight to prevent detection. Id., Exh. R at 70-72. The aggregate length of Petitioner's sentences is 106 years. Id., Exh. R.

Petitioner took a direct appeal of his convictions and sentences, arguing:

> The trial court erroneously replaced Defendant's first-degree murder conviction with a second-degree murder conviction because the conviction for that crime is not expressly allowed by the controlling extradition agreement between the United States and Mexico. And, the *Supremacy Clause* requires that the first-degree murder conviction be vacated because it conflicts with the controlling extradition agreement.

Id., Exh. CC at 32. Petitioner argued the State of Arizona had violated the extradition agreement between the United States and Mexico and the "doctrine of specialty" by reducing the charge after conviction and by imposing consecutive sentences. Id., Exh. CC. In his direct appeal Petitioner also argued that the trial court violated his *Sixth Amendment* right to a jury trial by enhancing his sentence using facts that were neither admitted by Petitioner nor found to be true beyond a reasonable doubt by a jury. Id., Exh. CC at 52.

The Arizona Court of Appeals affirmed Petitioner's convictions and sentences in a decision issued August 16, 2005. Id., Exh. EE. The Court of Appeals noted that Mexico had agreed to extradite Petitioner on a charge of first-degree murder. Id., Exh. EE. The Court of Appeals noted Mexico had agreed to extradite Petitioner on that charge if the State of

Arizona agreed to oppose the imposition of a life sentence if convicted. Id., Exh. EE. Additionally, the Arizona Court of Appeals reiterated the fact that, after Petitioner was convicted, his counsel notified the Mexican government of Petitioner's conviction. Id., Exh. EE. The Mexican government responded that it was not in favor of the imposition of a life sentence. Id., Exh. EE.

The Arizona Court of Appeals held that Petitioner's extradition, trial, and conviction on the charge of first degree murder was not in violation of the extradition agreement because the agreement specifically provided Petitioner could be extradited to face that charge. Id., Exh. EE. The appellate court concluded that the means used to bring the sentence mandated by the extradition agreement into compliance with Arizona law did not deprive Petitioner of any substantive right. Id., Exh. EE. Additionally, the Arizona Court of Appeals concluded that relief based on the application of the doctrine of specialty would depend on the wishes of Mexico, which country had indicated only a desire that Petitioner not be sentenced to life imprisonment if convicted of first-degree murder. Id., Exh. EE.

The Arizona Court of Appeals also determined that, if there had been any violation of the specialty doctrine, the error was invited by Petitioner because there was no contemporaneous objection to the state's motion for diminution of the murder count and because prior to trial and in closing argument Petitioner himself had argued for conviction on the lesser-included offense of second-degree murder. Id., Exh. EE.

Petitioner did not seek review of the Court of Appeals' decision in his direct appeal by the Arizona Supreme Court.

Petitioner initiated an action for state post-conviction relief pursuant to Rule 32, Arizona Rules of Criminal Procedure, on October 25, 2005. Id., Exh. HH. This action was dismissed on Petitioner's motion on November 14, 2005.

Petitioner filed another Rule 32 action on December 2, 2005. Id., Exh. KK. Petitioner was appointed counsel, who informed the state trial court on October 10, 2006, that she could not find any colorable claims to raise in a Rule 32 petition. Id., Exh. LL. Petitioner filed a pro per petition for relief, reasserting the claims raised in his direct appeal. Id.,

Exh. MM. The state trial court denied relief and the Arizona Court of Appeals denied review in a decision issued September 26, 2008. Id., Exh. PP & Exh. QQ.

Petitioner asserts he is entitled to relief from his convictions because the trial court's reduction of the first-degree murder conviction to second-degree murder was, he contends, erroneous. Petitioner asserts that "the conviction for that [second-degree murder] is not expressly allowed by the controlling extradition agreement between the United States and Mexico." Accordingly, he argues, "the *Supremacy Clause* requires that the first-degree [murder conviction] be vacated because it conflicts with the extradition agreement". Petitioner also contends his sentences must be vacated because the trial court aggravated his sentence based on facts not found by the jury, in violation of his *Sixth Amendment* rights.

Respondents maintain the petition must be denied and dismissed. Respondents assert that Petitioner's challenge to the reduction of his first-degree murder conviction to second-degree murder is procedurally barred because the Arizona Court of Appeals found that Petitioner invited any error by requesting the challenged reduction in charge. Respondents also contend this claim may be denied because the Arizona Court of Appeals' ruling on the merits was neither contrary to, nor an unreasonable application of, United States Supreme Court precedent. Respondents assert the second claim for relief must be denied because Arizona Court of Appeals' rejection of Petitioner's *Sixth Amendment* challenge was neither contrary to, nor an unreasonable application of, Supreme Court precedent.

II Analysis

....

Respondents argue that the Court should not review the merits of Petitioner's extradition-based claim regarding the propriety of his conviction for first-degree murder and the reduction in his conviction to second-degree murder because the state court's decision denying his specialty doctrine claim in Petitioner's direct appeal rested on an adequate and independent basis for barring federal habeas relief. Respondents contend the adequate and independent state basis for rejecting Petitioner's claim is that Petitioner waived the objection by inviting any error. Respondents cite to cases indicating the rule was clear, consistently applied, and well-established at the time of Petitioner's direct appeal. See Answer (Docket No. 12) at 51-52.

Some federal courts have concluded that a state's common law "invited error" rule is an independent and adequate state law that is sufficient to bar federal habeas review of a claim for relief. See *Leavitt v. Arave, 383 F.3d 809, 832-33 (9th Cir. 2004)* (stating "[t]here is no reason that we should treat the invited error rule differently from other state procedural bars"); *Wilson v. Ozmint, 357 F.3d 461, 467 (4th Cir. 2004); Coleman v. O'Leary, 845 F.2d 696, 699-701 (7th Cir. 1988); Francois v. Wainwright, 741 F.2d 1275, 1282 (11th Cir. 1984); Tillman v. Cook, 25 F. Supp. 2d 1245, 1274-76 (D. Utah 1998).*

However, it is at least arguable whether the Arizona Court of Appeals' decision denying this claim in Petitioner's direct appeal rested on the bar of invited error. The appellate court did begin discussion of the specialty doctrine claim by noting Petitioner had repeatedly sought the outcome achieved, i.e., conviction on second degree, rather than first degree, murder. After then thoroughly discussing the doctrine of specialty and applicable federal law and the merits of the claim, the Arizona Court of Appeals summarily stated that, "even if" Petitioner's conviction on second-degree murder had violated the specialty doctrine, any error was invited error and, accordingly, not reversible.

Because the claim may be denied on the merits and it is arguable if the state court decision may be affirmed based on the "adequate and independent" state bar, it is necessary to discuss whether the Court of Appeals' denial of the claim on the merits of the claim was clearly contrary to established federal law.

....

Violation of extradition agreement

Petitioner contends that the trial court violated the extradition treaty between the United States of America and Mexico by convicting him of first degree murder because, Petitioner argues, the governing treaty did not allow for a Mexican national's extradition for prosecution on an offense which could result in life imprisonment. Petitioner also contends that reducing the conviction from first-degree murder to second-degree murder violates the specialty doctrine, i.e., the doctrine that one can only be tried for the offense specified in the extradition agreement.

Petitioner raised these issues in a pre-trial motion. The motion was denied by the state trial judge after briefing and oral argument regarding the diplomatic note, the relevant treaty, the current status of the interpretation and extension of the treaty, the circumstance of Petitioner's case, including the exchange of notes between Mexican and United States officials regarding Petitioner's extradition agreement, and Arizona law. See Response, Exh. G.

The Arizona Court of Appeals denied the extradition-based claims on the merits when presented in petitioner's direct appeal. The Court of Appeals determined:

> The doctrine of specialty provides that a state that has obtained extradition of a person is prohibited from prosecuting that person "for any offense other than that for which the surrendering state agreed to extradite." *United States v. Andonian, 29 F.3d 1432, 1434-35 (9th Cir. 1994)* (internal citations omitted).

> An extradited person may be tried for offenses other than those for which the person was surrendered if the extraditing country consents. The proceedings did not violate the doctrine of specialty. Romero was extradited for first-degree murder, all in compliance with the extradition agreement and the doctrine of specialty. The subsequent reduction to the lesser-included offense of second-degree murder in order to comply with the sentencing provisions of the agreement does not mandate reversal of Romero's conviction.

***

> Extradition treaties are construed liberally to affect their purpose of surrendering fugitives to be tried for their alleged offenses. *United States v. Wiebe, 733 F.2d 549, 554 (8th Cir. 1984).* Under these circumstances, the reduction of Romero's conviction to a lesser-included offense constituted a

reclassification contemplated by the treaty. Romero does not contest that the charge of second-degree murder, as a lesser included offense of first-degree murder, was based on the same factual allegations as those established in the request for extradition based on first-degree murder, or that the punishment for second degree murder provided for a sentence of less than life imprisonment. Therefore, the treaty itself permitted a conviction for second-degree murder.

Answer, Exh. EE at 9-10.

In "*United States v. Rauscher, 119 U.S. 407, 7 S. Ct. 234, 30 L. Ed. 425 (1886)*, and *Johnson v. Browne, 205 U.S. 309, 27 S. Ct. 539, 51 L. Ed. 816 (1907)*, the Supreme Court set forth principles for interpreting extradition treaties and analyzed the effect of limitations on what offenses may be punished by the extraditing country." *Rodriguez Benitez v. Garcia, 495 F.3d 640, 643 (9th Cir. 2007)*. The Arizona Court of Appeals' decision denying Petitioner's claim was not an objectively unreasonable application of the holdings in these cases.

Rauscher established the doctrine of specialty, which provides that an extradited defendant may not be prosecuted for any offense other than that for which the surrendering country agreed to extradite.[].
...

In Browne, a defendant who was convicted in the United States of conspiracy to defraud the government fled the country and was extradited from Canada under a treaty which did not cover conspiracy. [] Because of the treaty's limitations, Canadian authorities surrendered the defendant for another offense but not for the conspiracy charge. [] The Supreme Court, looking to the agreed-upon terms of extradition and to the relevant treaty language, refused to uphold a reinstated conviction on the conspiracy charge.

Rodriguez Benitez, 495 F.3d at 643-44 (internal citations and quotations omitted).

Similar to the circumstance of the petitioner in *Rodriguez Benitez*, the terms of the agreement regarding the Petitioner's extradition indicated Mexico's concern about the sentence which could be imposed on Petitioner and not the degree of murder on which Petitioner could be tried. The Arizona trial court's reduction of the crime of conviction, which was supported by the evidence adduced at trial and which reduction was not contemporaneously opposed by Petitioner, did not deprive Petitioner of a substantive constitutional right. Cf. *United States v. Campbell, 300 F.3d 202, 211 (2d Cir. 2002)* (recognizing a difference between extradition terms limiting what sentence could be entered by the receiving state's courts and what sentence the receiving state could force the prisoner to serve).

The Ninth Circuit Court of Appeals concluded in Rodriguez Benitez that, because Supreme Court precedent, i.e., Rauscher and Browne, addressed limitations on charged offenses and the case before them involved limitations on the petitioner's sentence, it could not be said that the state court's opinion was contrary to clearly established federal law because to decide otherwise would have required an extension of the specialty doctrine. See *495 F.3d at 644.* "Only if the refusal to extend Rauscher's and Browne's holdings was objectively unreasonable must Benitez be granted a writ." Id. "Refusing to extend Supreme Court holdings governing limitations on charged offenses to unilaterally imposed sentencing conditions was not objectively unreasonable, and therefore AEDPA requires us to leave the decision of the California court undisturbed." *Id.* Similarly, the Arizona court's decision regarding Petitioner's claims based on the specialty doctrine and the reduction of Petitioner's conviction was not objectively unreasonable and Petitioner is not entitled to habeas relief on this claim.

Sixth Amendment sentencing claim

Petitioner asserts his aggravated prison terms violate his *Sixth Amendment* rights and the doctrine of Blakely v. Washington because the trial court, rather than a jury, found the existence of the six circumstances used to aggravate his sentence for second-degree murder.

In rejecting relief on this claim, the Arizona Court of Appeals applied the Arizona Supreme Court's decision in *Arizona v. Martinez, 210 Ariz.*

578, 115 P.3d 618 (2005), interpreting Blakely. Answer, Exh. EE at 16-17. The appellate court concluded that, pursuant to Martinez, Petitioner's constitutional rights were not violated because Petitioner had conceded at least one aggravating circumstance, i.e., the presence of an accomplice. The Court of Appeals reiterated the holding of Martinez that, once it was established that a single Blakely-compliant aggravating factor existed, i.e., a jury had found or the defendant had admitted the existence of an aggravating factor, the defendant's rights were not violated because the trial judge found additional aggravating factors.

The Arizona courts have interpreted Blakely to allow for the imposition of an aggravated sentence founded partially on facts not found by a jury if at least one aggravating factor is compliant with Blakely, i.e., found by a jury or admitted by the defendant. See *Arizona v. Martinez, 210 Ariz. 578, 115 P.3d 618 (2005)*; *Arizona v. Henderson, 210 Ariz. 561, 115 P.3d 601 (2005)*. The sentencing scheme iterated in Martinez was upheld upon review by the United States Supreme Court. See *Martinez v. Arizona, 546 U.S. 1044, 126 S. Ct. 762, 163 L. Ed. 2d 592 (2005)*.

Arizona's response to Blakely as explained in Martinez has been found to be not clearly contrary to federal law. See *Cunningham v. California, 549 U.S. 270, 294 n.17, 127 S. Ct. 856, 871 n.17, 166 L. Ed. 2d 856 (2007)* (finding California's sentencing process unconstitutional and analyzing the Colorado Supreme Court's response to Blakely in *Colorado v. Lopez, 113 P.3d 713, 716 (Colo. 2005)*; Colorado's Lopez decision is materially similar to the Arizona Supreme Court's Martinez opinion); *Stokes v. Schriro, 465 F.3d 397, 402-03 (9th Cir. 2006)* (holding "the Arizona state courts' interpretation of these [sentencing] provisions does not contradict clearly established federal law"). Accordingly, the Arizona court's decision denying this claim in Petitioner's direct appeal was not clearly contrary to federal law and Petitioner is not entitled to relief on this claim.

STATE OF ARIZONA, APPELLEE, V. MICHAEL CANALES, APPELLANT.
NO. 1 CA-CR 15-0100

COUNSEL: Arizona Attorney General's Office, Phoenix, By Joseph T. Maziarz, Counsel for Appellee. Maricopa County Public Defender's Office, Phoenix, By Spencer D. Heffel, Counsel for Appellant.

(Text added/modified for emphasis) Courts consistently allow the state to prevent defendants from presenting evidence. The same police and prosecutors consistently argue that there are confidential informants who will be jeopardized if disclosed, but do not provide case/fact specific evidence. By so doing they prevent examination. They vouch for witnesses and amend the charges so that convictions be obtained thereby preventing a meaningful defense. Courts consistently sanction this systematic practice refusing to find bad faith thereby condoning this misconduct which is on the rise . As it was never their intent to subject the state's case to a meaningful adversarial process, when viewed in the totality, and not in isolation, this should constitute fraud upon the court by these lawyers.

Michael Canales ("Appellant") appeals his convictions and sentences for two counts of sale or transportation of dangerous drugs. Appellant's counsel has filed a brief in accordance with *Smith v. Robbins, 528 U.S. 259, 120 S. Ct. 746, 145 L. Ed. 2d 756 (2000)*; *Anders v. California, 386 U.S. 738, 87 S. Ct. 1396, 18 L. Ed. 2d 493 (1967)*; and *State v. Leon, 104 Ariz. 297, 451 P.2d 878 (1969)*, stating that he has searched the record on appeal and found no arguable question of law that is not frivolous. Appellant's counsel therefore requests that we review the record for fundamental error. *See State v. Clark, 196 Ariz. 530, 537, ¶ 30, 2 P.3d 89, 96 (App. 1999)* (stating that this court reviews the entire record for reversible error). This court allowed Appellant to file a supplemental brief *in propria persona*, and he has done so, raising two issues that we address.

FACTS AND PROCEDURAL HISTORY
On September 5, 2013, a grand jury issued an indictment, charging Appellant with two counts of sale or transportation of dangerous drugs (methamphetamine), each a class two felony. *See A.R.S. § 13-3407*. The State later filed an allegation of historical priors, alleging Appellant had two historical prior felony convictions for enhancement purposes.

At trial, the State presented the following evidence: In March 2013, Phoenix police detectives Egea and Ayala were working undercover as narcotics officers, and they became aware of Appellant through Appellant's former girlfriend and a confidential informant. At approximately 4:30 p.m. on March 20, the detectives drove to an apartment complex in Phoenix, where the confidential informant introduced them to Appellant. The confidential informant walked away after the introduction, and the detectives, left alone with Appellant, inquired about purchasing methamphetamine. Appellant informed the detectives that he did not have the methamphetamine on his person, and the detectives agreed to drive Appellant to a different location, where Appellant would supply the methamphetamine.

The detectives drove Appellant to a second apartment complex. Detective Egea handed Appellant $110 to purchase the methamphetamine. Appellant exited the vehicle and entered a nearby apartment. When Appellant returned, he handed Detective Egea a Ziploc baggie containing a substance that appeared to be methamphetamine. Detective Egea gave Appellant an additional $20 for facilitating the deal, and the detectives drove Appellant back to the first apartment complex. The substance in the Ziploc baggie that Appellant handed Detective Egea was subsequently tested and determined to be 3.519 grams of methamphetamine, a usable quantity.

On April 10, 2013, the undercover detectives again arranged to purchase methamphetamine from Appellant. The detectives drove to a convenience store, where they met the confidential informant. Soon afterward, at approximately 3:40 p.m., Appellant arrived. Detective Ayala was the purchaser, and as Appellant approached Detective Ayala in the parking lot, the confidential informant walked away, while Detective Egea "kind of hung around [and] watched" the transaction between Appellant and Detective Ayala. Detective Ayala handed Appellant $150, and Appellant walked to a vehicle and retrieved a substance, which he gave to Detective Ayala. The substance was subsequently tested and determined to be 7.21 grams of methamphetamine in a usable condition.

The jury found Appellant guilty of both charged counts, and found the State had proved an alleged aggravating circumstance of pecuniary gain. Before sentencing, Appellant admitted he had two historical prior felony convictions for enhancement purposes. The trial court sentenced Appellant to concurrent, presumptive terms of 15.75 years' imprisonment in the Arizona Department of Corrections for each count, and credited him for 140 days of presentence incarceration. Appellant filed a timely notice of appeal.

ANALYSIS

I. Alleged Prosecutorial Misconduct/Vouching

Appellant argues his conviction must be reversed because the prosecutor committed misconduct during closing argument by vouching for the State's witnesses. We disagree.

"To prevail on a claim of prosecutorial misconduct, a defendant must demonstrate that '(1) misconduct is indeed present; and (2) a reasonable likelihood exists that the misconduct could have affected the jury's verdict, thereby denying [the] defendant a fair trial.'" *State v. Moody, 208 Ariz. 424, 459, ¶ 145, 94 P.3d 1119, 1154 (2004)* (citation omitted). Prosecutorial misconduct is not merely "legal error, negligence, mistake, or insignificant impropriety, but, taken as a whole, amounts to intentional conduct which the prosecutor knows to be improper and prejudicial." *Pool v. Superior Court, 139 Ariz. 98, 108, 677 P.2d 261, 271 (1984)* (footnote omitted). To justify reversal, the misconduct "must be 'so pronounced and persistent that it permeates the entire atmosphere of the trial.'" *State v. Lee, 189 Ariz. 608, 616, 944 P.2d 1222, 1230 (1997)* (citations omitted). Even then, reversal is not required unless the defendant was denied a fair trial. *State v. Bible, 175 Ariz. 549, 600, 858 P.2d 1152, 1203 (1993).*

It is improper for a prosecutor to vouch for the credibility of the State's witnesses. *State v. Salcido, 140 Ariz. 342, 344, 681 P.2d 925, 927 (App. 1984).* "Prosecutorial vouching occurs 'when the prosecutor places the prestige of the government behind its witness,' or 'where the prosecutor suggests that information not presented to the jury supports the witness's testimony.'" *State v. Garza, 216 Ariz. 56, 64, ¶ 23, 163 P.3d 1006, 1014 (2007)* (citing *State v. Dumaine, 162 Ariz. 392, 401, 783 P.2d 1184, 1193 (1989), disapproved on other grounds by State v. King, 225 Ariz. 87, 89-90, ¶¶ 9-12, 235 P.3d 240, 242-43 (2010)).*

We have reviewed the entirety of the prosecutor's closing arguments, and conclude that nothing in the prosecutor's remarks constitutes impermissible prosecutorial vouching. The prosecutor neither bolstered the detectives' credibility by referencing matters outside the record nor placed the prestige of the government behind the detectives by providing personal assurances of their veracity. *See State v. King, 180 Ariz. 268, 277, 883 P.2d 1024, 1033 (1994)* (citation omitted). Further, "during closing arguments counsel may summarize the evidence, make submittals to the jury, urge the jury to draw reasonable inferences from the evidence, and suggest ultimate conclusions." *Bible, 175 Ariz. at 602, 858 P.2d at 1205.* The prosecutor did exactly that. Moreover, viewed in context, the prosecutor's arguments made clear that it was for the jury alone to determine the witnesses' credibility and to "consider the evidence in light of reason, common sense, and experience." Finally, the prosecutor's subsequent characterization of the detectives' testimony as "reasonable" was fair rebuttal to defense counsel's argument challenging the detectives' credibility. *See State v. Duzan, 176 Ariz. 463, 468, 862 P.2d 223, 228 (App. 1993); see also State v. Martinez, 130 Ariz. 80, 82, 634 P.2d 7, 9 (App. 1981)* (concluding that prosecutorial comments that are a fair rebuttal to areas opened by the defense are proper). The prosecutor did not commit misconduct by her remarks, much less fundamental, reversible error.

II. The Confidential Informant

Appellant also argues the trial court abused its discretion and violated the *Confrontation Clause* in denying his pretrial motion to compel disclosure of the identity of the State's confidential informant, who did not testify at trial. We disagree.

Appellant's argument revolves around the following facts: Before trial, Appellant filed a motion to compel disclosure of the identity of the confidential informant who introduced the detectives to Appellant. The State responded that the informant was not present during the charged transactions and was not a material witness. At the evidentiary hearing on the motion, Detective Egea testified the confidential informant was not present during any drug-related conversations or transactions involving the detectives and Appellant. The prosecutor noted Appellant had not asserted the defense of entrapment, and after argument by counsel, the trial court denied Appellant's motion.

The only defense Appellant asserted in his notice of defenses was insufficiency of the State's evidence.

"Disclosure of the existence of an informant or of the identity of an informant who will not be called to testify" is not required if "disclosure would result in substantial risk to the informant or to the informant's operational effectiveness, provided the failure to disclose will not infringe the constitutional rights of the accused." *Ariz. R. Crim. P. 15.4(b)(2)*. A defendant seeking to overcome the State's policy of protecting an informant's identity bears the burden of demonstrating the informant "would be a material witness on the issue of guilt which might result in exoneration and that nondisclosure of his identity would deprive the defendant of a fair trial." *State v. Grounds, 128 Ariz. 14, 15, 623 P.2d 803, 804 (1981)* (quoting *State v. Tuell, 112 Ariz. 340, 343, 541 P.2d 1142, 1145 (1975)*, abrogated on other grounds by *State v. Duran, 233 Ariz. 310, 313, ¶¶ 17-18, 312 P.3d 109, 112 (2013)*); accord *State v. Robles, 182 Ariz. 268, 271, 895 P.2d 1031, 1034 (App. 1995)*. To make this showing, however, the defendant must provide evidence, such as "sworn affidavits, stipulated facts, depositions, and oral testimony." *Grounds, 128 Ariz. at 15, 623 P.2d at 804*; accord *Robles, 182 Ariz. at 271, 895 P.2d at 1034* (affirming the denial of a motion for disclosure for failure to present evidence in support of the appellant's claim that the confidential informant had entrapped him). "A mere possibility or speculative hope that an informant might have other information which might be helpful to the defendant is insufficient" to compel disclosure. *State ex rel. Berger v. Superior Court (Sorum), 21 Ariz. App. 170, 172, 517 P.2d 523, 525 (1974)*.

In this case, Appellant did not testify at the evidentiary hearing on the disclosure motion or present any affidavit, deposition testimony, or other evidence in support of his motion. Instead, as in *Grounds* and *Robles*, only defense counsel's argument was presented in support of the requested disclosure. Both of those courts found argument alone insufficient, and so do we. See *Grounds, 128 Ariz. at 15, 623 P.2d at 804*; *Robles, 182 Ariz. at 271, 895 P.2d at 1034*. Other than the testimony of Detective Egea, which supports the trial court's decision to deny Appellant's motion, the record is devoid of evidence on which this court can further review the trial court's ruling. Accordingly, on this record, disclosure of the confidential informant's identity would have been inappropriate, and Appellant has not sustained his burden of proving he was deprived of a fair trial by the denial of his motion. *See Grounds, 128 Ariz. at 15, 623 P.2d at 804.*

Further, the *Confrontation Clause* prohibits the admission of an out-of-court statement of a witness who does not appear at trial if the statement is testimonial, unless the witness is unavailable and the defendant had a prior opportunity to cross-examine the witness. *See Crawford v. Washington, 541 U.S. 36, 53-54, 124 S. Ct. 1354, 158 L. Ed. 2d 177 (2004).* Because no testimony of the confidential informant was offered against Appellant, Appellant's rights under the *Confrontation Clause* were not implicated. The trial court did not abuse its discretion, much less commit fundamental, reversible error in denying Appellant's motion to compel the identity of the State's confidential informant.

STATE OF ARIZONA, APPELLEE, V. EDGAR PABON GARCIA, APPELLANT.
NO. 1 CA-CR 14-0699

(Text added/modified for emphasis) Courts consistently allow the state to prevent defendants from presenting evidence. The prosecutors consistently delay charging thereby preventing a meaningful defense. Courts consistently sanction this systematic practice refusing to find bad faith thereby condoning this misconduct which is on the rise . As it was never their intent to subject the state's case to a meaningful adversarial process, when viewed in the totality, and not in isolation, this should constitute fraud upon the court by these lawyers.

COUNSEL: Arizona Attorney General's Office, Phoenix, By Joseph T. Maziarz, Counsel for Appellee. The Hopkins Law Office PC, Phoenix, By Cedric Martin Hopkins, Counsel for Appellant.

In August 2005, Garcia arrived at the home of an acquaintance, Fabian Mendez, in a Cadillac owned by the victim. According to

Mendez's testimony, Garcia knocked on his door and asked if he wanted to rob the victim, who was drunk in the back seat of the car. Mendez said no but asked Garcia for a ride to the mall. Garcia agreed to take Mendez to the mall and, while in the mall's parking lot, again tried to persuade Mendez to help rob the victim. Mendez again said no. Garcia then asked if Mendez would go with him to run some errands and buy beer. Mendez agreed, and they began driving west.

Mendez testified that Garcia pulled off the road around 339th Avenue and Indian School Road and asked Mendez to open the back door of the car. Mendez got out of the car and opened the back door, and Garcia dragged the victim out of the car. Garcia then told Mendez he was going to kill the victim and asked Mendez for help as he was dragging the victim away from the car. Mendez declined and stayed with the car.

Garcia returned to the car and grabbed a knife. After some time passed, Mendez started the car, honked the horn, revved the engine, and told Garcia he would leave if Garcia did not hurry up. Shortly thereafter, Garcia returned to the car with the victim's wallet, admitted to having killed the victim, and put the knife in the car's center console.

Garcia drove the car back toward Phoenix, stopping once for gas and beer. Shortly after leaving the gas station, a police officer pulled Garcia over for speeding. The officer approached the car and asked if there were any weapons in the car, whereupon Garcia turned over the knife which had no noticeable blood on it. Mendez then announced he was "going to run," grabbed his beer, exited the car, and ran away. Although Mendez was also charged with first-degree murder, kidnapping, and aggravated robbery, he pled guilty to manslaughter in exchange for testifying truthfully at Garcia's trial. Mendez successfully escaped but was later arrested.

Garcia was arrested for failing to present identification when requested by the officer, and the victim's wallet and identification were found in Garcia's pocket during a search incident to arrest. Mendez successfully escaped but was later arrested. When the officer asked Garcia why he was driving a car registered in someone else's name, Garcia told the officer the victim had sent Garcia and Mendez to Phoenix in the car following a drug transaction in California.

In October 2005, the Drug Enforcement Administration intercepted a telephone call between Garcia and another individual where Garcia discussed a need to bury a body. Based on this information, deputies with the Maricopa County Sheriff's Office were able to locate the victim's body. In November 2005, the victim's car was processed, and blood stains were found on the back side of the front passenger seat which contained the victim's DNA. The knife, which was mistakenly left in the trunk of the officer's car until November 2005, was tested in 2006 and 2010, but no blood was found.

On September 13, 2012, Garcia was indicted on one count of aggravated robbery in violation of *Arizona Revised Statutes (A.R.S.) section 13-1903(A)*, one count of kidnapping in violation of *A.R.S. § 13-1304(A)(6)*, and one count of first-degree murder in violation of *A.R.S. § 13-1105(A)(2)*. In December 2013, Garcia moved to dismiss the charges for pre-indictment delay "of almost seven years." The trial court denied the motion, and the case proceeded to trial. At trial, following the State's presentation of its case, Garcia's counsel moved for judgment of acquittal on all charges, pursuant to Arizona Rule of Criminal Procedure 20, which the court also denied. The jury convicted Garcia on all counts, and the trial court sentenced Garcia to concurrent sentences of fifteen years' imprisonment for aggravated robbery, twenty-one years' imprisonment for kidnapping, and life imprisonment for first-degree murder

....

I. The Trial Court Did Not Err in Denying Garcia's Motion to Dismiss for Pre-Indictment Delay.

The statute of limitations is a defendant's primary protection against due process violations arising from stale prosecutions. *See State v. Broughton, 156 Ariz. 394, 397, 752 P.2d 483 (1988)* (citing *United States v. Lovasco, 431 U.S. 783, 789, 97 S. Ct. 2044, 52 L. Ed. 2d 752 (1977)*, and *State v. Van Arsdale, 133 Ariz. 579, 581, 653 P.2d 36 (App. 1982)*). Here, Garcia's motion to dismiss was not premised upon expiration of the statute of limitations, but rather the State's pre-indictment delay of "nearly seven years."

Garcia does not dispute that the State filed the charges against him within the applicable limitations periods. *See A.R.S. § 13-107(A)* ("A prosecution for any homicide . . . may be commenced at any time."), (B)(1) (setting seven-year limitations period for aggravated robbery and kidnapping).

A dismissal for pre-indictment delay requires the defendant show "the prosecution intentionally delayed proceedings to gain a tactical advantage over the defendant or to harass him, *and* that the defendant has actually been prejudiced by the delay." *Id.* (citations omitted). While any delay in bringing criminal charges results in some degree of prejudice, the defendant "must demonstrate prejudice above and beyond that which is inherent in the workings of a clogged judicial system" by proof that is "definite and not speculative." *See id. at 397-98* (citations omitted).

Garcia fails to satisfy either requirement. Although Garcia argues at length that the State has failed to justify the delay, the burden is on Garcia, and he has presented no proof that the State intentionally delayed prosecution to obtain a tactical advantage or to harass him. *See State v. Lacy, 187 Ariz. 340, 346, 929 P.2d 1288 (1996)* (holding a motion to dismiss for pre-indictment delay must fail "[a]bsent proof of an intentional delay for strategic or harassment purposes") (citing *Stoner v. Graddick, 751 F.2d 1535, 1541 (11th Cir. 1985)*).

Moreover, the prejudice Garcia asserts is merely speculative. He contends "any evidence that could have been collected at or near the scene is lost," and "videos" were no longer available. There is no proof that on-the-scene evidence or unidentified video evidence ever existed, let alone any indication as to whether it would have bolstered Garcia's defense. Therefore, Garcia's argument fails, and the trial court did not err in denying Garcia's motion to dismiss for pre-indictment delay. Garcia also urges us to presume prejudice where he argues there were nearly seven years of pre-indictment delay. Garcia cites no support for this proposition, which is contrary to established case law. *See Broughton, 156 Ariz. at 397* ("[A] defendant has a heavy burden to prove pre-indictment delay caused actual prejudice.") (citing *United States v. Valentine, 783 F.2d 1413, 1416 (9th Cir. 1986)*).

STATE OF ARIZONA, APPELLEE, V. JAMAR DONTAE ROPER, APPELLANT.
NO. 1 CA-CR 14-0537

(Text added/modified for emphasis) Courts consistently allow the state to prevent defendants from presenting evidence. The prosecutors consistently conceal evidence thereby preventing a meaningful defense. Courts consistently sanction this systematic practice refusing to find bad faith thereby condoning this misconduct which is on the rise . As it was never their intent to subject the state's case to a meaningful adversarial process, when viewed in the totality, and not in isolation, this should constitute fraud upon the court by these lawyers.

COUNSEL: Arizona Attorney General's Office, Phoenix, By Joseph T. Maziarz, Counsel for Appellee. Maricopa County Public Defender's Office, Phoenix, By Carlos Daniel Carrion, Counsel for Appellant.

Jamar Dontae Roper ("Roper") appeals his convictions and sentences for two counts of aggravated assault. Roper's counsel has filed a brief in accordance with *Smith v. Robbins, 528 U.S. 259, 120 S. Ct. 746, 145 L. Ed. 2d 756 (2000)*; *Anders v. California, 386 U.S. 738, 87 S. Ct. 1396, 18 L. Ed. 2d 493 (1967)*; and *State v. Leon, 104 Ariz. 297, 451 P.2d 878 (1969)*, stating that he has searched the record on appeal and found no arguable question of law that is not frivolous. Roper's counsel therefore requests that we review the record for fundamental error. *See State v. Clark, 196 Ariz. 530, 537, ¶ 30, 2 P.3d 89, 96 (App. 1999)* (stating that this court reviews the entire record for reversible error). We allowed Roper to file a supplemental brief *in propria persona*, and he has done so, raising two issues that we address.

FACTS AND PROCEDURAL HISTORY

In 2009, a grand jury indicted Roper, charging him with two counts of aggravated assault--a class 2 felony, and one count of misconduct involving weapons--a class 1 misdemeanor. *See A.R.S. §§ 13-1203(A)(2) (Supp. 2015), -1204(A)(8)(a) (Supp. 2009), -3102(A)(2) (Supp. 2009)*. The State also alleged the two offenses were dangerous and the sentences for the aggravated assault offenses could not be less than the presumptive sentences and could only be in flat time because the offenses were committed against on-duty peace officers. *See A.R.S. §§ 13-105(13)* (Supp. 2015), -709.01 (Supp. 2009) ; *State v. Woodall, 155 Ariz. 1, 7, 744 P.2d 732, 738 (App. 1987)* (stating an automobile constitutes a dangerous instrument if used to commit an offense).

At trial, the State presented the following evidence: At approximately 11:40 a.m. on October 30, 2009, during a routine patrol, Officer Huptich and Officer Elfritz with the Phoenix Police Department-- traveling in a fully-marked police vehicle and dressed in clearly-marked uniforms--noticed a gold Ford Taurus backed in a parking slot of a motel parking lot with V.J. in the driver's seat and Roper in the front passenger's seat. The motel was known as a high-crime property, and stolen vehicles are often parked in that manner to hide the license plate from the view of patrolling officers. While the officers were approaching the car to check whether the occupants of the car were staying at the motel, they noticed movements from Roper that looked like he was tucking something between the console and his seat. Officer Huptich went to the driver's side and Officer Elfritz went to the passenger's side. Once the officers started to converse with the occupants, Roper immediately yelled at V.J. to roll up the window and reached over to lock the doors.

The officer changed his last name from Harris after the incident.

Officer Huptich commanded both to exit the car. V.J. eventually came out of the car, leaving the driver's side door open and handing the officers her driver's license and Roper's identification card. Once V.J. exited, Roper moved into the driver's seat. To better see what Roper was doing, Officer Elfritz walked to the front of the car. At that moment, Roper drove the car forward, almost hitting Officer Elfritz. The officer had to jump out of the way to avoid being struck by the vehicle. To block Roper from driving away, Officer Huptich ran to the patrol car and backed it close to the Taurus. As Officer Huptich was walking back to the Taurus, Roper drove the car forward again, forcing Officer Huptich to jump out of the way to avoid injury.

Both officers then stood next to the driver's side, keeping the door open, and commanded Roper to exit the car. Roper did not do so, and in a further attempt to stop Roper, Officer Huptich used pepper spray, but to no avail. Roper managed to slam the door shut--almost hitting Officer Huptich--and rammed the Taurus into the patrol car. The Taurus stalled as a result; Roper restarted it, backed it up quickly, and then moved it forward while turning right and scraping the rear driver's side of the patrol car. He then drove out of the parking lot. Officer Huptich radioed a description of Roper to the police dispatcher.

Approximately half an hour later, the Taurus was located in a parking lot of an apartment building less than two miles away from the motel. Shortly thereafter, Officer Kincannon with the Phoenix Police Department detained Roper at a nearby bus stop. Roper was later identified at the bus stop by both Officers Elfritz and Huptich. Officers Elfritz and Huptich went back to the parking lot of the apartment building, inspected the Taurus, and found a gun inside. At the police station, after being given his *Miranda* warnings, Roper admitted he owned that gun and that he had purchased it on "the street." When asked why he refused to obey the police and fled, Roper replied he did not want to go to jail.

During the first trial of this case in 2010, the trial court found it necessary to place Roper in Rule 11 proceedings to determine his competency to stand trial, and declared a mistrial. Over the next three and a half years, Roper went through restoration efforts and a series of Rule 11 hearings. Eventually in 2014, Roper was restored to competency and tried. The jury found Roper guilty as charged, and that his offenses were dangerous, and he had assaulted on-duty peace officers. The court sentenced him to concurrent terms of 10.5 years' imprisonment for the aggravated assault offenses with credit for 193 days of presentence incarceration.[8] Roper timely appealed.

I. Alleged Prosecutorial Misconduct

Roper argues his conviction must be reversed because the prosecutor committed misconduct by not disclosing and suppressing evidence favorable to him, allegedly violating *Brady v. Maryland, 373 U.S. 83, 83 S. Ct. 1194, 10 L. Ed. 2d 215 (1963)*. Roper contends the trial court abused its discretion in denying his motion to dismiss on these grounds. We disagree.

"To prevail on a claim of prosecutorial misconduct, a defendant must demonstrate that '(1) misconduct is indeed present; and (2) a reasonable likelihood exists that the misconduct could have affected the jury's verdict, thereby denying [the] defendant a fair trial.'" *State v. Moody, 208 Ariz. 424, 459, ¶ 145, 94 P.3d 1119, 1154 (2004).* For alleged misconduct to constitute a *Brady* violation, the evidence must be favorable to the defendant and have been suppressed by the prosecutor, and there is a reasonable probability that, had the evidence been disclosed to the defense, the result of the proceeding would have been different. *Strickler v. Greene, 527 U.S. 263, 280-81, 296, 119 S. Ct. 1936, 144 L. Ed. 2d 286 (1999)*; *Brady, 373 U.S. at 87 (1963)*.

After a hearing, the trial court found that the record did not support the allegation of a *Brady* violation. As he did before the trial court, Roper asserts on appeal that the State suppressed evidence of an interview that allegedly occurred approximately six months after the incident, where V.J. told a prosecutor and four police officers that Roper was not the person in the car with her during the incident. V.J., however, could not pinpoint when the interview took place or identify the prosecutor or the officers who conducted the interview. The defense first learned from V.J. about the alleged interview in April 2014--before the trial but almost four years after the purported interview. At the hearing for the motion, the State called two officers who had delivered a subpoena for V.J. and might be the officers to whom V.J. was referring. Both officers denied any interview had occurred. V.J. also testified at the hearing. Afterwards, the trial court concluded V.J.'s claim of an interview was not credible and, even assuming otherwise, the State was not trying to hide this witness because the State had disclosed V.J. as one of its witnesses back in 2010. Further, even assuming the State had suppressed the evidence of the alleged interview, the result of the proceeding would not have been different because the defense was free to conduct its own investigation or bring the evidence before the jury. We agree. The trial court did not err or abuse its discretion in denying the motion to dismiss based on alleged prosecutorial misconduct.

II. Favorable Evidence

Roper also argues this court should reverse the conviction and dismiss the case with prejudice because favorable evidence exists on record. The favorable evidence he refers to is the testimony from V.J., claiming Roper was not the person with her in the Taurus during the incident.

The mere existence of favorable evidence does not warrant a reversal of a conviction or dismissal of a case. The record shows the favorable evidence Roper refers to was presented to, and duly weighed by, the jury. Absent clear error, we defer to the jury's weighing of witness credibility and factual determinations of guilt and aggravating factors. We find no such error here.

THE STATE OF ARIZONA, APPELLEE, V. BRYAN LAMAR LEE, APPELLANT.
NO. 2 CA-CR 2014-0312

(Text added/modified for emphasis) Courts consistently allow the state to prevent defendants from presenting evidence. The prosecutors consistently present evidence that cannot be cross examined thereby preventing a meaningful defense. Courts consistently sanction this systematic practice refusing to find bad faith thereby condoning this misconduct which is on the rise . As it was never their intent to subject the state's case to a meaningful adversarial process, when viewed in the totality, and not in isolation, this should constitute fraud upon the court by these lawyers.

COUNSEL: Mark Brnovich, Arizona Attorney General, Joseph T. Maziarz, Section Chief Counsel, Phoenix, By Amy M. Thorson, Assistant Attorney General, Tucson, Counsel for Appellee. Steven R. Sonenberg, Pima County Public Defender, By Katherine A. Estavillo, Assistant Public Defender, Tucson, Counsel for Appellant.

After a jury trial, Bryan Lee was found guilty of first-degree murder and kidnapping. He was sentenced to life in prison without the possibility of release for twenty-five years on the murder conviction and a 10.5-year prison term for the kidnapping conviction. On appeal, he argues the trial court erred in denying his motion to preclude certain statements as inadmissible hearsay and in failing to instruct the jury on third-party culpability. For the following reasons, we affirm.

....

Lee first contends the trial court erred in denying his motions to preclude testimony about statements made during a conversation among Marrone, Brown, and Lee on the day J.P. was murdered. Specifically, he argues the inculpatory statements that Brown could not attribute with certainty to either Lee or Marrone lacked foundation and Marrone's admissions constituted inadmissible hearsay because the state failed to demonstrate Lee had adopted those admissions. "We review a trial court's evidentiary rulings for a clear abuse of discretion." *State v. Abdi, 226 Ariz. 361, ¶ 21, 248 P.3d 209, 214 (App. 2011).*

As noted above, Brown caused a mistrial in Lee's first trial after disclosing that he had not told the whole truth about J.P.'s death. During a later interview, Brown related for the first time that Marrone and Lee had described killing J.P. in detail on the night of the murder. When asked to attribute specific statements to Marrone or Lee, Brown said he was not sure if he would be able to differentiate among some of the statements.

Lee filed two motions to preclude, arguing that any statements made by Marrone to Brown should be barred as inadmissible hearsay and contending the statements Brown could not specifically attribute to either defendant lacked foundation. The state responded that any statements made by Marrone in Lee's presence were admissible as adopted admissions because Lee had actively participated in the conversation. The trial court agreed, noting Lee's participation "show[ed] that he adopted the statements made by . . . Marrone," and concluded the statements were not hearsay.

At trial, apparently consistent with his statements in an interview after the mistrial, Brown testified that on the day J.P. was murdered, he "showed up at [Marrone]'s house just like [he] would any other day," and noticed a truck outside that he did not recognize with Marrone's couch in it. Marrone and Lee were both in the house when Brown arrived. After "hanging out for a couple of minutes," Brown "felt a weird energy about the room" and asked "what was going on." After a private conversation, Lee and Marrone eventually revealed to Brown that "they had killed [J.P.]" and "he was in the back of the truck under the couch."

Lee takes issue with the state's reference to Brown's trial testimony and notes that this court "considers only the evidence . . . presented at the suppression hearing" when reviewing a pretrial ruling on a motion to suppress. *See State v. Becerra, 231 Ariz. 200, ¶ 4, 291 P.3d 994, 996 (App. 2013), review granted* (Ariz. May 29, 2013). But it appears Lee did not offer any evidence at the hearing on his motions, presenting only argument. And to the extent the trial court may have relied on portions of a transcript of Brown's pretrial interview, that transcript is not before us; we therefore presume it supports the trial court's ruling. *See State v. Villalobos, 114 Ariz. 392, 394, 561 P.2d 313, 315 (1977)* (appellate court presumes testimony or evidence not included in record on appeal supported trial court's rulings). In any event, Brown's statements as described at the hearing and in the motions to preclude were consistent with his trial testimony.

Furthermore, pretrial evidentiary rulings are generally subject to change when evidence is introduced at trial. *See* Bennett Cooper et al., *Arizona Practice Series: Trial Handbook* § 4:2 (2014) (rulings on motions in limine "interlocutory" and reconsideration not barred absent prejudice to party), *citing Henry ex rel. Estate of Wilson v. HealthPartners of S. Ariz., 203 Ariz. 393, ¶¶ 19-20, 55 P.3d 87, 93 (App. 2002).* Indeed, the record here strongly suggests the trial court did not deem its ruling to necessarily be final because it prefaced it with "[a]t this time it is the ruling of the Court as follows."

Brown testified "they [had] approached [him] with the idea to follow them out to Marana to get rid of the body." He recalled that Marrone "verbally" suggested the idea, but Lee was "present for the whole formation of the plan." Brown also stated "they had described . . . to [him] exactly what had happened," and provided details regarding how long it had taken for J.P. to die and how they had cleaned up afterwards. Brown "particularly remember [ed Marrone]" describing the events, but said they "were all three discussing it," and he specifically recalled Lee had said J.P. "immediately became weak in the knees," when he grabbed him, and that choking J.P. "was very hard and he had to call [Marrone] over to take turns." According to Brown, there were no signs of a struggle in the house because Lee and Marrone had cleaned up, wrapped J.P.'s body, and put him in the truck before Brown arrived.

Lee does not dispute that any statement attributed directly to him with certainty was admissible as a party admission. *See Ariz. R. Evid. 801(d)(2)*.

Brown followed Lee and Marrone to Marana, where he had left his car at a convenience store before joining them in J.P.'s truck. The three men then drove to a desert area where they dug a shallow grave, removed J.P.'s body from the truck, unrolled him from plastic sheeting he had been wrapped in, and buried him. After retrieving Brown's car, Lee and Marrone dumped the couch on the side of the road and left J.P.'s truck in a Marana neighborhood along with his keys and cell phone. The three then drove back to Marrone's house in Brown's car. On the way, Marrone reportedly stated "the situation was just so crazy and unreal," and Lee said he "didn't expect his hands to get so tired or [the murder] to take so long." At the house, Marrone gave Brown "a little bit of marijuana" and "[a] couple hundred dollars."

Adopted Admissions

Lee contends Marrone's statements were inadmissible hearsay because "the [s]tate did not make a sufficient showing that [he had] adopted [Marrone's] statements." Hearsay is inadmissible unless a rule, statute, or constitutional provision provides otherwise. *Ariz. R. Evid. 802*. An admission by a defendant is not hearsay. *Ariz. R. Evid. 801(d)(2)(A)*. Nor is a statement by a third party offered against a defendant who manifested an adoption or belief in the statement's truth. *Ariz. R. Evid. 801(d)(2)(B)*. Such a statement is adopted when a defendant affirmatively agrees with statements made in his presence or expounds upon the statements by adding his own comments or explanations. *State v. Anderson, 210 Ariz. 327, ¶ 36, 111 P.3d 369, 381 (2005)*; cf. *Taylor-Bertling v. Foley, 233 Ariz. 394, ¶¶ 14-16, 313 P.3d 537, 542 (App. 2013)* (statements by homeowner's father not adopted by homeowner when she made no statement of agreement and added no further explanation or comment).

Lee argues the state failed to make a sufficient showing that he was "actively participating" in the conversation with Brown and Marrone and, consequently, his participation did not rise to the level described in *State v. Daugherty*, in which the defendant "expressly agreed with . . . the statements made by her companion." *173 Ariz. 548, 550, 845 P.2d 474, 476 (App. 1992)*. Instead, Lee contends he was "merely present" when Marrone was speaking to Brown. The available record, however, refutes that contention.

According to Brown's version of the events, all of Marrone's statements discussed at the pretrial hearing and testified to at trial were made in Lee's presence, and Lee expounded on them by adding his own comments and observations throughout the conversation. *See Anderson, 210 Ariz. 327, ¶ 36, 111 P.3d at 381*. For example, at the house, Lee related that choking J.P. had been "very hard," and while driving back from Marana, Lee said he "didn't expect his hands to get so tired or [the murder] to take so long." Even if Lee's comments were not in direct response to Marrone's, they amply demonstrated his active participation in the conversation. Accordingly, we find no abuse of discretion in the trial court's admission of Marrone's statements as Lee's adopted admissions.

Lack of Foundation

In a related argument, Lee contends that statements Brown could not attribute to either Lee or Marrone with certainty lacked foundation, citing *State v. Wehrhan, 25 Ariz. App. 277, 542 P.2d 1157 (1975)* and *State v. Gaddy, 118 Ariz. 594, 578 P.2d 1023 (App. 1978)*. In *Wehrhan*, a witness testified she had heard either the defendant "or someone else" say a restaurant had been robbed. *25 Ariz. App. at 279, 542 P.2d at 1159*. According to the witness, even if the defendant did not say it, the statement was uttered in his presence, but she was unsure if the defendant had heard it. *Id.* This court determined the trial court had erred in admitting the statement because the witness could not state with certainty that it was made by the defendant or that he heard the statement. *Id.*

In *Gaddy*, the state sought to admit a portion of a medical report that stated the defendant had been injured by a nightstick after he had "cut somebody's throat." *118 Ariz. at 595, 578 P.2d at 1024*. The defendant objected on hearsay grounds. *Id.* A key issue was whether the defendant had been injured before or after the stabbing incident. *Id.* When the doctor was asked about the information contained in the report, he had difficulty remembering the facts and gave conflicting and confusing answers. *Id. at 596, 578 P.2d at 1025.* Nevertheless, the trial court admitted the exhibit into evidence. *Id.* In reversing its ruling, we concluded the statement lacked foundation to qualify as an exception to the hearsay rule because the source of the information was not established. *Id.*

At trial, Lee argued that the statements Brown could not specifically attribute to either him or Marrone lacked foundation because, without identifying the declarant, "we can't say which hearsay exception applies, and if we can't say which hearsay exception applies, then that statement remains hearsay if the [s]tate is offering it for the truth of the matter asserted." We disagree.

Unlike in *Wehrhan* and *Gaddy*, there is no foundational issue here because Brown was certain that the statements were made either by Lee or Marrone, in both their presence, with no one else present during the conversations. Thus, each statement was either made by Lee and constituted an admission by party opponent, or was made by Marrone in Lee's presence and impliedly adopted by him, as noted above. *See Ariz. R. Evid. 801(d)(2); cf. State v. John, 210 Conn. 652, 557 A.2d 93, 109 (Conn. 1989)* (that witness could not recall which defendant made statement not essential to admissibility because both defendants adopted it through responses to witness's subsequent questions). In either scenario, the statements would have been admissible non-hearsay. *See id.; see also Commonwealth v. Brown, 394 Mass. 510, 476 N.E.2d 580, 583 (Mass. 1985)* (statements not specifically attributable to particular defendant admissible where statement was either admission by defendant or implied adoption of codefendant's admission).

Confrontation clause

Lee also argues he was denied his constitutional right to confront witnesses against him when Marrone's out-of-court statements were admitted because he was "unable to cross-examine [Marrone] on th[o]se incriminating statements." *See U.S. Const. amend. VI.* "The *Sixth Amendment* prohibits a court from admitting testimonial hearsay statements made by a non-testifying witness unless that person is unavailable and the defendant had a prior opportunity for cross-examination." *State v. Forde, 233 Ariz. 543, ¶ 65, 315 P.3d 1200, 1218 (2014), citing Crawford v. Washington, 541 U.S. 36, 68, 124 S. Ct. 1354, 158 L. Ed. 2d 177 (2004).* A statement is testimonial if the "'primary purpose'" of the conversation was to "'creat[e] an out-of-court substitute for trial testimony.'" *Ohio v. Clark, U.S. , , 135 S. Ct. 2173, 2180, 192 L. Ed. 2d 306 (2015), quoting Michigan v. Bryant, 562 U.S. 344, 358, 131 S. Ct. 1143, 179 L. Ed. 2d 93 (2011).*

Ordinarily, we review an evidentiary issue that implicates the *Confrontation Clause* de novo. *See State v. Ellison, 213 Ariz. 116, ¶ 42, 140 P.3d 899, 912 (2006).* Lee, however, failed to object on this basis below, *see State v. Hamilton, 177 Ariz. 403, 408, 868 P.2d 986, 991 (App. 1993);* we thus review the issue only for fundamental error, *see State v. Henderson, 210 Ariz. 561, ¶ 19, 115 P.3d 601, 607 (2005)* (fundamental error review applies when defendant fails to object to alleged trial error).

We find no error here, much less fundamental error. Once Lee adopted Marrone's statements, they effectively became his own statements and were no longer hearsay. *See Ariz. R. Evid. 801(d)(2)(B)* (statement adopted by party not hearsay). Moreover, Marrone's statements were not testimonial. *See Clark, U.S. at , 135 S. Ct. at 2180* (statements not testimonial when made to persons outside of a law enforcement context and primary purpose not to create state's evidence). Thus, the *Confrontation Clause* is inapplicable. *See Crawford, 541 U.S. at 54; see also People v. Jennings, 50 Cal. 4th 616, 114 Cal. Rptr. 3d 133, 237 P.3d 474, 508 (Cal. 2010)* (when inculpatory statement made in defendant's presence is admissible as adoptive admission, court no longer concerned with credibility of original declarant; accordingly, no confrontation right impinged by its admission).

STATE OF ARIZONA, APPELLEE, V. WILLIE EARL KEY, APPELLANT.
NO. 1 CA-CR 14-0789

(Text added/modified for emphasis) Courts consistently allow the state to prevent defendants from presenting evidence. The prosecutors consistently present evidence that cannot be cross examined thereby preventing a meaningful defense. As it was never their intent to subject the state's case to a meaningful adversarial process, when viewed in the totality, and not in isolation, this should constitute fraud upon the court by these lawyers.

COUNSEL: Law Office of Nicole Farnum, Phoenix, By Nicole Farnum, Counsel for Appellant. Arizona Attorney General's Office, Phoenix, By Adele G. Ponce, Counsel for Appellee.

FACTS AND PROCEDURAL HISTORY

A fight broke out at the Terrace Park apartment complex on May 26, 2013, and escalated to a shooting. The residents who called 9-1-1 reported that an African-American man was carrying a laser pistol and gunshots were being fired; the man was between five feet, seven inches and five feet, nine inches tall; and he was huskily built, bald, between thirty and forty years old, and was wearing pajama bottoms, but no shoes or shirt.

After police officers arrived, they found a wounded man with a gunshot injury to his leg. During the search for the gunman, Officer Robles saw a barefoot and shirtless man matching the 9-1-1 description, who was later identified as Key, running with his right hand at his waistband. Officer Robles stopped Key and drew his weapon. Key let go of his waistband and raised his hands, and a gun moved down his right pajama leg and fell to the ground. When Key ignored the officer's instructions, Officer Robles radioed for assistance, holstered his gun, and took out his Taser.

Officers Gombar and Zamora responded, and saw Officer Robles holding his Taser and giving Key verbal instructions. Key was aggressive, yelling, moving around, and not following the instructions. When Key assumed a fighting stance, Officer Gombar tackled him, and the officers attempted to restrain Key, who was kicking and fighting. Only after Officer Gombar used a Taser were the officers able to control Key.

Once Key was handcuffed and in custody, the .45 caliber gun with a laser sight, which had slipped down his pajama pants leg, was collected. The crime scene technicians also collected other items, including a .45 caliber shell that had been fired from Key's gun.

Key was subsequently indicted for two counts of aggravated assault, misconduct involving weapons, unlawful discharge of a firearm, threatening or intimidating, and resisting arrest. The State later amended the indictment by dismissing one aggravated assault charge and the threatening or intimidating charge. The case went to trial and after the presentation of the evidence, closing arguments, and jury instructions, the jury convicted Key on all counts. The court then held a Phase II hearing, and after argument and instructions, the jury found beyond a reasonable doubt that the unlawful discharge of a firearm was a dangerous offense, and the unlawful discharge offense involved the infliction or threatened infliction of a serious physical injury, an aggravating circumstance.

....

Key also objects to the admission of the telephone call made by a lady who reported the sounds of gunshots and described the shooter. In making its pre-trial ruling, and despite the fact that no *Confrontation Clause*objection was raised, the court found the telephone call nontestimonial and ruled it did not violate the *Confrontation Clause*. And, as noted, we review an evidentiary ruling to which Key did not object for fundamental error, *see Valverde, 220 Ariz. at 585, ¶ 12, 208 P.3d at 236, Alvarez, 213 Ariz. at 469, ¶ 7, 143 P.3d at 670*, mindful that we normally review rulings that implicate the *Confrontation Clause* de novo. *State v. Ellison, 213 Ariz. 116, 129, ¶ 42, 140 P.3d 899, 912 (2006)* (citing *Lilly v. Virginia, 527 U.S. 116, 137, 119 S. Ct. 1887, 144 L. Ed. 2d 117 (1999)*).

The *Confrontation Clause* in the *Sixth Amendment to the United States Constitution* guarantees a criminal defendant the right to "confront [] [] the witnesses against him." *U.S. Const. amend. VI*. Confrontation means more than being allowed to confront, or see, the witness testifying in the courtroom, and includes the right to cross-examine witnesses. *Davis v. Alaska, 415 U.S. 308, 315, 94 S. Ct. 1105, 39 L. Ed. 2d 347 (1974)*. The confrontation right also precludes the government from using out-of-court testimonial statements made by witnesses who are not available for cross-examination unless it can be shown that a defendant had a prior opportunity to cross-examine that witness. *Crawford v. Washington, 541 U.S. 36, 68, 124 S. Ct. 1354, 158 L. Ed. 2d 177 (2004).*

A statement is testimonial if it is a "solemn declaration or affirmation made for the purpose of establishing or proving some fact." *State v. Boggs, 218 Ariz. 325, 337, ¶ 56, 185 P.3d 111, 123 (2008)* (quoting *Crawford, 541 U.S. at 51*). In examining whether a 9-1-1 call to the police or operator is testimonial or nontestimonial, the Court in *Davis v. Washington,* stated:

> Statements are nontestimonial when made . . . under circumstances objectively indicating that the primary purpose . . . is to enable police assistance to meet an ongoing emergency. They are testimonial when the circumstances objectively indicate that there is no such ongoing emergency, and that the primary purpose . . . is to establish or prove past events potentially relevant to later criminal prosecution.

547 U.S. 813, 822, 126 S. Ct. 2266, 165 L. Ed. 2d 224 (2006). As a result, the Court found that a 9-1-1 call is generally nontestimonial because it "is ordinarily not designed primarily to 'establis[h] or prov[e]' some past fact, but to describe current circumstances requiring police assistance." *Id. at 827* (alterations in *Davis*).

Then, in *Michigan v. Bryant,* the Court provided the analysis to determine when the "primary purpose" of any questioning or interrogation is to help police meet an ongoing emergency. *562 U.S. 344, 359, 131 S. Ct. 1143, 179 L. Ed. 2d 93 (2011).* The Court stated a court must "objectively evaluate the circumstances in which the encounter occurs and the statements and actions of the parties." *Id.* In fact, "the existence of an ongoing emergency at the time of an encounter between an individual and the police is among the most important circumstances informing the primary purpose of an interrogation." *Id. at 361* (internal quotation marks omitted). It is "relevant to determining the primary purpose" of the questioning "because an emergency focuses the participants on something other than 'prov[ing] past events potentially relevant to later criminal prosecution.'" *Id.* (quoting *Davis, 547 U.S. at 822*) (alteration in original). "[I]t focuses them on ending a threatening situation." *Id.* (internal quotation marks and citation omitted). As a result, "because the prospect of fabrication in statements given for the primary purpose of resolving th[e] emergency is presumably significantly diminished, the *Confrontation Clause* does not require such statements to be subject to the crucible of cross-examination." *Id.* Accordingly, statements made during a 9-1-1 call before the ongoing emergency is resolved are more likely to be nontestimonial.

Based on the Court's analytical framework, the caller in this case described an ongoing emergency -- she heard shots -- and described the person she thought to be the shooter to enable the police to respond. Her telephone call was made two minutes after the victim's call and less than two minutes after the shooting. The questions the 9-1-1 operator asked were for the purpose of determining the nature of the emergency, the location of the incident, the type of weapons, possible injuries, and a description of the perpetrator in order to dispatch police to the actual location. Because the caller's 9-1-1 statements were describing an ongoing emergency that focused on a threatening situation, the statements were nontestimonial and their admission, as a result, does not violate the *Confrontation Clause. Id.* Consequently, the court did not err by finding that the second telephone call was admissible.

STATE OF ARIZONA, APPELLEE, V. JOHNATHAN ANDREW DOODY, APPELLANT.
NO. 1 CA-CR 14-0218

(Text added/modified for emphasis) Courts consistently allow the state to prevent defendants from presenting evidence. The prosecutors consistently prevent evidence of third parties who committed crimes from being presented thereby preventing a meaningful defense. As it was never their intent to subject the state's case to a meaningful adversarial process, when viewed in the totality, and not in isolation, this should constitute fraud upon the court by these lawyers. The same prosecutors repeatedly do just that.

COUNSEL: Arizona Attorney General's Office, Phoenix, By Joseph T. Maziarz, Counsel for Appellee. The Hopkins Law Office, PC, Tucson, By Cedric Martin Hopkins, Counsel for Appellant.

Johnathan Andrew Doody murdered nine people inside a Buddhist temple in 1991. A jury found Doody guilty of nine counts of first degree murder, nine counts of armed robbery and one count each of first degree burglary and conspiracy to commit armed robbery and/or first degree burglary. The trial court sentenced Doody to nine consecutive terms of life imprisonment with a possibility of parole after twenty-five years for the murder counts and a consecutive, aggregate term of twelve years' imprisonment for the remaining counts. This was Doody's third trial in this matter. The United States Court of Appeals for the Ninth Circuit reversed Doody's original 1993 convictions after it found interrogators did not adequately inform Doody of his rights under *Miranda v. Arizona, 384 U.S. 436, 86 S. Ct. 1602, 16 L. Ed. 2d 694 (1966)*, and because the methods of interrogation rendered his confession to the murders involuntary. *Doody v. Ryan, 649 F.3d 986, 1023 (9th Cir. 2011)*. A second trial in 2013 resulted in a mistrial.

Doody does not challenge the sufficiency of the evidence to support his convictions. He contends, however, that the trial court erred when it denied Doody's motion in limine to admit evidence of a subsequent murder and when it failed to consider mitigating circumstances for sentencing purposes. For the reasons that follow, we affirm Doody's convictions and sentences. We have jurisdiction pursuant to *Arizona Constitution, Article 6, Section 9*, and *Arizona Revised Statutes (A.R.S.) sections 12-120.21(A)* (2003), 13-4031 (2010) and 13-4033 (2010).

I. Doody's Motion in Limine

Doody first argues the trial court erred when it denied his motion in limine to admit evidence of the details of a tenth murder that occurred approximately nine weeks after the "temple murders." We review a trial court's evidentiary rulings for abuse of discretion. *State v. Amaya-Ruiz, 166 Ariz. 152, 167, 800 P.2d 1260, 1275 (1990)*.

A. Background

We first clarify the record to put the issue and Doody's arguments in context. A second person, "Garcia," participated in the temple murders. In exchange for the state's agreement not to seek the death penalty, Garcia pled guilty to nine counts of first degree murder and agreed to testify truthfully in any proceedings against Doody. The court sentenced Garcia to nine consecutive terms of life imprisonment with a possibility of parole after twenty-five years. Garcia ultimately testified at trial that Doody shot each of the murder victims individually with a rifle as they lay on the floor and Garcia fired into the group of victims four times with a shotgun.

Doody filed a pretrial motion in limine to admit evidence of the details of a tenth murder Garcia participated in as an accomplice. Nine weeks after the temple murders, the sixteen-year-old Garcia and his fourteen-year-old girlfriend ran away together. They encountered the tenth victim at a campsite and borrowed matches from her. Garcia planned to rob the tenth victim shortly thereafter and repeatedly told his girlfriend there should be "no witnesses" once they did so. Garcia pressured his girlfriend to kill the tenth victim, and told her, "If you love me, you'll do this." The girlfriend shot the tenth victim twice in the back with a nine millimeter handgun, after which they took the victim's money and ATM card. The girlfriend admitted she shot the victim but claimed Garcia controlled everything, that it was all his plan and that he manipulated her. Garcia revealed the tenth murder to investigators as part of his plea agreement in the instant case. Garcia pled guilty to that murder as well and received a tenth, consecutive sentence of life imprisonment with a possibility of parole after twenty-five years.

Doody alleged in his motion in limine that there were similarities between the temple murders and the tenth murder. Relying on *Arizona Rule of Evidence 404(b)* (*Rule 404(b)*), Doody asserted these alleged similarities were relevant to Garcia's motive and intent and would impeach Garcia's trial testimony by showing Garcia's "common scheme or plan" to minimize his involvement in any murder he participated in, attribute the actual murder to another person and portray himself as simply a follower. At the hearing on the motion, Doody argued further that the evidence was relevant to show Garcia was a "serial killer" who "cuts deals with the state, implicates others in exchange for favorable outcome for himself, . . . minimizes his involvement in the crimes as he did in both the [tenth murder] and the temple murders and he manipulates people." He also argued the evidence showed Garcia has a "character trait for, basically, implicating other people; cutting deals; minimizing his involvement." Finally, Doody argued the evidence that Garcia used the phrase "no witnesses" in the tenth murder was most important because he would testify it was Doody who used that phrase during the temple murders.

The trial court denied the motion in limine in part and granted it in part. The court held it would allow some evidence of the tenth murder. The court held Doody could introduce evidence that Garcia participated in the tenth murder, "cut deals" with law enforcement, entered into plea agreements, implicated other people and minimized his involvement in all ten murders. The court would not, however, allow Doody to introduce evidence of the details of the tenth murder. The court held *Rule 404(b)* was not designed to permit a party to "dredge up every bad thing [a] person has done." The court found Doody's attempt to admit the details of the tenth murder was "simply an argument that, boy, Garcia is a bad guy; he's a bad guy, don't listen to him." The court also held it was "running into a big [Arizona Rule of Evidence] 403 wall" with the details of the tenth murder. Regarding Garcia's use of the phrase "no witnesses," the court held Doody could introduce evidence Garcia personally used the phrase after the temple murders, but not in the context of the details of the tenth murder. The court noted that this court addressed this final limitation on direct appeal in 1996 and found no reversible error.

Pursuant to the court's ruling, the jury heard evidence Garcia and his girlfriend committed the tenth murder nine weeks after the temple murders and that they both pled guilty and received prison sentences, including a life sentence for Garcia. The jury learned the murder also involved armed robbery. The jury learned the names of the victim and Garcia's girlfriend, Garcia's and his girlfriend's ages and the date and location of the murder. The jury also heard evidence that Garcia pled guilty to the tenth murder as part of the plea agreement in the temple murders and that he did so to avoid the death penalty in both the temple and tenth murders. Finally, the jury heard Garcia agree that he had benefited "greatly" from his plea bargains with the state. Despite the trial court's ruling, Doody never asked Garcia if he used the phrase "no witnesses" after the temple murders. Even so, the jury heard Garcia use the phrase during his testimony about the temple murders without attributing it to Doody and, therefore, knew the phrase and its use were not unique to Doody.

B. Discussion

On appeal, Doody continues to argue the details of the tenth murder were admissible pursuant to *Rule 404(b)* as evidence of the common scheme or plan allegedly evidenced in the facts of the temple and tenth murders. Doody argues the common scheme or plan was for Garcia to plan to kill people to steal their money, manipulate someone else into doing the killing and then, if caught, make a favorable deal with the state, minimize his involvement and deflect the blame for any murder to the other person. Doody's defense at trial was that he was not at the temple the day of the murders, was in no way involved in the murders and he was simply a "dupe" for Garcia.

The trial court did not abuse its discretion when it limited the evidence of the details of the tenth murder. First, combined with all of the evidence regarding Garcia's involvement in the temple murders and the details of the resulting plea agreement, the jury heard more than sufficient evidence about the tenth murder and Garcia's subsequent "deal" with the state to support Doody's position that Garcia was simply a ten-time murderer trying to keep his plea agreements intact by saying what the state wanted to hear and blaming Doody. It was well within the trial court's discretion to find that additional details such as how Garcia manipulated his girlfriend into shooting the victim and why they did so were of no additional probative value. Second, a trial court "has considerable discretion in determining whether the probative value of the evidence is substantially outweighed by its unfairly prejudicial effect." *State v. Gilfillan, 196 Ariz. 396, 405, ¶ 29, 998 P.2d 1069, 1078 (App. 2000)*. The court did not abuse its discretion when it held the probative value, if any, of the details of an unrelated murder that occurred more than two months later was outweighed by the considerations identified in *Arizona Rule of Evidence 403*.

Third, to admit another act as evidence of a common scheme or plan pursuant to *Rule 404(b)*, the other act must be "part of 'a particular plan of which the charged crime is a part.'" *State v. Ives, 187 Ariz. 102, 106, 927 P.2d 762, 766 (1996)* (quoting *State v. Ramirez Enriquez, 153 Ariz. 431, 433, 737 P.2d 407, 409 (App. 1987)*). It is not enough that other acts "'show similarities where one would expect differences' or demonstrate a 'visual connection' to the other charged offenses." *Ives, 187 Ariz. at 108, 927 P.2d at 768*. Nor is mere similarity sufficient to prove conduct was part of a common scheme or plan. *State v. Hughes, 189 Ariz. 62, 69, 938 P.2d 457, 464 (1997)*. "The common scheme or plan exception requires something more than mere criminal tendencies." *Id.* The evidence must be of a "commitment to a particular plan of which the charged crime is a part. It is a matter of the particularity of the plan and thus of the probative force of the connection between one crime and another." *Ramirez Enriquez, 153 Ariz. at 433, 737 P.2d at 409*. "The distinction is between proving a specific plan embracing the charged crime and proving a general commitment to criminality which might well have involved the charged crime." *Id.* (quoting Morris K. Udall & Joseph M. Livermore, Arizona Practice: Law of Evidence § 84, 184 n.17 (2d ed. 1982)).

Here, there is no common scheme or plan and there was otherwise no probative connection between the details of the temple murders and the tenth murder. While the tenth murder further established that Garcia had criminal tendencies and/or a general commitment to criminality that might involve murder and/or robbery, the tenth murder was not evidence of a "commitment to a particular plan of which the [temple murders and/or the tenth murder were] a part." It was not enough that both events involved robberies in which Garcia and/or his accomplice shot a victim and took the victim's money. The temple murders were a mass murder. Garcia and Doody planned the temple crimes over a period of months. They gathered information regarding the layout of the temple, possible security systems, whether doors would be locked, the presence and location of gold, money and other valuables they believed might be inside as well as who would be present. They drew a diagram of the temple. They obtained weapons. They wore clothing and equipment that concealed their identities and made them appear to be law enforcement officers. They planned who would go in first and continued the law enforcement ruse to control the occupants once inside the temple. The tenth murder was a crime of opportunity committed on the spur of the moment by two teenage runaways who blundered into an unfortunate victim's campsite.

There was also no common scheme or plan because Garcia never minimized his involvement in the tenth murder and did not unjustifiably deflect blame to his girlfriend. He did not need to because his girlfriend admitted she shot and killed the victim and Garcia's statements regarding the tenth murder matched the results of the investigation of that murder "to a T." Finally, Garcia's post-arrest actions to obtain a plea deal and/or make any deal more beneficial are in no way part of a "common scheme or plan" as contemplated by *Rule 404(b)*. Such actions do not demonstrate "commitment to a particular plan of which the charged crime is a part." Were we to hold otherwise, a defendant's attempts to minimize involvement and/or deflect blame during a criminal investigation or plea negotiations could be considered part of a common scheme or plan. *Rule 404(b)* and the case law that addresses the rule do not contemplate such absurd results.

Finally, in regard to the limitation of evidence regarding Garcia's use of the phrase "no witnesses" after the temple murders, this court addressed this same issue in Garcia's first appeal in 1996 and found that limitation was well within the trial court's discretion. *State v. Doody, 187 Ariz. 363, 375, 930 P.2d 440, 452 (App. 1996)*. It remains so. This court also addressed the exclusion of the other details of the tenth murder in the first trial and found no error. That resolution is not dispositive, however, because we addressed a different theory of admissibility than the theory Doody relied upon in the third trial. *Doody, 187 Ariz. at 374, 930 P.2d at 451*.

BLAINE KYLE MCNEESE, PETITIONER, V. CHARLES RYAN, ARIZONA ATTORNEY GENERAL, RESPONDENTS. CIV 12-00962 PHX FJM (MEA) UNITED STATES DISTRICT COURT FOR THE DISTRICT OF ARIZONA

(Text added and modified for emphasis) As a matter of regular practice the Attorney General's Office consistently fails to advise the federal courts that lawyers appointed to represent inmates do not as a matter of routine exhaust but procedurally default on federal claims. There are too many such incidents. The failure of the Attorney General to be candid constitute a pattern. As this is a pattern with the Arizona Attorney General's Office this should constitute fraud upon the court, because, they are concealing facts on a systemic basis, to defeat valid claims.

COUNSEL: Blaine Kyle McNeese, Petitioner, Pro se, BUCKEYE, AZ. For Charles L Ryan, named as Charles Ryan, Director of Department of Corrections, Attorney General of the State of Arizona, Respondents: Barbara Anne Bailey, LEAD ATTORNEY, Office of the Attorney General, Phoenix, AZ.

I Procedural History

A grand jury indictment returned December 18, 2008, charged Petitioner with one count of theft of at least $25,000, one count of forgery, and one count of identity theft. See Answer, Exh. B. The charges were based on the events of September 30, 2003, during which time Petitioner was an officer with the Arizona Department of Public Safety ("DPS"). The jury accepted the prosecution's theory of the case: Petitioner had arranged with a limousine driver that, acting in his capacity as a DPS officer, Petitioner would "pull over" the limousine on a particular date at a particular time while the driver was transporting particular passengers who would be carrying a large sum of cash. Petitioner would cite and arrest the driver and search the vehicle pursuant to the arrest, removing $45,000 in cash that Petitioner knew the passengers would have in the limousine. Petitioner used the name of another DPS officer on the citation and he and the limousine driver split the $45,000. The passengers reported the loss of the money, leading to the investigation. Petitioner resigned from the DPS in November of 2003.

In June 2005, Detectives Vern Alley and Larry Landers were investigating the robbery of $40,000 in cash from the passengers of a limousine whose driver was arrested during a traffic stop conducted by Petitioner on September 30, 2003. Id., Exh. S. The detectives went to Petitioner's home to confront him with the evidence regarding Petitioner's participation in the robbery. The detectives discussed the matter with Petitioner and his wife. During that conversation with the detectives Petitioner admitted that he had coordinated the traffic stop with the limousine driver and that he had obtained cash from the car. Petitioner also stated that he "got $20,000 out of it." Id., Exh. S. Petitioner later engaged in a "freetalk" with detectives; the detectives testified at Petitioner's trial that he admitted to the crimes during this "freetalk." Id., Exh. S. Attached to the state's sentencing recommendation as Exhibit 4 is a transcript of a portion (pages 32 through 42) of the "freetalk." Answer, Exh. F at Exhibit 4. On January 7, 2010, after four days of trial, a jury convicted Petitioner of all three counts alleged in the indictment. However, the jury found that the theft was based on a value of less than $25,000, rendering that offense a class 3 felony as opposed to the class 2 felony charged in the indictment. The evidence introduced at trial included phone records indicating Petitioner and the limousine driver had spoken by phone on 79 occasions in the four months prior to the robbery and sixteen times on the date of the robbery.

On February 9, 2010, the trial court sentenced Petitioner to an aggravated term of six years' imprisonment pursuant to his conviction on the theft charge and to an aggravated term of three years' imprisonment pursuant to his conviction on the charge of identity theft. Id., Exh. G. Petitioner was sentenced to the presumptive term of 2.5 years' imprisonment pursuant to his conviction for forgery. The trial court ordered that the forgery and identity theft sentences be served concurrently to each other and consecutively to the sentence imposed for theft.

Petitioner took a timely direct appeal of his convictions and sentences. In his direct appeal Petitioner asserted that the trial court abused its discretion when it permitted the use of his "free talk" statements for impeachment purposes; that the prosecutor engaged in misconduct when he referred to a "free talk agreement" in direct examination and closing argument; and that the trial court erred in admitting a copy of the traffic citation issued to the limousine driver during the robbery into evidence after the state had destroyed the original. Id., Exh. P.

The Arizona Court of Appeals denied relief in a decision entered June 21, 2011. The appellate court reviewed Petitioner's first claim for fundamental error, under state law. Id., Exh. S. The court held that, although the trial court erred by permitting the state to use Petitioner's statements during a "free talk" with police to impeach the testimony of Petitioner's wife at trial, the error was not fundamental. The court noted that Petitioner had argued that "his state and federal constitutional rights were violated in the heading for this issue in his opening brief," but that Petitioner had failed "to provide citation to any authority or argument" for the claim. Accordingly, citing *Arizona v. Moody, 208 Ariz. 424, 452 n.9, 94 P.3d 1119, 1147 (2004)*, the court held Petitioner had "abandoned these claims." The state appellate court analyzed Petitioner's claim of prosecutorial misconduct under state law and held that the prosecutor's statements in closing argument did not constitute fundamental error. The state court further held that, under state law, the trial court's admission of a photocopy of the citation on which Petitioner had forged the name of a fellow DPS officer was not reversible error. Id., Exh. S.

Petitioner sought review of the Arizona Court of Appeals' decision by the Arizona Supreme Court, which denied review on January 10, 2012. Id., Exh. T.

Petitioner initiated a state action for post-conviction relief pursuant to Rule 32, Arizona Rules of Criminal Procedure, on May 18, 2010, while his direct appeal was pending. Id., Exh. K. On June 16, 2010, Petitioner filed a motion "to withdraw [his] notice of post-conviction relief without prejudice so that it [could] be filed at a later date." Id., Exh. M. The trial court dismissed the Rule 32 action without prejudice on August 3, 2010. Id., Exh. O.

On July 15, 2011, Petitioner initiated a second Rule 32 action. Id., Exh. U. The state trial court appointed counsel to represent Petitioner in his Rule 32 proceedings. On January 3, 2012, Petitioner's appointed counsel informed the trial court that he had reviewed the trial and appellate proceedings and was "unable to find any claims for relief to raise in post-conviction relief proceedings." On May 12, 2012, the Rule 32 action was dismissed for Petitioner's failure to timely file a pro per pleading by February 21, 2012, as ordered by the state trial court. Id., Exh. FF.

In his federal habeas action Petitioner asserts:

1. His right to due process of law was violated because the state used Petitioner's statements during a "free talk" to impeach his wife's trial testimony;

2. The prosecutor committed misconduct by referring to Petitioner's "free talk" in direct examination and closing argument;

3. The trial court erred by admitting a photocopy of a traffic citation at trial after the state had destroyed the original;

4. The two detectives who testified at Petitioner's trial "perjured themselves" by testifying that Petitioner admitted to the crimes of conviction.

II Analysis

A. Exhaustion and procedural default

Petitioner did not present any claims to the Arizona Court of Appeals in a procedurally correct manner in his Rule 32 action, which was dismissed by the state trial court for Petitioner's failure to prosecute any specific claims in that action. Accordingly, because the Arizona Rules of Criminal Procedure regarding timeliness, waiver, and the preclusion of claims bar Petitioner from now returning to the state courts to exhaust any unexhausted federal habeas claims, Petitioner has exhausted, but procedurally defaulted, any claim not previously fairly presented to the Arizona Court of Appeals in his direct appeal. See *Insyxiengmay v. Morgan, 403 F.3d 657, 665 (9th Cir. 2005)*; *Beaty v. Stewart, 303 F.3d 975, 987 (9th Cir. 2002)*. See also *Stewart v. Smith, 536 U.S. 856, 860, 122 S. Ct. 2578, 2581, 153 L. Ed. 2d 762 (2002)* (holding Arizona's state rules regarding the waiver and procedural default of claims raised in attacks on criminal convictions are adequate and independent state grounds for affirming a conviction and denying federal habeas relief on the grounds of a procedural bar); *Ortiz v. Stewart, 149 F.3d 923, 931-32 (9th Cir. 1998)*.

E. Petitioner's claims for relief

1. Petitioner contends his right to due process was violated because the state used Petitioner's statements during a "free talk" to impeach his wife's trial testimony and because the state never "disclosed a copy of the 'freetalk.'"

In his direct appeal Petitioner asserted the trial court erred by allowing the introduction of statements he made during a "freetalk" to be used to impeach his wife's trial testimony. When discussing the merits of this claim the state court noted that, although Petitioner had stated in the heading of this section of his brief that his state and federal constitutional rights were violated by this error, Petitioner did not argue anywhere in the brief that these rights were violated, nor did he cite to any legal opinion so holding. Accordingly, the state court found Petitioner had abandoned any claim that this error by the trial court violated his state or constitutional rights. See Answer Exh. S at 18 n. 10.

The state court then reviewed the argument pursuant to state law and concluded that although the trial court erred, the error was not fundamental because it did not permeate the proceedings and deny Petitioner a fair trial, *inter alia*, given the "overwhelming" evidence of guilt.

Petitioner did not provide the state court the opportunity to review the merits of the federal constitutional claim presented in his *section 2254* petition. The state court decided the merits of the claim based solely on state law. Accordingly, Petitioner has procedurally defaulted this claim in the state courts. Because the state court's decision is an adequate and independent basis for declining to consider the merits of the federal habeas claim, the Court need not consider the merits of the claim absent a showing of cause and prejudice or that a fundamental miscarriage of justice will occur.

In his reply to the answer to his petition Petitioner contends:

> The Petitioner's claims are not procedurally barred.... Claims 1 through 3 were handled by a state appointed attorney []. He followed all appropriate rules and applications for the petitioner's state appeals. ... Since the Petitioner is not an attorney and has limited experience with the law the Petitioner

assumes all the correct procedures were followed. If this is not the case the Petitioner should not be responsible.

Doc. 16 at 2-3.

With regard to the merits of his claim, Petitioner contends that the use of the "freetalk" violated Petitioner's *Fifth Amendment* rights because it was plain error and prejudicial and in violation of the Arizona state rules regarding admission of evidence and his right to not be forced to incriminate himself. Doc. 16 at 5-6. Petitioner asserts repeatedly that because "the state never turned over a copy of Petitioner's 'freetalk'", that the "trial court erred by allowing the state to attempt to impeach Petitioner's wife with the 'freetalk," resulting in a violation of his constitutional rights. Petitioner further contends that he never voluntarily confessed to the alleged crimes. Petitioner alleges that the two detectives had a "vendetta" against him and lied and fabricated evidence to make him look guilty.

....

2. Petitioner contends the prosecutor committed misconduct by referring to Petitioner's "free talk" in direct examination and closing argument.

Petitioner presented a claim based on these facts to the Arizona state court in his direct appeal. The state court analyzed this claim pursuant to state law and held that the prosecutor's statements in closing argument did not constitute fundamental error. The state court examined the claim for fundamental error because Petitioner's counsel had not objected to the statements at trial as prosecutorial misconduct. The appellate court specifically found that there was no evidence that the prosecutor was "reading" from the "freetalk" during closing argument, but concluded that the "objectionable statements appear to be the State's somewhat overzealous characterizations of Defendant's admissions to Detectives A and L as well as to some of the other evidence introduced at trial...." Answer, Exh. S at 29-30 & n.15. The appellate court also concluded that any erroneously admitted statements were not prejudicial in light of the weight of the evidence against Petitioner. Id., Exh. S at 32. Counsel did object to the statements as assuming facts not in evidence.

Petitioner is not entitled to federal habeas relief on this claim for the reasons stated with regard to his first claim for habeas relief. Petitioner did not present any federal constitutional claim to the Arizona Court of Appeals in his direct appeal with regard to the arguments raised in his second claim for federal habeas relief. When raising this claim in the state courts Petitioner's brief did not state any federal claim and did not cite any federal constitutional provision or any federal case law. Petitioner has procedurally defaulted this claim in the state courts. Because he has not shown cause for nor prejudice arising from his default of this claim, nor has Petitioner established a fundamental miscarriage of justice as that term is defined in federal habeas law, he is not entitled to relief on this claim.

....

4. The two detectives "perjured themselves" by testifying that Petitioner admitted to the crimes and to other acts.

In his reply to the answer to his petition, Petitioner allows that he did not present this claim to the state courts. Petitioner asserts that he did not present the claim to the state courts because his counsel in his direct appeal advised him that the claim was not likely to succeed.

Petitioner did not properly exhaust this claim in the state courts. Petitioner contends: "[C]ounsel ... had all the information in relationship to Ground 4 and stated that I did not have a colorful claim. Since my claim in Ground 4 is one of the main causes that the Petitioner was convicted I believe that *Edwards v. Carpenter, 529 U.S. 446, 451, 120 S. Ct. 1587, 146 L. Ed. 2d 518 (2000)* applies." Doc. 16 at 3. Petitioner contends that failure to review this claim will result in a fundamental miscarriage of justice, notwithstanding that the state court found the error was not fundamental.

The ineffective assistance of appellate counsel is not sufficient cause to excuse the procedural default of a claim unless the habeas petitioner exhausted an ineffective assistance of appellate counsel claim in the state courts, which Petitioner has not done. Additionally, counsel's failure to raise what counsel considers to be a losing argument is not deficient performance and is generally not prejudicial.

Petitioner has not shown cause for nor prejudice arising from his procedural default of this claim. Additionally, no fundamental miscarriage of justice will occur absent consideration of this claim because there is sufficient evidence that Petitioner was not factually innocent. Although Petitioner alleges numerous legal errors in his habeas pleadings he does not argue his factual innocence nor discuss a plausible theory regarding the other evidence introduced against him at trial.

FAILURE TO EXHAUST REMEDIES

MIGUEL ANGEL PLATERO DIAZ, PETITIONER, V. CHARLES RYAN AND ARIZONA ATTORNEY GENERAL, RESPONDENTS. CIV 09-00725 PHX MHM (MEA) UNITED STATES DISTRICT COURT FOR THE DISTRICT OF ARIZONA

(Text added and modified for emphasis) In Arizona counsel routinely advise defendants the fact that defendants will receive a certain sentence to induce a guilty plea when as a matter of routine they do not as evidenced by the number of complaints. As a matter of regular practice the Attorney General's Office consistently fails to advise the federal courts that when lawyers are appointed in Arizona, they fail to advise defendants to take pleas by fully explaining the consequences. Hearings are held but these hearings are only formalities for Arizona judges do not spend the necessary time and effort explaining the consequences of rejecting pleas. As a direct consequence there are defendants serving life terms in Arizona prisons all because of the failure of the Attorney General to be candid. There are too many such incidents which constitute a pattern .As this is a pattern with the Arizona Attorney General's Office this should constitute fraud upon the court, because, they are concealing facts on a systemic basis, to defeat valid claims.

COUNSEL: Miguel Angel Plateo Diaz, also known as Miguel Angel Diaz, Petitioner, Pro se, WINSLOW, AZ.

For Charles Ryan, Arizona Attorney General, State of, Respondents: Julie Ann Done, Office of the Attorney General, Phoenix, AZ.

I Procedural History

A Maricopa County grand jury indictment issued May 26, 2006, in docket number CR2006-121919, charged Petitioner and a co-defendant with one count of burglary in the first degree, seven counts of aggravated assault, one count of assisting a criminal street gang, and one count of impersonating a peace officer. See Answer, Exh. B. The charges arose from a home invasion that occurred on or between April 21 and 22, 2006. Id., Exh. B & Exh. G at 10.

A settlement conference in CR2006-121919 and another case wherein Petitioner was the sole defendant, CR2006-140056, was set for November 14, 2006. See id., Exh. E. Docket number CR2006-140056 involved charges of possession of marijuana for sale, possession or use of marijuana, and misconduct involving weapons. See id., Exh. E. In Petitioner's settlement conference memoranda, he acknowledged possession of a large amount of marijuana and that a weapon was found during the execution of a search warrant at his home. Petitioner also acknowledged that, in docket number CR2006-121919, the home invasion crime, the "State has a cooperating co-defendant who places the defendant at the scene. The rest of the evidence against the defendant is somewhat circumstantial." Id., Exh. E.

In the settlement conference memorandum Petitioner averred he had no prior felony convictions. Id., Exh. E. Petitioner acknowledged he had been offered a plea agreement that provided he would plead guilty to one count of burglary in CR2006-121919 and be sentenced to a term of seven to 21 years' imprisonment. The plea offers provided the sentence for burglary would run concurrently with that imposed in CR2006-140056, in which Petitioner would plead guilty to one count of possession [*3] of marijuana for sale. Id., Exh. E.

The settlement conference memorandum states:

> The Defendant is not adamantly averse to a plea but he and his family understandably have reservations about the range which is up to 21 years in prison. No individuals were seriously injured in the home invasion and the defense does not believe the Defendant would necessarily receive more than 21 years after trial, however, does acknowledge some form of stacked sentences is a possibility.

Id., Exh. E.

On November 14, 2006, pursuant to a written plea agreement signed that same day, Petitioner pled guilty in CR2006-121919 to one count of burglary in the first degree. Id., Exh. G & Exh. I. The plea agreement provided Petitioner was "giving up [his] right to a determination of probable cause, to a trial by jury ... [his] right to jury determination of aggravating factors beyond a reasonable doubt, and right to appeal." Id., Exh. F. The written plea agreement provided the presumptive term of imprisonment for burglary was 10.5 years and that the maximum sentence was 21 years. Id., Exh. F. The plea agreement stipulated that Petitioner's sentence would not exceed 16 years' imprisonment. Id., Exh. F.

In the state's sentencing memorandum it argued Petitioner's sentence should be aggravated based on the emotional, physical, and financial harm to the victims, and the presence of an accomplice. Id., Exh. H. The state also asserted Petitioner was a threat to public safety, and argued there were a lack of mitigating factors. Id., Exh. H. The sentencing memorandum also alleged Petitioner was a documented member of a street gang involvement and provided general information regarding gang activity. Id., Exh. H.

A sentencing hearing was conducted February 8, 2007. Id., Exh. J. Two of the victims from the home invasion testified regarding the impact of that crime. See id., Exh. J at 3-10. Petitioner's counsel presented mitigation evidence at the sentencing hearing, asserting Petitioner's lack of an adult criminal record and the fact that he had relinquished his ties to a street gang weighed in favor of leniency. In response, the state maintained that, under the circumstances of the case, Petitioner was not deserving of any leniency. Id., Exh. J. at 14-15.

Before sentencing Petitioner, the state court asked if he was satisfied with his counsel's representation, to which question Petitioner responded, "Yes, sir." Id., Exh. J at 26. The trial court then found the following aggravating circumstances with regard to the burglary conviction: Petitioner was a documented gang member; the crime was committed for pecuniary gain; there were multiple victims; the extreme emotional and financial harm to the victims; the physical injuries suffered by the victims; and the presence of one or more accomplices.

Id., Exh. J at 27-28. The trial court determined that the aggravating circumstances substantially outweighed the mitigating circumstances and sentenced Petitioner to serve a term of 16 years' imprisonment pursuant to his conviction for burglary. The court sentenced Petitioner to a concurrent term of seven years' imprisonment in CR2006-140056 pursuant to his conviction for possession of marijuana for sale. Id., Exh. J at 28-29 & Exh. K.

On March 21, 2007, Petitioner initiated a timely state action for post-conviction relief pursuant to Rule 32, Arizona Rules of Criminal Procedure. See id., Exh. M. In Arizona this is the first appeal "as of right" for defendants who plead guilty and thereby waive their right to a direct appeal. Accordingly, Petitioner was appointed counsel to represent him in his post-conviction proceedings. Id., Exh. N. After reviewing the record, Petitioner's appointed counsel notified the state trial court that he was unable to find any claims for relief to raise on Petitioner's behalf. Id., Exh. O.

On November 14, 2007, Petitioner filed a *pro per* brief asserting he was entitled to post-conviction relief because his right to a fair trial was violated when the trial court imposed an improper aggravated sentence. Id., Exh. P. Petitioner also asserted Arizona's sentencing scheme was unconstitutional because it mandated that judges, rather than a jury, find the existence of aggravating sentencing factors. Additionally, Petitioner asserted he was denied his right to the effective assistance of counsel because his trial counsel failed to properly advise him regarding the plea agreement. Petitioner asserted his counsel assured Petitioner his sentence would not be greater than the presumptive sentence, i.e., 10.5 years' imprisonment. Petitioner also alleged his counsel was ineffective for failing to object to the sentence imposed by the trial court at the time Petitioner was sentenced. Id., Exh. P.

The state trial court summarily dismissed Petitioner's action for post-conviction relief, finding he had "failed to show any colorable claim for post-conviction relief." Id., Exh. S. Petitioner sought review of this decision by the Arizona Court of Appeals, which denied review on January 21, 2009. Id., Exh. W & Petition, Attach. Petitioner did not seek review of this decision by the Arizona Supreme Court.

In his federal habeas action Petitioner asserts he is entitled to relief because he was denied his right to the effective assistance of counsel. Petitioner also argues he was unconstitutionally sentenced to an aggravated term of imprisonment in violation of his *Sixth* and *Fourteenth Amendment* rights. Petitioner also contends his sentence for burglary must be vacated because he was sentenced pursuant to a state statute that violates the United States Constitution.

II Analysis

....

D. Petitioner's claims for relief

1. Petitioner asserts he is entitled to relief because he was denied his right to the effective assistance of counsel during his plea and sentencing proceedings.

Petitioner contends his counsel's performance was deficient because counsel assured Petitioner he would receive the presumptive sentence, i.e., 10.5 years' imprisonment. Petitioner also argues his counsel was ineffective for failing to lodge a contemporaneous objection to Petitioner's sentence went it was imposed by the trial court. Petitioner properly exhausted these ineffective assistance of counsel claims in the state courts by asserting the claims before the Arizona Court of Appeals in his state action for post-conviction relief. The state courts' determination that Petitioner's constitutional right to the effective assistance of counsel was not violated was not clearly contrary to federal law.

To state a cognizable claim that their counsel was unconstitutionally ineffective, a petitioner must show that his attorney's performance was deficient and that the deficiency prejudiced the petitioner's defense. See *Strickland v. Washington, 466 U.S. 668, 687, 104 S. Ct. 2052, 2064, 80 L. Ed. 2d 674 (1984)*. The petitioner must overcome the strong presumption that counsel's conduct was within the range of reasonable professional assistance required of attorneys in that circumstance. See id.

To prevail on the merits of a habeas claim of ineffective assistance of counsel the petitioner must show that the state court applied the doctrine of Strickland to the facts of his case in an objectively unreasonable manner. *Woodford v. Visciotti, 537 U.S. 19, 25, 123 S. Ct. 357, 360, 154 L. Ed. 2d 279 (2002)*. The United States Supreme Court has emphasized that "[a]n unreasonable application of federal law is different from an incorrect application of federal law." Id. (internal quotations omitted).

Ineffective assistance of counsel claims in the context of cases wherein the defendant pled guilty, rather than go to trial, are also governed by the doctrine of *Strickland*. See, e.g., *Hill v. Lockhart, 474 U.S. 52, 57, 106 S. Ct. 366, 369, 88 L. Ed. 2d 203 (1985)*; *Fields v. Attorney General, 956 F.2d 1290, 1296-97 (4th Cir. 1992)*. When a defendant raises a *Sixth Amendment* challenge to a conviction resulting from a plea agreement the "prejudice" prong of the *Strickland* test is modified; the defendant must show there is a reasonable probability that, but for counsel's alleged errors, he would not have pled guilty to the charges against him, but instead would have insisted on going to trial. See *Hill, 474 U.S. at 59, 106 S. Ct. at 370*. Accord *Fields, 956 F.2d at 1297*; *Craker v. McCotter, 805 F.2d 538, 542 (5th Cir. 1986)*.

Petitioner has not established that he was prejudiced by any alleged error in his counsel's prediction of the sentence ultimately imposed by the state trial court. The record in this matter, *inter alia* Petitioner's state trial court criminal case settlement conference memorandum, indicates Petitioner was entirely aware of the fact that his guilty plea could result in a maximum sentence of 21 years' imprisonment. Petitioner was also alerted to the potential consequences of his guilty plea, i.e., a statutory maximum sentence of 21 years' imprisonment and a maximum sentence of 16 years' imprisonment pursuant to the plea agreement, by the state trial court before the court accepted Petitioner's plea. See Answer, Exh. G at 5 & 9.

Even if defense counsel did inaccurately predict the sentence ultimately imposed this alleged deficiency would not, as a matter of law, constitute unconstitutionally ineffective assistance of counsel. See *Womack v. McDaniel, 497 F.3d 998, 1003-04 (9th Cir. 2007)* (holding a petitioner is not unconstitutionally prejudiced by their counsel's inaccurate predictions as to a sentence if the petitioner was informed of the potential sentence by a written plea agreement).

Petitioner also contends his counsel was ineffective because counsel did not object to the sentence imposed by the trial court. The state courts' determination that Petitioner's counsel's performance was not deficient nor prejudicial in this regard was not clearly contrary to federal law. To succeed on an assertion his counsel's performance was deficient because counsel failed to raise a particular argument the petitioner must establish the argument was likely to be successful, thereby establishing that he was prejudiced by his counsel's omission. See *Tanner v. McDaniel, 493 F.3d 1135, 1144 (9th Cir.)*, cert. denied, *552 U.S. 1068, 128 S. Ct. 722, 169 L. Ed. 2d 565 (2007)*; *Weaver v. Palmateer, 455 F.3d 958, 970 (9th Cir. 2006)*, cert. denied, *552 U.S. 873, 128 S. Ct. 177, 169 L. Ed. 2d 120 (2007)*. A defendant has no constitutional right to compel counsel to raise particular objections if counsel, as a matter of professional judgment, decides not to raise those objections. See *Jones v. Barnes, 463 U.S. 745, 751, 103 S. Ct. 3308, 3312, 77 L. Ed. 2d 987 (1983)* (declining to promulgate "a per se rule that the client, not the professional advocate, must be allowed to decide what issues are to be pressed"). Because an argument that the sentence imposed was not in accordance with the plea agreement or the United States Constitution would not be successful, Petitioner's *Sixth Amendment* rights were not violated by his counsel's failure to object to his sentence.

.....

3. Petitioner contends his sentence for burglary must be vacated because he was sentenced pursuant to a state statute that violates the United States Constitution.

Petitioner alleges that Arizona's sentencing scheme violates the *Sixth, Eighth*, and *Fourteenth Amendments to the United States Constitution*. Petitioner contends the statutes violates the Constitution because they require a judge, rather than a jury, to find factors used to aggravate a convicted defendant's sentence. Petitioner argues that because the statutes require a judge, rather than a jury, to find aggravating factors, the statutes violate the *Sixth Amendment* right to a jury trial.

Petitioner arguably raised this claim in his state action for post-conviction relief, asserting both that his sentence violated the United States Supreme Court's opinion in Blakely v. Washington and that *subsection 702(B)* and *subsection 702(C)* are unconstitutional. Answer, Exh. P. In his state action for post-conviction relief Petitioner argued the United States Constitution was violated by Arizona's determination that one Blakely-compliant factor was sufficient to aggravate a defendant's sentence when the other factors were found by a judge rather than a jury. The Arizona state courts' denial of relief on Petitioner's claim that his sentence violates his federal constitutional right to a determination by a jury of each factual element of the crime charged was not clearly contrary to federal law.

Petitioner was sentenced to a term of imprisonment above the presumptive term but below the maximum term. However, Petitioner's sentence was "aggravated" based on factors admitted by Petitioner, including the presence of an accomplice.

In *Blakely v. Washington, 542 U.S. 296, 303-04, 124 S. Ct. 2531, 2537-38, 159 L. Ed. 2d 403 (2004)*, the United States Supreme Court determined that a defendant in a criminal case is entitled to have a jury determine beyond a reasonable doubt any fact that increases his sentence beyond the "statutory maximum," unless the fact was admitted by the defendant or was based on a prior conviction. The United States Supreme Court clarified that the term "statutory maximum" was to be interpreted as the presumptive sentence, or the presumptive sentence given the facts as found by the jury or admitted by the defendant, rather than the maximum statutory sentence allowed. See *Allen v. Reed, 427 F.3d 767, 772 (10th Cir. 2005)* ("In other words, the relevant 'statutory maximum' is not the maximum sentence a judge may impose after finding additional facts, but the maximum he may impose without any additional findings.").

However, the maxim of *Blakely* does not provide relief to a defendant when the facts supporting the sentence enhancement are established by a plea of guilty or admitted by the defendant. Accordingly, the Arizona state courts' decision that Petitioner's *Sixth Amendment* right to have a jury find each fact used to aggravate his sentence was not clearly contrary to federal law.

In *Arizona v. Martinez, 210 Ariz. 578, 115 P.3d 618 (2005)*, the Arizona Supreme Court considered the impact of Blakely on Arizona's sentencing statutes. In Arizona, the statutory maximum sentence in a case where no Blakely-compliant or Blakely-exempt aggravating factors are present is the presumptive term. See *210 Ariz. at 583, 115 P.3d at 623*. However, because an Arizona defendant may receive an aggravated sentence based on a single aggravating factor, see *Arizona Revised Statutes Annotated § 13-702(B)*, a single Blakely-compliant or Blakely-exempt aggravating factor establishes the facts "legally essential" to punishment. See *Arizona v. Martinez, 210 Ariz. 578, 115 P.3d 618 (2005)*; *Arizona v. Henderson, 210 Ariz. 561, 115 P.3d 601 (2005)*. The sentencing scheme iterated in Martinez was upheld upon review by the United States Supreme Court. See *Martinez v. Arizona, 546 U.S. 1044, 126 S. Ct. 762, 163 L. Ed. 2d 592 (2005)*.

Because an Arizona defendant may receive an aggravated sentence based on a single aggravating factor, see *Arizona Revised Statutes Annotated § 13-702(B)*, the federal courts have concluded that if a single Blakely-compliant or Blakely-exempt aggravating factor establishes the facts "legally essential" to punishment, a defendant's constitutional right to a jury trial is not violated by the fact that other factors were found in the context of sentencing the defendant. See, e.g., *Stokes v. Schriro, 465 F.3d 397, 402-03 (9th Cir. 2006)*.

Arizona's response to Blakely as explained in Martinez has been found to be not clearly contrary to federal law. See *Cunningham v. California, 549 U.S. 270, 294 n.17, 127 S. Ct. 856, 871 n.17, 166 L. Ed. 2d 856 (2007)* (finding California's sentencing process unconstitutional and analyzing the Colorado Supreme Court's response to Blakely in *Colorado v. Lopez, 113 P.3d 713, 716 (Colo. 2005)*; Colorado's Lopez decision is materially similar to the Arizona Supreme Court's Martinez opinion); *Stokes, 465 F.3d at 402-03* (holding "the Arizona state courts' interpretation of these [sentencing] provisions does not contradict clearly established federal law"). Accordingly, the Arizona court's decision denying this claim in Petitioner's direct appeal was not clearly contrary to federal law and Petitioner is not entitled to relief on this claim.

KEITH R. STOKES, PETITIONER, V. CHARLES L. RYAN, TERRY GODDARD, MRS. DAIELL, RESPONDENT. CIV 08-02362 PHX DGC (MEA) UNITED STATES DISTRICT COURT FOR THE DISTRICT OF ARIZONA

(Text added and modified for emphasis) In Arizona counsel routinely advise defendants the fact that defendants will receive a certain sentence to induce a guilty plea when as a matter of routine they do not as evidenced by the number of complaints. As a matter of regular practice the Attorney General's Office consistently fails to advise the federal courts that when lawyers are appointed in Arizona, they fail to advise defendants to take pleas by fully explaining the consequences. Hearings are held but these hearings are only formalities for Arizona judges do not spend the necessary time and effort explaining the consequences of rejecting pleas. As a direct consequence there are defendants serving life terms in Arizona prisons all because of the failure of the Attorney General to be candid. There are too many such incidents which constitute a pattern. As this is a pattern with the Arizona Attorney General's Office this should constitute fraud upon the court, because, they are concealing facts on a systemic basis, to defeat valid claims.

COUNSEL: Keith R Stokes, Petitioner, Pro se, SAFFORD, AZ. For Terry L Goddard, Arizona Attorney General, State of, Charles L Ryan, K. Daniel, Warden of ASPC-Safford, Respondents: Laura Patrice Chiasson, Office of the Attorney General, Tucson, AZ.

I Procedural History

......In April of 2003, a jury found Petitioner guilty of one count of second-degree murder, two counts of attempted first-degree murder, and one count of aggravated assault, the result of events occurring in 1999. Petitioner was sentenced to aggravated terms of, respectively, twenty years, fifteen years, and twelve years' imprisonment, on the first three counts. Petitioner was sentenced to a presumptive term of seven and one-half years' imprisonment pursuant to his conviction for aggravated assault. The state trial court ordered the sentences be served consecutively. See Answer, Exh. A (Arizona v. Stokes, No. 1 CA-CR 03-0397 (Ct. App. Feb. 24, 2004)). The Arizona Court of Appeals affirmed

Petitioner's convictions and sentences in a decision issued on February 24, 2004. Id., Exh. A. Petitioner did not seek review of this decision by the Arizona Supreme Court.

Petitioner filed a timely state action seeking post conviction relief pursuant to Rule 32, Arizona Rules of Criminal Procedure, on March 17, 2004. Id., Exh. C. The state trial court dismissed the petition on March 1, 2005. Id., Exh. D. The Arizona Court of Appeals denied review of that decision on August 14, 2006. Id., Exh. E. On January 22, 2008, Petitioner filed a "Supplemental to My Petition for Review" in the Arizona Supreme Court. Id., Exh. F.

On April 21, 2008, Petitioner filed a petition seeking a writ of coram nobis. Id., Exh. G. The state trial court treated this writ as a second petition for post-conviction relief. In a decision issued June 3, 2008, the state trial court found all the claims stated were precluded, and dismissed the petition. Id., Exh. H.

In his amended habeas petition Petitioner contends he is entitled to federal habeas relief because, he asserts, perjured testimony was presented to the grand jury in violation of his right to due process of law. Petitioner further contends his conviction for murder violates his right to due process because the victim's death, ten months after he was shot by Petitioner, was not the result of Petitioner's actions. Petitioner also maintains his *Eighth Amendment* rights were violated because he was charged with attempted first degree murder and convicted of second degree murder. Additionally, Petitioner contends his sentence violates the separation of powers doctrine because the trial court's application of Arizona's sentencing statutes was "manifest injustice." Petitioner also alleges his trial counsel was unconstitutionally ineffective.

II Analysis

The petition seeking a writ of habeas corpus is barred by the applicable statute of limitations found in the Antiterrorism and Effective Death Penalty Act ("AEDPA"). The AEDPA imposed a one-year statute of limitations on prisoners seeking federal habeas relief from their state convictions. See, e.g., *Lott v. Mueller, 304 F.3d 918, 920 (9th Cir. 2002)*. The AEDPA provides that a petitioner is entitled to tolling of the statute of limitations during the pendency of a "properly filed application for state post-conviction or other collateral review with respect to the pertinent judgment or claim." *28 U.S.C. § 2244(d)(2)(2006 & Supp. 2009).* See also *Artuz v. Bennett, 531 U.S. 4, 8, 121 S. Ct. 361, 363-64, 148 L. Ed. 2d 213 (2000); Harris v. Carter, 515 F.3d 1051, 1053 (9th Cir.),* cert. denied, *129 S. Ct. 397, 172 L. Ed. 2d 323 (2008).*

Petitioner's conviction became "final" at the conclusion of his direct appeal proceedings, at which time Petitioner had a properly-filed petition for post-conviction relief pending in the state trial court. The Arizona Court of Appeals denied review of the decision dismissing Petitioner's first action for post-conviction relief on August 14, 2006. Answer, Exh. E. Petitioner had thirty days to appeal that decision to the Arizona Supreme Court. See Ariz. R. Crim. P. (2009). Therefore, the statute of limitations on Petitioner's federal habeas action began to run on September 15, 2006, and expired on or about September 16, 2007. See *Tillema v. Long, 253 F.3d 494, 498 (9th Cir. 2001); Bowen v. Roe, 188 F.3d 1157, 1159 (9th Cir. 1999).* Compare *Hemmerle v. Schriro, 495 F.3d 1069, 1077 (9th Cir. 2007); Riddle v. Kemna, 523 F.3d 850, 855 (8th Cir. 2008).*

Petitioner did not file his federal habeas action until April 30, 2009, approximately nineteen months after the statute of limitations expired.

.....

In response to the answer to his petition, Petitioner filed an "Amended" section 2254 petition which is two pages. The second page states:

> Petitioner was tried, convicted and sentence[d] in violation of Arizona legislative statues (sic) *13-110 (13-111) 13-1150 CB)* and *13-116.* Prosecution created his own interpretation of charges before trial court, and persuaded courts to apply its interpretation beyond legislative intent as a fermented statues (sic) plainly state manifest in just has occurred in this cause (sic).

Docket No. 13.

Petitioner has not established that he is entitled to equitable tolling of the statute of limitations because he has not presented evidence of due diligence or a factor outside the defense which resulted in his failure to timely file his habeas action. Even if the "fundamental miscarriage of justice" standard for excusing procedural default of habeas claims were applicable as a reason for tolling the statute of limitations, Petitioner has not established that the failure to consider his habeas claims on their merits would result in a fundamental miscarriage of justice. Cf. *Hayman v. Pennsylvania, 624 F. Supp. 2d 378, 394 (E.D. Pa. 2009)* (discussing case law on when equitable tolling is warranted).

ANDREW J. ALLERDICE, PETITIONER - APPELLANT, V. CHARLES L. RYAN, DIRECTOR OF THE ARIZONA DEPARTMENT OF CORRECTIONS, AND ARIZONA ATTORNEY GENERAL, RESPONDENTS - APPELLEES. NO. 08-17281 UNITED STATES COURT OF APPEALS FOR THE NINTH CIRCUIT

(Text added and modified for emphasis) As a matter of regular practice the Attorney General's Office consistently fails to advise the federal courts that lawyers appointed to represent inmates do not as a matter of routine exhaust but procedurally default on federal claims. There are too many such incidents. The failure of the Attorney General to be candid constitute a pattern. As this is a pattern with the Arizona Attorney General's Office this should constitute fraud upon the court, because, they are concealing facts on a systemic basis, to defeat valid claims.

COUNSEL: For ANDREW J. ALLERDICE, Petitioner - Appellant: David Eisenberg, I, Esquire, Attorney, David Eisenberg, PLC, Phoenix, AZ. For CHARLES L. RYAN, Director of the Arizona Department of Corrections, ARIZONA ATTORNEY GENERAL, Appellee - Respondents: Joseph Thomas Maziarz, ARIZONA ATTORNEY GENERAL'S OFFICE, Phoenix, AZ.

Petitioner-Appellant Andrew Allerdice timely appeals the district court's denial of his habeas corpus petition. Because the parties are familiar with the facts and procedural history of this case, we will discuss them only as necessary to explain our decision.

We review the denial of a petition for writ of habeas corpus de novo. *Holley v. Yarborough, 568 F.3d 1091, 1098 (9th Cir. 2009)* (citation omitted). A writ may only be granted on a claim adjudicated in state court if the state court proceeding applied a legal rule that contradicts controlling Supreme Court authority, comes to a different conclusion when presented with materially indistinguishable facts, or identifies the correct legal standard but applies it in an objectively unreasonable manner to the facts. *28 U.S.C. § 2254(d)*; *Williams v. Taylor, 529 U.S. 362, 404-13, 120 S. Ct. 1495, 146 L. Ed. 2d 389 (2000)*. We have jurisdiction pursuant to *28 U.S.C. §§ 1291* and *2253*.

Allerdice first argues that his trial counsel's stipulations constituted ineffective assistance of counsel. To prevail on an ineffective assistance claim, a petitioner must show that his counsel's performance was deficient and that the deficient performance prejudiced the defense. *Strickland v. Washington, 466 U.S. 668, 687, 104 S. Ct. 2052, 80 L. Ed. 2d 674 (1984)*. Allerdice argues that prejudice should be presumed, because his lawyer failed to subject the state's case to "meaningful adversarial testing." *United States v. Cronic, 466 U.S. 648, 659-60, 104 S. Ct. 2039, 80 L. Ed. 2d 657 (1984)*. For prejudice to be presumed, counsel's failure must be complete. *Bell v. Cone, 535 U.S. 685, 696-98, 122 S. Ct. 1843, 152 L. Ed. 2d 914 (2002)*. Here, although counsel stipulated to certain facts, he also obtained stipulations from the state regarding defense exhibits, offered evidence, cross-examined witnesses, elicited favorable testimony, and presented a coherent if ultimately unsuccessful defense in closing argument. This is not a complete failure to test the State's case. Thus, *Strickland,* rather than *Cronic,* governs assessment of Allerdice's ineffective assistance of counsel claim.

Counsel was not ineffective. Strategic choices as to how to defend a case are "virtually unchallengeable." *Strickland, 466 U.S. at 690*. Counsel chose a strategy of defending on lack of intent to defraud, bolstered by claims of poor police work, after an adequate investigation; given the facts, the choice fell within a "wide range of reasonable professional assistance." *Id. at 689*. Moreover, Allerdice cannot show that he was prejudiced, as his claim that the State was unprepared to prove its case absent the stipulations is speculative. The Mohave County Superior Court's rejection of Allerdice's ineffective assistance of counsel claim was not objectively unreasonable. *Williams, 529 U.S. at 409*.

Allerdice next contends that the stipulations, entered over his express objection, constituted the "practical equivalent of a plea of guilty." *Brookhart v. Janis, 384 U.S. 1, 86 S. Ct. 1245, 16 L. Ed. 2d 314 (1966)*. A plea of guilty is not just an admission of guilt, but an agreement that no further proof by the prosecution is required; there is nothing to do but impose judgment. *Boykin v. Alabama, 395 U.S. 238, 242, 89 S. Ct. 1709, 23 L. Ed. 2d 274 (1969)*.

The Arizona court did not unreasonably reject this claim. First, it was not fairly presented in state court. *Picard v. Connor, 404 U.S. 270, 275-76, 92 S. Ct. 509, 30 L. Ed. 2d 438 (1971)*. Instead of relying on *Brookhart,* Allerdice framed his claim as an ineffective assistance of counsel claim, predicated on a failure to reasonably inform. This was inadequate to alert the state court to the controlling legal principles that he now relies on. *Anderson v. Harless, 459 U.S. 4, 6, 103 S. Ct. 276, 74 L. Ed. 2d 3 (1982)* (per curiam); *Rose v. Palmateer, 395 F.3d 1108, 1111-12 (9th Cir. 2005),* cert. denied, *545 U.S. 1144, 125 S. Ct. 2971, 162 L. Ed. 2d 896 (2005); see also Picard, 404 U.S. at 277* (rejecting as procedurally defaulted an equal protection claim that "entered this case only because the Court of Appeals injected it"). Accordingly, Allerdice did not exhaust this claim. *Id. at 275.* Because the time for Allerdice to raise this claim in state court has expired, *Ariz. R. Crim. P. 32.4, 32.1,* he has procedurally defaulted it, and federal habeas relief is unavailable absent cause and prejudice or a fundamental miscarriage of justice, which Allerdice has not attempted to demonstrate. *Engle v. Isaac, 456 U.S. 107, 125 n.28, 129, 102 S. Ct. 1558, 71 L. Ed. 2d 783 (1982); Beaty v. Stewart, 303 F.3d 975, 987 (9th Cir. 2002)*.

Second, even if not procedurally defaulted, Allerdice's claim lacks merit. The stipulations did not compare to a guilty plea. Defense counsel still vigorously contested the state's evidence, especially with respect to Allerdice's mental state. Moreover, counsel's conduct in Allerdice's trial was more like that in *Florida v. Nixon, 543 U.S. 175, 188?89, 125 S. Ct. 551, 160 L. Ed. 2d 565 (2004),* than it was like that in *Brookhart.* In *Nixon,* counsel conceded his client's guilt in order to preserve his credibility to argue mitigation at the penalty phase. The *Nixon* court determined that there was no *Brookhart* violation, and that counsel's actions did not violate the defendant's constitutional rights.

Allerdice's original claim of failure to reasonably inform was equally unmeritorious. The record demonstrated that counsel began negotiating the stipulations, with Allerdice's knowledge, six months before trial. Further, although Allerdice objected to the stipulations, he simultaneously rejected any plea deal. He did not show lack of consultation or prejudice. However, denominated, the Mohave County Superior Court reasonably rejected Allerdice's claim.

JAMES E. ROBINSON, PETITIONER, VS. CHARLES L. RYAN, ET AL., RESPONDENTS.
CIV 11-1383-PHX-GMS (MHB) UNITED STATES DISTRICT COURT FOR THE DISTRICT OF ARIZONA

(Text added/modified for emphasis) Arizona state courts decline to afford litigants who have evidence of actual innocence evidentiary hearings/their day in court. Instead they insist on maintaining convictions of those innocent.
COUNSEL: James E Robinson, Petitioner, Pro se, KINGMAN, AZ. For Charles L Ryan, named as Charles Ryan, Attorney General of the State of Arizona, Respondents: William Scott Simon, Office of the Attorney General, Criminal Appeals, Phoenix, AZ.

BACKGROUND

On December 6, 2007, Petitioner pled guilty to one count of theft of a means of transportation. (Exh. A.) As part of the plea, Petitioner admitted to having committed one historical prior felony offense. (Exh. A.) On December 20, 2007, the trial court sentenced Petitioner to a term of 6.5 years' imprisonment. (Exh. B.)
Nearly two years later, on September 22, 2009, Petitioner filed a notice of post-conviction relief alleging newly discovered evidence of actual innocence, stating:

Defendant claims innocence in the matter of CR 2007-13870-001 DT. Defendant's belated post-conviction relief is due to discovery of [a] new material fact on August 28, 2009. Defendant, now, exercises due diligence to bring the matter forward to [the] court's attention, praying for relief under Arizona Rules of Criminal Procedure, Rule 32.

(Exh. C.)

The trial court subsequently dismissed the petition as untimely filed, finding:

> This is Defendant's first Rule 32 notice. However, an "of right" Rule 32 notice must be filed within 90 days of sentencing. … Because Defendant's notice was not filed within 90 days of sentencing, Defendant's notice is untimely.

(Exh. D.) The court further noted that despite Petitioner's claim of newly discovered evidence, the claim was nevertheless untimely because "Defendant [had] not set forth any facts in support of [his] claim." (Exh. D.) Petitioner did not file a petition for review in the Arizona Court of Appeals.

On April 28, 2010, the Arizona Court of Appeals declined to accept jurisdiction of Petitioner's request for special action jurisdiction. (Exh. E.)

On July 12, 2011, Petitioner filed the instant Petition for Writ of Habeas Corpus raising three grounds for relief. (Doc. 1.) In Ground One, Petitioner claims that he was denied his *Fourteenth Amendment* right to have the state court judge review an affidavit that allegedly demonstrates that Petitioner was actually innocent of theft of a means of transportation. He notes that the order dismissing his notice of post-conviction relief did not mention the affidavit and incorrectly stated that Petitioner's claim of actual innocence was not supported by any facts. In Ground Two, Petitioner contends he was denied his *Sixth Amendment* right to "have fair trial court proceedings" because the state court judge did not review the affidavit. In Ground Three, he asserts that he is being incarcerated in violation of the *Eighth Amendment* because "[s]entencing an 'actually innocent' defendant to a prison term is illegal on its face."

DISCUSSION

In their Answer, Respondents contend that the habeas petition is untimely. As such, Respondents argue that Petitioner's habeas petition must be denied and dismissed.

The Antiterrorism and Effective Death Penalty Act of 1996 ("AEDPA") imposes a statute of limitations on federal petitions for writ of habeas corpus filed by state prisoners. See *28 U.S.C. § 2244(d)(1)*. The statute provides:

> A 1-year period of limitation shall apply to an application for a writ of habeas corpus by a person in custody pursuant to the judgment of a State court. The limitation period shall run from the latest of --
> (A) the date on which the judgment became final by the conclusion of direct review or the expiration of the time for seeking such review;
> (B) the date on which the impediment to filing an application created by State action in violation of the Constitution or laws of the United States is removed, if the applicant was prevented from filing by such State action;
> (C) the date on which the constitutional right asserted was initially recognized by the Supreme Court, if the right has been newly recognized by the Supreme Court and made retroactively applicable to cases on collateral review; or
> (D) the date on which the factual predicate of the claim or claims presented could have been discovered through the exercise of due diligence.

An "off-right" petition for post-conviction review under Arizona Rule of Criminal Procedure 32, which is available to criminal defendants who plead guilty, is a form of "direct review" within the meaning of *28 U.S.C. § 2244(d)(1)(A)*. See *Summers v. Schriro, 481 F.3d 710, 711 (9th Cir. 2007)*. Therefore, the judgment of conviction becomes final upon the conclusion of the Rule 32 of-right proceeding, or upon the expiration of the time for seeking such review. See id.

Additionally, "[t]he time during which a properly filed application for State post-conviction or other collateral review with respect to the pertinent judgment or claim is pending shall not be counted toward" the limitations period. *28 U.S.C. § 2244(d)(2)*; see *Lott v. Mueller, 304 F.3d 918, 921 (9th Cir. 2002)*. A post-conviction petition is "clearly pending after it is filed with a state court, but before that court grants or denies the petition." *Chavis v. Lemarque, 382 F.3d 921, 925 (9th Cir. 2004)*. A state petition that is not filed, however, within the state's required time limit is not "properly filed" and, therefore, the petitioner is not entitled to statutory tolling. See *Pace v. DiGuglielmo, 544 U.S. 408, 413, 125 S. Ct. 1807, 161 L. Ed. 2d 669 (2005)*. "When a post conviction petition is untimely under state law, 'that [is] the end of the matter' for purposes of § 2244(d)(2)." *Id. at 414*.

In Arizona, post-conviction review is pending once a notice of post-conviction relief is filed even though the petition is not filed until later. See *Isley v. Arizona Department of Corrections, 383 F.3d 1054, 1056 (9th Cir. 2004)*. An application for post-conviction relief is also pending during the intervals between a lower court decision and a review by a higher court. See *Biggs v. Duncan, 339 F.3d 1045, 1048 (9th Cir. 2003)* (citing *Carey v. Saffold, 536 U.S. 214, 223, 122 S. Ct. 2134, 153 L. Ed. 2d 260 (2002)*). However, the time between a first and second application for post-conviction relief is not tolled because no application is "pending" during that period. See id. Moreover, filing a new petition for post-conviction relief does not reinitiate a limitations period that ended before the new petition was filed. See *Ferguson v. Palmateer, 321 F.3d 820, 823 (9th Cir. 2003)*.

The statute of limitations under the AEDPA is subject to equitable tolling in appropriate cases. See *Holland v. Florida, U.S. , , 130 S.Ct. 2549, 2560, 177 L.Ed.2d 130 (2010)*. However, for equitable tolling to apply, a petitioner must show "'(1) that he has been pursuing his rights diligently and (2) that some extraordinary circumstances stood in his way'" and prevented him from filing a timely petition. *Id. at 2562* (quoting *Pace, 544 U.S. at 418*).

Petitioner was sentenced under the plea agreement on December 20, 2007. Petitioner had 90 days to file an "of-right" petition for post-conviction relief pursuant to the Arizona Rules of Criminal Procedure. See *Ariz.R.Crim.P. 32.4(a)*. He failed to file a petition within that time period and, thus, the statute of limitations began to run on March 20,

2008 -- one day after the 90-day period expired. The statute of limitations then expired one year later -- on March 20, 2009.

Petitioner filed an untimely notice of post-conviction relief on September 22, 2009 -- more than six months after the statute of limitations expired. Because the statute of limitations had passed by the time Petitioner filed his notice of post-conviction relief, the petition (or request for special action filed thereafter) did not toll the limitations period. See *Pace, 544 U.S. at 417* (holding that time limits for filing a state post-conviction petition are filing conditions which, if not met, preclude a finding that a state petition was properly filed). An untimely state post-conviction petition does not restart an already expired statute of limitations. See *Jiminez v. Rice, 276 F.3d 478, 482 (9th Cir. 2001)*. Petitioner filed the instant habeas petition on July 12, 2011 -- well over two years after the limitations period expired. The habeas petition is therefore untimely.

The Ninth Circuit recognizes that the AEDPA's limitations period may be equitably tolled because it is a statute of limitations, not a jurisdictional bar. See *Calderon v. United States Dist. Ct. (Beeler), 128 F.3d 1283, 1288 (9th Cir. 1997)*, overruled in part on other grounds by *Calderon v. United States Dist. Ct. (Kelly), 163 F.3d 530, 540 (9th Cir. 1998)*. Tolling is appropriate when "'extraordinary circumstances' beyond a [petitioner's] control make it impossible to file a petition on time." Id.; see *Miranda v. Castro, 292 F.3d 1063, 1066 (9th Cir. 2002)* (stating that "the threshold necessary to trigger equitable tolling [under AEDPA] is very high, lest the exceptions swallow the rule") (citations omitted). "When external forces, rather than a petitioner's lack of diligence, account for the failure to file a timely claim, equitable tolling of the statute of limitations may be appropriate." *Miles v. Prunty, 187 F.3d 1104, 1107 (9th Cir. 1999)*. A petitioner seeking equitable tolling must establish two elements: "(1) that he has been pursuing his rights diligently, and (2) that some extraordinary circumstance stood in his way." *Pace, 544 U.S. at 418*. Petitioner must also establish a "causal connection" between the extraordinary circumstance and his failure to file a timely petition. See *Bryant v. Arizona Attorney General, 499 F.3d 1056, 1060 (9th Cir. 2007)*.

The circumstances in this case do not support a finding that Petitioner pursued his rights diligently or that extraordinary circumstances prevented him from filing a timely habeas petition. In his Traverse and memorandum in support thereof, Petitioner submits:

> It would take almost two years for Petitioner to find the whereabouts of witness who had [possession] of [the] motorcycle at the time Petitioner borrowed it, and for Petitioner to get [an] affidavit from him. ... Petitioner is aware that a lot of time had gone by from sentencing date and date he received evidence, but there was no way he could have predicted when or where he would find his witness.

Later in his pleading Petitioner states:

> As evidence from the Petitioner has shown there was no way for the Petitioner to show evidence of innocence because there was no way to get [a hold] of his witness [;] the reason being was that witness Rosenthal was under conditions of release and could not be in contact with police for any reason.

The Court finds Petitioner's reasoning specious and contradictory. While he may not have had Rosenthal's affidavit in hand, Petitioner has undoubtedly been aware of the essential facts presented in the affidavit since the date of his arrest. Further, although a review of the affidavit suggests that Petitioner knew Rosenthal (in that Petitioner merely "borrowed" his motorcycle), Petitioner, nevertheless, failed to meet the state court deadlines for seeking review of his case contending that it took two years to find him. Within the same pleading Petitioner states that Rosenthal was under conditions of release and there was no way to get in contact with him. Petitioner filed an untimely notice of post-conviction relief, and after that proceeding was dismissed, failed to seek appellate review of the dismissal by filing petition for review -- even after he claims to have acquired the evidence at issue. The Court additionally notes that the record is void of any requests for extensions of time. This is not a case where Petitioner has been diligently pursuing his rights, and Petitioner has not described any extraordinary circumstance which prevented him from filing a timely habeas petition.

Despite the Court finding that Petitioner has not been diligently pursuing his rights and has failed to establish extraordinary circumstances, Petitioner contends that the "actual innocence gateway" of *Schlup v. Delo, 513 U.S. 298, 115 S. Ct. 851, 130 L. Ed. 2d 808 (1995)*, applies to him and warrants equitable tolling. A credible claim of actual innocence can constitute an equitable exception to the AEDPA's limitations period. See *Lee v. Lampert, 653 F.3d 929, 932 (9th Cir. 2011) (en banc)*. However, in order to present otherwise time-barred claims to a federal habeas court under Schlup, Petitioner has the heavy burden of producing "new reliable evidence -- whether it be exculpatory scientific evidence, trust-worthy eyewitness accounts, or critical physical evidence -- that was not presented at trial" that so strongly shows his actual innocence "that it is more likely than not that no reasonable juror would have convicted him in light of the new evidence." *Id. at 938* (quoting *Schlup, 513 U.S. at 324, 327)*. The Court finds that Petitioner lacks such evidence.

As previously indicated, Petitioner attempts to support his claim of actual innocence with an affidavit, which appears to be penned by Petitioner and signed by Howard Rosenthal. The affidavit states the following:

> On June 13, 2007, I was in [the] process of purchasing a 2003 Triumph motorcycle, with 1100CC capacity, and black in color. On June 14, 2007, the motorcycle was in my garage at my residence ... awaiting final transaction. When Mr. James Robinson arrived at my house, while I was asleep, he asked my room[m]ate ... if he could use the motorcycle in question to facilitate purchasing food; he assumed the motorcycle belong[ed] to me -- therefore, with no illegality attached to it. Subsequent to Robinson's return, my home was raided by Phoenix police [and] Robinson was arrested and charged for "theft -- means of transportation." Neither I nor Robinson had any knowledge [that] said motorcycle was stolen. In fact, initial police investigation at the scene did not reveal the motorcycle was stolen. Robinson was unaware of any illegality, if it in fact existed and he used it for legitimate purposes. I further offer my full cooperation to state authorities to resolve this matter, in any way necessary, for Mr. Robinson is completely innocent of

this crime. I am writing this of sound mind and under no duress or threats of any sort.

Initially, the Court notes that affidavits alone are not a promising way to demonstrate actual innocence. Though sworn, affidavits are not convincing evidence of innocence because "the affiants' statements are obtained without the benefit of cross-examination and an opportunity to make credibility determinations." *Herrera v. Collins, 506 U.S. 390, 417, 113 S. Ct. 853, 122 L. Ed. 2d 203 (1993)*. In addition to the inherent weakness of an affidavit, the affidavit at issue is particularly unhelpful and does not have the indicia of reliability sufficient to make out a claim of actual innocence in that the statements set forth therein are based on layers of hearsay, opinions, inference, and conclusory assertions -- not particularized facts. Moreover, actual innocence evidence "must be considered in light of the proof of Petitioner's guilt at trial." *Id. at 418*. Where, as in this case, Petitioner pled guilty, such admission of culpability mitigates strongly against a subsequent finding of actual innocence, particularly given the unreliable nature of the evidence submitted by Petitioner. See id. (finding "troubling" petitioner's failure to offer an explanation as to why he, "by hypothesis an innocent man, pleaded guilty").

The Court finds that the Rosenthal affidavit simply fails to qualify as "exculpatory scientific evidence, trustworthy eyewitness accounts, or critical physical evidence," such that it would establish a gateway actual innocence claim as contemplated by Schlup. Accordingly, Petitioner is not entitled to equitable tolling and his habeas petition is untimely.

ROGER DALE CASEY, PETITIONER, VS. CHARLES L. RYAN, ET AL., RESPONDENTS.

CIV 11-00155-PHX-NVW (MHB) UNITED STATES DISTRICT COURT FOR THE DISTRICT OF ARIZONA

(Text added/modified for emphasis) Arizona changes its sentencing laws but does not provide for a remedy to those who may benefit from such changes.

COUNSEL: Roger Dale Casey, Petitioner, Pro se, FLORENCE, AZ. For Charles L Ryan, named as Charles Ryan, Attorney General of the State of Arizona, Respondents: Adriana Marie Rosenblum, Office of the Attorney General, Phoenix, AZ.

BACKGROUND

On September 17, 1976, Petitioner was charged by information in the Maricopa County Superior Court with one count of escape from a community correctional center in CR 94403; one count of burglary in the second degree while armed with a gun or deadly weapon, one count of assault with intent to commit rape in CR 94424; one count of rape, one count of lewd and lascivious acts, and one count of crime against nature in CR 94425; and one count of theft of a motor vehicle in CR 94426. (Doc. 14, Exhs. A, D.) Following jury trials, Petitioner was convicted as charged in all four cases. (Doc. 14, Exhs. B, C, D.)

On May 11, 1977, the state court sentenced Petitioner to 4.5 to 5 years' imprisonment in CR 94403; 25 years to life on both counts in CR 94424 to run concurrently to each other but consecutively to the sentence in CR 94403; 25 years to life, 9 to 10 years, and 18 to 20 years in CR 94425 to run concurrently to each other but consecutively to the sentences in CR 94424; and 9 to 10 years in CR 94426 to run consecutively to the sentences in the other cause numbers. (Doc. 14, Exh. D.)

Petitioner filed a timely notice of appeal from the convictions and sentences in all four cases on May 12, 1977. (Doc. 14, Exhs. E, F.) Petitioner, however, moved to dismiss his appeal, and the Arizona Supreme Court granted his motion on September 6, 1977. (Doc. 14, Exh. G.)

More than 15 years later, on October 8, 1992, Petitioner filed a notice of post-conviction relief in cause numbers CR 94425 and 94426. (Doc. 14, Exhs. H, I.) On March 15, 1993, Petitioner filed his petition for post-conviction relief arguing that he received ineffective assistance from his trial counsel in violation of the *Sixth Amendment of the United States Constitution* and *Article II, Section 24 of the Arizona Constitution* because trial counsel failed to object to the alleged misconduct of the prosecutor during closing argument. (Doc. 14, Exh. I.) On May 26, 1993, the state court issued a minute entry dismissing

Petitioner's petition. (Doc. 14, Exh. M.) The state court found that Petitioner's claims of prosecutorial misconduct and ineffective of assistance of counsel were precluded because they could have been addressed had Petitioner not voluntarily dismissed his direct appeal. (Doc. 14, Exh. M.) The state court further determined that, even if Petitioner's claims were not precluded, he had failed to present a material question of law or fact that would entitle him to relief. (Doc. 14, Exh. M.) While there appears to be a subsequent notice of post-conviction relief in cause number CR 94424, (Doc. 14, Exh. J), there is no indication in the record that Petitioner pursued this matter.

On July 8, 1993, Petitioner filed a petition for review in the Arizona Court of Appeals. (Doc. 14, Exh. N.) In his petition, he argued that the state court incorrectly found that: (1) preclusion prohibited litigation of his "impermissible comment" issue in post-conviction relief proceedings by virtue of his voluntary dismissal of his appeal; and (2) the comments made by the prosecutor during closing argument were not comments directing the jury's attention to Petitioner's failure to testify at trial. (Doc. 14, Exh. N.) On March 8, 1994, the Arizona Court of Appeals issued a memorandum decision affirming the state court's findings. (Doc. 14, Exh. O.) In so doing, the court found that Petitioner had waived his prosecutorial misconduct claim when he failed to raise it on direct appeal. (Doc. 14, Exh. O.) The court, however, disagreed that Petitioner had waived his ineffective assistance of counsel claim and instead concluded that he had failed to present a material question of fact or law that would entitled him to relief in post-conviction proceedings. (Doc. 14, Exh. O.)

Petitioner filed a petition for review in the Arizona Supreme Court raising the same issues. (Doc. 14, Exh. P.) The Arizona Supreme Court issued an order denying review on November 1, 1994. (Doc. 14, Exh. P.)

Almost 14 years later, on July 22, 2008, Petitioner filed a second petition for post-conviction relief in cause numbers CR 94403, 94424, 94425, and 94426. (Doc. 14, Exh. Q.) In his second petition for post-conviction relief, Petitioner argued that: (1) the state court failed to consider any mitigating facts and, as a result, his sentences were cruel and unusual in violation of the *Eighth Amendment of the United States Constitution*; and (2) given the substantial changes in Arizona's sentencing law over the past 30 years, Petitioner today would not receive such a harsh and excessive sentence. (Doc. 14, Exh. Q.) The state court denied the successive petition on February 19, 2009, finding that such relief was precluded pursuant to *Rule 32.2(a)(1)* because issues relating to Petitioner's allegedly unjust and excessive sentences were issues that could have been raised on direct appeal. (Doc. 14, Exh. R.) Although Petitioner's pleading was entitled "Writ of Habeas [sic] Corpus," the state court construed the pleading as a successive petition for post-conviction relief. (Doc. 14, Exhs. Q, R.)

On March 19, 2009, Petitioner filed a petition for review in the Arizona Court of Appeals. (Doc. 14, Exh. S.) In his petition, he argued that the state court incorrectly found his sentencing claims precluded. (Doc. 14, Exh. S.) He reasoned that he could not have raised his claims until the sentencing laws were changed. (Doc. 14, Exh. S.) He further reasoned that his *Eighth Amendment* cruel and unusual punishment claim could be raised at any time as long as the violation of his constitutional right was ongoing. (Doc. 14, Exh. S.) The Court of Appeals summarily denied review of the petition on April 13, 2010. (Doc. 14, Exh. T.)

Thereafter, Petitioner filed a petition for review in the Arizona Supreme Court raising the same issues. (Doc. 14, Exh. U.) The Arizona Supreme Court issued an order summarily denying review on September 30, 2010. (Doc. 14, Exh. U.)

On January 24, 2011, Petitioner filed the instant habeas petition alleging the following grounds for relief: (1) excessive sentence in violation of the *Eighth Amendment*; and (2) "substantial changes in Arizona sentencing laws" have rendered Petitioner's sentence excessive. (Doc. 1.) Respondents filed an Answer (Doc. 14), and Petitioner filed a Reply (Doc. 15).

DISCUSSION

In their Answer, Respondents contend that Petitioner's habeas petition is untimely. In the alternative, Respondents assert that Petitioner claims are procedurally defaulted. Respondents request that the habeas petition be denied and dismissed with prejudice.

....

The Court's review of Petitioner's post-conviction relief proceedings reveals that Petitioner's Amended Petition for Writ of Habeas Corpus is untimely. Petitioner filed a notice of appeal from his convictions and sentences. (Doc. 14, Exhs. E, F.) Petitioner, however, moved to dismiss his appeal, rendering his judgment of conviction and sentence final on September 6, 1977 -- the date the Arizona Supreme Court granted his motion. (Doc. 14, Exh. G.) Because Petitioner's conviction became final before April 24, 1996, the effective date of the AEDPA, the statute of limitations for Petitioner to file his federal habeas petition began to run on April 25, 1996, and expired on April 24, 1997. See *Patterson, 251 F.3d at 1247*. Therefore, absent any tolling, Petitioner was required to file the instant habeas petition on or before April 24, 1997. See *28 U.S.C. § 2244(d)(1)(A)*; *Malcom v. Payne, 281 F.3d 951, 955 (9th Cir. 2002)*; *Patterson, 251 F.3d at 1245-46*. Assuming Petitioner could have filed a petition for review from the dismissal of his direct appeal by the supreme court, his judgment of conviction and sentence would still have become final on October 6, 1977 -- well before the effective date of AEDPA. See Ariz.R.Crim.P. (establishing 30-day time limit from the filing of a decision for filing petition for review in Arizona Supreme Court).

Petitioner's commencement of his first post-conviction relief proceeding did not toll the limitations period as it concluded on January 30, 1995 -- 90 days after the Arizona Supreme Court denied review -- more than a year before the one-year period under the AEDPA commenced. See *Bowen v. Roe, 188 F.3d 1157, 1158-59 (9th Cir. 1999)* (ruling that the period of "direct review" under *§ 2244(d)(1)(A)* includes 90-day period during which defendant can file petition for writ of certiorari from United States Supreme Court). Likewise, Petitioner's commencement of a second post-conviction relief proceeding on July 22, 2008, did not toll the limitations period. Since the second petition for post-conviction relief was filed after the AEDPA statute of limitations ended, it could not restart the expired one-year limitations period. See *Ferguson, 321 F.3d at 823* ("Like the Eleventh Circuit, we hold that *section 2244(d)* does not permit the reinitiating of the [federal one-year] limitations period that has ended before the state petition was filed."). In sum, Petitioner filed the instant habeas petition on January 24, 2011 -- 13 years and 9 months after the one-year limitations period expired on April 24, 1997. The Petition is therefore untimely and should be dismissed with prejudice, absent any equitable tolling.

As previously indicated, the AEDPA's statute of limitations is subject to equitable tolling in appropriate cases. See *Holland, 130 S.Ct. at 2560.* In Holland, the Court reiterated its position "that a 'petitioner' is 'entitled to equitable tolling' only if he shows '(1) that he has been pursuing his rights diligently, and (2) that some extraordinary circumstance stood in his way' and prevented timely filing." *Id. at 2562* (quoting *Pace, 544 U.S. at 418*). "To apply the doctrine in 'extraordinary circumstances' necessarily suggests the doctrine's rarity, and the requirement that extraordinary circumstances 'stood in his way' suggests that an external force must cause the untimeliness, rather than ... merely 'oversight, miscalculation or negligence on the petitioner's part, all of which would preclude the application of equitable tolling.'" *Waldron-Ramsey v. Pacholke, 556 F.3d 1008, 1011 (9th Cir. 2009)* (citation omitted).

Petitioner suggests that his untimeliness should be excused because significant changes in the sentencing law have occurred that render his sentences cruel and unusual. Moreover, Petitioner suggests that as long as he is serving a cruel and unusual sentence, he should be able to challenge that sentence under the *Eighth Amendment*. Petitioner, however, does not identify what sentencing laws have changed, whether they apply to his case, and if applicable, how they render his sentences cruel and unusual. Petitioner, thus, has not suggested any extraordinary circumstance that would justify equitable tolling, let alone demonstrated that an external impediment stymied the diligent pursuit of his rights. Accordingly, Petitioner is not entitled to equitable tolling and his habeas petition is therefore untimely.

DINO WAYNE KYZAR, PETITIONER-APPELLANT, V. CHARLES L. RYAN; STATE OF ARIZONA ATTORNEY GENERAL, RESPONDENTS-APPELLEES. NO. 12-17564 UNITED STATES COURT OF APPEALS FOR THE NINTH CIRCUIT

(Text added and modified for emphasis)As a matter of regular practice the Attorney General's Office consistently misrepresents to federal courts that inmates have failed to exhaust administrative remedies knowing this not to be true. They fail to disclose the fact that lawyers representing the defendants and appointed by the state refuse to preserve and present federal issues. They also fail to advise the court that Arizona prisons do not have law books and materials which inmates may use to exhaust remedies, that they have a system of paralegals which is a sham. These paralegals are not allowed to assist inmates in presenting claims, ADOC Policy DO 902. As this is a pattern with the Arizona Attorney General's Office this should constitute fraud upon the court, because, they are misrepresenting facts on a systemic basis, to defeat valid claims. There are too many such incidents which constitute a pattern.

COUNSEL: Tara K. Hoveland (argued), South Lake Tahoe, California, for Petitioner-Appellant. David A. Simpson (argued), Deputy Attorney General; Thomas C. Horne, Attorney General; Joseph T. Maziarz, Chief Counsel, Criminal Appeals Section; and David A. Sullivan, Assistant Attorney General, Arizona Attorney General's Office, Phoenix, Arizona, for Respondents-Appellees.

....

A. Facts

At the time of the murder, Cropper lived in Building 26 of the San Juan unit at Perryville prison. The building was divided into four pods--A, B, C, and D--with each pod having an upper and lower tier. Cropper lived in Cell No. 258 on the D pod's upper tier. Cropper's cellmate was Lloyd Elkins. Cropper and Elkins had been cellmates for about one month in Building 24 before they were transferred to Building 26 on March 3, 1997, four days before the murder.

While Cropper was living in Building 24--but before he was cellmates with Elkins--Kyzar gave him a nine to twelve inch steel knife with electrical tape wrapped around the base to form a handle. A few weeks later, after Cropper and Elkins became cellmates, Elkins saw Cropper in possession of a second knife with a serrated blade. According to Elkins, Cropper generally knew where to find knives buried around the prison yard. With respect to the prevalence of knives at Perryville, Cropper testified at trial that "[e]verbody on the yard ha[d] some type of weapon."

On the day of the murder, Deborah Landsperger, a correctional officer assigned to Building 26, discovered that mops and brooms were missing from the equipment room. Around 10:30 A.M., Landsperger and Brent Lumley, another correctional officer, decided to conduct a cell-to-cell search for the missing items. They started searching in the D pod's upper tier of cells.

Cropper and Elkins lived in the second cell searched. After Landsperger noticed tattoo patterns on top of a cabinet, she ordered Cropper and Elkins to exit the cell. Lumley did a pat down search of the inmates. The officers ordered Cropper and Elkins to wait outside the cell until the search was over.

Landsperger and Lumley confiscated several items of contraband during their search of Cell No. 258, including more tattoo paraphernalia, a serrated knife blade without a handle, and either a "cement nail," or a four to six inch "railroad spike." At some point during the search, Cropper came back into his cell and called Landsperger a "corncob cunt" and a "bitch." Lumley told Cropper, "Don't be doing that," which prompted Cropper to curse at Lumley too. Cropper acknowledged that his tirade was so loud that other inmates in D pod probably heard him.

Landsperger and Lumley ordered Cropper to sit in the dirt area on the bottom tier of the D pod for the remainder of the search. Joshua "Tiny" Brice, an inmate who lived in the B pod of Building 26, saw Cropper standing by the stairs during the search. As Brice walked by, Cropper said that his cell was being shaken down. The search concluded around 11:30 A.M. because Landsperger and Lumley needed to count the inmates and take them to lunch.

Landsperger showed her supervisor, Lieutenant Hugh Matson, the knife she had confiscated from Cropper's cell and recounted his verbal tirade. Matson, Landsperger and one or two sergeants went to Cropper's cell to address his behavior. When asked if he had been verbally abusive towards Landsperger, Cropper said, "Fuck that bitch. She doesn't know what she's doing." Cropper told Matson, "Fuck you, punk. Get out of my fucking house, you little punk. Step off. I've got nothing to say to you." *Id.* Cropper also declared, "It's on," which Matson interpreted as a direct threat of violence. Cropper agreed that his words were a threat of revenge. Matson placed Cropper and Elkins on lockdown pending a disciplinary investigation. Cropper kicked or punched his cell door as the officers were leaving. *Id.*

After the correctional officers left, Cropper had a conversation with Eugene Long through the vent between their cells. Long lived in the neighboring cell, No. 257, with Bruce Howell. According to Elkins, Long characterized the shakedown of Cropper's cell as a form of harassment and said there "needed to be a fallout on the yard." Elkins testified that Cropper was acting "like a maniac" after this conversation and ranting about how the correctional officers had disrespected him.

About twenty minutes after his first conversation with Long, Cropper said through the vent, "Hey, homeboy, go get Dino and Blue for me." Dino Kyzar and Sean "Blue" Gieslin were inmates who lived together in the A pod of Building 26 and exercised authority over the other white prisoners. A week or two before the murder, Gieslin told Dave Fipps, another inmate in Building 26, that Kyzar was running the yard to deflect attention from Gieslin. According to Fipps, Kyzar and Gieslin were the people to see if you needed a weapon because they were effectively in charge among the white inmates.

Shortly after lunch, Kyzar and Gieslin arrived at Cropper's cell. Elkins, who was sitting on his bed, overheard the conversation that took place through the cell door window. Cropper told Kyzar, "I want the good one," while making a stabbing motion. A "good one" is prison slang for a knife or "shank" with a handle on it. Kyzar responded, "I ain't got it. You got it." Cropper replied, "Give me any one." Kyzar then cautioned Cropper about his apparent intentions, "Well, are you sure about this? How much time you got, homeboy?" Cropper said, "It don't fucking matter. I'm a career criminal anyway." *Id.* As Kyzar and Gieslin were leaving, Cropper said, "You guys need to get off the yard," an expression that was not defined at trial. The entire conversation between Cropper and Kyzar lasted about two minutes.

As Joshua Brice was returning from lunch, Gieslin, Kyzar, and Long approached him near a picnic table in the B pod. Kyzar instructed Brice to "[s]how Eugene [Long] where the shank is." Brice responded that he did not know exactly where to find a knife. Kyzar replied, "Just show him the general area." *Id*. Brice complied because of the respect Kyzar commanded among the white inmates.

Brice indicated to Long a dirt area in the B pod where another inmate had buried a knife about one month earlier. Brice watched for guards while Long started digging in that area. As Long was digging, Clifford Settle, an inmate who lived on the B pod's bottom tier near where Long was digging, asked Brice if he was looking for a knife. Brice said no, but indicated that Long was trying to find a shank. After Brice summoned Long, Settle told them a knife was hidden between two concrete slabs outside his cell. Long straddled the concrete slabs, pulled out a knife, and concealed it in his pants. Brice and Long then walked back to their respective cells.

Meanwhile, Kyzar and Gieslin encountered Dave Fipps in the yard as they were heading to the administration building. Gieslin cryptically instructed Fipps to go to Long's cell to see if everything had been handled. When Fipps arrived at Cell No. 257, Howell was standing outside keeping watch while Long and Brice were inside the cell. Fipps reported that Kyzar and Gieslin wanted to know if everything was being handled. Brice said yes.

According to Brice, Fipps held two flyswatters that Long had taped together while Long taped the knife he had retrieved to the flyswatters. Long stood on the toilet in his cell and called through the vent, "Hey, Padlock," which was Cropper's nickname. Elkins heard Long tell Cropper, "I got it," to which Cropper responded, "Let me see it." After Long showed Cropper the knife, Cropper said, "That ain't the good one. Fuck it. Send it through." *Id*. Elkins testified that Long used the flyswatters to pass the knife to Cropper through the vent between their cells. Cropper also asked for a right-handed glove, which Long passed through the vent using the same technique. After wrapping a boot lace around the bottom of the knife, Cropper asked Long to spin the lock on his cell. Long complied. Elkins then heard either Long or Howell say, "It's open. Go, go, go."

Landsperger, who had just finished writing a report in the control room for the C and D pods about the items confiscated from Cropper that morning, saw Long playing with the lock on Cropper's cell. When Landsperger heard Long say, "Oh shit," she ordered him to come down and talk with her. As Long was talking to Landsperger, whose back was turned to the control room where Lumley was writing his own report, Cropper escaped from his cell. Cropper went directly to the control room and stabbed Lumley to death with the knife Long had passed to him only a few minutes earlier. All four pods in Building 26 were immediately placed on lockdown.

Brice was in the administration building when the lockdown was ordered. As Brice was walking back to Building 26, Gieslin and Kyzar approached him in the main recreation yard. All three men were detained in a fenced in area outside Building 26 along with other inmates. As Brice, Gieslin, and Kyzar were waiting to reenter the building, they saw Howell, Long, Cropper, and Elkins escorted across the yard in restraints. The guards were yelling at Cropper and crying as they brought him out of Building 26. Brice, Gieslin, and Kyzar also saw an ambulance and helicopter arrive and then leave. Shortly before Brice was removed from the fenced in area, Kyzar told him to keep his mouth shut.

B. Procedural History

The State of Arizona charged Kyzar with conspiring to commit a deadly or dangerous assault by a prisoner (Count I); aiding a dangerous or deadly assault by a prisoner (Count II); and promoting prison contraband (Count III).

On September 13, 1999, a Maricopa County jury found Kyzar guilty on Count I, but acquitted him on Counts II and III. After denying Kyzar's motion for a new trial, the trial judge sentenced him to twenty-one years in prison. Kyzar's arguments on direct appeal to the Arizona Court of Appeals were unsuccessful. The Arizona Supreme Court denied Kyzar's petition for review on November 1, 2001.

About one year later, in October 2002, Kyzar filed a *pro se* petition for post-conviction relief arguing, *inter alia*, that the State had not introduced sufficient evidence to convict him of conspiring to commit a dangerous or deadly assault on a prison guard under the standard recently announced in *Evanchyk v. Stewart, 202 Ariz. 476, 47 P.3d 1114 (Ariz. 2002)*. In denying Kyzar's post-conviction petition, the trial court held that *Evanchyk* was "inapposite" to his case. Kyzar renewed his argument based on *Evanchyk* before both the Arizona Court of Appeals and the Arizona Supreme Court, which summarily denied Kyzar's petitions for review on March 24, 2004 and November 9, 2004, respectively. Kyzar's subsequent motion in state court is irrelevant to his sufficiency of the evidence claim.

On August 21, 2006, Kyzar filed a *pro se* federal habeas petition arguing, as its third ground for relief, that the evidence admitted at trial was constitutionally insufficient to support his conviction. The district court, adopting a magistrate judge's report and recommendation, denied Kyzar's habeas petition in its entirety in February 2008. After issuing a certificate of appealability on Kyzar's challenge to the trial court's denial of his motion to sever and his sufficiency of the evidence claim, we vacated in part and remanded only on the latter issue. *See Kyzar v. Ryan, 430 F. App'x 630 (9th Cir. 2011), cert. denied, 132 S. Ct. 431, 181 L. Ed. 2d 280.*

On remand, the district court rejected Kyzar's sufficiency of the evidence claim. *See Kyzar v. Ryan, No. CV 06-2015-PHX-SRB, 2012 U.S. Dist. LEXIS 162054, 2012 WL 5497805 (D. Ariz. Nov. 13, 2012).* We granted a certificate of appealability on this issue. *See 28 U.S.C. § 2253(c)(2).*

II. Exhaustion of Remedies

Respondent's first argument on appeal is that Kyzar failed to exhaust available state remedies because he did not fairly present his sufficiency of the evidence claim to the Arizona courts in a timely fashion. Our review is de novo. *See Chambers v. McDaniel, 549 F.3d 1191, 1195 (9th Cir. 2008).*

Kyzar's claim is governed by the Anti-Terrorism and Effective Death Penalty Act of 1996 ("AEDPA"), which requires petitioners to exhaust the remedies available to them in state court. *28 U.S.C. § 2254(b)(1)(A).* "[T]he exhaustion doctrine is designed to give the state courts a full and fair opportunity to resolve federal constitutional claims before those claims are presented to the federal courts." *O'Sullivan v. Boerckel, 526 U.S. 838, 845, 119 S. Ct. 1728, 144 L. Ed. 2d 1 (1999).* In practical terms, "state prisoners must give the state courts one full opportunity to resolve any constitutional issues by invoking one complete round of the State's established appellate review process." *Id.* A habeas claim is procedurally defaulted if it was not fairly presented to the state courts in a timely fashion. *Id. at 848.*

"[E]xcept in habeas petitions in life-sentence or capital cases, claims of Arizona state prisoners are exhausted for purposes of federal habeas once the Arizona Court of Appeals has ruled on them." *Swoopes v. Sublett, 196 F.3d 1008, 1010 (9th Cir. 1999)* (per curiam). Kyzar was charged with three class 2 felonies under Arizona law: conspiracy to commit a dangerous or deadly assault by a prisoner; aiding a dangerous or deadly assault by a prisoner; and promoting prison contraband. The statutory maximum sentence for a class 2 felony in Arizona is thirty-five years. *Ariz. Rev. Stat. Ann. § 13-704(E).* Because Kyzar did not face a possible life sentence or the death penalty, our exhaustion analysis focuses on whether he fairly presented his sufficiency of the evidence claim to the Arizona trial court and the Arizona Court of Appeals. *See O'Sullivan, 526 U.S. at 845* (holding that petitioners must "invoke[e] one *complete round* of the State's established appellate review process" (emphasis added)). *See Ariz. Rev. Stat. Ann. §§ 13-1206* (categorizing "dangerous or deadly assault by a prisoner" as a class 2 felony), *Ariz. Rev. Stat.* (categorizing "promoting prison contraband" as a class 2 felony if contraband is a "deadly weapon" or "dangerous instrument"); *see also id.* at §§ 13-303(B) (subject to qualifications not relevant here, aiding an offense is treated the same as committing the underlying substantive offense), *13-1003(D)* (except for class 1 felonies, "conspiracy is an offense of the same class as the most serious offense which is the object of or result of the conspiracy").

"In order to 'fairly present' an issue to a state court, a [habeas] petitioner must 'present the substance of his claim to the state courts, including a reference to a federal constitutional guarantee and a statement of facts that entitle the petitioner to relief.'" *Gulbrandson v. Ryan, 738 F.3d 976, 992 (9th Cir. 2013)* (quoting *Scott v. Schriro, 567 F.3d 573, 582 (9th Cir. 2009)*). "[F]or the purposes of exhaustion, pro se petitions are held to a more lenient standard than counseled petitions." *Sanders v. Ryder, 342 F.3d 991, 999 (9th Cir. 2003)* (citing *Peterson v. Lampert, 319 F.3d 1153, 1159 (9th Cir. 2003)* (en banc)); *see also Slack v. McDaniel, 529 U.S. 473, 487, 120 S. Ct. 1595, 146 L. Ed. 2d 542 (2000)* ("[T]he complete exhaustion rule is not to 'trap the unwary *pro se* prisoner.'" (quoting *Rose v. Lundy*, 455 U.S. 509, 520, 102 S. Ct. 1198, 71 LEd. 2d 379 (1982))).

Applying these principles, we conclude that Kyzar's pro se filings before the Arizona trial court and Arizona Court of Appeals fairly presented his sufficiency of the evidence claim. In his petition for post-conviction relief, Kyzar argued that *Evanchyk* constituted a significant change in Arizona conspiracy law insofar as it required the State to prove "*both* that the perpetrator ha[d] an intent to promote or aid commission of a specific offense and that he agree[d] with another person that the offense be committed." *47 P.3d at 1117*. In Kyzar's view, the State failed to prove at trial that he "premeditated an agreement to conspire [sic] dangerous or deadly assault [on] Officer Lumley inside of the prison officers control room or any other officer or person(s) before or on March 7, 1999." Kyzar argued that the absence of evidence showing an agreement violated his due process rights. *Id.*

MATTHEW RONALD CREAMER, PETITIONER - APPELLANT, V. CHARLES L. RYAN, INTERIM DIRECTOR OF ADOC AND STATE OF ARIZONA ATTORNEY GENERAL, RESPONDENTS - APPELLEES. NO. 09-16425 UNITED STATES COURT OF APPEALS FOR THE NINTH CIRCUIT

(Text added and modified for emphasis) As a matter of regular practice the Attorney General's Office consistently fails to advise the federal courts that due to Arizona prisons not having law libraries and the prohibition by their policy DO 902 of inmates being assisted by paralegals, inmates are not aware that they must use the special action procedure to exhaust remedies. There are too many such incidents. The failure of the Attorney General to be candid constitute a pattern. As this is a pattern with the Arizona Attorney General's Office this should constitute fraud upon the court, because, they are concealing facts on a systemic basis, to defeat valid claims.

COUNSEL: MATTHEW R. CREAMER, Petitioner - Appellant, Pro se, Tucson, AZ. For CHARLES L. RYAN, Interim Director of ADOC, STATE OF

ARIZONA ATTORNEY GENERAL, Respondent - Appellee: Aaron Jay Moskowitz, Assistant Attorney General, ARIZONA ATTORNEY GENERAL'S OFFICE, Phoenix, AZ.

Arizona prisoner Matthew Ronald Creamer appeals pro se from the district court's dismissal of his *28 U.S.C. § 2254* habeas petition for failure to exhaust. We have jurisdiction under *28 U.S.C. § 2253*, and we affirm.

Creamer contends that because Arizona law does not provide for judicial review of prison disciplinary proceedings, he was not required to exhaust his claims in state court.

In Arizona, state court review of an inmate disciplinary decision may be obtained by filing a petition for special action. *See Rose v. Ariz. Dep't of Corrections, 167 Ariz. 116, 804 P.2d 845, 849 (Ariz. Ct. App. 1991).* Contrary to Creamer's argument, Arizona Revised Statutes ("A.R.S.") *§ 31-201.01(L)* does not bar the initiation of a special action by a prisoner, because it only applies to tort claims. Likewise, *A.R.S. § 12-302* does not prevent the filing of a special action by a prisoner. *See A.R.S. § 12-302(E)* (inability to pay filing fees does not prevent filing of an action).

Because Creamer did not challenge his disciplinary proceedings by filing a special action in state court, the district court properly dismissed his claims as unexhausted. *See 28 U.S.C. § 2254(b)(1)(A), (c).*

The district court did not abuse its discretion by denying Creamer's motion for reconsideration because he did not identify any new evidence, change in law, clear error, or manifest injustice in the court's order. *See Sch. Dist. No. 1J, Multnomah County, Or. v. ACandS, Inc., 5 F.3d 1255, 1262-63 (9th Cir. 1993)* (setting forth standard of review and grounds for reconsideration).

PLEAS

JAMES EARL FOX, Petitioner - Appellant, v. CHARLES L. RYAN; STATE OF ARIZONA ATTORNEY GENERAL, Respondents - Appellees. No. 09-15834 UNITED STATES COURT OF APPEALS FOR THE NINTH CIRCUIT

(Text added and modified for emphasis) As a matter of regular practice the Attorney General's Office consistently fails to advise the federal courts that when lawyers are appointed in Arizona, they fail to advise defendants to take pleas by fully explaining the consequences. Hearings are held but these hearings are only formalities for Arizona judges do not spend the necessary time and effort explaining the consequences of rejecting pleas. As a direct consequence there are defendants serving life terms in Arizona prisons all because of the failure of the Attorney General to be candid. There are too many such incidents which constitute a pattern. As this is a pattern with the Arizona Attorney General's Office this should constitute fraud upon the court, because, they are concealing facts on a systemic basis, to defeat valid claims.

COUNSEL: For JAMES EARL FOX, Petitioner - Appellant: Rubin Salter, Jr., Esquire, Attorney, LAW OFFICE OF RUBIN SALTER, JR., Tucson, AZ. JAMES EARL FOX, Petitioner - Appellant, Pro se, Florence, AZ. For CHARLES L. RYAN, STATE OF ARIZONA ATTORNEY GENERAL, Respondents - Appellees: Alan L. Amann, Assistant Attorney General, AGAZ - OFFICE OF THE ARIZONA ATTORNEY GENERAL (TUCSON), Tucson, AZ.

Fox turned down a favorable plea deal and, after he was convicted by a jury and sentenced to 27 years in custody, moved for post-conviction relief, arguing that his trial counsel was ineffective for failing to warn him that his sentences on the multiple counts could be consecutive. What occurred following the state court's grant of post-conviction relief was unusual. The post-conviction court vacated Fox's sentence of 15.75 years for trafficking in stolen property and 11.25 years for attempted trafficking, both sentences to run consecutively-- but the court did not vacate his convictions following a jury trial. The court then conducted a plea colloquy where Fox pleaded guilty to a count of which he had already been convicted, which conviction was still valid. When the state post-conviction court subsequently realized it made a mistake, it vacated the "second" guilty plea and resentenced Fox on the original convictions so that the 15.75 year term and the 11.25 year term would run concurrently. The end result of the court's actions is that Fox's total sentence was reduced from 27 years to 15.75 years.

The state appellate court's determination that the *Double Jeopardy Clause* was not violated by the court's *sua sponte* vacatur of the "second," accepted guilty plea, followed by its resentencing Fox pursuant to the original convictions, was reasonable. *See 28 U.S.C. § 2254(d)(1)*. There is currently a split of authority in the circuits as to whether jeopardy automatically attaches in every case immediately upon a court's acceptance of a guilty plea. *See United States v. Patterson, 406 F.3d 1095, 1100 (9th Cir. 2005)* (Kozinski, C.J., dissenting from denial of rehearing en banc) (discussing circuit split on this issue). As the Supreme Court has told us, divergent treatment by different circuit courts may "[r]eflect[] the lack of guidance from [the Supreme] Court." *Carey v. Musladin, 549 U.S. 70, 76, 127 S. Ct. 649, 166 L. Ed. 2d 482 (2006)*. That is the case here: there is no clearly established federal law as established by the Supreme Court on this issue. *See 28 U.S.C. § 2254(d)(1)*. Further, the reinstatement of convictions on charges of which Fox had already been found guilty by a jury beyond a reasonable doubt, followed ultimately by a *reduction* in his overall sentence, does not implicate any of the purposes of the *Double Jeopardy Clause* as stated in *Ohio v. Johnson, 467 U.S. 493, 501, 104 S. Ct. 2536, 81 L. Ed. 2d 425 (1984)*. The district court properly declined to grant habeas on this issue.

JEFFREY A. HERALD, PETITIONER, V. CHARLES L. RYAN, ARIZONA ATTORNEY GENERAL, RESPONDENTS. NO. CV 14-2188 PHX DLR (MEA) UNITED STATES DISTRICT COURT FOR THE DISTRICT OF ARIZONA

(Text added and modified for emphasis) In Arizona counsel fail to get full discovery from the state, counsel lying as to the factual basis, counsel fail to interview witnesses and investigate and pursue facts, and counsel failed to present evidence of mitigating factors at sentencing, evidenced by the number of complaints. As a matter of regular practice the Attorney General's Office consistently fails to advise the federal courts that when lawyers are appointed in Arizona, they fail to advise defendants to take pleas by fully explaining the consequences. Hearings are held but these hearings are only formalities for Arizona judges do not spend the necessary time and effort explaining the consequences of rejecting pleas. As a direct consequence there are defendants serving life terms in Arizona prisons all because of the failure of the Attorney General to be candid. There are too many such incidents which constitute a pattern. As this is a pattern with the Arizona Attorney General's Office this should constitute fraud upon the court, because, they are concealing facts on a systemic basis, to defeat valid claims.

COUNSEL: Jeffrey Allen Herald, also named as Jeffrey A Herald and Jeffrey Herald, Petitioner, Pro se, TUCSON, AZ. For Charles L Ryan, named as Charles Ryan of Arizona Department of Corrections, Attorney General of the State of Arizona, Respondents: William Scott Simon, LEAD ATTORNEY, Office of the Attorney General, Criminal Appeals, Phoenix, AZ.

I Procedural background

A grand jury indictment returned September 17, 2008, charged Petitioner (using his own and an additional nine "aka" identities) with 39 counts of fraudulent schemes and artifices, class 2 felonies, and 39 counts of theft, class 2, 3, 4, 5, and 6 felonies (based upon the amount allegedly stolen). See Doc. 13 (Answer), Exh. A. Thirteen of the counts, encompassing seven victims, involved Petitioner's "legal services" business and alleged he misrepresented to clients that he was a licensed attorney. Id., Exh. A. The remaining counts pertained to a "loan origination" business. Id., Exh. A.

Petitioner was initially represented in his criminal proceedings by retained counsel, who subsequently withdrew from representation. Id., Exh. B & Exh. C. The state trial court thereafter appointed Mr. Wallin as Petitioner's defense counsel. On August 3, 2009, Petitioner sought to remove Mr. Wallin as counsel because he "considered [Petitioner] guilty without going through several boxes of evidence;" he had interviewed "several witnesses," including family members, but "came up with a total different story than reality;" and because he had "no clue about [Petitioner's] case." Id., Exh. D. On December 29, 2009, Petitioner again moved to substitute counsel. Id., Exh. E. The state trial court denied these motions, finding that there was no legal basis to justify a change in defense counsel. Id., Exh. F.

On May 18, 2010, Petitioner again sought to remove Mr. Wallin as counsel, asserting that Mr. Wallin had interviewed only one of Petitioner's proposed witnesses and that he had "corrupted the case" by interviewing state witnesses. Id., Exh. H. Petitioner filed two additional motions to remove Mr. Wallin. Id., Exhs. I & J. Mr. Wallin subsequently filed ten motions in limine, addressing multiple evidentiary issues. Id., Exhs. K-T. The trial court eventually granted Petitioner's motion to change counsel and directed that Mr. Wallin "meet and confer with the newly assigned attorney to discuss the history and progress of this case, its charges, and interviews thus far conducted." Id., Exh. U.

On October 25, 2010, Ms. Shoemaker was appointed to represent Petitioner. Id., Exh. V. On January 11, 2011, with the trial scheduled to begin on February 14, 2011, Ms. Shoemaker filed a motion pursuant to *Rule 11, Arizona Rule of Criminal Procedure*, requesting that Petitioner undergo a mental evaluation, although Petitioner had previously been found competent in July 2010. Id., Exh. W & Exhs. X & Y. Ms. Shoemaker argued that she had personally witnessed Petitioner suffer extreme mood swings during legal visits and phone calls. Id., Exh. X. The motion was granted, Petitioner was determined to be competent, and the trial was re-set for November 7, 2011. Id., Exh. Z. Ms. Shoemaker then re-urged all of Mr. Wallin's previously filed motions. Id., Exh. AA

On May 2, 2011, Petitioner filed a "petition to compel," asking the state court to order defense counsel "to work with [Petitioner]." Id., Exh. BB. Petitioner avowed that he did not want to dismiss counsel, "as she seems capable to handle [his] case." Id., Exh. BB. Petitioner averred, however, that counsel had not visited him often enough and that counsel "[had] not moved forward on this case much at all to prepare for trial." Id., Exh. BB. Petitioner further alleged that he and his counsel suffered from a lack of communication and that he had not received certain documents he had requested from her. Id., Exh. BB. In a minute entry dated June 2, 2011, in response to Petitioner's request, the trial court stated that its practice was to avoid involvement in the attorney-client relationship unless there was a motion to change counsel before the court. Id., Exh. CC. Petitioner then avowed to the trial court that the issues raised in his motion to compel had been "satisfactorily resolved, except for an issue regarding counsel obtaining Petitioner's 'Quick Books.'" Id., Exh. CC.

On August 9, 2011, the parties averred they were ready for a trial commencing November 7, 2011. Id., Exh. DD On August 26, 2011, a settlement conference was conducted, during which the settlement judge reviewed with Petitioner the charges against him and the potential sentences he faced if found guilty. Id., Exh. EE at 4-6. At that time the state offered Petitioner a plea agreement that would allow Petitioner to plead guilty to three counts of fraudulent schemes as class 2 felonies with one prior conviction, with a sentencing range of 10 to 20 years on each count, with the court retaining discretion to decide whether the sentences would be concurrent or consecutive. Id., Exh. EE at 5. The plea agreement also required Petitioner to plead guilty to five additional counts of fraudulent schemes and receive sentences of probation on those convictions, to be commenced after Petitioner served the terms of imprisonment. Id., Exh. EE at 5-6. The court advised Petitioner at that time that, if he proceeded to trial and was convicted on most or all of the charges, he could potentially spend the rest of his life in prison. Id., Exh. EE at 6.

Petitioner initially responded that he was legally innocent of the charges because he had run an "honest business" and that was merely the victim of a recession and clients who had falsified information. Id., Exh. EE at 8-9. The prosecutor then summarized the evidence against Petitioner regarding both the legal services and loan businesses. Id., Exh. EE at 13-18. Petitioner disputed the state's allegations and noted he had witnesses who said that he had actually closed some loans, thereby providing the agreed-upon services and arguing that, therefore, he could not be guilty of fraud. Id., Exh. EE at 18-25. The judge (J. Schwartz) advised Petitioner that "the risk [was] huge" if Petitioner went to trial, particularly in light of his multiple prior felonies. Id., Exh. EE at 30. Petitioner said "I'm totally innocent in this case," but stated that he and his lawyer would have to discuss the plea deal. He stated "it would be better if we could come down a little bit." Id., Exh. EE at 33.

Petitioner brought "witnesses" with him to the settlement conference in an effort to bolster his argument that he had run a legitimate business and that he had not defrauded his clients. Id., Exh. EE at 11-14. The prosecutor again summarized the evidence that would be presented against Petitioner, including the fact that he had previously been imprisoned for fraud schemes and theft. Id., Exh. EE at 13 & 16. The prosecutor noted Petitioner had represented to his victims that he was a licensed attorney. Id., Exh. EE at 13-14. The prosecutor delineated Petitioner's mortgage "scheme," noting that he had represented to victims that he could fund their multi-million dollar projects "in house" if he failed to acquire financing for the projects through third-parties. Id., Exh. EE at 13-17. Petitioner again offered the "testimony" of an individual at the settlement conference who stated that they had given Petitioner $80,000 and he had returned the loan amount in full. Id., Exh. EE at 20. Petitioner again asserted that he had "closed" the loans his victims complained of but that he had not done it in a sufficiently timely fashion or at an interest rate sufficiently low enough to keep his clients from asserting they had been defrauded. Id., Exh. EE at 18-22.

The settlement conference was continued on September 16, 2011. Id., Exh. FF.

The court stated:

> [O]bviously the worst case scenario is if the Judge gave a 23-year term and did three of them consecutively. That can add up to 69 years. I mean we have to have that possibility. But the best case scenario is a five year term on each count, all three of them to run concurrently. That's a five-year term.

Id., Exh. FF at 4. Petitioner stated that he was 53 years of age and also noted the possibility that he could get "five times three which is 15 years." Id., Exh. FF at 5. At the beginning of the settlement conference the court discussed with Petitioner potential sentencing judges, noting the parties had agreed that Judge Barton, who had been the assigned trial judge, would not sentence Petitioner. The prosecutor allowed that, if Petitioner would accept the plea agreement they would expand the "bottom" of the sentencing range in the plea agreement on each of the three counts to five years, and that she had "twisted arms" to get the five year "bottom". Id., Exh. FF at 3-4 & 15-16.

After a recess to consult with his counsel and his wife, who was also present, and in the presence of the Deputy (because Petitioner was in custody), Petitioner agreed to the plea deal. Exh. FF at 20-21. At that time the parties agreed Petitioner would be sentenced by Judge Granville. Id., Exh. FF at 22. Petitioner then entered a guilty plea. Id., Exh. GG.

The plea agreement, dated September 16, 2011, stipulated that Petitioner would plead guilty to Amended Counts 1, 3 and 5, charging fraudulent schemes and artifices as class 2 felonies with one prior felony conviction, and Counts 7 and 13, charging fraudulent schemes and artifices as class 2 felonies. Id., Exh. HH. Counts 1, 3 and 5 carried a presumptive sentence of 9.25 years, a minimum of 6 years (4.5 if the court made exceptional circumstances findings), and a maximum of 18.5 years. Id., Exh. HH at 18-25.

The presentence report recommended Petitioner be sentenced to concurrent, presumptive terms of imprisonment on each count of conviction. Id., Exh. II. The state's sentencing recommendation detailed Petitioner's history of arrests on fraud charges and eight felony convictions in four states since 1979. Id., Exh. JJ.

Defense counsel filed a sentencing memorandum, which stated that the five guilty pleas involved legal practices counts that had already been resolved by the Arizona State Bar Association, and that the victims had received refunds of any fees paid to Petitioner. Id., Exh. KK. Counsel further stated that Petitioner took responsibility for misleading those victims. Id., Exh. KK at 2. With regard to the counts involving the commercial loans, counsel averred Petitioner had "worked to get the loans funded," but that those clients "were not always happy with the loan terms." Id., Exh. KK at 3. Counsel cited two clients for whom Petitioner believed that he had earned the fees paid to Petitioner. Id., Exh. KK at 4. Counsel also provided information on mitigating sentencing factors such as Petitioner's family support, mental health concerns, and remorse. Id., Exh. KK at 5.

At Petitioner's sentencing on November 18, 2011, the state court (Judge Granville) heard from two character witnesses for Petitioner, then entered judgment on the five counts set forth in the plea agreement. Id., Exh. LL. The prosecutor made additional statements regarding Petitioner's conduct, including comments from victims. Id., Exh. LL at 13-21. Petitioner responded that the prosecutor's facts were inaccurate and disputed the victims' comments. Id., Exh. LL at 21-25. Petitioner asserted that the prosecutor could not "open my QuickBooks on the computer," which would have showed that he had refunded money on loan contracts. Id., Exh. LL at 22. Petitioner stated that defense counsel "has the files" and "has gone through them," and that the court should look at his spreadsheet showing he had made partial payments of monies owed to his victims. Id., Exh. LL at 24. Petitioner asked the court to follow the presentence report with regard to imposing sentence. Id., Exh. LL at 21-25.

Defense counsel then spoke on Petitioner's behalf and averred she had acquired fifteen boxes of documents from Mr. Wallin, which documents were obtained from Petitioner's business office. Id., Exh. LL at 26. She argued that Petitioner's company had actually tried to assist the victims, although the victims did suffer harm. Counsel noted the court had a list of victims whose money had been returned to them. Id., Exh. LL at 24-32. She then noted Petitioner's medical problems and argued the presumptive term of imprisonment be imposed. Id., Exh. LL at 24-32.

Before imposing sentence, the state court cited as mitigating factors Petitioner's age, that Petitioner had repaid many of the victims, his acknowledgment of responsibility, and health issues. Id., Exh. LL at 34. The court then sentenced Petitioner to mitigated terms of eight years' imprisonment on Counts 1, 3 and 5, with the term on Count 1 consecutive to Count 3 and the term on Count 5 concurrent with Count 3 and consecutive to Count 1. Id., Exh. LL at 34. The court imposed a term of five year's probation each on Counts 7 and 13, to begin after Petitioner's discharge from prison. Petitioner also received credit for 984 days of presentence incarceration. After sentence was imposed, Petitioner clarified with the court that his aggregate sentence was 16 years. Id., Exh. LL at 36.

On December 27, 2011, Petitioner filed a timely notice of post-conviction relief pursuant to *Rule 32, Arizona Rules of Criminal Procedure*, and counsel was appointed to represent him in his Rule 32 proceedings. Id., Exh. MM. On June 29, 2012, Petitioner's appointed counsel filed notice avowing that they had reviewed the record, transcripts, and correspondence from Petitioner, trial counsel's files, and a draft Rule 32 petition prepared by Petitioner, and that after doing so he was unable to find any colorable claims for relief to present in a Rule 32 petition. Id., Exh. NN.

Petitioner filed a pro per Rule 32 petition asserting he received ineffective assistance of counsel because counsel failed to obtain "full discovery," did not interview witnesses, and "never worked with Petitioner to prepare for trial." Petitioner also alleged his counsel failed to prepare mitigating factors at sentencing and gave Petitioner erroneous advice which prevented him from making an informed decision on whether to accept the plea agreement. Petitioner also argued that the state had violated his right to due process by failing to provide "full disclosure" and that the state trial court had violated his right to due process by failing to consider a motion to change counsel that he alleged was filed at sentencing. Id., Exh. OO.

The state trial court denied relief in Petitioner's *Rule 32* action in a decision entered January 11, 2013. Id., Exh. TT. The court concluded that relief was precluded pursuant to *Rule 32.2(a)(3), Arizona Rules of Criminal Procedure*, because Petitioner had waived the enumerated claims "when he validly entered into the plea agreement." Id., Exh. TT. The court found the *Rule 32* action was, therefore, subject to summary dismissal pursuant to Arizona Rule of Criminal Procedure 32.6. Id., Exh. TT.

Petitioner sought review of this decision by the Arizona Court of Appeals. Petitioner argued his trial counsel rendered ineffective assistance by failing to "get full discovery" from the state and by not meeting with him often enough. Petitioner alleged counsel failed to present mitigating evidence at sentencing and erroneously advised him that he would receive a term of no more than seven or eight years' imprisonment if he entered into the plea agreement. Petitioner further alleged counsel lied when she provided the factual basis for the plea. Petitioner also asserted he was denied his right to the effective assistance of counsel because counsel appeared at sentencing even though he had "fired" her two weeks prior and because she failed to investigate facts and interview witnesses. Petitioner also alleged the state did not provide full disclosure and that the trial court erred because it failed to consider a motion for a change of counsel that was allegedly filed after Petitioner pled guilty. Petitioner also asserted that the trial judge should have recused himself because the judge allegedly knew Petitioner's uncle. Petitioner also argued he was innocent of the charges against him because there was insufficient evidence to support his convictions. Id., Exh. UU.

Attached to Petitioner's pleading to the Arizona Court of Appeals in his Rule 32 action, and offered as evidence in this habeas action, is a typescript of a "report" from Joseph Kalcantu of Houston, Texas, which avers that he was retained by a former Governor of Texas to investigate the bringing of criminal charges against Petitioner by Maricopa County. Id. (Answer), Exh. WW, Attach. The letter avers that the fraud charges against Petitioner were the result of corporate materials stolen by Jeffrey Stallcup, a former employee, and provided to a Maricopa County detective "without a search warrant." Id., Exh. WW, Attach. The letter references taped telephone conversations from 2006 in which a Maricopa County investigator conveyed to Petitioner's clients that he was defrauding them. Id., Exh. WW, Attach. The letter averred it was "known" that Mr. Wallin and Ms. Shoemaker (Petitioner's plea and sentencing counsel) "made a deal with Ms. Van Wie [the prosecutor] on other clients in order to sacrifice Mr. Herald's case..." Id., Exh. WW, Attach. The letter concludes that, having been an FBI investigator on fraud cases for twenty-five years, Mr. Kalcantu had determined Petitioner had not committed fraud. Id., Exh. WW, Attach. The letter is signed as "signature on file," and is not notarized nor sworn. See id., Exh. WW, Attach.

The Arizona Court of Appeals granted review but denied relief. Id., Exh. XX. The appellate court found that Petitioner's ineffective assistance claims were without merit. The court also concluded Petitioner had waived any claim regarding the state's discovery when he pled guilty and that there was no evidence in the record regarding Petitioner's alleged motion to change counsel after sentencing. Id., Exh. XX. The Court of Appeals further determined that Petitioner had failed to support his judicial bias claim and that he had failed to demonstrate any potential prejudice. Id., Exh. XX. The court also determined

Petitioner's insufficient evidence claim was without merit because Petitioner had provided a sufficient factual basis to support his guilty pleas on the counts of conviction. Id., Exh. XX.

On October 2, 2014, Petitioner filed the instant petition seeking a writ of habeas corpus. Petitioner asserts he is entitled to federal habeas relief because he was denied his right to the effective assistance of counsel and because he was subjected to an illegal search and seizure. Petitioner further argues he is entitled to relief because the prosecutor and defense counsel engaged in "corruption" and because there was "corruption and [a] major conflict of the sentencing judge". Doc. 1.

II Analysis

A. Exhaustion and procedural default

....

Because Petitioner pled guilty and waived his right to a direct appeal and because Petitioner has now completed a Rule 32 action, the Arizona Rules of Criminal Procedure regarding timeliness, waiver, and the preclusion of claims, which have been found to be consistently applied and well-established, bar Petitioner from now returning to the state courts to exhaust any unexhausted federal habeas claims, Accordingly, Petitioner has exhausted, but procedurally defaulted, any claim not fairly presented to the Arizona Court of Appeals in his Rule 32 action. See *Hurles, 752 F.3d at 780*; *Insyxiengmay v. Morgan, 403 F.3d 657, 665 (9th Cir. 2005)*; *Beaty v. Stewart, 303 F.3d 975, 987 (9th Cir. 2002)*. See also *Stewart v. Smith, 536 U.S. 856, 860, 122 S. Ct. 2578, 2581, 153 L. Ed. 2d 762 (2002)*.

B. Cause and prejudice

....

E. Waiver of claims upon entry of guilty plea

Petitioner agreed to plead guilty to the charges against him in a written plea agreement. The United States Supreme Court limited the grounds upon which a state prisoner may seek habeas relief after entering a voluntary and intelligent guilty plea in *Tollett v. Henderson, 411 U.S. 258, 93 S. Ct. 1602, 36 L. Ed. 2d 235 (1973)* (holding that a knowing and voluntary guilty plea waives all non-jurisdictional defects occurring prior to the entry of the guilty plea). Other than a challenge to the voluntary and intelligent character of the plea itself, a defendant's guilty plea bars federal habeas relief based on pre-plea non-jurisdictional constitutional claims. See *Haring v. Prosise, 462 U.S. 306, 319-20, 103 S.Ct. 2368, 2376-77, 76 L. Ed. 2d 595 (1983)* ("Our decisions subsequent to Tollett make clear that a plea of guilty does not bar the review in habeas corpus proceedings of all claims involving constitutional violations antecedent to a plea of guilty"); *Moran v. Godinez, 57 F.3d 690, 700 (9th Cir. 1994)* (foreclosing pre-plea ineffective assistance of counsel claim); *Ortberg v. Moody, 961 F.2d 135, 137-38 (9th Cir. 1992)*; *Hudson v. Moran, 760 F.2d 1027, 1029-30 (9th Cir. 1985)* ("As a general rule, one who voluntarily and intelligently pleads guilty to a criminal charge may not subsequently seek federal habeas corpus relief on the basis of pre-plea constitutional violations."); *Mitchell v. Superior Court, 632 F.2d 767, 769 (9th Cir. 1980)*. Pre-plea error is considered "jurisdictional" when it implicates the government's power to prosecute the defendant. *United States v. Johnston, 199 F.3d 1015, 1019 n.3 (9th Cir.1999)*. See also *United States v. Broce, 488 U.S. 563, 574-76, 109 S.Ct. 757, 765, 102 L. Ed. 2d 927 (1989)*. For example, Tollett does not foreclose a claim that: a defendant was vindictively prosecuted, see *Blackledge v. Perry, 417 U.S. 21, 30-31, 94 S.Ct. 2098, 2103-04, 40 L. Ed. 2d 628 (1974)*, that the indictment under which a defendant pled guilty placed him in double jeopardy, see *Menna v. New York, 423 U.S. 61, 62, 96 S.Ct. 241, 242, 46 L. Ed. 2d 195 (1975)*, or the statute under which the defendant was indicted is facially unconstitutional. See *United States v. Garcia-Valenzuela, 232 F.3d 1003, 1006 (9th Cir. 2000)*.

The federal courts have concluded that a plea colloquy must satisfy several requirements in order for a guilty plea to be considered voluntary and knowing. See, e.g., *Loftis v. Almager, 704 F.3d 645, 647-48 (9th Cir. 2012)*; *Tanner v. McDaniel, 493 F.3d 1135, 1146-47 (9th Cir. 2007)*. A guilty plea is not considered voluntary and knowing unless a defendant is informed of and waives his privilege against self-incrimination, his right to trial by jury, and his right to confront witnesses. *Tanner, 493 F.3d at 1147*, citing *Boykin v. Alabama, 395 U.S.*

238, 243-44, 89 S. Ct. 1709, 1712-13, 23 L. Ed. 2d 274 (1969). A defendant must understand the consequences of his plea, including "the range of allowable punishment that will result from his plea." *Little v. Crawford, 449 F.3d 1075, 1080 (9th Cir. 2006).*

The transcripts of the settlement hearings in this matter and Petitioner's plea colloquy indicate Petitioner's guilty plea was entered knowingly and voluntarily. At the time he entered his guilty plea the state court found the plea was knowing and voluntary. A state court's factual finding that a plea was voluntary and knowing is entitled to a presumption of correctness by a federal habeas court. See *Lambert v. Blodgett, 393 F.3d 943, 982 (9th Cir. 2004); Cunningham v. Diesslin, 92 F.3d 1054, 1060 (10th Cir. 1996).* Factual findings of a state court are presumed to be correct and can be reversed by a federal habeas court only when the federal court is presented with clear and convincing evidence. See *Miller-El v. Dretke, 545 U.S. 231, 125 S. Ct. 2317, 2325, 162 L. Ed. 2d 196 (2005); Vega v. Ryan, 757 F.3d 960, 965 (9th Cir. 2014).* Petitioner's after-the-fact conclusory allegations that he was incorrectly advised as to the consequences of his guilty plea are not clear and convincing evidence which can overcome the weight of his contemporaneous statements regarding his understanding of the plea agreement. A petitioner's contemporaneous statements carry substantial weight in determining if his entry of a guilty plea was knowing and voluntary. See *Blackledge v. Allison, 431 U.S. 63, 74, 97 S. Ct. 1621, 1629, 52 L. Ed. 2d 136 (1977)*("Solemn declarations in open court carry a strong presumption of verity. The subsequent presentation of conclusory allegations unsupported by specifics is subject to summary dismissal, as are contentions that in the face of the record are wholly incredible"); *Doe v. Woodford, 508 F.3d 563, 571 (9th Cir. 2007); Restucci v. Spencer, 249 F. Supp. 2d 33, 45 (D. Mass. 2003)* (collecting cases so holding).

Because Petitioner entered a knowing and voluntary guilty plea, federal habeas relief is precluded with regard to any pre-plea non-jurisdictional habeas claims, such as allegations of ineffective assistance of counsel which occurred prior to Petitioner's entry of a guilty plea and his allegation that he was denied his *Fourth Amendment* rights in the investigation of the alleged crimes.

F. Petitioner's claims for relief

1. Ineffective assistance of counsel

Petitioner argues that he was deprived of his right to the effective assistance of counsel because counsel did not meet with Petitioner often enough, counsel failed to get full discovery from the state, counsel failed to interview witnesses and investigate and pursue facts, and because counsel failed to present evidence of mitigating factors at Petitioner's sentencing. Petitioner also alleges counsel was lying when she provided the factual basis for the plea and that counsel provided erroneous information regarding the plea and the maximum sentence that could be imposed. Petitioner raised these claims before the Arizona Court of Appeals in his pro per petition in his state action for post-conviction relief pursuant to *Rule 32*, Arizona Rules of Criminal Procedure, and the Court of Appeals found the claims without merit. To the extent any of these claims are not precluded by the entry of Petitioner's guilty plea, they are without merit and the Arizona Court of Appeals' decision denying relief on Petitioner's allegation that he was denied his right to the effective assistance of counsel was not clearly contrary to nor an unreasonable application of federal law.

The Supreme Court established a two-part test for evaluating ineffective assistance of counsel claims in *Strickland v. Washington, 466 U.S. 668, 687, 104 S. Ct. 2052, 80 L. Ed. 2d 674 (1984)*. The Strickland test applies to a federal habeas petitioner's challenge to a conviction entered upon a guilty plea. See, e.g., *Hill v. Lockhart, 474 U.S. 52, 106 S. Ct. 366, 88 L. Ed. 2d 203 (1985)*; *Washington v. Lampert, 422 F.3d 864, 872 (9th Cir. 2005)*. In such a context, "the ineffectiveness inquiry probes whether the alleged ineffective assistance impinged on the [petitioner's] ability to enter an intelligent, knowing and voluntary plea of guilty." *Lambert, 393 F.3d at 980*. To prevail on this claim, Petitioner must show that his counsel's representation fell below the range of competence demanded of counsel in criminal cases and that he suffered actual prejudice as a result of counsel's incompetence. *Id. at 873*. Because a petitioner's failure to make the required showing of either deficient performance or prejudice defeats the claim, the court need not address both factors where one is lacking. *Strickland, 466 U.S. at 697-700.*

In Hill, the Supreme Court adapted the two-part Strickland standard to challenges to guilty pleas based on ineffective assistance of counsel, holding that a defendant seeking to challenge the validity of his guilty plea on the ground of ineffective assistance of counsel must show that (1) his "counsel's representation fell below an objective standard of reasonableness," and (2) "there is a reasonable probability that, but for [his] counsel's errors, he would not have pleaded guilty and would have insisted on going to trial." *474 U.S. at 57-59, 106 S. Ct. 366.*

Womack v. McDaniel, 497 F.3d 998, 1002 (9th Cir. 2007).
Petitioner was not prejudiced by what he asserts was his counsel's prediction of the sentences that might be imposed pursuant to the plea agreement because the state court clearly and repeatedly alerted Petitioner to the potential consequences of his guilty plea, including clarifying with Petitioner that he could be sentenced to a term of sixteen years' imprisonment if the sentences were ordered to be served consecutively. See *Womack, 497 F.3d at 1003,* citing *Doganiere v. United States, 914 F.2d 165, 168 (9th Cir. 1990)* (holding that the petitioner "suffered no prejudice from his attorney's prediction because, prior to accepting his guilty plea, the court explained that the discretion as to what the sentence would be").

The record in this matter belies all of Petitioner's claims of ineffective assistance of counsel. Petitioner offers only vague and conclusory allegations with regard to any possible prejudice he might have suffered as a result of counsel's alleged inadequacies, as Petitioner faced a total sentence of 63 years imprisonment had he chosen to reject the plea agreement and proceed to trial. See *Greenway v. Schriro, 653 F.3d 790, 804 (9th Cir. 2011)* ("[Petitioner]'s cursory and vague [ineffective assistance of counsel claim] cannot support habeas relief."). Accordingly, the state court's decision that Petitioner was not denied his right to the effective assistance of counsel was not clearly contrary to nor an unreasonable application of *Strickland* and *Hill* and Petitioner is not entitled to federal habeas relief on this claim.

BOY WHITE, PETITIONER, V. CHARLES RYAN, ARIZONA ATTORNEY GENERAL, RESPONDENTS.
CIV 11-02126 PHX GMS (MEA) UNITED STATES DISTRICT COURT FOR THE DISTRICT OF ARIZONA

(Text added and modified for emphasis) In Arizona counsel routinely have incompetent people plead guilty, counsel lying as to the factual basis, counsel fail to interview witnesses and investigate and pursue facts, evidenced by the number of complaints. As a matter of regular practice the Attorney General's Office consistently fails to advise the federal courts that when lawyers are appointed in Arizona, they fail to advise defendants to take pleas by fully explaining the consequences. Hearings are held but these hearings are only formalities for Arizona judges do not spend the necessary time and effort explaining the consequences of rejecting pleas. As a direct consequence there are defendants serving life terms in Arizona prisons all because of the failure of the Attorney General to be candid. There are too many such incidents which constitute a pattern. As this is a pattern with the Arizona Attorney General's Office this should constitute fraud upon the court, because, they are concealing facts on a systemic basis, to defeat valid claims.

COUNSEL: Boy White, Petitioner, Pro se, KINGMAN, AZ. For Charles L Ryan, Attorney General of the State of Arizona, Respondents: Craig William Soland, LEAD ATTORNEY, Office of the Attorney General, Phoenix, AZ.

I Procedural History
A grand jury indictment returned July 12, 2006, charged Petitioner with three counts of fraudulent schemes and artifices, class 2 felonies (counts 1, 5, and 8), seven counts of burglary in the second degree (counts 2, 4, 6, 7, 9, 10, and 11), and one count of theft (count 3). See Answer, Exh. A.

In a written plea agreement signed by Petitioner on February 16, 2007, Petitioner agreed to plead guilty to one count of theft (count 3), with one prior felony conviction; one count of burglary in the second degree (count 6); and one count of burglary in the second degree (count 9). See id., Exh. E. The plea agreement provided, inter alia, that, with regard to the sentence to be imposed on count 3, the charge of theft, the crime carried a "presumptive sentence of 6.5 years; a minimum sentence of 4.5 years (3.5 years if the Court makes an exceptional circumstances finding); and a maximum sentence of 13.0 years (16.25 years if the trial court makes an exceptional circumstances finding)", and that Petitioner would serve "not less than 6.5 years in the Department of Corrections." Id., Exh. E.

At a change of plea proceeding, the trial court reviewed the plea agreement with Petitioner and advised him of the range of possible sentences. Id., Exh. F & Exh. G. Petitioner's counsel advised the court at the beginning of the proceeding that Petitioner was illiterate and could not read nor write English. The court informed Petitioner that the maximum sentence he could receive based on a guilty plea to count 3 was 13 years imprisonment, which could be increased to a term of 16 years upon a finding of special circumstances. The court noted that Petitioner would not be sentenced to less than 6.5 years imprisonment.

At the change of plea proceeding Petitioner told the court the plea agreement had been read to him and that his lawyer had explained the plea agreement to Petitioner. Petitioner was told he was waiving his right to a jury trial and to have a jury find him guilty beyond a reasonable doubt. Petitioner stated that he had not consumed any drugs or alcohol prior to entering the plea. Petitioner admitted the factual basis for the crimes to the court.

On April 12, 2007, the trial court entered judgment pursuant to Petitioner's guilty plea, and sentenced Petitioner to an aggravated term of eleven years imprisonment pursuant to his conviction for theft (count 3). The court suspended imposition of sentence on the other two counts and ordered that Petitioner be placed on concurrent terms of probation for four years upon his discharge from prison. Id., Exh. H & Exh. I at 12-14.

On May 9, 2007, Petitioner filed a petition for post-conviction relief, seeking a reduction in his sentence, in which he alleged:

Defendant was told by his attorney that upon a plea of guilty, Defendant would receive a sentence of 6.5 years. When the Court sentenced Defendant to 11 years and Defendant asked his counsel why he didn't get the 6.5 years sentence promised by counsel, counsel snidely remarked, "Be glad you didn't get 13 (years)." Defendant signed off on the plea and initialed each paragraph only because counsel explained it meant a 6.5 year sentence. Defendant signed where counsel indicated--because Defendant is illiterate! A test administered by the Arizona Dept. of Corrections 5 days after sentencing indicates Defendant reads at a sub-first grade level and that his language skills are at a first grade level. (See: Exhibit "A", attached hereto and made a part hereof.) The words and language of the plea are far too technical for a 6 year old (--or first grader) mind to comprehend. Defendant signed and initialed where counsel indicated after counsel said it meant a 6.5 year sentence. Based on the facts of this case, it is clear that the Plea was coerced and/or induced by counsel and that it was not knowingly and intelligently entered by Defendant in violation of his constitutional rights where defendant received an 11 year sentence after being promised a 6.5 year sentence. The facts also appear to raise the argument that Defendant also was denied effective assistance of counsel.

Id., Exh. N.

Petitioner was appointed counsel to represent him in his Rule 32 proceedings. See id., Exh. O. On August 10, 2007, Petitioner's appointed counsel informed the state court that she was unable to find any claims for relief to raise on Petitioner's behalf. See id., Exh. P. The state Superior Court ordered counsel to remain in an advisory capacity and granted Petitioner 45 days in which to file a pro per petition for post-conviction relief. See id., Exh. Q.

On October 31, 2007, the state trial court dismissed Petitioner's Rule 32 proceedings because Petitioner had failed to file a petition for post-conviction relief by the deadline imposed by the court. Id., Exh. R.

Petitioner did not seek review of this decision by the Arizona Court of Appeals.

On July 10, 2008, Petitioner initiated a second action for state post-conviction relief pursuant to *Rule 32, Arizona Rules of Civil Procedure*. Id., Exh. S & Exh. T. In attempting to justify the successive and untimely nature of the action Petitioner claimed "newly-discovered material facts exist which probably would have changed the verdict or sentence"; "the defendant's failure to file a timely notice of post-conviction relief ... was without fault on the defendant's part"; and "there has been a significant change in the law that would probably overturn the conviction or sentence." Id., Exh. S. See also id., Exh. T.

Petitioner asserted in the second Rule 32 action that:

> 1. Defendant is illiterate and requires assistance as he cannot read or write and was put in solitary confinement with no assistance when he previously filed a "NOTICE of POST-CONVICTION Relief." Defendant received legal mail from the Court and an attorney but could not read it and waited months for legal assistance. Defendant has recently been moved to a new unit (Santa Rita) at ASPC Tucson, where help is available.
>
> 2. Stokes v. Schrio, Apprendi, Blakely, State v. Honorable Michael J Brown and the statutory changes to *A.R.S. 13-702* prescribe the factors used by a judge to aggravate his sentence must be determined by "trier of fact" (jury) first.
>
> 3. A new witness has been located.

Id., Exh. S.

On July 25, 2008, the state Superior Court dismissed Petitioner's second Rule 32 action because he failed to demonstrate that he was entitled to an exception under *Rule 32.1(f)*; he failed to demonstrate a significant change in the law; he had waived his right to a jury determination of aggravating factors in his plea agreement; and he had not demonstrated that newly-discovered material facts exist that would probably have changed the verdict or sentence. Id., Exh. U. Petitioner did not seek review of this decision by the Arizona Court of Appeals.

On March 13, 2009, Petitioner filed a third notice of post-conviction relief, seeking review based on newly-discovered evidence. Id., Exh. V.

The Superior Court found that Petitioner had sufficiently raised a claim to allow an untimely filing, and gave Petitioner 60 days in which to file a pro per petition for post-conviction relief. Id., Exh. W.

Petitioner's pro per Rule 32 petition, filed January 4, 2010, alleged:

> The appointed legal advocate, Scott Allen, requested a mitigation hearing. Theresa Sanders, the sentencing judge, refused.
>
> Petitioner is diagnosed schizophrenic. He was untreated at the time of the burglary giving rise to the imprisonment. He was diagnosed and put on medication while awaiting trial.

Id., Exh. Y.

On March 29, 2010, the state trial court dismissed Petitioner's third Rule 32 action, determining he had failed to show any colorable claim for relief pursuant to *Rule 32.1 of the Arizona Rules of Criminal Procedure*. Id., Exh. CC. Petitioner sought review of this decision by the Arizona Court of Appeals, which rejected the petition as untimely filed. Id., Exhs. DD, FF, GG, JJ.

On February 25, 2011, Petitioner filed another notice of post-conviction relief which alleged:

> Defendant is illiterate, and an inmate reviewing his "plea agreement" saw that the stipulated sentence was not followed. Defendant was diagno[s]ed as schizophrenic, which contributed to his lack of understanding of the plea and sentencing process. His counsel was ineffective, and did not follow through on the stipulated sentence, nor did he bring a m[i]tigating specialist. His Rule 32 counsel was ineffective, and did not evaluate defendant's illiteracy, mental condition, and the sentence stipulation. Defendant respectfully requests that a lawyer be appointed to review this case and represent him in a post-conviction relief.

Id., Exh. KK.

On March 28, 2011, the state Superior Court dismissed Petitioner's fourth Rule 32 action as untimely, finding that Petitioner had "failed to state a claim for which relief could be granted in an untimely Rule 32 proceeding." Id., Exh. LL. Petitioner sought review of this decision by the Arizona Court of Appeals, which dismissed the petition for review as untimely filed. Id., Exh. NN.

On August 11, 2011, Petitioner filed another notice of petition for post-conviction, alleging:

> Defendant/Petitioner White was sentenced in 2007. He is illiterate. Another inmate at the [illegible] unit looked at his time comp, release date does not compute. He should have been given credit for more days served in Maricopa County Jail. Petitioner respectfully requests that this court appoint an attorney to help correct this error.

Id., Exh. OO.

On September 2, 2011, the state Superior Court dismissed the petition on the merits, stating: "the defendant is not being held beyond the expiration of his sentence." Id., Exh. PP. Petitioner did not seek review of this decision.

In his federal habeas petition Petitioner asserts he is entitled to relief because he was denied his right to the effective assistance of counsel because his counsel allowed Petitioner, who is illiterate, to sign a plea agreement understanding that the agreement provided for a maximum sentence of 6.5 years and Petitioner received a sentence of eleven years. Petitioner also alleges counsel was ineffective because he did not assert Petitioner's incompetence; Petitioner avers he was diagnosed as schizophrenic two years after his legal proceedings. Petitioner contends he did not knowingly and voluntarily enter the plea agreement. Petitioner alleges he was heavily medicated at the time the plea agreement was explained to him by his counsel. Petitioner asks, as relief, that his sentence be reduced to the 6.5 years specified in the plea agreement. Attached to the pleadings is a form dated April 17, 2007, and a letter dated September 15, 2008, indicating Petitioner does not have a GED or high school diploma and that Petition has learning disabilities as a result of schizophrenia because his medications interfere with his focus.

II Analysis

A. Statute of limitations

....

Allowing that Petitioner's diagnosis of mental illness and the fact that he diligently pursued post-conviction remedies warrants equitable tolling, the Magistrate Judge will consider Respondents' argument that Petitioner failed to properly exhaust his federal habeas claims in the state courts. Respondents contend that the claims for relief are also barred by the doctrine of exhaustion and procedural default.

B. Exhaustion and procedural default

....

Petitioner does not contend that he is actually innocent of the crimes of conviction, accordingly, no fundamental miscarriage of justice will occur absent a consideration of the merits of Petitioner's habeas claims.

Additionally, even if Petitioner's mental disabilities constitute cause for his procedural default of his habeas claims, Petitioner cannot show prejudice arising from the procedural default of his claims.

The "clearly established Federal law, as determined by the Supreme Court of the United States" at issue in this case is the test for ineffective assistance of counsel claims set forth in *Strickland v. Washington, 466 U.S. 668, 104 S. Ct. 2052, 80 L. Ed. 2d 674, [] (1984)*, and in *Hill v. Lockhart, 474 U.S. 52, 106 S. Ct. 366, 88 L. Ed. 2d 203, [] (1985)*. Under Strickland, to establish a claim of ineffective assistance of counsel, the petitioner must show (1) grossly deficient performance by his counsel, and (2) resultant prejudice. *466 U.S. at 687, 104 S. Ct. 2052*. In Hill, the Supreme Court adapted the two-part Strickland standard to challenges to guilty pleas based on ineffective assistance of counsel, holding that a defendant seeking to challenge the validity of his guilty plea on the ground of ineffective assistance of counsel must show that (1) his "counsel's representation fell below an objective standard of reasonableness," and (2) "there is a reasonable probability that, but for [his] counsel's errors, he would not have pleaded guilty and would have insisted on going to trial." *474 U.S. at 57-59, 106 S. Ct. 366.*

Womack v. McDaniel, 497 F.3d 998, 1002 (9th Cir. 2007).

To establish deficient performance, a person challenging a conviction must show that counsel's representation fell below an objective standard of reasonableness. A court considering a claim of ineffective assistance must apply a strong presumption that counsel's representation was within the wide range' of reasonable professional assistance. The challenger's burden is to show that counsel made errors so serious that counsel was not functioning as the "counsel" guaranteed the defendant by the *Sixth Amendment.*

Premo v. Moore, 131 S. Ct. 733, 739, 178 L. Ed. 2d 649 (2011) (internal citations and quotations omitted), citing *Harrington, 131 S. Ct. at 788* ("The question is whether an attorney's representation amounted to incompetence under 'prevailing professional norms,' not whether it deviated from best practices or most common custom."). Counsel's performance is not deficient nor prejudicial when counsel "fails" to raise an argument that counsel reasonably believes would be futile. See *Premo, 131 S. Ct. at 741; Harrington, 131 S. Ct. at 788.*

Furthermore, to succeed on a claim that his counsel was constitutionally ineffective regarding a guilty plea, a petitioner must show that his counsel's advice as to the consequences of the plea was not within the range of competence demanded of criminal attorneys. See, e.g., *Hill v. Lockhart, 474 U.S. 52, 58, 106 S. Ct. 366, 369, 88 L. Ed. 2d 203 (1985).* Although the Court may proceed directly to the prejudice prong when undertaking the Strickland analysis, the Court may not assume prejudice solely from counsel's allegedly deficient performance. See *Jackson v. Calderon, 211 F.3d 1148, 1155 n.3 (9th Cir. 2000).*

Petitioner has not established that his counsel's performance was deficient, or that any alleged deficiency prejudiced Petitioner. The plea agreement was beneficial to Petitioner and Petitioner indicated both in the written plea agreement, which was read to him, and at the plea colloquy that he understood the terms of the plea agreement and was pleading guilty voluntarily and knowingly. Petitioner has not demonstrated that, but for counsel's advice with regard to the plea agreement, Petitioner would have chosen to go forward to trial on all of the counts charged in the indictment. Nowhere in his pleadings does Petitioner contend that he could not be found guilty of the other charges stated in the indictment and Petitioner fully understood that, if convicted of the other charges in the indictment, Petitioner faced a lengthy sentence.

Petitioner's unsupported statements in his federal habeas pleadings that his guilty plea was not voluntary do not supply the "clear and convincing evidence" standard necessary for the Court to conclude that Petitioner's plea was not knowing or voluntary. Petitioner's contemporaneous statements regarding his understanding of the plea agreement carry substantial weight in determining if his entry of a guilty plea was knowing and voluntary. See *Blackledge v. Allison, 431 U.S. 63, 74, 97 S. Ct. 1621, 1629, 52 L. Ed. 2d 136 (1977)* ("Solemn declarations in open court carry a strong presumption of verity. The subsequent presentation of conclusory allegations unsupported by specifics is subject to summary dismissal, as are contentions that in the face of the record are wholly incredible"); *Doe v. Woodford, 508 F.3d 563, 571 (9th Cir. 2007)*; *Restucci v. Spencer, 249 F. Supp. 2d 33, 45 (D. Mass. 2003)* (collecting cases so holding).

CHARLES ANTHONY MCDONALD, PETITIONER, VS. CHARLES L. RYAN, ET AL., RESPONDENTS.

NO. CV-10-1513-PHX-DGC (LOA) UNITED STATES DISTRICT COURT FOR THE DISTRICT OF ARIZONA

(Text added/modified for emphasis) The Attorney General failed to disclose that in Arizona defense counsel do not thoroughly disclose plea offers and there are too many such incidents. Failure to disclose this systemic problem is fraud upon the court.

....

I. Factual and Procedural Background

A. Charges, Trial and Sentencing

On January 29, 2004, the State of Arizona filed an indictment in the Arizona Superior Court, Maricopa County, charging Petitioner with burglary in the second degree, a Class 3 felony, and possession of burglary tools, a Class 6 felony. (Respondents' Exh. A at 5) The State amended the indictment to allege 23 historical prior felony convictions, commission of the offenses while released from confinement, and aggravating circumstances other than prior convictions. (Respondents' Exh. A at 14, 15, 44)

Following a mistrial, on December 8, 2004, a second trial commenced on December 9, 2004. On December 14, 2004, the jury found Petitioner guilty as charged. (Respondents' Exh. B at 89, 91, 110; Exh. A 105, 109) The jury subsequently found that the State had established several aggravating circumstances beyond a reasonable doubt. (Respondents' Exh. B at 117) On March 2, 2005, the trial court sentenced Petitioner as a repetitive offender to an aggravated 20-year term of imprisonment on the second-degree burglary conviction and an aggravated concurrent 4.5-year term of imprisonment on the possession of burglary tools conviction. (Respondents' Exh. B at 126)

B. Direct Appeal

Petitioner timely appealed. Appellate counsel filed a brief pursuant to *Anders v. California, 386 U.S. 738, 87 S. Ct. 1396, 18 L. Ed. 2d 493 (1967)*. (Respondents' Exh. C) Thereafter, Petitioner filed a *pro se* brief asserting that: (1) the trial court denied Petitioner the right to self-representation; (2) the trial court considered improper aggravating circumstances when sentencing Petitioner; (3) the trial court improperly admitted a victim impact statement during sentencing; (4) the trial court denied Petitioner the opportunity to review the pre-sentence report; and (5) the trial court imposed an excessive sentence. (Respondents' Exh. D)

On March 2, 2006, the Arizona Court of Appeals affirmed Petitioner's convictions and sentences. (Respondents' Exh. E) Petitioner filed a motion for reconsideration which the appellate court denied. (Respondents' Exhs. F, G) Petitioner filed a petition for review in the Arizona Supreme Court, which was summarily denied on August 17,

2006. (Respondents' Exhs. H, I) Petitioner did not petition the United States Supreme Court for a *writ of certiorari*.

C. Post-Conviction Review

On August 25, 2006, Petitioner, proceeding *pro se*, filed a notice of post-conviction relief in the trial court pursuant to Ariz.R.Crim.P. 32. (Respondents' Exh. J) Petitioner filed a petition for post-conviction relief, raising the following claims:

> 1. Trial counsel was ineffective for failing to request a mistrial based on juror bias.
> 2. Trial counsel was ineffective for failing to properly advise Petitioner on the merits of a plea offer.
> 3. Trial counsel was ineffective for failing to object to statements made by the prosecution on behalf of the victim's son at the sentencing hearing.
> 4. Trial counsel was ineffective for failing to effectively cross-examine state witnesses.
> 5. Trial counsel was ineffective for failing to adequately investigate and interview corroborating witnesses.
> 6. Trial counsel was ineffective for failing to present meaningful mitigation evidence at the sentencing hearing.

(Respondents' Exh. K) After the petition was fully briefed, the trial court conducted an evidentiary hearing on the issue of counsel's failure to adequately advise Petitioner of the strength and weaknesses of his case in association with a plea offer. (Respondents' Exh. B at 185, Exh. N) At the conclusion of the evidentiary hearing, on May 21, 2008, the court denied the petition. (Exh. N at 48)

Petitioner petitioned the Arizona Court of Appeals for review of the denial of post-conviction relief. The appellate court summarily denied review on November 24, 2009. (Respondents' Exhs. O, P) On December 18, 2009, the Arizona Supreme Court likewise denied review. (Respondents' Exh. Q)

D. Federal Petition for Writ of Habeas Corpus

Thereafter, Petitioner filed a timely Petition for Writ of Habeas Corpus pursuant to *28 U.S.C. § 2254* in this District Court. (Doc. 3) Petitioner raises the following claims for relief:

1. The trial court denied Petitioner his right to self-representation.
2. Petitioner's sentence violated the *Sixth Amendment* because the court submitted improper aggravating circumstances to the jury and the trial court considered an aggravating factor not submitted to the jury.
3. Petitioner's aggravated sentences violate the *Eighth Amendment*.
4. Trial counsel was ineffective for failing to advocate on Petitioner's behalf at sentencing.
5. Trial counsel was ineffective for failing to conduct reasonable pretrial investigation.
6. Trial counsel was ineffective for failing to raise the issue of juror bias.
7. Trial counsel was ineffective for failing to properly advise Petitioner regarding the merits of a plea offer.
8. Petitioner's right to due process was violated during post-conviction proceedings.

(Doc. 3) The Court previously dismissed Ground 8 and directed Respondents to answer the remaining grounds for relief. (Doc. 4) Respondents have filed an Answer to the Petition, to which Petitioner has replied. For the reasons set forth below, the Petition should be denied. Respondents concede that the Petition is timely; thus, the Court will not further address this issue. (Doc. 12 at 5)

II. Exhaustion and Procedural Bar

G. Ground Seven - Failure to Adequately Advise on Merits of Plea Offer

In Ground Seven, Petitioner argues that counsel was ineffective for failing to properly advise him of a plea offer, and failing to adequately inform him of risks of going to trial and his sentencing exposure. (Doc. 3 at 12)

Petitioner raised this claim during post-conviction proceedings and the State court conducted an evidentiary hearing. (Respondents' Exh. K) At the evidentiary hearing, trial counsel testified that the State had extended several plea offers but that the first, mandating a term of 7 years' imprisonment, was withdrawn by the State shortly after it was extended. (Respondents' Exh. N at 35, 37) The plea was withdrawn on March 22, 2004 after the police detective investigating the case objected to the plea offer as too lenient. (Respondents' Exh. N at 17-18, 37) A second plea offer was extended for a sentencing range of 10 to 13 years imprisonment, but Petitioner rejected that offer after informing counsel that he had given a free-talk in a murder case that the State could not prove without his testimony, and he thought the State would extend a better offer. (Respondents' Exh. N at 28, 37) Petitioner told defense counsel that he was telling the truth, that he wanted to go to trial, and that he thought he would be acquitted. (*Id.* at 28, 30) Petitioner asked counsel about the substantial difference in the proposed sentences between the two offers and asked what had happened to the offer for a term of 7-years' imprisonment. (*Id.* at 36-37)

Defense counsel testified that she explained the terms of the plea offer to Petitioner, discussing the impact of his 20-plus prior felony convictions on the sentencing range, and informed Petitioner that he would be subject to "an extremely aggravated sentence" if convicted at trial, "which was much worse than we get under the plea offer." (Respondents' Exh. N at 27) Defense counsel also explained that the plea offer was for a sentencing range of not less than 10 years and no more than 13 years, and that it "was better than what he was going to get from [the trial judge]." (*Id.* at 31) Petitioner never conveyed to counsel that he interpreted the sentencing range to be an additional 13-year sentence. (*Id.*) Defense counsel testified that she reviewed the merits of the case with Petitioner, and informed him that his version of the events could not be corroborated and that she "didn't think the jury was going to believe his story. His story was simply beyond belief." (Respondents' Exh. N at 28) Defense counsel confirmed with the prosecutor and the previous defense attorney that Petitioner had had discussions with the State about testifying in a murder case. (*Id.* at 33)

The State offered Petitioner an "8 to 11-year" plea offer if Petitioner cooperated in the murder case. (*Id.* at 34, 37) Petitioner rejected the offer, stating that it was "still too much time." (*Id.* at 37)

Counsel further testified that, on the first day of trial which ended in a mistrial, Petitioner gave counsel the name of a woman he said would corroborate his story. Counsel called the woman, but she hung up the phone once counsel explained the nature of her call. (Respondents' Exh. N at 28-29) After the mistrial, the attorneys talked to the jurors who conveyed that they did not believe Petitioner's version of the events. (Respondents' Exh. N at 29) After speaking to the jurors, the State notified defense counsel that it would re-extend the "10 to 13-year" plea offer, but that Petitioner would have to accept it immediately. (Respondents' Exh. N at 29-30) Defense counsel conveyed the jurors' impressions to Petitioner, and Petitioner stated that he did not care and wanted to select a new jury. (*Id.* at 30) Defense counsel told Petitioner that the State had re-extended the "10 to 13-year" plea offer. (*Id.* at 31) Defense counsel's discussion with Petitioner was brief and focused on the length of the sentence offered. (*Id.*) Petitioner rejected the plea offer because the sentence was too long. (*Id.* at 32)

At Petitioner's first trial, when the court decided that it would grant a mistrial, the judge asked the prosecutor how quickly she could retry the case. (Respondents' Exh. Y at 40) The prosecutor responded that Petitioner could accept the plea offer, or the trial would commence the following day. (*Id.*) The court asked about the terms of the plea offer and defense counsel stated that it was a "10 to 13-year" plea. (*Id.* at 41) As the parties discussed an additional term of the plea offer, defense counsel interrupted and stated, "my client just informed me that he's continuing to reject that offer." (Respondents' Exh. N at 42) The jury returned to the courtroom and the trial court declared a mistrial. (*Id.*)

At the evidentiary hearing on Petitioner's petition for post-conviction relief, Petitioner testified that he first became aware of a plea offer including a 7-year term of imprisonment after he received the file from appellate counsel. (Respondents' Exh. N at 7-9) Petitioner also stated that he did not hear about the "10 to 13-year" plea offer until a mistrial was declared. (*Id.* at 9-11) Petitioner stated that he and counsel had a brief conversation about the plea offer at the defense table and it was the only conversation he ever had with counsel about that plea offer. (*Id.* at 11-13) Petitioner testified that he understood the "10 to 13-year" plea offer to mean that the trial court could "give [him] up to 13 plus years" or "the top was 13 and aggravated meant that [the court] could go over the 13 and give [him] a few years on top of it." (Respondents' Exh. N at 10-11)

At the conclusion of the evidentiary hearing, the post-conviction court found that Petitioner had not met his burden of establishing that trial counsel rendered ineffective assistance. The State court explained:

> The testimony from Ms. Todd (defense counsel) indicates that she did in fact, have a conversation with Mr. McDonald in the jail regarding the plea agreement, that she had the plea agreement with her, that she advised the defendant of the stipulations in the plea agreement for an aggravated term of 10 to 13 years and that there was some discussion regarding the 7 years being withdrawn.
>
> So it sounds like based on her testimony, Mr. McDonald also knew about the seven-year offer and I don't need to reach the second prong unless I find that counsel's performance was deficient.
>
> I find that the defendant has not proved by a preponderance that defense counsel's performance was deficient and he was aware of the offer and communicated to him in the jail and communicated again to him after the mistrial, as reflected in the transcript and the resuscitation of the conversation between the prosecutor, the Court and defense counsel on page 12 of Mr. Beene's response [to the petition for post-conviction relief.]
>
> Petition for Post-Conviction Relief is dismissed.

(Respondents' Exh. N at 47-48)

Petitioner has not shown that the State court's ruling was contrary to, or an unreasonable application of, federal law. The relevant federal law governing ineffective assistance of counsel claims is *Strickland v. Washington, 466 U.S. 668, 104 S. Ct. 2052, 80 L. Ed. 2d 674 (1984)*, which requires a showing of "both deficient performance by counsel and prejudice." *Knowles v. Mirzayance, 556 U.S. 111, 129 S.Ct. 1411, 1420, 173 L. Ed. 2d 251 (2009)*. The *Sixth Amendment* guarantees a criminal defendant effective assistance of counsel during all critical stages of the criminal process, including plea negotiations. *Hill v. Lockhart, 474 U.S. 52, 57, 106 S. Ct. 366, 88 L. Ed. 2d 203 (1985); United States v. Leonti, 326 F.3d 1111, 1116 (9th Cir. 2003).* Thus, *Strickland's* two-prong test applies to ineffectiveness claims in connection with the plea process. *Hill, 474 U.S. at 57.* The first part of the inquiry is whether counsel's performance was "within the range of competence demanded of attorneys in criminal cases." *Id.* (quoting *McMann v. Richardson, 397 U.S. 759, 771, 90 S. Ct. 1441, 25 L. Ed. 2d 763 (1970)).* The second part focuses on whether counsel's deficient performance affected the outcome of the plea process. *Id., 474 U.S. at 59.* Petitioner must establish that he was prejudiced by counsel's deficient performance, *i.e.*, that "there is a reasonable probability that, but for counsel's unprofessional errors, the result of the proceeding would have been different." *Id. at 694.* A reasonable probability is a probability sufficient to undermine confidence in the outcome. *Id.*

"'Surmounting *Strickland's* high bar is never an easy task.'" *Richter, 131 S. Ct. at 788* (quoting *Padilla v. Kentucky, 559 U.S. , 130 S.Ct. 1473, 1485, 176 L. Ed. 2d 284 (2010)).* "The question is whether an attorney's representation amounted to incompetence under 'prevailing professional norms,' not whether it deviated from best practices or most common custom." *Richter, 131 S. Ct. at 788* (quoting *Strickland, 466 U.S. at 690*). Establishing that a state court's application of *Strickland* was unreasonable under § 2254(d) is even more difficult, because both standards are "highly deferential," *466 U. S. at 689*, and *Strickland's* general standard has a substantial range of reasonable applications. The issue under § 2254(d) is not whether counsel's actions were reasonable, but whether there is any reasonable argument that counsel satisfied *Strickland's* deferential standard. *Richter, 131 S. Ct. at 788.* The Supreme Court recently addressed the reasons for a "most deferential" standard for judging counsel's performance:

> Unlike a later reviewing court, the attorney observed the relevant proceedings, knew of materials outside the record, and interacted with the client, with opposing counsel, and with the judge.

Premo v. Moore, U.S. , 131 S.Ct. 733, 739-40, 178 L. Ed. 2d 649 (2011). The Court also recognized that "[p]lea bargains are the result of complex negotiations suffused with uncertainty, and defense attorneys must make careful strategic choices in balancing opportunities and risks" of a plea. *Id. at 741*. Considerations surrounding these strategic choices in the pre-trial context "make strict adherence to the *Strickland* standard all the more essential when reviewing the choices an attorney made at the plea bargain stage." *Id*. Mindful of these principles, the Court will consider whether the State court unreasonably applied *Strickland* to the facts of this case. *28 U.S.C. § 2254*.

A. Whether Counsel's Performance was Deficient

To establish a claim of ineffective assistance of counsel under *Strickland*, a petitioner must establish that his counsel's errors were so serious that counsel was deficient, and that counsel's "deficient performance prejudiced the defense." *Strickland, 466 U.S. at 687*. To be deficient, counsel's representation must have fallen "below an objective standard of reasonableness," *Id., 466 U.S. at 688*, and there is a "strong presumption" that counsel's representation is within the "wide range" of reasonable professional assistance. *Id. at 689; see also Kimmelman v. Morrison, 477 U.S. 365, 381, 106 S. Ct. 2574, 91 L. Ed. 2d 305 (1986)* (quoting *Strickland, 466 U.S. at 689*). *Strickland* mandates a "strong presumption of competence." *Cullen v. Pinholster, U.S. , 131 S.Ct. 1388, 1407, 179 L. Ed. 2d 557 (2011)*. This Court must "'give [counsel] the benefit of the doubt." *Id*. (citations omitted). As stated above, the post-conviction court found that there was no evidence that trial counsel's performance was deficient. (Respondents' Exh. N) During the evidentiary hearing on post-conviction review, the trial court found that counsel discussed the plea offers with Petitioner. On habeas corpus review, this Court defers to the State court's factual findings.

The State court record establishes that the State extended several plea offers in this case and that Petitioner was aware of the offers. The State court's record further establishes that Petitioner rejected the plea offers because the sentences were too long and he thought he would be acquitted. (Respondents' Exh. N) Petitioner has not met his high burden of establishing that the State court's conclusion that trial counsel's performance was not deficient was based on an unreasonable determination of the facts, or was contrary to, or an unreasonable application of, clearly established federal law. Moreover, as discussed below, even assuming counsel's performance was deficient, Petitioner has not established prejudice.

B. Prejudice

Even if counsel's performance was constitutionally deficient, Petitioner is not entitled to habeas corpus relief because he fails to demonstrate prejudice. *Strickland, 466 U.S. at 687.* [HN39] Petitioner must "show that there is a reasonable probability that, but for counsel's unprofessional errors, the result of the proceeding would have been different." *Id., 466 U.S. at 694.* "A reasonable probability is a probability sufficient to undermine confidence in the outcome." *Id.* "That requires a 'substantial,' not just 'conceivable,' likelihood of a different result." *Pinholster, 131 S.Ct. at 1403* (quoting *Richter, 562 U.S. , 131 S. Ct. at 791*).

The United States Supreme Court has not specifically addressed what constitutes prejudice when a criminal defendant rejects a plea offer and proceeds to trial. The parties' briefing does not specifically address this issue. Rather, Petitioner appears to argue that, to establish prejudice, he must establish a reasonable likelihood he would have accepted a plea offer. Respondents appear to agree with this statement of the law.

The Supreme Court has held that *Strickland* applies in the context of plea bargaining. *Hill v. Lockhart, 474 U.S. 52, 106 S. Ct. 366, 88 L. Ed. 2d 203 (1985).* However, the Supreme Court has not addressed the specific question of what constitutes prejudice when a petitioner rejects a plea offer and proceeds to a fair trial. The Supreme Court has interpreted the *Sixth Amendment's* right to effective assistance of counsel as ensuring a criminal defendant receives a fair trial. *Strickland, 466 U.S. at 687.* The Supreme Court reiterated in *Pinholster* that, "'the purpose of the effective assistance guarantee of the *Sixth Amendment* is not to improve the quality of legal representation . . . [but] simply to ensure that criminal defendants receive a fair trial.'" *Pinholster, 131 S.Ct. at 1403* (quoting *Strickland, 466 U.S. at 689*). The Supreme Court has never held that a defendant who foregoes a plea bargain and is later convicted after a fair trial has suffered a constitutional violation. *See Nunes v. Mueller, 350 F.3d 1045, 1052-53 (9th Cir. 2003)*. Rather, the Supreme Court's cases interpreting the *Sixth Amendment* in the context of plea bargaining have involved cases where the petitioner waived the right to a fair trial by accepting a plea offer, not a case where the petitioner rejected a plea and exercised his right to a fair trial. *Premo v. Moore, 562 U.S. , 131 S.Ct. 733, 737-40, 178 L. Ed. 2d 649 (2011); Wright v. Van Patten, 552 U.S. 120, 124-25, 128 S. Ct. 743, 169 L. Ed. 2d 583 (2008); Hill v. Lockhart, 474 U.S. 52, 59, 106 S. Ct. 366, 88 L. Ed. 2d 203 (1985); McMann v. Richardson, 397 U.S. 759, 760-66, 90 S. Ct. 1441, 25 L. Ed. 2d 763 (1970)*. Although circuit courts, including the Ninth Circuit, have discussed *Strickland's* prejudice prong in the context of a rejected plea offer, the lack of any Supreme Court holding on that issue precludes a finding that the State court's decision in this case was contrary to, or an unreasonable application of, clearly established Supreme Court precedent. *Pinholster, 131 S.Ct. at 1399* ([HN41] "State court decisions are measured against [the United States Supreme Court's] precedents as of the 'time the state renders its decision.'") (quoting *Lockyer v. Andrade, 538 U.S. 63, 71-72, 123 S. Ct. 1166, 155 L. Ed. 2d 144 (2003)); Ponce v. Felker, 606 F.3d 596, 604 (9th Cir. 2010)* ("If Supreme Court cases 'give no clear answer to the question presented,' the state court's decision cannot be an unreasonable application of clearly established federal law.") (quoting *Van Patten, 552 U.S. at 126); Moses v. Payne, 555 F.3d 742, 754 (9th Cir. 2009)* ("In light of *Musladin, Panetti*, and *Van Patten*, we conclude that when a Supreme Court decision does not 'squarely address[] the issue in th[e] case' or establish a legal principle that 'clearly extend[s]' to a new context to the extent required by the Supreme Court in these recent decisions . . . , it cannot be said, under [the] AEDPA, there is 'clearly established' Supreme Court precedent addressing the issue before us, and so we must defer to the state court's decision.") (quoting *Van Patten, 552 U.S. 120, 125, 128 S. Ct. 743, 169 L. Ed. 2d 583 (2008)* (alterations in original); *see also Earp v. Ornoski, 431 F.3d 1158, 1184 n. 23 (9th Cir. 2005)* (describing habeas petitioner's reliance on circuit-court authority as "futile" because, "post-AEDPA [,] only

Supreme Court holdings are binding on state courts.") (citing *Lambert v. Blodgett, 393 F.3d 943, 974 (9th Cir. 2004)).* The Supreme Court has recently granted certiorari to determine, "What remedy, if any should be provided for ineffective assistance of counsel during plea bargain negotiations if the defendant was later convicted and sentenced pursuant to constitutionally adequate procedures?" *Lafler v. Cooper, U.S. , 131 S.Ct. 856, 178 L. Ed. 2d 622 (January 7, 2011).*

Nevertheless, for purposes of analyzing Petitioner's claim, the Court will consider Ninth Circuit authority. The Ninth Circuit has held that to establish prejudice from incorrect advice resulting in rejection of a plea offer, Petitioner "must show that there is a reasonable probability that he would have accepted the plea agreement had he received accurate advice from his attorney." *Hoffman v. Arave, 455 F.3d 926, 941-942 (9th Cir. 2006), judgment vacated in part on other grounds by Arave v. Hoffman, 552 U.S. 117, 128 S. Ct. 749, 169 L. Ed. 2d 580 (2008); see also Nunes, 350 F.3d at 1052.* However, as discussed below, while the Ninth Circuit has discussed *Strickland's* prejudice prong in the context of a rejected plea offer, the lack of any Supreme Court holding on that issue precludes a finding that the State court's decision in this case was contrary to, or an unreasonable application of, clearly established Supreme Court precedent. *Pinholster, 131 S.Ct. at 1399* ("State court decisions are measured against [the United States Supreme Court's] precedents as of the 'time the state renders its decision.'") (citations omitted).

Undoubtedly, Petitioner would prefer a lesser sentence than the one he received. The Court, however, must look to Petitioner's statements and beliefs at the time of the trial to determine whether there is a reasonable probability that Petitioner would have pled guilty absent counsel's alleged deficient performance. The record here reflects that Petitioner was committed to his defense that he was merely present at the scene and did not commit any crimes. When discussing plea offers with his trial counsel, Petitioner expressed his belief that he thought he would be acquitted. Before and during his trial, during his post-conviction proceedings in State court, and in this Petition, Petitioner has consistently maintained that he was merely present at the scene and did not commit any crimes. (Doc. 3 at 10) Additionally, the record reflects that Petitioner felt that the plea offers were for too much time. (Respondents' Exh. N) Petitioner does not offer any support for his contention that he would have accepted a plea offer. The Ninth Circuit has stated that such self-serving statements are viewed with skepticism:

> [The petitioner's] self-serving statement, made years later, that [defense counsel] told him that 'this was not a death penalty case' is insufficient to establish that [the habeas petitioner] was unaware of the potential death verdict. If the rule were otherwise, every rejection of a plea offers, viewed perhaps with more clarity in the light of an unfavorable verdict, could be relitigated upon the defendant's later claim that had his counsel better advised him, he would have accepted the plea offer.

Turner v. Calderon, 281 F.3d 851, 881 (9th Cir. 2002) (internal citations omitted).

Petitioner's consistent belief that he was merely present at the scene and had not committed a crime, does not support his contention that he would have accepted any plea offer. *See Smith v. United States, 348 F.3d 545, 552 (6th Cir. 2003)* (stating that, although not dispositive, "[p]rotestations of innocence throughout trial are properly a factor" in determining whether a defendant would have accepted a plea agreement).

In sum, Petitioner has not shown that the State court's rejection of his claim of ineffective assistance of counsel was contrary to, or an unreasonable application of, clearly established federal law, or that it was based on an unreasonable determination of the facts. *28 U.S.C. § 2254.* Thus, Petitioner is not entitled to habeas corpus relief on this claim.

MICHAEL JOE MURDAUGH, PETITIONER, VS. CHARLES L. RYAN, ET AL., RESPONDENTS.

NO. CV 09-831-PHX-FJM UNITED STATES DISTRICT COURT FOR THE DISTRICT OF ARIZONA

(Text added/modified for emphasis) The Attorney General failed to disclose that in Arizona defense counsel do not thoroughly disclose plea offers, advise their clients to lie to the court , say yes to everything, and there are too many such incidents. Failure to disclose this systemic problem is fraud upon the court.

COUNSEL: For Michael Joe Murdaugh, Petitioner: Jon M Sands, LEAD ATTORNEY, Paula K Harms, Therese Michelle Day, Federal Public Defenders Office, Phoenix, AZ. For William White, Warden, Arizona State Prison - Eyman Complex, Charles L Ryan, Director, Arizona Department of Corrections (Predecessor to Dora Schriro), Respondents: Jeffrey Alan Zick, Melissa Alice Parham, Office of the Attorney General, Phoenix, AZ.

....

III. CLAIMS

....

A. Guilty Pleas: Claims 8-11

Petitioner contends that he was mentally incompetent to enter a knowing, voluntary, and intelligent guilty plea, that defense counsel performed ineffectively in handling the issue, and that the trial court failed to make an adequate competency determination before accepting the guilty pleas.

Background

At trial and sentencing Petitioner was represented by Jess Lorona, pursuant to Lorona's contract with the Maricopa County Office of Court Appointed Counsel ("OCAC"). Lorona was assisted by co-counsel (first Patricia Gitre, then Peter Claussen), investigators (Stella Salinas and Jeff Bachtle), and a mitigation specialist (first Holly Wake, then Linda Christianson).

On November 20, 1998, at the request of defense counsel, the trial court ordered that Petitioner undergo a competency screening evaluation "in preparation for a possible Change of Plea." (Doc. 35, Ex. 132.) On December 9, 1998, Dr. Jack Potts, a forensic psychiatrist, conducted the evaluation. (Doc. 35, Ex. 68.) Dr. Potts reviewed the court's minute entry ordering the evaluation, a police report regarding the Reynolds murder, a copy of the indictment, and Petitioner's Correctional Health Services medical records. (*Id.* at 1.)

According to Dr. Potts, Petitioner was "fully alert and oriented to his name, our location, and the general reason for our interview." (*Id.* at 2.) Petitioner's thought processes were "goal-directed and intact throughout" and there was "absolutely no evidence that he was suffering from perceptual disturbances such as auditory or visual hallucinations during the time of [the] evaluation." (*Id.*) Petitioner denied having any "special powers," his memory was "grossly intact for both recent and remote events," his "cognitive abilities appeared to be consistent with that of the general population, if not slightly above average," and "his abilities to abstract and conceptualize appeared to be grossly intact." (*Id.*)

Dr. Potts noted that Petitioner had "some beliefs that may be considered 'fringe.'" (*Id.*) Petitioner described having "out of body experiences." (*Id.*) He claimed to have knowledge of the Buddhist monk killings in Phoenix. (*Id.*) Petitioner also informed Dr. Potts that he believed he was "being monitored through telephone wiretaps and surveillance." (*Id.*) Petitioner was concerned that when he underwent leg surgery while incarcerated, "a location transmitting device had been implanted in his skull"; he wanted to get a CT scan or skull x-ray to confirm this suspicion. (*Id.*) Dr. Potts noted, however, that "when questioned further, the defendant said these concerns and knowledge of surveillance activities" had "nothing to do with his taking a plea." (*Id.*)

Dr. Potts determined that Petitioner understood the charges against him, was aware of his constitutional rights, knew that the prosecution would be seeking the death penalty, and understood the ramifications of pleading guilty. (*Id.*) Petitioner maintained that he was "not desirous of putting his family or the alleged victim's families through the trauma of a trial." (*Id.* at 3.)

Dr. Potts opined that Petitioner would likely be found competent. (*Id.*) His "initial impression" was that Petitioner's "belief systems do not impact on his rational or factual understanding of the proceedings he is facing, his ability to effectively assist his attorney, or his understanding of waiving his rights by entering a plea." (*Id.*)

However, while noting that Petitioner had never evidenced "any major mental illness" to the court or to the attorneys, Dr. Potts explained that Petitioner had a long history of "abusing methamphetamine" and might suffer from "a paranoid delusional disorder secondary to his past use." (*Id.*) Therefore, Dr. Potts recommended that Petitioner's competency be evaluated further, out of concern that Petitioner's paranoia might impair his judgment and could prompt him to plead guilty whether or not doing so was in his best interest. (*Id.*)

On December 10, 1998, the trial court granted Petitioner's motion for a competency determination and transferred the case to a Commissioner for further Rule 11 proceedings. (Doc. 35, Ex. 133.) The court appointed Drs. John Scialli, a psychiatrist, and Scott Sindelar, a clinical psychologist, to examine Petitioner and evaluate his competency to stand trial or plead guilty. (*Id.*, Ex. 134.) The doctors were ordered to evaluate Petitioner's "present competency," including whether he was "able to understand the nature and object of the proceeding" and "able to assist in [his] defense." (*Id.*) They were also instructed to address "whether mental illness, defect or disability has substantially impaired [Petitioner's] ability to make a competent decision concerning a waiver of rights and to have a rational, as well as factual understanding of the consequences of entering a plea of guilty," and whether Petitioner understood the constitutional rights he would give up by pleading guilty. (*Id.*)

Dr. Sindelar examined Petitioner on January 19, 1999. (Doc. 35, Ex. 69.) He determined that Petitioner was "competent to stand trial," "able to understand the nature of the proceedings against him," and "currently able to assist counsel in the preparation of his defense." (*Id.* at 1.) Dr. Sindelar noted that Petitioner had a "long history of multiple substance abuse," including intravenous injection of methamphetamine. (*Id.*) Nonetheless, Dr. Sindelar believed that Petitioner could make a competent decision concerning the waiver of his rights and that he had a "factual and a rational understanding of the consequences of pleading guilty." (*Id.* at 2.) Petitioner "appeared very knowledgeable about his alternatives and the reasons for his choices." (*Id.*) His "thought content was logical and connected except when he attempted to convince [Dr. Sindelar] that he might have an electronic device implanted in his skull"; according to Dr. Sindelar, this "content sounded delusional." (*Id.*) However, Dr. Sindelar did not believe this delusion affected Petitioner's competency or his "ability to help his attorney." (*Id.*)

Dr. Scialli examined Petitioner and also concluded that he was competent to stand trial and to plead guilty. (Doc. 35, Ex. 70 at 1.) Dr. Scialli interviewed Petitioner on January 12, 1999. (*Id.* at 1.) He reviewed police reports from Petitioner's offenses, medical records from Correctional Health Services, Dr. Potts' pre-screening report, and news stories regarding the charges against Petitioner. (*Id.* at 2.) Dr. Scialli noted that Petitioner had one prior "known psychiatric contact," an incident in 1978 when Petitioner was briefly hospitalized in Indiana while intoxicated with amphetamines. (*Id.*) In 1997, while incarcerated on the present charges, Petitioner had informed jail staff that he was depressed, suicidal, and had a sleep disorder. (*Id.*) No medication was prescribed at the time, but subsequently he was diagnosed with anxiety disorder and prescribed anti-anxiety medication. (*Id.*) Dr. Scialli indicated that he had spoken to Petitioner's ex-wife, who said that Petitioner "had been making comments about the CIA for around the year prior to his incarceration," and that Petitioner believed a tracking device had been implanted in his leg. (*Id.* at 2.)

Dr. Scialli determined that Petitioner was "criminally competent to stand trial," explaining that Petitioner was able to "understand the nature of the proceedings against him" and "assist counsel in the preparation of his own defense." (*Id.* at 2-3.) Although Petitioner possessed the "fringe" beliefs noted by Dr. Potts, Dr. Scialli found "no evidence of illogical thoughts, delusions or hallucinations." (*Id.*) Dr. Scialli also found that Petitioner's beliefs did not interfere with his reasoning ability. (*Id.*)

According to Dr. Scialli, if Petitioner "chooses to plead guilty, mental illness has not substantially impaired [his] ability to make a competent decision concerning waiver of rights, and to have a rational, as well as factual, understanding of the consequences of pleading guilty." (*Id.*) Petitioner was aware of the details of his plea agreement, which he had discussed with counsel; he specifically acknowledged to Dr. Scialli that he would still "get the death penalty even with the plea deal." (*Id.*)

Petitioner's motivation for accepting the plea deal was that "death row has a better quality of life" than that of the general prison population, and that he wanted to "spare others from the stress of a trial." (*Id.* at 4.) He also believed that the outcome would be the same whether he pled guilty or went to trial. (*Id.*) Dr. Scialli found "nothing illogical" about Petitioner's reasoning. (*Id.*) When Dr. Scialli explained "possible defense and/or mitigating factors" available in a trial, Petitioner indicated that he was "not previously aware of these things" but even with that information he would still choose to plead guilty. (*Id.*)

Finally, Dr. Scialli discussed Petitioner's desire to obtain an x-ray to identify the tracking device he believed was in his skull, and the possible effect of this desire on his decision to plead guilty. (*Id.*) Petitioner told Dr. Scialli that when he discussed the plea agreement with Lorona, Lorona told him he would get the x-ray if he signed the agreement. (*Id.*) Dr. Scialli found that Petitioner's discussion of the issue was "done in a logical way, notwithstanding no information from his attorney as to whether the skull x-ray had been discussed when discussing the plea agreement." (*Id.*) Dr. Scialli found that Petitioner's beliefs about the implant did not "interfere [] with his ability to enter a plea of guilty" and concluded that "[w]hat was more convincing was that the defendant said that he would still enter a plea(s) of guilty even if getting an x-ray were not part of the deal." (*Id.*) Dr. Scialli also noted that Petitioner would "drop" the issue if he received an x-ray and it showed no evidence of an implant. (*Id.*) According to Dr. Scialli, "This sort of reasoning is not typical of a paranoid delusion." (*Id.*)

On January 26, 1999, the parties stipulated to a determination of Petitioner's competency based on Dr. Sindelar and Dr. Scialli's reports. RT 1/26/99 at 3-4; ROA 178. The Commissioner found Petitioner competent to stand trial, concluding that he was "competent in assisting counsel in his own defense, and making rational decisions reference the handling of this matter." RT 1/26/99 at 4-5; ME 179. The Commissioner then remanded the case to the trial court for a status conference. RT 1/26/99 at 5-6; ME 179.

....

On February 1, 1999, the State filed a motion requesting that the court order Correctional Health Services to provide Petitioner with a skull x-ray. ROA 182. The prosecutor stated that the x-ray would "reassure [Petitioner] that no tracking device exists" and "alleviate any potential coercive allegations raised at any future plea proceedings." *Id.* at 2. The court granted the State's motion and ordered Correctional Health Services to perform a skull x-ray. RT 2/2/99 at 2-3.

On May 3, 1999, Lorona orally requested that Petitioner be sent back to Dr. Potts for an additional Rule 11 competency evaluation; the court granted the request. RT 5/3/99 at 3; ROA 191. Thereafter, the court granted a number of continuances for Dr. Potts to complete the evaluation. *See* RT 7/7/99 at 3-4; RT 8/11/99 at 3-4.

Dr. Potts visited Petitioner again on August 19, 1999, eight months after his initial interview, and found that Petitioner "continues to present as he has." (Doc. 35, Ex. 71 at 1.) Dr. Potts again opined that Petitioner was "very well aware of the charges he is facing" and "well aware that he has been offered a plea agreement wherein, on at least one of the cases he would be sentenced to life, and in the other case, he might receive the death penalty." (*Id.*) Dr. Potts noted that Petitioner continued to desire testing to "see if there is an implant in his brain." (*Id.*) Petitioner had already undergone a CT scan, which was "reported as negative," but, "as is not uncommon with paranoid individuals," Petitioner believed that the results might have been doctored and now wanted an MRI. (*Id.*) As discussed below, the record presented during the PCR proceedings indicates that on July 30, 1999, jail staff discovered that Petitioner had cut himself on his left wrist and elbow and on the top of both feet. (Doc. 35, Ex. 103 at 2.) He was escorted on his own power to the jail clinic where he received stitches. (*Id.*) After assuring staff that he would not harm himself further, he returned to his cell. (*Id.*) Petitioner stated that he was upset over the anniversary of his father's death. (*Id.*) Staff also found a "suicide note." (*Id.*)

Although Petitioner still believed he had a tracking device in his head, Dr. Potts stated that Petitioner did not "believe that the implant has anything to do with the legal proceedings he is facing." (*Id.* at 2.) Dr. Potts also noted that Petitioner continued to claim knowledge of the Buddhist temple murders but opined that those beliefs did not "impact on his offenses or the proceedings he is presently facing." (*Id.*)

Dr. Potts found that Petitioner was "continuing to experience paranoid beliefs and delusions secondary to his past amphetamine abuse," noting that it is not uncommon for such symptoms to persist "even for years after the cessation of amphetamines." (*Id.*) He reiterated that Petitioner's presentation was "consistent with delusions secondary to past chronic methamphetamine abuse." (*Id.* at 2.) Dr. Potts indicated, based on the information he had, that Petitioner had functioned "relatively well" before he became an addict. (*Id.*) He concluded that it was likely that Petitioner's methamphetamine use "greatly contributed to the alleged offenses having occurred." (*Id.*)

Dr. Potts again determined that Petitioner fully appreciated the rights he would waive by pleading guilty and that Petitioner was "capable of weighing various options." (*Id.* at 3.) He noted that one of Petitioner's stated reasons for entering a guilty plea was to spare the victims' families additional suffering. (*Id.*) According to Dr. Potts, a more extensive competency evaluation was not warranted, because Petitioner's delusions were "relatively circumscribed" and seemed to have little if any bearing on the proceedings. (*Id.* at 2-3.)

On October 8, 1999, Lorona informed the trial court that Dr. Potts had again found Petitioner competent and did not recommend any further competency proceedings. The trial court denied the defense motion for a full competency evaluation. RT 10/8/99 at 3-4; ROA 196.

Petitioner's change of plea hearing occurred on January 10, 2000. The trial court questioned Petitioner to determine whether he understood the proceedings. RT 1/10/00 at 10-28. The court asked Petitioner about his age, education level, whether he had difficulty reading or understanding English, and whether he was taking any medications. *Id.* at 10. Petitioner informed the court that he had taken Klonopin for anxiety and Elavil for back pain. *Id.* at 11. He stated that the medications helped him to understand the proceedings and that he understood "everything very clearly." *Id.*

The court asked Petitioner if his attorney had discussed the plea agreement with him; Petitioner stated that he had. *Id.* at 11-12. The court then informed Petitioner of the charges against him and the potential sentence on each charge. *Id.* at 12-24. Petitioner stated that he understood all of the charges and possible sentences. *Id.* at 13-17. When asked if any promises or guarantees had been made to him in exchange for his pleas, Petitioner replied, "None at all." *Id.* at 15-16, 25. Petitioner expressed a desire that the court and the State avoid speaking to the media about the offenses, but indicated that he had received no guarantees from anyone regarding media coverage. *Id.* at 20.

The court asked Petitioner if he had signed each of the plea agreements because he "understood them and agreed with them." *Id.* at 26. Petitioner responded, "Yes, ma'am." *Id.* When the court asked Petitioner if there was anything in the agreements that he did not understand, Petitioner replied, "No, ma'am." *Id.*

The court then informed Petitioner that he had a right to a separate jury trial in each of his cases, in which the "obligation would be on the state to prove [his] guilt to a jury beyond a reasonable doubt as to each count in each case." *Id.* at 27. Petitioner stated that he understood that right. *Id.* The court told Petitioner that if the case went to trial, the State would call witnesses and his attorney could cross-examine those witnesses and call witnesses on Petitioner's behalf. *Id.* at 27. The court informed Petitioner that he could choose whether or not to testify at trial and if he chose not to testify the jury could not use his silence against him. *Id.* Petitioner stated that he understood those rights. *Id.*

Petitioner pled guilty to kidnapping and first degree murder in the Eggert case and aggravated robbery, kidnapping, and first degree murder in the Reynolds case. *Id.* at 28-34. As the prosecutor described the factual bases of the charges, Petitioner occasionally interrupted to correct what he considered to be factual errors. *Id.* at 29-34. When the court questioned him regarding the factual bases of the charges, Petitioner again answered the questions clearly and offered corrections. *Id.* at 34-38. The trial court found that Petitioner's guilty pleas were knowing, intelligent, and voluntary. *Id.* at 42-43.

On appeal, during oral argument before the Arizona Supreme Court, Petitioner's appellate counsel asserted for the first time that Petitioner had been incompetent to plead guilty. *Murdaugh, 209 Ariz. at 27, 97 P.3d at 852.* Because Petitioner did not raise the claim in his opening brief, the court reviewed the claim only for fundamental error, concluded there was none, and found the claim waived. *Id.* The court explained:

> In this case, the trial judge found that Murdaugh was competent to plead guilty and that there was a sufficient factual

basis to support the plea. The judge questioned Murdaugh directly about his agreement with the State, and Murdaugh responded that he understood both the nature and the consequences of his plea. He also told the judge that he was not under the influence of alcohol at the time of the plea and that the drugs he was taking to control anxiety and back pain did not impair his ability to understand the plea proceedings. In addition, Murdaugh stated that his attorney had gone over all the terms of the plea agreement with him and that he fully understood the implications of the plea.

The trial judge did not inquire further into whether Murdaugh was mentally competent to enter the plea agreement. A year before the plea proceedings, however, Drs. Sindelar and Scialli had evaluated Murdaugh's competency to stand trial. Relying on the reports prepared by these doctors, the court had found Murdaugh competent to stand trial. Dr. Potts re-evaluated Murdaugh approximately four months before he entered into his plea agreements. Murdaugh's counsel informed the court that Dr. Potts did not recommend any further competency evaluation. From this we can infer that Dr. Potts found Murdaugh competent to understand the proceedings and assist in his defense. Finally, neither Murdaugh nor his trial counsel raised any claim, either during the change of plea or during the sentencing hearing, that Murdaugh may have been incompetent to plead guilty.

Viewing this evidence in the light most favorable to sustaining the trial court's decision, reasonable evidence supports the trial court's finding that Murdaugh was competent to enter a plea of guilty and that he entered the plea knowingly, intelligently, and voluntarily.

Id.

(1) Claim 8

Petitioner alleges that trial counsel performed ineffectively by failing to ensure that his guilty pleas were knowing, intelligent, and voluntary and by inducing him to plead guilty by making promises based on his delusions. (Doc. 35 at 168.) Respondents concede this claim is exhausted.

Clearly established federal law

Claims of ineffective assistance of counsel are governed by the principles set forth in *Strickland v. Washington, 466 U.S. 668, 104 S. Ct. 2052, 80 L. Ed. 2d 674 (1984).* To prevail under *Strickland,* a petitioner must show that counsel's representation fell below an objective standard of reasonableness and that the deficiency prejudiced the defense. *Id. at 687-88.*

The inquiry under *Strickland* is highly deferential and "every effort [must] be made to eliminate the distorting effects of hindsight, to reconstruct the circumstances of counsel's challenged conduct, and to evaluate the conduct from counsel's perspective at the time." *Id. at 689; see Wong v. Belmontes, 130 S. Ct. 383, 384, 175 L. Ed. 2d 328 (2009)* (per curiam); *Bobby v. Van Hook, 130 S. Ct. 13, 16, 175 L. Ed. 2d 255 (2009)* (per curiam). Thus, to satisfy *Strickland's* first prong, a defendant must overcome "the presumption that, under the circumstances, the challenged action might be considered sound trial strategy." *Id.* "The test has nothing to do with what the best lawyers would have done. Nor is the test even what best lawyers would have done. We ask only whether some reasonable lawyer at the trial could have acted, in the circumstances, as defense counsel acted at trial." *Id. at 687-88.*

With respect to *Strickland's* second prong, a petitioner must affirmatively prove prejudice by "show[ing] that there is a reasonable probability that, but for counsel's unprofessional errors, the result of the proceeding would have been different. A reasonable probability is a probability sufficient to undermine confidence in the outcome." *Strickland, 466 U.S. at 694.*

Because an ineffective assistance of counsel claim must satisfy both prongs of *Strickland,* the reviewing court "need not determine whether counsel's performance was deficient before examining the prejudice suffered by the defendant as a result of the alleged deficiencies." *Id. at 697.* Therefore, "if it is easier to dispose of an ineffectiveness claim on the ground of lack of sufficient prejudice . . . that course should be followed." *Id.*

Under the AEDPA, this Court's review of the state court's rulings on Petitioner's ineffective assistance claims is subject to another level of deference. *Bell v. Cone, 535 U.S. 685, 698-99, 122 S. Ct. 1843, 152 L. Ed. 2d 914 (2002); see Knowles v. Mirzayance, 129 S. Ct. 1411, 1420, 173 L. Ed. 2d 251 (2009)* (noting that a "doubly deferential" standard applies to *Strickland* claims under the AEDPA). Therefore, to prevail on this claim, Petitioner must make the additional showing that the PCR court, in ruling that trial counsel was not ineffective, applied *Strickland* in an objectively unreasonable manner. *28 U.S.C. § 2254(d)(1).*

Analysis

Petitioner sets forth a number of specific challenges to Lorona's performance. He alleges that counsel spent insufficient time working on the case, did not visit him regularly in jail, and did not consult with him. (Doc. 35 at 170-71, 175-76.) He contends that his "paranoid and disturbed" behavior should have alerted Lorona to "possible mental health and competency issues." (*Id.* at 70.) He argues that Lorona failed to provide defense experts with information regarding his interactions with Petitioner. (*Id.* at 171.) He claims that Lorona did not personally review the plea agreement with him. (*Id.* at 181.) Finally, he asserts that Lorona induced him to plead guilty by promising that he would receive a head x-ray. (*Id.* at 181.)

The PCR court rejected these allegations of ineffective assistance, finding that Petitioner's guilty plea was knowing and voluntary and noting that Petitioner appeared coherent and rational in his interactions with the trial court and assured the court that he "understood the proceedings as well as the consequences." (Doc. 31, Ex. 93 at 17.) This ruling was neither contrary to nor an unreasonable application of *Strickland,* nor was it based on an unreasonable determination of the facts. Petitioner's allegations, some of which are contrary to the record, are insufficient to establish that Lorona performed at a constitutionally ineffective level with respect to Petitioner's guilty pleas.

First, far from ignoring signs that Petitioner had mental health issues, Lorona secured examinations from three experts, all of whom found Petitioner competent to plead guilty. The court rejects

Petitioner's assertion that Lorona performed ineffectively by failing to argue that Petitioner was incompetent to enter a plea. Drs. Potts, Scialli, and Sindelar examined Petitioner and "provided detailed, reasoned reports which contained their individual opinions that [he] was competent." *Moran v. Godinez, 57 F.3d 690, 699-700 (9th Cir. 1994)*. Because Lorona was "entitled to rely on these reports," it was unnecessary for him to investigate the issue further. *Id. at 700*.

In *Taylor v. Horn, 504 F.3d 416, 438-39 (3d Cir. 2007)*, the Third Circuit held that the petitioner could show neither deficient performance nor prejudice based on counsel's failure to request a competency examination. Prior to his guilty plea, the petitioner had been found competent by two experts. *Id. at 421*. The court determined that "counsel's interactions with Taylor - paired with both the . . . reports concluding that Taylor was competent - were sufficient for counsel to reasonably forego a competency hearing." *Id. at 438*. In addition, because there was no reasonable probability that the petitioner was incompetent, counsel's failure to request a competency hearing was not prejudicial. *Id. at 439*. Similarly, in Petitioner's case, there were "sufficient indicia of competence," *id. at 438*, such that Lorona's failure to pursue an argument that Petitioner was incompetent to plead guilty did not constitute deficient performance and did not result in prejudice.

Also unavailing is Petitioner's assertion that Lorona failed to provide the Rule 11 experts with records necessary for their evaluations. Although Dr. Potts stated in his pre-screening competency report that he did not receive any information from the defense, investigator Jeff Bachtle recalled delivering documents about Petitioner's background to Dr. Potts. RT 4/29/08 at 42-43. At the evidentiary hearing before the PCR court on Petitioner's claims of ineffective assistance of counsel, Dr. Potts testified that he spoke with Lorona concerning the pre-screening evaluation but could not remember if they had further contact, nor could he recall if Bachtle had provided him with additional records. RT 5/14/08 at 37-41. Dr. Scialli testified that while he received no materials from defense counsel, he had enough information before him to make a determination. RT 4/28/08 at 30-31. Neither Dr. Potts nor Dr. Scialli suggested that their evaluations were compromised due to a lack of documentary evidence.

Next, Petitioner fails to show that Lorona performed ineffectively with respect to Petitioner's desire for a head x-ray. Petitioner himself indicated to Drs. Potts and Scialli that an x-ray was not a necessary condition of his guilty plea. (Doc. 35, Ex's. 68, 70.) In addition, prior to pleading guilty Petitioner received an x-ray at the State's request. *See* ROA 182; ME 181. Therefore, Lorona's promise of an x-ray did not serve as an inducement for Petitioner's plea.

Petitioner's complaints about counsel's lack of effort and infrequent jail visits are not sufficient to establish ineffective assistance of counsel. Although Lorona only visited Petitioner in jail five or six times over the course of his representation, he spoke to Petitioner on the phone two to three times every week and discussed the case with Petitioner during court appearances. RT 4/29/08 at 108-10, 129-30. In addition, defense investigator Bachtle visited Petitioner in jail more than 20 times and spoke with him on the phone several times a week. *Id.* at 43-45. The mitigation specialists also had contact with Petitioner in jail. *See* RT 4/28/08 at 39; RT 4/30/08 at 129.

Even if Lorona's infrequent jail visits constituted deficient performance, "the mere fact that counsel spent little time with [petitioner] is not enough under *Strickland,* without evidence of prejudice or other defects." *Bowling v. Parker, 344 F.3d 487, 506 (6th Cir. 2003).* While Petitioner alleges generally that Lorona had a duty to engage in more frequent personal contact with him, he has provided "no explanation how additional meetings with his counsel, or longer meetings with his counsel, would have led to new or better theories of advocacy or otherwise would have created a 'reasonable probability' of a different outcome." *Hill v. Mitchell, 400 F.3d 308, 325 (6th Cir. 2005); see Lenz v. Washington, 444 F.3d 295, 302-03 (4th Cir. 2006).*

Petitioner argues that the numerous delays in the proceedings reflect the extent of Lorona's other commitments and his lack of focus on Petitioner's case. However, the record indicates that Lorona requested continuances primarily to prepare for trial, because discovery was not complete, because the parties were attempting to settle the case, or because reports from the defense experts were not yet available. *See* RT 9/17/97, 4/6/98, 4/1/99, 6/7/99, 8/11/99, 10/24/00.

Other continuances were requested by the State. *See* RT 2/19/98, 6/16/98, 12/10/99. Moreover, it was Petitioner's express desire that Lorona "stretch out" the case for "as long as possible." (Doc. 35, Ex. 44; *see id.,* Ex. 6.)

Likewise, Petitioner's contention that Lorona did not discuss the plea agreement with him are not well-founded. During the PCR evidentiary hearing, Bachtle testified that Lorona, who had already reviewed the plea agreement with Petitioner, requested that he go to the jail and again discuss the agreement with Petitioner. RT 4/29/08 at 65-66; *see* Doc. 35, Ex. 76. Lorona testified that either he or co-counsel went to the jail to review the plea agreement with Petitioner. *Id.* at 150-51. Lorona also discussed the agreement with Petitioner while they were together in court. *Id.* Moreover, after being presented with the plea agreement, Petitioner wrote Lorona a letter discussing changes he would like made and concluding, "Get these matters taken care of and I will then sign the plea deals to avoid the trauma of trials on my own and the victim's families." (Doc. 35, Ex. 47.) Such statements are inconsistent with the assertion that Petitioner was unfamiliar with the terms of the plea agreement.

It is clear that from an early point in the case Petitioner expressed a desire to plead guilty in order to spare his and the victims' families the ordeal of a trial. For example, on April 18, 1996, Bachtle wrote a memo to Lorona noting that "Petitioner stated that he does NOT want to go to trial regarding his murder charges. He does NOT want to bring the victim's family or his own family into court to listen to the allegations pertaining to the victim's death." (*Id.,* Ex. 18.)

The Ninth Circuit recently reiterated that "prejudice does not generally exist when a defendant chooses to plead guilty." *Smith v. Mahoney, 596 F.3d 1133, 1146 (9th Cir. 2010)* (citing *Lambert v. Blodgett, 393 F.3d 943, 980 (9th Cir. 2004); Langford v. Day, 110 F.3d 1380, 1383-84 (9th Cir. 1996)*). Petitioner, like the defendants in *Langford* and *Smith,* "strongly and repeatedly insisted on pleading guilty and seeking the death penalty." *Langford, 110 F.3d at 1386.* He was "determined and unequivocal in his decision to plead guilty," *id. at 1388,* consistently citing as the reason for his plea a desire to spare the families the trauma of a trial. As the court stated in *Smith,* "In such cases, where 'the defendant has his own reasons for pleading guilty,' relief is not warranted." *596 F.3d at 1147* (quoting *McMann v. Richardson, 397 U.S. 759, 767, 90 S. Ct. 1441, 25 L. Ed. 2d 763 (1970)).*

Conclusion

Petitioner wanted to plead guilty, and the uncontradicted opinions of the mental health experts indicated that he was competent to do so. Lorona's performance was neither deficient nor prejudicial. Therefore, the PCR court's rejection of this claim was not objectively unreasonable and Petitioner is not entitled to relief. Claim 8 is denied.

Claude Raymond Dove, Petitioner -vs- Charles L. Ryan, et al., Respondents

CV-08-1914-PHX-MHM (JRI) UNITED STATES DISTRICT COURT FOR THE DISTRICT OF ARIZONA

(Text added/modified for emphasis) The Attorney General failed to disclose that in Arizona defense counsel do not thoroughly disclose plea offers and there are too many such incidents. Failure to disclose this systemic problem is fraud upon the court.

COUNSEL: Claude Raymond Dove, Petitioner, Pro se, TUCSON-AZ-TUCSON-ASPC-CIMARRON, TUCSON, AZ.For Dora B Schriro, Director, Attorney General of the State of Arizona, Charles L Ryan, Interim Director of AZ Department of Corrections, Respondents: Julie Ann Done, ATTORNEY, Office of the Attorney General, Phoenix, AZ.

....

3. Plea Negotiations and Burden of Proof on Prior Convictions

Settlement Conference - Prior to trial, on October 8, 2004, a consolidated settlement conference was held in both cases. (Exhibit KK, R.T. 10/8/4.) The conference began with the judge reviewing the charges and noting that the State had alleged "two prior felony convictions." (*Id.* at 2.) In reviewing the potential sentencing on the felony charges, the judge stated:

if you're convicted at trial and the State proves the prior felony convictions, <u>and the State would have to prove those at the trial beyond a reasonable doubt</u>, the absolute minimum prison sentence for each of the Class 2 felonies is 10.5 years. The standard minimum is 14 years.

(*Id.* at 2-3 (emphasis added).)

The court went on to discuss the sentencing on the other charges, and the State's offer to allow Petitioner to plead to just the two class two felonies with an agreement to cap the sentence at concurrent presumptive sentences. (*Id.* at 3-4.) The court went on to explain the sentencing effect of the proffered plea:

So the maximum you'd be facing would be nine-and-a-quarter years for everything all wrapped up instead of 35 years on each of the Class 2 felonies. These occurred on separate occasions, so you could be sentenced to consecutive sentences if you're convicted of all this at a trial or trials, and the judge would be able to do that.

(*Id.* at 4.)

Petitioner declined to accept the offer. (*Id.* at 17-18.)

<u>Priors Trial</u> - At the bench trial on the historical priors, the State proffered evidence of four prior convictions. A trial was held on the priors, with the defense opposing two as stale and asserting that the state had failed to meet its burden of proving all but one of the others beyond a reasonable doubt. (Exhibit LL R.T. 7/15/05 at 24-27, 30.) During the course of the proceeding, defense counsel argued that the State was required to prove the priors beyond a reasonable doubt, and that the State had failed to do so because fingerprints were provided only with respect to a single prior, and the use of a "pen pack" was improperly replied upon to prove the balance. The Arizona Court of Appeals described the "pen pack" as including "a certified 'Automated Summary Record' which summarized Dove's prior convictions and sentences, a certified prior conviction record, a series of photographs of Dove, a complete set of Dove's fingerprints. and a certification that all

of these documents came from Dove's DOC master record file." (Exhibit U, Mem. Dec. at 2.)

The judge disagreed on the burden of proof, but eventually recessed to research the matter. (*Id.* at 14-15, 30.) Eventually, the judge determined that the "the burden of proof on historical convictions is clear and convincing." (*Id.* at 31.)

The judge found that the state had "proved that the defendant has actually four prior felony convictions by clear and convincing evidence." (*Id.* at 32.) Nonetheless, Petitioner was sentenced on the basis of "two historical prior convictions" (*id.* at 33), which was sufficient to trigger the enhanced sentencing (*see* Exhibit U, Mem. Dec. at 3, n. 3, citing *Ariz. Rev. Stat. § 13-604(D)* ("two or more historical prior felony convictions")).

B. CONSOLIDATED PROCEEDINGS ON DIRECT APPEAL

Petitioner filed notices of appeal in both cases. (Exhibits O and P.) New counsel was appointed. (Exhibit Q, M.E. 8/8/5.) The appeals were consolidated, and a combined Opening Brief was filed by counsel, asserting insufficient evidence of the prior felony convictions, and abuse of discretion in failing to consider mitigating factors. (Exhibit R.) The Arizona Court of Appeals rejected both claims, and affirmed Petitioner's sentences. (Exhibit U, Mem. Dec.) Petitioner did not seek further review, and the mandate (Exhibit V) was issued on July 7, 2006.

C. CONSOLIDATED PROCEEDINGS ON POST-CONVICTION RELIEF

In both cases, Petitioner then filed Notice of Post-Conviction Relief. (Exhibits W and X.) The Office of the Public Defender was appointed to represent Petitioner, and the proceedings were consolidated. (Exhibit Y, M.E. 6/26/6.) Petitioner filed a PCR Petition (Exhibit X) raising a single claim of ineffective assistance of counsel, asserting that trial counsel had incorrectly advised Petitioner during plea negotiations on the state's burden of proof on prior convictions. Petitioner cited no federal authority in support of his Petition. The Petition was summarily denied on December 8, 2006. (Exhibit CC, Ruling.)

Petitioner filed through counsel a Petition for Review (Exhibit DD), again raising the single claim of ineffective assistance of trial counsel. Petitioner cited a single federal authority, *U.S. v. Day, 969 F.2d 39 (3rd*

Cir. 1992) for the proposition that relief on the claim was available even if Petitioner received a fair trial. (Exhibit DD at 7.) The Arizona Court of Appeals summarily denied review. (Exhibit FF, Order 10/19/07.)

Petitioner then filed a *pro se* Petition for Review by the Arizona Supreme Court (Exhibit GG). Petitioner again raised the same claim of ineffective assistance. The Arizona Supreme Court summarily denied review. (Exhibit II, Order 4/1/8.)

....

B. GROUND ONE - INEFFECTIVE ASSISTANCE OF COUNSEL

In his Ground One, Petitioner asserts that trial counsel was ineffective in failing to properly advise Petitioner on the burden of proof for prior convictions, resulting in Petitioner rejecting a favorable plea offer. (Petition, #1 at 6.)

1. Standard of Review

The AEDPA creates a limit on what errors entitle a state prisoner to relief. Relief is only warranted if the state court's decision of a matter was "contrary to, or an unreasonable application of, clearly established Federal law, as determined by the Supreme Court of the United States." *28 U.S.C. §2254(d)(1)*

This claim was presented in Petitioner's first PCR proceeding. (Exhibit X, PCR Pet.; Exhibit DD, Pet.Rev.) The trial court issued a summary denial (Exhibit CC, Order 12/8/6), as did the Arizona Court of Appeals (Exhibit FF, Order 10/19/07) and the Arizona Supreme Court (Exhibit II, Order 4/1/8).

Where there is no reasoned rejection of the claim, it is impossible to ascertain whether the state court identified the correct law, or whether they applied it reasonably. This Court is left to applying its own evaluation, comparing the outcome to that of the state court, and only then if there is a discrepancy can this court begin to evaluate whether the state court outcome was "contrary to [*36] or an unreasonable application of" Supreme Court law. *See Himes v. Thompson, 336 F.3d 848, 853 and n.3 (9th Cir. 2003)* ("Independent review of the record is not de novo review of the constitutional issue, but rather, the only method by which we can determine whether a silent state court decision is objectively unreasonable"). *See also Wilson v. Czerniak, 355 F.3d 1151, 1154 (9th Cir. 2004).*

In *Nunes v. Mueller*, the Ninth Circuit acknowledged that Supreme Court law has never explicitly addressed whether the right of effective assistance of counsel extends to a decision to reject a plea offer, and thus a state court decision rejecting such a claim could not be "contrary to" Supreme Court law. *350 F.3d 1045, 1053 (9th Cir. 2003).* Nonetheless, the *Nunes* court recognized that such a claim is cognizable under *Strickland* and went on to evaluate the state court's decision under the "unreasonable application" prong of § 2254(d)(1).

Because there was no reasoned rejection of Petitioner's claim, this Court must undertake its own evaluation of Petitioner's claim.

2. Standard for Ineffective Assistance

Generally, claims of ineffective assistance of counsel are analyzed pursuant to *Strickland v. Washington, 466 U.S. 668, 104 S. Ct. 2052, 80 L. Ed. 2d 674 (1984).* In order to prevail on such a claim, Petitioner must show: (1) deficient performance - counsel's representation fell below the objective standard for reasonableness; and (2) prejudice - there is a reasonable probability that, but for counsel's unprofessional errors, the result of the proceeding would have been different. *Id. at 687-88.* Although the petitioner must prove both elements, a court may reject his claim upon finding either that counsel's performance was reasonable or that the claimed error was not prejudicial. *Id. at 697.*

3. Application to Petitioner's Claim

Respondents contend that this clam is without merit because: (1) the erroneous advice on the burden of proof on prior convictions came after the plea agreement expired; (2) there is no evidence to support Petitioner's contention that the erroneous advice affected his decision to reject the plea offer, because Petitioner rejected the plea on the basis that it would result in a nine year sentence. (Supp. Answer, #16 at 13-16.) Moreover, Respondents contend that the state court's decision must be upheld because the result reached was not objectively unreasonable.

Method of Applying *Strickland* Unreasonable - However, a tenable conclusion is not the only the hallmark of an objectively reasonable decision. As recognized in *Nunes v. Mueller, 350 F.3d 1045 (9th Cir. 2003)*, "[u]nder the AEDPA standard of review, it is entirely appropriate-even necessary-that federal courts ask whether the state court applied correct legal principles (in this case, the *Strickland* analysis) in an objectively unreasonable way, an inquiry that requires analysis of the state court's *method* as well as its result." *Id. at 1054* (citations omitted, emphasis in original). The *Nunes* court found that the California court had applied *Strickland* unreasonably because it summarily rejected the petitioner's claim of ineffectiveness in a rejected plea despite the fact that the Petitioner had "clearly made out a prima facie case of ineffective assistance of counsel under *Strickland.*" (*Id.*)

Here, the trial court rejected Petitioner's ineffective assistance claim on the basis that Petitioner "failed to present a colorable claim for relief." (Exhibit CC, Order 12/8/6.) As a result, Petitioner was not permitted an evidentiary hearing, and the court did not evaluate the evidence underlying his claims.

However, Petitioner's assertion that trial counsel rendered defective advice and resulted in his rejection of a plea he would have otherwise accepted, laid out an ineffective assistance claim under *Strickland.* No other fact need have been alleged to make out such a claim.

An Arizona PCR petition is not required, under the Arizona Rules of Criminal Procedure to contain conclusive evidence supporting a claim nor even all evidence a petitioner hopes to present in support of his claim.

> A defendant is entitled to an evidentiary hearing when he presents a colorable claim, that is a claim which, if defendant's allegations are true, might have changed the outcome. When doubts exist, "a hearing should be held to allow the defendant to raise the relevant issues, to resolve the matter, and to make a record for review."

State v. Watton, 164 Ariz. 323, 328, 793 P.2d 80, 85 (1990) (internal citations omitted). The PCR court was "obligated to treat his factual allegations as true." *State v. Jackson, 209 Ariz. 13, 15-16, 97 P.3d 113, 115-116 (App. 2004). See also State v. Richmond, 114 Ariz. 186, 194, 560*

P.2d 41, 49 (1976), overruled on other grounds, State v. Salazar, 173 Ariz.399, 416, 844 P.2d 566, 583 (1992) ("To be colorable, a claim has to have the appearance of validity, i.e., if the defendant's allegations are taken as true, would they change the verdict?").

The evidentiary requirements for supporting a petition are far from strenuous:

> Facts within the defendant's personal knowledge shall be noted separately from other allegations of fact and shall be under oath. Affidavits, records, or other evidence currently available to the defendant supporting the allegations of the petition shall be attached to it.

Ariz. R. Crim. P. 32.5.

Here, Petitioner made out essentially the same allegations as the petitioner in *Nunes*:

> With Nunes' claims being taken at face value as the state court claimed it had done, the factual scenario was (1) that Nunes' attorney gave him the wrong information and advice about the state's plea offer and (2) that if Nunes had instead been informed accurately, he would expressly have taken the bargain.

350 F.3d at 1054. The only difference in Petitioner's allegations were that the claimed error was not on the plea offer itself, but on the alternatives to that offer. Despite those allegations, the Arizona court concluded that Petitioner had failed to make out a colorable claim. "With the state court having purported to evaluate [Petitioner's] claim for sufficiency alone, it should not have required [Petitioner] to prove his claim without affording him an evidentiary hearing." *Nunes, 350 F.3d at 1054.* Refusing to do so was an objectively unreasonable application of *Strickland.*

However, while an unreasonable application of Supreme Court law is necessary to habeas relief, it is not sufficient. Petitioner must still show to this Court that his claim is meritorious. In *Nunes*, the district court had concluded that the ineffective assistance claim was meritorious, and thus the dispute on appeal focused on whether the requirements of *28 U.S.C. § 2254(d)* had been met.

<u>Defective Performance</u> - Petitioner contends that he rejected the plea offer of a maximum of 9.25 years in prison based upon trial counsel's advice that the state would have to prove his prior convictions "beyond a reasonable doubt" and that the evidence they had available, *i.e.* the ADC "pen pack" would not meet that burden. As it turned out, some three months before Petitioner's settlement conference, the Arizona Court of Appeals had determined that the actual burden of proof was "clear and convincing." *See State v. Cons, 208 Ariz. 409, 94 P.3d 609 (App. 2004)* (decided July 22, 2004).

Timing of Advice - Respondents contend that the erroneous advice came after the plea offer had already expired. They point to the fact that the only time this advice was given on the record was at the sentencing proceedings in July, 2005, long after the plea offer purportedly had expired. [5] (Suppl. Ans. #16 at 14.) They argue that Petitioner "rejected" the offer at the settlement conference on October 8, 2004. At the settlement conference, the prosecutor agreed to extend the deadline for excepting the offer through the following Monday. (Exhibit KK, R.T. 10/8/4.) It is not clear to the undersigned that the plea was "rejected." The transcript simply reveals that Petitioner declined to accept it at the time of the hearing. The conclusion of the hearing was:

> THE COURT: I take it you don't want to accept it today?
> THE DEFENDANT: No, No.
> THE COURT: All right. Have a nice weekend.
> THE DEFENDANT: All right. You, too.

However, the advice need not have been on the record to support Petitioner's claim. *See Nunes, 350 F.3d at 1055, n.6* (observing the tension between *Strickland* and a rule requiring evidence beyond a defendant's own statement). Petitioner points to the fact that prior to Petitioner's declining to accept the plea offer, the trial judge had advised Petitioner, without correction by trial counsel, that "the State would have to prove [the prior felony convictions] at trial beyond a reasonable doubt." (Exhibit KK, R.T. 10/8/04 at 2-3.) (*See* Petition, #1 at

7.) Corroboration of Petitioner's allegations flows from the fact that counsel continued to argue the erroneous position at sentencing. Nonetheless, the undersigned is not prepared to finally determine the timing (or even the existence) of such advice without an evidentiary hearing to evaluate Petitioner's credibility, and without any testimony by trial counsel.

Regardless, this Court need not resolve the timing issue to resolve Petitioner's claim.

Prejudice - Petitioner must not only show deficient performance, but prejudice. To establish prejudice from incorrect advice resulting in rejection of a plea offer, Petitioner "must show that there is a reasonable probability that he would have accepted the plea agreement had he received accurate advice from his attorney." *Hoffman v. Arave, 455 F.3d 926, 941-942 (9th Cir. 2006), judgment vacated in part on other grounds by Arave v. Hoffman, 552 U.S. 117, 128 S.Ct. 749, 169 L. Ed. 2d 580 (2008).* Respondents argue that Petitioner would have rejected the plea offer even with the correct advice, pointing to his aversion to going "to prison for nine years, signing my life away for nine years." (Exhibit KK, R.T. 10/8/4 at 16.)

Of course, in his verified Petition (#1 at 6) and in his verified Supplemental Reply, Petitioner avows that "[h]ad petitioner been furnished accurate information before and at his Settlement Conference Hearing, this petitioner would have accepted the State's Plea Offer." (#17 at 21.) However, this Court is not obligated to accept Petitioner's bare, after-the-fact assertion, but is required to evaluate all the circumstances. *Cf. Hill v. Lockhart, 474 U.S. 52, 59, 106 S. Ct. 366, 88 L. Ed. 2d 203 (1985)* (court required to assess likelihood of different decision in instance where plea *accepted* on basis of bad advice).

Here, Petitioner's underlying contention is that he decided to go to trial on the erroneous conclusion that he could get a better deal at trial by, in part, successfully defeating the State's allegations of prior convictions because the State's offer of evidence, namely the ADC "pen pack", did not provide proof beyond a reasonable doubt of all the prior convictions alleged. However, Petitioner specifically argues that trial counsel "had explained to petitioner prior to the Settlement Conference, 'that he should not take that particular plea offer of the pleading guilty to the two (2) Class-II felony's with One (1) prior conviction for the presumptive term of Nine-and-a-Quarter (9.25) years where the State's Pen Pack (in presumed error) only contained one (1) photograph, One (1) Set of Finger-prints, of One specific Conviction which could only prove One (1) Prior Conviction.' " (Supp. Reply, #17 at 10.) Thus, under Petitioner's version of the facts, he proceeded to trial on the assumption that the state would only be able to prove one prior conviction.

Plea Range - The plea offers provided for Petitioner to plead to the two Class 2 felony charges with one prior felony conviction, dismiss the Class 6 paraphernalia charge, and stipulate to concurrent sentences capped at the presumptive. That resulted in an effective sentencing range of 4.5 to 9.25 years, with a presumptive concurrent sentence of 9.25 years. (Exhibit KK, R.T. 10/8/4 at 3-4.)

Assumed Range - Petitioner claims that he was led to believe that if he rejected the plea offer and was convicted, he would face sentencing on the basis of only one prior felony. With just one prior conviction, Petitioner would have faced sentences of 4.5 to 23.25 years on each Class 2 felony, and .75 to 2.75 years on the Class 6 felony, which if consecutive would be a sentencing range of 5.25 to 49.25 years, with a presumptive concurrent sentence of 9.25 years. (Supp. Rep. Exh. G, Sentencing Table) *See also Ariz. Rev. Stat. § 13-702.01 (2003)* (repealed effective 1/1/09). Arizona courts have discretion to select either consecutive or concurrent sentences. *State v. Garza, 192 Ariz. 171, 174-175, 962 P.2d 898, 901-901 (1998).*

Actual Range - Finally, based upon the finding of two or more priors, Petitioner ultimately faced a sentencing range of 10.5 to 35 years on each Class 2 felony, and 2.25 to 5.75 years on the Class 6 felony, for an effective range of 12.75 to 75.75 years, with a concurrent presumptive sentence of 15.75 years. (Supp. Rep. Exh. G, Sentencing Table; Exhibit KK, R.T. 10/8/4 at 3.) *See also Ariz. Rev. Stat. § 13-702.01 (2003)* (repealed effective 1/1/09).

Given the disparity between the assumed sentencing range at trial and the actual range, and the lack of disparity between the offered plea sentencing range and the assumed trial range, it is not unreasonable to believe that a defendant might elect trial under the assumed trial sentencing range, but would have chosen the plea had he known the actual sentencing range.

That is particularly so where, as here, the defendant believed there were substantive defenses to be exploited at trial. For example, at the settlement conference, Petitioner, counsel and the court discussed the potential for a motion to suppress, and an entrapment defense. (Exhibit KK, R.T. 10/8/4 at 14-17.) Petitioner goes to some lengths to explain why there was no assertion by him or counsel of the lack of evidence on the prior convictions, arguing that to do so would have alerted the prosecution to the weakness in their evidence on the priors while they still had time to shore it up. (Supp. Reply, #17 at 8-15.) That explanation is plausible, but does not alter the undersigned's conclusions.

Based solely upon the foregoing, the undersigned might be able to conclude that there is a reasonable probability that but for counsel's erroneous advice Petitioner would have accepted the plea offer.

However, by the time that trial was prepared to begin, Petitioner had experienced a change of heart and was seeking to revive the plea offer. (Supp. Reply, #17 Exhibit H, R.T.17/25/05 at 6-10; Exhibit LL R.T. 7/15/05 at 50-51.) Other than the proximity of trial, the only thing that had changed was Petitioner's loss of his suppression motion. (Exhibit A, Docket at items 30-32.) Petitioner (and, based upon his arguments at sentencing, counsel) continued to believe at that time that the priors required proof beyond a reasonable doubt. This suggests that the burden of proof issue was at least not the sole basis for declining the plea offer.

Moreover, the record reflects that Petitioner and counsel were not focused on the potential exposure at trial, but were preoccupied with the belief that the prosecutor was being unusually harsh in his dealings with Petitioner, and that a better plea offer could eventually be obtained. That was a centerpiece of Petitioner's explicit reasoning in declining the plea at the settlement conference:

THE DEFENDANT: . . . It was like nine people that has been arrested at the same time as I was, and none of them have gotten nine years for the little rock they had. People have gone home on probation.

(Exhibit KK, R.T. 10/8/4 at 8.)

THE DEFENDANT: . . .But yet you want to lock me away forever. But people who have pounds, tons of cocaine are getting probation. I don't think it's fair.

THE COURT: Well, let me interrupt you, Mr. Dove, because your argument isn't with me. Your argument is with them. I understand I asked you if you had any questions, but they control the plea offer that they make. I can't tell the State what to offer you, and this is the best they are offering. And if they don't --

MR. TERPSTRA [defense counsel]: I'm sorry, judge. I think it should be clear, as I have told your Honor and Mr. Dove, and the record should be clear, the things Mr. Dove is saying I have brought to the attention of [the prosecutor] Mr. Yost. And the names he's given me of the other people arrested, I followed up on and talked to their attorneys and brought it to the attention of Mr. Yost to show just these things.

(*Id.* at 9.)

THE DEFNDANT: Okay, I understand what you just said. But if they are so bad on drug offenders, why the people that got arrested with me went home on probation? If they so bad on drug offenders, they should be locked up along with me. That's all I am saying. I just think there is favoritism being played here. Something is going on here.

(*Id.* at 11.)

Even at the time of trial, it was suggested that the reason for the rejection of the plea was not based upon an evaluation of the plea versus trial, but on the belief that a better plea would be offered.

MR. TERPSTRA: . . . We had a settlement conference previously with Judge Howser [sic] and Mr. Dove rejected the offer at that time. We've had a further discussion, myself and Mr. Yost and Mr. Dove about trying to make an improvement on the offer. Mr. Yost has consistently not be [sic] willing to improve on the offer that had been extended.

Today, the morning of trial, Mr. Dove expressed to me that he would like to take that offer, would like to take that plea bargain as it had been offered. I explained to him, as he knew, the deal had been off the table. I also told him that we could try and get it back.

(Supp. Reply, #17, Exhibit H, R.T. 1/25/05 at 7-8.)

THE WITNESS [Petitioner]: Yes. I really don't have no excuse for what I did, I was suffering from a disease. I'm not a drug seller at all, I was hooked on crack cocaine. I didn't quite understand what was going on because it was a sting operation that got a lot of smokers off the street, like ten of us got locked up the same day. *All the people that got locked up, the most any of them got was three years or probation and they wanted me to do nine years, that's why I didn't want to take the plea bargain.* I thought they would give me three years, too. The rest of the people involved was smoking drugs just like me and they got three years and two years and they want to give me nine years.

I would like to take, if I could, take the plea bargain now because if I lose, I'm going to get more than nine years so --

(*Id.* at 9 (emphasis added).)

At sentencing, trial counsel pursued this line so far as to suggest that the individual prosecutor, Mr. Yost, had some special animus in these types of cases that resulted in unfavorable plea offers. Counsel argued that most similar cases resulted in much more favorable plea offers. (Exhibit LL, R.T. 7/15/05 at 45-48.) He argued that in another case he defended in which the same prosecutor had prosecuted, a similar offer had been made by Mr. Yost.

MR. TERPSTRA: . . . Same offer, plead to nine and a quarter years or prior with class two with a prior and he didn't budge from that offer either. . . . Never budged from the offer.

Went to a different prosecutor, settlement conference, easily dropped another prior, pled without a prior, got a super mitigated sentence three years after Mr. Yost was off the case.

THE COURT: Was there a settlement conference in this case?

MR. TERPSTRA: Absolutely, before Judge Hauser. Mr. Yost never budged from the offer.

I don't think Mr. Yost is a bad guy. When he says he was reasonable, I never believe that Mr. Dove, compared to other defendants or circumstances of this case should have got the offer that he did but that was the offer and clearly it was better than losing at trial.

Clearly he did reject it and he was let out of custody in November by Judge Hicks on both cases and Mr. Yost says he's not numb to certain things. He's certainly numb to the situation that someone that does have an addiction like Mr. Dove and how they process information. He's not the same person as you or me, come on dummy, nine and a quarter versus 15. If you reject it, how could you be so stupid. Look at the obvious differences --

THE COURT: I don't know what you're saying, is he not competent?

MR. TERPSTRA: He's perfectly competent. He doesn't view reality in the same ways. He's desperate. *He kept believing through the whole thing it would get better*, I'm telling him --

(*Id.* at 48-51 (emphasis added).)

All of this suggests that Petitioner's rejection of the plea was not a weighing of the plea versus the potential outcomes at trial (and thus dependent upon counsel's defective advice on the priors), but was instead based upon a weighing of the plea against the potential that a better plea would eventually be forthcoming. Testimony from counsel or Petitioner at any habeas evidentiary hearing would have to be weighed against these statements on the record, and Petitioner suggests no reason to believe they would eliminate the reasonableness of a decision to rely instead upon the inferences from the existing record.

Given the record of the proceedings in this case, the undersigned cannot conclude that there is a reasonable probability that the defective advice made the difference in Petitioner's decision to let the plea offer pass unaccepted.

REFERENCES

1 U.S. Supreme Court Justice Anthony Kennedy, Address at American Bar Association Annual Meeting (Aug. 9, 2003) (transcript available at http://www. abanow.org/2003/08/speech-by-justice-anthony-kennedy-at-aba-annual-meeting/).

2 Harmelin v. Michigan, 501 U.S. 957 (1991). The Supreme Court upheld a life without parole sentence for simple possession of a little more than a pound of cocaine, a non-violent offense. The case involved Michigan's "650 Lifer Law," which made LWOP mandatory for any offender possessing more than 650 grams of cocaine or heroin. The law resulted in overcrowding in prisons, requiring many to be granted commutations by the state's governor.

3 Ewing v. California, 538 U.S. 11 (2003). Ewing was convicted of felony grand theft for stealing three golf clubs, worth $399 a piece. Because Ewing had been convicted previously of four felonies, he received a 25 years to life sentence pursuant to California's three strikes law.

4 Rummel v. Estelle, 445 U.S. 263 (1980). The defendant was convicted in Texas for two felonies (fraudulent use of a credit card to obtain $80 worth of goods or services, and passing a forged check in the amount of $28) and was convicted of a third felony, obtaining $121 by false pretenses, and received a mandatory life sentence under Texas's recidivist statute.

5 Jacob Carpenter, *East Naples Man's Life Sentence for Child Porn Too Harsh, Attorney Says*, Naples News, Nov. 3, 2011, http://www.naplesnews.com/ news/2011/nov/03/east-naples-mans-life-sentence-child-porn-too-hars/.

6 Testimony of Michelle Collette, (Sep. 20, 2011). http://www.famm.org/Repository/Files/COLLETTE%20TESTIMONY%209-20-11.pdf (last accessed April 3, 2012). Arrested in Massachusetts in possession of 607 Percocet pills, a prescription painkiller, Collette faced a 15-year minimum under Massachusetts' mandatory minimum for drug trafficking.

7 Graham v. Florida, 130 S.Ct. 2011, 2026 (2010). The Court noted that "even a 5-year-old, theoretically" could be prosecuted criminally. The word "theoretically" denotes that prosecutors refraining from prosecuting juveniles of especially young age is a matter of practice rather than law. Although criminal prosecutions of very young offenders may not be practiced currently, the lack of statutory definitions of age of criminal responsibility could permit this practice to change over time.

8 Berkus v. Illinois, 359 U.S. 121, 124, 128-129 (1959); Abbate v. United States, 359 U.S. 187 (1959).

9 1 U.S.C.A. § 109 (West 2012); S. David Mitchell, *In with the New, Out with the Old: Expanding the Scope of Retroactive Amelioration*, 37 Am. J. Crim. L. 1, 5 (2009).

10 International Covenant on Civil and Political Rights, Dec. 16 1966, S. Treaty Doc. No. 95-20 (1992), art. 10(3), 999 U.N.T.S. 171.

11 Ashley Nellis & Ryan S. King, The Sentencing Project, No Exit: The Expanding Use of Life Sentences in America, (2009).

12 John L. Anderson, The Label of Life Imprisonment in Australia: A Principled or Populist Approach to an Ultimate Sentence 1 (2012) (unpublished manuscript) (on file with authors). This figure refers to known cases in five of eight jurisdictions in Australia.

13 Vinter and Others v. United Kingdom, Apps. Nos. 66069/09 and 130/10 and 3896/10, Eur. Ct. H.R., para. 37 (2012) (this figure refers to cases of "whole life orders" in England and Wales).

14 Dirk van Zyl Smit, *Outlawing Irreducible Life Sentences: Europe on the Brink?* 23 Fed. Sent. R. 39, 41 (2010).

15 U.S. Population as 313,292,000. *Resident Population of the United States,* United States Census Bureau, http://www.census.gov/population/www/ popclockus.html (last visited Apr. 12, 2012); Australia's population as 22,876,120. *Population Clock,* Australian Bureau of Statistics, http://www.abs.gov.au/ ausstats/abs@.nsf/94713ad445ff1425ca256820 00192af2/1647509ef7e25faaca2568a900154b63?OpenDocument (last visited Apr.

12, 2012); England and Wales as 54,072,000. Simon Rogers, *England and Wales' population broken down by race, sex, age, and place*, The Guardian (Feb. 26, 2010, 12:06PM), http://www.guardian.co.uk/news/datablog/2010/feb/26/population-ethnic-race-age-statistics#data (last visited Apr. 12, 2012); Netherlands as 16,728,091. *Statline,* Central Bureau voor de Statistiek, http://statline.cbs.nl/StatWeb/publication/?VW=T HYPERLINK "http://statline.cbs.nl/StatWeb/publication/?VW=T&DM=SLEN&PA=37943eng&LA=EN"& HYPERLINK "http://statline.cbs.nl/StatWeb/publication/?VW=T&DM=SLEN&PA=37943eng&LA=EN"DM=SLEN HYPERLINK "http://statline.cbs.nl/StatWeb/publication/?VW=T&DM=SLEN&PA=37943eng&LA=EN"& HYPERLINK "http://statline.cbs.nl/StatWeb/publication/?VW=T&DM=SLEN&PA=37943eng&LA=EN"PA=37943eng HYPERLINK "http://statline.cbs.nl/StatWeb/publication/?VW=T&DM=SLEN&PA=37943eng&LA=EN"& HYPERLINK "http://statline.cbs.nl/StatWeb/publication/?VW=T&DM=SLEN&PA=37943eng&LA=EN"LA=EN.

16 *Rough Justice in America, Too Many Law, Too Many Prisoners,* The Economist, Jul. 22, 2010, *available at,* http://www.economist.com/node/16636027 (last visited Apr. 9, 2012); Emily Bazelon, *Arguing Three Strikes,* N.Y. Times, May 21, 2010, *available at,* http://www.nytimes.com/2010/05/23/ magazine/23strikes-t.html (last visited Apr. 9, 2012).

17 Jacqueline E. Ross, *Damned Under Many Headings: The Problem of Multiple Punishment,* 29 Am. J. Crim. L. 245, 249 (2002).

18 MaryBeth Lipp, *A New Perspective on the "War on Drugs": Comparing the Consequences of Sentencing Policies in the United States and England,* 37 Loy. L.A. L. Rev. 979, 1014 (2004).

19 Don Cipriani, Children's Rights and the Minimum Age of criminal Responsibility 221-222, (Ashgate, 2009).

20 Committee on the Rights of the Child, General Comment No. 10: Children's Rights in Juvenile Justice, para. 33, U.N. Doc. CRC/C/GC/10 (April 25, 2007).

21 Connie de la Vega and Michelle Leighton, *Sentencing our Children to Die in Prison: Global Law and Practice*, 42 U.S.F. L. Rev. 983 (2008).

22 U.N. Convention on Rights of the Child, GA Res. 44/25, Annex, U.N. GAOR, 44th Sess., Supp. No. 49, U.N. Doc. A/44/49 (Nov. 20, 1989). It is important to note that although a transitional government has been in place since 2004, Somalia's regions are controlled through other local governing bodies who act independently of one another without a central governing body. *The World Factbook*, The CIA, https://www.cia.gov/library/publications/the-worldfactbook/ geos/so.html (last visited Apr. 11, 2012). Additionally, South Sudan is a newly formed country, gaining independence on July 9th, 2011. *The World Factbook*, The CIA, https://www.cia.gov/library/publications/the-world-factbook/geos/od.html (last visited Apr. 11, 2012).

23 Bartkus v. Illinois, 359 U.S. 121, 124, 128-129 (1959); Abbate v. United States, 359 U.S. 187 (1959); Jeffrey S. Raynes, *Federalism vs. Double Jeopardy: A Comparative Analysis of Successive Prosecutions in the United States, Canada, and Australia*, 5 Cal. W. Int'l L. J. 399 (1974); Micronesia, Trust Territory Controlled Substances Act, Pub. L. No. 5-110, §299.

24 1 U.S.C.A. § 109 (West 2012); S. David Mitchell, *In with the New, Out with the Old: Expanding the Scope of Retroactive Amelioration*, 37 Am. J. Crim. L. 1, 5 (2009).

25 Lauren E. Glaze, Bureau of Justice Statistics, Correctional Population in the United States, 2010 3 (Dec. 2011), *available at* http://bjs.ojp. usdoj.gov/content/pub/pdf/cpus10.pdf; International Centre for Prison Studies, Entire world - Prison Population Rates per 100,000 of the national population, *available at* http://www.prisonstudies.org/info/worldbrief/wpb_stats.php?area=all HYPERLINK "http://www.prisonstudies.org/info/worldbrief/wpb_stats.php?area=all&category=wb_poprate"& HYPERLINK "http://www.prisonstudies.org/info/worldbrief/wpb_stats.php?area=all&category=wb_poprate"category=wb_poprate.

28 Adam Liptak, *Inmate Counts in U.S. Dwarfs Other Nations'*, N.Y. Times, Apr. 23, 2008, http://www.nytimes.com/2008/04/23/us/23prison.html.

29 Arnold Schwarzenegger, State of the Union Address (Jan. 6, 2010) (transcript available at http://www.cahcc.com/index.php/the-news/150-transcript-ofgov-arnold-schwarzenegger-delivering-state-of-the-state-address).

30 Liptak, *supra* note 28.

31 For example, burglary convicts serve on average 16 months in prison in the United States, compared to five months in Canada or seven months in England. *Id.* (citing Marc Mauer, Executive Director of The Sentencing Project).

32 International Covenant on Civil and Political Rights, *supra* note 10, art. 10(3).

33 The Pew Center on the States, Public Opinions on Sentencing and Corrections Policy in America (2012), *available at* http://www. pewcenteronthestates.org/uploadedFiles/wwwpewcenteronthestatesorg/Initiatives/PSPP/PEW_NationalSurveyResearchPaper_FINAL.pdf.

34 *See, e.g.*, Principled Sentencing: Readings on Theory and Policy vi (Andrew von Hirsch, Andrew Ashworth & Julian Roberts eds., Hart Publishing, 2nd ed. 1998); Anthony Bottoms, *The Philosophy and Politics of Punishment and Sentencing, in* The Politics of Sentencing Reform 18 (Chris Clarkson & Rod Morgan eds., 1995), Julian Roberts et al., Penal Populism and Public Opinion: Lessons from Five Countries 5-8 (2003); Anderson, *supra* note 12.

35 The Institute on Money in State Politics, Policy Lockdown: Prison Interests Court Political Players (2006), *available at* http://www. followthemoney.org/press/Reports/200605021.pdf; Martha Elena Menendez, Human Rights Advocates Prison Privatization and Prison Labor: The Human Rights Implications, 6-7 (2012), *available at* http://www.humanrightsadvocates.org/wp-content/uploads/2010/05/Prison- Privatization-and-Forced-Prison-Labor-2012.pdf.

36 Corrections Corporation of America contributed $1.1 million and GEO Group $880,000. The Institute on Money in State Politics, Policy Lockdown: Prison

Interests Court Political Players (2006), *available at* http://www.followthemoney.org/press/Reports/200605021.pdf.

37 American Civil Liberties Union, Banking on Bondage: Private Prisons and Mass Incarceration (2011), http://www.aclu.org/prisonersrights/banking-bondage-private-prisons-and-mass-incarceration (last accessed April 11, 2012); Brian Gran & William Henry, *Holding Private Prisons Accountable: A Socio-Legal Analysis of "Contracting Out" Prisons*, 34 Social Justice 173 (2007-2008), *available at* http://www.case.edu/artsci/soci/Gran/documents/Gran_Henry.pdf.

38 Joan Petersilia, *California's Correctional Paradox of Excess and Deprivation*, 37 Crime & Just. 207, 224 (2008).

39 Alexander Volokh, *Privatization and the Law and Economics of Political Advocacy*, 66 Stan. L. Rev. 1197 (2008).

40 Id.

41 Tim Kowal, *The Role of the Prison Guards Union in California's Troubled Prison System*, League of Ordinary Gentlemen, (June 5, 2011), http://ordinarygentlemen.com/blog/2011/06/05/the-role-of-the-prison-guards-union-in-californias-troubled-prison-system/; Volokh, *supra* note 39, at 1197.

42 Volokh, *supra* note 39, at 1197.

66 *See, e.g.*, International Covenant on Civil and Political Rights, *supra* note 10, art. 7; Universal Declaration of Human Rights, art. 5, December 10, 1948, G.A Res. 217A (III), U.N. Doc. A/810 at 71 (1948); European Convention on Human Rights, art. 3, Nov. 4, 1950, 213 U.N.T.S. 221; Charter of Fundamental Rights of the European Union, art. 4, Dec. 7, 2000, C 364/1; Convention Against Torture, art. 16, Dec. 10, 1984, 1465 U.N.T.S. 85, 113; Dirk van Zyl Smit and Andrew Ashworth, *Disproportionate Sentences as Human Rights Violations*, 67 Mod. L. Rev. 541, 543 (2004).

67 Adam Gopnick, *The Caging of America,* The New Yorker, Jan. 30, 2012; Nancy J. King, *Portioning Punishment: Constitutional Limits on Successive and Excessive Penalties*, 144 U. Pa. L. Rev. 101 (1995).

68 Nancy J. King, *Portioning Punishment: Constitutional Limits on Successive and Excessive Penalties*, 144 U. Pa. L. Rev. 101 (1995).

69 Coker v. Georgia, 433 U.S. 584 (1977); Kennedy v. Louisiana, 128 S. Ct. 2641 (2008).

70 Roper v. Simmons, 543 U.S. 551 (2005).

71 Atkins v. Virginia, 536 U.S. 304 (2002).

72 Roper, 543 U.S. at 563-64.

73 *See* Rummel v. Estelle, 445 U.S. 263 (1980) (allowing life with parole for obtaining money under false pretenses under a recidivist statute); Harmelin Michigan, 501 U.S. 957 (1991) (allowing life without parole for possession of cocaine); Ewing v. California, 538 U.S. 11 (2003) (allowing 25 years to life under a "three strikes" recidivism statute); Hutto v. Davis, 454 U.S. 370 (1982) (allowing forty years imprisonment for selling marijuana). *See also,* Solem v. Helm, 463 U.S. 277 (1983) (striking down LWOP for passing a worthless check); Youngjae Lee, *The Purposes of Punishment Test*, 23 Fed. Sent. Rep. 58 (2011). The proportionality analysis consists of two tests, the culpability test and the purposes of punishment test.

74 Roper, 543 U.S. at 572.

75 Graham v. Florida, 130 S. Ct. 2011 (2010).

76 *See* Amnesty International, et al. as Amici Curiae Supporting Petitioners, Miller v. Alabama (2012) (No. 10-9646), 2012 WL 174238 for a more thorough treatment of the 8th Amendment jurisprudence citing international and foreign law and practice.

77 Amnesty International, et al. as Amici Curiae Supporting Petitioners, Miller v. Alabama (2012) (No. 10-9646), 2012 WL 174238.

78 Trop v. Dulles, 356 U.S. 58, 102 (1958).

79 Coker v. Georgia, 433 U.S. 584, 596 n. 10. (1977).

80 Edmund v. Florida, 458 U.S. 782, 798 (1982).

81 Thompson v. Oklahoma, 487 U.S. 815, 830 (1988).

82 Atkins v. Virginia, 536 U.S. 304, 315 n. 21 (2002).

83 Roper v. Simmons, 543 U.S. 551, 578 (2005).

84 Graham v. Florida, 130 S. Ct. 2011, 2034 (2010).

85 International Covenant on Civil and Political Rights, *supra* note 10, art. 10(3).

86 International Covenant on Civil and Political Rights, *supra* note 10, art. 10(3).

87 U.N. Human Rights Committee, *General Comment 21, art. 10*, 33, U.N. Doc. HRI/GEN/1/Rev.1 (1994).

88 Medellin v. Texas, 552 U.S. 491, 536 (2008) (Stevens, J. concurring): "One consequence of our form of government is that sometimes States must shoulder the primary responsibility for protecting the honor and integrity of the Nation." In a follow-up opinion on the denial of habeas corpus relief, Justice Stevens again emphasized the point: "I wrote separately to make clear my view that Texas retained the authority and, indeed, the duty as a matter of international law to remedy the potentially significant breach of the United States' treaty obligations . . ." Medellin v. Texas, 129 S.Ct. 360, 362, (2008) (Stevens, J.,dissenting).

89 138 Cong. Rec. S4781 (daily ed. Apr. 2, 1992).

90 United Nations Standard Minimum Rules for the Treatment of Prisoners, adopted Aug. 30, 1955 by the First United Nations Congress on the Prevention of

Crime and the Treatment of Offenders, U.N. Doc. A/CONF/611, annex I, E.S.C. res. 663C, 24 U.N. ESCOR Supp. (No. 1) at 11, U.N. Doc. E/3048 (1957), amended E.S.C. res. 2076, 62 U.N. ESCOR Supp. (No. 1) at 35, ¶ 56-59, U.N. Doc. E/5988 (1977).

91 Basic Principles for the Treatment of Prisoners, G.A. Res. 45/11, U.N. Doc. A/RES/45/111 (Dec. 14, 1990).

92 African Commission on Human and Peoples' Rights, *Report of the Special Rapporteur on Prisons and Conditions in Africa, Mission to the Republic of South Africa,* (June 14-30, 2004), *available* at http://www.achpr.org/english/Mission_reports/South%20Africa/Special%20Rap _Prisons_South%20Africa.pdf.

www.ingramcontent.com/pod-product-compliance
Lightning Source LLC
Chambersburg PA
CBHW071535210326
41597CB00019B/3005